Basel III and Beyond

Basel III and Beyond
A Guide to Banking Regulation after the Crisis

Francesco Cannata and Mario Quagliariello

Riskbooks

Published by Risk Books, a Division of Incisive Financial Publishing Ltd

Haymarket House
28–29 Haymarket
London SW1Y 4RX
Tel: +44 (0)20 7484 9700
Fax: +44 (0)20 7484 9800
E-mail: books@riskwaters.com
Sites: www.riskbooks.com
www.incisivemedia.com

© Incisive Media Investments Ltd.

ISBN 978 1 906348 60 1

British Library Cataloguing in Publication Data
A catalogue record for this book is available from the British Library

Publisher: Nick Carver
Commissioning Editor: Sarah Hastings
Editorial Development: Alice Levick
Managing Editor: Lewis O'Sullivan
Designer: Lisa Ling

Typeset by Mark Heslington Ltd, Scarborough, North Yorkshire

Printed and bound in the UK by Berforts Group Ltd

Conditions of sale
All rights reserved. No part of this book may be reproduced in any material form whether by photocopying or storing in any medium by electronic means whether or not transiently or incidentally to some other use for this book without the prior written consent of the Editor and copyright owner except in accordance with the provisions of the Copyright, Designs and Patents Act 1988 or under the terms of a licence issued with the written consent of the Author or Editor by the Copyright Licensing Agency Limited, 90, Tottenham Court Road, London W1P 0LP.

Warning: the doing of any unauthorised act in relation to this book may result in civil and criminal liability.

Every effort has been made to ensure the accuracy of the text at the time of publication. However, no responsibility for loss occasioned to any person acting or refraining from acting as a result of the material contained in this publication will be accepted by the Editor or the named Authors or Incisive Media Plc.

This book is current as at July, 2011 and represents the personal views of the Editor and the named Authors and not their organisations or colleagues. Reasonable care has been taken in the preparation of this book, but this book is not specific legal advice on which persons may rely. No responsibility can be or is accepted for any omissions, errors or for any loss sustained by any person placing reliance on its contents.

To our families

Contents

About the Editors		xi
About the Authors		xiii
Foreword by Mario Draghi		xxi
Introduction		xxiii

PART I: BASEL IN THE SHADOW OF THE CRISIS

1 The Big Financial Crisis   3
   Paul Collazos
   Bank of England

2 The Policy Response: From the G20 Requests to the FSB Roadmap; Working Towards the Proposals of the Basel Committee   45
   Patrizia Baudino
   European Central Bank

PART II: THE NEW CAPITAL STANDARDS

3 The New Definition of Regulatory Capital   73
   Laetitia Meneau; Emiliano Sabatini
   French Prudential Supervisory Authority; Bank of Italy

4 A New Framework for the Trading Book   99
   Federico Cabañas
   Bank of Spain

5 Counterparty Credit Risk and Other Risk-Coverage Measures   137
   Akhtar Siddique
   Office of the Comptroller of the Currency

| 6 | Tools for Mitigating the Procyclicality of Financial Regulation
Mario Quagliariello
European Banking Authority | 155 |

PART III: COMPLEMENTING CAPITAL REGULATION

| 7 | The Regulatory Leverage Ratio
Alan Adkins
Financial Services Authority | 185 |

| 8 | The New Framework for Liquidity Risk
Gianluca Trevisan
Bank of Italy | 207 |

| 9 | The Discipline of Credit Rating Agencies
Luca Giordano, Valerio Novembre, Neomisio Susi
CONSOB | 243 |

| 10 | Systemically Important Banks
Daryl Collins, David Rule
UK Financial Services Authority | 289 |

| 11 | Regulating Remuneration Schemes in Banking
Isabel Argimón, Gerard Arqué, Francesc Rodríguez
Bank of Spain | 301 |

PART IV: THE EMERGING REGULATORY LANDSCAPE

| 12 | Crisis Management and Resolution
Giovanni Bassani; Maurizio Trapanese
UK Financial Services Authority; Bank of Italy | 339 |

| 13 | The Impact of the New Regulatory Framework
Francesco Cannata; Ulrich Krueger
Bank of Italy; Deutsche Bundesbank | 375 |

| 14 | A Brazilian Perspective on Basel III
Lucio Rodrigues Capelletto, Paula Cristina Seixas de Oliveira
Central Bank of Brazil | 397 |

15 **A New Institutional Framework for Financial Regulation and Supervision**   421
Andrea Enria; Pedro Gustavo Teixeira
European Banking Authority; European Central Bank

Annex A: Structural Regulation Redux: The Volcker Rule   469
Marco Bevilacqua
Bank of Italy

Annex B: The Changing Uses of Contingent Capital under the Basel III Framework   485
Massimo Libertucci
Bank of Italy

Index   497

About the Editors

Francesco Cannata is the head of the regulatory impact assessment unit in the regulation and supervisory policies department of Bank of Italy, the Italian central bank. He has been the bank's representative in a number of international working groups dealing with Basel II issues (IRB, Pillar II, LGD, double default), supervisory cooperation (colleges of supervisors) and impact studies at the European Central Bank (ECB), the committee of European Banking Supervisors (CEBS) and the Basel and the Basel Committee on Banking Supervision (BCBS). More recently, at the Basel Committee and CEBS he has been closely involved in the quantitative impact studies conducted on the Basel III reform. He is also coordinating at national level the monitoring activity that international regulators conduct on a regular basis on bank's minimum requirements and prudential standards. His interests concern mainly the regulation of banks' capital adequacy, economics of financial regulation, and risk management. He has published several articles in Italian and international journals, including the *Journal of Financial Services Research*, the *Journal of Banking Regulation* and *Risk*. He is also the editor of a comprehensive book on internal ratings. He holds an MSc in finance from the Cass Business School (UK) and a PhD in banking and finance from III University of Rome (Italy).

Mario Quagliariello is currently a principal bank sector analyst at the European Banking Authority. He previously served as a senior economist in the regulation and supervisory policies department of Bank of Italy, the Italian central bank. He has been the representative of Bank of Italy in a number of international working groups dealing with financial stability issues at the ECB, CEBS, International Monetary Fund (IMF) and the Basel Committee. His interests concern macroprudential analysis and stress tests, banks' capital regulation, procyclicality and the economics of financial regulation. At the Basel Committee and the European commission, he has been involved in the work on countercyclical capital buffer. Mario has published several articles in Italian and international journals, including the *Journal of Banking and Finance*, the *Journal of Financial Services Research*, the *Journal of International Financial Markets, Institutions and Money*, *Applied Economics*, *Applied Financial Economics* and *Risk*, and edited the volume *Stress Testing the Banking System: Methodologies and Applications*. He holds a PhD. in economics from the University of York (UK).

About the Authors

Alan Adkins is responsible for the prudential cross-sectoral policy department at the Financial Services Authority, and chairs the Basel Committee for Banking Supervision (BCBS) trading book group and the leverage ratio sub-group of the committee's policy development group. Prior to working with the Financial Services Authority (FSA), Adkins worked for RiskMetrics Group in New York and London. He studied physics at Cambridge University.

Isabel Argimón is head of the banking analysis and regulatory policy division in the directorate general of regulation of the Bank of Spain, in charge of the development of the agenda for cost–benefit analysis. Her research interests are in the area of the impact of financial regulation. Previously, she was chief economist of the public sector and fiscal policy unit at the research department of the Bank of Spain, where she was involved in the assessment of Spanish public finances and managed both the research and short-term analysis of fiscal policy. Argimón also spent several years at HM Treasury, as economic adviser for public expenditure policy and financial regulation, and was head of the group of economic advisers working in the UK FSA. She graduated in economics from the University of Barcelona, where she was born, holds a master's from the University of California, San Diego, and has a PhD in economics from the Universidad Complutense.

Gerard Arqué works as a research assistant in the financial stability department at the Bank of Spain, and is doing research on financial regulation and its relation with bank capital and risk behaviour. He joined the Bank of Spain in 2009 after pursuing an MSc in macroeconomics and finance from the Barcelona GSE. In 2008 Arqué also worked as an intern in the international banking division at Criteria CaixaCorp.

Giovanni Bassani has been working in the financial stability division at the UK FSA since April 2008. He is dealing with cross-border coordination in crisis management and resolution and macroprudential regulation. Before joining the UK FSA, Giovanni worked for a decade in the Bank of Italy on international cooperation in banking regulation and supervision. He is a qualified lawyer in Italy and holds a Master of Laws Degree (LLM) in International Banking and Financial Law from the University of London.

Patrizia Baudino is a principal financial stability expert in the directorate general financial stability of the European Central Bank. She joined the ECB in 2002, and has held a number of positions since then, both in the international and in the financial stability directorates. Her work focuses on banking-sector stability, primarily in mature financial systems. Baudino spent three years (2007–2010) on secondment at the Financial Stability Board (FSB) – formerly the Financial Stability Forum (FSF) – where she was deeply involved in the FSB/FSF work in response to the financial crisis. She holds a PhD in economics from Princeton University.

Marco Bevilacqua is a policy analyst at the regulation and supervisory policies department of the Bank of Italy. His main interests concern banking regulation, financial system structure and regulatory impact assessment. He holds an MSc in finance from Bocconi University (Italy) and an MSc in economics from Univesitat Pompeu Fabra (Spain).

Federico Cabañas has been working for the directorate of supervision in the Bank of Spain for more than 13 years as a bank examiner. In 2001 he joined the risk management models division, where he is in charge of the validation of VaR models for capital purposes. He also coordinates specialised inspections in the treasury and capital markets divisions of large banks. From 2005 to 2007 Cabañas worked for the Basel Committee on Banking Supervision (BCBS) Secretariat, where, among other projects, he supported the update of the Basel Core Principles as well as the work of the Core Principles liaison group, accord implementation group and joint forum subgroups. He has represented Spain in several international groups both at European and Basel levels. A member of the BCBS TBG and EBA

SGMR and was also involved in the design of the market-risk component of the 2010 Stress Test conducted by the EBA. He is responsible for the training of new recruits in the supervision department in the area of treasury activities. He also gives in-house seminars to longer-standing inspectors and has collaborated in several workshops organised by the Financial Stability Institute and IOSCO. Cabañas holds degrees in business administration and psychology. He is also a registered actuary.

Lucio Rodrigues Capelletto holds a PhD in accounting from Universidade de São Paulo (2006) and an MSc in administration from Universidade de Brasília (1995). He specialised in banking and financial law at Boston University (2001), graduated in accounting (1999), and in administration (1989). He has had professional experience in banking supervision at the Central Bank of Brazil (BCB) since 1992 and expertise in international accounting standards (IFRS), financial system and banking supervision. Capelletto is currently deputy head of the department of financial system surveillance and information management at the BCB and professor and researcher at the doctorate programme at Universidade de Brasília.

Paul Collazos has been an economist at the financial stability directorate of the Bank of England since 2007. In this capacity, he has represented the bank in the capital monitoring group of the Basel Committee on banking supervision and the subgroup on credit risk of the European banking authority. He is also a member of the credit risk standing group and the prudential standards sub-board of the UK Financial Services Authority. Before joining the Bank, between 1995 and 1996 Collazos worked at the Office of the Chief Adviser of the Ministry of the Economy of Peru. He then served as an economist at the research department of the Peruvian Financial Services Authority (1996–2007). He graduated from the Pontifical Catholic University of Peru in 1993 with a BSc in economics. In August 2000, Collazos earned a master's degree in finance from the Universidad Pacifico. In 2002 the British Council awarded him with the Chevenning Scholarship to take a master of science in economics at the London School of Economics and Political Science. Collazos also taught monetary economics and macroeconomics at the Pontifical Catholic University of Peru and the Universidad del Pacifico respectively.

Daryl Collins works in the macroprudential policy department at the UK's Financial Services Authority and has recently been contributing to the work of the Financial Stability Board and the Basel Committee on banking supervision to develop a methodology for assessing the systemic importance of globally active banks. Collins joined the FSA in October 2007. Prior to that he worked at HM Treasury in the UK and the New Zealand Treasury. Born in New Zealand, he has a first class postgraduate degree in economics from the University of Auckland and a degree in international business.

Andrea Enria was recently appointed chairperson of the newly established European Banking Authority (EBA). He studied economics at the Bocconi University in Milan. He started his career at the Bank of Italy in the supervisory department and later worked in the research department, dealing mainly with regulatory issues, supervisory cooperation, analytical issues on banking supervision and financial stability. In 1999, he joined the ECB, where he was involved in macro-prudential analysis and banking regulation, working also as secretary of the ESCB banking supervision committee and then as head of the financial supervision division. In 2004, Enria became the first secretary general of the committee of European banking supervisors (CEBS), where he dealt with technical aspects of EU banking legislation, supervisory convergence and cooperation within the EU. In 2008, he went back to the Bank of Italy as head of the regulation and supervisory policy department.

Luca Giordano works as an economist at the economic research department at CONSOB. He has worked as a financial officer at the department of international financial affairs of the Italian Ministry of Economy and Finance and spent two years developing macroeconomic short-term analysis and microeconomics of banking. He holds a PhD in economics from the University of Naples Federico II and a master's degree in economics and finance (MEF) from the department of economics of the same university. He has published in banking, econometrics, and empirical macroeconomics.

Ulrich Krüger joined the Deutsche Bundesbank in 1999 after completing his PhD in mathematics at the University of Halle. He works as a senior economist and carries out quantitative research related to the impact of capital regulation. He spent several years in the banking supervision department. As a member of the capital monitoring group, the task force on the impact of the new capital framework and the quantitative impact study working group, Krüger was involved in the quantitative impact studies and monitoring projects organised by the Basel Committee and the committee of European banking supervisors when the regulatory reforms of Basel II/III were being developed. He joined the financial stability division in 2010 and is responsible for leading a unit dealing with macroprudential databases.

Massimo Libertucci works as an economist in the regulation and supervisory policies department of the Bank of Italy, the Italian central bank. He holds an MSc in economics from the University of Warwick (UK). Prior to joining the Bank of Italy, he worked as an analyst at CONSOB, the Italian financial services commission. His professional interests span most aspects of the economics of financial markets and prudential regulation.

Laetitia Meneau has been deputy head of the international affairs department, insurance of the French Prudential Supervisory Authority (ACP) since January 2011, particularly involved in "group's issues": group supervision and convergence of practices for supervisory colleges in Solvency II as well as the setting up of a common framework for internationally active insurance groups. Prior to that, she was deputy head of the international affairs department, banking, following the Basel III package. From 2007 to 2009, being the French delegate to the working group on the definition of capital and to the contingent capital working group of the Basel Committee, she was actively involved in the discussions on the new definition of capital. From 2004 to 2007, she was in the CEBS Secretariat in London. From 2000 to 2004, she was an offsite examiner at the French Commission Bancaire. Meneau is a graduate from ESSEC (Ecole Supérieure des Sciences Economiques et Commerciales) and from Sciences Po Paris.

Valerio Novembre is an economist at the economic research department at CONSOB and an adjunct lecturer in banking risk management at the University of Florence. Prior to that, he was a research fellow in banking and finance at the University of Florence and a visiting researcher at the CEBS and at the Queen Mary College in London. Novembre holds a PhD in economics, markets and institutions from the IMT Institute for Advanced Studies in Lucca and an MSc in finance and regulation from the London School of Economics and Political Science. He has published policy-oriented research in corporate governance and finance.

Paula Cristina Seixas de Oliveira has been the head of the liquidity and market risks monitoring division at the department of financial system surveillance and information management of the BCB since July 2006. In 2009, she joined the BCBS working group on liquidity and has participated in the development of the document "Basel III: International Framework for Liquidity Risk Measurement, Standards and Monitoring Acts", published in December 2010. Before being appointed with risks monitoring activities, Oliveira was part of the team responsible for the definition and implementation of the new Brazilian payment system (2000–2002). She has a degree in civil engineering. In March 2005, Oliveira earned her master's degree in economics from the Universidade de Brasília. Prior to joining the Central Bank in 1992, she worked as civil engineer for six years.

David Rule joined the UK's FSA in August 2009 and is head of the macroprudential department. He represents the FSA on the macroprudential working group of the Basel Committee on banking supervision and the advisory technical committee of the European systemic risk board. In May 2011, he became a head of department for the prudential supervision of major UK banks. Before joining the FSA, Rule worked for a financial trade association and spent 15 years at the Bank of England, including roles in banking supervision, debt management, market infrastructure analysis and financial stability analysis. His final role at the Bank of England was as head of the sterling markets division, where he led the bank's reforms of the sterling money markets. Rule has a master's degree in economics from Cambridge University and degrees in political theory and modern history.

Emiliano Sabatini works in the Bank of Italy, banking and financial supervision department. His career has included experience in the financial advisory and banking sectors. Sabatini joined the Bank of Italy in January 2009 and his topic is the prudential regulation of banks, investment firms, UCITS, payment institutions and IMEL. He holds a master's degree in quantitative finance form CORIPE (Turin).

Akhtar Siddique is the deputy director of the enterprise risk analysis division at the Office of the Comptroller of the Currency (OCC), Washington, DC, where he has worked since 2003. He provides technical assistance for examinations of national banks in valuation and risk models and capital-adequacy assessment. He has represented the OCC in intra- and interagency initiatives on counterparty credit risk management, Pillar II initiatives etc. Siddique has authored numerous papers published in peer-reviewed journals, including the *Journal of Finance*, *Review of Financial Studies*, *Management Science* and the *Journal of Accounting Research*. He holds a PhD. in finance from Duke University and taught finance at Georgetown University prior to joining the OCC.

Neomisio Susi works in the markets department at CONSOB, where he is responsible for coordinating preliminary analyses on market abuse cases and for the assessment of the applications for registration by CRAs. He has participated – by representing CONSOB in the meetings of the European Council – in the drafting of Regulation 1060/2009 and his amended version. He is a member of the European Securities and Markets Authority (ESMA) standing committee on credit rating agencies. Susi has previously worked in the economic research department of CONSOB, elaborating and developing research analyses, especially on asset management, private equity, initial public offerings and holding companies. He holds a degree in economics from the Luiss University and a master's in finance from the London Business School.

Pedro Gustavo Teixeira is counsellor to the vice-president of the European Central Bank (ECB) and lecturer on European financial regulation at the Institute for Law and Finance of the Goethe-Universität, Frankfurt am Main. Previously, he was an adviser at the Directorate-General Financial Stability of the ECB, which he joined in 1998 after his PhD studies at the Law Department of the European University Institute. He was secretary of the banking supervision committee of the European System of Central Banks (ESCB) as well as of several high-level ECB and EU committees dealing with financial crisis management. He also practised law in Lisbon, Portugal, and was an adviser at the Lisbon Stock Exchange. He has a number of publications on EU law and financial regulation.

Francesc Rodríguez Tous works as a research assistant in the financial stability department at the Bank of Spain. His research focuses on the effects of financial regulation on bank capital and risk behaviour. He joined the Bank of Spain in 2009 after pursuing an MSc in economics from the London School of Economics. He previously worked as a teacher assistant at the Universitat Pompeu Fabra.

Maurizio Trapanese is vice-director in the regulation and supervisory policies department of the Bank of Italy. His main areas of responsibility concern financial stability, macroprudential analysis and crisis management. He is involved in the negotiations with the EU commission to introduce into European legislation the new regulatory framework defined by the Basel Committee on banking supervision at the global level. Trapanese has been the representative of the Bank of Italy in a number of international working groups within the European System of Central Banks (ESCB), the European Central Bank (ECB), the committee of European banking supervisors (CEBS), the economic and financial committee (EFC) and the European Union. He holds an MSc in economics from the University of Warwick (UK) and a laurea in economics, *cum laude*, from the Bocconi University of Milan.

Gianluca Trevisan is a senior financial analyst in the banking supervision area at the Bank of Italy. He has been the representative of the Bank of Italy in several international working groups dealing with financial stability issues and has published several articles in refereed Italian journals. His interests concern liquidity, stress tests and cross-border cooperation on crisis management.

Foreword

One central lesson we have learnt is that the financial system entered the crisis with too little capital, liquidity buffers that were far too small, and a capital and valuation regime with significant procyclical consequences. Buoyant economic conditions and loopholes in regulation led inexorably to imprudent risk taking in the financial sector.

The response of the authorities has been prompt, with emergency interventions followed by a comprehensive roadmap for reforming financial regulation at the global level. I often recall the drivers of the reform; the novelties that have played a key role in getting us to where we are now. We have certainly come a long way towards strengthening the financial system since the crisis began. This has been achieved through (i) the newly developed consciousness that we all sit in the same boat because the financial systems are integrated and strongly correlated; (ii) the guidance of the G20 in agreeing objectives and timelines for substantial changes; and (iii) the establishment of mechanisms, such as the Financial Stability Board (FSB), to speed up and coordinate the policy development and technical work that is necessary in order to meet these objectives.

The outcome of this process is palpable.

As for regulatory policies, a fundamentally revised global bank capital framework has been endorsed. It aims at achieving stronger protection through improved risk coverage, greater and higher-quality capital, countercyclical buffers and constraints on the build-up of excessive leverage. Capital rules have been complemented by global liquidity standards, which will promote higher liquidity buffers and limit maturity mismatches that so extensively contributed to the crisis. In addition, standards on governance, risk management and remuneration have been radically improved so as to remove misaligned incentives.

Advances have been made in policy frameworks and tools to contain the moral-hazard risks posed by systemically important institutions. Mechanisms for cross-border oversight, crisis management and resolution have been agreed at the global level so as to expand the capacity of the authorities to resolve "too-big-to-fail" institutions.

The architecture for financial regulation and oversight has also been deeply revised. Top-down, system-wide oversight arrangements have been put in place at the national, regional and international levels. These include a reinforced international cooperation as well as a more all-encompassing surveillance, with broadened macroprudential perspectives. In Europe, the European Systemic Risk Board and the European Supervisory Authorities are fully operational within the new European System of Financial Supervisors; in the US, a Financial Services Oversight Council has been established; finally, the mandates of the International Monetary Fund and the FSB have been broadened.

This book provides the reader with a comprehensive discussion of the contents of the regulatory reform, taking advantage of the knowledge of experts who contributed to shaping the new rules. The editors – Francesco Cannata and Mario Quagliariello – have selected contributors from all over the global regulatory community. This is a vivid example of the unprecedented amount of international dialogue and cooperation that eventually led to substantive changes to financial regulation.

International consensus and coordination remain crucial in dealing with the challenges we have ahead of us to finalise the reform. We must not only reaffirm our commitment to global solutions, but demonstrate our willingness to reach agreement on the remaining open issues. We also need to maintain the momentum of consistent implementation to preserve a level playing field across national financial sectors. In fact, full and consistent implementation will take time and perseverance over the coming years. In the process, we must guard against pressures to water down the reform or allow for untenable national discretions, which would leave the entire regulatory repair effort in vain.

Mario Draghi
Governor of the Bank of Italy and chairman of the Financial
Stability Board
May 2011

Introduction

Francesco Cannata; Mario Quagliariello

Bank of Italy; European Banking Authority

"My voice may sound to you harsh, and I may too severely insist on proclaiming the necessity of virtue and sacrifice; but I know, and you too – untainted by false doctrine, and unspoiled by wealth – will soon know also, that the sole origin of every Right is in a Duty fulfilled."
Giuseppe Mazzini (1860)

The financial crisis erupted in 2007 in the US subprime mortgage market – a relatively small business segment of the global financial system – galvanised into existence an unprecedented period of financial instability in the international markets and the most severe economic recession since the Great Depression of the 1930s. After much debate, a consensus regarding the origins of the crisis has emerged. The list of factors is long, ranging from long-lasting macroeconomic imbalances to microeconomic failures.

Financial regulation, or the lack thereof, must also take responsibility. Prudential and accounting rules did not adequately mitigate excessive risk-taking. In some cases, they in fact provided bankers with wrong incentive structures, fostering weak lending standards and perverse behaviours.

In the aftermath of the crisis, an intense discussion concerning the responsibilities of regulation brought together both policymakers and academics. Solutions have proven hard to identify and consensus difficult to achieve. Some arguments – such as the incomplete implementation of Basel II (entered into force in most jurisdictions at the very moment when the crisis was breaking out) and the interaction of the prudential rules with the accounting standards – were initially underestimated. Basel II has therefore become a sort of scapegoat for such gaps in the regulation. It is however, fair to acknowledge that the debate allowed the parties involved to challenge certain standards of modern financial regulation, such as the ability of the market to automatically correct its "failures".

The post-mortem of the financial crisis clearly points to some major shortcomings in the regulatory framework: the low loss-absorbing capacity of capital instruments held by many banks; the lack of a harmonised framework for liquidity risk; an insufficient toolkit to address the procyclicality of the financial sector; weak arrangements for crisis management, especially for cross-border groups; and the moral hazard posed by bail-outs of several large players. A deep rethinking of the rules for banks and other financial intermediaries has been envisaged along these lines since the early phases of the financial crisis. A first report published in March 2008 by the Financial Stability Forum, now Financial Stability Board, provided the Basel Committee on Banking Supervision (BCBS) and the other international standard setters with a detailed roadmap, endorsed by the G20 leaders.

Overall, the policy response has been swift. In the first place, emergency measures aimed at avoiding the collapse of the international financial system, reducing panic and restoring ordered conditions in the financial markets have been adopted. The proposal for a comprehensive revision of financial regulation represents the longer-term response. Such a goal, which includes (but is not limited to), the new prudential framework for banks (ie, Basel III), has been achieved rapidly: in about two years, most of the shortcomings of the pre-crisis international framework have been addressed. As a comparison, the design of the Basel II framework was started in 1999 and finalised in 2006.

The regulatory process has been supported by an intense and far-reaching consultation with the banking industry and other relevant stakeholders, and by comprehensive impact assessments, which helped to identify the likely effects of the new rules on banks and on the economy as a whole.

International coordination – at both the political and technical levels – has also been a key element of the reform process. All authorities involved in the negotiations were well aware that the ultimate and ambitious objective of creating a true level playing field in the financial system might have implied some costs in terms of reduced national discretions. Indeed, the most apparent lesson of the crisis is that jurisdictions with more prudent regulatory and supervisory frameworks are also exposed to the risks posed by the institutions operating in other jurisdictions. This notwithstanding, there have been compromise solutions and some revival of national interests. After all, any international negotiation – especially where the political pressure is particularly high – implies some degree of compromise.

The regulatory reform addresses most drawbacks in financial regulation. Some interventions – such as the revision of the definition of regulatory capital – were already in the policy agenda before the crisis and had been temporarily postponed to allow for the implementation of the Basel II framework. Other measures – such as the introduction of harmonised quantitative standards for managing liquidity risk as well as of a leverage ratio – have become a top priority after the crisis. The introduction of explicit tools for smoothing the possible cyclical effects of capital regulation represents a genuinely new approach to financial regulation. These tools complement the traditional microprudential rules with a macroprudential approach.

Some bricks of the reform – stricter and harmonised rules on banking managers' remunerations, more effective arrangements for crisis management, a stronger discipline of rating agencies and a revision of the institutional settings for the regulatory and supervisory activity – go beyond the Basel III framework and contribute to a safer financial system. This last piece of reform represents a crucial condition for the success of the wider global reform: history in Europe and other jurisdictions, for instance the US, shows that an ambiguous and sometimes cumbersome organisation of the regulatory and supervisory activity may jeopardise the effectiveness of any new rule or regulation, even if they are comprehensive and well designed.

Some final pieces are under discussion at the time of writing, among them the prudential treatment of systemically relevant institutions and a proper definition of the scope of application of financial regulation. However, the backbone of a more sound and prudent financial system has been established.

It is now time for the implementation of the new rules in the various jurisdictions. Past experience suggests that this is a challenging and tricky task: a homogeneous transposition of the international rules at regional level and an adequate enforcement by supervisors are necessary conditions for the success of the reform. Otherwise, not only will the huge regulatory effort lack effectiveness but the credibility of the entire regulatory community will be seriously compromised.

This book provides a timely and accurate picture of all the components of the global reform, devoting particular attention to the Basel III framework – which represents the major regulatory response to the crisis – but also providing a discussion of the other elements of the policy agenda.

The title of the book reflects our objective. "Basel III" is clearly the focus, but we do not neglect other elements of the reform package that go "beyond" prudential rules. Originally we intended to refer explicitly to Basel II in the title of the book, since the transition from the 1988 first Capital Accord to a risk-sensitive capital regulation still represents – in our view – a landmark in the evolution of modern banking regulation. In fact, the Basel III rules go beyond Basel II but they have not altered the philosophy – the link between risk and capital – that lies at the heart of Basel II. However, since the Basel Committee has officially named the new framework "Basel III", we could not but respectfully accept this definition.

The book provides the reader with a detailed and comprehensive explanation of the reform, which will undoubtedly shape the financial landscape and "banking regulation" for the foreseeable future. Its publication closely follows the final endorsement of the Basel Committee proposals, which were released in December 2010. Notwithstanding the timely publication, *Basel III and Beyond: A Guide to Banking Regulation after the Crisis*, rather than being an "instant" book, is instead targeted at representing a robust and rigorous reference for the years ahead.

A big asset we, as editors, were able to rely on was the unique and very committed team of experts in financial regulation all over the world. All contributors are regulators who have been involved, in different ways and various capacities, in the discussion, design, test and assessment of the rules. In their chapters, they thus provide an insider view of the rationale behind the proposals and the description of the main policy options, in addition to their own explanations and examples. Views from a high number of international bodies and national financial regulators are reflected in the text. In order of appearance: the Bank of Italy, the European Banking Authority, the Bank of England, the European Central Bank, the Banque de France-Commission Bancaire, the Bank of Spain, the US Office of the Comptroller of the Currency, the UK Financial Services Authority, the CONSOB (the Italian securities commission), the Deutsche Bundesbank and the Central Bank of Brazil.

Notwithstanding the large variety of topics and their high degree of technical complexity, our intention was to edit a straightforward book where a technical approach is appropriately merged with plain language so as to serve a wide readership. On the one hand, beginners should be able to understand the different facets of financial regulation even with a basic knowledge of it. On the other hand, more advanced readers will find all the details they need for understanding the implications of the new pieces of regulation from both regulatory and banks' standpoints. To this end, every chapter explains why there was a need for a given piece of regulation, how rules were before the crisis, and how they have been revised as the result of the financial turmoil.

The book is organised into four parts.

Part I, "Basel in the Shadow of the Crisis", contains two chapters, which represent the essential background for a better understanding of the rationale of the global regulatory reform. For this reason, references to both chapters are spread around the whole text.

Chapter 1, "The Big Financial Crisis", written by P. Collazos, discusses the origins and the dynamics of the financial crisis, by focussing on the macroeconomic background of the turmoil as well as on the financial practices that contributed to the crisis. Chapter 2, "The Policy Response: From the G20 Requests to the FSB Roadmap; Working Towards the Proposals of the Basel Committee" from P. Baudino, contains a comprehensive discussion of the overall policy response that the G20 leaders and the Financial Stability Board (FSB) have designed to address the shortcomings of financial regulation highlighted during the crisis.

Part II, "The New Capital Standards", focuses on the components of the Basel III reform aimed at revising the already existing Basel II rules.

Chapter 3, "The New Definition of Regulatory Capital", by L. Meneau and E. Sabatini, discusses the rationale of one of the major changes introduced to the current rules: the definition of supervisory capital, which still represents the key parameter for both supervisors and market analysts to assess the solvency of a financial institution. The discussion of the limitations of the current framework that emerged during the crisis is followed by a detailed and well-explained illustration of the rationale and contents of the new rules.

Chapter 4, "A New Framework for the Trading Book", by F. Cabañas, addresses the very first response (in mid-2009) of international regulators to the financial crisis, in the form of the strengthening of the market risk framework. Banks' business in trading-book activities has been one of the main features of the crisis: the prudential rules were clearly inadequate in capturing the effective risk profile of such activity. The chapter illustrates the changes introduced to the 1996 market risk regulation (from the "stressed VaR" to the incremental risk charge), which requires an earlier implementation than the rest of the regulatory package.

The second "leg" of the changes introduced to the way risk-weighted assets are computed, the denominator of the solvency ratios, is represented by an articulated range of measures aimed at strengthening the prudential treatment of counterparty credit risk. The rationale and contents of these measures, together with a further set of new rules, are explained in Chapter 5, "Counterparty Credit Risk and Other Risk-Coverage Measures" by A. Siddique.

Chapter 6, "Tools for Mitigating the Procyclicality of Financial Regulation", by M. Quagliariello, provides a systematic discussion of one of the most debated topics of the reform package, ie, the range of instruments that the Basel Committee has introduced to mitigate the potential effects of procyclicality of financial regulation. These include the tools for smoothing the cyclicality of minimum capital requirements, an incentive mechanism for capital conservation, more forward-looking provisions and a rule to allow banks to build-up more capital buffers during an excessive credit growth. As discussed in this chapter, not all of these measures – even though they were originally designed as complementary rules – have received the same attention in the final rules text. Moreover, the challenges of their practical implementation in the coming years suggest that much work has still to be done. However, the somehow revolutionary principle that a macroprudential approach is a necessary complement to the traditional capital regulation has been introduced.

As mentioned above, Basel III introduces also a set of totally new rules, at least at the international level, which are aimed at complementing the function and role of the capital solvency ratios. These are discussed in Part III of the book, "Complementing Capital Regulation".

The first of these measures is the leverage ratio, described and discussed in Chapter 7, "The Regulatory Leverage Ratio", by A. Adkins. The chapter provides a detailed explanation of the policy choices adopted by regulators in defining this measure, also comparing the relevant options that have been discussed in the consultative phase and analysing the interaction between the leverage ratio and the risk-sensitive capital requirements, which is the key issue to ensure the proper functioning of such a tool.

A second stream of rules that significantly strengthen the current international framework is represented by the standards on liquidity risk, described in Chapter 8 "The New Framework for Liquidity Risk", written by G. Trevisan. After providing an overview of the recommendations for liquidity risk management that international regulators had issued in 2008 and reviewing the goal and design of the two liquidity standards (a short-term coverage ratio and a structural ratio), the chapter focuses on the challenging implementation phase.

The set of measures introduced to make the discipline of credit rating agencies more rigorous is described by L. Giordano, V. Novembre and N. Susi in Chapter 9, "The Discipline of Credit Rating Agencies". The issue is not new in the debate on financial regulation, since the behaviour and performance of rating agencies are harshly questioned every time a financial or corporate crisis occurs. However, the central role of external ratings in the sub-prime turmoil has made the topic even more crucial. The chapter provides a broad perspective of the different market failures and describes the solutions adopted by international standard setters and regulators.

Chapter 10, "Systemically Important Banks", contributed by D. Collins and D. Rule deals with the regulation of systemic institutions. This is the most hotly contested topic (not only for regulators but also at a political level) in the regulatory debate after the crisis. The contents of the chapter are wide-ranging, and include: the identification of systemically important banks, the introduction of capital and liquidity surcharges, structural regulations aiming at avoiding the creation of too-big-to-fail banks and crisis-management procedures. A careful reading of the chapter will certainly allow the reader to better follow the development of the debate in the coming months, until the finalisation of the rules by the end of 2011.

The last chapter of part III, "Regulating Remuneration Schemes in Banking", written by I. Argimón, G. Arqué and F. Rodriguez, is devoted to the remuneration mechanisms in the financial sector. There is a wide consensus that they have contributed to the alteration of the bank manager incentives, and represent a short-sighted approach to the setting-up of the business strategies. The chapter describes and comments on the initiatives adopted by the FSB, the Basel Committee and the European Commission in order to ensure that remuneration policies are less affected by short-term interests. The advantages and disadvantages of different policy options are also analysed.

Part IV, "The Emerging Regulatory Landscape", deals with a variety of topics which complete the picture drawn in the preceding sections.

The controversial issue of crisis management is addressed in Chapter 12, "Crisis Management and Resolution", contributed by G. Bassani and M. Trapanese. The discussion focuses on the new framework for crisis management and resolution at both the global and the EU levels. The analysis covers the different facets of crisis management, including international cooperation, emergency plans and burden-sharing agreements.

A detailed overview of the impact analyses that international authorities have carried out while defining the Basel III rules is provided in Chapter 13, "The Impact of the New Regulatory Framework", authored by F. Cannata and U. Krueger. The discussion of the effects of the introduction of the new framework has accompanied the entire reform process and provided different views. The simulations carried out by international regulators, even though they should be interpreted with caution, do represent a unique starting point for a deep understanding of the implications, both quantitative and strategic, of the new rules on banks and the economy as a whole. The chapter describes the main results of the quantitative impact studies carried out at G20 and EU level as well as of the macroeconomic analyses made both on the transitional period and in the long run.

With respect to previous regulatory interventions, the negotiations of Basel III have involved a higher number of countries. However, the different characteristics and business practices of the various banking systems make the implementation challenges in some countries even more interesting. Chapter 14, "A Brazilian Perspective on the Revised Basel Framework", from L. Cappelletto and P. C. Seixas de Oliveira, addresses this issue by discussing the possible implications of the new regulatory framework in Brazil.

The final chapter, written by A. Enria and G. Texeira, entitled "A New Institutional Framework for Financial Regulation and Supervision", switches to more institutional issues: sound rules may turn out to be ineffective if accompanied by a weak supervisory framework. The future architecture of financial supervision and regulation is described and commented on, including the role of the FSB and the IMF at the global level and the establishment of the European System of Financial Supervisors in Europe.

The book is enriched by two Annexes. The first, "Structural Regulation Redux: the Volcker Rule", comes from M. Bevilacqua and describes the main contents of the US Dodd-Frank Act with a special focus on the Volcker Rule. The second, entitled, "Contingent Capital", and written by M. Libertucci, focuses on the debate on possible uses of contingent convertible debt for regulatory purposes.

This book is the result of teamwork and the project would have not been finalised without the contribution and help of many people.

First of all, the contributors. We had the pleasure to interact with a group of motivated and committed friends and colleagues, who, even under heavy workloads, accepted to dedicate their time – very often their holidays and weekends – to drafting their chapters. We are grateful to A. Adkins, I. Argimon, G. Arqué, G. Bassani, P. Baudino, M. Bevilacqua, F. Cabañas, P. Collazos, D. Collins, A. Enria, L. Giordano, U. Krueger, M. Libertucci, L. Meneau, V. Novembre, L. Rodrigues Cappelletto, F. Rodriguez, D. Rule, E. Sabatini, P. C. Seixas de Oliveira, A. Siddique, N. Susi, P. Texeira, M. Trapanese and G. Trevisan for their support and invaluable help.

Second, we are happy to thank all the staff at Risk Books. Sarah Hastings and Lewis O'Sullivan provided us with helpful comments and suggestions for fine-tuning the proposal and finalising the book. We are more than grateful to Alice Levick, our editorial assistant, for her help, careful reading of the whole manuscript and (incredible) patience.

The opinions expressed are those of the authors and do not necessarily reflect those of the Bank of Italy, or the European Banking Authority.

Part 1

Basel in the Shadow of the Crisis

1

The Big Financial Crisis

Paul Collazos

Bank of England

1.1 INTRODUCTION

This chapter analyses the origins and dynamics of the financial crisis that erupted in 2007 and led to a deep rethinking of the regulatory framework at international level. The discussion focuses on both the financial practices that contributed to the financial turmoil and their macroeconomic context.

There are various estimates of the length of the financial crisis.[1] This chapter defines the big financial crisis as the period from the first announcements of write-offs in subprime assets[2] (early 2007) to the publication of the US stress test results (May 2009).

Section 1.2 studies the genesis of the crisis. The turmoil was caused by the crystallisation of subprime losses at a time of severe deterioration of the safety cushions that protected investors and creditors from bank failures. This was a relatively short period (from 2002 to 2006) in which several large financial firms rapidly ran down their reserves of provisions and buffers of capital, becoming vulnerable to systemic shocks.

Section 1.3 analyses the dynamics of the crisis. During most of the period between early 2007 and mid-2009, markets observed a slow realisation of losses together with episodes of public intervention – mainly through the provision of loans of last resort – and private recapitalisations, which provided temporary relief to creditors and investors. The analysis also covers the panic after the collapse of Lehman Brothers (on September 15, 2008) and the series of measures taken by authorities, bank managers and investors to boost financial firms' solvency ratios and restore market confidence.

The chapter concludes with a brief review of the secondary effects of the crisis on the credit supply, including the consequences that affected the global economy several years after the onset of the crisis.

1.2 THE ORIGINS OF THE CRISIS: 2002–2006

Across countries and ages, financial systems have suffered a series of aggregate shocks, typically in the form of bursts of asset-price bubbles. The last two centuries provide dozens of examples, including the collapse of Peruvian bonds that triggered the crisis of the British banking system in 1825, the crash of 1929 that started the Great Depression and the speculative investments in Asia that originated the 1999 turmoil in emerging markets.[3] In all these cases initial shocks were both systemic and cyclical.

To protect itself against these types of shock, the banking industry has rarely reduced the scale or the scope of its operations. Instead banks have managed aggregate risks through a regulated "safety net" aimed at protecting shareholders, debt holders and depositors from the losses of bank failures. The definition of safety net typically includes deposit insurance, loans of last resort and early intervention,[4] but this chapter extends this concept to reserves of provisions, buffers of capital and capital requirements. The instruments comprising such a safety net can then be classified in five categories.

1. Provisions: This accounting allowance or expense is the first line of protection against future losses. Provisions are deducted from profits to build up a reserve that can be drawn down when write-offs occur (Fernández de Lis, Martínez Pagés and Saurina 2000; Cavallo and Majnoni 2002).
2. Capital buffers: Surpluses of regulatory capital[5] over minimum requirements are the second instrument of the safety net. Such buffers prevent banks from breaching the minimum if either extreme losses occur or the amount of required capital increases in the future (Kashyap, Rajan and Stein 2008).
3. Capital requirements: This instrument is intended to protect creditors rather than investors. It covers losses that occur after the bank has been placed into liquidation. It also serves as the trigger for transfer of control rights from managers and shareholders to supervisors before insolvency becomes imminent (Dewatripont and Tirole 1994).

4. Deposit insurance funds: This element aims at protecting uninformed depositors, preventing inefficient bank runs (Diamond and Dybvig 1983). The fund, which is built up through deposit insurance premiums in certain jurisdictions, compensates depositors in the event of bank failure.
5. Early intervention: This is the final line of protection for all creditors before the use of resolution tools (such as balance-sheet restructuring, property transfer and liquidation). Under an early intervention regime, supervisors can impose restrictions on dividends, permissions or remunerations and even replace banks' management (Mayes 2004).

These five elements prevent banks from being unsafely exposed to aggregate shocks, increasing the resilience of the financial system and reducing the likelihood of systemic crisis. This chapter argues that the big financial crisis observed between 2007 and 2009 was the consequence of both an accelerated deterioration of the safety net in most developed economies and the occurrence of a shock originated in the subprime sector.

1.2.1 The rapid detriment to the financial safety net

The increasing systemic fragility that caused the big financial crisis affected all the components of the safety net in a very short timeframe. Such a speed of deterioration was caused not only by management and accounting practices that sought to ensure large bonuses and dividend payouts rather than increase the amount of provisions and capital reserves, but also by audit and supervisory cultures that did not safeguard the level of these reserves.

The primacy of short-term goals explains why these practices became very common. The benefits of the safety net are evident in the long run when prudential regulations reduce the probability of a banking crisis and its adverse effects on the economy.[6] But, in the short run, the implementation of a proper safety net is usually seen as costly. The maintenance of buffers and reserves reduces profits, dividends and bonuses and a close monitoring of the different components of the safety net may require significant supervisory effort and resources. The perception of excessive costs explains the lack of focus on the fragility of the safety net, which in turn explains the vulnerability of the banking sector in the run-up to the crisis.

1.2.1.1 Shortfalls of provisions

Bank managers and shareholders have few incentives to improve a safety net that – in the short run – will reduce net profits, dividend payouts and managerial bonuses. In contrast, they seek to maximise earnings and reduce costs and allowances, particularly those related to loan provisions.

The reduction of provisions occurred systematically between 2001 and 2006 (Figure 1.1). The shortfall of provisions was evident at the end of 2008 when banks disclosed figures that compared the level of provisions against expected losses. With the exception of a few Spanish institutions, major European banks showed significant shortfalls of provisions (Figure 1.2).

The shortage of provisions not only affected loan allowances. Other asset classes also lacked proper levels of provisions. For instance, bank managers were systematically too optimistic about the valuation of deferred taxes and intangible assets.[7] The crisis showed that, under stressed situations, banks needed to write down significant portions of these assets.

The fact that managerial bonuses were linked to short-term profits created an incentive structure where higher provisions resulted in lower bonuses. The international accounting standards based on

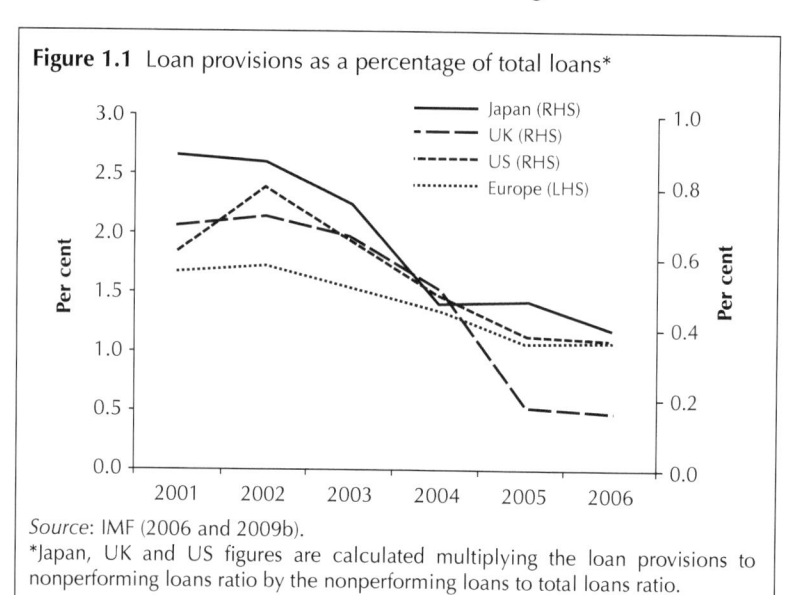

Figure 1.1 Loan provisions as a percentage of total loans*

Source: IMF (2006 and 2009b).
*Japan, UK and US figures are calculated multiplying the loan provisions to nonperforming loans ratio by the nonperforming loans to total loans ratio.

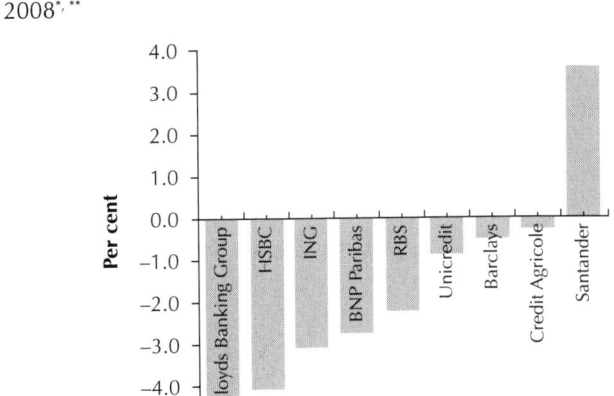

Figure 1.2 Difference between provisions and Basel II expected losses in 2008*,**

[Bar chart showing Per cent on y-axis ranging from -6.0 to 4.0, with bars for: Lloyds Banking Group (~-5.5), HSBC (~-4.0), ING (~-3.0), BNP Paribas (~-2.5), RBS (~-1.5), Unicredit (~-0.5), Barclays (~-0.5), Credit Agricole (~-1.5), Santander (~3.7)]

Source: Annual reports and Pillar III disclosures of above mentioned Banks.
*Figures are expressed as percentages of total capital.
**Santander's expected losses are calculated multiplying the expected loss rate to the total amount of exposures at default that corresponds to portfolios under the internal rating-based approach of Basel II.

incurred rather than long-run expected losses were also consistent with the incentives created by these remuneration schemes. In Spain, where higher provisions are required, regulators faced strong criticism from market analysts and accountants who complained that these provisions were neither transparent nor compatible with international financial reporting standards. Both issues were resolved through additional disclosure and reporting (Saurina 2009).

1.2.1.2 Depletion of capital buffers

Corporate finance dictates that the volume of external funds a firm can attract depends positively on its levels of equity capital.[8] Creditors have neither perfect information about the value of the firm's assets, nor the ability to enforce repayment before liquidation. So the amount that a firm can borrow from debt markets will increase with its ability to protect debt holders from losses, which in turn will depend on its levels of equity capital.[9]

This principle is very relevant during bad times, when external funds are scarce and the cost of debt is high. But, in good times, firms can fuel asset growth with cheap debt and little equity.[10] During booms, bond issuances are more frequent and regular than seasoned equity offerings. For instance, corporate and financial firms issued ten times more debt than equity in the years prior to the crisis (Figure 1.3).

Even in stressed scenarios, voluntary (as opposed to enforced) equity capital offerings have been penalised by existing investors because markets believe that such issuances provide signals of poor expected performance. Profitable firms would instead prefer to increase their capital cushions through earnings retention.[11]

The availability of external funds and the reluctance to issue additional equity explain the rapid depletion of bank capital buffers. A few years before the crisis bank managers and investors realised there was no need for significant capital cushions in order to obtain cheap funds from debt markets.[12] Berróspide and Edge (2010) found that, in just a couple of years, buffers of bank Tier 1 capital, ie, surpluses above the 4% international standard, fell from 10% to 8% of risk-weighted assets (RWAs) as shown in Figure 1.4.

The emergence of the so-called hybrid instruments (neither pure debt nor equity) can be explained by the increasing demand for fixed-income products, and the advantage that these instruments

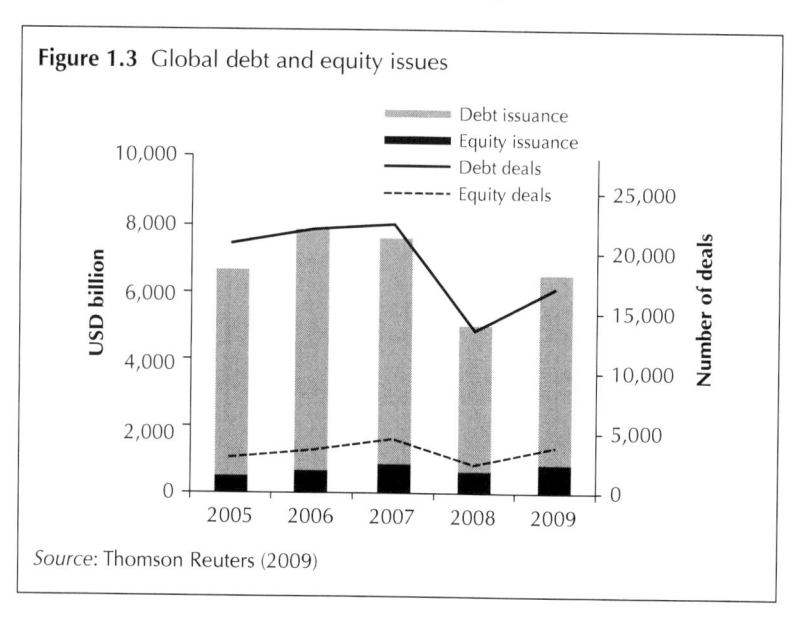

Figure 1.3 Global debt and equity issues

Source: Thomson Reuters (2009)

Figure 1.4 US Tier 1 capital ratios

Source: Berrospide and Edge (2010)

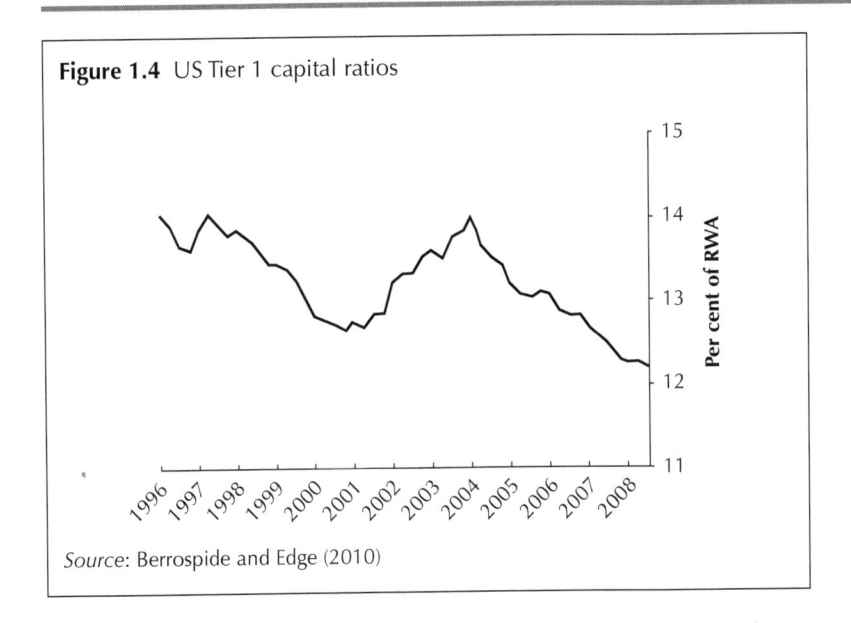

had the same regulatory treatment as equity (ie, they qualify as regulatory capital). The aforementioned depletion of buffers would have been more pronounced if the calculation of Tier 1 capital had deducted these hybrid instruments before the crisis.[13]

1.2.1.3 Reduction of capital charges
Between 2002 and 2007, the growth of capital requirements was lower than the increase in banks' balance sheets (Figure 1.5). Such a fall in capital charges per unit of asset was not driven by a fundamental improvement in banks' portfolio quality. The evolution of capital requirements suggests that, in the run-up to the crisis, large banks reallocated their portfolios towards exposures with low capital charges (mainly trading, interbank and sovereign positions). They also used risk-transfer mechanisms such as securitisations and credit derivatives as well as models that underestimated the risk in the trading book.

The emergence of the market for risk transfer products started in the mid-1990s. Figure 1.6 shows the rapid increase in yearly issuances of securitisations, which evolved from US$1.5 trillion in 2000 to US$4.7 trillion in 2006. Figure 1.7 reports a similar evolution for the nominal amount of outstanding derivative contracts, which grew from US$100 trillion in 1998 to US$600 trillion in 2007. Most of

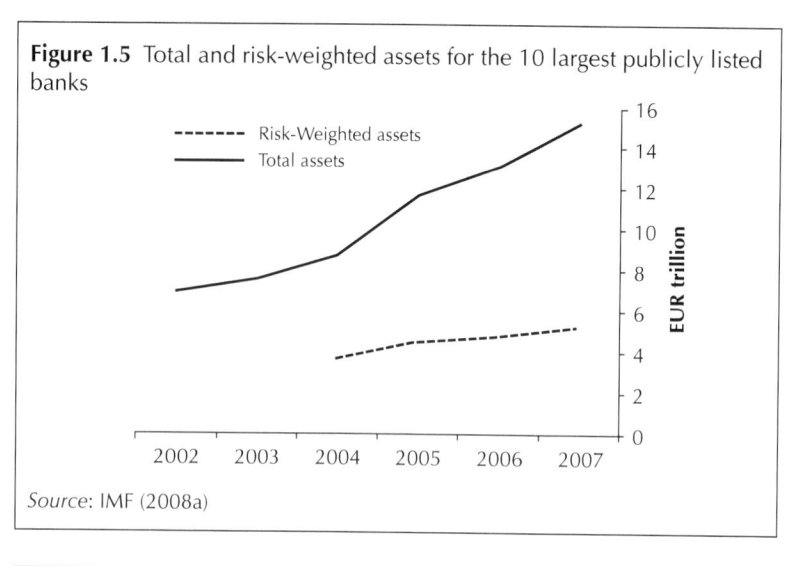

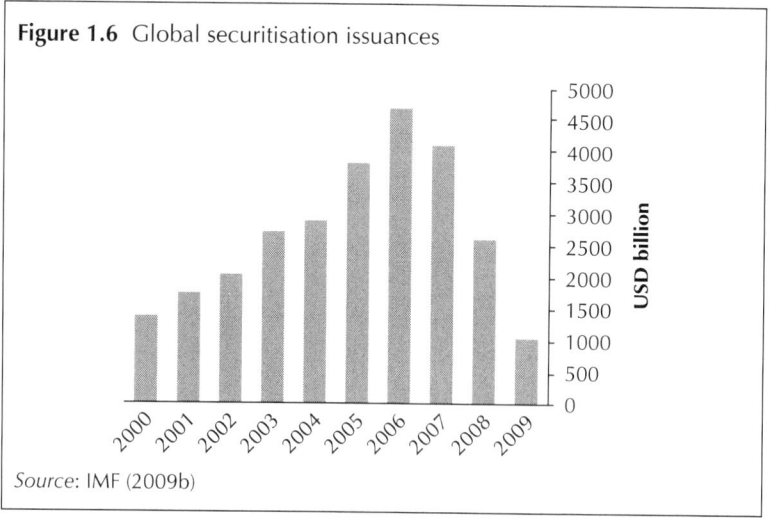

Figure 1.5 Total and risk-weighted assets for the 10 largest publicly listed banks

Source: IMF (2008a)

Figure 1.6 Global securitisation issuances

Source: IMF (2009b)

these products provided insurance to productive firms but some of them, particularly credit derivatives and synthetic securitisations, also operated as devices to minimise capital charges.

After 20 years under the same capital framework, Basel I, banks learned how to use risk-transfer mechanisms to reduce their capital requirements. Banks became increasingly better at measuring their exposures collateralised by financial assets and guaranteed by banks or governments, which enabled them to attract the low capital

Figure 1.7 Global nominal value of derivatives

Source: IMF (2010a)

Figure 1.8 Size of the trading book*

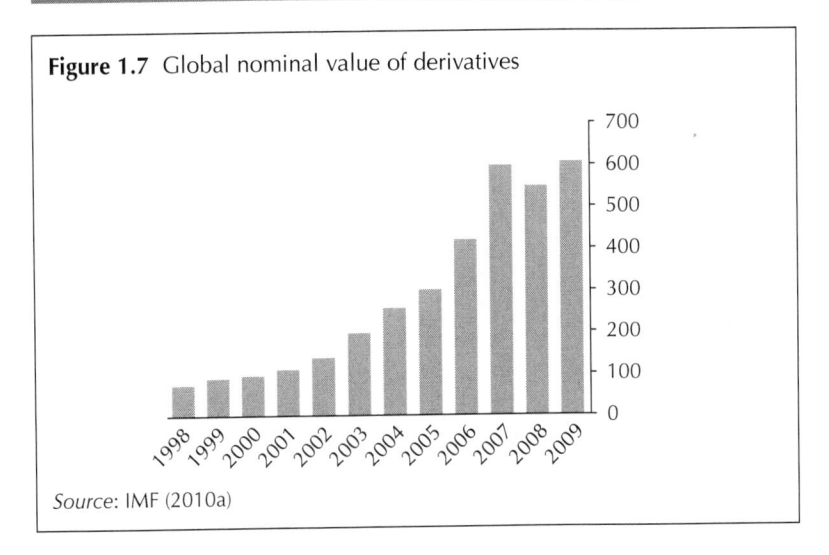

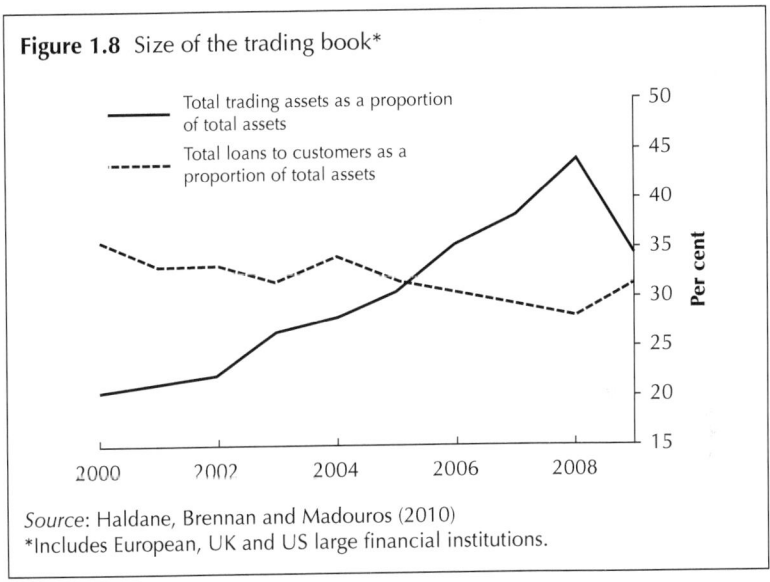

Source: Haldane, Brennan and Madouros (2010)
*Includes European, UK and US large financial institutions.

charges given to sovereigns and financial exposures and therefore to reduce their capital requirements per unit of asset. For example, leveraging up on assets with high intrinsic credit risk but low regulatory measures of risk (either low credit conversion factors or low risk weights) would have resulted in high returns without incurring high capital charges.

The boundary between the trading book and the banking book

also created opportunities to reduce capital requirements. Since the introduction of the trading book, banks moved certain assets into this book to reduce their capital charges. Figure 1.8 shows the rapid increase in the size of the trading book in the US, UK and EU.

The invention of the trading book was one of the most effective devices for regulatory arbitrage. The vague definition of "trading intent", created in order to define the boundary between the banking and trading books for regulatory purposes, also contributed to the increase in traded exposures. The extended use of fair-value[14] accounting and market risk modelling also provided a useful framework to reclassify some banking book items into the trading book, with the subsequent reduction in capital charges. The regulatory trading book was used to separate the part of the portfolio that is subject to credit risk (the banking book) from the portion that is marked to market or bears market risks, so that banks could apply the low capital charges corresponding to traded exposures.

Panel 1.1 describes in more detail how and why the trading book came into being in Europe (through the Capital Adequacy Directive of March 1993) and more globally (through the Basel Committee's Amendment of January 1996). The origins of the trading book were closely linked to three factors: the introduction of standards that allowed banks to publish their statements using fair-value accounting for certain items; risk-modelling trends such as the value-at-risk method; and level-playing-field considerations (ie, the fact that Europe lacked an equivalent to the Glass–Steagall Act).

PANEL 1.1 THE INVENTION OF THE TRADING BOOK

The separation of commercial and investment banks introduced in the US by the Glass–Steagall Act of 1933 can be seen as the first distinction between bankers' and brokers' activities. But it was just after the crash of 1987 that most international banks began to use market prices (to value their trading positions, and models to manage their market risks).

A few years later, between 1989 and 1992, European authorities introduced rules that allowed banks to use an accounting trading book, which can be broadly defined as a section of the financial statements where items are valued using either market prices (mark-to-market) or models (mark-to-model).

In September 1989 Spain introduced an asset class for securities that could be marked to market (the so-called held-for-trading category). In

↓

1990, the British Bankers' Association issued guidelines that formally recommended the valuation of trading book securities at market prices. The same year, France approved rules that introduced an accounting trading book. In Germany, the 1991 Commercial Code allowed exceptions to accounting regulations that required valuation at historical costs. And similar regulations were introduced in Italy in 1992.[15]

The development of fair-value accounting standards and the innovations in market risk modelling prompted the introduction of the trading book for capital requirement purposes. In 1993 the European Commission introduced the concept of trading book in Article 2 (6a) of the Capital Adequacy Directive, defining it as "proprietary positions in financial instruments which are held for resale and/or which are taken on by the institution with the intention of benefiting in the short term from actual and/or expected differences between their buying and selling prices, or from other price or interest-rate variations" (Council Directive 93/6/EEC 1993).

Three years later, the Basel Committee transposed this text into the 1996 Amendment to the first capital accord (Basel I). The Basel II capital framework of 2006 maintained the criterion of trading intent to define the boundaries of the trading book, allowing banks to reallocate their assets towards this book and benefit from lower (market risk) capital charges. The fact that capital charges are lower for the trading book is discussed further in Chapter 3.

1.2.1.4 Arbitrage of deposit insurance

Deposit insurance was another tool of the safety net that was perceived as costly. As it implies stricter regulation, regular supervision and in certain jurisdictions the payment of insurance premiums, the costs of deposit insurance were avoided by potential entrant firms and financial entrepreneurs through another form of regulatory arbitrage: shadow banking.

The modern definition of shadow banks includes either instruments or firms that mimic the two key functions of banks: maturity and credit risk transformation. It therefore includes money market funds, asset-backed commercial paper issuers, finance companies, structured investment vehicles, credit hedge funds,[16] securities lenders and government-sponsored enterprises. Like banks, these entities capture resources from creditors and invest these funds into long-term projects whose cashflow and collateral allow them to expand their portfolio. But, unlike banks, they are unregulated entities, so their customers are not protected by deposit insurance and, more importantly, their managers are not subject to banking supervision.

With neither deposit insurance fees nor regulatory constraints, the business model of shadow banks became extremely popular (Adrian and Shin 2009). Between 1995 and 2007, the amount of funds collected by these entities in the US increased four times, becoming larger than the banking system (Figure 1.9). In just two years, the crisis eroded up to 25% of the value of their assets. Given the lack of a safety net for these entities, their investors absorbed all these losses. Many of these investors were commercial banks whose clients in turn were depositors. The consequence of the collapse of many US money market funds in September 2008 illustrates the spillover effects of losses in the shadow banking sector.

1.2.1.5 Lack of early intervention

Early intervention procedures seek to minimise the dead-weight losses associated with bank failures, particularly bankruptcy costs and intangible assets depreciations (eg, qualitative information about borrowers' reputations). Early intervention also operates as a disciplining device that provides bank managers and shareholders with incentives to comply with the minimum requirements. Without this form of enforcement, the minimum requirements will be simple indicators of performance, mere tools of market discipline.

But, like any other safety-net component, early-intervention regimes were perceived as costly tools. This is because early intervention requires close monitoring of bank activities, which consumes significant resources and effort from supervisors.

The rapid erosion of capital buffers between 2002 and 2006 reveals the lack of active early-intervention regimes in certain jurisdictions.[17] If early-intervention regimes had been effective, regulators would have enforced earlier recapitalisations, higher retention rates and larger provisions. In contrast, markets observed a period of low conservation of capital, poor levels of provisions and infrequent equity raises. The absence of early-intervention processes was also evident from the high payout ratios of the last decade (Figure 1.10). Managers and shareholders were reluctant to retain more earnings despite the evident decrease in capital buffers.

Early intervention would have also mitigated moral hazard. Rather than a one-period game, the relationship between the super-

Figure 1.9 US shadow banks' liabilities

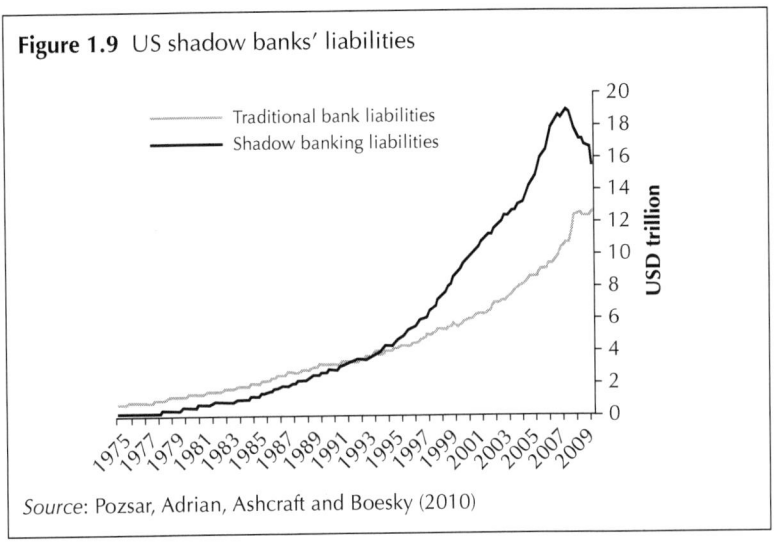

- Traditional bank liabilities
- Shadow banking liabilities

USD trillion

Source: Pozsar, Adrian, Ashcraft and Boesky (2010)

Figure 1.10 Dividend payout ratios[*,**]

Per cent

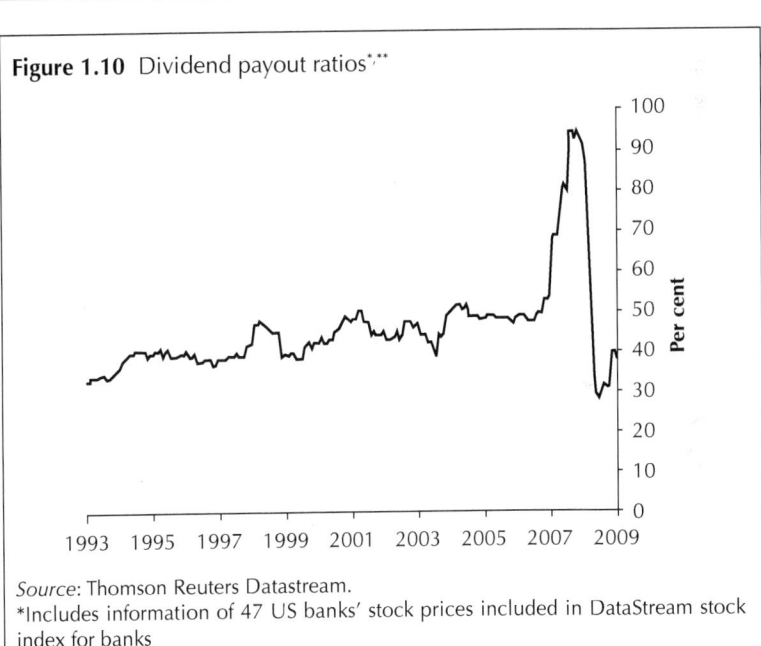

Source: Thomson Reuters Datastream.
*Includes information of 47 US banks' stock prices included in DataStream stock index for banks
**Dividend payout ratios are calculated as the ratio of dividend yields to earnings per share

visor and the supervisee should be analysed as a dynamic process where every fault in the safety net should be detected and a rapid correction enforced.

The absence of such a dynamic process was evident during the crisis and its sequence of bailouts and loans of last resort. Some authors have argued this type of support was also evident prior to the crisis. Roubini and Mihm (2010), for instance, provide a couple of examples of pre-crisis "regulatory forbearance".[18]

Early intervention bears the costs of intrusive supervision but also yields the benefits of lower probabilities of bank failure. Before the crisis, regulators traded off between safety and costs. Their decisions resulted in low levels of effective supervisory effort (evident from the low and decreasing levels of capital buffers) and higher probabilities of bank resolution (evident from the number of bankruptcies reported during the turmoil).

1.2.2 The nature of the shock of 2007

In the early 2000s, a shock in the market of subprime mortgages would have been an idiosyncratic disturbance, but at the beginning of 2007 it was a fully formed aggregate shock. During the 10 years before the crisis the size of subprime annual issuances had grown from US$50 billion in 1997 to US$600 billion in 2005 (Figure 1.11). By the beginning of 2006 all the large and internationally active banks were exposed (directly or not) to these assets.

The banking sector was vulnerable to this aggregate shock. The

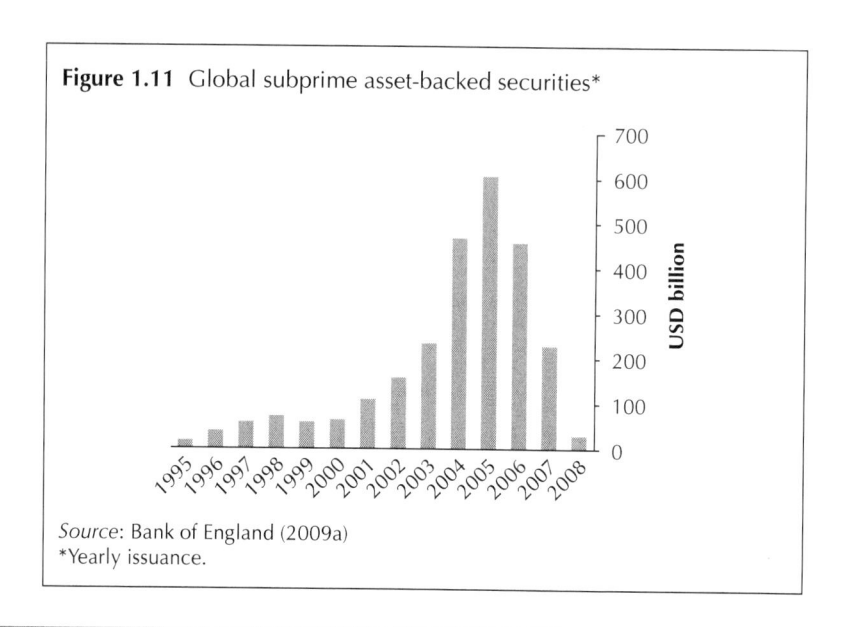

Figure 1.11 Global subprime asset-backed securities*

Source: Bank of England (2009a)
*Yearly issuance.

Figure 1.12 Sovereign debt*

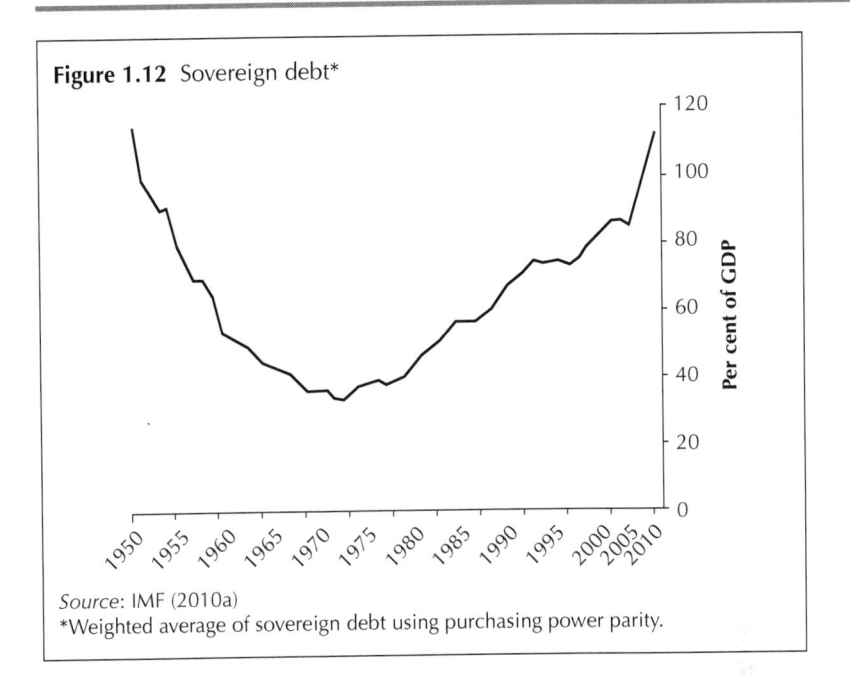

Source: IMF (2010a)
*Weighted average of sovereign debt using purchasing power parity.

fragile status of the safety net was unable to provide the financial system with enough cushions to absorb the losses originated in this sector. But this was just one dimension of the problem. On the real side of the economy, households and firms were unprotected from the amplification effects of such a systemic shock. There were failures in the dual task described by Gieve (2009): managers and investors failed at "protecting the banks from the cycle" and regulators failed at "protecting the cycle from the banks". If the former refers to the need for a safety net, the latter relates to the necessity of policy instruments to mitigate the potential adverse effects of financial amplifiers.

Conceptually, the persistence and amplification of shocks that affect financial systems depend on the state of the macroeconomy. The impact of aggregate shocks on the economy will be more severe in the presence of global imbalances, distortions in the yield-curve and credit market frictions. All these elements were present when the world's largest economies were hit by the shock in the subprime sector.

❏ Global imbalances: The flow of funds coming from China, Japan and other surplus economies distorted the usual transmission

Figure 1.13 Nominal official interest rates

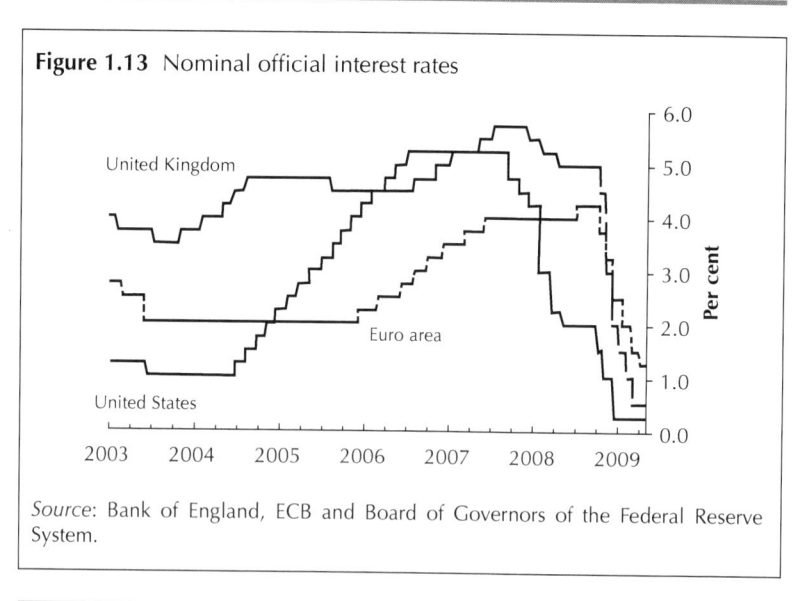

Source: Bank of England, ECB and Board of Governors of the Federal Reserve System.

Figure 1.14 Long-term versus short-term real interest rates

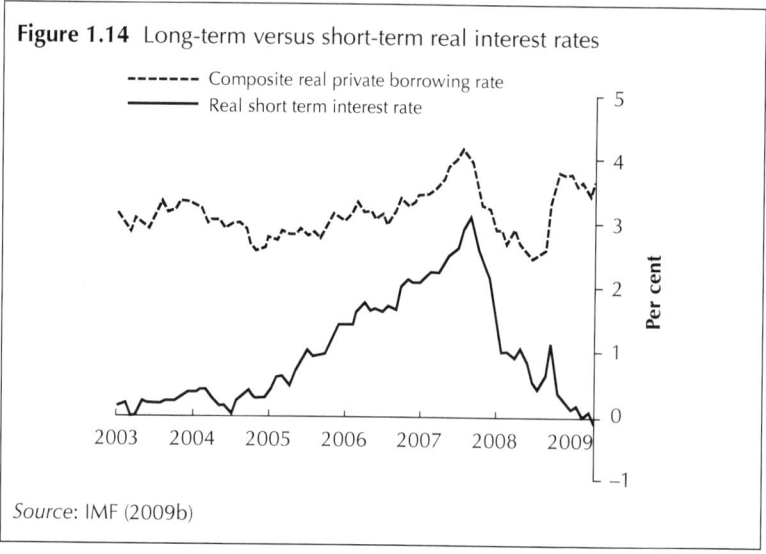

Source: IMF (2009b)

mechanism of monetary policy in the US, UK, EU and other deficit economies. Such savings had created a growing demand for assets supported by governments in developed economies, including both sovereign bonds and asset-backed by governmental guarantees (Figure 1.12).

❑ Yield-curve distortions: The world's economy was exposed to a prolonged period of low interest rates that fuelled an excessive supply of credit. When central bankers attempted to correct these trends (Figure 1.13), they found that the usual transmission mechanism did not work. Despite the increase in short-term interest rates, long-term interest rates remained unaltered (Figure 1.14) and the lending supply continued its spiral of excessive growth.

❑ Credit cyclicality: The possibility of default imposes constraints on the terms of lending (eg, collateral requirements and rating limits). These constraints produce cyclicality in the supply of lending as adverse shocks will reduce the value of borrowers' collateral and raise the number of rating downgrades, which in turn will tighten credit standards (Figures 1.15 and 1.16).

There are various views on how these factors were interconnected. For instance, Bernanke (2005) and King (2011) argue the distortion in the yield curve occurred because of excessive savings from surplus countries flowing into deficit countries. Alternatively, Schiller (2000, 2008) considers that such a distortion occurred because market participants suffered from "irrational exuberance", so they believed the upswing would continue for ever.

But the ability to identify these imbalances, distortions and

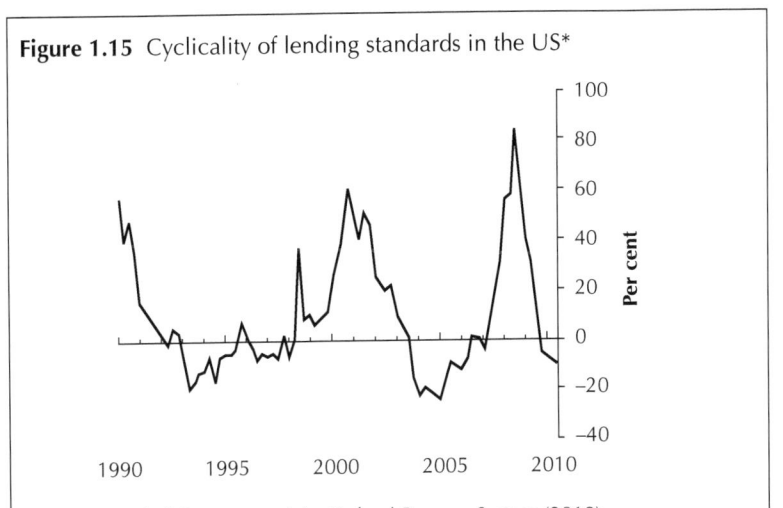

Figure 1.15 Cyclicality of lending standards in the US*

Source: Board of Governors of the Federal Reserve System (2010)
*The series corresponds to the percentage of a sample of banks operating in the US that tighten standards for commercial and industrial loans to large and medium-sized firms.

Figure 1.16 Lending to the private sector*

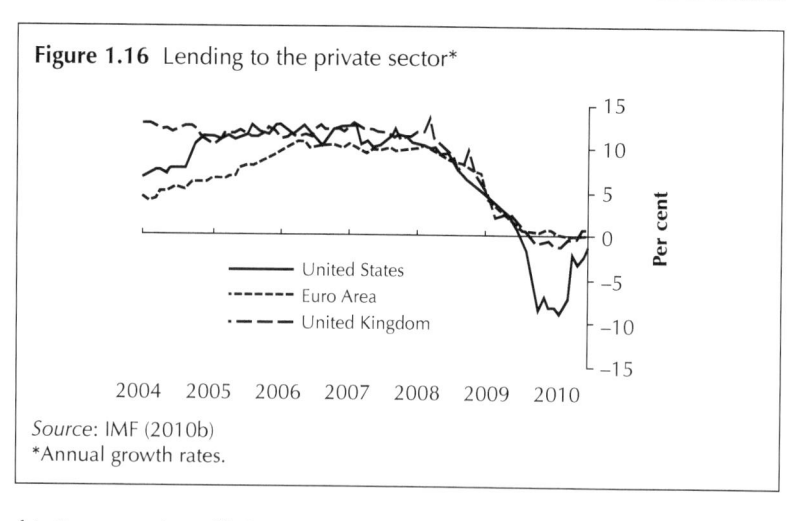

Source: IMF (2010b)
*Annual growth rates.

frictions was insufficient, since neither regulators nor central bankers had policy instruments to mitigate the effects of such distortions. It is unclear whether prudent banking rules and conventional monetary policies would have been enough to dampen the cyclicality of the lending supply.[19]

1.3 DYNAMICS OF THE CRISIS: 2007–2008

This section describes how the fragility of the safety net and the occurrence of a systemic shock turned into a systemic crisis. At the end of 2006, major institutions in the US, UK and EU were vulnerable to losses that were going to occur between 2007 and 2009. Figure 1.17 shows that capital surpluses above the minimum ranged from 3% to 7% of risk-weighted assets, while losses to be realised varied from 7% to 15% of risk-adjusted assets. The limited amounts of capital buffers reported as of the end of 2006 were inadequate to resist losses above 7% of total risk-weighted assets. At the start of 2007, the largest financial firms were indeed fragile.

The financial turmoil of 2007 and 2008 occurred in at least three stages: the systemic shock (from early 2007 to the collapse of Lehman Brothers); the panic of autumn 2008; and the recapitalisation at the end of 2008. Each stage implied a combination of public and private reactions that sought to restore the strength of the safety net.

Figure 1.17 Pre-crisis capital adequacy

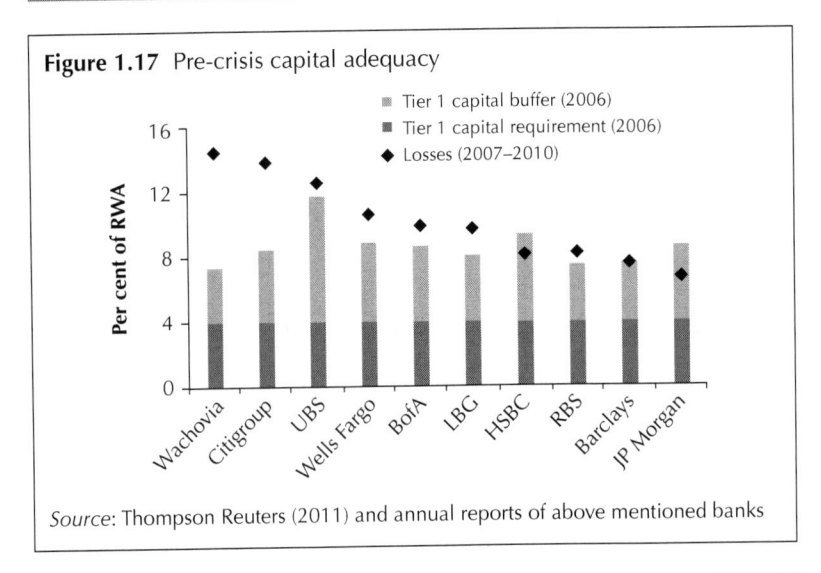

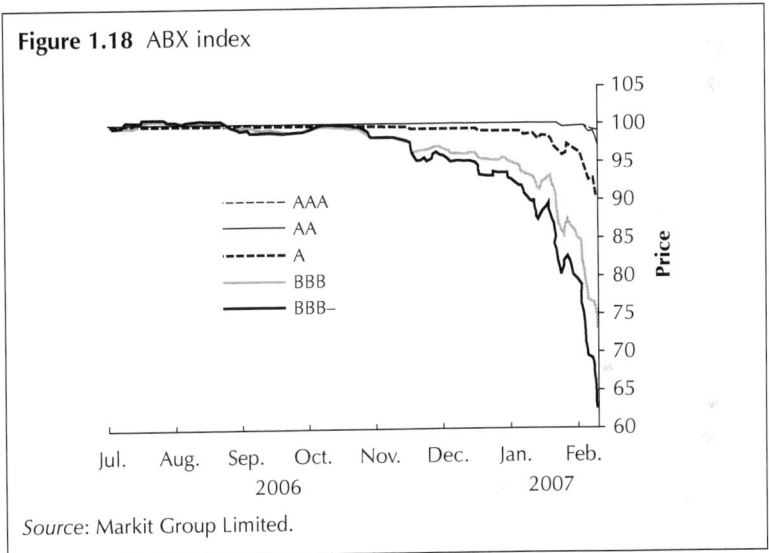

Legend:
- Tier 1 capital buffer (2006)
- Tier 1 capital requirement (2006)
- Losses (2007–2010)

Banks (x-axis): Wachovia, Citigroup, UBS, Wells Fargo, BofA, LBG, HSBC, RBS, Barclays, JP Morgan

Y-axis: Per cent of RWA

Source: Thompson Reuters (2011) and annual reports of above mentioned banks

Figure 1.18 ABX index

Series: AAA, AA, A, BBB, BBB–

X-axis: Jul. – Feb. 2006–2007
Y-axis: Price (60–105)

Source: Markit Group Limited.

1.3.1 The systemic shock

Subprime losses built up slowly from January 2007 to the end of 2009. The process of loss crystallisation started with a series of reports that predicted write-offs followed by announcements that confirmed such predictions. By June 2008, the balance sheets of small money market funds, monoline insurers (ie, insurers that guarantee the repayment of bonds), and small and large banks were all exposed to subprime losses. This subsection covers the first reactions from both private and public sector to the long chain of announcements of credit and market losses related to subprime operations. It also highlights the first public interventions aimed at protecting depositors and creditors. Panel 1.2 summarises the timeline of loss announcements during this crisis.

1.3.1.1 Crystallisation of losses

The subprime shock started with early announcements of larger-than-expected defaults in subprime mortgages. In February 2007, HSBC was the first large and internationally active bank that reported that its subprime mortgage portfolio showed delinquencies of US$10.5 billion. But subprime losses (ie, write-offs of subprime assets) were no news. At the end of March 2007, more than 50 small non-bank mortgage lenders in the US had collapsed due to subprime losses.[20]

During the first half of 2007, similar reports had been issued by Bear Stearns and IKB Deutsche Industriebank, which then were followed by a series of market reports that anticipated significant charge-offs (ie, provisions for losses) of subprime assets and subsequent falls in profitability rates. That period also coincided with the introduction of Markit's ABX.HE index: a synthetic credit default price index referencing a basket of 20 subprime mortgage-related securities. This simple statistical device exacerbated the demand for information on the value of collateralised debt obligations, revealing to their subscribers a fall in every segment of these asset-backed securities (Figure 1.18).

This first stage of the crisis also observed profit cut announcements from the largest international banks. Citigroup, Merrill Lynch and UBS were the first banks announcing severe write-downs and quarterly losses by the end of 2007. Their warnings were followed, from January to June 2008, by loss recognitions made by Société Générale, Credit Suisse, Morgan Stanley and Lehman Brothers.

By mid-2008, the bad news had moved towards the monoline sector, a segment of the insurance industry that provided guarantees to bonds and securities backed by mortgages. And in August 2008 Fannie Mae and Freddie Mac, two US government-sponsored entities aimed at providing funds to mortgages lenders, announced larger-than-expected quarterly losses, after a long period of increasing credit spreads (Figure 1.19).

Figure 1.19 Credit default spreads of government-sponsored enterprises*

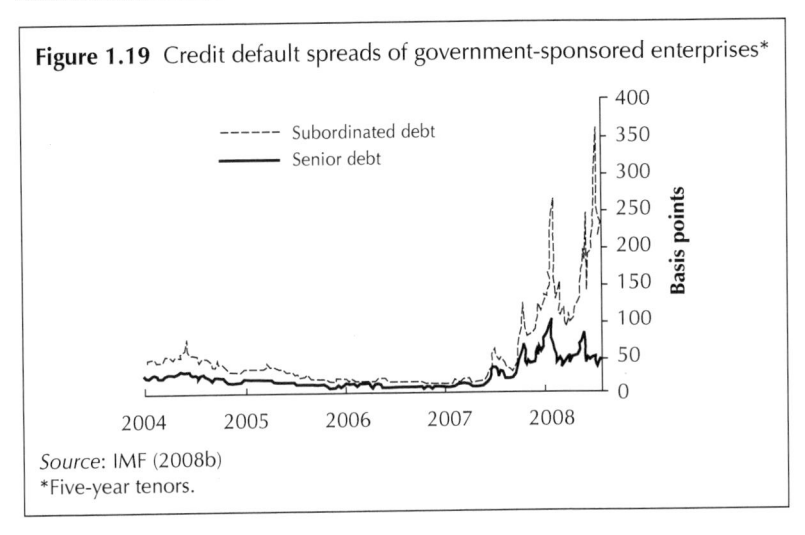

Source: IMF (2008b)
*Five-year tenors.

Figure 1.20 Libor to Overnight Index Swap spreads

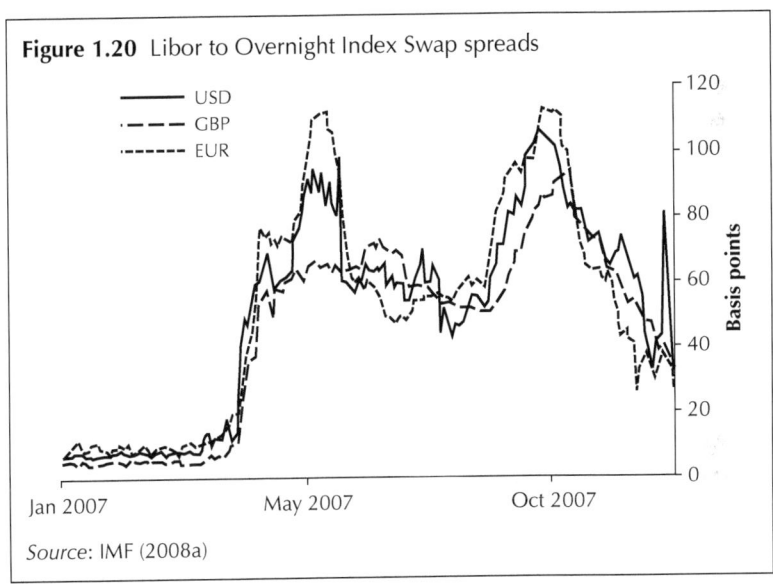

Source: IMF (2008a)

Overall, by mid-2008, the world's 10 largest financial institutions had accumulated subprime losses of US$490 billion. The losses for the 30 largest firms summed up to US$790 billion by the end of 2008 and mushroomed to over US$1.2 trillion by mid-2010.

1.3.1.2 Rescue of depositors

Despite all these announcements and reports, the subprime losses were not translated into dividend cuts. The largest banks continued releasing dividends and there was no evidence of coupon cancellations or payment deferrals. The lack of loss absorbency (ie, the ability to suspend the release of dividends or coupons) was also evident from the calls of hybrid instruments with incentives to redeem.[21] The immediate effect of such payments was a further reduction in the volume of liquid assets and capital buffers below the levels observed previously.

But the "timely payment" of dividends and coupons did not prevent investors from flying out of the institutions most exposed to subprime mortgages. Such withdrawal of funds caused a severe shortage of liquidity in August 2007, which easily spilled over into interbank markets (Figure 1.20).

The shortage of liquidity was evident in both Europe and the US and required consecutive liquidity injections of €156 billion from the European Central Bank (ECB) and US$60 billion from the Fed. These decisions were followed by a 50-basis-point reduction in the discount window interest rate of the Fed and an extension of the range of reserve targets set by the Bank of England.

Liquidity problems associated with investors' concerns about the effect of bad mortgages did not affect only small firms. In September 2007, Northern Rock, the fifth largest bank in the UK, and

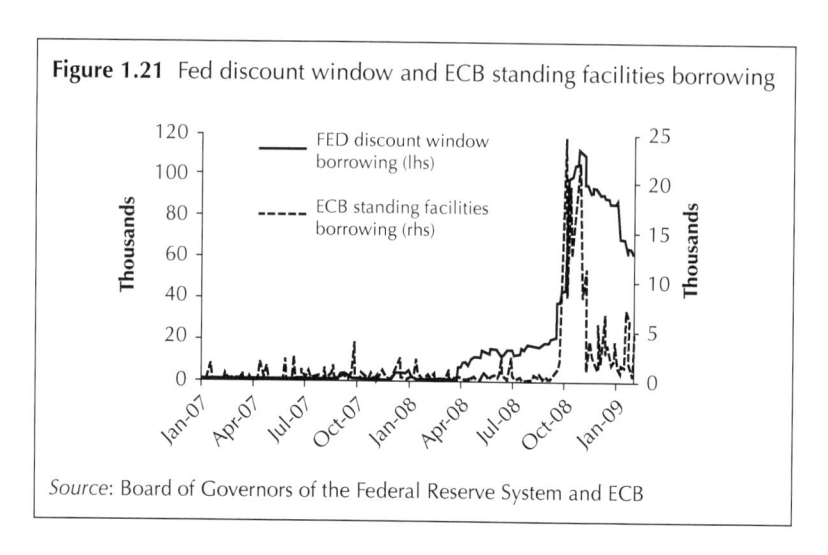

Figure 1.21 Fed discount window and ECB standing facilities borrowing

Source: Board of Governors of the Federal Reserve System and ECB

Figure 1.22 Write-offs and capital injections

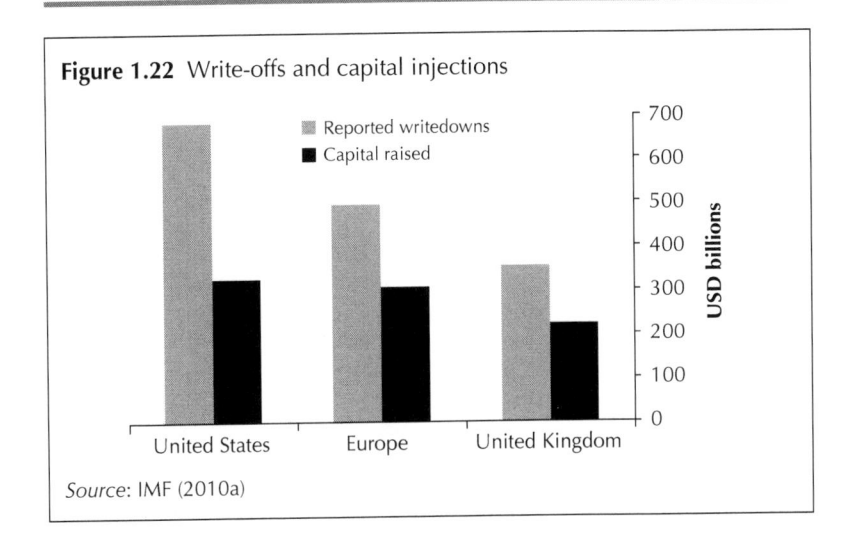

- Reported writedowns
- Capital raised

Source: IMF (2010a)

Countrywide, the largest mortgage lender in the US, suffered retail deposit runs that required rapid assistance from the Bank of England and the Fed, respectively. Such loans of last resort were followed by the announcement of a governmental unlimited guarantee for existing deposits in the case of Northern Rock.

The demand for public liquidity assistance continued during this period. By the end of 2007, the Bank of England, the Fed, the ECB and the Swiss National Bank (SNB) announced measures designed to tackle these short-term funding pressures. In April 2008 the Bank of England launched the Special Liquidity Scheme to allow banks to swap high-quality mortgage-backed securities for UK treasury bills. In May 2008, the Fed, the ECB and the SNB announced coordinated additional measures to provide further liquidity and ensure depositors' protection (Figure 1.21).

PANEL 1.2 SUBPRIME LOSSES

The following list summarises the main announcements of subprime losses either incurred or anticipated between March 2007 and August 2008.[22]

- ❏ March 5, 2007: HSBC reported they found evidence that one of their subprime mortgages portfolios evidenced delinquency rates that were higher than expected.

↓

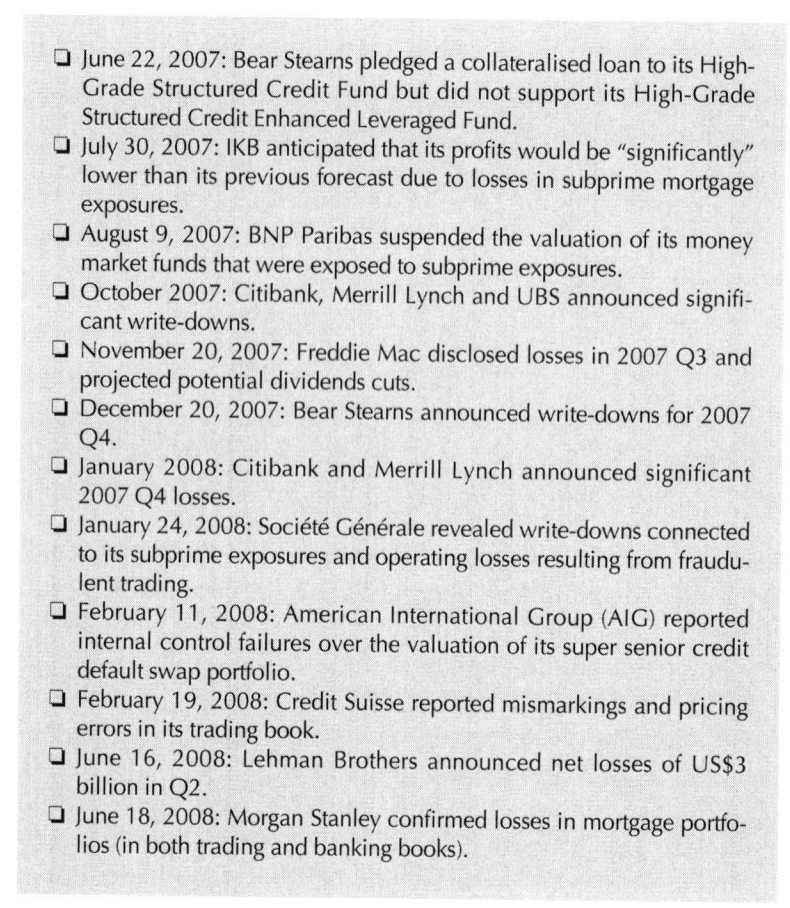

- ❏ June 22, 2007: Bear Stearns pledged a collateralised loan to its High-Grade Structured Credit Fund but did not support its High-Grade Structured Credit Enhanced Leveraged Fund.
- ❏ July 30, 2007: IKB anticipated that its profits would be "significantly" lower than its previous forecast due to losses in subprime mortgage exposures.
- ❏ August 9, 2007: BNP Paribas suspended the valuation of its money market funds that were exposed to subprime exposures.
- ❏ October 2007: Citibank, Merrill Lynch and UBS announced significant write-downs.
- ❏ November 20, 2007: Freddie Mac disclosed losses in 2007 Q3 and projected potential dividends cuts.
- ❏ December 20, 2007: Bear Stearns announced write-downs for 2007 Q4.
- ❏ January 2008: Citibank and Merrill Lynch announced significant 2007 Q4 losses.
- ❏ January 24, 2008: Société Générale revealed write-downs connected to its subprime exposures and operating losses resulting from fraudulent trading.
- ❏ February 11, 2008: American International Group (AIG) reported internal control failures over the valuation of its super senior credit default swap portfolio.
- ❏ February 19, 2008: Credit Suisse reported mismarkings and pricing errors in its trading book.
- ❏ June 16, 2008: Lehman Brothers announced net losses of US$3 billion in Q2.
- ❏ June 18, 2008: Morgan Stanley confirmed losses in mortgage portfolios (in both trading and banking books).

1.3.1.3 Rescue of creditors

The liquidity crisis in late 2007 was the consequence of fundamental problems that became obvious in early 2008, when central banks and governments realised that the major financial institutions in their jurisdictions required significant recapitalisations. The goal of such capital injections was to prevent future write-offs from eroding the precarious capital buffers, triggering a chain of resolutions. But these capital injections were accompanied by public statements indicating that only creditors, not shareholders, should be rescued if public capital injections were necessary.

The initial attempts to recapitalise banks were a combination of modest private capitalisation efforts, sponsored acquisitions and nationalisations.

- Modest capitalisations: These include capital injections made by investors of Citigroup in January 2008 (US$14.5 billion), HBOS and the Royal Bank of Scotland (RBS) in April 2008 (£16 billion), Barclays in June 2008 (£15 billion) and the small rise of US$4 billion of convertible preferred stock made by Lehman Brothers in March 2008.
- Sponsored acquisitions: This comprises the acquisition of Bear Stearns by JP Morgan in March 2008; the takeover of Washington Mutual, also acquired by JP Morgan in September 2008; the sale of Merrill Lynch to Bank of America in November 2008; the absorption of Wachovia by Wells Fargo in December 2008; and in Europe the acquisition of HBOS by Lloyds TSB in September 2008, which formed the Lloyds Banking Group (LBG).
- Partial and temporary nationalisation: This includes the US federal government decision to place Fannie Mae and Freddie Mac in conservatorship in September 2008 and the UK Treasury decision to inject up to £37 billion of new capital to RBS, Lloyds and HBOS in October 2008.[23]

All these efforts had two common features. First, they were aimed at protecting creditors rather than shareholders. Post-crisis, equity investors either absorbed losses or were wound up. Second, these efforts resulted in a temporary increase in capital buffers, which provided an ephemeral calm in financial markets. The remaining losses that occurred in the autumn of 2008 rapidly depleted these insufficient buffers (Figure 1.22).

1.3.2 The Panic of 2008
In spring 2008 most banks observed that expected losses exceeded their initial level of capital reserves. Many banks would have triggered the point of intervention without some form of capital injection. In some cases, public and private aid was received opportunely. In other cases, investors fled abruptly before their financial institutions could recapitalise. That was the case for Lehman Brothers, whose failure initiated an episode of financial panic that spread rapidly and globally.

1.3.2.1 The collapse of Lehman Brothers

The historic case of Lehman Brothers illustrates the mechanical sequence of loss crystallisation, capital erosion and bankruptcy procedures in the case of a financial firm that is severely undercapitalised.

In 2007 Lehman Brothers had just US$25 billion of capital to finance US$700 billion of assets (Valukas 2010). The difference was funded mainly through short-term liabilities, particularly repo transactions (ie, sales of collateral with a promise of repurchase). Moreover, Lehman's business model allowed using the liquidity obtained from these operations to expand – even after the start of the crisis – its already significant exposures in subprime assets.

The stressed market conditions that preceded the sale of Bear Stearns and the crystallisation of losses that occurred in the summer of 2008 affected any attempt from Lehman's management to obtain more liquidity and capital, raising serious concerns about the viability of the firm.

During its last six months, the investment bank had failed in a series of attempts to attract fresh capital from internal and external investors. Between April and September 2008, Bank of America, Barclays, Korea Development Bank, Goldman Sachs and Morgan Stanley were among the institutions that rejected the possibility of a privately funded recapitalisation.

The prospects for public capital injections were also unfavourable. From the beginning of the crisis until September 2008, the US Treasury had operated under the assumption that banks should dilute the value of their investors' equity shares (ie, shareholders should be "winded-up") in order to receive public capital. Even the decision to place Fannie Mae and Freddie Mac in conservatorship was an example of public rescue operations focused on creditors' rather than shareholders' interests. The combination of Lehman management's reluctance to accept a winding-up scenario for its investors and the fact that the Fed did not have the authority to provide capital or unsecured guarantees[24] did prevent a solution based on either private or public capital injections.[25] Then, on September 9, 2008, Lehman Brothers announced quarterly losses and six days later the emblematic investment firm filed for bankruptcy.

Figure 1.23 Money market funds assets

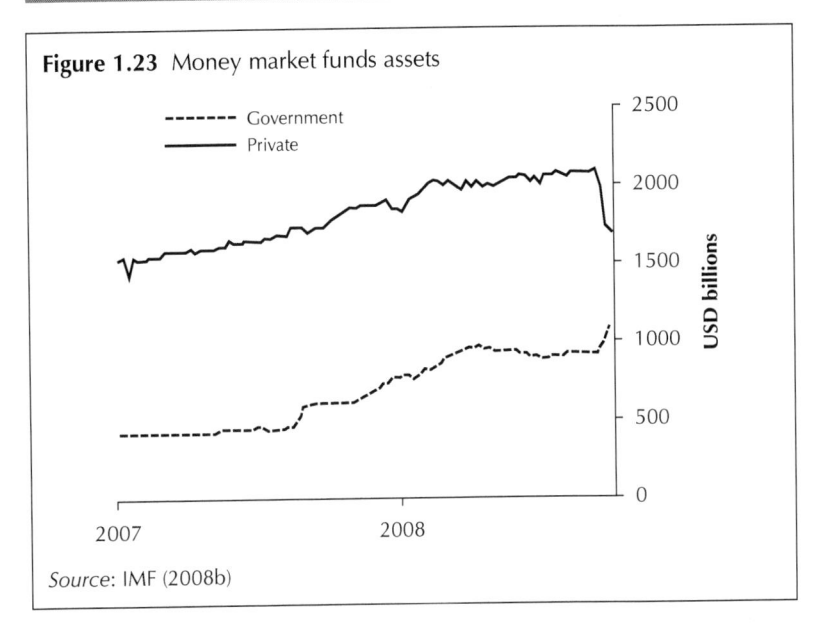

Source: IMF (2008b)

Figure 1.24 Outstanding amounts of US commercial paper issuance

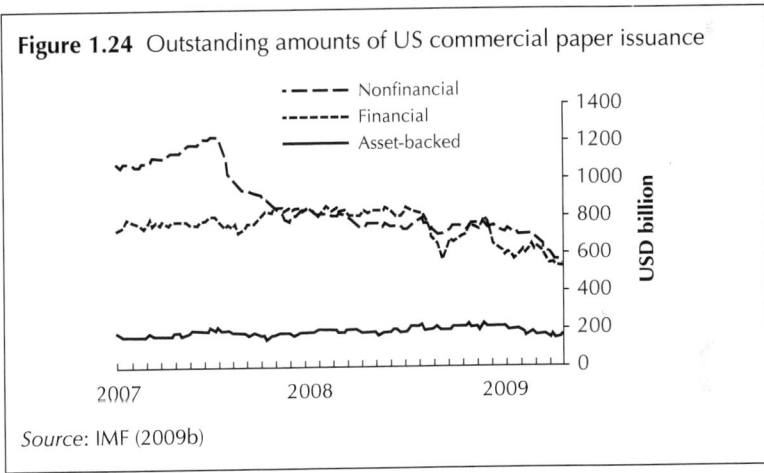

Source: IMF (2009b)

1.3.2.2 The systemic crisis

The immediate effect of the failure of Lehman Brothers was a run on money market funds, which triggered the subsequent collapse of both commercial debt and interbank markets internationally.

❏ Run on money market funds: Immediately after the collapse of Lehman Brothers, shareholders of these funds withdrew over US$500 billion. In just three days, the outflow reached 25% of

these funds (Figure 1.23) whose portfolios comprised securities issued by high-quality firms and banks (the so-called "prime" funds).
- ❏ Run on short-term debt instruments: The next episode of the systemic crisis was the rapid liquidation of US$200 billion of short-term commercial paper (Figure 1.24) and repo instruments. Most of these sales were led by money market funds that required cash to repay their obligations.
- ❏ Run on interbank markets: The limited ability to issue commercial paper with maturities beyond 4–8 days (Figure 1.25) led to the collapse of corporate borrowing and triggered several runs on bank deposits and corporate credit lines. First small firms and then large corporations sought immediate access to liquidity to the "fullest extent possible"[26] at the same time as bank funds were experiencing shortages.

Money market fund investors and short-term debt markets were the vehicles through which the systemic crisis affected interbank markets, but they were not the cause of the crisis. The fundamental reasons behind why the collapse of individual institutions had turned into a systemic crisis include not only the damages in the

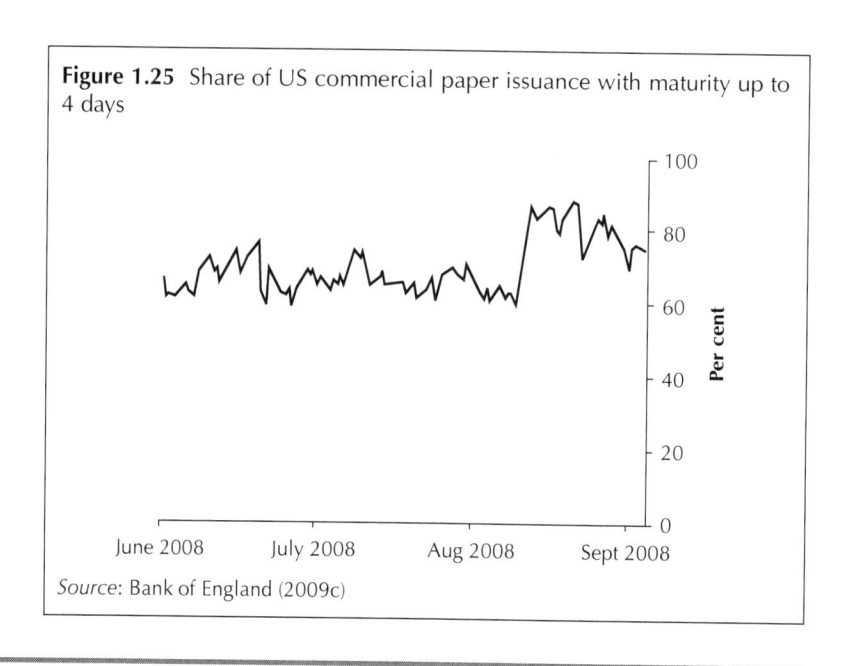

Figure 1.25 Share of US commercial paper issuance with maturity up to 4 days

Source: Bank of England (2009c)

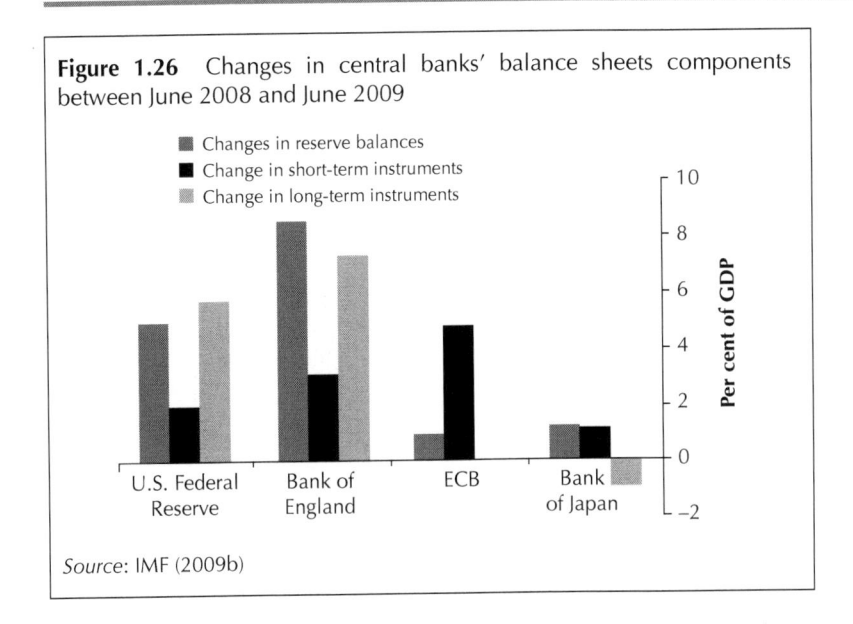

Figure 1.26 Changes in central banks' balance sheets components between June 2008 and June 2009

- Changes in reserve balances
- Change in short-term instruments
- Change in long-term instruments

Per cent of GDP

U.S. Federal Reserve, Bank of England, ECB, Bank of Japan

Source: IMF (2009b)

safety net that should ordinarily cushion credit shocks but also global imbalances and credit frictions that amplified the subprime losses into a system-wide shock. All of these failures forced national authorities to explore radical policies to restore market confidence, including options such as public capital injections and direct lending to the private sector.

1.3.3 The restoration of market confidence

The extension of liquidity facilities to non-bank financial institutions was the initial form of public intervention to stop the shortage of funds exacerbated by the systemic crisis. By the end of September 2008, the US government allowed the transformation of investment firms into banks. The conversions of Goldman Sachs and Morgan Stanley into supervised entities allow them to access public funds. These measures were supplemented with unconventional monetary injections to non-bank financial firms, including a US$85 billion credit facility for AIG in exchange for an 80% stake.

This subsection describes how national authorities prevented a further deterioration in market confidence by restoring the main components of the safety net. The set of policy measures included public provision of liquidity, equity capital and credit risk insurance. Ultimately, it also required direct lending to the non-financial sector.

Figure 1.27 Government-guaranteed and non-guaranteed bonds issuance in matured markets

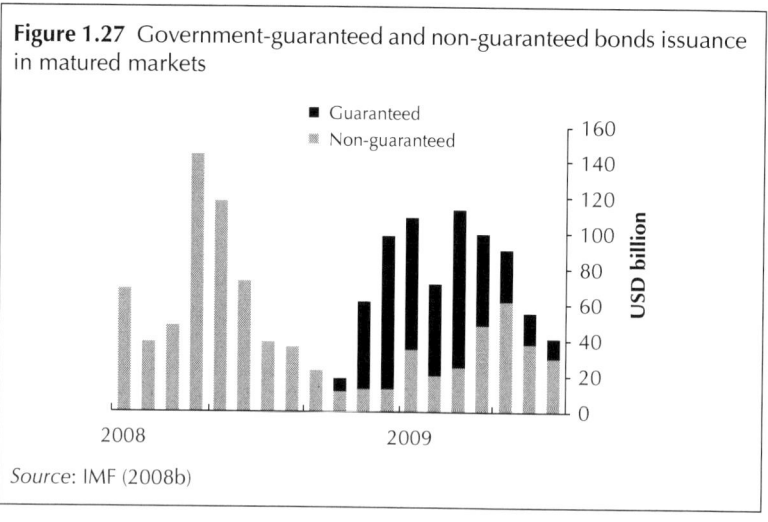

Source: IMF (2008b)

Figure 1.28 Public interventions* in the US and UK as a percent of GDP**

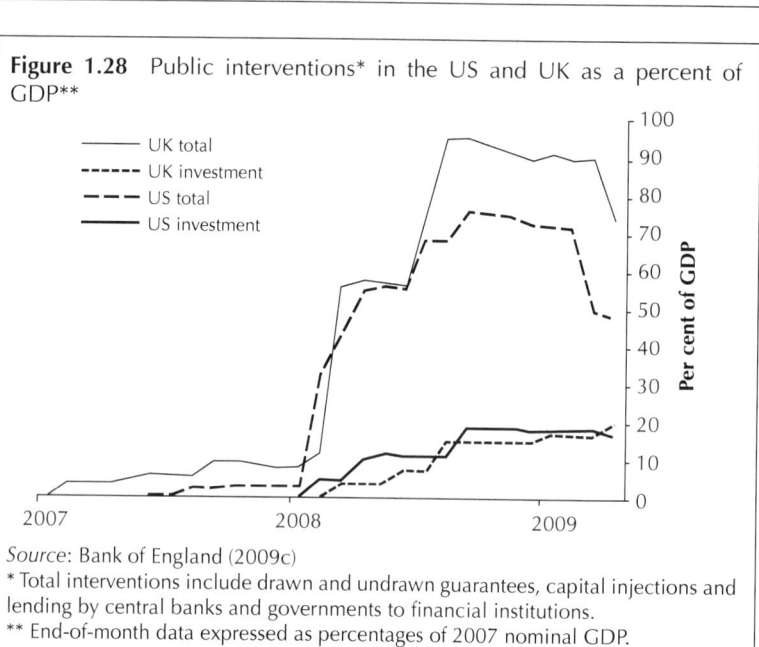

Source: Bank of England (2009c)
* Total interventions include drawn and undrawn guarantees, capital injections and lending by central banks and governments to financial institutions.
** End-of-month data expressed as percentages of 2007 nominal GDP.

1.3.3.1 Rescue of bank shareholders

While the provision of vast amounts of liquidity restarted the functioning of interbank operations, it did not reverse the stress observed in other financial markets. In early October 2008, both the US and the UK treasuries introduced measures to provide banks with credit risk insurance through governmental guarantee programmes.[27] These programmes effectively reactivated the issuance of corporate debt (Figure 1.27), which recovered their pre-crisis levels in early 2009.

In terms of capital requirements, the provision of public credit insurance implied an artificial reallocation towards safer assets. Loans guaranteed by the government could be classified as "sovereign exposures" under the so-called substitution approach[28] of the capital framework. The result was an opportune reduction in the value of banks' risk-weighted assets and the subsequent decrease in their capital requirements.

These interventions did not impose constraints to shareholders' interests. In contrast, they provided liquid resources and reduced capital charges, allowing shareholders to release dividends and increase payout ratios just after the worst financial crisis since the Great Depression.[29]

1.3.3.2 Rescue of non-bank shareholders

The artificial reallocation of portfolios created by governmental guarantees was followed by further measures aimed at minimising the impact on the real sector. The collapse of the market for commercial paper pushed highly rated firms to use their credit lines and revolving credit facilities to obtain more funds. This reaction reduced the availability of new lending to other firms. Ivashina and Scharfstein (2010) analyse this crowding-out effect and reported a significant fall in the flow of new productive[30] loans between August and October 2008.

The use of unconventional liquidity lines for non-financial firms was seen as a necessary remedy to mitigate this type of secondary effect. The introduction in the US of the Term Asset-Backed Securities Loan Facilities programme (TALF), with resources of US$1 trillion, and the announcement in the UK of the Asset Purchase Scheme, with an initial £175 billion credit line, initiated a series of unconventional measures (known as credit easing) aimed at providing funds to both banks and the real economy (Figure 1.28). In May 2009, the ECB introduced a similar programme, which offered €60 billion.

Acharya *et al* (2011) highlight that between 2007 and 2008 the 25 largest financial firms raised US$238 billion of common equity and reported US$1,146 billion of incurred losses. The need for additional capital injections promoted the creation of the Troubled Asset Relief Program (TARP) in October 2008. TARP provided US$700 billion of public funds to corporations and banks (which used half of these funds). By the end of 2009, 686 US financial institutions had received funds from TARP.

It was the combination of all these factors – as well as the measures described in previous sections – that finally contained the financial turmoil. In February 2009, the Fed conducted a comprehensive stress test for the major US financial institutions (including investment banks that had recently joined the list of supervised institutions). The results of the Supervisory Capital Assessment Program (SCAP) showed that most of the largest US financial firms had held enough capital buffers to absorb stressed losses under a hypothetical adverse scenario (Figure 1.29). One year later a similar exercise conducted by the Committee of European Banking Supervision (CEBS) also suggested that the largest banks in Europe had a sufficient amount of capital cushions (Figure 1.30).

Although this event can be referred to as the end of the period known as the big financial crisis, the negative effects of the crisis did

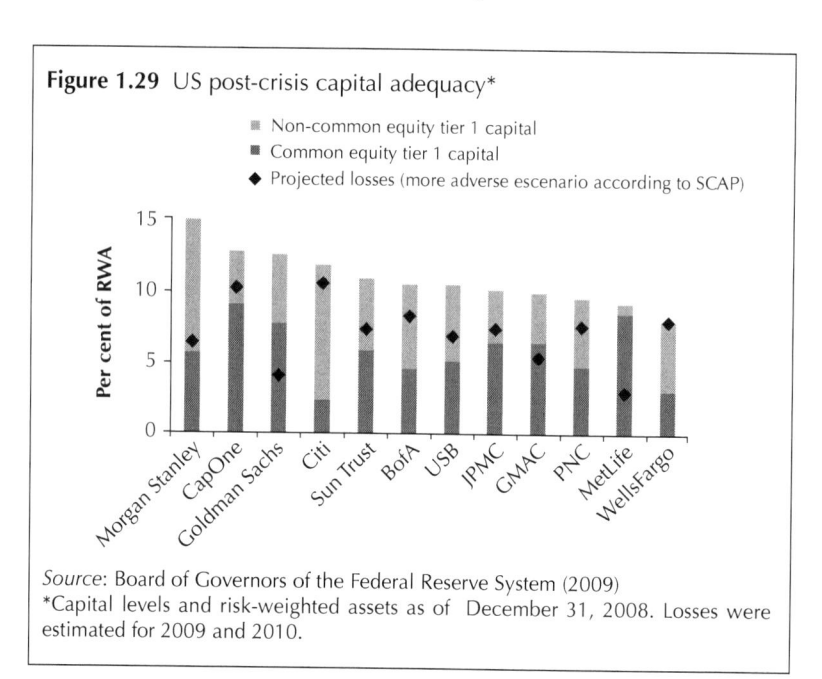

Figure 1.29 US post-crisis capital adequacy*

- Non-common equity tier 1 capital
- Common equity tier 1 capital
- ◆ Projected losses (more adverse escenario according to SCAP)

Source: Board of Governors of the Federal Reserve System (2009)
*Capital levels and risk-weighted assets as of December 31, 2008. Losses were estimated for 2009 and 2010.

Figure 1.30 EU post-crisis capital adequacy*

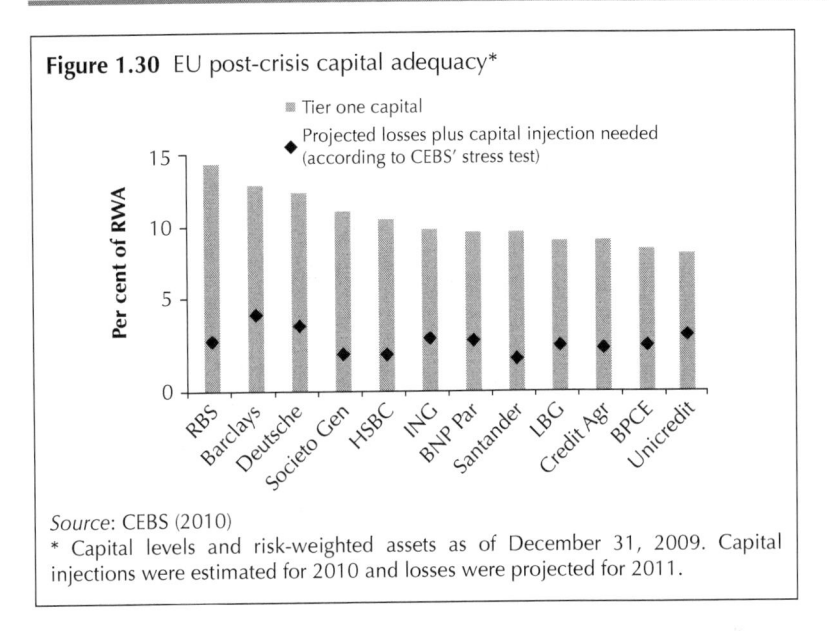

Source: CEBS (2010)
* Capital levels and risk-weighted assets as of December 31, 2009. Capital injections were estimated for 2010 and losses were projected for 2011.

not stop at that point. In fact, the crisis continued to affect the real side of the global economy for several years. The financial turmoil of 2007 and 2008 reversed the trends of global GDP and initiated a deep credit cycle that is now described as the Great Recession.[31]

1.4 CONCLUSIONS

Through an analysis of both the financial practices that contributed to the financial turmoil and their macroeconomic context, this chapter discussed the origins and dynamics of the financial crisis of 2007 and 2008.

When the genesis of the crisis is scrutinised, it becomes clear that the rapid deterioration of the different components of the safety net, coupled with the increasing prominence of global imbalances and the crystallisation of subprime losses, led to a global systemic crisis. The crisis was rooted in two different but intertwined factors. First, the fragility of the safety net – driven by different forms of regulatory arbitrage and forbearance – set up a scenario of financial market deregulation. Second, the aggregate nature of the subprime shock, which rapidly evolved from a sectoral problem to a systemic phenomenon due to a series of imbalances and distortions, as well as a lack of policy tools to minimise the effects.

An analysis of the dynamics of the crisis identified three different stages that began in 2007 and came to an end in 2009: the period covered by consecutive write-downs and losses reports; the interim stage that observed the collapse of Lehman Brothers and the subsequent systemic crisis triggered by runs on money market funds; and finally the process of restoration of market confidence through a series of attempts to protect depositors, creditors and ultimately shareholders.

This chapter has emphasised the evolution of the objectives of public intervention throughout these stages of the crisis: from the initial intention to rescue depositors and creditors through the public provision of liquidity facilities to the final goal of ensuring a stable supply of credit to the real economy. Ultimately, this objective justified the introduction of unconventional policies such as governmental guarantees and credit easing. In the longer run, a comprehensive reform of financial regulation has been started. The following chapters describe the outcome of this process.

ANNEX 1: (LACK OF) EVIDENCE OF LOSS ABSORPTION

An analysis of the dividend history of the largest US banks between January 2007 and December 2009 reveals there was limited evidence of loss absorption in capital instruments issued by financial institutions in the US. The following tables show that dividends cuts were few and late, with mandatory coupon deferrals imposed by the US Treasury as a part of TARP.

Table 1.A covers those firms that have received more than US$10 billion through the capital purchase programme (CPP) – one of the specific components of TARP. Table 1.B includes other (non-bank) financial institutions (such as AIG, Freddie Mac and Fannie Mae), recent mergers and acquisitions and also a couple of failed banks.

Before the implementation of TARP (October 2008), no major US bank cancelled, deferred or cut dividends for common equity; moreover, the largest US banks redeemed hybrid instruments (as defined in Subsection 1.2.1.2) on their earliest call dates. But at the end of 2008 the shareholders of Citigroup, Bank of America, Morgan Stanley and JP Morgan agreed to decrease their quarterly dividends by at least 50%, in order to meet the conditions imposed by the Treasury in order to access TARP funds.

The use of TARP funds imposed severe constraints on US banks' capital management. Banks under TARP were prohibited from repurchasing, redeeming or paying any dividend for common stock, other junior securities or preferred stock as long as accrued dividends for the capital funded via TARP needed to be paid.

These conditions did not prevent banks with access to TARP funds from continuing to pay out significant dividends (Acharya *et al* 2011), but provided these banks with strong incentives for an early repayment of capital issued via the TARP. On June 17, 2009, Morgan Stanley and JP Morgan redeemed their preferred shares funded with TARP. They were followed by Bank of America's decision to repay their preferred instruments and Citigroup's decision to raise common stock to repay the US$20 billion to the TARP fund.

Although all these redemptions and repayments were good news for US taxpayers, they allowed major US banks to release larger dividends and redeem their hybrid instruments, adversely affecting the prospects of capital conservation and the (necessary) boost in the level of capital reserves.

BASEL III AND BEYOND: A GUIDE TO BANKING REGULATION AFTER THE CRISIS

Table 1.A Dividend history of selected going-concern US financial institutions

Institutions		Period[a]	Core Tier 1	Hybrids			
				Preferred shares[b]	Innovative Tier 1	Upper Tier 2	Lower Tier 2
Banks under TARP	Citigroup	before TARP	still paid/redeemed				Citigroup agreed not to redeem the junior subordinated debt securities before 15/03/2057.
		after TARP	Citigroup agreed not to pay dividends above US$0.01 per share per quarter for 3 years (beginning in 2009).	In February 2009, Citigroup exchanged shares of new preferred stock for an equal number of shares of old preferred stock, which then was cancelled.			
	Wells Fargo	before and after TARP	still paid/redeemed				
	JP Morgan	before TARP		still paid/redeemed			
		from TARP to SCAP	JP Morgan reduced quarterly dividends from US$0.38 to US$0.05 per share, effective from 30/04/09.				
		after SCAP	On 17/06/09 JP Morgan repaid TARP funds				
	Bank of America (BoA)	before TARP	still paid/redeemed	still paid/redeemed			
		from TARP to SCAP	In October 2008, BofA reduced its quarterly cash dividends by 50%. In January 2009, it further reduced them to US$0.01 per share.				
		after SCAP	On 09/12/09 BoA repaid TARP funds				
	Morgan Stanley	before TARP	still paid/redeemed				
		from TARP to SCAP	Morgan Stanley agreed not to increase the current dividend (US$0.27) on its common stock as long as any preferred stock issued under TARP remains outstanding. Morgan Stanley was prohibited from repurchasing, redeeming or paying any dividend for common stock, other junior securities or preferred stock ranking equally with the Series D Preferred Stock unless all accrued and unpaid dividends for these series are paid.				
		after SCAP	On 17/06/09 Morgan Stanley paid TARP funds				
	Goldman Sachs	before and after TARP	still paid/redeemed (on 17/06/09 Goldman Sachs repaid TARP funds)				

Source: Annual reports of above mentioned institutions
(a) TARP was approved on 3 October 2008 and SCAP was released on 7 May 2009
(b) This includes trust preferred securities (TRUPS)

THE BIG FINANCIAL CRISIS

Table 1.B Dividend history of selected gone-concern and non-bank US financial institutions

Institutions		Period[a]	Core Tier 1[b]	Hybrids			
				Preferred shares[c]	Innovative Tier 1	Upper Tier 2	Lower Tier 2
Mergers and acquisitions	Bear Stearns (now JPMC)	until 30/05/2008		still paid/redeemed until acquisition			
	Merrill Lynch (now BoA)	until 1/1/2009					
	Washington Mutual (now JP Morgan)	until 25/09/2008					
	Wachovia (now Wells Fargo)	until 3,12/2008					
Closures	Indy Mac	until 11/07/2008	In September 2007, Indy Mac reduced its quarterly stock dividend from 0.50 to 0.25 per share.	still paid/redeemed until closure			
	Lehman Brothers	until 15/09/2008	Lehman cut dividend by 93% on 10/09/08.	still paid/redeemed until closure			
Non-banks under TARP	AIG	Before TARP		still paid/redeemed			
		After TARP		Suffered losses/cancellations of dividends		still paid/redeemed	
	Freddie Mac	Before TARP					
		After TARP					
	Fannie Mae	Before TARP					
		After TARP					

Source: Annual reports of above-mentioned institutions
(a) TARP was approved on October 3, 2008, and SCAP was released on May 7, 2009
(b) This includes cooperative shares in the case of a mutual
(c) This includes trust-preferred securities (TRUPS)

39

I am indebted to Tamiko Bayliss, José Berróspide, Charles Calomiris, Christian Castro, Victoria Ivashina, Alice Levick, Mario Quagliarello, Victoria Saporta and Jochen Schanz for their useful comments and suggestions on earlier drafts. The views expressed here are those of the author and not necessarily those of the Bank of England.

1. For instance, the "heat map" produced by the International Monetary Fund (IMF) (2010b) shows that, in certain markets, the period of excessive price volatility (greater than nine standard deviations) continued since March 2007 until late 2010. The Bank for International Settlements (2009) identifies five stages of the crisis, covering from June 2007 to mid-March 2009. The Bank of England (2009a) report the key events of the crisis occurred between spring 2007 and summer 2009.
2. Subprime assets not only comprise mortgage loans to borrowers with poor or bad credit records but also securities collateralised with these types of loan.
3. Kindleberger (1978) and Calomiris (2009) provide a comprehensive list of cases with the recurrent pattern of asset-price boom and bust. The crises of 1825, 1929 and 1999 are described by Neil (1998), Bernanke (2000) and Roubini and Setser (2004) respectively.
4. See, for instance, Admati *et al* (2010) or Calomiris (1999).
5. Regulatory capital comprises both equity and debt instruments that qualify as capital according to the regulator. It also includes reserves of retained earnings net of certain assets that – according to the regulator – are subject to uncertain valuation or double-counting of capital. These deducted assets are usually dubbed capital deductions.
6. Schanz *et al* (2011) estimate that a one-percentage-point reduction in the probability of crises leads to an annual benefit of between about 0.5% and 1.4% of GDP.
7. Based on the case of Japanese banks, Skinner (2008) found evidence that bank managers' estimates of profits were systematically optimistic, so deferred tax assets were overestimated. Moreover, his study reveals a negative correlation between these earnings forecast errors and banks' regulatory capital positions, suggesting managers of banks with the weakest capital positions were the most optimistic. Quoting the case of Countrywide, Gorton (2008) illustrates how mortgages servicing rights, a particular type of intangible asset in the US, suffered significant write-downs during the crisis.
8. There are several frictions that affect the Modigliani and Miller (1958, 1963) theorem where a firm's capital structure does not affect the value of its assets, so total funding costs remain unaltered. Such frictions could be corporate income taxes, bankruptcy costs or information asymmetries between managers and shareholders or between shareholders and bond holders.
9. Gertler (2010) stresses that the role of equity capital as a cushion for creditors is particularly relevant for banks. This is because information asymmetries and enforcement barriers between equity and debt holders are more severe in banking.
10. The procyclical evolution of the leverage ratio has been reported and analysed extensively. See, for instance, Adrian and Shin (2010), Brunnermeier (2009), Gorton and Metrick (2009), Geanakoplos (2010) and Acharya and Schnabal (2009).
11. Cornett and Tehranian (1994) provide further detail and evidence in the case of banks of New England during the 1990s.
12. The low price of debt was driven by the persistent inflows of capital caused by growing current account imbalances (a point to be discussed in Subsection 1.2.2).
13. Huizinga and Laeven (2009) provide evidence suggesting that banks used accounting discretion to overstate the book value of capital.
14. Fair value can be broadly defined as either the market value or the price at which willing and knowledgeable parties could trade an asset.
15. Enria *et al* (2004) describe these regulatory developments and the debate on fair-value accounting in the European Union.

16 Credit hedge funds are investments funds that buy collateralised debt obligations, which allow them to leverage up on the collateral to obtain additional liquidity.
17 Intervention regimes vary across jurisdictions. Some national authorities were more diligent than others in enforcing early capitalisations.
18 In 1998, the US Federal Reserve System (Fed) sponsored private capital injections to rescue banks from the Long Term Capital Management crisis. In 2000, when the dotcom bubble turned into a bust, the Fed provided banks with additional liquidity through interest-rate cuts. Whether these actions are instances of regulatory forbearance is subject to debate.
19 In Spain, dynamic provisioning rates would have needed to be much higher to smooth the supply of credit. In the UK, monetary policy would have needed to slow money spending in the economy, below levels consistent with meeting the inflation target in order to curb growth in banks' balance sheets (Bank of England 2009b).
20 The effects of the subprime crisis in Europe lagged those in the US. In September 2007 occurred the first failure of a UK mortgage company: the Victoria Mortgage Funding.
21 The Annex reports that there was limited evidence of loss absorption before the US public recapitalisation programme.
22 Based on Bank of England (2009a).
23 The inclusion of AIG in this group is subject to debate. The AIG case is briefly discussed in Subsection 1.3.3.
24 Bernanke (2010) indicates that the Fed understood the consequences of Lehman Brothers' failure but the only policy tools available at that time were short-term liquidity facilities against acceptable collateral.
25 The US supervisor of Lehman's core subsidiaries, the Securities and Exchange Commission (SEC), issued an emergency order to enhance investor protection against "naked short-selling", but this measure did not prevent the investment bank's failure.
26 Ivashina and Scharfstein (2010) quote this excerpt from the 8-K report of Dana Holding Corporation.
27 Similar measures had also been taken in the case of Hypo Real Estate, Dexia, Fortis, and Bradford and Bingley.
28 The substitution approach allows loans or other exposures guaranteed by third parties to attract the capital charge assigned to a direct claim on the guarantor.
29 See Figure 1.10.
30 Rather than synthetic conduits, these loans funded productive investments in physical and working capital.
31 See, for instance, Kiyotaki, Gertler and Queralto (2010).

REFERENCES

Acharya V., I. Gujral, N. Kulkarni and H. Song Shin, 2011, "Dividends and Bank Capital in the Financial Crisis of 2007–2009", National Bureau of Economic Research Working Paper No. 16896, Cambridge MA.

Acharya, V., and P. Schnabl, 2009, "How Banks Played the Leverage 'Game'?", *Financial Markets, Institutions and Instruments* 18, pp. 144–5.

Admati, A., et al, 2010, "Fallacies, Irrelevant Facts, and Myths in the Discussion of Capital Regulation: Why Bank Equity is Not Expensive", Rock Center for Corporate Governance at Stanford University Working Paper Series No. 86 and Stanford GSB Research Paper No. 2063, October.

Adrian, T., and H. S. Shin, 2009, "The Shadow Banking System: Implications for Financial Regulation", Federal Reserve Board of New York, Staff Report No. 382, July.

Adrian, T., and H. S. Shin, 2010, "Liquidity and leverage", *Journal of Financial Intermediation* 19(3), pp. 418–37, July.

Bank of England, 2008, "Financial Stability Report", London, October.

Bank of England, 2009a, "Financial Stability Report", London, June.

Bank of England, 2009b, "The role of macroprudential policy: a discussion paper", London, November.

Bank of England, 2009c, "Financial Stability Report", London, December.

Bank for International Settlements, 2009, "79th Annual Report: 1 April 2008–31 March 2009", Basel, June.

Bernanke, B., 2004, *Essays on the Great Depression* (Princeton, NJ: Princeton University Press).

Bernanke, B., 2005, "The Global Saving Glut and the US Current Account Deficit", speech delivered at the Sandridge Lecture, Virginia Association of Economists, Richmond, March.

Bernanke, B., 2010, "Lessons from the Failure of Lehman Brothers", testimony before the Committee on Financial Services, US House of Representatives, Washington, DC, April.

Berróspide, J., and R. Edge, 2010, "The Effects of Bank Capital on Lending: What Do We Know, and What Does It Mean?", *International Journal of Central Banking* 6(4), December.

Board of Governors of the Federal Reserve System, 2009, "The Supervisory Capital Assessment Program: Overview of Results", Washington, DC, May.

Board of Governors of the Federal Reserve System, 2010, "Senior Loan Officer Opinion Survey on Bank Lending Practices", Washington, DC, October.

Brunnermeier, M., 2009, "De-ciphering the credit crisis of 2007", *Journal of Economic Perspectives* 23(1), pp. 77–100.

Calomiris, C., 1999, "Building an incentive-compatible safety net", *Journal of Banking & Finance* 23(10), October.

Calomiris, C., 2009, "Banking Crises and the Rules of the Game", National Bureau of Economic Research Working Paper No. 15403.

Cavallo, M., and G. Majnoni, 2002, "Do banks provision for bad loans in good times?: Empirical evidence and policy implications", in R. Levich, G. Majnoni and C. Reinhart (eds), *Ratings, Rating Agencies and the Global Financial System* (Boston, MA: Kluwer Academic Publishers).

Cornett, M., and H. Tehranian, 1994, "An examination of voluntary versus involuntary security issuances by commercial banks: the impact of capital regulation on common stock returns", *Journal of Financial Economics* 35.

Council Directive 93/6/EEC on the capital adequacy of investments firms and credit institutions, 1993, Official Journal, Series L 141.

Dewatripont, M., and J. Tirole, 1994, *The Prudential Regulation of Banks* (Cambridge, MA: MIT Press).

Diamond, D., and P. Dybvig, 1983, "Bank Runs, Deposit Insurance and Liquidity", *Journal of Political Economy* 91.

Enria., A., *et al*, 2004, "Fair Value Accounting and Financial Stability", European Central Bank, Occasional Paper Series No. 13, April.

Fernández de Lis, S., J. Martínez Pagés and J. Saurina, 2000, "Credit Growth, Problem Loans and Credit Risk Provisioning in Spain", Bank of Spain Working Paper No 0018, October.

Geanakoplos, J., 2010, "The leverage cycle", in D. Acemoglu, K. Rogoff and M. Woodford (eds), *National Bureau of Economic Research Macroeconomics Annual*, 2009, *Volume 24* (Chicago: Chicago University Press).

Gertler, M., 2010, "Banking Crises and Real Activity: Identifying the Linkages", *International Journal of Central Banking* 6(4), December.

Gieve, J., 2009, "Seven lessons from the last three years", speech at the London School of Economics, London, February.

Gorton, G., 2008, "The Panic of 2007", Yale International Center for Finance, Working Paper No. 08–24, August.

Gorton, G., and A. Metrick, 2009, "Securitized Banking and the Run on Repo", National Bureau of Economic Research, Working Paper No. 15223.

Haldane, A., S. Brennan and V. Madouros, 2010, "The contribution of the financial sector – miracle or mirage?" in *The Future of Finance: The LSE Report* (London: London School of Economics and Political Science).

Huizinga, H., and L. Laeven, 2009, "Accounting Discretion of Banks During a Financial Crisis", IMF Working Paper No. 09/207.

International Monetary Fund, 2006, "Global Financial Stability Report: Market Developments and Issues", Washington, September.

International Monetary Fund, 2008a, "Global Financial Stability Report: Containing Systemic Risks and Restoring Financial Soundness", Washington, DC, April.

International Monetary Fund, 2008b, "Global Financial Stability Report: Financial Stress and Deleveraging Macro-Financial Implications and Policy", Washington, DC, October.

International Monetary Fund, 2009a, "Global Financial Stability Report: Responding to the Financial Crisis and Measuring Systemic Risks", Washington, DC, April.

International Monetary Fund, 2009b, "Global Financial Stability Report: Navigating the Financial Challenges Ahead", Washington, DC, October.

International Monetary Fund, 2010a, "Global Financial Stability Report: Meeting New Challenges to Stability and Building a Safer System", Washington DC, April.

International Monetary Fund, 2010b, "Global Financial Stability Report: Sovereigns, Funding, and Systemic Liquidity", Washington, DC, October.

Ivashina, V., and D. Scharfstein, 2010, "Bank Lending During the Financial Crisis of 2008", *Journal of Financial Economics* 94(3), September.

Kashyap., A., R. Rajan and J. Stein, 2008, "Rethinking Capital Regulation", Federal Reserve Bank of Kansas City, Economic Policy Symposium, pages 431–471.

Kindleberger, C., 1978, *Manias, Panics, and Crashes: A History of Financial Crises* (New York: Basic Books).

King, M., 2011, "Global imbalances: the perspective of the Bank of England", *Banque de France Financial Stability Review* (15), February.

Kiyotaki, N., M. Gertler and A. Queralto, 2010, "Financial Crises, Bank Risk Exposure and Government Financial Policy", manuscript.

Mayes, D. G., 2004, "The role of the safety net in resolving large financial institutions", in D. Evanoff and G. Kaufman (eds), *Systemic Financial Crises: Resolving Large Bank Insolvencies* (Chicago: Federal Reserve Bank of Chicago).

Modigliani, F., and M. Miller, 1958, "The cost of capital, corporation finance, and the theory of investment", *American Economic Review* 48(3).

Modigliani, F., and M. Miller, 1963, "Corporate income taxes and the cost of capital: A correction", *American Economic Review* 53(3).

Neil, L., 1998, "The Financial Crisis of 1825 and the Restructuring of the British Financial System", *Federal Reserve Bank of St Louis Review* 80(3), May–June.

Pozsar, Z., T. Adrian, A. Ashcraft and H. Boesky, 2010, "Shadow Banking", Federal Reserve Bank of New York Staff Report No. 458. New York, July.

Roubini, N., and B. Setser, 2004, *Bailouts or Bail-ins? Responding to Financial Crises in Emerging Economies* (Washington, DC: Institute for International Economics).

Roubini, N., and S. Mihm, 2010, *Crisis Economics: a crash course in the future of finance* (London: Allen Lane).

Saurina, J., 2009, "Dynamic Provisioning: The Experience of Spain", World Bank Crisis Response Note 7, Washington, DC, July.

Schanz, J., *et al*, 2011, "The long-term economic impact of higher capital levels", Bank of England Working Paper, forthcoming.

Schiller, R., 2000, *Irrational Exuberance* (Princeton, NJ: Princeton University Press).

Schiller, R., 2008, *The Subprime Solution: How Today's Global Financial Crisis Happened, and What to Do about It* (Princeton, NJ: Princeton University Press).

Skinner, D., 2008, "The Rise of Deferred Tax Assets in Japan: The Role of Deferred Tax Accounting in the Japanese Banking Crisis", *Journal of Accounting and Economics* 46.

Thomson Reuters, 2009, "Equity Capital Markets Review: Fourth Quarter 2009." Accessed May 15, 2011. http://www.thomsonfinancial.jp/pdf/TR/LTs/4Q09%20Equity%20Capital%20Markets%20Review.pdf

Thompson Reuters, 2011, "Fact Box – European, US writedowns, credit losses." Accessed May 15, 2011. http://uk.reuters.com/article/2011/02/24/banks-writedowns-losses-idUKLDE71N1J720110224

Valukas, A., 2010, "Lehman Brothers Holdings Inc. Chapter 11 Proceedings: Examiner's Report", Jenner and Block, Chicago.

2

The Policy Response: From the G20 Requests to the FSB Roadmap; Working Towards the Proposals of the Basel Committee

Patrizia Baudino

European Central Bank

2.1 INTRODUCTION

This chapter provides an overview of the various supervisory and regulatory policies for the financial sector that have been set in motion following the financial crisis that started in 2007. In particular, it discusses the overall policy response that the G20, alongside the Financial Stability Board (FSB) and its member bodies, designed in order to address the shortcomings of pre-crisis financial supervision and regulation. The policy changes described in the chapter cover both the global institutional arrangements and the nature and scope of regulation and supervision.

Substantial changes to the institutional structure at a national and international level have been undertaken since 2007, not only to match the needs generated by the regulatory changes, but also to respond to a call for more inclusiveness and better cross-border cooperation among supervisory authorities. The latter was a response to the systemic impact of a financial crisis that originated in a few countries but had global repercussions. This chapter presents these changes within the framework of the G20 activities.

Concerning the changes to regulation and supervision, the chapter aims at setting the stage for the remainder of the book and at placing the proposals of the Basel Committee, which are described in more detail in the following chapters and are at the core of the changes affecting banks, within the broader context of the overall financial sector regulatory reforms underway. It thus describes in broad terms the components of the overall reform activities: improvement in prudential rules; the associated shift to a more effective supervisory model and the special attention devoted to systemically important financial institutions; the issue of the perimeter of regulation and the role of more lightly or unregulated parts of the financial system; and the interplay between prudential and accounting standards. In addition, the chapter discusses a major change in the nature of regulation presently at the centre of the regulatory reform, namely the need to complement the traditional microprudential approach, ie, institution-focused, with a macroprudential approach, ie, system-wide-focused. This change in approach does not apply only to banks, as it is more general in nature. It also goes beyond the microprudential changes that underlie the revisions to banking regulation undertaken by the Basel Committee. However, it is crucial, as it marks a change in approach. In fact, this new approach puts emphasis on the systemic impact of financial institutions' activities and the regulation that applies to them, thus responding to one of the main weaknesses of pre-crisis regulation for the financial sector.

Several of the regulatory and supervisory initiatives reviewed in the chapter are very complex and cannot be completed in a short period of time. To keep momentum, and to ensure that the reforms will be implemented – and, most importantly, that they will become part of regulatory and supervisory practices – the G20 process has been activated, and timelines for implementation agreed (see Section 2.5 for an overview, and individual chapters of the book for details on each strand of work). The concluding section reflects on the next steps in the G20 agenda in relation to the financial sector and remaining open issues.

The rest of the chapter is organised as follows: Section 2.2 introduces the two themes of the chapter, ie, the institutional changes and the changes in the nature of regulation and supervision. Section 2.3 deals with the institutional changes at the international level, building on the G20 processes and the FSB activities. Section 2.4 deals with the changes to regulation and supervision: these are divided between the micro- and macroprudential changes, as explained in Section 2.2. Section 2.5 concludes.

2.2 THE MAIN LESSONS FROM THE 2007 FINANCIAL CRISIS

There is no shortage of insightful analyses regarding the causes of the recent financial crisis that started in the second half of 2007[1], and other chapters in this book provide a rich overview. Taking this analysis as given, this chapter aims to give an overview of the regulatory and supervisory response, according to two main themes:

1. the changes in the institutional arrangements at the national and international level; and
2. the changes in regulation and supervision of financial firms, and the adoption of a macroprudential approach.

These themes reflect the two-pronged approach that authorities have adopted in response to the crisis. On the one hand, institutional arrangements had to be modified. This was needed both to respond to the call for greater inclusiveness in the international groupings where the new international regulatory architecture was being framed, and to support the adoption of a macroprudential approach to supervisory policies, at the national and international level (see Section 2.3).

On the other hand, as shortcomings in regulation and supervision were identified, it became increasingly clear that their nature and scope needed to be revised. This was not only to respond to the crisis, but also to create the foundations of a financial system that would be more resilient, less leveraged and less prone to financial instability. This change required both improved and more effective microprudential measures (see Subsection 2.4.1), and the adoption of a macroprudential approach to supervision and regulation, with its focus on systemic risk (see Subsection 2.4.2).

2.3 THE NEW INSTITUTIONAL ARRANGEMENTS

The review of existing institutional arrangements has been undertaken at both national and international levels. The focus here, however, will be on the international dimension, given its relation with the design of the new regulatory and supervisory framework undertaken at the international level. Chapter 15 provides more information about regional and national initiatives.

2.3.1 The G20 process and expanded membership of international groupings

At the international level, the G20[2] has become a centrepiece of the response to the financial crisis and the development of a new regulatory framework. The G20 was established in 1999 at the suggestion of the G7 finance ministers, and it was designed as a mechanism to respond to the global financial crisis of 1997–1999. Since then G20 finance ministers and central bankers have met annually. The G20 first became involved in the response to the 2007 financial crisis in late 2008, when leaders of the G20 countries were invited to a summit in Washington, DC, to coordinate the global policy response. The decision to meet at the leader's level was commensurate with the gravity of the crisis and the need for the highest level of political commitment in the response to it. After the Washington 2008 summit, the G20 started to have regular meetings at the leader's level, with at least one annual meeting until the end of 2010. In 2010, an agreement[3] was reached to continue such meetings at a regular annual frequency in the future.[4]

Notwithstanding the more important profile assumed by the G20 in the international arena, it retains a very lean institutional structure,[5] it does not have a permanent secretariat or a chairperson, and its organisation is managed on a rotation basis by the country taking over the presidency and hosting the meetings each year. This reflects the fact that the G20 is a mechanism to discuss issues and reach broad policy consensus, but not to design specific rules and to actively monitor their implementation.[6] Rather, the G20 tasks its members with the implementation and fulfilment of its recommendations. In the Declarations published after each summit since 2008, the G20 leaders have addressed their recommendations to national authorities, as well as to international institutions such as the International Monetary Fund (IMF), the Organisation for Economic and Cooperation Development (OECD) and the Bank for International Settlements (BIS), and international standard setters such as the Basel Committee on Banking Supervision (BCBS) and the International Organisation of Securities Commissions (IOSCO). It is in this context that the FSB has come to play an especially important role for the G20. The FSB regularly submits implementation reports to the G20, coordinates the initiatives of its members and undertakes ad hoc studies in response to G20 requests.

The relation between the FSB and the G20 can be traced back to the Washington G20 summit in 2008, when the G20 leaders, while recognising the important role played by the precursor of the FSB (ie, the Financial Stability Forum), called for a more inclusive international grouping to organise the regulatory response to the financial crisis. The transformation from the Financial Stability Forum (FSF) to the FSB, which was completed with the formal establishment of the FSB in April 2009, and its endorsement by G20 leaders at the London summit in 2009, involved a stronger institutional setup and an expanded membership. In particular, the FSB would comprise all G20 countries, former FSF members, Spain and the European Commission, a significant expansion from the FSF membership, which was formed around the G7 and by early 2009 counted representatives from only 12 countries.[7] Although the FSF had already been steering the regulatory and supervisory response to the crisis since late 2007,[8] the FSB was established with a mandate to reshape the global regulatory system. In particular, at the London Summit Communiqué in 2009 (paragraph 15), the Leaders stated,

... In particular we agree:

- to establish a new Financial Stability Board (FSB) with a strengthened mandate, as a successor to the Financial Stability Forum (FSF), including all G20 countries, FSF members, Spain, and the European Commission;
- that the FSB should collaborate with the IMF to provide early warning of macroeconomic and financial risks and the actions needed to address them;
- to reshape our regulatory systems so that our authorities are able to identify and take account of macroprudential risks;
- to extend regulation and oversight to all systemically important financial institutions, instruments and markets. This will include, for the first time, systemically important hedge funds;
- to endorse and implement the FSF's tough new principles on pay and compensation and to support sustainable compensation schemes and the corporate social responsibility of all firms;
- to take action, once recovery is assured, to improve the quality, quantity, and international consistency of capital in the banking system. In future, regulation must prevent excessive leverage and require buffers of resources to be built up in good times;
- to take action against non-cooperative jurisdictions, including tax havens. We stand ready to deploy sanctions to protect our public finances and financial systems. The era of banking secrecy is over. We note that the OECD has today published a list of countries assessed by the Global Forum against the international standard for exchange of tax information;

❑ to call on the accounting standard setters to work urgently with supervisors and regulators to improve standards on valuation and provisioning and achieve a single set of high-quality global accounting standards; and
❑ to extend regulatory oversight and registration to Credit Rating Agencies to ensure they meet the international code of good practice, particularly to prevent unacceptable conflicts of interest.

The close cooperation between the FSB and the G20 is expected to continue in the future, as indicated in the Seoul Summit Document (paragraph 40) issued by the leaders at the end of the summit in Seoul in November 2010. The leaders stated, "We reaffirmed the FSB's role in coordinating at the international level the work of national financial authorities and international standard setting bodies in developing and promoting the implementation of effective regulatory, supervisory and other financial-sector policies in the interest of global financial stability".

As part of the same drive towards a greater inclusiveness that led to the expansion of the FSF to the FSB, changes took place in other key international groups. In particular, the BCBS (a member of the FSB that holds a key position in the regulatory and supervisory changes under way, given the importance of the banking sector) also expanded its membership in 2009 to a wider constituency that includes all G20 countries, as well as some non-G20 countries that were already BCBS members.[9] On a national level, new institutional setups relating to the adoption of a macroprudential approach to supervision and regulation have been created. Good examples of these changes are the US Financial Stability Oversight Committee,[10] the UK Financial Policy Committee[11] and the European Union's European Systemic Risk Board.[12] The FSB has been a promoter of these changes, and the G20 agenda has further supported them.[13]

Finally, changes in the governance of the IMF and the representation of member countries – which have been under way for several years – have been accelerated in the context of the wider institutional changes in the aftermath of the crisis. In the Seoul Summit Declaration (Paragraph 16), the leaders laid out the ground rules for modernising the IMF governance, and indicated a stringent timeline for the completion of the necessary steps, which are expected to be accomplished by the time the next general review of quotas will have to be completed, ie, January 2014. Although the reforms in the IMF governance are not a product of the 2007 financial crisis, the response to the crisis has given new impetus to these changes, due to need for more inclusiveness of international decision making, and the need to draw on the support of those countries not originally part of the main international decision making bodies.

2.3.2 Interaction among national authorities during crises

Other important aspects of the strengthening of the international arrangements for supervision and regulation of financial firms include the efforts in the area of crisis prevention and crisis resolution of cross-border firms, especially banks. The 2007 crisis clearly showed the deficiencies of pre-existing arrangements for cooperation in normal times between home and host supervisors, as well as for coordination of policy interventions during a crisis. Progress in this area can only be slow, given the existing differences in rules and regulations across countries, as enshrined in national laws, and the difficulties involved in devising international agreements for burden sharing in the resolution of cross-border banks (see chapter 12). Nonetheless, efforts have been made to improve the conditions for cross-border cooperation in relation to the largest international financial firms, along two dimensions: crisis prevention and crisis management. In relation to the first the Basel Committee on Banking Supervision (2010a) identified a number of areas for improvement in national resolution powers and their implementation, and in better information sharing among the key national authorities of the countries where the firm operates. In particular, 10 areas were selected where concrete recommendations could be made: effective national resolution powers; frameworks for a coordinated resolution of financial groups; convergence of national resolution measures; cross-border effects of national resolution measures; reduction of complexity and interconnectedness of group structures and operations; planning in advance for orderly resolution; cross-border cooperation and information sharing; strengthening risk mitigation mechanisms; transfer of contractual relationships; exit strategies; and market discipline. While many of the BCBS (2010a) recommendations refer to national arrangements, they can help to improve cross-border cooperation by better defining national frameworks for crisis prevention and management. In this spirit, it is worth mentioning the FSB work in the area of supervisory practices (FSB 2010e). There, the FSB put forward recommendations to strengthen the intensity and effectiveness of supervision. Adherence to them can help foster alignment in supervisory practices across countries and facilitate cross-border interaction. Such "common language" across supervisors can enhance communication during normal times and possibly also in crisis times.

With regard to crisis management, the FSF (2009b) issued principles for cooperation during crisis times to enhance the preparation of modalities for better cross-border interaction among home and host authorities, and their activation during a crisis. These principles were received and endorsed by the G20 leaders at the London summit in 2009, and since then the FSB has been engaged in work to make them operational. The details of these arrangements will be discussed in Chapter 12, but at a general level they can be seen as part of the efforts to strengthen the international infrastructure for information sharing and coordination across countries. In particular, crisis management groups (CMGs), comprising a small number of authorities from the home and the largest host countries, were created according to these principles. These groups are expected to focus on crisis preparation and crisis management, thus fostering cooperation and information sharing.[14] Furthermore, the FSB (2010f) recommended that each country have a designated resolution authority responsible for exercising resolution powers over financial institutions, with a mandate that fully obliges each resolution authority to seek cooperation with its foreign counterparts.

Efforts to improve supervisory cooperation across borders have produced more specific requirements by the FSB (2010d) in the case of the very largest and systemically relevant cross-border financial institutions, the so-called Systemically Important Financial Institutions (SIFIs), or the Global-SIFIs (G-SIFIs).[15] G-SIFIs must prepare recovery and resolution plans under a scenario of severe stress. As these plans include the review of business decisions over operations across all the countries where G-SIFIs are active, they bring to the fore the issue of the cross-border implications of recovery and resolution plans. For each G-SIFI, the FSB (2010f and 2010g) recommended that there be institution-specific cooperation agreements between home and host authorities, which should clarify the roles and responsibilities in planning for and managing the resolution of the institution.

2.3.3 The FSB "peer reviews"

The design of policy recommendations is only the first step in the improvement of the regulatory framework, and their adoption in supervisory practices is the second, essential, step. However, considering the very high number of recommendations put forward since the financial crisis of 2007 by the FSB and its member bodies, there is an inevitably high risk of failure in consistent implementation across countries, or of only partial or delayed implementation.

To respond to this risk, the FSB and G20 process created new tools as described in the G20 Pittsburgh statement of September 2009, in which the G20 leaders tasked the FSB "to monitor the implementation of FSB standards". These tools are the "peer reviews" (FSB 2010a), divided into "thematic reviews" and "country reviews". They are exercises in which FSB member jurisdictions review both the achievement of others in their implementation of financial-sector standards and policies as agreed within the FSB, and the effectiveness of these standards in their jurisdiction. The peer reviews should not duplicate existing assessment mechanisms, such as IMF–World Bank's Financial Sector Assessment Program (FSAP) and Reports on the Observance of Standards and Codes (ROSCs),[16] but should build on them, so that the systematic and timely monitoring of the implementation of the relevant recommendations from the FSAPs can feed into the peer review. The specific contribution of the FSB peer reviews arises from the cross-sector, cross-functional, system-wide perspective brought by its members.

As part of their membership commitments, all FSB member jurisdictions have to undergo periodic peer reviews to evaluate their adherence to international standards in the regulatory and supervisory area. The FSB regards the initial coverage of peer reviews of only member jurisdictions as a way of leading by example, thus encouraging non-FSB member jurisdictions to undergo similar evaluations.

Thematic peer reviews focus on the implementation of policies or standards agreed within the FSB, with particular attention paid to consistency in cross-country implementation and the effectiveness of the policy or standard in achieving the intended results. Country peer reviews focus on the implementation and effectiveness of financial-sector standards and policies agreed within the FSB within a specific member jurisdiction. These reviews also monitor the systematic and timely pursuit of the relevant recommendations arising from a FSAP or ROSC.

The first thematic review (FSB 2010b) was completed in March 2010, to implement the FSB Principles and Implementation Standards for Sound Compensation Practices, and two more were launched in the same year (one on the implementation of the 2008 FSF Report's recommendations concerning risk disclosures by market participants, and the other on mortgage underwriting practices, based on the relevant recommendations in the Joint Forum Report, 2010). Concerning the country reviews, in 2010 they were undertaken for Mexico, Spain and Italy (see, eg, FSB 2010c), and the other three, for Australia, Canada, and Switzerland, are scheduled for 2011, with more to be planned for subsequent years. Moreover, as announced by the FSB in the run-up to the Seoul G20 summit of November 2010, an FSB Peer Review Council will be established and will be especially tasked with the peer reviews of the effectiveness and consistency of national policy measures for G-SIFIs, which were expected to start no later than the end of 2012 (FSB 2010g).

2.3.4 Outreach beyond the G20 membership

Finally, as part of the efforts for the greater inclusiveness of the international regulatory agreements, and the recognition of the importance of consulting widely and engaging a broad range of countries, the FSB has made strides to take account of the perspectives of emerging-market countries, also going beyond those that are FSB members. To this end, at the Seoul G20 summit the FSB submitted a proposal to G20 leaders for the establishment of a regional consultative group structure that will expand and formalise outreach efforts already in place under the FSF, and which is scheduled to hold meetings starting in 2011.

2.4 THE CHANGES TO REGULATION AND SUPERVISION

The institutional changes mentioned in the first part of the chapter are the canvas for the activities of a more efficient and more inclusive international supervisory community. However, the regulatory and supervisory failures that emerged during the crisis imposed a need to improve the nature and scope of financial regulation and supervision as well.

The FSB has spearheaded the process to change the supervision and regulation of the financial sector,[17] covering both the "micro" aspect of these activities (the traditional microprudential approach) and the "macro" aspect (labelled the macroprudential approach), which is novel and will be explained here. The rest of the book will provide details on the initiatives on both the micro- and macroprudential initiatives, but here we can provide a roadmap for interpreting and connecting these various initiatives.

2.4.1 Microprudential changes[18]
Regulation and supervision have traditionally had a microprudential orientation, ie, they have focused on individual institutions, and set out guidance and requirements for banks, insurance companies and other types of financial firms without focusing on the system-wide impact of such guidance. This approach still has merit, and is useful for the supervision of individual firms, as it is the action of each firm and its financial standing that is the basis for any assessment of its robustness and its capacity to provide financial services in a prudent manner and according to its mandate. However, the crisis has shown the need for innovations within the microprudential approach. This has become especially evident in the area of SIFIs, the capital and liquidity requirements for banks, and in the regulatory initiatives covering the unregulated financial sector.

2.4.1.1 SIFIs
The crisis clearly showed the systemic costs associated with weak and failing financial firms. In particular, it led to the reckoning of the need for more demanding regulatory and supervisory requirements for SIFIs, to reflect the systemic costs associated with the potential failure of any of them. The form that such requirements are going to take – eg, capital surcharges, contingent capital or bail-in debt for higher loss absorbency – remains to be decided and Chapter 10 reviews the state of play on the treatment of SIFIs. But what matters here is the emphasis on systemic risk that drives the emphasis on SIFIs.

As already mentioned, microprudential regulation does not aim to address the systemic implications of the activities of individual firms, and considers the operating environment of each firm as exogenous. This approach continues to be valid for the smaller firms, which, on an individual basis, are highly unlikely to affect the functioning of the financial system as a whole. But, for SIFIs, the working assumption underlying microprudential regulation has been shown to be flawed. Indeed, the sophisticated financial firms that were expected to better manage their risk and to benefit from the differentiation of their activities, were more risky and eventually became the very centre of the crisis. Similarly, market mechanisms failed to correctly price the systemic impact of SIFIs on financial stability, possibly under the assumption that the very systemic significance of SIFIs would activate official interventions at times of stress. While large and interconnected firms are not exclusive to the financial sector, the externalities they impose on a whole sector are much higher in the case of financial firms, given leverage in the financial system and in each SIFI, balance-sheet mismatches (eg, in terms of maturity or currency) and the way in which interconnectedness can compound the strains in the system when combined with leverage.

The FSB, jointly with the IMF and the BIS (IMF *et al* 2009), formulated guidelines on how national authorities can assess the systemic importance of financial institutions, markets and products.[19] Since then, efforts have been made both to identify ways to improve the intensity and effectiveness of SIFIs' supervision (FSB 2010e), and to operationalise the guidelines and produce a list of institutions to which the FSB recommendations for G-SIFIs would initially apply. Over time, the experience gained in the regulation of G-SIFIs is expected to provide sufficient guidance to applying similar regulatory provisions to the other SIFIs as well.

2.4.1.2 Capital and liquidity requirements for the banking sector

At the very core of the present changes in financial regulation and supervision is the overhaul of banking regulation, via the introduction of a new set of rules known as Basel III (BCBS 2010b). The crucial importance of the new bank regulatory package by the BCBS reflects both banks' traditional role at the core of the financial system and the way in which they contributed to the 2007 financial crisis (see Chapter 1).

The new regulatory provisions for banks fall squarely in the traditional microprudential approach to regulation and supervision, given the continued importance of firm-based supervision. But, even as they remain steeped in the supervisory tradition, they are characterised by three main innovations: (i) they include an element of counter-cyclicality, which recognises how the loss-absorption capacity of a financial institution varies with the economic cycle, and that good times should be used to set aside buffers to be used in bad times; (ii) they introduce a leverage ratio, which does not grade banks' positions according to their risk content, and can thus complement more sophisticated measures of risk, especially as banks may struggle to correctly measure risk when its nature is not well understood; and (iii) they introduce minimum liquidity standards, which were not traditionally part of the regulatory requirements for banks, but can help banks to fare better during stress in funding markets. In addition, they not only increase the minimum level of capital, but they refine the requirements over its components – their nature and related minimums – as well as extending the risk coverage of the bank capital framework.

Overall, these features are expected to produce a regulatory framework that is more stringent and more robust against measurement error. Higher capital and liquidity buffers should also ensure that banks have more resources to draw upon in stress times, without creating negative spillover effects on the rest of the banking or financial sector.

While a higher regulatory burden on banks should provide them with the incentives to better internalise the cost of their operations, the BCBS and the FSB have been especially careful not to trigger a relapse in market instability with the introduction of the new regulations. To this end, they have proposed to the G20 leaders, winning their support in the Seoul summit, not to introduce these measures before the financial system has managed to exit from the depths of the financial crisis. As a result, their introduction is staggered and planned over a relatively long-term horizon, stretching into 2019. As shown in a joint BCBS–FSB report (2010a and 2010b) on the cost of the transition to higher capital requirements, an implementation over no less than four years is not expected to derail the economic recovery (see Chapter 13).

2.4.1.3 The scope of regulation
As regulatory efforts in the aftermath of the 2007 financial crisis centred on banks, there was a risk that financial intermediation would move increasingly away from the regulated to the unregulated sector, a fact that would defy the objective of reducing systemic

risk. And as seen in that financial crisis, which was precipitated by funding difficulties in the so-called "shadow" banking sector, systemic risk became more difficult to monitor when concentrated in the unregulated financial sector. In this context, and responding to the request from the G20 summit in Washington in 2008 for a review of the differentiated nature and scope of regulation, Joint Forum (2010) outlined the main concerns along two avenues: (i) the risk of inconsistencies across the regulation of banks, insurance companies and securities markets, and associated regulatory arbitrage; and (ii) the risk of gaps arising due to the scope of financial regulation for each subsector, which might leave certain activities only lightly regulated, or outside of the scope of regulation altogether. While the specifics of the regulatory gaps across sectors and the associated issue of the boundary of the scope of regulation will inevitably vary over time, as the financial system and its regulation evolve, the Joint Forum report developed some general principles to inform the continuous monitoring and reviewing of the scope of financial regulation. In particular, it argued for consistency in regulation across the three sectors (banking, insurance, securities) and across jurisdictions, and for the application of regulation according to activities, products, and markets in a similar way – subject to similar minimum supervision and regulation – irrespective of whether the activities are associated with different types of financial firms. Besides reducing opportunities for regulatory arbitrage and contributing to greater efficiency and stability in the global financial system, adoption of these two guiding principles is also expected to facilitate a coordinated approach to assess the cross-sectoral implications of the regulatory gaps of systemic risk, something that was clearly lacking prior to the 2007 crisis.

Efforts are now under way to increase transparency and reduce the origination of risks in the unregulated sector.[20] Starting with the shadow banking sector, due to its large size, the FSB pledged (2010f) to assess the appropriateness of the regulatory scope, and to expand the regulatory perimeter to it. The FSB committed to develop specific recommendations by mid 2011.[21] These recommendations must balance two conflicting elements: on the one hand, allowing for a more lightly regulated quasi-banking sector that banks can use, combined with heavier demands on the banks as enshrined in the Basel III proposal; and, on the other hand, concerns of risks shifting outside of the scope of supervision and becoming undetectable.

2.4.1.4 Accounting standards

The international efforts in this area are twofold: convergence across different accounting standards and better interaction between prudential considerations and accounting standards. Convergence – primarily in relation to accounting standards by the International Accounting Standards Board (IASB) and the US Financial Accounting Standards Board (FASB) – is an important issue from the perspective of a level playing field for financial firms, and of avoiding regulatory arbitrage across regions. But it is the improved interaction with prudential issues that is more important in relation to the new regulatory framework for banks.

Two accounting issues are especially relevant from a supervisory perspective: the treatment of the impairment of financial assets, and of valuation uncertainty in fair value measurements.[22] Both issues were brought to the fore during the financial crisis. On the one hand, pre-crisis provisioning requirements were found *ex post* to be inadequate for absorbing mounting financial losses. One of the drivers of the discrepancy was the accounting standard requiring that provisions be set according to the concept of incurred rather than expected loss – a way to improve transparency in banks' financial accounts. However, restricting provisions to incurred losses made it impossible for banks to reflect any early assessment of expected losses, and thus to limit the impact of increasing losses on the capital buffers. On the other hand, the crisis had also induced very high volatility in asset values, where valuations were made according to the measurement known as "fair value", which is based on prices in financial markets, if available. Such volatility was problematic for the banks at the peak of the crisis, as they struggled to respond to its impact on their balance sheet. Moreover, it was recognised that high initial asset valuations that could revert in adverse market conditions, could distort incentives in the origination of derivative financial assets and their placement with bank customers.[23]

Although full convergence between the accounting and prudential perspectives may not be possible, given their different driving principles – in a nutshell, transparency for one and prudence for the other – it is also the case that the crisis has led relevant authorities to recognise the need for taking into better account the systemic implications of accounting and prudential standards. Although both sets of standards are by design of a microprudential nature, awareness of the costs of a narrow interpretation of a microprudential approach has increased, thus creating room for reducing adverse impacts on the financial system.

Concerning the convergence between IASB and FASB standards, it has progressed more slowly than initially requested by the G20 leaders, at the summits in 2009 in Pittsburgh and again in 2010 in Toronto, but a new completion date for convergence was announced in mid-2010 and was set to the second half of 2011.

2.4.2 A change in the approach: macroprudential considerations

An important part of the debate on how to enhance the regulation and supervision of financial institutions has focused on the need to adopt a macroprudential approach.[24] This approach requires that the monitoring and assessment of conditions of each financial institution take into account conditions in the financial sector as a whole. Clearly, when considering a small and very simple financial institution, the two-way link between it and the financial system is unlikely to be strong, as even its default would have only a limited systemic impact. But, for larger and/or interconnected firms, these links are significantly stronger, becoming clearly of a systemic nature for SIFIs and G-SIFIs.

The concept of a macroprudential approach to regulation and supervision is not new,[25] but the very costly failures in the 2007 crisis have imposed a forceful rethink of its adoption. Calling for such an approach in regulation and supervision clearly implies a more radical change than the incremental changes discussed in the previous section on microprudential issues.

A simple way to understand the difference between the micro- and macroprudential approaches is to consider the so-called fallacy of composition, ie, the assumption that the system as a whole is safe when the individual components – in this case, banks – are safe. The reason why this may not be the case follows from the fact that, while individual banks may take actions that are prudent from their own point of view, in aggregate, these actions can be destabilising. For instance, selling an asset when the price of risk increases, can be an appropriate response for an individual firm. But, if many firms act in the same way, the asset price will collapse, forcing institutions to take even more steps to reduce their exposures to the same risk factors. Another example is the case of a bank that decides to respond to a worsening in its capital adequacy, on the back of weaker macroeconomic conditions, by deleveraging. However correct this may be from the bank's perspective, if all banks take the same action, lower availability of credit will worsen the macroeconomic contraction and further reduce the quality of banks' credit portfolio and strain their capital-adequacy ratios.

As a result, adopting a macroprudential approach requires that the interlinkages within the financial system, and between it and the real economy, be explicitly taken into account. The challenge facing policymakers is to find ways to translate the concept of a macroprudential approach into a more operational framework. Given the underlying assumption of a need to better integrate macroeconomic and financial-sector imbalances, two options can be identified: a revision of the regulatory and supervisory framework for financial institutions, and a change in macroeconomic policies so that they more closely reflect imbalances in the financial sector. In line with the focus of this publication on policies for the financial system, the second option is discussed only briefly at the end of this section, while the first is explored in further detail below.

2.4.2.1 The macroprudential approach and systemic risk

The concept of systemic risk[26] underpins the adoption of a macroprudential approach, but a well-established definition has not been attempted as part of the development of the policy agenda. This partly reflects the multidimensionality of systemic risk. On the one hand, it is a risk that affects the financial system as a whole, but on the other it also has repercussions on the real economy. For instance, FSF (2009c) indicates that "A macroprudential orientation focuses policy on avoiding damage to the financial system as a whole with an eye to the impact on the real economy."

While a working definition of systemic risk has not been officially endorsed by the international regulatory community, various efforts are under way to measure systemic risk, especially in relation to the banking sector. IMF (2009) presents a range of methodologies to better identify systemic linkages, so as to better monitor which institutions may turn out to be "too interconnected to fail". These tools help to enhance surveillance and regulation of systemic-risk. IMF (2009) also discusses methodologies based on financial market signals that can be used as indicators of overall systemic stress. As already mentioned in the context of the discussion on SIFIs, an important issue is the identification of those institutions that carry a higher impact on systemic risk. IMF–FSF–BIS (2009) outlines the concepts along which the systemic importance of an individual firm can be identified.

Within the spectrum of regulatory and supervisory policies, the feedback mechanisms between the real and financial sectors has been addressed along two dimensions: the evolution of aggregate risk over time and in synchrony with the economic cycle (ie, the time dimension), and the distribution of risk across the financial system at a given point in time (ie, the cross-sectional dimension). The FSB adopted this taxonomy, launching, for the time dimension, work streams on procyclicality (FSF, 2009c), and, for the cross-sectional dimension, work streams on the reduction of data gaps that limit authorities' capacity to monitor systemic risk at any point in time (FSB and IMF, 2009). Progress has been occurring in both areas (see FSB, 2010f and Chapter 6 on procyclicality).

Separately, some of the initiatives to develop the macroprudential approach are not related to the microprudential policies under development (for example, the CGFS (2010) study on policy options over margins requirements and haircuts for financial assets), while others build on the microprudential measures and add to them an overlay of macroprudential considerations (for example, the countercyclical capital buffers in the BCBS proposals). Where it *can* exist, the overlap with microprudential policies helps to strengthen the consistency between the micro- and the macroprudential approaches, which is essential to produce an overall regulatory package that is internally consistent. It is in fact the combined impact of all regulatory changes that determines their effectiveness, as well as the regulatory burden for financial firms. To this end, the FSB can be an effective mechanism to ensure consistency across all policy proposals, and to calibrate their impact in such a way that their combined effect is not detrimental to the real economy.

An important aspect of the adoption of a macroprudential approach to supervision and regulation is the institutional changes that must accompany it, as already mentioned in Section 2.3. Suffice it to say, these institutional changes are important to ensure that (i) there is a reference authority in charge of the adoption of the macroprudential policies, and (ii) that it will be accountable for that. This substantially increases the likelihood that macroprudential policies will be implemented at national and regional levels. At the same time, as experience is gained in the conduct of macroprudential policies in supervision and regulation, forums such as the FSB can be used by national authorities to exchange information and experience and identify best practices. Going forward, the FSB, in consultation with the BIS and the IMF, is committed to further consider the scope to develop principles for effective macroprudential policies (FSB 2010f).

2.4.2.2 Other policies
As the interaction between the macroeconomy and the financial sector may also inform the design of macroeconomic policies, a short reference can be made to the lively debate in the academic and policy circles. To begin with, it must be recognised that this debate started well before the 2007 financial crisis. For instance, White (2006) discussed a proposal for an "augmented inflation target", which would require that concerns about financial-sector imbalances be expressed in terms of price objectives, although over a rather longer policy horizon than what is typically used in monetary policy. This approach could allow for financial stability considerations to be incorporated in the decision-making framework used by central banks. Adrian and Shin (2008) discussed how the level of the interest-rate target affects the intensity of financial intermediation, via the fluctuations in the level of financial leverage, thus amplifying the transmission channel typically associated with monetary policy. Similarly, Blanchard *et al* (2010) put forward a proposal that central banks adopt a higher inflation target, for example, not the more typical 2% but 4%, so as to have more room to respond to financial-sector stress. This reflects the realisation that the effectiveness of monetary policy is limited when nominal interest rates are close to zero, where the traditional channels through which monetary policy can affect the economy become ineffective. However, from this very selective review of the discussion in macroeconomic policy circles, it is clear that there is yet no consensus on the best way to

adjust macroeconomic policies, if ever, and more explorations of the issue by academics and policymakers are likely to continue.

2.5 CONCLUSIONS AND OPEN ISSUES

This chapter has provided an overview of the main policy changes under way at international and national levels. The sheer number of initiatives suggests that the implementation of these policies will need time, for which it will be essential that the highest level of political commitment remains in place. The Seoul Document concluding the Seoul 2010 summit also commits the G20 jurisdictions to the implementation of the new regulatory provisions within the agreed timelines. In particular, G20 leaders are committed to the translation of these provisions into national laws, and to start the implementation of the new bank regulation, which was scheduled to begin on January 1, 2013 and with a completion date of January 1, 2019. The document also sets clear timelines for the completion of the work by the relevant international groupings: for instance, the leaders encouraged the FSB, BCBS and other relevant bodies to complete their remaining work on SIFIs in accordance with the endorsed work processes and timelines in 2011 and 2012; they called on the FSB to build on this work and develop attributes of effective resolution regimes by 2011, and they called on the IASB and the FASB to complete their convergence project by the end of 2011. These explicit and stringent timelines are useful to create references for achieving the milestones in the revision of the regulatory framework.

At the same time, challenges clearly remain. In particular, efforts must be made to ensure that the implementation of the new regulatory provisions are consistent across countries and regions. The Seoul Document recognises the challenge, by stating, "It is essential that we fully implement the new standards and principles, in a way that ensures a level playing field, a race to the top and avoids fragmentation of markets, protectionism and regulatory arbitrage. We recognised different national starting points." It is also important that the dialogue with the industry does not interfere with a stringent implementation of the regulation. While some market commentaries were very critical of Basel III prior to the final agreement at the end of 2010, due to fears of a very high burden on banks, the analysis of Basel III by the regulatory community was less pessimistic (BIS–FSB, 2010a and 2010b) and provided a useful counterpoint to such concerns. Moreover, negotiations among authorities will already introduce adjustments to the recommendations received from technical reports where there is a fear that the impact of new regulations may be uneven across countries, and may be generally costly. Such negotiations are inherent to the achievement of a global consensus, with the Seoul Document also stressing the commitment of the G20 to better reflect the perspective of emerging-market economies in financial regulatory reforms. But it is important that the final quality of the regulatory package remains high, and therefore adequate to meet the very demanding needs of an increasingly complex financial system. The rest of the book will provide in-depth analysis of the specific regulatory changes applying to banks under the Basel Committee framework, which are at the core of a successful implementation of the overhaul of financial regulation reviewed in this chapter.

More broadly, the success of the many initiatives discussed here in strengthening the foundations of the financial system will hang on their capacity to not only address the failures that have emerged, but to be sufficiently broad in scope that they can address more fundamental fault lines and contribute to the reduction of the likelihood and severity of potential future crises.

> The opinions expressed are those of the authors and do not necessarily reflect those of the European Central Bank (ECB). This chapter was written while the author was on secondment at the Secretariat of the Financial Stability Board (FSB), and it does not necessarily represent the views of the FSB and its members, or of the ECB.

---

1   See, for instance, Financial Stability Forum (2008) and International Monetary Fund (2008), as well as Chapter 1. Levine (2010) is an example of the discussion over the policy failures.
2   The term G20 refers to the number of member jurisdictions. They are: Argentina, Australia, Brazil, Canada, China, France, Germany, India, Indonesia, Italy, Japan, Mexico, Russia, Saudi Arabia, South Africa, Korea, Turkey, the United Kingdom, the United States, and (represented by the rotating Council presidency and the European Central Bank) the European Union. Other countries may join the meetings at the discretion of the host country. The managing director of the International Monetary Fund (IMF) and the president of the World Bank, the chairs of the International Monetary and Financial Committee and Development Committee of the IMF and World Bank participate in G20 meetings on an *ex officio* basis.
3   In January 2010, at a technical-level meeting of the G20, it was decided that, after the Seoul meeting in November 2010, the G20 leaders would meet annually, in the autumn, and that the regular meetings at the level of G20 finance ministers and central bank governors would continue to take place, typically during the spring and sometimes also the autumn meetings of the International Monetary Fund and the World Bank, as well as in the final weeks before each G20 leaders' summit.

4 The following G20 summits took place in the following order: the second, hosted by the UK in London on April 1–2, 2009; the third hosted by the US in Pittsburgh on September 24–25, 2009; the fourth (co-chaired by Canada and Korea) in Toronto on June 26–27, 2010; the fifth hosted by Korea on November 11–12, 2010. The next summits (at the time of writing) will be hosted by France (in November 2011) and Mexico (in 2012).

5 Material for each G20 meeting is posted on ad-hoc websites that are prepared by each host country. However, a collection of main documents over the history of the G20 is available from the G20 Information Centre, at the University of Toronto (available at http://www.g20.utoronto.ca). An overview of G20 activities is available on a dedicated website: www.g20.org.

6 The G20 also deals with issues that are unrelated to financial-sector policies, but in this chapter all references to the G20 are in relation to its activities related to the financial sector only.

7 The 12 countries were Canada, France, Germany, Japan, Italy, the United Kingdom, the United States, Australia, Hong Kong, Netherlands, Singapore and Switzerland. The G20 countries that were not members of the FSF and that joined the FSB are Argentina, Brazil, China, India, Indonesia, Korea, Mexico, Russia, Saudi Arabia, South Africa and Turkey. The international financial institutions, international regulatory and supervisory groupings and committees of central bank experts that are members of the FSB are: the Bank for International Settlements, the European Commission, the International Monetary Fund, the Organisation for Economic Cooperation and Development, the World Bank, the Basel Committee on Banking Supervision, the Committee on the Global Financial System, the Committee on Payment and Settlement Systems, the International Association of Insurance Supervisors, the International Accounting Standards Board and the International Organisation of Securities Commissions. The European Central Bank is also a member of the FSB.

8 See, in particular, FSF (2008).

9 See the BCBS (2009), where the members in the new configuration of the BCBS are listed to be Argentina, Australia, Belgium, Brazil, Canada, China, France, Germany, Hong Kong SAR, India, Indonesia, Italy, Japan, Korea, Luxembourg, Mexico, the Netherlands, Russia, Saudi Arabia, Singapore, South Africa, Spain, Sweden, Switzerland, Turkey, the United Kingdom and the United States.

10 See Dodd–Frank Act (2010), Title I, Subtitle A.

11 See the report by HM Treasury (2011).

12 See Council of the European Union (2010). See Chapter 15 for further details on the ESRB.

13 For instance, see the G20 Communiqué after the Washington, DC, November 15, 2008 meeting: "The IMF, with its focus on surveillance, and the expanded FSF, with its focus on standard setting, should strengthen their collaboration, enhancing efforts to better integrate regulatory and supervisory responses into the macro-prudential policy framework and conduct early warning exercises." Or the Communiqué after the London, April 2, 2009, meeting: "We will amend our regulatory systems to ensure authorities are able to identify and take account of macro-prudential risks across the financial system including in the case of regulated banks, shadow banks, and private pools of capital to limit the build up of systemic risk. We call on the FSB to work with the BIS and international standard setters to develop macro-prudential tools."

14 The CMGs are different from supervisory colleges, which have been in existence for longer and are primarily tasked with the sharing of information as part of the routine supervisory monitoring of institutions. However, the two may overlap depending on the national or regional legal frameworks (eg, in the European Union, supervisory colleges are also responsible for crisis prevention and crisis management).

15 See Chapter 10.

16 FSB member jurisdictions are committed to undergoing a FSAP every five years.

THE POLICY RESPONSE

17 See Financial Stability Board (2010f) for a review of progress in the various FSB initiatives.
18 This chapter focuses on the main regulatory initiatives in the context of banking-sector reforms, but several others are also under way, concerning, for instance, deposit insurance standards, infrastructure for payment and securities settlement, and the use of ratings. Some of these initiatives are discussed in the following chapters, but for a full overview see Financial Stability Board (2010b).
19 The academic community has also been active in the debate over SIFIs. See, eg, Duffie (2011).
20 Other initiatives cover hedge funds (especially in terms of reporting to supervisors and investor protection) and over-the-counter derivatives contracts (requiring that standardised contracts trade on exchanges or electronic trading platforms, and are cleared through central counterparties), but are not discussed here, given the book's focus on banks. The term "shadow banking sector" refers to the fact that the financial institutions involved (typically, structured investments vehicles – SIVs) were closely intertwined with banks. However, while banks are always regulated, SIVs were only lightly or not regulated at all.
21 The G20 reaffirmed the need to analyse the shadow banking sector in the Communiqué following the Meeting of Finance Ministers and Central Bank Governors on February 18–19, 2011.
22 Other issues that the FSB is monitoring refer to the derecognition of repurchase agreements and the netting/offsetting of financial instruments (see Financial Stability Board, 2010f).
23 For details, see Financial Stability Forum (2009a), the joint CGFS-FSF Report (2009) and Chapter 1.
24 The concept of a macroprudential approach was widely present in speeches from the heads of several national and international authorities, so that an exhaustive reference would be too long for this chapter. A useful reference to review the debate over a macroprudential approach is Brunnermeier *et al* (2009).
25 Borio (2009) discusses the origin of the term and its first appearance in the policy circles, where, for instance at the BIS, its use started already in the late 1970s, and was beginning to appear in publications from the policy community already in the mid-1980s. See also Borio (2003) for an early analysis of the concept of macroprudential regulation.
26 See Brunnermeier *et al.* (2009).

REFERENCES

Adrian T., and H. Shin, 2008, "Financial Intermediaries, Financial Stability and Monetary Policy", paper delivered at the Economic Policy Symposium of the Federal Reserve Bank of Kansas City, "Maintaining Stability in a Changing Financial System", August.

Bank for International Settlements and Financial Stability Board, 2010a, "Assessing the macroeconomic impact of the transition to stronger capital and liquidity requirements", interim report, Basel, August.

Bank for International Settlements and Financial Stability Board, 2010b, "Assessing the macroeconomic impact of the transition to stronger capital and liquidity requirements" – final report, Basel, December.

Basel Committee on Banking Supervision, 2009, "Basel Committee broadens its membership", press release, Basel, June

Basel Committee on Banking Supervision, 2010a, "Report and recommendations of the Cross-border Bank Resolution Group", final paper, Basel, March.

Basel Committee on Banking Supervision, 2010b, "The Basel Committee's response to the financial crisis", report to the G20, Basel, October.

Blanchard O., G. Dell'Ariccia and P. Mauro, 2010, "Rethinking macroeconomic policy", IMF Staff Position Note No. 2010/03, February.

Borio C., 2003, "Towards a macroprudential framework for financial supervision and regulation?", BIS Working Papers No. 128, February.

Borio C., 2009, "The macroprudential approach to regulation and supervision", *VOX*, April 14.

Brunnermeier M., A. Crockett, C. Goodhart, A. Persaud and H. Shin, 2009, "The fundamental principles of financial regulation", *Geneva Reports on the World Economy* 11.

Committee on the Global Financial System and Financial Stability Forum, 2009, "The role of valuation and leverage in procyclicality", Basel, March.

Committee on the Global Financial System, 2010, "The role of margin requirements and haircuts in procyclicality", CGFS Publications No. 36, Basel, March.

Council of the European Union, 2010, 3045th Council Meeting, press release, Economic and Financial Affairs Committee, Brussels, November.

Dodd–Frank Wall Street Reform and Consumer Protection Act, 2010, Congress of the United States of America.

Duffie, D., 2011, *How Big Banks Fail and What to Do About It* (Princeton, NJ: Princeton University Press).

Financial Stability Board, 2010a, "FSB Framework for Strengthening Adherence to International Standards", Basel, March.

Financial Stability Board, 2010b, "Thematic Review on Compensation", peer-review report, 2010, Basel, March 30.

Financial Stability Board, 2010c, "Country Review of Mexico", peer-review report, Basel, September.

Financial Stability Board, 2010d, "Reducing the moral hazard posed by systemically important financial institutions – FSB Recommendations and Time Lines", Basel, October.

Financial Stability Board, 2010e, "Intensity and Effectiveness of SIFI Supervision Recommendations for enhanced supervision", Basel, November.

Financial Stability Board, 2010f, "Progress since the Washington summit in the Implementation of the G20 Recommendations for Strengthening Financial Stability – Report of the Financial Stability Board to G20 leaders", Basel, November.

Financial Stability Board, 2010g, "Progress of Financial Regulatory Reforms", letter to G20 leaders, Basel, November.

Financial Stability Board and International Monetary Fund, 2009, "The Financial Crisis and Information Gaps – Report to the G-20 Finance Ministers and Central Bank Governors", October.

Financial Stability Forum, 2008, "Report on Enhancing Market and Institutional Resilience", Basel, April.

Financial Stability Forum, 2009a, "Report of the FSF Working Group on Provisioning", Basel, March.

Financial Stability Forum, 2009b, "FSF Principles for Cross-border Cooperation on Crisis Management", Basel, April.

Financial Stability Forum, 2009c, "Report of the Financial Stability Forum on Addressing Procyclicality in the Financial System", Basel, April.

HM Treasury, 2011, "A new approach to financial regulation – building a stronger system", February

International Monetary Fund, 2008, "Global Financial Stability Report – Containing Systemic Risks and Restoring Financial Soundness", IMF, April.

International Monetary Fund, 2009, "Global Financial Stability Report – Responding to the Financial Crisis and Measuring Systemic Risks", IMF, April.

International Monetary Fund, Financial Stability Board, Bank for International Settlements, 2009, "Guidance to Assess the Systemic Importance of Financial Institutions, Markets and Instruments: Initial Considerations", background paper, report to the G-20 finance ministers and central bank governors, October.

Joint Forum, 2010, "Review of the Differentiated Nature and Scope of Financial Regulation", Basel, January.

Levine, R., 2010, "The governance of financial regulation: reform lessons from the recent crisis", BIS Working Papers No. 329, Basel, November.

White W., 2006, "Procyclicality in the financial system: do we need a new macrofinancial stabilisation framework?", BIS Working Papers No. 193, January.

Part II

The New Capital Standards

3

The New Definition of Regulatory Capital

Laetitia Meneau; Emiliano Sabatini

French Prudential Supervisory Authority; Bank of Italy

3.1 INTRODUCTION

Since the early 1980s, minimum capital requirements for banks have gained a pivotal role in financial regulation. With financial innovation and the input of international regulators, banking regulation evolved in most jurisdictions towards prudential approaches that allowed banks to carry out any type of financial business provided they were able to cover the corresponding risks by setting aside capital.

According to economic theory, the rationale for minimum capital requirements stems from the incentive structure entailed by banks' safety-net systems. On the one hand, deposit insurance may give banks an incentive to increase risk, if the insurance premium is flat. On the other, since depositors are partially or fully insured, they have no incentive to monitor the bank. Therefore, requiring banks to hold minimum capital as a percentage of risk-adjusted assets prevents them from excessive risk taking. In addition, capital serves as a buffer against possible losses and thus banks' default, externalities and contagion.

Obviously, to be fully effective, a ratio of capital to risk-weighted assets must be correctly designed: the quality of capital needs to be satisfactory from a prudential point of view, ie, capital should absorb losses when they materialise, and risk weights must reflect the true riskiness of assets.

Neither the numerator nor the denominator of the solvency ratio proved, however, fully adequate (as discussed in Chapter 4). In principle, capital should absorb banks' losses, protecting depositors and other senior creditors from the adverse consequences of a failure. In practice, there are different types of regulatory capital. Common shares represent the strongest protection: they are the first line of defence against losses, by ensuring that a bank can overcome negative shocks while remaining in a going-concern status. Nonetheless, lower-quality capital instruments – eg, hybrid instruments and subordinated debts – were considered as eligible for the purpose of prudential regulation, since they could contribute to absorbing losses in a gone-concern scenario, before depositors and senior creditors are involved. Non-harmonised regulatory adjustments have also made it possible for some banks to display strong capital ratios with limited tangible common equity. Finally, the crisis revealed the inconsistency in the definition of regulatory capital across jurisdictions and the lack of disclosure that would have enabled the market to assess the true quality of regulatory capital of banks.

Some of these inconsistencies were as a matter of fact known to regulators even before the crisis and, indeed, the Basel Committee for Banking Supervision (BCBS) had already planned major changes to the definition of regulatory capital. However, these inconsistencies turned out to be devastating during the crisis, demanding a prompt and profound regulatory repair and becoming a top priority in the policy agenda. Therefore, the G20 and the Financial Stability Board (FSB) called on the Basel Committee for a reform able to deliver an increase in the quality, consistency and transparency of the capital base of banks.

All these issues are discussed in this chapter,[1] which is organised as follows: Section 3.2 details the definition of capital under the previous regimes (Basel I and Basel II); Section 3.3 contains a definition of capital under Basel III; Section 3.4 discusses the quantity of capital under Basel III; Section 3.5 analyses the transitional arrangements and grandfathering mechanisms; Section 3.6 concludes.

3.2 THE DEFINITION OF REGULATORY CAPITAL UNDER BASEL I AND BASEL II

The capital adequacy framework agreed in 1988 by the Basel Committee for Banking Supervision (Basel I) – which envisages minimum capital requirements that banks have to meet vis-à-vis risk-weighted exposures – consists of three components: (i) the eligibility criteria for regulatory capital; (ii) the risk-weights attached to the exposures (risk-weighted assets, otherwise known as RWA); (iii) the minimum requirements, such as the fact that the banks must always comply with the solvency ratio (regulatory capital/risk-weighted assets) of 8%.

As for the eligibility criteria, Basel I provides for the following architecture: regulatory capital is divided into two tiers, depending on the quality – ie, the capacity of absorbing losses – of the different components. Tier 1 capital – the highest-quality tier, since it covers losses in a going-concern scenario – consists largely of shareholders' equity and reserves. Some other instruments – whose nature is close to that of common equity – can also be counted, within specific limits. Tier 2 capital (ie, the second tier) is made of subordinated debts that bear losses mainly in liquidation (ie, gone concern).

At least 50% of the regulatory capital base must consist of equity and reserves (Tier 1). The other elements of capital are admitted into Tier 2 up to an amount equal to that of Tier 1, with a sub-category (subordinated term debt) limited to a maximum of 50% of Tier 1. Items that do not contribute to the coverage of losses, such as goodwill and investments in the capital of other banks and financial institutions, are to be deducted in order to avoid the double use of capital known as "double gearing" of capital, ie, the use of the same amount of capital for covering risks in different parts of the financial system. Double gearing occurs whenever one entity holds regulatory capital issued by another entity and the issuer is allowed to count the capital in its own balance sheet.

Some changes to the international rules on capital were introduced after 1988. In 1996, with the Market Risk Amendment, another category of regulatory capital, called "Tier 3", was designed to cover market risks. In 1998, as financial innovation developed, the Basel Committee published a press release (the 1998 Press Release) setting out the characteristics capital instruments that combine features of both equity and debt should meet in order to be counted as Tier 1, subject to a 15% limitation. Such instruments are generally referred to as "innovative hybrid instruments".

Due to the increasing financial innovation, the consistent application of Basel I and of its subsequent amendments was more and more difficult to achieve. Cross-jurisdictional differences were particularly relevant in the following fields.

❏ The definition of "Equity". Some countries considered non-cumulative perpetual preferred stock as being regulatory capital on the grounds that it was considered as "equity" in accounting standards. Others did not.
❏ The interpretation of the 1998 Press Release. The diversity of instruments arose mainly as a result of the particular features of local markets and differences in national tax and company laws. For instance, in Europe, in the absence of an EU-wide legal text, competent authorities built on their assessment of hybrids' eligibility on qualitative requirements that were very similar or complementary to the 1998 Press Release. But, as the features attached to these instruments differ, the eligibility and the limits to the inclusion of such instruments in Tier 1 varied from country to country (Committee of European Banking Supervisors 2006).
❏ With regard to the deduction of investments in banks and other financial institutions, the situation varied between Europe and the US. In particular, following the Core Principles of the Joint Forum,[2] Europe put in place a regulatory regime that paid due consideration to the increasing interconnection between the banking and the insurance activities within the same groups, called financial conglomerates.

Such different definitions of regulatory capital inevitably led to an increasingly uneven playing field among financial institutions. A review was therefore very much needed.

As we mentioned, although Basel II focused on putting in place a risk-sensitive framework and did not touch upon the definition of regulatory capital, such a review was already in the pipeline: "converging on a uniform international capital standard under this Framework will ultimately require the identification of an agreed set of capital instruments that are available to absorb unanticipated losses on a going-concern basis". (Basel Committee on Banking Supervision 2004)

The financial crisis accelerated the review. Allowing for high regulatory ratios with so little common equity and non-fully harmonised regulatory capital structure prompted investors to lose confidence.

Facing difficulties to compare and have a clear and transparent view on the solvency situation of the banks, market participants disregarded the regulatory ratios and used their own metrics such as "Core Tier 1" ratios to try to measure the share of "real capital" compared with risk-weighted assets. The irony was that the definition of these alternative measures varied from one analyst to the other and was not comparable, either; the implementation of the market's own metrics did not help the solvency situation.

3.3 THE DEFINITION OF REGULATORY CAPITAL IN BASEL III

In the above-mentioned context, there was an urgent need to address the combined shortcomings of insufficient quality, lack of harmonisation and low quantity, by raising both the quality and quantity of capital. In 2010 the Basel Committee introduced a new set of guidelines (Basel Committee on Banking Supervision 2010), which can be summarised as follows:

- the regulatory capital structure is simplified (Subsection 3.3.1);
- the quality of regulatory capital is improved and harmonised (Subsection 3.3.2):
  - Common Equity Tier 1 (CET 1) is clearly defined;
  - stricter eligibility criteria are devised for all Tiers; and
  - deductions are made entirely and directly from CET 1, and the list of items to be deducted is reviewed and made more rigorous; and
- the quantity of regulatory capital is increased: higher levels of ratios are to be met and a new form of instrument is to be used in case of distressed situations.

3.3.1 The new regulatory capital structure

The structure of regulatory capital is divided into two tiers:

- Tier 1, composed of CET 1 and Additional Tier 1, which covers losses on going concerns and whose predominant form must be CET 1; and
- Tier 2, which has loss-absorbency in gone concerns.

However, rules are significantly simplified with respect to the current framework. The distinction between Upper and Lower Tier 2 is removed as well as the reference to Tier 3. The former amendment to Basel II is due to the fact that, in practice, most banks did not issue Upper Tier 2 in vast amounts, as the cost of issuing Tier 1 was equivalent but the regulatory benefit higher. The latter amendment is linked to the increased role of market risk during the last decade. However, now that market risk is, under Basel II, a Pillar I risk there were no reasons to cover it with a specific and lower-quality capital instrument.

However, the main innovation of Basel III is a harmonised definition of Common Equity Tier 1 (CET 1), the component of Tier 1 capital composed of the highest-quality capital instruments. As the crisis has shown, the lack of homogeneity has represented an element of uncertainty and an uneven playing field across countries and institutions. Therefore CET 1 is the metric that regulators have identified to assess the solvency situation of the banks.

Under Basel II, the 8% minimum capital requirements were to be met mainly with Tier 1 and Tier 2 capital, with the latter counting up to 100% of the former. In practice, this implied that banks could meet the regulatory minimum, holding Tier 1 capital equal to 4% of risk-weighted assets (RWAs). Since hybrid capital instruments could count for up to 50% of Tier 1 itself in some countries, banks could implicitly be holding common equity representing only 2% of

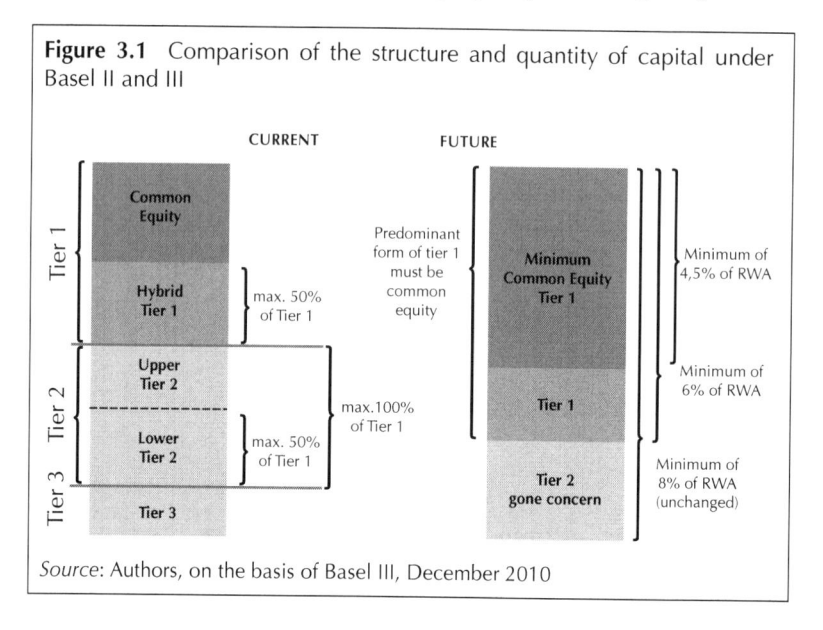

Figure 3.1 Comparison of the structure and quantity of capital under Basel II and III

Source: Authors, on the basis of Basel III, December 2010

RWAs. Under Basel III, while the minimum total capital ratio is kept at 8% of RWAs, the minimum Tier 1 ratio is increased to 6% and an explicit requirement – 4.5% of RWAs – is set for the CET 1 ratio.

3.3.2 Raising the quality of regulatory capital: eligibility criteria and deductions

Basel III provides for a common and more rigorous definition of regulatory capital. First, the eligibility criteria, that an instrument must respect in order to be included in regulatory capital, (in CET 1, Additional Tier 1 or Tier 2) have been completely revised. Second, to strengthen the reliability of CET 1 the list of deductions is more comprehensive and the following rule is adopted: the items are deducted from CET 1, while the Basel II 50:50 rule is no longer applied.[3]

Three main criteria are identified to assess the quality of capital instruments to be eligible for prudential purposes: (i) loss absorbency; (ii) flexibility of payments; (iii) permanence.

We analyse below the main eligibility criteria for each Tier.

3.3.2.1 Common Equity Tier 1 (CET 1).
To be included in CET 1, an instrument must meet 14 criteria (see Panel 3.1). The Basel Committee devised these criteria with a view to replicating the characteristics of common shares, as these are of the highest quality: available at any time and the most loss-absorbent.

As the idea is to identify the most reliable form of capital, an instrument must be classified as equity both under the relevant accounting standards and for determining balance-sheet insolvency (Criteria 9 and 10); moreover, it has to be clearly and separately disclosed in the bank's balance sheet (Criterion 14).

In terms of loss absorbency, CET 1 holders must be the first to absorb losses that exceed current earnings, allowing the bank to continue its activities in times of poor performance (Criterion 8). Consistently, CET 1 instruments are the most deeply subordinated claim also in liquidation (Criteria 1 and 2).

As regards permanence, it is necessary that CET 1 instruments be perpetual and never repaid outside liquidation (Criterion 3). This provision aims to ensure a stable and solid equity base, mitigating the risk that banks need to raise new capital in downturns or distressed conditions when the cost of capital increases. Permanence also implies that money is immediately available; therefore the instruments must be directly issued and fully paid (Criterion 11). Only by satisfying these conditions can capital really be available at any time to cover the bank's losses.

Finally, several requirements in terms of flexibility of payment are introduced. CET 1 instruments must leave full discretion to the bank over the amount and timing of dividend distributions. In that respect, the bank should be free to decide on whether or not to pay any dividend to CET 1 holders. Suspension of dividends does not represent an event of default (Criterion 6). Moreover, a cap on dividends is not allowed because it may generate market expectations that can affect the banks' dividend policy strategy (Criterion 5). These provisions aim to maintain the hierarchy among different capital holders, avoiding the high level of loss absorbency being compensated through preferential rights that might either undermine bank's solidity or affect its business strategy.

For joint-stock companies, the 14 criteria must be met solely with common shares, ie, only a common share that meets the 14 eligibility criteria can be included in CET 1. This is an approach of form (common shares) plus substance (eligibility criteria). In cases where institutions issue non-voting common shares, they must be identical to voting common shares in all respects except the absence of voting rights.

The criteria also apply to non-joint-stock companies, such as mutuals, cooperatives and savings institutions, taking into account their specific constitution and legal structure. The application of the criteria should preserve the quality of the instruments by requiring that they be deemed fully equivalent to common shares in terms of their capital quality as regards loss absorption, and do not possess features that could cause the condition of the bank to be weakened as a going concern during periods of market stress. Supervisors will exchange information on how they apply the criteria to non-joint-stock companies in order to ensure consistent implementation.

Another debated issue is represented by the treatment of minority interests. The extent to which they are included in the predominant form of capital varies from one country to another under Basel II. Indeed, whereas minority interests representing the indirect issuance of Tier 1 hybrid instruments are treated fairly consistently and are excluded from the predominant form of regulatory capital,

PANEL 3.1 ELIGIBILITY CRITERIA FOR COMMON EQUITY TIER 1

1. Represents the most subordinated claim in liquidation of the bank.
2. Entitled to a claim on the residual assets that is proportional with its share of issued capital, after all senior claims have been repaid in liquidation (ie, has an unlimited and variable claim, not a fixed or capped claim).
3. Principal is perpetual and never repaid outside of liquidation (setting aside discretionary repurchases or other means of effectively reducing capital in a discretionary manner that is allowable under relevant law).
4. The bank does nothing to create an expectation at issuance that the instrument will be bought back, redeemed or cancelled, nor do the statutory or contractual terms provide any feature that might give rise to such an expectation.
5. Distributions are paid out of distributable items (retained earnings included). The level of distributions is not in any way tied or linked to the amount paid in at issuance and is not subject to a cap (except to the extent that a bank is unable to pay distributions that exceed the level of distributable items).
6. There are no circumstances under which the distributions are obligatory. Non-payment is therefore not an event of default.
7. Distributions are paid only after all legal and contractual obligations have been met and payments on more senior capital have been made. This means that there are no preferential distributions, including in respect of other elements classified as the highest-quality issued capital.
8. It is issued capital that takes the first and proportionately greatest share of any losses as they occur. Within the highest-quality capital, each instrument absorbs losses on a going-concern basis proportionately and equally with all the others.
9. The paid-in amount is recognised as equity capital (ie, not recognised as liability) for determining balance-sheet insolvency.
10. The paid-in amount is classified as equity under the relevant accounting standards.
11. It is directly issued and paid in and the bank cannot directly or indirectly have funded the purchase of the instrument.
12. The paid-in amount is neither secured nor covered by a guarantee of the issuer or related entity or subject to any other arrangement that legally or economically enhances the seniority of the claim.
13. It is issued only with the approval of the owners of the issuing bank, either given directly by the owners or, if permitted by applicable law, given by the board of directors or by other persons duly authorised by the owners.
14. It is clearly and separately disclosed on the bank's balance sheet.

Source: Basel III, December 2010

> **PANEL 3.2 PRUDENTIAL REGULATION AND CORPORATE LAW**
>
> Basel III requires that joint stock companies include in CET 1 only common shares that are compliant with all the identified criteria and that other institutions include only the highest-quality capital instruments, which also fulfil the 14 criteria listed in Panel 3.1. The aim is clear and everyone agrees with it. However the application of this provision may face difficulties because the definition of common shares is not homogeneous across jurisdictions.
>
> In practice, there is a balance to be reached between transparency, which is guaranteed looking at the legal form of the instrument, and consistency, which is preserved looking at the substance. Under a formal approach based on the legal definition of common shares, only common shares are included in CET 1, but they can have different economic features according to the different definitions included in national corporate laws. By contrast, if the attention is on the economic substance, all the instruments included in CET 1 need to meet the 14 criteria, but they may not only be common equity according to corporate laws, thus reducing transparency. As a consequence, there is a need to reach a harmonisation, not only of the prudential regime, but also of the corporate law (see Panels 3.3 and 3.4).

the minority interests arising from the consolidation of "operating" subsidiaries are subject to heterogeneous treatments. Some countries included the full amount of such minority interest while some did not at all; others did not recognise the surplus of minority interest (ie, the amount of minority interest exceeding the minimum requirements of the subsidiary).

Under Basel III the treatment is harmonised. Capital instruments issued by a fully consolidated subsidiary of a bank or institution that is subject to the same minimum prudential standards and level of supervision, to third-party investors, receive recognition according to the quality of the instrument in a so-called "corresponding approach" only if (i) the instrument meets all the criteria for classification in the relevant tier (ie, as CET 1, Additional Tier 1 or total capital – the sum of all the tiers) and (ii) the subsidiary that issued the instrument is a bank. Capital issued to third-party investors out of a special-purpose vehicle (SPV) is excluded from CET 1, but can be included in consolidated Additional Tier 1 or Tier 2, subject to certain conditions being met.

The idea is to recognise subsidiaries' capital only to the extent that it effectively covers consolidated risks and therefore it can be considered as capital that face consolidated losses. To reach this goal Basel III provides for a calculation procedure whose target is to identify the level of subsidiaries' capital requirement relevant at the consolidated level.

That procedure can be summarised as follows:

- total minority interest meeting the two criteria above (the subsidiary is a bank and capital instrument that satisfies all the criteria to be eligible) minus the amount of the surplus CET 1 of the subsidiary issued to the third parties;
- the surplus is calculated as the CET 1 of the subsidiary minus the lower of (i) the minimum Tier 1 requirement of the subsidiary plus the 2.5% capital conservation buffer (see Chapter 7), that is to say 7% of the risk-weighted assets (individual basis); and (ii) the portion of the consolidated minimum CET 1 requirement plus the capital buffer that relates to the subsidiary (consolidated basis – contribution approach); and
- the amount of the surplus that is attributable to the third parties is calculated by multiplying the surplus CET 1 by the percentage of CET 1 attributable to third parties.

The same calculation applies to Additional Tier 1 and Tier 2 instruments issued by a fully consolidated subsidiary of the bank to third-party investors, by using, as threshold, 8.5% Tier 1 and 10.5% total capital.

The concrete calculation of minorities would have to be further elaborated, for instance, with simplified numerical examples to avoid miscalculations.

In summary, CET 1 consists of the sum of the following items:

- common shares (or the equivalent for non-joint-stock companies);
- stock surplus (share premium) resulting from the issue of instruments included in CET 1;
- retained earnings and other comprehensive income, including interim profits or losses;
- accumulated other comprehensive income and other disclosed reserves;

❏ common shares issued by consolidated subsidiaries of the bank and held by third parties (ie, minority interest) that meet the criteria for inclusion in CET 1 capital; and
❏ regulatory adjustments applied in the calculation of CET 1.

In addition, a number of adjustments will have to be made out of CET 1.

First, compared with the situation, whereby banks make different regulatory adjustments depending on the country in which they operate, there is a significant improvement in harmonising the types of deductions to be made. For instance, under Basel III, not only is goodwill to be deducted, but all the intangible assets. We must note, however, a specific opt-out provision for countries such as Japan in which, subject to prior supervisory approval, banks that report under local Generally Accepted Accounting Principles (GAAP) may use the International Financial Reporting Standards (IFRS) definition of intangible assets to determine which assets are required to be deducted.

Second, the new definition of regulatory capital is now composed only of elements that fully reflect the solvency situation of each institution. In particular, learning from the crisis, all unrealised gains and losses that result from changes in fair value of liabilities due to changes in the bank's own credit risk are not taken into account in the calculation of CET 1. This aims at avoiding situations where the depreciation of the value of the liability due to changes in own credit risk led to an increase of own funds.

Third, as already mentioned, no item is deducted 50% from Tier 1 and 50% from Tier 2 anymore. Instead certain securitisation exposures, shortfall,[4] certain equity exposures under the PD/LGD approach, the non-payment/delivery on non-delivery-versus-payment and non-payment-versus-payment transactions (DvP and PvP respectively) and significant investments in commercial entities, will be risk-weighted 1250%.

Fourth, two main changes have been introduced in the treatment of holdings in financial institutions. In the Basel II definition of regulatory capital, such holdings are deducted 50% from Tier 1 and 50% from Tier 2. This treatment did not adequately address the issue of double gearing in the financial sector. In Basel III, the deductions are thus applied to CET 1.

THE NEW DEFINITION OF REGULATORY CAPITAL

Table 3.1 List of adjustments to be made out of CET 1

	Deducted from CET (see para 78 in Basel III published document)
Investment in own shares	Shall be deducted from CET, net of any associated tax liability that would be extinguished if goodwill becomes impaired or derecognised.
Goodwill and other intangibles (but MSR)	Allow IFRS treatments where different from national GAAP (eg, software).
Deferred tax assets Tax loss carry forward	Those that on future profitability of the institution to be realised receive limited recognition in CET (net of deferred tax liabilities). Other DTA should be assigned relevant sovereign risk weighting. For DTA arising from temporary differences, text below table.
Unconsolidated investments in financials	If a bank's holdings of common stock in other financial institutions in aggregate exceed 10% of the common equity, then the amount above 10% should be deducted. Netting of positions; underwriting exemptions (also, see text below).
Shortfall of provisions to expected losses	Deducted.
Cashflow hedge reserve	The positive and negative cash flow hedge is removed from CET where it relates to the hedging of projected cashflows that are not recognised on the balance sheet.
Gains and losses due to changes in own credit risk	All gains and losses resulting from changes in the fair value of liabilities that are due to changes in institution's own credit risk are removed from CET.
Defined-benefit pension fund	Assets should be deducted from CET1. Assets to which the bank has unrestricted and unfettered access can, with supervisory approval, offset the deduction.

Source: Authors, on the basis of Basel III, December 2010

However, acknowledging some diversification benefits in insurance and other financial entities' holdings, those investments are deducted only above a threshold. In particular, significant investments in the common shares of unconsolidated financial institutions (banks, insurance and other financial entities) receive recognition (ie, are not to be deducted) with a cap at 10% of the bank's common equity (after deduction of items that do not depend on the threshold). Such treatment is applied together with other assets such as mortgage-servicing rights (MSRs) and deferred-tax assets (DTAs) that arise from temporary differences.

However, the sum of these three items eligible in regulatory capital cannot exceed a threshold of 15% and it is subject to full disclosure. The amount not deducted is risk-weighted at 250%.[5]

The original treatment of holdings in financials (the Basel Committee's Consultation paper of December 2009 foresaw a deduction in full) was heavily criticised by a number of representatives from the industry. In particular, they pointed out that such a rule penalises the business model of "bank insurance carried out by financial conglomerates. This was considered unfair, as such a business model proved to be resilient in the crisis. Furthermore, we may wonder why intangible assets such as MSRs are treated in the same way as investments in other financial institutions, which are very

---

PANEL 3.3 PRUDENTIAL REGULATION AND FISCAL REGIMES

Only DTAs (deferred-tax assets) that arise from temporary differences are recognised in CET 1 up to the limit of 10%.[6] Limiting the recognition to this kind of DTA is due to the fact that, while DTAs that arise from carry-forward losses can be considered a "dilution of losses" over coming years, DTAs that arise from temporary differences represent an ahead payment generated by the interaction between accounting and fiscal regimes. In order to realise this "potential" credit, through a reduction in future tax payments, only one condition must be satisfied: bank makes profit. When a bank makes profits, these items represent a positive amount that can be used to offset the tax debit that arises from the accounting year. However, if a bank reports losses, then DTAs eligible to be used cannot be used to offset the tax debit. (ie, they are not "permanent" credit).

This treatment will affect jurisdictions in an inhomogeneous way because fiscal regimes differ from one country to another so that (i) not only the amount of DTAs but also (ii) the period that a DTA can be used as a "tax credit" will vary.

The more fiscal and accounting regimes diverge from one another, the greater the relevance of this phenomenon.

We should be very cautious as to the possible impact of this treatment on a bank's provisioning policy, for instance in cases where fiscally eligible provisions are lower than the accounting provisions. Moreover, the fiscal rate being fixed, the difference between the fiscal data and the accounting data is higher in downturn (when accounting provisions increase to cover the high risk embedded in loans portfolios) and lower in upturn (when the risk in loan portfolios is lower or less perceived), therefore leading to potential undesirable procyclical effects.

tangible assets. The measure was also considered as disproportionate. In Europe, the European Commission, which is planning to transpose Basel III into European legislation, is keen to ensure that the reality of conglomerates is properly taken into consideration.

3.3.2.2 The new set of eligibility criteria for Additional Tier 1
Tier 1 includes, in addition to CET 1, other capital instruments (Additional Tier 1), which are subject to strict eligibility criteria. The aim of these instruments is to strengthen ongoing prudential capital by giving banks a complementary tool to raise capital. Under current rules, the only existing internationally agreed regulatory guidance to assess whether an instrument is eligible for prudential purposes is the 1998 Press Release. At the European level this guidance has been used to take, under the aegis of the Committee of European Banking Supervisors (CEBS – now the European Banking Authority – EBA), the necessary steps to set out more detailed eligibility criteria. Leveraging on this work, the European Union adopted a directive setting out eligibility criteria for Tier 1 hybrid instruments. The Directive came into force as of December 31, 2010.

Basel III goes further. Compared with the current situation, the criteria are more detailed and very much tightened, notably due to the elimination of "innovative" (ie, instruments with incentives to redeem) and dated hybrid instruments, currently eligible for up to 15% of Tier 1. There is consequently no longer any distinction between "innovative" and "non-innovative" (ie, instruments without incentives to redeem). The associated limitations are no longer valid.

Furthermore, Basel III requires that:

❏ dividend pushers[8] and payment of coupons in kind[9] be prohibited; and
❏ Additional Tier 1 instruments classified as liabilities must encompass a loss-absorption mechanism – this requirement is in addition to the cancellation of coupons.

With regard to the loss-absorption mechanism, three situations are considered by Basel III: (i) should the bank go into liquidation, the claim of the holder is not at par but at the reduced amount; (ii) should the bank proceed to a write-down of its liabilities and need to call its

Table 3.2 A reinforced set of eligibility criteria for Additional Tier 1 instruments: comparison between CRD 2 and Basel III

	CRD2	Basel III
Permanence	30 year permitted for 15% bucket only. Incentive to redeem permitted in 15% bucket only. Callable in 15% and 35% buckets after respectively minimum 10/5 years. Not permitted in 50% bucket. Requires supervisory approval.	It is perpetual, ie, There is no maturity date and there are no incentives to redeem. May be callable at the initiative of the issuer only after a minimum of 5 years and under conditions.
Flexibility of payments	Cancellation of coupon whenever necessary and mandatory when in breach. ACSM (Alternative Coupon Settlement Mechanism) and dividend pusher acceptable under certain conditions.	Dividend/coupon discretion. a. The bank must have full discretion at all times to cancel distributions/payments. b. Cancellation of discretionary payments must not be an event of default. c. Banks must have full access to cancelled payments to meet obligations as they fall due. d. Cancellation of distributions/payments must not impose restrictions on the bank except in relation to distributions to common stockholders. ACSM and dividend pusher are not acceptable.
Loss absorbency	Adequate mechanism CEBS examples of a) conversion, b) write-down with write-up on *pari passu* basis.	Instruments classified as liabilities must have principal loss absorption through either (i) conversion to common shares at an objective pre-specified trigger point or (ii) a write-down mechanism which allocates losses to the instrument at an objective pre-specified trigger point. The write-down will have the following effects: a. reduce the claim of the instrument in liquidation b. reduce the amount re-paid when a call is exercised c. partially or fully reduce coupon/dividend payments on the instrument
Limits	50% convertible in emergency situation 35% non innovative 15% innovative	4,5% CET 6,0% Tier 1

Source: Authors, on the basis of the Directive 2006/48/EC, 2006 and Basel III, December 2010

instruments, the reimbursed amount is the written-down amount; (iii) should the bank decide to "pay coupons" (ie, pay the interest of the debt instrument) or dividend on the instruments, then the amount of the coupons to be paid must also be reduced.

With regard to flexibility of payment, Basel III provides for a set of rules that aim to leave to the bank the necessary freedom to manage its earnings and reserves without jeopardising or worsening its financial situation.

Finally, Basel III requires instruments to be perpetual, which implies that dated instruments that exist in some countries will no longer be eligible. The issuer can, however, foresee that the instrument be called after a certain period of time (minimum five years), but this can only happen at the sole initiative of the issuer and subject to the prior supervisory approval. Once more the idea is to ensure a solid capital base, while leaving some flexibility for banks' capital management.[10]

3.3.2.3 The new set of eligibility criteria for Tier 2
While Tier 1 is to be used in going-concern scenarios, Tier 2 is meant to cover losses on a gone-concern basis, ie, when a bank enters a liquidation process. Compared with the current situation, the criteria have been reinforced, notably by excluding incentives to redeem from this category (see Panel 3.5).

Considering the Tier 2 role, from a loss-absorbency point of view, Tier 2 holders are subordinated only to depositors and senior creditors.

The instrument cannot be repaid or reimbursed in the first five years. Availability and fully paid-in conditions (Criteria 1 and 9) are required in order to ensure that a bank has concrete control of the money in order to face any potential losses.

An additional crucial requirement for all classes of capital instruments, put forward on January 2011 by the Basel Committee (Basel Committee on Banking Supervision 2011), is that they should be able to fully absorb losses at a point where a bank is no longer viable, in order to avoid taxpayers being exposed to losses (or to reduce the burden of public bailouts). The overarching principle is that taxpayers are and should remain senior to all capital holders, regardless of the tier. Indeed, during the financial crisis a number of distressed banks were rescued by the public sector injecting funds in

PANEL 3.5 CRITERIA FOR INCLUSION IN TIER 2 CAPITAL

1. Issued and paid-in.
2. Subordinated to depositors and general creditors of the bank.
3. Is neither secured nor covered by a guarantee of the issuer or related entity or other arrangement that legally or economically enhances the seniority of the claim vis-à-vis depositors and general bank creditors.
4. Maturity:
    a. minimum original maturity of at least five years;
    b. recognition in regulatory capital in the remaining five years before maturity will be amortised on a straight line basis;
    c. there are no step-ups or other incentives to redeem.
5. May be callable at the initiative of the issuer only after a minimum of five years:
    a. to exercise a call option a bank must receive prior supervisory approval;
    b. a bank must not do anything that creates an expectation that the call will be exercised; and
    c. banks must not exercise a call unless:
        i. they replace the called instrument with capital of the same or better quality and the replacement of this capital is done at conditions that are sustainable for the income capacity of the bank; or
        ii. the bank demonstrates that its capital position is well above the minimum capital requirements after the call option is exercised.
6. The investor must have no rights to accelerate the repayment of future scheduled payments (coupon or principal), except in bankruptcy and liquidation.
7. The instrument cannot have a credit-sensitive dividend feature, that is to say a dividend/coupon that is reset periodically based in whole or in part on the banking organisation's credit standing.
8. Neither the bank nor a related party over which the bank exercises control or significant influence can have purchased the instrument, nor can the bank directly or indirectly have funded the purchase of the instrument.
9. If the instrument is not issued out of an operating entity or the holding company in the consolidated group (eg, an SPV), proceeds must be immediately available without limitation to an operating entity or the holding company in the consolidated group in a form that meets or exceeds all of the other criteria for inclusion in Tier 2 Capital.

Source: Basel III, December 2010

the form of common equity and other forms of Tier 1. While this had the effect of supporting depositors, it also implied that subscribers of Tier 2 subordinated debt, and in some cases of Additional Tier 1 instruments, did not absorb losses incurred by certain large internationally active banks, which would have been liquidated had the public sector not provided support.

Therefore, the following seven requirements have been introduced:

1. The terms and conditions of all Additional Tier 1 and Tier 2 instruments issued by an internationally active bank must have a provision that requires such instruments, at the option of the relevant authority, to either be written off or converted into common equity upon the occurrence of the trigger event unless:
    a. the governing jurisdiction of the bank has in place laws that (i) require such Tier 1 and Tier 2 instruments to be written off upon such an event, or (ii) otherwise require such instruments to fully absorb losses before taxpayers are exposed to loss;
    b. peer-group review confirms that the jurisdiction conforms with clause (a); and
    c. it is disclosed by the relevant regulator and by the issuing bank, in issuance documents going forward, that such instruments are subject to loss under clause (a) in this paragraph.
2. Any compensation paid to the instrument holders as a result of the write-off must be paid immediately in the form of common stock (or its equivalent in the case of non-joint-stock companies).
3. The issuing bank must maintain at all times all prior authorisation necessary to immediately issue the relevant number of shares specified in the instrument's terms and conditions, should the trigger event occur.
4. The trigger event is either the earlier of (i) a decision that a write-off, without which the firm would become non-viable, is necessary, as determined by the relevant authority; and (ii) a decision to make a public-sector injection of capital, or equivalent support, without which the firm would have become non-viable, as determined by the relevant authority.

5. The issuance of any new shares as a result of the trigger event must occur prior to any public-sector injection of capital so that the capital provided by the public sector is not diluted.
6. The relevant jurisdiction in determining the trigger event is the jurisdiction in which the capital is being given recognition for regulatory purposes. Therefore, where an issuing bank is part of a wider banking group, and if the issuing bank wishes the instrument to be included in the consolidated group's capital in addition to its solo capital, the terms and conditions must specify an additional trigger event. This trigger event is the earlier of (i) a decision that a write-off, without which the firm would become non-viable, is necessary, as determined by the relevant authority in the home jurisdiction; and (ii) a decision to make a public-sector injection of capital, or equivalent support, in the jurisdiction of the consolidated supervisor, without which the firm receiving the support would have become non-viable, as determined by the relevant authority in that jurisdiction.
7. Any common stock paid as compensation to the holders of the instrument must be common stock of either the issuing bank or the parent company of the consolidated group (including any successor in resolution).

3.4 THE QUANTITY OF REGULATORY CAPITAL

As discussed in previous sections, one of the main objectives of the Basel III regulatory reform was to strengthen the quality of capital instruments that supervisors allow banks to include in the regulatory definition of capital. In this respect, both the introduction of a narrower layer of capital (ie, CET 1) and the agreement on eligibility criteria that are stricter than the current rules, do represent a remarkable achievement. In parallel, it has been decided to increase also the level of capital (so-called "calibration"). Indeed, the financial crisis has also put in evidence that a higher level of capital should be kept by institutions in order to properly face losses.

Basel III has introduced new standards that cannot be put in place overnight. Therefore, a transitional phase has been planned. With regard to the levels of the ratios (4.5% for CET 1, 6% for Tier 1 and 8% for total capital), the new framework should be fully implemented within five years, starting 2013.

In addition, two capital buffers have been introduced: a capital conservation buffer and a countercyclical buffer so that the level of capital of institutions can reach a maximum of 13% (see Chapter 6). The FSB is also discussing the issue of systemically important financial institutions (SIFIs) and the measures to mitigate the impact of their failure on the real economy (for example in terms of domestic economy stability or unemployment rate) while avoiding the moral-hazard risk – a sort of "public guarantee" that affects stakeholders' involvement and biases their risk perception.

Requiring an additional capital surcharge is one of the possible measures under discussion (See Chapter 10).

3.5 TRANSITIONAL ARRANGEMENTS AND GRANDFATHERING MECHANISMS

Basel III will be applied gradually in order to provide banks with sufficient time to adjust their capital structures and to avoid jeopardising the economic recovery.

The phase-in process is represented in Figure 3.2.

In detail, the regulatory adjustments (ie, deductions and prudential filters) will be fully deducted from CET 1 by January 1, 2018. Prior to that date, 20% of the required deductions will be made from CET 1 on January 1, 2014, 40% on January 1, 2015, 60% on January 1, 2016, 80% on January 1, 2017, and reach 100% on January

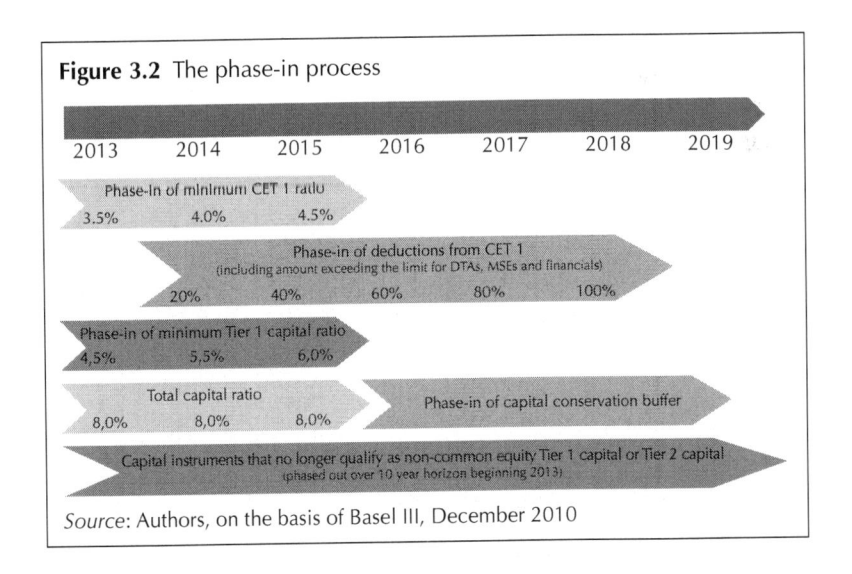

Figure 3.2 The phase-in process

	2013	2014	2015	2016	2017	2018	2019
Phase-in of minimum CET 1 ratio	3.5%	4.0%	4.5%				
Phase-in of deductions from CET 1 (including amount exceeding the limit for DTAs, MSEs and financials)		20%	40%	60%	80%	100%	
Phase-in of minimum Tier 1 capital ratio	4.5%	5.5%	6.0%				
Total capital ratio	8.0%	8.0%	8.0%				
				Phase-in of capital conservation buffer			
Capital instruments that no longer qualify as non-common equity Tier 1 capital or Tier 2 capital (phased out over 10 year horizon beginning 2013)							

Source: Authors, on the basis of Basel III, December 2010

1, 2018. During the transition period, the remainder not deducted will continue to be subject to existing national treatments.

Second, with regard to the instruments that do not meet the eligibility criteria, the following measures will be applied.

❏ Existing public capital injections are grandfathered until 2018.
❏ Capital instruments that do not meet the criteria for inclusion in CET 1 will be excluded as of January 1, 2013. However, instruments meeting the following three conditions will be phased out over a 10-year horizon beginning January 1, 2013: (i) they are issued by a non-joint-stock company; (ii) they are treated as equity under the prevailing accounting standards; and (iii) they receive unlimited recognition as part of Tier 1 capital under current national banking law. Their recognition will be capped at 90% of their nominal amount (outstanding on January 1, 2013) from January 1, 2013 with the cap reducing by 10 % in each subsequent year.
❏ The treatment of minority interest will also be phased in: when minority interests are included under the existing national treatment but are no longer eligible under Basel III, 20% of their amount (the 20% here refers to the amount of minorities included in CET 1 under each national prudential regime) should be excluded from the relevant component of capital on January 1, 2014, 40% on January 1, 2015, 60% on January 1, 2016, 80% on January 1, 2017, and reach 100% on January 1, 2018.
❏ Capital instruments that no longer qualify as Additional Tier 1 capital or Tier 2 capital will be phased out beginning January 1, 2013. Fixing the base at the nominal amount of such instruments outstanding on January 1, 2013, their recognition will be capped at 90% from January 1, 2013, with the cap reducing by 10% in each subsequent year. This cap is applied to Additional Tier 1 and Tier 2 separately. It refers to the total amount of instruments outstanding that no longer meet the relevant entry criteria. To the extent that an instrument is redeemed, or its recognition in capital is amortised, after January 1, 2013, the nominal amount serving as the base is not reduced.
❏ In addition, instruments with an incentive to be redeemed that are not called at their effective maturity date are treated differently, depending on whether the instruments meet, on a forward-

looking basis, the new eligibility criteria as set out in paragraph 94 (g) of Basel III.
❏ Instruments issued on or after January 1, 2013 must meet the criteria to be included in regulatory capital. Instruments issued prior to January 1, 2013 that do not meet those criteria will be phased out from January 1, 2013.
❏ Finally, the minimum CET 1 Ratio is to be progressively increased, from 3.5% in 2013, to 4% in 2014 and to 4.5% in 2015; so is the minimum Tier 1 ratio, which will increase from 4.5% in 2013, 5.5% in 2014 to 6% in 2015.

3.6 CONCLUSION

Basel III comprises a fundamental reform in three interrelated respects regarding the definition of regulatory capital. First, it introduces a tightening of the definition of capital, in particular with a strong focus on common equity and stricter and more harmonised eligibility criteria with regard to all capital instruments. Second, it represents a move away from complex hybrid instruments, by disallowing the recognition of a number of features that did not prove to be loss-absorbing in periods of stress. Finally, all capital instruments must now absorb losses at the point of non-viability, which was not the case before or during the financial crisis.

Moreover, one of the key lessons from the financial crisis has been that a common understanding of the new rules will facilitate a true level playing field. With Basel III, regulatory capital, strengthened both in quality and quantity, should represent a more effective tool to bear banking losses in going concerns and in gone concerns, mitigating the risk of default and/or the need for state aid. However, it is already possible to identify some particularly sensitive issues for the future: for example, how will capital markets be able to meet the new demand for capital by banks?

Basel III has already put in place measures in order to address these questions, through transitional arrangements. Moreover, monitoring the new framework and financial innovation will help to assess whether the new capital framework needs to be further reviewed. However, it remains to be seen whether further efforts in other fields, such as accounting rules, fiscal regimes and corporate law, will help to achieve full harmonisation

All in all, the regulatory reform, including the definition of regulatory capital, was endorsed at the Seoul G20 meeting and is on track. The key challenge is to ensure a consistent implementation at an international level, bearing in mind that not all the countries have yet implemented Basel II, while Europe often leads the pack.

The views expressed in this chapter are the authors' and do not reflect those of the French Prudential Supervisory Authority nor of the Bank of Italy.

1. For a discussion on the changes to the denominator, see Chapter 4.
2. See http://www.bis.org/publ/bcbs47.pdf.
3. Under Basel II some deductions were made 50% from Tier 1 and 50% from Tier 2.
4. With regard to banks that use the IRB method to assess credit risk, the amount of shortfall/excess reserve is defined by comparing provisions to expected losses.
5. On January 1, 2013, a bank must deduct the amount by which the aggregate of the three items above exceeds 15% of its CET 1, calculated prior to the deduction of these items but after application of all other regulatory adjustments applied to CET 1. As of January 1, 2018, the amount of the three items that remains recognised after the application of all regulatory adjustments must not exceed 15% of the CET 1, calculated after all regulatory adjustments. The items included in the 15% limit are subject to full disclosure.
6. DTAs are generated by the application of different rules between fiscal and accounting regimes in order to define the earning before taxes. Where the accountant earning is lower the fiscal one, DTAs are reported in the balance sheet.
7. See IAS/IFRS 7 for further information.
8. This is a feature whereby the payment of a coupon/dividend of instrument A automatically triggers the payment of the coupon/dividend of an instrument that is senior to instrument A.
9. The coupon is paid out of shares rather than by cash.
10. For instance, a bank may benefit from favourable market conditions, exercising the call to substitute cheaper instruments for costly capital.
11. This document has been incorporated in the comprehensive version of "International Convergence of Capital Measurement and Capital Standards: A Revised Framework", including the June 2004 Basel II Framework (see also later reference), the 1996 Amendment to the Capital Accord to Incorporate Market Risks (see also later reference), and the 2005 paper on "The Application of Basel II to Trading Activities and the Treatment of Double Default Effects".

REFERENCES

Basel Committee on Banking Supervision, 1988, "International convergence of capital measurement and capital standards", July.[11]

Basel Committee on Banking Supervision, 1996, "Amendment to the capital accord to incorporate market risks, updated version in 2005". January.

Basel Committee on Banking Supervision, 1998 "Instruments eligible for inclusion in Tier 1 capital", press release, October.

Basel Committee on Banking Supervision, 2004, "Basel II: International Convergence of Capital Measurement and Capital Standards: a Revised Framework", June.

Basel Committee on Banking Supervision, 2009, "Strengthening the resilience of the banking sector", consultative document, December.

Basel Committee on Banking Supervision, 2010, "Basel III: A global regulatory framework for more resilient banks and banking systems", December.

Basel Committee on Banking Supervision, 2011 "Final elements of the reforms to raise the quality of regulatory capital", press release, January.

Committee of European Banking Supervisors, 2006, "Current rules on own funds and market trends in the new capital instruments" June.

Committee of European Banking Supervisors, 2007, "A quantitative survey on hybrid capital instruments", March.

Joint Forum on Financial Conglomerates, 1999, "Supervision of financial conglomerates", February.

4

A New Framework for the Trading Book

Federico Cabañas
Bank of Spain

4.1 INTRODUCTION

Throughout 2009 and 2010 most public attention has focused on the completion of the Basel III package of regulatory measures, which were published in December 2010. Basel III raises the resilience of the banking sector by strengthening the Basel II regulatory capital framework.

Traditionally, regulation had been designed with a purely microprudential (institution-specific) perspective and relied almost entirely on individual capital-adequacy indicators. Regulation was constructed mainly around each individual institution's capital ratio without taking into account a "macro" view (see Chapter 2). The focus on capital also implied that regulation largely ignored other risks, which had no direct impact on losses, such as liquidity.

Basel III does widen the traditional scope of regulation, including for the first time macroprudential elements, such as the introduction of a leverage ratio, a new 2.5% conservation buffer or, for globally systemic banks, establishing additional capital buffers. Basel III also introduces for the first time a global liquidity standard to supplement capital measures.

However, it is worth noting that the introduction of these new macroprudential and liquidity components to the regulatory framework does not imply the elimination of the existing Basel II micro-, institution-specific regulation. Basel II remains largely unchanged as a key part of the new Basel III framework, though some enhancements have also been introduced.

4.1.1 Evolution of the capital ratio: from Basel I to Basel III.

Basel I had introduced a simple capital ratio between a financial firm's capital (numerator) and its credit assets multiplied by a limited set of risk weights (denominator).

Until the implementation of the 1996 Market Risk Amendment (MRA), which made compulsory for banks to set minimum capital requirement for market risks as well, the ratio (well known as "solvency ratio") took only credit risk into account. It is worth highlighting that the 1996 MRA also introduced for the first time the possibility of using a bank's internal model for capital purposes (of course, subject to supervisory validation and approval). The rule also contained a standardised approach as a fallback option.

The Basel II framework, finalised in 2004 and entered into force in most jurisdictions between 2007 and 2008, changed the credit risk component of the denominator of the solvency ratio and extended to credit risk the possibility (already introduced for market risk by the 1996 MRA) of using institutions' internal models for regulatory capital purposes. However, the numerator (the capital definition) and the actual level of the ratio remained unchanged.

The Basel III reform has changed the two components of the solvency ratio that remained in a Basel I world: (i) the definition of capital, which is now much stricter as regards the quality of capital instruments to be eligible; and (ii) the level of the ratio itself, which has been increased (see Chapter 3).

However, there are two elements of the capital reform that do modify the way in which the denominator of the ratio is calculated. These changes relate to (i) the trading book and (ii) counterparty risk frameworks. In both cases, the basic logic behind the adjustments has been to incorporate risk components that were absent from the denominator of the current capital ratio.

4.1.2 Link between the Market Risk Framework and the Regulatory Trading Book

Paragraph 683(i) of the Basel Accord text defines market risk as the risk of losses in on- and off-balance-sheet positions arising from movements in market prices. The rule establishes that the instruments subject to this requirement are those that incorporate risks pertaining to interest-rate-related instruments and equities in the trading book (TB) and foreign exchange (FX) risk and commodities risk throughout the bank, regardless of whether they have been booked in the TB or in the banking book (BB).

In general, the positions held in a bank's TB portfolio are identified as the ones subject to market-risk requirements. Accordingly, in this chapter we will generally refer to "TB positions" when describing the scope of instruments subject to the market-risk framework. However, it is worth highlighting that, for FX and commodity risk, we must consider all positions, regardless of its trading- or banking-book nature.

Regarding the BB–TB boundary, one of the most controversial elements of the existing regulation is that, according to the definition, what makes a position part of a bank's TB portfolio is the intention[1] that the institution has. Paragraph 685 states that a trading book consists of positions in financial instruments and commodities held either with trading intent[2] or in order to hedge other elements of the trading book.

This chapter discusses the rationale and explains the main changes introduced in the market-risk framework,[3] which are often labelled as "Basel 2.5", given that this area of work started just after

Figure 4.1 New elements added to the Market Risk (MR) framework

Previous market risk framework,	New market risk framework,
The capital requirements for market risk are calculated as the **sum** of the following elements	The capital charge according to the internal models approach, which is the SUM of
❏ The capital charge according to the standardised measurement method to the extent a bank does not use internal models, covering: • general and specific interest rate risk; • general and specific equity position risk; • Foreign exchange risk; • commodities risk.	1. the **higher** of (1) its previous day's VaR number; and (2) an average of the daily VaR measures on each of the preceding 60 b.d. multiplied by a factor.
❏ The capital charge according to the internal models approach, which is the **higher** of (1) its previous day's VaR number; and (2) an average of the daily VaR measures on each of the preceding 60 b.d. multiplied by a factor.	2. The **higher** of (1) its latest available stressed-VaR numbers over the preceding 60 b.d. multiplied by a factor; plus
To the extent a banks' internal model does not cover specific risk, the specified risk capital charges of the standardised measurement method apply	3. The incremental or comprehensive risk capital charge.

2 new "components" ("blocks" or "patches") for
General (Stressed VaR) and Specific (IRC + CRM) market risk modelling.

Source: Analysis of the TB QIS: available at http://www.bis.org/publ/bcbs163.pdf

the finalisation of the Basel II framework (in 2005) and was finalised just before the Basel III reform (in 2009). The new requirements for counterparty risk are contained in Chapter 5.

The text is organised as following. Section 4.2 provides a general view of the reform; Section 4.3 discusses the main developments that have taken place both in banks' TB activities and in regulation since the 1996 MRA was first implemented; Section 4.4 describes the lengthy "Basel 2.5" rulemaking process that has included several consultation rounds; Sections 4.5 and 4.6 explain the new treatment for specific risk and the new stressed VaR (sVaR) capital measure respectively; finally, Section 4.7 provides some conclusions.

4.2 SYNOPSIS OF THE MAIN CHANGES

Figure 4.1 shows the new elements added to the Market Risk (MR) framework. As it can be seen, the changes affect only the internal-models approach; the Standardised approach remains virtually unchanged.[4]

The old "daily VaR" measure, which is widely used by financial institutions in their internal modelling, is still in place as a basic element of the market-risk framework; however, two additional components have been incorporated:

❏ a "stressed VaR" (sVaR) measure; and
❏ an "incremental" (IRC) or "comprehensive" (CRM) risk capital charge.

The new components of the framework have to be summed to the old VaR-based capital charge. This approach is similar to the so-called "building block" that is used under the market-risk standardised rules. This type of aggregation is conservative in general terms, since it allows offsetting and diversification benefits only inside each one of the "blocks", but not within the different "blocks".

In addition to the conservativeness in the aggregation, some banks have noted that the different capital components are quite divergent in nature, with each having to be calculated based on different levels of confidence (eg, 99 to 99.9%) or different holding and capital horizons[5] (eg, 10 days for VaR and sVaR versus a 3–12-month holding period for the Incremental Risk Charge (IRC)). Thus, instead of using the "building block" term, some practitioners have suggested the alternative wording "patchwork"[6] when referring to the new MR framework.

4.3 A FLASHBACK: DEVELOPMENTS IN THE TRADING BOOK UNDER THE 1996 FRAMEWORK

In order to understand the different components of the July 2009 TB package, it is worth taking a look at both market and regulatory developments that have taken place since the 1996 MRA was first introduced. The need to introduce some enhancements to the TB framework has been widely discussed since the implementation of the 1996 Market Risk Framework (MRF). However, some of the well-known flaws of the framework have become more prominent due to changes in the composition of banks' TB portfolios.

4.3.1 Evolution in banks' TB portfolios.

As we have seen, the 1996 Amendment to the Basel Capital Accord allowed, subject to supervisory approval, the use of internal models to calculate regulatory capital requirements for market risk. Since then, the composition of the trading book of banks has nevertheless changed substantially, incorporating increasingly more and more credit-related products, such as credit derivatives and tranches of collateralised debt obligations (CDOs), as well as other complex products such as hedge funds or fund-of-funds products (this was clearly a main driver behind the crisis – see Chapter 1).

In this respect, a survey published in April 2005 conducted jointly by the Basel Committee on Banking Supervision (BCBS) and the International Organisation of Securities Commissions (IOSCO) (BCBS–IOSCO 2005a) showed the growing importance of credit, structured products, hedge funds and securitisations in banks' TB portfolios. The survey actually concluded, "By and large, the current trading book definition, based on trading intent, is challenged by instruments for which liquidity is questionable and/or that are held for medium or long-term periods."

Of course, these market developments led to an increase in credit risk in the trading book and a concomitant rise in other risks such as default risk, event risk, liquidity risk, concentration risk and correlation risk, which were not adequately captured when market-risk regulations were devised.

4.3.2 Treatment of specific risk in the 1996 framework

Under the 1996 MRF for interest-rate risk and equity-position risk, a distinction was made between general risk, ie, the risk arising from general market movements (fluctuations in the level of interest rates or general equity market movements), and specific risk, ie, the risk related to the credit quality of issuers.

While the 1996 trading-book regime aimed to cover both general risk and specific risk, banks' market-risk internal models were primarily designed to provide an alternative to the standardised measure of general risk and allow the effects of correlations across and within risk factors to be taken into account.

The original text (BCBS 1996) of the 1996 MRA actually states in Paragraph 11:

> The focus of most internal models is a bank's general market risk exposure, typically leaving specific risk (i.e. exposures to specific issuers of debt securities or equities) to be measured largely through separate credit risk measurement systems. Banks using models should be subject to capital charges for the specific risk not captured by their models. Accordingly, a separate capital charge for specific risk will apply to each bank using a model to the extent that the model does not capture specific risk.

Although measuring specific risk under the internal models approach was in practice allowed, it clearly presented difficulties in terms of modelling a number of key variables such as event risk, defined as a significant and/or sudden change in the price of a security in the wake of events[7] affecting the issuer and often beyond the assumptions of VaR models (ie, 99% confidence interval, 10-business-day holding period), or default risk, associated in particular with the sudden failure of an issuer (ie, jump-to-default risk).

Thus, it was established that the use of internal models for measuring specific risk could be acceptable only when subject to additional conditions. In order to use an internal estimate, the model had to be able to explain *ex ante* historical changes in the value of the portfolio and capture concentrations[8] in the composition of the portfolio. It also had to demonstrate that it remained reliable in an adverse environment and that it could be validated by backtesting.

As a fallback option, a risk-capital surcharge was established. A k factor of 1, ie, a multiplier of four – instead of three[9] – had to be applied to the specific VaR measure, if the internal model did not fully capture event and default risk.

Despite the fact that banks have significantly improved their modelling of market risk (both in terms of risk sensitivity and completeness) since the 1996 Amendment to the Capital Accord was approved, to date no institution has been authorised to apply a multiplier of less than four for their specific risk modelling. Thus, the capture of event and default risk was still missing from banks' models or, at best, remained partial.

Of course, this could be interpreted as the result of an excessive meticulousness from supervisors. However, taking into account the initial results for the new IRC obtained from the several quantitative impact studies (QISs) conducted to date, it seems implicit that during all these years there has been no capital incentive to develop such models (BCBS 2009e).

It is clear that applying a four instead of a three multiplier to the specific VaR measure was a bargain in terms of capital compared with a full modelling charge for both default and migration risks.[10]

4.4 "BASEL 2.5" – FROM JULY 2005 TO JUNE 2010
4.4.1 July 2005

In July 2005, the Basel Committee and IOSCO (BCBS–IOSCO 2005b) proposed a series of measures, known already at that time as "Basel 2.5", aimed at enhancing the trading-book regulatory regime. The proposed improvements were intended to clarify the types of exposure that qualify for inclusion in the trading book, to provide further guidance on prudent valuation methods for these exposures and stress testing, and to strengthen modelling standards for market risk (Prato 2006).

Banks were required to implement a clear set of policies and procedures for determining which positions could be included in, and which should be excluded from, the trading book.[11] The regulatory standards also included prudent valuation guidance for less liquid trading-book positions and, where necessary, higher valuation adjustments than those made under standard accounting practice.

As regards modelling standards, the July 2005 package (ie, "Basel 2.5") focused on the capture of event risk by internal models used to measure specific risk, the use of more robust standards for specific risk and the conduct of more complete backtesting and model-validation tests; and, in terms of capital impact, established for the first time the obligation to calculate an Incremental capital charge for Default Risk (IDR) not captured in the VaR-based calculation.

Those institutions that had already received specific risk-model recognition would have to meet the new requirements by January 1, 2010. If they failed to do so, they would have to use the standardised rules for specific risk. However this package was directly applicable to new models, ie, any institution that would ask for the first time to use its specific risk internal model for capital purposes had to meet the new standards from the beginning.

As discussed below, the IDR charge was expanded during the consultation process and, finally, the July 2009 IRC has superseded the July 2005 IDR, with the January 2010 deadline postponed (twice) until December 2011. Consequently, to date, only those institutions that have asked to use their specific risk internal model for capital purposes after 2005 have been obliged to implement an IDR-type charge.[12]

It is worth remembering that, apart from the requirement to incorporate an IDR charge for default risk in the trading book, the July 2005 package included two additional sets of measures with a capital impact: (i) a new treatment for counterparty credit risk for over-the-counter derivatives, repo-style and securities financing transactions, which allowed the use of effective positive exposure (EPE) types of internal model (see Chapter 5); and (ii) the recognition of double-default effects for covered transactions. Contrary to what occurs with the IDR charge, these two measures implied a reduction in capital requirements, and (also contrary to the IDR) both have already been implemented, together with the rest of the Basel II Accord.[13]

Thus, it seems fair to conclude that the "new" regulatory treatment for TB-specific risk is far from being "new", and, though some changes and refinements have been introduced since 2005, banks have been given reasonable time to implement the new standards.

4.4.2 July 2008–January 2009 first and second consultative documents

Building on the lessons learned from the financial crisis, the Basel Committee decided to expand the scope of the incremental default capital charge to capture not only defaults but a wider range of incremental risks (including event risks). Two "consultative packages" were published, in July 2008 and January 2009 (BCBS 2008a, 2008b, 2009a, 2009b).

4.4.2.1 From "Incremental Default Risk" to "Incremental Risk Charge"

One of the lessons derived from the crisis was that most of the TB credit losses did not arise from actual defaults, but rather from credit migrations (ie, an unexpected upgrade or downgrade in the issuer's rating) combined with widening of credit spreads (ie, an increase in an issuer credit spread in the absence of a rating change) and the loss of liquidity. Thus, covering only the default risk stemming from TB portfolios no longer appeared adequate. The updated framework incorporated migration risk to the IDR charge, which was renamed accordingly as "Incremental Risk Charge" (IRC).

In the July 2008 consultative documents banks were allowed one more year from the original January 1, 2010, implementation deadline established for the IDR (eg, until January 1, 2011) to incorporate into their internal models all risks covered by the IRC. In addition to the changes to the IRC, the consultative documents included enhanced guidelines to improve the internal VaR models for market risk and updated the July 2005 prudent valuation guidance for positions subject to market risk of the Basel II Framework.

4.4.2.2 Proposed treatment for TB securitisations

While the Committee decided to expand the IRC to incorporate migration risk, it also agreed to narrow the scope of application of the new IRC charge, excluding securitisations from its potential scope. The January 2009 Consultative Document established that, while a firm could choose to model specific risk for securitisation products for the calculation of the 10-day VaR estimate (as discussed in the introduction to this chapter), it would still be subject to a specific risk capital charge calculated according to the standardised method.

It is worth noting that securitisations included in the TB have been widely identified as one of the main loss drivers in banks' portfolios.[14] In this regard it seems fair to state that the transfer of credit risk from the banking book (BB) to the TB led to a risk undercapitalisation, and this risk transfer across books had been achieved via the securitisation process.

It may be concluded that the securitisation process allowed the possibility of regulatory arbitrage by enabling the transformation of BB risk (eg, loans, mortgages or credit cards) into TB "assets" (eg, securities), with a lower capital charge.

Of course, the application of the standardised charges for securitisations eliminated the possibility of regulatory arbitrage between BB and TB for these instruments; however, the exclusion of the securitisations (and resecuritisations, ie, securitisations whose underlyings are other securitisations) from the scope of the IRC was caused primarily by a lack of trust in the ability of banks to model default and migration risk for these instruments.

In this respect, it is worth noting that, during the consultation process, the banking industry recognised that, for the time being, securitisations presented serious IRC modelling challenges.[15] For instance, the joint comment letter from the International Swaps and Derivatives Association (ISDA), the Institute of International Finance (IIF), the London Investment Banking Association (LIBA) and the International Banking Federation (IBFed) (2008) to the July 2008 Consultative Package stated:

> Structured products – The draft guidelines require banks to have in place a model for "credit default and migration risks for positions subject to credit risk" by 1 January 2010. It should be feasible for most large banks to implement such a model by that date for their corporate credit portfolios, where the concepts of default and migration risk are relatively well understood and where banks have been working on IDR models for some time. Firms are much less likely to be in a position to implement a model for default and migration risks on structured products by that date, as the behavior of such assets over the economic cycle is less well understood. Moreover, recent market events have demonstrated that a default-migration-spread risk framework may not be the most appropriate for structured products. Prescribing a model incorporating "migration risk" would force banks to use credit ratings to model the risk on structured finance products. It is unlikely that such an approach would have captured the trading losses of 2007 and 2008, and firms may prefer to model the risk of such assets on a price basis . . .

The BCBS encouraged banks to further develop their models for securitisation products. However, until a methodology robust enough to adequately capture incremental risks for securitised products was developed, the Committee established that the capital charges of the standardised measurement method would be applied to these products.

4.4.2.3 Correlation trading "carve-out"

During the consultation of the January 2009 documents (which had excluded securitisations from the IRC scope), industry groups unanimously emphasised that the application of the standardised rules for so-called "correlation trading"[16] activities (which fall under the scope of the "securitisation" definition) would have unintended consequences (BCBS, various commentators, 2009).

Correlation trading positions are most often unrated – in line with the underlying, unrated but liquid corporate credit default swap (CDS) names they reference – and would have attracted an inappropriate level of capital requirements under the proposed amendments.

Banks noted that, under the standardised rules, in most cases the only possible treatment for these "correlation trading" portfolios would have been full deduction from capital (ie, the capital would decrease by the position's full amount), since most positions were unrated and the application of the Supervisory Formula was not possible in practice due to data constrains (usually this means a lack of data).

According to banks, the amendments would have required full deduction for many tranches, even where most credit risk is hedged, either with offsetting tranche positions or via the underlying single-name CDS markets. Banks alleged that without the ability to offset long and short positions in correlation books under the standardised approach for specific risk (Paragraph 709 (iii) and Paragraphs 713–17) a capital charge would have been levied against the full notional amount of both long and short positions.

Thus, the main risk drivers of the actual exposure of the correlation book would have been inaccurately represented and the capital charge severely distorted: both the original correlation positions and the hedges (whether in the form of CDS index trades, standard index tranche trades or single-name CDS trades) would have been recognised as separate, speculative positions, with no permitted offset for capital purposes.

Regarding the deduction treatment for unrated tranches, it is worth noting that, previously, the rule (Paragraph 718 (xciv) of Basel II) already established that any securitisation position subject to a deduction treatment under the securitisation framework should receive the same treatment under TB specific rules.

However, this rule also allowed "securitisation exposures where a two-way [eg, liquid] market exists for the exposures [eg, the securitisations themselves] or, in the case of synthetic securitisation, all their constituent risk components" (Paragraph 718 (xcv) of Basel II) to be carved out from the scope of the deduction rule.

Based on the liquidity of the underlying markets, many firms made use of this carve-out for calculating the capital requirement of correlation transactions forming part of their derivative business, including, in particular, trading activity relating to standard and bespoke tranches based on market standard CDS indexes.

In addition, the banking industry highlighted that the characteristics of correlation trading positions had little in common (apart from being categorised as securitisations) with the sorts of opaque, leveraged collateral debt obligations (CDOs) and CDOs squared (ie, resecuritisation) or cubed (ie, re-resecuritisation), which were the source of large trading losses in 2007/08.[17]

As a result, the impact of the proposed revisions for the calculation of the additional regulatory capital requirements with respect to the sole specific risk on the actively managed single tranches referencing single-name liquid corporate CDSs would have rendered the tranche-derivative business uneconomic.

According to the industry (ISDA–IIF–LIBA–IBFed 2009a), the demise of correlation trading activity would have materially impacted banks' capacity to hedge the concentration and corporate portfolio risks arising from their loan books and significantly inhibit new corporate lending. Overall, liquidity of the CDS market would also be expected to be severely affected as correlation credit hedging accounts for a large part of the corporate single-name CDS and corporate CDS index trading volumes.

Industry groups requested to maintain the carve-out that was established in Paragraph 718 (xcv) of Basel II for securitisation positions actively managed and hedged.

4.4.3 The final rule

In response to the dialogue with the industry, a revised proposal was released in July 2009 (BCBS 2009c, 2009d). The final proposal allowed banks to conduct their own modelling for correlation trading activities under strict minimum requirements and subject to additional stress-test requirements as well as to a regulatory floor. The new capital charge, applicable solely to correlation trading portfolios, was called the "Comprehensive Risk Measure" (CRM).

On 18 June 2010, the BCBS (2010a) published a press release introducing some fine-tuned adjustments to the July 2009 package. In particular, the Committee agreed to a coordinated start date of not later than December 31, 2011 (eg, one additional year from the already delayed calendar), for all elements of the July 2009 trading-book package.[18] The Committee also clarified that the specific capital charge for an individual position in a credit derivative or securitisation instrument may be limited to the maximum possible loss.

Following the publication in December 2010 of the results of the Comprehensive Quantitative Impact Study (QIS) (BCBS 2010b) exercise conducted to assess the impact of both Basel 2.5 and Basel III, the BCBS also announced that it had agreed to set the level of the regulatory floor for the "Comprehensive Risk Measure" at 8% of the capital charge that would result from the application of the standardised measurement method to the Bank's Correlation Trading portfolio.

In February 2011 the Basel Committee published an updated version of the "revisions to the Basel II market risk framework" document (BCBS 2011a). The document reflects the adjustments announced in the above-mentioned press release as well as the stress-testing guidance for the correlation trading portfolios.

BOX 4.1 BASEL III PHASE-IN VERSUS BASEL 2.5 "EARLY" IMPLEMENTATION

The BCBS has agreed that the Basel III standards will be phased in gradually (to be completed in 2018), so that the banking sector can move to the higher capital standards while supporting lending to the economy. Standards where there is a lack of experience, such as the liquidity and leverage ratios, will be phased in gradually. This should enable the BCBS to address any unintended consequences.

However, the new TB regulation envisaged to be implemented by the end of 2011, long before the rest of the regulatory measures were due to be adopted. Due to this "early" implementation some practitioners labelled the new TB rules as "Basel 2.5". Of course, this tighter calendar has been one of the common complaints from the industry.

Regarding this "early" implementation, some industry representatives have argued that the Basel 2.5 rules were created in something of a hurry, in response to the sense that the overall capital for the trading

↓

book was too low and needed to be fixed, rather than based on a precise, careful analysis of the risks and an equally careful decision as to how to capitalise them.

It is fair to state that some of the changes to the framework had been introduced as a quick fix for some of the flaws and gaps embedded in the TB framework that were dramatically highlighted by the financial crisis. But we must also remark that other elements of the reform, such as the need to have a sound and prudent treatment for specific risk, were well known, and supervisors were discussing these issues with the industry long before the crisis erupted.

Therefore, although some institutions may argue that the "2.5" label reflects the tighter calendar compared with the one established for Basel III, it might be worth remembering that, back in 2005, the "2.5" label had exactly the opposite meaning: "2.5" did reflect the delayed introduction (that for specific risk was never fulfilled) of some necessary enhancements to the Basel II framework.

4.5 NEW TREATMENT FOR SPECIFIC RISK IN THE MARKET RISK FRAMEWORK

According to the final rule the treatment of specific (credit) risk comprises the application of the following:

❏ an "incremental risk charge" (IRC) for all non-securitisation credit positions in the TB, which has to incorporate both default and migration risks;
❏ a "comprehensive risk measure" (CRM) for securitisations included in the correlation trading portfolio; and
❏ the standardised rules for the rest of the securitisations.

We will discuss each one of these three new components of the specific risk treatment separately, but first we need to describe some minor changes introduced in the specific VaR capital charge.

4.5.1 Changes in specific VaR

4.5.1.1 Positions subject to specific VaR

As explained in Subsection 4.3.2 of this chapter, it may be worth reminding the reader that, despite the introduction of an IRC and a CRM charge, the "old" specific VaR charge is still in place. Therefore, all TB credit (and equity) positions authorised by the supervisor, to be computed under a specific risk model, remain subject to a specific VaR (and sVaR) capital charge. However, due to the introduction of the new IRC and CRM capital charges, as well as the new treatment for TB securitisations mentioned above, some minor changes have been produced in the old "specific VaR" component of the internal model framework.

First, the July 2009 rule obliges banks to apply the BB capital charges for all TB securitisation positions. To avoid piling up both BB and TB specific charges for these portfolios, the final rule also establishes that TB securitisations are not subject, in principle, to a "specific VaR" capital charge.

However, on a consistent basis, the rule allows a bank to include all securitisations in its specific VaR calculation. This clause was introduced to avoid penalising those portfolios where TB securitisations are managed together with other credit-related instruments. Some banks alleged that these portfolios would render an inaccurate risk position in case securitisations hedging other positions were eliminated. Nevertheless, the BB capital charges must always be applied to all securitisations.

4.5.1.2 Event risk

As noted previously, the 1996 MRA stated that banks' specific risk models should be able to capture "event" risk. What was meant exactly by "event" risk was established in a footnote (No. 5): "Where the price of an individual debt or equity security moves precipitously relative to the general market, eg, on a take-over bid or some other shock event; such events would also include the risk of default."

Thus, according to the 1996 definition, "event risk" was part of "specific risk" and affected both equity and credit positions. If we examine the capital charges introduced by the July 2009 rule, it is clear that the credit component of event risk (eg, default) must be captured by the new IRC.

Accordingly, a new footnote (No. 15) has been added to paragraph 718 (Lxxxviii) of the solvency rule to clarify that banks do not need to capture default and migration risks on their VaR-specific models for positions subject to the IRC. So, for credit positions, VaR-specific models do not need to capture event risk any more. However, it is worth noting that, at least for equity positions (which are not included in the scope for IRC), VaR models must still capture event risk, which has been defined (see Footnote 20 of the July 2009 regulatory package) thus: "Events that are reflected in large changes or jumps in prices must be captured, eg, merger break-ups/takeovers. In particular, firms must consider issues related to survivorship bias."

Finally, it is important to underline that the IRC substitutes the specific risk capital surcharge that was explained in Subsection 4.3.2 of this chapter. Thus, the fallback option of using a multiplier of four (instead of three) for the specific VaR measure, if the internal model did not capture adequately event and default risk, has been eliminated.

4.5.2 Incremental risk charge
4.5.2.1 Rationale

The IRC introduces additional standards intended to complement the VaR modelling framework. One of its basic objectives is to address a number of perceived shortcomings in the current 99% 10-day VaR framework.

For instance, VaR ignores differences in the underlying liquidity of trading-book positions. In addition, VaR calculations are typically based on a 99% one-day VaR, which is scaled up to 10 days, thus the VaR capital charge may not fully reflect large daily losses that occur less frequently than two to three times per year.

The IRC represents an estimate of the default and migration risks of unsecuritised credit products over a one-year capital horizon at a 99.9% confidence level, taking into account the liquidity horizons of individual positions or sets of positions.

As there is no single industry standard for addressing the trading-book issues noted above, the IRC guidelines generally take the form of high-level principles, giving banks considerable flexibility in terms of how to operationalise these principles. The guidelines even allow banks' internal approaches for measuring trading-book risks not to fully map into the high-level supervisory principles in terms of capital horizon, constant level of risk, rollover assumptions or other factors.

Nevertheless, in order to apply any alternative treatment, the bank must demonstrate that the resulting internal capital charge would deliver a charge at least as high as that produced by a model that directly applies the supervisory principles.

4.5.2.2 Scope

The IRC encompasses all positions subject to a capital charge for specific interest-rate risk according to the internal models approach to specific market risk. However, a bank is not permitted to incorporate into its IRC model any securitisation positions, even when securitisation positions are viewed as hedging underlying credit instruments held in the trading account.

The IRC focuses entirely on credit risk and thus equities are, as a general rule, excluded from its potential scope. However, during the consultation process some banks argued that the exclusion of equities would produce an inaccurate picture of their credit portfolio, since they were managing credit positions together with equity cash and derivative instruments.

Accordingly, the final rule has allowed banks (subject to supervisory approval) to include consistently all listed equity and derivatives positions based on listed equity in their incremental risk models when such inclusion is consistent with how the bank internally measures and manages this risk at the trading-desk level. If equity securities are included in the computation of incremental risk, the rule states that default is deemed to occur if the related debt defaults.

There are still a few open issues related to the scope of the IRC: for instance, whether intergroup credit exposures or defaulted credits must be subject to an IRC charge. In addition, firms have also asked whether some non-equity capital instruments or sovereign positions should be included in the IRC scope.

Regarding these and other open implementation issues, the BCBS (2011b) published in February 2011 a document that provides an answer to some of the interpretative issues related to the implementation of the new TB framework. Updated versions of the document will be published on the Committee's website if and when additional interpretive issues arise.

4.5.2.3 Risks captured by the IRC

The IRC must capture the following credit-related risks:

❏ default risk: this means the potential for direct loss due to an obligor's default as well as the potential for indirect losses that may arise from a default event; and

❏ credit migration risk: this means the potential for direct loss due to an internal/external rating downgrade (for long positions) or upgrade (for short positions) as well as the potential for indirect losses that may arise from a credit migration event.

One of the underlying objectives of the reform was to eliminate (or at least mitigate) regulatory arbitrage possibilities, achieving broad consistency between capital charges for similar positions (adjusted for illiquidity) held in the banking and trading books. Since the Basel II Framework reflects a 99.9% soundness standard over a one-year capital horizon, the IRC is also described in those terms. Thus, the guidelines clearly establish that the IRC must meet a standard of soundness that is equivalent to the internal ratings-based approach (IRB).

The precise implications of the "IRB-soundness" overarching principle raise several implementation issues. For instance, it may be subject to interpretation whether IRB parameters (probabilities of default (PDs) and loss-given defaults (LGDs)) can be directly used for IRC calculations, or, alternatively, to what extent may "IRC" parameters be estimated based mainly (if not entirely) on external ratings. In addition, how to deal with unrated credit exposures, as well as how IRB and IRC parameters should be combined as inputs for IRC calculations, may also raise implementation issues. However, these issues are under discussion and there is no clear answer at the time of writing.

Regarding rating migrations and jumps in credit spreads, it is not always the case that a downgrade (or upgrade) precedes a sharp movement in spreads: in many occasions the rating migration occurs after the jump in spread, or there is no market reaction to a migration. This means that the precise definition of "credit migration" might be subject to interpretation. On the other hand, for many credit spreads there is limited data (the five-year CDS is generally the most liquid one, but for other maturities liquidity is scarce), thus the economical effect of a rating migration might not be consistently applied.

4.5.2.4 Assumptions and regulatory parameters for computing the IRC

As we have seen, a bank's IRC model must measure losses due to default and migration at a 99.9% confidence interval based on (i) the assumption of a constant level of risk over a capital horizon of one year, and taking into account (ii) the liquidity horizons applicable to individual trading positions or sets of positions. For each IRC-covered position the model should also capture the impact of rebalancing positions at the end of their liquidity horizons so as to achieve a constant level of risk over a one-year capital horizon.

(i) The assumption of a constant level of risk implies that a bank rebalances, or rolls over, its trading positions over the one-year capital horizon in a manner that maintains the initial risk level, as indicated by a metric such as VaR or the profile of exposure by credit rating and concentration. This means incorporating the effect of replacing positions whose credit characteristics have improved or deteriorated over the liquidity horizon with positions that have risk characteristics equivalent to those that the original position had at the start of the liquidity horizon. The frequency of the assumed rebalancing must be governed by the liquidity horizon for a given position (see (ii) below).

Rebalancing positions does not imply, as the IRB approach for the banking book does, that the same positions will be maintained throughout the capital horizon. Particularly for more liquid and more highly rated positions, this provides a benefit relative to the treatment under the IRB framework. However, a bank may use a one-year constant position assumption, as long as it does so consistently across all portfolios.

(ii) The liquidity horizon represents the time required to sell the position or to hedge all material risks covered by the IRC model in a stressed market. The liquidity horizon must be measured under conservative assumptions and should be sufficiently long that the act of selling or hedging in itself does not materially affect market prices.

In general, within a given product type, a non-investment-grade position[19] is expected to have a longer assumed liquidity horizon than an investment-grade position. Firms also need to apply conservative liquidity horizon assumptions for products, regardless of rating, where secondary market liquidity is scarce, particularly during periods of financial market volatility and investor risk-aversion. The application of prudent liquidity assumptions is particularly important for rapidly growing product classes that have not been tested in a downturn.

A bank can assess liquidity by position or on an aggregated basis (eg, using so-called "buckets"). If an aggregated basis is used (eg, investment-grade European corporate exposures not part of a core CDS index), the aggregation criteria should be defined in a way that meaningfully reflects differences in liquidity.

How this bucket aggregation "mapping" is done in practice might also raise several implementation issues. The number of "buckets" used (granularity – generally speaking more buckets means more granularity and fewer buckets means less granularity) is another open issue that might have significant effects in the final capital outcome.

A bank's IRC model must appropriately reflect issuer and market concentrations. Thus, all other things being equal, a concentrated portfolio should attract a higher capital charge than a more granular portfolio. In particular, due to the longer period needed to liquidate such positions, the liquidity horizon is expected to be greater for positions that are concentrated. The longer liquidity horizon for concentrated positions is necessary to provide adequate capital against two types of concentration: issuer and market concentration.

4.5.2.5 Correlations and diversification

Economic and financial dependence among obligors causes a clustering of default and migration events. Accordingly, the IRC charge must include the impact of correlations between default and migration events among obligors and a bank's IRC model must include the impact of such clustering of default and migration events.

However, the impact of diversification between default or migration events and other market variables would not be reflected in the computation of capital for incremental risk.[20] Accordingly, the capital charge for incremental default and migration losses has to be added to the VaR-based capital charge for market risk (eg, similar to the standardised "building block" approach).

4.5.2.6 Offsetting and hedging

The guidelines establish that exposure amounts may be netted only when long and short positions refer to the same financial instrument. Otherwise, exposure amounts must be captured on a gross (ie, non-netted) basis. Thus, hedging or diversification effects associated with long and short positions involving different instruments or different securities of the same obligor (ie, "intra-obligor hedges"), as well as long and short positions in different issuers (ie, "inter-obligor hedges"), may not be recognised through netting of exposure amounts.

Of course, this does not mean that there is no risk benefit, but any positive effect can be recognised only by capturing and modelling separately the gross long and short positions in the different instruments or securities.

4.5.2.7 Maturity mismatches within the liquidity horizon
If an instrument has a shorter maturity than the liquidity horizon (or if a maturity longer than the liquidity horizon is not contractually assured), the IRC must, where material, include the impact of potential risks that could occur during the interval between the maturity of the instrument and the liquidity horizon.

4.5.2.8 Optionality
The IRC model must reflect the impact of optionality.[21] Accordingly, banks' models should include the nonlinear impact of options and other positions with material nonlinear behaviour with respect to price changes. In addition, for TB positions that are typically hedged via dynamic hedging strategies, a rebalancing of the hedge within the liquidity horizon of the hedged position may also be recognised.

Such recognition is admissible only if the bank (i) chooses to model rebalancing of the hedge consistently over the relevant set of TB risk positions, (ii) demonstrates that the inclusion of rebalancing results in a better risk measurement and (iii) demonstrates that the markets for the instruments serving as hedge are liquid enough to allow for this kind of rebalancing even during periods of stress. Any residual risks resulting from dynamic hedging strategies must be reflected in the capital charge.

4.5.3 Securitisation treatment: correlation trading carve-out
As it has been already noted, in the January 2009 Consultative Documents, the BCBS decided to exclude all securitisations (and re-sec) from the scope of the IRC. However, the final rule released in July 2009 introduced a limited exception, allowing banks to conduct their own modelling for so-called correlation trading activities. The new capital charge, which was called "Comprehensive Risk Measure" (CRM), must meet strict minimum requirements and is

subject to additional stress-test requirements as well as to a regulatory floor.

4.5.3.1 Description of the correlation trading business
Correlation trading books typically combine trading in liquid CDS Index tranches and bespoke tranches with hedging in corporate CDS indexes (such as iTraxx and CDX[22]) and liquid, single-name, corporate CDSs. Both tranche products are OTC products with an active inter-dealer market.

Bespoke tranche trades are typically traded with non-financial clients. Corporate CDS index tranches are traded with funds (including regulated funds) as well as with bank trading desks. Correlation desks typically hedge the core credit risk inherent in their activity with corporate CDS index tranches, corporate CDS indexes and single-name corporate CDSs. The desks remain exposed to a certain level of basis risk, for example between bespoke and index tranches.

4.5.3.2 Scope of the "Comprehensive Risk Measure"
Positions. Banks can include in their correlation trading portfolios solely those securitisation exposures and nth-to-default[23] credit derivatives where all reference underlying entities are single-name products,[24] including single-name credit derivatives, for which a liquid two-way market[25] exists. This will include commonly traded indexes based on these reference entities.

The rule excludes explicitly from the potential scope those positions that are resecuritisation, or derivatives of securitisation exposures that do not provide a *pro rata* share in the proceeds of a securitisation tranche. This therefore excludes options on a securitisation tranche, or a synthetically leveraged super-senior tranche.

In addition, positions that reference a claim on a special-purpose entity, or include an underlying that would be treated as a retail exposure, a residential mortgage exposure or a commercial mortgage exposure under the standardised approach to credit risk cannot be included either in the correlation trading portfolio.[26]

Risks to be included. Regarding the risks to be covered by the CRM, it is worth highlighting that any internally developed approach must adequately capture not only incremental default and migration risks (eg, credit), but all price risks.[27]

Paragraph 718 (xcv) lists the credit-related risks that have to be included in the "comprehensive risk measure":

1. the cumulative risk arising from multiple defaults, including the ordering of defaults, in tranched products;
2. credit spread risk, including the gamma and cross-gamma effects;[28]
3. volatility of implied correlations, including the cross effect between spreads and correlations;
4. basis risk, (ie, risk stemming from not perfectly correlated "hedges") including both the basis between the spread of an index and those of its constituent single names; and the basis between the implied correlation of an index and that of bespoke portfolios;
5. recovery-rate volatility, as it relates to the propensity for recovery rates to affect tranche prices; and
6. to the extent the comprehensive risk measure incorporates benefits from dynamic hedging, the risk of hedge slippage and the potential costs of rebalancing such hedges.

In addition, since the CRM has to capture "all price risks", a bank may also include in the correlation trading portfolio positions that hedge other risks (apart from credit) that stem from the securitisation positions subject to inclusion in the scope of the CRM, and which are neither securitisation exposures nor nth-to-default credit derivatives. Nevertheless, the overarching principle is that there must always be a liquid two-way market for the instrument or its underlying risks.

4.5.3.3 Additional requirements

For a bank to apply the CRM carve-out, it must have sufficient market data to ensure that it fully captures the salient risks of these exposures. It must also be able to demonstrate (for example, through backtesting) that its risk measures can appropriately explain the historical price variation – ie, that the risk measures explain (or, rather, "measure") the right levels of risk (eg, price variation) observed in the past – of these products.

Regarding the scope of the model, the institution must ensure that it can separate the positions for which it holds approval to incorporate them into its comprehensive risk measure from those positions for which it does not hold this approval.

Ad hoc stress tests. In addition, banks must regularly apply a set of specific, predetermined stress scenarios to the portfolio. In February 2011 the BCBS (2011a) published (as an annex to the main market risk framework document) guidance for the stress testing that has to be applied for the correlation trading portfolio.

The goal of predetermined stress testing is to provide estimates of the mark-to-market (MTM) changes that would be experienced by the Correlation Trading Portfolio in the event of credit-related shocks. In particular the scenarios have been designed to examine the implications of stresses to (i) default rates, (ii) recovery rates, (iii) credit spreads and (iv) correlations, on the trading desk's profit-and-loss.

The prescribed stress tests are bidirectional (ie, they reflect widening and tightening of the risk factors) and refer to specific historical reference periods. These periods correspond to historical intervals of three months or less over which spreads for single-name and tranched credit products have exhibited very large, broad-based increases or decreases.

Each stress scenario involves replicating historical movements in all credit-related risk factors over the reference period. In these exercises, only credit-related risk factors are shocked; non-credit-related risk factors (which are part of the scope of the CRM, since "all risks" should be incorporated) driving default-free term structures of interest rates and foreign-exchange rates should be fixed at current levels.

The predetermined stress scenarios encompass changes in credit spreads, but abstract from defaults of individual firms. Thus, in addition to movements in spreads, the guidance incorporates assumptions of actual defaults into the sector shock scenarios. For each of the seven historical scenarios four jump-to-default (JTD) stress tests should be performed.

The bank must apply the predetermined stress scenarios at least weekly and report the results, including comparisons with the capital charges implied by the banks' internal model for estimating comprehensive risks, at least quarterly to its supervisor. Any instances where the stress tests indicate a material shortfall of the "comprehensive risk measure", it must be reported to the supervisor in a timely manner.

Based on the stress-testing results, the supervisor may impose a supplemental capital charge against the correlation trading portfolio, to be added to the bank's internally modelled capital requirement.

Internal stress test. In addition to these prescribed regulatory stress scenarios, the standards encompass more flexible high-level principles governing a bank's internal stress testing. In this respect, a bank is expected to implement a rigorous internal stress-testing process to address other potential correlation trading risks, including bank-specific risks related to its underlying business model and hedging strategies.

Regulatory floor. In June 2010, following the QIS exercise conducted to assess the impact of the new regulation, the BCBS announced it had agreed to set the level of the floor for the "Comprehensive Risk Measure" at 8% of the charge resulting from the application of the standardised measurement method.

4.5.3.4 Issues around the application of the standardised approach for TB securitisations

As a consequence of the calculation basis used for the CRM regulatory floor, all institutions will have to calculate the capital requirements for all securitisation exposures included in their trading books according to the standardised rules, either because the standardised approach is the only one available (which is the case for non-CT exposures) or because the internal model-based CRM is subject to the 8% regulatory floor, which is based on the standardised measure.

As has been mentioned before, the standardised approach for securitisations is mainly a ratings-based approach designed for long-only positions. Therefore, the treatment of TB unrated tranches or short positions poses several implementation issues.

Treatment of short positions. Banks have strongly complained about the basis of the calculation of the floor and defend that the standardised rules don't make economical sense. According to banks, the way positions are factored can even penalise hedging strategies (as explained in Section 4.3).

To avoid unduly penalising hedging, the final rule establishes that the specific risk capital charge for the correlation trading portfolio should be calculated as the larger of (i) the total specific charges that would apply just to the net long positions and (ii) the total specific risk capital charges that would apply just to the net short positions under the standardised rules.

The industry has argued that this maximum of long/short treatment should also be extended to the non-correlation trading securitisation exposures that have no alternative to the standardised rules. However, in its June 2010 press release the Committee reconfirmed that the capital charge for non-correlation trading securitisation positions should be based on the sum of the capital charges for net long and net short positions.

Regardless, in order to give firms some time to rebalance their portfolios, it was agreed that, for a transition period of two years following the implementation of the market risk revisions (ie, until the end of 2013), the charges may be based on the larger of the capital charges for net long and net short positions.[29]

Unrated securitisations. Banks allege that the application of the Banking Book (BB) standardised capital charges to TB securitisation portfolios doesn't make economical sense, since they are arbitrarily high (eg, deduction) for unrated positions.

According to the BB rules, the specific risk charge for an unrated position has to be calculated based both on the creditworthiness of the underlying positions of the securitisation and the tranche's level of seniority in the securitisation's structure. This is done via the Supervisory Formula Approach (SFA), which is defined in Paragraphs 623 to 636 of the Basel II framework.[30]

Under the SFA, the capital charge for a securitisation tranche depends on five bank-supplied inputs: the IRB capital charge, had the underlying exposures not been securitised (KIRB);[31] the tranche's credit enhancement level (L); its thickness (T); the pool's effective number of exposures (N); and the pool's exposure-weighted average loss-given-default (LGD).

Thus, in order to use the SFA, the firm must obtain these parameters for the underlying exposures. In this regard, Paragraph 712 (vi) establishes the following possibilities.

❏ If a bank has approval for the IRB approach for the asset classes that include the underlying exposures, then the bank may factor its IRB PDs and LGDs into the SFA. Of course, when estimating PDs and LGDs for calculating KIRB, the bank must meet all the minimum requirements for the IRB approach.
❏ If IRB parameters are not available, but the bank has a VaR measure that incorporates specific risk that has been authorised by the supervisor,[32] and the bank derives estimates for PDs and LGDs according to the IRC standards (specified in Paragraphs 718 (xcii) and 718 (xciii)) that are in line with the quantitative standards for the IRB approach, the bank may use these estimates for calculating KIRB and, consequently, for applying the supervisory formula approach.
❏ In all other cases the capital charge can be calculated as 8% of the weighted-average risk weight that would be applied to the securitised exposures under the standardised approach, multiplied by a concentration ratio.[33] If the concentration ratio is 12.5 or higher, the position has to be deducted from capital as defined in Paragraph 561.

The resulting specific risk capital charge must not be lower than any specific risk capital charge applicable to a rated, more senior tranche. If a bank is unable to determine the specific risk capital charge as described above, or prefers not to apply the treatment described above to a position, it must fully deduct that position from capital.

In other words, if a bank is an IRB institution, and the underlying exposures are internally rated, then the bank may use these IRB parameters. If this is not the case but the bank is authorised to use its internal model for general and specific market risks and has an IRC model approved by its supervisor, then it can use these IRC parameters. If no IRB or IRC parameters are available, then the standardised rules apply, which in practice means positions will have to be deducted.

It is worth remembering that the IRC guidelines state that IRC parameters must nevertheless be "in line with the quantitative standards for the internal ratings-based approach". Of course, what "in line with the quantitative standards for the internal ratings-based approach" means exactly is subject to interpretation and, as has been noted in the IRC section (see 4.5.2), is one of the IRC open implementation issues.

4.5.4 Summary of the new treatment of specific risk in the Market Risk Framework

Table 4.1 summarises the new treatment for specific risk, both under the standardised measurement method and the internal models approach.

4.6 STRESSED VALUE-AT-RISK
4.6.1 Rationale

One of the key lessons derived from the crisis was that losses in banks' trading books were significantly higher than the minimum capital requirements under the Pillar I market risk rules. In fact, these capital requirements were based on VaR-type loss estimations, which reflected the low levels of volatility that were present in financial markets prior to the crisis, and did not capture default and migration risks, which were a main driver behind bank's losses.

As a regulatory response to these flaws and gaps, in its January 2009 Consultative Document, the Committee decided to introduce an sVaR capital requirement. The proposed sVaR had to be calculated taking into account a one-year observation period relating to significant losses, and the resulting capital charge had to be added to the traditional VaR requirement based on the most recent one-year observation period.

The introduction of an sVaR requirement was aimed both at increasing the overall level of capital for TB activities and at reducing the procyclicality of the minimum capital requirements for market risk, which was one of the overall objectives of the reform.

4.6.2 Industry concerns

During the consultation, the banking industry pointed out that the inclusion of a sVaR component into the capital requirements as an addition to the current VaR element necessarily double-counts risk. In general, banks understood the need to introduce a measure to dampen cyclicality, but argued that a weighted average of VaR and

Table 4.1 New treatment of specific risk

Instrument type	Standardised measurement method	Internal models approach
Unsecuritised credit products that are not included in the correlation trading portfolio.	Specific risk capital charges according to the standardised measurement method (unchanged).	99%/10-day VaR-specific risk measure times three* plus 99%/10-day sVaR-specific risk measure times three* plus IRC charge including default and migration risks at a 99.9% confidence level and a one-year capital horizon.
Securitisation products that are not included in the correlation trading portfolio.	New capital charges for securitised products under the standardised measurement approach, independent of whether a bank otherwise uses the standardised measurement method or the internal models approach. Transitional Arrangement: maximum of the net long/short capital requirements till December 2013.	
Products that are included in the correlation trading portfolio (Paragraph 689 (iv)).	New capital charges for securitised products under the standardised measurement approach, calculated as the maximum of (i) the total specific risk capital charges that would apply just to the net long positions from the net long correlation trading exposures combined, and (ii) the total specific risk capital charges that would apply just to the net short positions from the net short correlation trading exposures combined (Paragraph 709 (ii)).	99%/10-day VaR-specific risk measure times three* plus 99%/10-day sVaR-specific risk measure times three* plus comprehensive risk capital charge including default and migration risks at a 99.9% confidence level and a one-year capital horizon.**
Equity products.	Current specific risk capital charges according to the standardised measurement method. The reduced specific risk capital charge of 4% for equities in liquid and well-diversified portfolios (Paragraph 718 (xxii)) has been eliminated, ie, an 8% specific risk capital charge applies.	99%/10-day VaR specific risk measure times three* plus 99%/10-day sVaR-specific risk measure times three.

* The multiplier may be adjusted up to 4 based on backtesting results. Banks may use one VaR model jointly modelling general and specific risk.
** The Committee set up a floor for the comprehensive risk capital charge of an 8% of the charge applicable under the SMM.
Source: Analysis of the TB QIS: available at http://www.bis.org/publ/bcbs163.pdf (updated to reflect June 2010 press release)

sVaR would be a conceptually more correct means of increasing the current market risk charge.

In addition, industry groups highlighted that the proposed market risk formula did not incentivise firms to improve their VaR models. Banks argued that, since the sVaR was bound to become the main capital driver in the near future, an institution with a more prudent model (for example, one with fewer backtesting exceptions) would be unduly penalised, since the number of backtesting exceptions would affect only the regular VaR and not the stressed one.

A firm with a less prudent VaR would have more backtesting exceptions, but the "add-on" factor would have a very limited influence in the final capital figure. In practice this discrepancy would be even greater, as sVaR is also likely to be higher for a firm that uses a more prudent model.

To address this issue, the Basel Committee changed this element in the final July 2009 regulation. According to the final rule, the backtesting exception add-on (which is calculated based on the regular VaR and thus ensures the quality of the model) should also be added to the sVaR multiplier. Therefore, banks will still have an incentive to have a prudent model in place, since an excess in the number of exceptions would be factored directly into the main capital driver (ie, the sVaR).

4.6.3 SVaR specificities

In principle, the sVaR should be calculated under the same assumptions and applying the same methodology as used for the regular VaR; however, there are some exceptions to this general rule.

The rationale behind the sVaR charge is to reflect the volatility of a continuous 12-month stressed period; therefore, the calculation of the sVaR using any kind of weighting scheme[34] doesn't seem to make economical sense, even if the regular VaR is calculated using such a scheme.

In addition, it is worth noting that no backtesting is requested for the sVaR, since it does not make any sense from a methodological perspective. However, the sVaR is subject to similar "use test"[35] requirements to those used for the ordinary VaR.

4.6.4 Implementation issues

The sVaR measure is intended to replicate a VaR calculation that would be generated on the bank's current portfolio if the relevant market factors were experiencing a period of stress. This should therefore be based on the 10-day, 99th-percentile, one-tailed confidence interval (ie, 99% measured in one of the two tails of the normal distribution) VaR measure of the current portfolio, with model inputs calibrated to historical data from a continuous 12-month period of significant financial stress relevant to the bank's portfolio.

The rule states that the period must be approved by the supervisor and regularly reviewed. As an example, Paragraph 718 (Lxxvi-(i)) notes that for many portfolios, a 12-month period relating to significant losses in 2007/2008 would adequately reflect a period of such stress, but other periods that might be relevant to the current portfolio must be considered by the bank. Thus, the determination of the period that should be used in each case is one of the main open implementation issues.

In principle, it seems that choosing a generic "stressed period", such as the one provided as an example by the rule, should be relatively straightforward. However, if banks were requested to find the worst period of all possible periods, the computational task would significantly increase. In addition, it is clear that the quality of the information would worsen as we moved backwards, and banks would be forced to use more and more proxies due to lack of relevant data. Finally it is clear that we should define a moment in the past where banks would "draw the line".

Some practitioners have even questioned whether market participants should use different stressed periods for different business lines (ie, each one of the lines that a firm has defined as a source of income on its trading activities, which depends on the business structure and internal policies of the firm in question). This would make things even more complicated, since there would be a need to define each business line in detail and banks would have to aggregate different sVaR calculations in a meaningful way.

Of course, this approach would produce a more significant period that would depend on each bank's TB business model, but it is not clear whether it would entirely fit in regulation. The final TB rule refers to a single sVaR calculation obtained from "a continuous 12-month period of significant financial stress relevant to the bank's portfolio". Thus, in principle, the data series used in the calculation must come from a single historical period, not an aggregation depending on each business line or risk factor. This kind of approach would also make a consistent implementation of the new rules more challenging.

A second element to be taken into account in the implementation process would be how often banks (and supervisors) should revise the relevance of the stressed period and whether this should be done based on a more formulaic or judgemental process.

On the one hand, considering that one of the intentions behind the sVaR is to dampen cyclicality, it seems logical to assume that the time-series data on which the sVaR is calculated should be stable. However, on the other hand, the rule also states clearly that the period used must be regularly reviewed by the bank and approved by the supervisor to ensure that it still represents a period of significant financial stress relevant to the bank's portfolio.

In addition, the rule is mindful of the possibility that the composition and direction of some of the TB portfolios might mean that the application of some stress scenarios will not deliver meaningful results. To address this issue, the rule suggests that banks could use antithetic data or apply absolute, rather than relative, movements in risk factors. "Antithetic" in this context means that price movements are considered relevant irrespective of their direction. The basic idea is that the sVaR should reflect that open risk positions (in either direction) are vulnerable to stressed variables.

One area of concern where firms are requesting specific guidance would be the inclusion in the sVaR of new risk factors and products that have emerged after the stressed period applied by the bank (or markets where the bank was not present at that time and, thus, had no historical data to apply). Methodological changes in the main VaR engine might also raise similar issues.

Finally, it is worth considering the possibility that the sVaR requirement might work *de facto* as an "entry barrier" for institutions that are introducing an internal model for the first time. The institution must have data on the stressed period in order to comply with the new rules, but this might not be the case – for instance, if the firm did not exist in 2008.

Unfortunately, it is likely that all these data constraints will grow in importance in the future, and the reliance on proxies for sVaR calculations is bound to increase as methodological changes and new products are introduced in the TB portfolios.

4.7 CONCLUSIONS

During the big financial crisis, trading-book exposures and the build-up of leverage represented important sources of losses. A main contributing factor was that the capital framework for market risk, based on the 1996 Amendment to the 1988 Capital Accord, did not capture some key risks. These regulatory gaps led to an under-capitalisation of trading books of financial institutions and incentivised the possibility of regulatory arbitrage between trading and banking books.

Thus, most of the changes in the trading-book framework reflect primarily the idea of better capturing those key risks that were missing in the 1996 rules. In this regard, it is true that some of the regulatory flaws present in the current TB framework have become prominent due to the crisis; however, to a large extent, they were known. For instance, the need to enhance the treatment of specific risk for credit has been discussed since the 1996 MRA was approved. In addition, it is obvious that these known flaws became more significant due to market developments that have led to a structural change in the composition of banks' TB portfolios compared with 1996. To confirm this, the 2005 Trading Book Review already contained significant changes to the market risk framework and paved the way for the 2009 regulatory changes.

Indeed, to address the regulatory shortcomings, the Basel Committee agreed to supplement the current VaR-based trading book framework with an incremental risk capital charge, which includes default risk as well as migration risk, for unsecuritised credit products. Due to a lack of trust in banks' modelling of securitisation positions, it was decided that the capital charges of the banking book would apply to all securitisation products held in the TB with a limited exception for certain so-called correlation trading activities. In this regard, banks may be allowed by their supervisor to calculate a comprehensive risk capital charge subject to strict qualitative minimum requirements as well as to predetermined stress testing and a supervisory floor. An additional response to the crisis is represented by the introduction of an sVaR requirement. Losses in most banks' trading books during the financial crisis have been significantly higher than the minimum capital requirements under the former Pillar I market risk rules. The additional sVaR requirement should also help reduce the procyclicality of the minimum capital requirements for market risk.

All these measures (known as "Basel 2.5") were set to be implemented by the end of 2011 in order to reduce the incentive for regulatory arbitrage between the banking and trading books. Basel 2.5 has a "tighter" calendar than the one established for Basel III, and this has been criticised by banks, despite the fact that the need to enhance significant parts of the market risk framework has been discussed with the industry for years (long before the crisis erupted in mid-2007), and the calendar suffered several postponements. Although agreeing to a large extent with most of the overarching objectives of the reform, the financial industry has often defined the final outcome as a so-called "patchwork", a fragmented and complex regulatory framework that might actually leave risks to "fall between the cracks" of the different measures. In addition, banks highlighted that, due to the overlap of the different charges, there is capital "double counting" (ie, asking capital twice for the same risk). The measures have also been criticised for being calculated based on different assumptions regarding levels of confidence or risk distributions, as well as using diverse capital and liquidity horizons.

To a large extent, this heterogeneity in the modelling assumptions is the result of differences both in risk nature as well as in the underlying characteristics (such as endogenous liquidity) of the positions held in TB portfolios. It is also worth remembering that all these model nuances were not taken into account in the old 1996 one-day VaR framework, which, alas, treated different risks and positions with different features in a homogeneous (and, thus, wrong) way, leading to a risk undercapitalisation of complex, stale and illiquid instruments, as well as credit-related positions more generally.

In conclusion, our impression is that the new framework on the trading book represents a necessary improvement in the regulatory treatment of market risk. The changes take into account some of the key lessons drawn from the financial crisis, such as the need to calculate capital under stress conditions and reintroduce other longstanding elements, such as the correct capture of specific risk.

At the same time, there are some elements of the reform that are not fully satisfactory and may need some rethinking. For example, the different capital charges that comprise the new framework may not be entirely consistent and may also produce clear overlaps between them (for instance, between VaR and sVaR). However, we should not forget that most of the inconsistencies and capital overlaps are a consequence of the need to address different supervisory goals. As an example, it is clear that the TB framework must be risk-sensitive and risk-comprehensive but, at the same time, it should help to dampen procyclicality and avoid an undercapitalisation of positions during low-volatility periods in the markets.

In this respect, the Basel Committee announced a project aimed at conducting a fundamental review of the whole market risk framework, in the direction of addressing any unintended consequences of the "Basel 2.5" package but, more importantly, aimed at addressing any remaining regulatory flaws and shortcomings of the revised regulatory framework. In particular, one of the overarching objectives of the fundamental review would be to eliminate the possibility of regulatory arbitrage between banking and trading books.

The opinions expressed here are those of the author and do not necessarily represent the views of the Bank of Spain.

1 The rule is mindful of the fact that it is quite questionable whether "a bank" can actually have intentions and provides some specific requirements (in terms of internal policies and type of business model) to operationalise this "intent" criterion. The current flaws in the existing TB–BB boundary are one of the elements to be addressed in the fundamental review of the market risk framework mentioned in Section 4.7 of this chapter.
2 According to Paragraph 687, positions held with trading intent are those held intentionally for short-term resale and/or with the intent of benefiting from actual or expected short-term price movements or to lock in arbitrage profits.
3 As has just been noted, the MR framework is to be applied to all the risks that stem from TB positions as well as for FX and commodities risk throughout the whole balance sheet.
4 In this regard, the only change introduced in the standardised approach is to increase from 4% to 8% the risk weight applicable to the equity-specific risk component. Previously, a 4% charge could be applied only if the portfolio was liquid and well diversified and subject to supervisory approval. The capital impact of this minor change is quite negligible.
5 Though this is factually true, and some inconsistencies may be unintended, it is also true that most of them do reflect differences in risk nature (such as endogenous liquidity or risk distribution) or are a consequence of the need to address different supervisory objectives, such as the need to have a risk-sensitive framework and, at the same time, dampen cyclicality from the TB capital framework.
6 Patchwork or "pieced work" is a form of needlework that involves sewing together pieces of fabric into a larger design.
7 Any "event" that has a significant influence in the price of a security as soon as it is disclosed (eg, a merge, an unexpected loss, an internal fraud or "rogue trader" case etc).

133

8   The model must reflect that any concentrated portfolio is more risky than a diversified one, even if the creditworthiness of all individual names is similar.
9   The general criterion is that, for capital calculation purposes, the ten-day-VaR measure has to be multiplied by a minimum of three plus an add-on factor that takes into account the number of backtesting exceptions that have been observed during the last year. However, for specific risk, banks have been widely using the four multiplier.
10 According to the TB QIS results published in October 2009, relative to the specific risk surcharge, the incremental risk capital charge is on average nine times as high.
11 In this respect, the committee decided that open equity stakes in hedge funds should be booked in the banking book, considering that their very limited liquidity and the uncertainty surrounding their daily marking-to-market meant that they rarely qualify for inclusion in the trading book.
12 Nevertheless, some jurisdictions have maintained the original implementation calendar.
13 As noted in the introduction to this chapter, it is true that counterparty credit risk standards are currently under revision, among other things, to incorporate credit valuation adjustment to the current framework.
14 For example, according to a loss-data collection exercise conducted during 2009 by the UK FSA (UK FSA 2010), the three largest categories of loss during the crisis (accounting for 75% of the total) were attributable to structured finance activities (eg, securitisations), which included positions held in "securitisation warehouses" and retained tranches from completed securitisations or holdings of ABSs and CDOs in trading portfolios. Securitisations incorporate, by all means, credit risk.
15 At the same time, banks argued that they could model simpler and better-understood securitisations, while the sorts of opaque, leveraged securitisations and resecuritisations that were the source of large trading losses in 2007/08 should therefore be subject to the standardised methodology for the foreseeable future.
16 See 4.5.3.1 for a description of this type of business.
17 In particular, its underlying risks could be identified and there were liquid instruments available that would allow banks to price those risks and hedge them.
18 To facilitate consistency, the committee also agreed to permit the flexibility to implement the Revisions to Pillar I of the document "Enhancements to the Basel II framework" (released in July 2009) at the same time as the trading-book reforms.
19 Rating below BBB (Fitch & Standard & Poor's), Baa3 (Moody's).
20 This is consistent with the Basel II Framework, which does not allow for the benefit of diversification when combining capital requirements for credit risk and market risk.
21 An option is a derivative financial instrument that establishes a contract between two parties concerning the buying or selling of an asset at a reference price. The buyer of the option gains the right, but not the obligation, to engage in some specific transaction (eg, buy or sell) on the asset, while the seller incurs the obligation to fulfil the symmetric transaction (eg, sell or buy) if so requested by the buyer of the option.
22 CDX and iTraxx: CDX indexes contain North American and emerging-market companies and are administered by CDS Index Company (CDSIndexCo) and marketed by Markit Group Limited; and iTraxx contain companies from the rest of the world and are managed by the International Index Company (IIC), also owned by Markit.
23 A credit derivative in which the payout is linked to one in a series of defaults (such as first-, second- or third-to-default), with the contract terminating at that point. Nth-to-default baskets have similar characteristics to synthetic securitisation tranches, in terms of leverage and exposure to correlation.
24 Ie, each of them references a single name.
25 A two-way market is deemed to exist where there are independent bona fide offers to buy and sell so that a price reasonably related to the last sales price or current bona fide competitive bid and offer quotations can be determined within one day and settled at such a price within a relatively short time conforming to trade custom.

26 To a large extent, this exclusion is redundant, since none of these securitisations would meet the "two-way liquid market" criterion.
27 This is why the new model was called "comprehensive risk measure".
28 Gamma: second derivative of a function to a variable. Its absolute value shows how accurate the delta (first derivative) is and its sign shows whether a "delta dynamic hedging" is over- or underestimating risk. Cross-Gamma: second derivative of the function to other variables, reflects correlation. It is the rate of change of delta of one underlying with respect to the change in price of another underlying, applicable on multi-underlying instruments such as securitisations.
29 During this transition period, there is a need to ensure that there is not undue recognition of hedging between economically unrelated positions.
30 In addition Paragraph 619 establishes that banks may use an internal-assessment approach (IAA) of the credit quality of the securitisation exposures, but solely to liquidity facilities and credit enhancements of asset-backed commercial paper (ABCP) programmes, provided the bank meets some operational requirements.
31 KIRB is the ratio of the IRB capital requirement including the EL portion for the underlying exposures in the pool to the exposure amount of the pool (eg, the sum of drawn amounts related to securitised exposures plus the EAD associated with undrawn commitments related to securitised exposures).
32 The supervisor must determine that the bank meets all the qualitative and quantitative requirements for general and specific (Paragraphs 718 (Lxxxviii) to 718 (xci-2-) market-risk models.
33 This concentration ratio is equal to the sum of the nominal amounts of all the tranches divided by the sum of the nominal amounts of the tranches junior to or *pari passu*. Pari passu is a Latin phrase that literally means "equal footstep" or "equal footing." In finance, this term refers to two or more loans, bonds, classes of shares having equal rights of payment or level of seniority with the tranche in which the position is held, including that tranche itself.
34 A weighting scheme generally implies that the most recent data is made more relevant for VaR calculation purposes, while an equal weighting of all data points included in the historical scenario implies that the model does not discriminate between recent scenarios and scenarios further back in time (eg, all scenarios (implicitly) carry the same probability of occurrence).
35 The so called "use test" implies that the bank must really use the model for management purposes and not just to comply with regulation.

REFERENCES

BCBS, 1996, "Amendment to the capital accord to incorporate market risks," January, available at http://www.bis.org/publ/bcbs24.pdf.

BCBS, 2008a, "Proposed revisions to the Basel II market risk framework – 1st consultative version", July, available at http://www.bis.org/publ/bcbs140.pdf.

BCBS, 2008b, "Guidelines for Computing Capital for Incremental Risk in the Trading Book – 1st consultative version", July, available at http://www.bis.org/publ/bcbs141.pdf.

BCBS, 2009a, "Revisions to the Basel II market risk framework – 2nd consultative version", available at http://www.bis.org/publ/bcbs148.pdf.

BCBS, 2009b, "Guidelines for computing capital for incremental risk in the trading book – 2nd consultative version", available at http://www.bis.org/publ/bcbs149.pdf.

BCBS, 2009c, "Revisions to the Basel II market risk framework", final version, July, available at http://www.bis.org/publ/bcbs158.pdf.

BCBS, 2009d, "Guidelines for computing capital for incremental risk in the trading book", final version, July, available at http://www.bis.org/publ/bcbs159.pdf.

BCBS, 2009e, "Trading book quantitative impact study by the Basel Committee: results", October, available at http://www.bis.org/publ/bcbs163.pdf.

BCBS, various commentators, 2009, "Comments received on 'Revisions to the Basel II market risk framework' and 'Guidelines for computing capital for incremental risk in the trading book' ", January, available at http://www.bis.org/publ/bcbs14849/cacomments.htm.

BCBS, 2010a, "Adjustments to the Basel II market risk framework announced by the Basel Committee", press release, June, available at http://www.bis.org/press/p100618.htm and, Annex, http://www.bis.org/press/p100618/annex.pdf.

BCBS, 2010b, "Results of the comprehensive quantitative impact study", December, available at http://www.bis.org/publ/bcbs186.htm

BCBS, 2011a, "Revisions to the Basel II market risk framework", updated as of December 31, 2010, February, available at http://www.bis.org/publ/bcbs193.htm.

BCBS, 2011b, "Interpretive issues with respect to the revisions to the MR framework", February, available at http://www.bis.org/publ/bcbs193a.pdf.

BCBS–IOSCO, 2005a, "Trading Book Survey: A Summary of Responses", April, available at http://www.bis.org/publ/bcbs112.pdf.

BCBS–IOSCO, 2005b, "The Application of Basel II to Trading Activities and the Treatment of Double Default Effects", July, available at http://www.bis.org/publ/bcbs116.pdf.

ISDA–IIF–LIBA–IBFed, 2008, "Comments received on 'Proposed revisions to the Basel II market risk framework' and 'Guidelines for Computing Capital for Incremental Risk in the Trading Book' ", available at http://www.bis.org/publ/bcbs14041/cacomments.htm.

Prato, Oliver, 2006, "Better capturing risks in the trading book" available at http://www.banque-france.fr/gb/publications/telechar/rsf/2006/etud1_0506.pdf.

UK FSA, 2010, "The prudential regime for trading activities: A fundamental review" August, available at http://www.fsa.gov.uk/pubs/discussion/dp10_04.pdf.

5

Counterparty Credit Risk and Other Risk-Coverage Measures

Akhtar Siddique

Office of the Comptroller of the Currency

5.1 INTRODUCTION

This chapter covers the revisions to the counterparty credit risk (CCR) capital rules in the Basel III framework. Counterparty credit risk is the risk that counterparties will fail to meet their obligations. It most commonly arises in over-the-counter (OTC) derivatives transactions that have promised cashflows in the future and whose payment depends on the creditworthiness of the counterparty. Canabarro and Duffie (2003) provide the following definition: "counterparty risk is the risk that a party to an OTC derivatives contract may fail to perform on its contractual obligations, causing losses to the other party."

Such a definition contains all the key features of counterparty credit risk and helps to highlight the difference with "traditional" credit risk. On the one hand, the fact that, for both risks, the cause of economic loss is the obligor's default makes them very similar. On the other hand, counterparty credit risk has two specific features, represented by the uncertainty of the exposure and the bilateral nature of the risk; in other words, in a derivatives transaction, risk (of non-payment) is borne by both the parties, whereas in a loan the risk is typically borne only by the lender. Such a risk matters less in transactions of exchange-traded derivatives, where the exchange guarantees the cashflows promised by the derivative to the counterparties and functions as the counterparty to all the clearing members of the exchange.

The regulations on minimum capital requirements for counterparty credit risk have evolved from simple to complex since 1988 (the year that the Basel I Capital Accord was introduced), paralleling the development of derivatives markets; moving from lookup tables, common across all institutions, to formulas relying on complex computations carried out internally and individually by the institutions. The Basel II framework already introduced significant improvements with respect to Basel I, making it consistent with the greater risk-sensitivity of the overall Basel II Capital Accord. This framework has been significantly strengthened by the Basel III global reform. Building on the experience gained during the financial crisis, the Basel Committee on Banking Supervision (BCBS) has intervened in a wide range of areas of risk coverage focusing on the denominator of the capital ratio (ie, a bank's capital divided by its risk weighted assets) by enhancing the risk weighted asset calculations. This includes the prudential treatment of market risk in the trading book (see Chapter 4) and counterparty credit risk.

This chapter, which focuses on the latter, is organised as follows. Section 5.2 describes the regulatory capital framework for counterparty credit risk under Basel I and Basel II; Section 5.3 provides an understanding of the rationale and the main features of the new Basel III rules; Section 5.4 discusses the other significant measures on risk coverage; Section 5.5 provides some conclusions.

5.2 REGULATORY CAPITAL FOR COUNTERPARTY CREDIT RISK BEFORE THE FINANCIAL CRISIS
5.2.1 Capital charges under Basel I
This section describes the counterparty credit risk capital charges in the Basel I framework followed by the revisions in Basel II. In the simple Basel I framework, regulatory capital for counterparty credit risk was based on the exposures' notional values (ie, the face amount of the instruments used rather than their market values). The rule was straightforward: for an OTC derivative, the exposure was calculated as the current mark-to-market, plus notional, times the following add-on factor (Table 5.1). Risk weights of 0% (for sovereigns and supranationals), 20% (for Organisation for Economic Cooperation and Development (OECD) Banks) or 50% (for all others) were applied, so as to determine the risk-weighted assets (RWAs) as the denominator of the capital ratio. Netting was recognised via net gross ratio. As a general rule, minimum capital charge was set at 8% of RWA.

Table 5.1 Add-on factors for counterparty credit risk under Basel I

Residual maturity	Interest rates	FX and gold	Equities	Precious metals (except gold)	Other commodities
< 1 year	0%	1%	6%	7%	10%
1–5 years	0.5%	5%	8%	7%	12%
> 5 years	1.5%	7.5%	10%	8%	15%

5.2.2 Capital charges under Basel II

The rules for the calculation of minimum capital requirements for credit risk represent one of the main changes introduced by Basel II (BCBS 2006). In that context counterparty credit risk was intended as an element of credit risk, in particular when measured with the internal ratings-based (IRB) approach, ie, using risk parameters such as probability of default (PD), loss-given default (LGD) and exposure at default (EAD).

The capital charge is provided by the following formula:

$$K = LGD \times \left[N\left(\frac{N^{-1}(PD) + \sqrt{R} \times N^{-1}(0.999)}{\sqrt{1-R}} \right) - LGD \times PD \right] \left(\frac{1 + (M - 2.5) \times b}{1 - 1.5 \times b} \right)$$

Capital = $K \times EAD$

$R = 0.12w + 0.24(1 - w)$ $w = \dfrac{1 - e^{-50PD}}{1 - e^{-50}}$

$b = (0.11852 - 0.05478 \ln(PD))^2$

where:

- K = capital charge per unit
- PD = probability of default
- LGD = loss-given default = (1 − recovery rate)
- R = asset correlation
- w = factor loading
- b = maturity adjustment

The major adaptation of the IRB algorithm for counterparty credit risk for the wholesale portfolio is in the calculation of the EAD and how M, the maturity adjustment, is defined.

EAD can be calculated using three alternative methodologies: current exposure method (CEM), standardised method (SM) and internal-models method (IMM).

Under the CEM (ie, Basel I with adjustments for credit derivatives), EAD is defined as the sum of the current positive replacement cost (by marking to market) and potential future exposures as a percentage of the notional using the supervisory schedules.

According to the SM, EAD is computed as the following:

$$\beta Max(\text{Current Market Value} - \text{Current Value of Collateral}; | RPT_{ij} - RPC_{ij} | \times CCF_j)$$

where RPT_{ij} and RPC_{ij} are "risk positions" transactions and collateral respectively, computed generally as notional values for linear positions and delta times notional values for nonlinear positions.

β and credit conversion factor (CCF) are supervisory scaling parameters and supervisory credit conversion factors respectively.

Under the IMM, EAD is computed using the effective expected positive exposure (EEPE) over a one-year horizon. Among the three methods, the IMM represents the most prominent element of the Basel II counterparty credit risk framework. The reason is that the most sophisticated and large financial institutions were expected to adopt IMM. It was viewed as being aligned with the true risks for institutions with counterparty credit risk. IMM capital charges were also generally believed to be significantly lower than the other two methods, because of its greater risk sensitivity.

IMM introduced the concept of an EEPE over a one-year horizon at the level of a netting set.[1] EAD was defined as $EAD = \alpha \times EEPE$, where α is the ratio of the internal economic capital computed using a full simulation to economic capital computed using EEPE. This was set at a regulatory level of 1.4 with the possibility that institutions (with supervisory approvals) would use internal models to decrease it to 1.2.

Thus, IMM effectively provided a bridge between the credit-risk and market-risk worlds since EEPE relies on concepts in the market-risk value-at-risk (VaR) world. It also permitted the introduction of the use of internal economic capital models to adjust the regulatory multiplier, α, downwards. The other element of the IRB formula where IMM differs from the rest of the credit risk framework is in M, the maturity adjustment. The maturity adjustment for derivatives transactions can be less than one year, unlike most regular credit exposures.

5.3 REVISIONS TO THE COUNTERPARTY CREDIT RISK CHARGES

5.3.1 Counterparty credit risk in the financial crisis

As discussed in Chapter 1, the origins and the dynamics of the financial crisis are very complex. Risk management in financial institutions has certainly played a key role in the way risk was perceived, measured and managed. A supervisory report published in 2008 (Senior Supervisors Group 2008) contains observations on the risk-management practices that have enabled some firms to weather the financial turmoil better than others, highlighting the "effectiveness of market and credit risk management practices in understanding and managing the risks in retained or traded exposures as well as in counterparty exposures, in valuing complex and increasingly illiquid products, and in limiting or hedging exposures to credit and market risk".

Focusing on credit-related losses during the crisis, a significant portion arose from counterparty credit risk. These losses were derived largely from credit valuation adjustment (CVA) of derivative positions, ie, as the credit quality of the counterparties deteriorated, banks were required to mark their positions down. Table 5.2 reports CVA losses that major international banks have disclosed in their financial statements for 2008.[2] In fact, significant proportions of the losses that banks suffered from subprime (ie, low-rated borrowers) loans as well as exposures to specialised bond insurance companies (ie, so-called monolines) occurred through derivatives positions, even when the counterparties had not defaulted. This was because credit valuation adjustments needed to be made when the creditworthiness of the counterparties declined.

The significant attention that the Basel Committee has decided to pay to the area of risk coverage derives from the wide range of shortcomings found in the current regulatory framework. As highlighted in the 2009 Consultative Document (BCBS 2009), during the financial crisis

> a key observation was that defaults and deteriorations in the creditworthiness of trading counterparties occurred precisely at the time when market volatilities, and therefore counterparty exposures, were higher than usual. Thus, observed generalised wrong-way risk was not adequately incorporated into the framework. Mark-to-market losses due to credit valuation adjustments (CVA) were not directly capitalised. The current framework addresses CCR as a default and

Table 5.2 CVA losses at year-end 2008

Bank	CVA Loss (millions USD)
JPMC	7,561
Citigroup	10,107
Bank of America	3,200
Morgan Stanley	3,800*
Deutsche Bank	1,730
Commerzbank/Dresdner	7,074**
HSBC	1,145*
RBS	11,502
BNP Paribas	1,407
Credit Suisse	10,234**
UBS	6,100

*CVA adjustments only for exposures to monoline insurers.
**Total fair-value adjustments (including CVA)

credit migration risk, but does not fully account for market value. Large financial institutions were more interconnected than currently reflected in the capital framework. As a result, when markets entered the downturn, banks' counterparty exposure to other financial firms also increased. The evidence suggests that the asset values of financial firms are, on a relative basis, more correlated than those of non-financial firms. As such, this higher degree of correlation with the market needs to be reflected in the asset value correlations.

Finally, central counterparties (CCPs) were not widely used to clear trades. The use of CCPs has been viewed as mitigating counterparty credit risk, as the CCP acts as a counterparty to the other participants.

5.3.2 Changes in the default-risk charge

The first element of the reform on counterparty risk has been enhancements to the risk measures that were in place to make them more robust in stressed environments. As discussed above, an important element of the Basel II counterparty credit risk framework is that the capital charge is a charge for default risk alone. Since the exposure (EEPE, as defined below) is quite similar, in the manner it is computed, to the VaR in the market-risk arena, several of the shortcomings of VaR were also understood to be applicable to the EEPE. Therefore, a significant change in Basel III has been the requirement that firms compute the EEPE with stressed inputs. For example, exposures may be computed using a Monte Carlo simulation assuming that the underlying risk factors have normal distributions.

Banks are now required to use stressed volatilities and correlations in their simulations. This is a stressed calibration of the exposures-generation systems. In other words, when the exposures are generated, the parameters reflect stressed environments.

The default-risk capital charge is therefore the larger of two capital charges, one computed with calibration using the current market data and the other computed using stress calibration. The new rules require the bank to identify a single stress for all the counterparties rather than defining the stresses counterparty by counterparty.

When the EEPE model is calibrated using historic market data, banks will have to use current market data to compute current exposures and at least three years of historical data to estimate parameters of the model. Alternatively, market-implied data (ie, using the current market prices) will have to be used to estimate parameters of the model. In all cases, data must be updated quarterly or more frequently if market conditions warrant, ie, if the parameter estimates are likely to have changed substantially. To calculate the EEPE using a stress calibration, banks will also have to either calibrate EEPE using three years of data that includes a period of stress to the credit default spreads of a bank's counterparties, or calibrate EEPE using market-implied data from a suitable period of stress.

In assessing the adequacy of the stress calibration, banks will have to take into account what factors drive their risk exposures. First of all, they will have to use a representative selection of the bank's counterparties with traded credit spreads. Both the identification of the representative selection of the counterparties and the identification of the stress period will require careful thought on the part of the bank as well as the supervisors. In particular, for the institutions that use implied market data such as implied volatilities, availability of the implied inputs from a stressed period may pose a challenge. Additionally, the stress period may always remain in the bank's dataset.

Banks are also required to develop benchmark portfolios, which have to be designed to be vulnerable to the same main risk factors as the bank, so that the shortcomings identified via the benchmark portfolios will be applicable to the full set of portfolios as well. Capital charges on these benchmark portfolios will be used by the supervisors to gauge the effectiveness of the stressed exposures calculation. The benchmark portfolio construction will also likely require substantial interactions between institutions and supervisors.

A possible conundrum is that, when exposures are monitored for risk-management purposes, banks are more likely to use market-implied inputs such as implied volatilities rather than historical volatilities. Thus, using exposure-monitoring systems for risk-management purposes may start to differ from the systems used to generate exposures for regulatory capital.

5.3.3 Capitalisation of credit valuation adjustment charges

A second piece of the regulatory reform on counterparty credit risk is represented by the capitalisation of credit valuation adjustments, ie, the mark-to-market losses using the market-risk framework. Many of the largest banks have developed internal models for computing the VaR of credit valuation adjustments. The Basel capital charge for CVA is a supervisory formula for the same VaR. Given the complexities of calculating VaR, internal models of VaR are not likely to be very comparable.

This charge is in addition to the default-risk capital charge. The CVA capital charge takes advantage of the existing VaR modelling for market risk. Banks are generally not required to compute CVA capital charges on the securities financing transactions and transactions with central counterparties.

The new capitalisation for CVA effectively sets out three regimes, depending on the approved method of calculating capital charges for counterparty credit risk and specific interest-rate risk. The distinction is between banks with IMM approval and approval of internal models for the specific risk for bonds in the market-risk framework, on the one hand, and all other institutions (standardised CVA capital charge) on the other.

For banks with IMM approval for counterparty credit risk and approval to use the market-risk internal-models approach for the specific risk in bonds, the CVA capital charge is meant to be calculated using the bank's specific risk model. The CVA capitalisation charge has led to intense discussion in the industry (among others, Rebonato *et al* 2010).

In the Basel III text (BCBS 2010a), regulators set out in great detail how the CVA for regulatory capital purposes is meant to be computed. They also specified how hedges for the CVA risk are meant to be handled into the capital charge. The CVA uses only the credit spreads of the counterparties and the regulatory expected exposure profiles. This VaR model is restricted to changes in the counterparties' credit spreads and does not model the sensitivity of CVA to changes in other market factors, such as changes in the value of the reference asset, commodity, currency or interest rate of a derivative. Importantly, the bank regulatory CVA capital model can differ from the accounting valuation method for determining CVA. The CVA capital-charge calculation also specifies a given regulatory formula for the CVA:

$$CVA = (LGD_{MKT}) \cdot \sum_{i=1}^{T} Max\left[0; exp\left(-\frac{s_{i-1} \cdot t_{i-1}}{LGD_{MKT}}\right) - exp\left(-\frac{s_i \cdot t_i}{LGD_{MKT}}\right)\right] \cdot \left(\frac{EE_{i-1} \cdot EE_i \cdot D_i}{2}\right)$$

where

- t_i is the time of the i-th revaluation time bucket, starting from,
- t_T is the longest contractual maturity across the netting sets with the counterparty,
- s_i is the credit spread of the counterparty at tenor t_i, used to calculate the CVA of the counterparty – it is the credit default swap (CDS) spread if it is available or a suitable proxy rating based on the rating, industry and region of the counterparty,

LGD_{MKT} is the loss-given default of the counterparty and should be based on the spread of a market instrument of the counterparty.[3]

The first factor within the sum represents an approximation of the market-implied marginal probability of a default occurring between times t_{i-1} and t_i. This is based on market prices and is generally different from the real-world probability of default.

EE_i is the regulatory expected exposure to the counterparty at revaluation time t_i,

D_i is the default-risk-free discount factor at time t_i, where $D_0 = 1$.

This is a definition that was introduced in a variety of industry approaches. However, it is important to note that this is a somewhat simplified approach in computing CVA. Looking at the individual components of the CVA calculations, it is important to note that LGD_{MKT} is the loss-given default of the counterparty and should therefore be based on the spread of a market instrument of the counterparty (or, where a counterparty instrument is not available, based on the proxy spread that is appropriate based on the rating, industry and region of the counterparty).

The formula above is the basis for all inputs into the bank's approved VaR model for bonds when calculating the CVA risk capital charge for a counterparty. For example, if the VaR model is based on full repricing (ie, not using approximations), then the formula must be used directly. In other cases, if, for example, the model is based on credit spread sensitivities, the Basel III rules text, BCBS (2010a) provides detailed rules on how to compute the credit-spread sensitivities.

Like the revised market-risk capital charge (see Chapter 4), the CVA capital charge is the sum of general and specific credit-spread risks, with both non-stressed and stressed VaR multiplied by three as in the market-risk rule. However, this excludes the IRC (incremental risk charge). Banks are required to compute non-stressed VaR using the current parameter calibrations (ie, using the last three years or market prices) for expected exposure. In computing the stressed VaR, the period of stress for the credit-spread parameters should be the most severe one-year stress period contained within the three-year stress period used for the exposure parameters.

As far as the portfolios to which the CVA capital charge applies, the CVA capital charge is a standalone market-risk charge, calculated on the set of CVAs for all OTC derivatives counterparties, collateralised and uncollateralised, together with eligible CVA hedges.

When banks do not have the required approvals to calculate a CVA capital charge for their counterparties according to the provisions set below, they will have to calculate a portfolio capital charge using the following formula:

$$2.33\sqrt{h}\sqrt{\left(\sum_i 0.5w_i\left(M_i EAD_i^{total} - M_i^{hedge} B_i\right) - \sum_{ind} w_{ind} M_{ind} B_{ind}\right)^2 + \sum_i 0.75 w_i^2 \left(M_i EAD_i^{total} - M_i^{hedge} B_i\right)^2}$$

where

h is the one-year risk horizon (in units of a year), h = 1,

w_i is the weight applicable to counterparty 'i', from one of seven weights based the counterparty's external rating (see Table 5.3) or, in the absence of an external rating, the internal rating mapped to the one of the external ratings subject to supervisory approval,

EAD_i^{total} is the exposure at default of counterparty 'i' (summed across its netting sets), including the effect of collateral as per the existing IMM, SM or CEM rules as applicable to the calculation of counterparty risk capital charges for such counterparty by the bank,

B_i is the notional of purchased single name CDS hedges (summed if more than one position) referencing counterparty 'i', and used to hedge CVA risk,

B_{ind} is the full notional of one or more index CDS of purchased protection, used to hedge CVA risk,

w_{ind} is the weight applicable to index hedges, mapped via the average spread of the index,

M_i is the effective maturity of the transactions with counterparty 'i',

M_i^{hedge} is the maturity of the hedge instrument with notional B_i,

M_{ind} is the maturity of the index hedge 'ind'.

Finally, specific rules have been defined for the calculation of the aggregate CCR and CVA risk capital charges. As an example, institutions with IMM approval and market-risk internal-models approval for the specific interest-rate risk of bonds, the total CCR capital charge is determined as the sum of the following components: (i) the higher of its IMM capital charge based on current parameter calibrations for EAD and its IMM capital charge based on stressed parameter calibrations for EAD; (ii) the combined advanced CVA risk capital charge for all the counterparties where the advanced CVA capital charge is computed counterparty by counterparty.

5.4 OTHER MEASURES FOR IMPROVING RISK COVERAGE

The other measures for risk coverage introduced by Basel III include: increased asset-value correlation in the IRB framework for financial

Table 5.3 Weights for the standardised CVA capital charge

Rating	Weight w_i (%)
AAA	0.7
AA	0.7
A	0.8
BBB	1.0
BB	2.0
B	3.0
CCC	18.0

counterparties (see subsection 5.4.1); increased margin period of risk (5.4.2); central counterparties (5.4.3) and enhanced counterparty credit-management requirements (5.4.4).

5.4.1 Increased asset-value correlation for financial counterparties

The asset-value correlation (AVC) is one of the key variables in the formula that determines the risk weight applied to the exposures under the Internal Ratings-Based Approach introduced by Basel II for computing the credit-risk capital requirements. In the light of the high interconnection shown among financial institutions during the financial crisis, the Basel Committee decided to increase this parameter in certain situations described below so as to increase the capital charge.

In particular, the increased AVC value applies to all transactions with financial counterparties and not only for OTC derivatives transactions. In particular, a 1.25 multiplier is applied to the correlation parameter of all exposures to financial institutions that are:

❏ regulated financial institutions with assets greater than or equal to US$100 billion, which applies to prudentially regulated insurance companies, brokers/dealers, banks, thrifts and futures commission merchants;
❏ unregulated financial institutions, regardless of size – unregulated financial institutions are legal entities whose main business includes: the management of financial assets, lending, factoring, leasing, provision of credit enhancements, securitisation, investments, financial custody, central counterparty services, proprietary trading and other financial services activities identified by supervisors.

The asset value correlation is given by the following formula:

$$R = 1.25 \times \left[0.12w + 0.24(1-w)\right], \qquad w = \frac{1-e^{-50PD}}{1-e^{-50}}$$

This effectively increases the capital charge for financial institutions, particularly those which may also be classified as systematically important financial institutions (SIFIs). Given the dependence on PD, the capital charge can increase by as much as 35% for a low-PD counterparty.

5.4.2 Collateralised counterparties and margin period of risk.

The revisions to the counterparty credit-risk framework also introduced explicit floors on the margin period of risk in the computation of EAD for margined transactions where there is daily remargining and revaluations. The floor is set at five days for repo-style transactions and ten days for OTC derivatives transactions.

However, where there are more than 5,000 transactions in a netting set or the transactions have illiquid collateral or complex trades, the margin period of risk is doubled to twenty days.

5.4.3 Central counterparties

The prudential treatment of CCPs represents a component of a wider reform on the OTC derivatives market, which was a milestone in the agenda of G20 leaders. The financial crisis exposed weaknesses in the structure of the OTC derivatives markets that had contributed to the build-up of systemic risk. While markets in certain OTC derivatives asset classes continued to function well throughout the crisis, the crisis demonstrated the potential for contagion arising from the interconnectedness of OTC derivatives market participants and the limited transparency of counterparty relationships.

At the 2009 G20 Pittsburgh meeting, it was stated,

> All standardised OTC derivative contracts should be traded on exchanges or electronic trading platforms, where appropriate, and cleared through central counterparties by end-2012 at the latest. OTC derivative contracts should be reported to trade repositories. Non-centrally-cleared contracts should be subject to higher capital requirements. We ask the FSB [Financial Stability Board] and its relevant members to assess regularly implementation and whether it is sufficient to improve transparency in the derivatives markets, mitigate systemic risk, and protect against market abuse.

Under the auspices of the FSB, in April 2010, a working group led by representatives of the Committee on Payment and Settlement Systems (CPSS), the International Organisation of Securities Commissions (IOSCO) and the European Commission was formed to make recommendations on the implementation of the G20 objectives. Several issues have been put on the table: standardisation of derivatives contracts, central clearing, exchange or electronic platform trading and reporting to trade repositories.

To help mitigate systemic risk in the OTC derivatives markets, the

G20 leaders agreed that all standardised derivatives contracts should be cleared, ie, the settlements carried out, through central counterparties by end-2012 at the latest. They also agreed that non-centrally-cleared contracts should be subject to higher capital requirements. In combination with setting mandatory clearing requirements and raising capital requirements for non-centrally-cleared contracts to reflect their risks, including systemic risks, the use of central clearing should be expanded through industry commitments to increasing standardisation and volumes of centrally cleared transactions.

To this end, the Basel Committee separately issued for public consultation a set of rules relating to the capitalisation of bank exposures to central counterparties (BCBS 2010c). This set of standards has been slated to be finalised in 2011, once consultation and an impact study have been completed and after CPSS-IOSCO has completed the update of its standards as applicable to CCPs. The committee has expressed its intention for these standards to come into effect at the same time as other counterparty credit-risk reforms, ie, a targeted date of January 2013.

The Basel Committee on Banking Supervision (BCBS) proposals have two sets of capital charges for a bank's exposures to regulated central counterparties. The first set is for the collateral (initial margin) held by the CCP without the use of a bankruptcy-remote vehicle and the mark-to-market exposures. The proposal makes this subject to a low risk weight, proposed at 2%.

The second set consists of default fund exposures to CCPs that will be subject to risk-sensitive capital requirements. Unlike in the case of bilateral OTC derivatives transactions, exposures to CCPs are not subject to the CVA capital charge. These criteria, together with strengthened capital requirements for bilateral OTC derivative exposures, will create strong incentives for banks to move exposures to such CCPs.

5.4.4 Enhanced counterparty credit-management requirements

As mentioned before, the analyses conducted on the financial crisis highlighted the importance of risk management (see, among others, Senior Supervisors Group 2008). In a similar manner, the Basel III rules also require better governance and risk management on stress testing, backtesting and model validation.

The new framework encourages a stress-testing programme that ensures that the risk measures used in counterparty credit risk such as expected positive exposure (EPE) perform as expected. The risk measures are usually computed using risk factors, generally with a Monte Carlo approach. The stress-testing framework is supposed to be for single factors (ie, the risk factors separately) as well as multi-factor (ie, several risk factors at once.) The exposures are also supposed to be stress-tested. The stress tests are meant to identify concentrations across several risk factors. Additionally, stress tests are meant to capture the possibility that stressed market movements will impact not only on the counterparty exposures, but also the credit quality of the counterparties. The revised rules also require that stress test results should be integrated into regular reporting to senior management.

In accordance with the enhanced requirements on stress testing, the reform also requires banks to conduct a regular programme of backtesting, ie, an *ex post* comparison of the risk measures generated by the model against realised risk measures, as well as comparing hypothetical changes based on static positions with realised measures. The bank must carry out an independent initial validation and an ongoing periodic independent review of the IMM model and the risk measures generated by it. Along with the revised capital framework, BCBS (2010b) has also been released. That is a much more detailed guidance on enhanced and sound practices for backtesting counterparty credit risk models.

5.5 CONCLUSIONS

Once the objective of the global reform was defined by G20 leaders and the Financial Stability Board (ie, to address the shortcomings of the regulatory framework that was in place, while keeping the risk-sensitivity principle embedded in the Basel II paradigm unchanged), the regulatory interventions aimed at strengthening risk coverage were considered as a key priority by the Basel Committee. The wide range of topics addressed and the degree of articulation of the solutions that have been envisaged confirm the willingness of international regulators to achieve such a result.

Counterparty credit risk, which before the financial crisis had been simply perceived as a type of credit risk and consequently treated from a prudential point of view, has been deeply discussed in the post-crisis regulatory debate and, as such, received an ad hoc treatment in the new framework. The high losses reported by many financial institutions arising from counterparty risk confirmed the central role that an adequate treatment of derivatives transactions can play in the measurement of overall capital adequacy of a bank.

All the changes that have been introduced go in the direction of making the prudential metrics more robust to stressed conditions, maintaining the possibility for less sophisticated institutions to rely on standardised methodologies. Other measures, such as a revised treatment of banks' exposures to central counterparties, are part of the revision of wider areas of the Basel II regulatory framework, such as the OTC derivatives market. Some of these measures were slated to be finalised throughout 2011 due to their complex nature.

At the time of writing it was not possible to fully assess the overall impact of these measures. On the one hand, as mentioned, some of these still have to be finalised and specific impact assessments are currently under way; on the other hand, banks' reactions to the new framework will represent a key driver with regard to portfolio strategies and business opportunities, as well as by the supervisory validation of internal metrics estimated by banks. Finally, data quality issues will have to be better addressed in order to get a more reliable picture of the likely effects of the new rules.

What is more certain is that risk coverage rules will play an even greater role in the assessment of banks' capital adequacy for both supervisors and institutions themselves, also because – unlike other Basel III components, such as the leverage ratio and the liquidity standards – they will enter into force at the beginning of 2013. If it transpires that the local implementation of the Basel III framework reflects the original intention of international regulators and the rules are adequately enforced in single jurisdictions (also relying on a credible peer-review mechanism across countries), the final objective of making the financial system more robust to stress scenarios and banks' behaviour more prudent will be achieved in coming years.

This chapter represents the views of the author alone and does not necessarily represent the views of the comptroller of the currency.

1. In the Basel II Capital Accord a netting set is a group of transactions with a single counterparty that are subject to a legally enforceable bilateral netting arrangement and for which netting is recognised for regulatory capital purposes.
2. Siddique (2010). Losses reported in other currencies are converted to USD using 1.3919 USD/EUR, 1.4619 USD/GBP and 0.93694 USD/CHF.
3. This LGD, which inputs into the calculation of the CVA risk capital charge, is different from the LGD that is determined for the IRB and CCR default risk charge, as it is a market assessment rather than an internal estimate.

REFERENCES

Basel Committee on Bank Supervision, 2006, "International Convergence of Capital Measurement and Capital Standards: A Revised Framework", Rules Text: comprehensive version.

Basel Committee on Bank Supervision, 2009, "Strengthening the resilience of the banking sector" Consultative Document, December.

Basel Committee on Bank Supervision, 2010a, "Basel III: A global regulatory framework for more resilient banks and banking systems" Rules Text, December

Basel Committee on Bank Supervision, 2010b, "Sound practices for back-testing counterparty credit risk models", Guidance, December.

Basel Committee on Bank Supervision, 2010c, "Capitalisation of bank exposures to central counterparties", Consultative Document, December.

Canabarro, E., and D. Duffie, 2003, "Measuring and Marking Counterparty Risk", in L. M. Tilman (ed.), *Asset/Liability Management of Financial Institutions*. Euromoney Books: London,

Financial Stability Board, 2010, "Implementing OTC Derivatives Market Reforms", October.

Rebonato, R., M. Sherring and R. Barnes, 2010, "CVA and the equivalent bond", *Risk*, September, pp. 118–21.

Senior Supervisors Group, 2008, "Observations on Risk Management Practices during the Recent Market Turbulence", March.

Siddique, A., 2010, "Dissecting the Financial Crisis of 2008: the Role of Credit Valuation Adjustments", mimeo.

6

Tools for Mitigating the Procyclicality of Financial Regulation

Mario Quagliariello

European Banking Authority

6.1 INTRODUCTION

This chapter deals with the issue of procyclicality in the financial sector. First, it describes how capital regulation can amplify the natural fluctuations of bank intermediation. Second, it provides a comprehensive overview of the measures adopted by the Basel Committee on Banking Supervision (BCBS) for mitigating procyclicality as well as tackling the shortcomings of the Basel II framework.

The nature of credit markets and their imperfections make banks' activity inherently cyclical. Unquestionably, a certain degree of cyclicality is expected and somehow desirable since it reflects the link between the banking and the nonfinancial sectors. Cyclicality turns into a policy concern – procyclicality – when it contributes to the amplification of economic cycle fluctuations and undermines the stability of the financial system. Indeed, the crisis has shown with dramatic clarity to what extent flawed regulatory frameworks and poor supervision can reinforce the cyclicality of the financial sector. In the aftermath of the crisis, when recessionary conditions spread worldwide, it also became perceptible that the possibility of cyclicality turning into procyclicality is not just an issue for textbooks.

The stylised facts are well known (see Chapter 1). In the boom preceding the turmoil, investors underestimated the potential risks implied in certain products. Banks relaxed the selection criteria of their borrowers – the subprime lending is the most crystalline example – and did not make provisions against future losses. Profitability was more than satisfactory and capital levels appeared consistent with risk exposures, which were perceived as very low. After the peak of the upturn, the ability of customers – in the beginning, the subprime clients – to repay their debts started worsening, the creditworthiness of borrowers deteriorated markedly, and nonperforming assets were revealed, causing significant losses in the balance sheets of banks. Death spirals determined a domino effect from one financial market to another, across jurisdictions and categories of intermediaries. The fall of the price of assets, along with the uncertainty of their true value, further affected customers' financial wealth and depressed the value of any collateral. The exposure of banks to credit, market and liquidity risks increased, requiring larger provisions, liquidity and capital buffers. This happened at the very moment when capital and liquidity were more expensive or simply not available. Intermediaries reacted by deleveraging and reducing credit supply, thus exacerbating the effects of the crisis and contributing to the deepest recession since the Great Depression in the 1930s.

The role of financial regulation – particularly of Basel II rules – in contributing to these events has been debated at both the political and the technical levels. The Financial Stability Forum (FSF 2009) highlighted "the disruptive effects of procyclicality" and issued specific recommendations in order to ensure that the Basel II framework promotes prudent capital buffers over the credit cycle, and mitigates the risk that the regulatory capital framework amplifies the transmission of shocks between the financial and real sectors. In particular, the Forum mandated the BCBS to strengthen the regulatory capital framework so that the quality and level of capital in the banking system increase during strong economic conditions and can be drawn down in periods of distress. The recommendations of the FSF – now renamed the Financial Stability Board (FSB) – have been endorsed by the G20 leaders, and they became the cornerstone of the Basel Committee for designing the suite of measures to work against the cyclical tendencies of credit markets (hereafter, the countercyclical package).

The chapter is organised as follows. Section 6.2 illustrates how capital regulation can contribute to procyclicality, underscoring the differences between Basel I and Basel II. Section 6.3 provides an overview of the countercyclical mechanisms already envisaged under the Basel II framework. Section 6.4 summarises the policy debate on possible new measures for dealing with procyclicality and Section 6.5 explains the new rules for mitigating procyclicality. The conclusions present a first assessment of the countercyclical package.

6.2 CAPITAL REGULATION AND PROCYCLICALITY
6.2.1 Cyclicality in Basel I

Any prudential rule aiming at ensuring that banks hold a minimum amount of capital can have cyclical effects. Indeed, in a recession, the number of borrowers that are not able to honour their financial obligations increases, reducing the revenue of banks and calling for higher levels of loan-loss provisions, which should be aligned with the increasing default rates. If bank profits are not sufficient to cover the extra credit losses due to the downturn, they need to deplete their own funds.

In principle, when risk weights are not linked to the actual riskiness of the counterparties – as in Basel I – the risk-weighted assets are not affected (Figure 6.1). Rather, they tend to increase during upturns as a consequence of the willingness of banks to expand credit supply (and, thus, nominal assets), adopting less rigorous selection standards for borrowers. Therefore, when the economic cycle inverts, banks may have riskier portfolios. In other words, under Basel I, cyclicality risk does not affect the minimum requirement, but it is

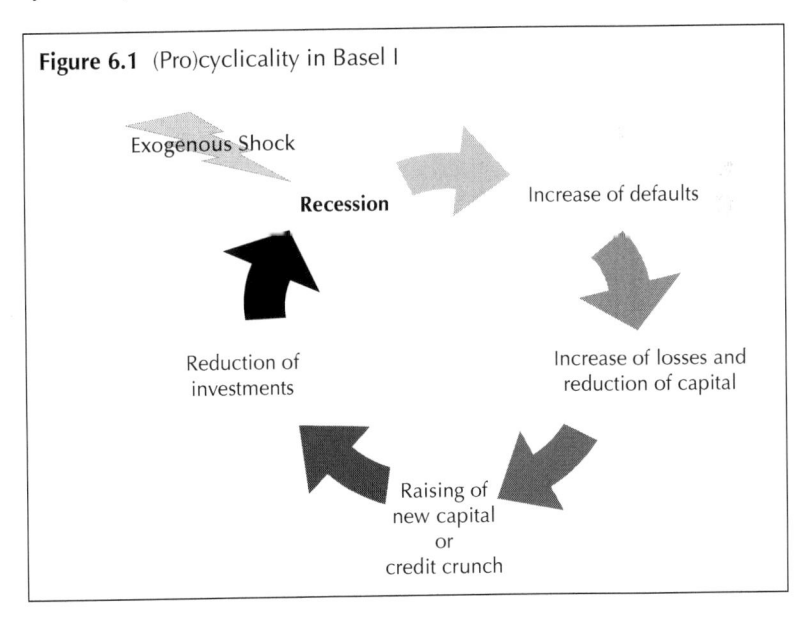

Figure 6.1 (Pro)cyclicality in Basel I

Exogenous Shock → Recession → Increase of defaults → Increase of losses and reduction of capital → Raising of new capital or credit crunch → Reduction of investments → (back to Recession)

limited to capital levels, which can decrease when profits cannot absorb credit losses.

If the reduction of capital is large, banks – particularly less capitalised ones – have to implement proper strategies in order to keep meeting the minimum requirements. Such strategies may consist of either raising new capital or cutting risky assets, ie, loans to customers. What banks will actually choose depends upon the cost and the effectiveness of the different options. Since in adverse economic conditions fundraising is typically more costly than in normal times, many intermediaries may decide to contain credit supply. As a result, cyclical effects may also emerge when capital requirements are not sensitive (or only slightly sensitive) to risk.

Clearly, feedback from the banking sector to the real economy (ie, procyclicality) is not automatic, but rather depends on whether capital requirements are binding for banks, and the degree to which nonfinancial firms rely on bank loans for financing investments.

6.2.2 Cyclicality in Basel II

With respect to Basel I, Basel II makes minimum capital requirements more sensitive to the riskiness of banks portfolios. This is the

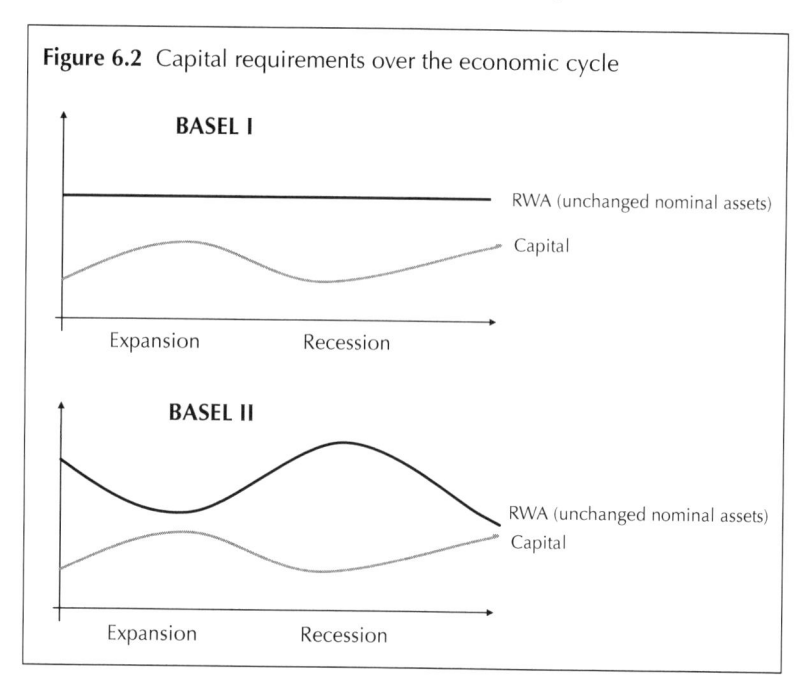

Figure 6.2 Capital requirements over the economic cycle

consequence of using risk parameters – particularly the probability of default (PD) – that may be affected by the economic conditions. In such a framework, the cyclical effect is not transmitted merely through the absolute level of capital, but also via the change of the riskiness of the assets held in banks' portfolios (Figure 6.2), measured by the migration of customers across rating buckets.

In fact, when minimum capital requirements depend on risk weights based on ratings – either internal or external – the deterioration of economic conditions leads to a higher frequency of rating downgrading, and to the worsening of capital requirements (Figure 6.3). By contrast, in expansionary phases, risk-weights improve as a consequence of better credit quality, capital ratios become less stringent, free capital increases and, therefore, the willingness and ability of banks to lend becomes stronger.

The fluctuations of the minimum capital requirement depend on the sensitivity of risk weights and on rating stability. Therefore, the minimum requirements for banks that adopt the standardised approach tend to be more stable than those based on internal ratings, since rating agencies are relatively through-the-cycle (TTC).

However, banks also adopting internal-ratings-based (IRB) approaches can show different degrees of cyclicality of capital

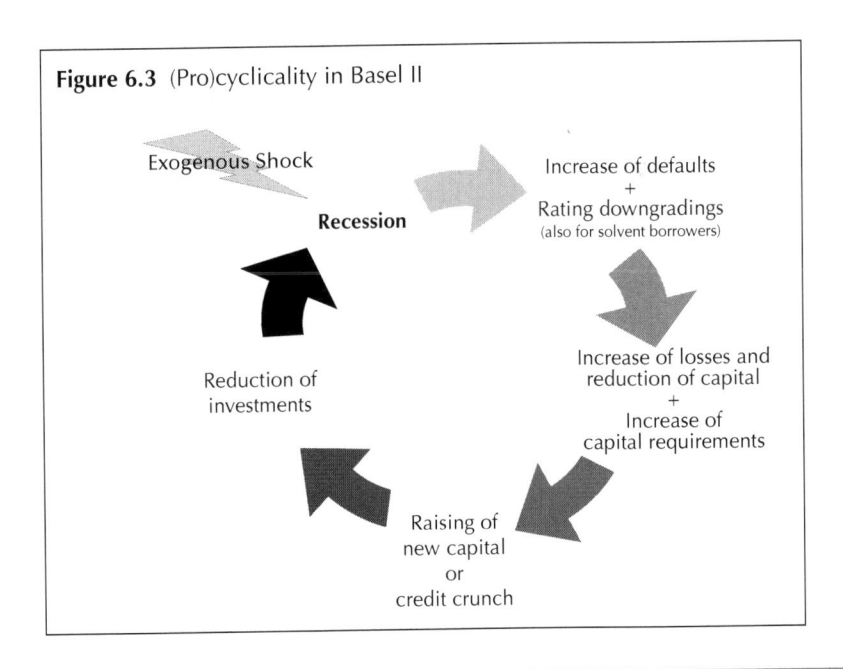

Figure 6.3 (Pro)cyclicality in Basel II

Exogenous Shock

Recession

Increase of defaults
+
Rating downgradings
(also for solvent borrowers)

Increase of losses and reduction of capital
+
Increase of capital requirements

Raising of new capital or credit crunch

Reduction of investments

requirements, depending on the philosophy behind ratings estimation.

In most rating systems, probabilities of default (PDs) are assigned in a two-stage process. First, an individual PD is assigned to a counterparty (this is known as PD assignment); next, counterparties are assigned to rating grades and a PD is estimated for each rating grade (known as PD quantification). The latter is used for calculating the minimum required capital of each exposure. Procyclicality can result from: (i) migrations (ie, individual counterparties are assigned better or worse PDs as the cycle improves or deteriorates); and (ii) recalibration of grade PDs (ie, grade PDs are updated as the cycle reverses); (iii) from a combination of the two.

In point-in-time (PiT) rating systems, banks seek to estimate default risk over a future limited period, typically one year, looking at current conditions. In such systems, the role of factor (ii) as a driver of procyclicality will typically be negligible, whereas factor (i) will be important: in a downturn a large number of borrowers migrate to worse grades, resulting in higher capital requirements (and vice versa in an expansion). By contrast, in TTC rating systems, debtors are assigned to rating grades based on the evaluation of their ability to remain solvent at the trough of a business cycle or during stress events. Thus, migrations to different rating grades are rare and their role as a driver of procyclicality tends to be negligible. In TTC systems some volatility of capital requirements might derive from factor (ii), as actual defaults do vary throughout the cycle. Table 6.1 summarises the impact of different rating system on the cyclicality of the minimum capital requirement.

Table 6.1 Impact on cyclicality of different rating systems

Degree of minimum capital requirement volatility	Statistical PD attached to individual borrowers is PiT	Statistical PD attached to individual borrowers is TTC
Grade-PD based on short-term average of default rates (not allowed by the EU Capital Requirement Directive)	+++	++
Grade-PD based on long-term average of default rates	+++	+

6.3 BASEL II COUNTERCYCLICAL RULES

The Basel II framework already includes mechanisms to reduce the possible procyclical impact of a risk-based capital regulation. They include provisions on the estimation of risk parameters, the treatment of some categories of counterparties, and Pillar II instruments. While their actual success in achieving this objective is still debated, it is important to briefly review their rationale in order to better understand the novelty of the Basel III rules.

6.3.1 Risk parameters

In the IRB approach, Basel II envisages specific provisions on the estimation of risk parameters in order to alleviate the fluctuations of capital requirements over different phases of the business cycle.

As far as the PD is concerned, the framework encourages banks to adopt TTC methodologies in the process of PD assignment. As for the PD quantification, grade PDs need to be a long-run average of the one-year default rates. Also, banks are expected to use time series of at least five years, which should, ideally, cover an entire business cycle. In this way, the volatility of the PD assigned to each rating class is reduced. However, as already discussed, the migration of the counterparties across different rating classes – which is likely if individual PDs are the results of non-genuinely TTC methodologies – leaves room for increases of the capital requirement when economic conditions deteriorate.

For the other risk parameters, specific guidelines are provided for mitigating procyclicality risk. Both the loss-given default (downturn LGD) and the exposure at default (EAD) should be estimated at the facility level and in such a way as to reflect recessionary conditions. In particular, the LGDs cannot be less than the long-run, default-weighted, average loss-rate-given default. This implies that banks are required to identify the appropriate downturn conditions and possible correlations between default rates and recovery rates, and, thus, incorporate them in the quantification of the LGD as to produce parameters that are consistent with downturn conditions.

Furthermore, the shape of the regulatory functions, which allow for the calculation of capital requirements using the estimated risk parameters as inputs, addresses the need to alleviate the cyclical effects on capital requirements. In particular, the concavity of the curves makes the elasticity of the capital requirements to PD changes lower as the PD increases, making the capital requirements less sensitive to rating downgrades. In other words, the slope of the curves implies that the capital requirements for high-quality portfolios are more sensitive to PD changes than those of riskier counterparties.

6.3.2 The treatment of less-cyclical borrowers

The implications of the new rules on the access to bank credit for small and medium-sized enterprises (SMEs) has been a key issue in shaping Basel II. In the consultative paper presented in 2001, the Basel Committee had introduced, under the IRB approach, a single weight curve for all portfolios. Also, in the standardised approach, a 100% risk weight was assigned to the loans to nonrated firms, regardless of their size. These provisions might have penalised SMEs, which are typically riskier than larger firms, unrated and largely dependent on bank loans.

Therefore, in the final rules, the slope of the regulatory curves was significantly reduced in order to lessen procyclicality risk for a large proportion of borrowers. This revision has led to a relevant reduction of the capital requirement associated with the different PD classes.

Second, under the IRB approach for corporate credits, banks were allowed to distinguish loans to SME borrowers (ie, those with less than €50 million in annual sales) from those to larger firms, with the former benefiting from lower capital requirements, all things being equal. The reduction in the required amount of capital can be as high as 20%, depending on the size of the borrower, and should result in an average reduction of approximately 10% across the entire set of SME borrowers.

Third, banks that manage small-business-related exposures in a manner similar to retail exposures were authorised to apply the retail IRB treatment to such exposures. This was allowed, provided that the total exposure of a bank to an individual SME is less than €1 million.

Finally, risk weights for non-mortgage retail exposures (thus including retail SME exposures) were reduced from 100% to 75% in the standardised approach.

6.3.3 Pillar II and stress tests

The concept of capital buffering was already envisaged in Basel II. In particular, stress tests were thought of as a valuable tool for making capital planning more forward-looking and, thus, contributing to dampen the cyclicality of capital needs.

In fact, in the Basel II discipline, stress tests address two distinct needs. First, they are a tool that allows banks to determine whether, and to what extent, the estimation of the risk parameters depends on the economic conditions prevailing in the time period used for the estimation, ie, they allow measuring the degree of cyclicality of the capital requirements implied by the estimation process. Second, they can be employed in order to quantify the amount of extra capital that banks may need in extreme, but still plausible, market conditions. The presence of adequate stress-testing methodologies is a prerequisite for the supervisory validation of IRB systems.

It is difficult to say whether Pillar II provisions might have contributed to the reduction in the impact of the crisis. Unquestionably, a proper use of stress tests would have warned banks about the need to build up capital buffers in excess of regulatory minimums. Unfortunately, as noted by Cannata and Quagliariello (2009), the focus of intermediaries and regulators in the first-time application stage was – somehow naturally – on the correct implementation of Pillar I provisions. Then, the timing of the crisis has prevented intermediaries from fully carrying out this self-assessment and increasing capital cushions, and has prevented supervisory authorities from checking their adequacy.

6.4 THE DEBATE AFTER THE CRISIS

In the aftermath of the crisis, the Basel II countercyclical measures have been considered – rightly or wrongly – unsatisfactory and ineffective. In their January 30, 2008, column in the *Financial Times*, Charles Goodhart and Avinash Persaud claimed that "the main problem is … the lack of counter-cyclical control mechanisms or instruments. Having foreseen the danger, the regulatory authorities did not have the instruments to do much about it. The Basel regime for capital adequacy does nothing to constrain credit booms. Its effect, if any, on the crunch will be to deepen it further."

There was therefore a strong consensus regarding the need to correct the procyclicality of financial regulation. However, there was much less agreement on the way forward. And the uncertainty as to the practical importance of the procyclical effects of the risk-sensitive capital regulation did not help in drafting concrete proposals.

Widely discussed options – which are not necessarily mutually exclusive – focused on methodologies for estimating risk parameters (primarily the probabilities of default), characteristics of the regulatory formulas and refinements to the Pillar II instruments.

6.4.1 Binding rules on the estimation of probabilities of default

As described in Section 6.2, Basel II favours TTC rating systems, but it does not force banks to adopt them. In Europe, for instance, most banks implemented hybrid solutions, including both PiT and TTC components. Therefore, a possible way for dealing with the cyclicality of risk-sensitive capital requirements is to explicitly require banks to adopt TTC systems. In fact, many observers – and banks themselves – have advocated regulatory requirements on TTC ratings as the preferred solution to cyclicality. It is, however, inexplicable why supervisors did not impose such requirements under Basel II, and why banks did not freely adopt TTC methodologies. It is puzzling that, while they had not voluntarily developed such systems in implementing Basel II, most banks strongly supported this policy option in drafting Basel III.

The truth is that the advantages of TTC approaches do not come without costs in terms, for instance, of comparability across time of the capital requirements. Moreover, their implementation may make it difficult to infer changes in portfolio risk from changes in banks' capital ratios.[2] For the same reasons, TTC ratings tend to be poorly suited for internal pricing and risk-management purposes and may fail the "use test" provided for by the Basel II framework, which envisages that risk estimates used for the calculation of capital requirements be effectively employed for internal risk-management purposes. The introduction of the "use test" has been a major achievement of Basel II and it still represents the first proof of the validity of the rating system and a prerequisite for internal and supervisory validation.

6.4.2 Strengthening stress tests

Another option, which can go together with more TTC ratings, and is one that also received support from banks, is to strengthen Pillar II provisions, particularly stress tests. Bank supervisors already have the responsibility of assessing capital adequacy in the light of analyses of the economic cycle and of macroprudential concerns. In particular, Pillar II gives supervisors the discretion to require banks to increase capital resources above the Pillar I minimum. While not limited to this purpose, Pillar II rules have been designed also for reducing cyclicality (this is the reason why stress tests should consider, at a minimum, the impact of a recession on capital adequacy). Banks can be required, for instance, to run stress tests based on common recessionary scenarios set by supervisors, and to adjust their capital buffers according to the results of such simulations.

6.4.3 Time-varying capital functions

Basel II aims at ensuring that the PD of a single bank stays below a given threshold, regardless of economic conditions. As noted by some academics (Kashyap and Stein 2004), the time invariance of the rule implies that in a recession the objective of reducing a bank's PD is overweighted, and that of keeping sufficient credit flows to the economy is underweighted (and vice versa during expansions). Therefore, it has been suggested that a policymaker who cares about both objectives could adopt confidence intervals that change over the business cycle. Another option is the adjustment of the asset correlation parameter in the IRB algorithm: the correlation would be adjusted downwards in bad times and upwards in booms.

It is clear that any attempt to modify elements of capital functions – for instance introducing time-varying confidence levels – implies new and lengthy quantitative analyses. Moreover, as business cycles differ across countries, a common recalibration would probably be inappropriate, and country-specific adjustments would need to be applied. This would significantly reduce cross-country comparability of the minimum capital requirements of banks. In addition, establishing an automatic link between capital requirements and forward-looking measures of economic conditions, such as equity prices, could have useful countercyclical properties, but would also make capital requirement heavily dependent on the volatility of stock prices. Other financial variables (such as spreads on credit-default swaps) are likely to suffer from similar problems. Furthermore, market variables are not necessarily robust indicators of credit cycles for jurisdictions where banks are mainly involved in retail segments and loans to SMEs and relevant markets are less liquid (Conciarelli and Quagliariello 2009).

6.4.4 Smoothing the output of the capital function

Another option for mitigating procyclicality while preserving the informative value of PiT rating systems is to smooth the output of the capital requirements formula (Gordy and Howells 2006), either through an autoregressive time-series filter that smoothes capital requirements at the individual bank level, or through applying a non-bank-specific, time-varying multiplier (higher than one in good times and smaller than one in bad times) to the output of the regulatory formulas. This multiplier could be linked, for example, to equity values or to credit growth and should be announced in each period by the national regulators and applied to all banks under their jurisdiction.[3]

Adjusting the output also has drawbacks, particularly in terms of perverse incentives for intermediaries. In fact, weak banks may be encouraged to increase portfolio risk rapidly – in the attempt to gamble for resurrection – because required capital would adjust only slowly. Moreover, the calibration of the speed of adjustment would pose practical challenges. In fact, the timing of capital restoration after a crisis would largely depend on the choice of this parameter, which may be difficult to estimate.

6.4.5 Countercyclical provisioning

Countercyclical provisioning does not directly amend the procyclicality of capital requirements, but could indeed contribute to the building-up of resources in good times, to be used to shelter loan losses during recessions. Regrettably, current accounting standards – whose goal is to ensure the transparency of financial statements, not conservatism – allow banks to provision only at the very moment when losses are actually incurred. This can have procyclical effects, since bad loans accumulate during good times but losses materialise in bad times.

The most cited practical example of countercyclical provisions is the Spanish system of dynamic (or "statistical") provisioning. The Spanish approach links provisions to banks' historical loan-loss experience. At an early stage of the debate, the EU Commission (2009) and the UK Financial Services Authority (2009) have also put forward proposals for introducing similar systems in the EU. Another possible mechanism for correcting this rules-driven procyclical effect would be to align provisions to expected losses, estimated through-the-cycle. This proposal has been sketched by the International Accounting Standard Board (IASB) (2009). In particular, provisions should reflect losses that banks estimate will be produced by a portfolio of loans, to be recognised in the income statement on an accrual basis or at origination. Such provisions would then be changed through time to reflect updated estimates of expected losses. The model would require the calculation of the net present value of the expected cashflows (ie, the difference between contractual cashflows and expected credit losses).

The effectiveness of this approach depends on how expected losses are estimated. The 2009 IASB proposal – which was under revision at the time of writing – was based on banks' internal estimates of expected losses, which tend to be PiT. Therefore, such specification might be as procyclical as the current method based on incurred losses: for PiT banks provisions would indeed continue to rise during downturns, thus restraining banks' lending capacity, while their low levels during upswings would contribute to sustained profits and lending booms.

6.5 THE BASEL III COUNTERCYCLICAL FRAMEWORK

Since no single solution is available for overcoming the different aspects of procyclicality, the Basel Committee opted for a set of complementary tools. In particular, the consultative document published in December 2009 envisaged measures for: (i) mitigating the cyclicality of the minimum capital requirements; (ii) promoting more forward-looking provisions; (iii) inducing banks to conserve capital; and (iv) achieving the goal of protecting the banking sector from excessive credit growth.

These measures were thought to be able to overcome the shortcomings of the Basel II framework and link more clearly the micro- and macroprudential perspectives, while reinforcing the incentives to sound and prudent risk management. This building-block approach represented a reasonable and pragmatic way of meeting the ambitious mandate agreed by the G20 leaders in April 2009 and the FSB roadmap. Unfortunately, not all of these measures have been fully finalised in their operational details. In some cases, such as for the tools that reduce the cyclicality of the minimum requirements, the disagreement within the Basel Committee on specific solutions led to conclusions that leave room to manoeuvre for national jurisdictions. In other cases, such as for provisioning rules, the policy discussion was still ongoing at the time of writing, since it involved both prudential regulators and accounting standard setters, which had no fully consistent missions. For this reason, the rest of the chapter deals with prudential countercyclical mechanisms, while the debate on dynamic provisions – and more generally accounting matters – are not discussed.

6.5.1 Tools for mitigating the cyclicality of the minimum capital requirements

Smoothing the fluctuations of the minimum capital requirements over the credit cycle is the natural starting point for a toolkit aiming at containing the cyclicality of Basel II. In fact, as underlined in Section 6.2, this is the only aspect of cyclicality that can be directly ascribed to a risk-sensitive capital regulation and very much depends on the rating philosophy of banks.

Throughout the reform process, the Basel Committee (2009, 2010a) did consider two concrete proposals – put forward by the Committee of European Banking Supervisors (CEBS) (already in 2009) and by the UK FSA (2009) – for mitigating the cyclicality of the minimum required capital for credit risk.

In their basic design, both proposals envisage a bank-specific mechanism that takes into account the historical changes in PDs estimated by banks in order to build buffers against recessionary conditions. The starting point is the PD of each regulatory portfolio. At time t, this PD is calculated as the average of grade PDs weighted by the number of counterparties in each grade:

$$\text{Time } t: \text{portfolio } PD = \frac{\sum_{g=1}^{k} PD^g N^g}{\sum_{g=1}^{k} N^g}$$

where PD^g is the PD of each grade g (1, ... , k) and N^g is the number of counterparties in grade g. The use of the number of counterparties instead of the exposures gives the same weights to all borrowers and reduce the impact of idiosyncratic factors.

The PD of the portfolio would obviously change over the cycle as the result of two different factors: (i) transition of borrowers across grades (which is more pronounced in more PiT rating systems); and (ii) change of grade PD (which may exist in TTC rating systems, depending on the calibration process). The methodology guarantees that the more PiT the rating, the greater the adjustment.

The original CEBS proposal was based on a mechanism for quantifying, for each regulatory portfolio, the gap between current PD and the downturn PD, ie, the highest PD over a given time span. The quantification of the buffer is straightforward. For each portfolio, a scaling factor is calculated as the ratio between the downturn PD and the current PD: the scaling factor is expected to be greater than 1 at all times but downturn periods. Then, for each rating grade, the scaling factor is used for adjusting the current-grade PDs. Accordingly, for each grade the capital buffer is determined as the difference between the amount of capital computed using the current PD and the one computed using the PD adjusted with the downturn scaling factor. Finally, for each portfolio, the buffer is the sum of grade-level buffers and would increase in expansion and decrease in recession.

This approach is equivalent to transforming portfolio PDs into recessionary PDs, which, in turn, implies that banks build up buffers that reflect the impact of stress scenarios. Given the goals and the characteristics of the other components of the countercyclical toolkit, which already incorporate stress scenarios, the alternative option envisages the use of the long-term average PDs. Under this approach, portfolio PDs estimated through a PiT rating system would be transformed into through-the-cycle PDs; for already through-the-cycle PDs the impact is expected to be fairly limited. While the final outcome is a TTC capital requirement, this approach avoids the shortcomings of a TTC rating system. In fact, the bank can continue estimating PiT PDs, if it so wishes, and using them for internal purposes, but the capital requirement is then computed by inputting the rescaled PDs in the regulatory formula. In that respect, the value of the use test is preserved. On the other hand, such an option is more suited for a Pillar I implementation, since it determines negative buffers (ie, the release of capital) in bad times, when the unadjusted PDs are above the long-term average.

Both proposals entail various benefits. First of all, the adjustment is bank-specific and based on risk-sensitive conditioning variables. This ensures that the incentive structure provided for by Basel II is met: TTC banks are required to hold lower buffers than those adopting PiT systems, which have more pronounced cyclical fluctuations of capital requirements. These features reduce the risk of regulatory arbitrage, which is likely to arise if non-risk-sensitive adjustments are applied without being complemented by tools for smoothing the minimum required capital. In other words, the proposal would level the playing field among PiT and TTC banks, making the other components of the countercyclical package – namely, the capital conservation buffer and the countercyclical buffer – really successful.

In addition, there is no need for supervisors to define recessions/expansions, since PD fluctuations and, thus, the dynamics of the scaling factor approximate the evolution of the business cycle. More generally, the approach does not require any calibration of the buffer; in fact, each bank would be required to hold buffers that are consistent with the cyclicality of its capital requirements: if cyclicality is a small problem, the solution would be small and vice versa (Angelini *et al* 2010).

This notwithstanding, the scaling-factor approach has been heavily criticised by banks and some supervisors as well. To be fair, data limitations – particularly the time-series for portfolios' PDs – can reduce the accuracy of the countercyclical adjustments. Also, to the extent that banks are allowed to use time series of different length, level-playing-field issues can arise. Other detractors of such a tool emphasised the risk of unreliable outcomes for banks that experienced significant structural changes in portfolio composition – eg, through Mergers and Acquisitions (M&As) – and would face requirements based on past measures of risk that can be addressed and overcome.

The result of this debate has been a compromise solution. The Basel Committee confirmed the need to introduce measures to achieve a better balance between risk sensitivity and the stability of capital requirements, but it also left the concrete implementation of such devices to national authorities, "should this be viewed as necessary". The approach based on automatic scaling factors has been therefore considered one of the possible tools that supervisors may activate should they consider the cyclicality of the minimum requirement to be excessive.

6.5.2 Capital conservation buffer

The capital conservation buffer is a target capital ratio, above the minimum requirements, aiming at ensuring that banks build up capital buffers outside periods of stress that can be run down as losses are incurred. The requirement is based on a capital conservation rule linking the ability of banks to distribute profits – dividends, discretionary bonuses and share buybacks – to the distance from the target ratio.

The rationale of the buffer is explained by the Basel Committee (2010b). The guiding principle is that banks should not be allowed – as sometimes happened before the crisis – to use the distribution of capital as a way to signal financial strength. "Not only is this irresponsible from the perspective of an individual bank, putting shareholders' interests above depositors', it may also encourage other banks to follow suit. As a consequence, banks in aggregate can end up increasing distributions at the exact point in time when they should be conserving earnings." Therefore, the obligation to meet a conservation buffer reduces the discretion of banks that have depleted their capital base to further reduce it via profit distribution.

A key point for understanding the design of the overall countercyclical toolkit is that – with respect to the devices for smoothing the minimum – the conservation buffer does not address explicitly the cyclicality of Basel II, but rather the natural cyclicality of the credit cycles. In other words, they are not a substitute, but are complementary: one cannot be used without the other.

The functioning of the mechanism is relatively plain. Banks are required to target a conservation ratio of 2.5% of the risk-weighted assets, to be met by common-equity Tier 1. If they are not able to do so, they face limits to distribution policies, with constraints that increase as the banks' capital levels approach the minimum requirements (Table 6.2). In other words, the further a bank is from the target level, the more severe the restrictions on profit distribution are.

The Basel Committee highlights that the target level is not intended as a new minimum, as some banks have argued during the public consultation.

First of all, by design, banks with capital levels at the top of the range would be subject to minimal constraints. In fact, conservation ratios of about 40% tend to be negligible for most banks that – voluntarily – retain such a share of their profits.

Table 6.2 Individual bank minimum capital conservation standards

Common-equity Tier 1 Ratio	Minimum capital conservation ratios (expressed as a percentage of earnings)
4.5–5.125%	100%
>5.125–5.75%	80%
>5.75–6.375%	60%
>6.375–7.0%	40%
>7.0%	0%

Second, with respect to breaches of minimum requirements, banks will not deal with any further sanction when their capital levels fall into the conservation range and, thus, they will be able to conduct business as usual. This clearly does not preclude further supervisory actions under Pillar II.

Third, a bank willing to make payments in excess of the restrictions would have alternative options, such as raising new capital. Since this is relatively easy in favourable economic conditions – and much less in a recession – the likely outcome is that banks will meet the buffer in good times, when the opportunity cost of cutting dividends is significant and capital is cheap, and they will use it in bad times, when profits are low and risk premiums increase markedly.

While the overall picture is well defined, there are some elements of the discipline that deserve some attention and room for possible improvements.

To start with, there are some definitions that remain too general. For instance, according to the Basel Committee the items that are subject to the restrictions are dividends and share buybacks, discretionary payments on additional Tier 1 capital instruments and discretionary bonus payments to staff. Behind this general principle, there are several open issues, particularly related to bonuses. For instance, it is still undefined whether the reference to the staff should be intended as the whole personnel of the bank or, rather, just the senior management; whether bonuses to be blocked are those to be awarded or those already awarded but subject to clawback clauses (see Chapter 11).

There are also more substantial matters. The rules text clarifies that the restrictions would apply at the consolidated level – ie, allowing minority interests to be distributed out of the group. The interaction with the scope of application can, however, become more complex should national authorities require – along with the consolidated – a solo level application.

More importantly, in terms of regulatory design, the inclusion of payments on additional Tier 1 does not appear well grounded. Indeed, since Tier 1 hybrids are by definition noncumulative (see Chapter 3), including them in the conservation measures would result – in the case of instruments accounted for as debt – in a transfer of wealth from Tier 1 subscribers to shareholders (the owners of retained earnings). This means that both equity holders and noncore Tier 1 investors would be subject to payment restrictions, but only the latter would lose their interests permanently, while the former would benefit from the increase of the capital base (and possibly higher dividends in the future).

Finally, decisions regarding how the restrictions would apply in practice are still to be taken. Indeed, while any breach of minimum capital requirements – which banks are required to notify to supervisors – entails a sanction that is applicable simultaneously with the breach, this is not necessarily the case for the buffer, since dividend distribution is a discrete event. An obvious solution is requiring banks to notify the supervisor of their ability to meet the buffer prior to any distribution. Since this information would possibly be based on non-audited data, supervisors should maintain the power to ask banks to postpone the distribution until official reporting is available. On the other hand, conservatism suggests that capital conservation constraints apply until the bank's capital increases to the top of the buffer range according to audited financial statements, even though this implies that a bank could have capital above the buffer level but still be subject to the capital conservation constraints. This is just an example of possible implementation problems when converting Basel principles into national legislations.

6.5.3 Countercyclical buffer

While the capital conservation buffer focuses on idiosyncratic problems, the rationale of the countercyclical buffer is much more linked to the need to introduce a genuine macroprudential view in banking regulation. As explained by the Basel Committee on Banking Supervision (2010b),

> the financial crisis has provided a vivid reminder that losses incurred in the banking sector can be extremely large when a downturn is preceded by a period of excess credit growth. These losses can destabilise the banking sector and spark a vicious circle, whereby problems in the financial system can contribute to a downturn in the real economy that then feeds back on to the banking sector.

The buffer is to be deployed when national authorities consider aggregate credit growth to be excessive, thus determining an unacceptable build-up of system-wide risk. However, and this is a central point, the main goal of the buffer is not to manage the credit cycle, but – much more pragmatically – to ensure that the banking system accumulates a buffer of capital in (very) good times to protect it against future potential losses.

> In addressing the aim of protecting the banking sector from the credit cycle, the countercyclical capital buffer regime may also help to lean against the build-up phase of the cycle in the first place. This would occur through the capital buffer acting to raise the cost of credit, and therefore dampen its demand, when there is evidence that the stock of credit has grown to excessive levels relative to the benchmarks of past experience. This potential moderating effect on the build-up phase of the credit cycle should be viewed as a positive side benefit, rather than the primary aim of the countercyclical capital buffer regime [BCBS 2010c].

The countercyclical buffer does not take into account the conditions of every single bank, but it looks at the situation of the banking sector as a whole. In that respect, the nature of the buffer is inherently macroprudential. This feature, on the other hand, has been a primary source of complaints for banks, which criticised heavily the lack of any bank-specific criterion in setting the buffer (see Box 6.1).

National authorities – whether central banks, banking supervisors or new macroprudential bodies, depending on national institutional architectures – have to switch the buffer requirement on when there are signals of excessive credit growth. In other words, national authorities are responsible for setting the buffer requirement applicable to credit exposures to counterparties in their jurisdiction. This decision is to be updated on a quarterly basis.

The most striking characteristic of the countercyclical buffer is precisely the identification of good and bad macroprudential conditions, ie, when the buffer has to be respectively turned on and off. This is much easier to say than to do.

BOX 6.1 THE INDUSTRY REACTION TO THE COUNTER-CYCLICAL BUFFER

In July 2010, the proposal for introducing in Basel III a countercyclical capital buffer has been subject to public consultation. This box summarises the feedback of the industry to the consultation. The list is not exhaustive, but limited to either the most relevant or most frequently raised comments.

EFFECTIVENESS OF THE BUFFER: A first criticism refers to the actual counter-cyclical function that the buffer can play. With no automatic rules, authorities can be reluctant to switch the buffer on in good times since they would penalise their banking sector and make it less competitive. Accordingly, they may fail to promptly switch the requirement off when a crisis is approaching because this can transmit dangerous signals, thus determining panic or self-fulfilling prophecies. On the other hand, banks themselves may be reluctant to allow their capital ratios to fall in times of financial stress, because of possible market pressures on less capitalised banks.

RESTRICTIONS ON DISTRIBUTIONS: Constraints on capital distributions can cause a rise in cost of capital and pose legal uncertainties regarding the contractual arrangements between credit institutions and investors. Banks wanting to maintain full flexibility on dividend and bonus policies may also decide to meet the buffer at all times, transforming them *de facto* into new minimum requirements. This criticism also applies to the capital conservation buffer.

INTERACTION WITH PILLAR II: The countercyclical buffer – along with other components of the reform package – may result in a duplication of Pillar II provisions. After the introduction of such measures, the remaining role of Pillar II ICAAP and stress tests is unclear.

SCOPE OF APPLICATION, DISINTERMEDIATION AND ARBITRAGE: The effectiveness of the buffer could be undermined if non-bank financial institutions are not subject to countercyclical buffer requirements. This may determine disintermediation phenomena towards those intermediaries or the shadow banking system at large.

LIMITS OF ONE-SIZE-FITS-ALL MEASURES: Requiring all banks in a jurisdiction to meet the same countercyclical buffer, regardless of their actual contribution to credit growth, tends to penalise banks with more prudent lending practices. A bank-specific buffer would be therefore a preferable option as well as sectoral approaches, targeted to those economic sectors that show signals of overheating.

PRACTICAL DIFFICULTIES IN ALLOCATING EXPOSURES AMONG JURISDICTIONS: The allocation of exposures to multinational companies could be problematic. Particularly for more complex financial products, information exposures on an ultimate risk basis can be difficult to gauge.

The decision should be, first of all, based on the dynamics of the ratio of credit to GDP, a benchmark variable that the Basel Committee selected as the most informative indicator for identifying the build-up of risk. In practice, when the credit-to-GDP ratio is above its long-term trend – by at least two percentage points (BCBS 2010c) – authorities should consider switching the buffer on. As an example, Figure 6.4 depicts the actual credit-to-GDP ratio, its trend and the gap for the UK between 1980 and 2010.

However, the benchmark variable is only the starting point and should not be used mechanically. Authorities are thus requested to apply judgement in adopting their decisions – on the activation as well as the level of the buffer – after using the best information available to identify the rise of systemic risk.

Hence, the decision-making process is partly rule-based and partly judgemental. A "guided" (or "constrained") discretion approach should guarantee, on the one hand, that the decisions are to some extent constrained and predictable – avoiding forbearance and unwarranted surprise effects – and, on the other, that sufficient flexibility is left to the authorities to avoid the adoption of inappro-

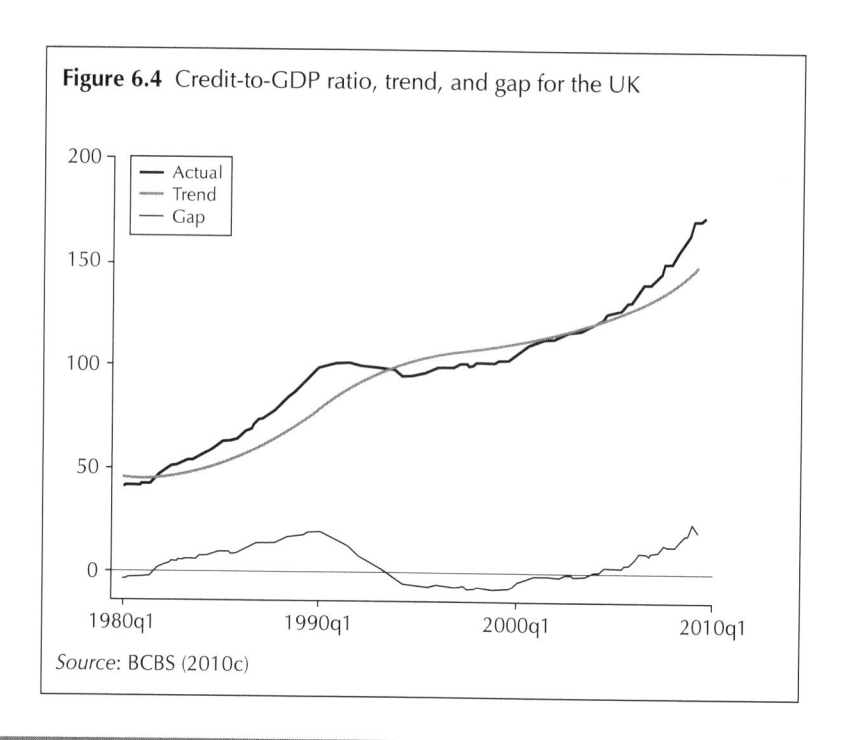

Figure 6.4 Credit-to-GDP ratio, trend, and gap for the UK

Source: BCBS (2010c)

priate countermeasures when the benchmark variable fails to transmit correct signals. The risk that excessive discretion undermines the cross-border level playing field is dealt with through specific obligations on communication and transparency as well as peer reviews on the implementation of the buffer.

From the activation of the buffer onwards, banks have to meet a countercyclical buffer up to 2.5% of the risk-weighted assets, to be met by common-equity Tier 1 or other fully loss-absorbent capital instruments.[4] The countercyclical buffer sits on the top of the capital conservation buffer. Therefore, banks whose capital level falls within the cumulative buffer range are subject to the same constrains on capital distributions described for the capital conservation buffer, unless they are able to get their capital level at the top of the range within 12 months from the announcement of the buffer decision.

As for the release phase, when the credit cycle turns, authorities can switch – promptly or gradually, depending on the severity of the crisis – the buffer requirement off. This decision is purely discretionary, since there is not an internationally agreed benchmark variable to be monitored. However, the Basel Committee has also outlined some principles that should assist national authorities, making the drivers of their pronouncements internationally harmonised.

From the release on, the capital surplus can be used by banks for covering losses and, possibly, to continue granting credit to the real economy.[5] The actual ability of banks to employ the excess capital is also linked to their expectations on the possible reactivation of the requirement. Therefore, when a decision is taken to release the buffer, authorities should also indicate how long they expect the release to last.

Looking at the micro level, the buffer is calculated according to the exposures of each bank vis-à-vis different borrowers. This implies that for internationally active banks the buffer must reflect the geographic composition of the credit portfolio. Banks will therefore be asked to look at the geographic location of their credit exposures and calculate the countercyclical capital buffer as a weighted average of the buffers that are applied in jurisdictions where they have exposures.

Exposures include all private sector exposures that attract a credit-risk capital charge or the risk-weighted-equivalent trading-book capital charges for specific risk, incremental risk charge and securitisation. While the identification of the weights to be attributed to each jurisdiction's buffer is limited to credit risk, the 2.5% add-on is computed on the entire amount of risk-weighted assets, thus including market and operational risks.

By construction, the buffer levels for cross-border banks depend to a large extent on the decision of the host-authorities. This general principle is somehow mitigated by leaving home authorities with the possibility of requiring banks to maintain higher – but not lower – buffers than those decided by host authorities.[6]

As for the capital conservation buffer, the scope of application is consolidated. However, host authorities have the right to demand that the countercyclical capital buffer be held at the individual legal entity level or subconsolidated level within their jurisdiction.

The bottom line is devoted to a more philosophical question. During the entire process that eventually led to the endorsement of the countercyclical buffer, it has been discussed whether this instrument is a Pillar I or a Pillar II mechanism. On the one hand, the decision on the buffer level is not bank-specific and it is fully transparent, pointing to Pillar I; on the other, the use of discretion resembles Pillar II tools. To be honest, neither of the two solutions sounds completely convincing. In fact, the countercyclical buffer is a macroprudential tool that hardly fits into Basel II categories. Instead it should be defined as a Pillar IV mechanism – something beyond microprudential regulation.

6.6 CONCLUSIONS

In the debate that followed the financial crisis, the introduction of countercyclical measures has been advocated as one of the possible solutions to the risk of procyclicality in the financial system. In December 2009, the Basel Committee announced a set of complementary tools. The first building block is represented by devices for mitigating the fluctuations of the capital requirements, particularly if calculated according to point-in-time methodologies. The second component is the adoption of more forward-looking provisions in order to overcome the shortcomings of the incurred-loss accounting. The third and fourth elements are capital reserves – the capital conservation and the countercyclical buffers – to be built up in good times and employed in less favourable conditions, either idiosyncratic or systemic. In July 2010, all the components of the countercyclical toolkit were endorsed by the Group of Governors and Heads of Supervision (GHoS 2010), the oversight body of the Basel Committee.

Thereafter, while some bricks of the countercyclical construction have been carefully designed, intensely discussed and eventually agreed upon, others have been overlooked or completely neglected when shaping the final reform package. In particular, consensus has been reached on the two buffers, whereas the disagreement over the devices for smoothing the minimum capital requirements determined their relegation to unharmonised Pillar II measures. The debate on forward-looking provisions is still open.

The measures eventually introduced by the BCBS are one-size-fits-all kinds of instruments. This clearly reflects the great appetite for macroprudential tools, almost entirely missing before the crisis. While there are still various implementation issues to be addressed, the potential of these tools should not be underestimated. In particular, the development of a countercyclical buffer that aims at becoming a key macroprudential instrument is undoubtedly an important achievement. The undeniable uncertainty over its possible role and real effectiveness is not a robust argument for postponing its introduction.

On the other hand, it is fair to acknowledge that the missing pieces leave the entire countercyclical mosaic incomplete. A major source of concern is the lack of adequate devices for mitigating the cyclicality of the regulatory minimums. Addressing the cyclicality of minimum requirements is the most crucial component of the work, without which the other measures may amount to very little (Enria and Quagliariello 2010). Patricia Jackson (2010) emphasises the unintended consequences of an incomplete countercyclical package with an example:

> for a traditional mortgage book, point-in-time PDs can increase by five from boom to recession, and the increase can be even sharper for riskier buy-to-let mortgage books. So far, the Basel Committee hasn't stabilised minimum requirements before putting on the counter-cyclical buffer, which provides perverse incentives for banks to make their risk estimates more point-in-time to offset the counter-cyclical add-on during good times.

Missing pieces may thus leave room for an unwarranted regulatory failure. Looking ahead, it is thus clear that the definition of the Pillar

II supervisory tools for dealing with the cyclicality of the minimum capital requirement should be a top priority, not only at the G20 level, but also for the EU implementation of the new rules. The proposals put forward by the CEBS and the UK FSA may be not the panacea, but they seem fit for purpose. They may certainly be discussed, criticised and improved, but should not be discarded or left to national discretion. For the same token, it is key that proper rules on provisions be established, trading off the need of accounting standard setters for transparency and the eagerness of prudential regulators for conservatism.

The opinions expressed are those of the author and do not necessarily reflect those of the European Banking Authority (EBA).

1 See Gordy and Howells (2006).
2 Gordy and Howells (2006) mention a multiplier tied to a moving average of the aggregate default rate for commercial bank borrowers. Repullo and Suarez (2008) propose a multiplier based on the deviation of GDP growth from trend. Brunnermeier *et al* (2009) propose to use credit growth. Himino (2009) proposes equity prices.
3 The debate on the possible use of contingent capital for meeting the countercyclical buffer is still ongoing. See De Martino *et al* (2010).
4 Since there are no longer restrictions on distributions, banks can also use the surplus for paying out dividends. Needless to say, should such distribution of capital be considered imprudent, the authorities can prohibit it under Pillar II.
5 Authorities can also impose a buffer in excess of 2.5% or risk-weighted-assets, if this is deemed necessary. This would apply to all domestic banks – thus including domestically incorporated subsidiaries of foreign banks – but the reciprocity provisions would not apply to the amount of the buffer in excess of 2.5%.

REFERENCES

Angelini, P., A. Enria, S. Neri, M. Quagliariello and F. Panetta, 2010, "Procyclicality of capital regulation: is it a problem? How to fix it?", Bank of Italy Occasional Paper No. 74.

Basel Committee on Banking Supervision, 2009, "Strengthening the resilience of the banking sector", consultative document, December.

Basel Committee on Banking Supervision, 2010a, "Instructions for the comprehensive quantitative impact study", February.

Basel Committee on Banking Supervision, 2010b, "Basel III: A global regulatory framework for more resilient banks and banking systems", December.

Basel Committee on Banking Supervision, 2010c, "Guidance for national authorities operating the countercyclical capital buffer", December.

Brunnermeier, M., A. Crockett, C. Goodhart, M. Hellwig, A. Persaud and H. Shin, 2009, "The Fundamental Principles of Financial Regulation", Geneva Report on the World Economy, No.11.

Cannata, F., and M. Quagliariello, 2009, "The Role of Basel II in the Subprime Financial Crisis: Guilty or Not Guilty?" Carefin Working Paper No. 3.

Committee of European Banking Supervisors, 2009, "Position paper on a counter-cyclical capital buffer", July.

Conciarelli, A., and M. Quagliariello, 2009, "A variable response to procyclicality", *Risk*, October.

De Martino, G., M. Libertucci, M. Marangoni and M. Quagliariello, 2010, "Countercyclical Contingent Capital, CCC: Possible Use and Ideal Design," Bank of Italy Occasional Paper No. 71.

Enria, A., and M. Quagliariello, 2010, "Is the countercyclical toolkit incomplete?", *Risk*, December.

European Commission, 2009, "Public Consultation regarding further possible changes to the Capital Requirements Directive, CRD" , July.

Financial Services Authority, 2009, "The Turner Review: A regulatory response to the global banking crisis", March.

Financial Stability Forum, 2009, "Report of the Financial Stability Forum on Addressing Procyclicality in the Financial System".

GHoS, 2010, press releases, July and September

Goodhart, C., and A. Persaud, 2008, "A Proposal for How to Avoid the Next Crash", *Financial Times*, January 30.

Gordy, M., and Howells B., 2006, "Procyclicality in Basel II: Can we treat the disease without killing the patient?", *Journal of Financial Intermediation* 15, pp. 395–417.

Himino R., 2009, "A counter-cyclical Basel II", *Risk* 22(3).

International Accounting Standard Board, 2009, "Request for Information, 'Expected Loss Model', Impairment of Financial Assets: Expected Cash Flow Approach", June.

Jackson, P., 2010, "A False Sense of Security: Lessons for Bank Risk Management from the Crisis", SUERF working paper.

Kashyap, A. K., and C. Stein, 2004, "Cyclical Implications of the Basel II Capital Standard", Federal Reserve Bank of Chicago Economic Perspectives, First Quarter, pp. 18–31.

Repullo, R., and J. Suarez, 2008, The Procyclical Effects of Basel II, CEPR Discussion Paper No. DP6862.

Part III

Complementing Capital Regulation

7

The Regulatory Leverage Ratio

Alan Adkins

Financial Services Authority

7.1 INTRODUCTION

This section examines the notion of leverage in the context of bank regulation and introduces the rest of the chapter.

What is leverage? What is a leverage ratio?

The etymology of the word "leverage" refers to the action of a lever. In finance, the term has been adopted to refer to various techniques by which cashflows, gains or losses are multiplied to provide proportionately larger returns to the owners or investors of a company, instrument or fund.

With regard to banking[1] the term "leverage" is generally used to relate the extent to which the assets (and to some extent the off-balance-sheet commitments) of a bank are funded by equity, as opposed to deposit or other debt liabilities. The maturity transformation function that the banking sector performs means that it is an inherently leveraged industry. Therefore, the question for bank management and regulators is not whether leverage is desirable, but, rather, what is the appropriate degree of leverage, either for an individual bank or for the system as a whole?

The market failure that exists in the banking industry and which justifies regulation (and the employment of regulators) has been well documented (Santos 2000). Bank managers acting as agents of the bank owners have an incentive to benefit from the asymmetric payoff, thus they take excessive risks. One of the easiest ways of doing this is to increase leverage. (There are a variety of possible strategies that were adopted in the run-up to the crisis to exploit the asymmetric payoff, of which increasing leverage was but one (Alessandri and Haldane 2009).

So we should not be surprised that regulators, acting on behalf of society, will have a different view from bankers on the maximum appropriate leverage of a bank or deposit-taking institution. Consequently the role of a leverage ratio, in a regulatory context, is to measure and limit the maximum allowed bank leverage.

Prior to the 2007 financial crisis the established general consensus (albeit with some exceptions) among many members of the Basel Committee on Banking Supervision (BCBS), was that a regulatory leverage ratio was crude, non-risk-based, and, if applied, would undermine the Committee's Basel II efforts to introduce risk-based capital requirements. For example in 2006, John Tiner, then chief executive of the UK's Financial Services Authority (FSA), said that "there have been suggestions that a US-style leverage ratio be incorporated into the Basel II framework, in effect creating a capital floor for banks which is not risk-based, and this idea worries me for that reason" (Tiner 2006).

In general terms, a leverage ratio can be defined as a measure of capital (eg, equity, Tier 1 or total capital), a measure of assets or exposures, and/or a limit imposed on the ratio between the two measures.[2] The measure of capital is often the "numerator" of the expression, and the assets measure the "denominator". Where the leverage ratio is expressed in these terms, the ratio will be a percentage: for example, a 5% ratio is equivalent to a leverage multiple of 20.

Given the simplicity of the concept, it is perhaps surprising that there have been so many leverage ratio definitions in practical use. Some of the more common definitions are discussed in Section 7.3, which is preceded in Section 7.2 by a discussion of why regulators have now revisited the use of a regulatory leverage ratio. Section 7.4 seeks to expand on the G20 regulatory reform process and discusses the key design elements of the Basel Committee's leverage ratio, while Section 7.5 considers the possible undesirable side effects of a regulatory leverage ratio.

7.2 WHY CAN'T WE RELY SOLELY ON THE RISK-BASED RATIOS?

This section examines the reasons why regulators should be cautious before relying solely on risk-based ratios and discusses two broad responses to the issues raised. Depressingly for supervisors, the ability of the risk-weighted capital ratios to distinguish between good and bad banks seems to have been rather limited. As the secretary general of the Basel Committee, Stefan Walter, noted (2010), "A recent study of the Basel Committee's Top-down Capital Calibration Group showed that the leverage ratio did the best job in discriminating between banks that ultimately required official sector support and those that did not!" Walter went on to say that the only risk-based ratio that performed well was tangible common equity to risk-based assets, which indicates that at least part of the problem was on the capital side rather than in the risk-weighted asset calculation. However, given the immense efforts by regulators and firms to invest in risk-based technology, and the comparative simplicity of the leverage ratio calculation, this is still a disturbing finding.

A good example of the potential for the risk-based requirements to underestimate risk dramatically is UBS (See Figure 7.1). This is one example of many, but it serves as a useful illustration. From 1998 to the peak at the end of 2006, UBS's balance sheet size increased by almost 150%. During this time, Tier 1 leverage more than doubled to almost 60 times (using a simple measure of on-balance sheet assets divided by Tier 1 capital), but the risk-weighted assets increased only modestly (by around 12%), and the Tier 1 risk-based ratio itself actually increased to around 12% (within the capital component of this ratio were an increasing number of hybrid capital instruments). Perhaps most strikingly, the average risk-weight (calculated as the ratio of risk-weighted assets to total assets) halved from 32% to 15%. Was the reduced average risk weight reflective of lower risk? At least for some assets, it was reflective of deficient risk capture, especially of highly rated structured products in the trading book, which attracted low risk weights. UBS's published report (UBS 2008) provides a detailed assessment of "what went wrong". The report states that UBS ultimately reported net losses of US$18.7 billion in relation to US residential mortgage sector exposures for the year ending December 31, 2007. It goes on to state that losses on "Super Senior" positions (defined in the report as the highest AAA-rated tranche of a CDO) contributed approximately 50% of UBS's total losses as at December 31, 2007.

To some extent, the shortcomings in the current risk-weighted assets should be in the process of being addressed. In June 2010 (Basel Committee on Banking Supervision 2010a), the Committee finalised significant adjustments to the July 2009 market-risk

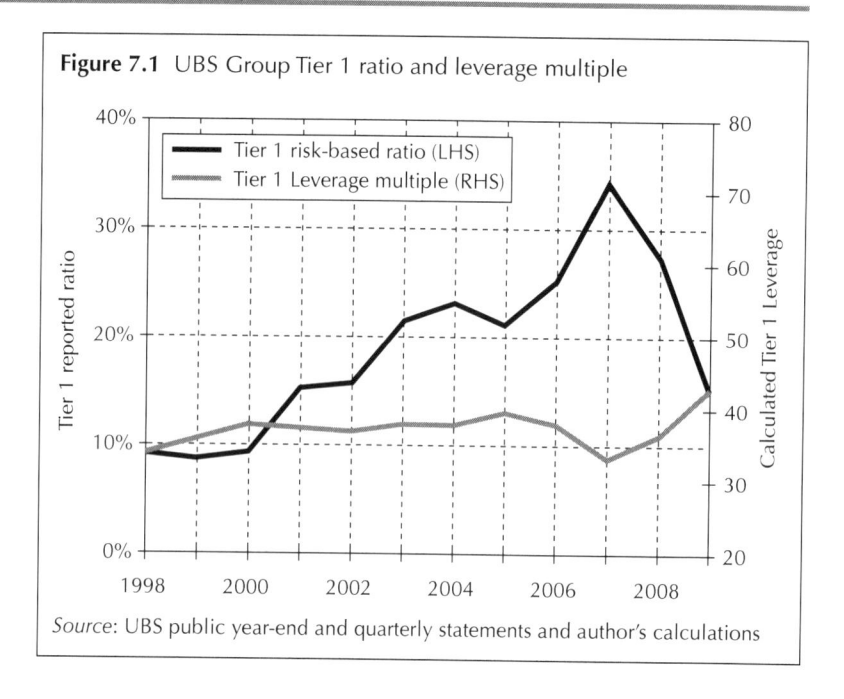

Figure 7.1 UBS Group Tier 1 ratio and leverage multiple

Source: UBS public year-end and quarterly statements and author's calculations

framework amendments. The associated quantitative impact study indicated that market risk capital requirements would increase by an average of 3–4 times the previous amount for the large, internationally active banks, which typically have the most significant trading-book activities. Similarly, there have been amendments to increase risk capture for counterparty credit risk and resecuritisations (in early 2011, the Committee was considering the calibration of the securitisation framework).

But, fundamentally, there are reasons why regulators should be cautious before relying solely on risk-based ratios. The reasons are fairly basic, but are worth rehearsing nonetheless:

1. The risk-based approaches (and the model-based approaches in particular) tend to be conditioned at some level on historical data. So any asset class that has historically performed relatively well will tend to have lower capital requirements, even if it has become more risky over time. This can lead to undercapitalisation and consequent incentives for banks to take excessive exposure to the asset class.

2. The risk-based modelled approaches tend to be based on a (notional) probability distribution function that is conditioned on data that in turn is often derived mainly from "good times". This leaves them vulnerable to the weakness that real-world financial distributions tend to have "fat tails" in times of stress, which are difficult to model accurately.
3. In relation to the above, many of the risk-based approaches tend to be based on a "cut-off" of a particular percentile. Even if it were possible to assess the probability distribution in the tail for a particular set of assets, there is no differentiation in the capital framework between different distributions beyond the cut-off point. So, in practice, banks have an incentive to take additional systemic tail risk without a compensating regulatory capital charge.
4. Especially in the trading book, there is fairly generous recognition of hedging in the capital framework. From a firm perspective, this makes sense: a particular exposure may exceed a firm's risk-tolerance and it can therefore be sensible to reduce it by hedging. Also, from a microprudential perspective, hedging is surely good practice (as long as the resulting counterparty risks are well managed). This reduces an individual firm's probability of loss, or size of loss, and is deserving of regulatory-capital benefits. But hedging in aggregate can make it less clear where the risk in the system actually lies and increases interconnectedness (and therefore risk) within the financial system. In times of stress, hedges can fail to perform, and what was previously regarded as "acceptable" basis risk becomes "significant" instead.
5. With regard to the point about hedging, the capital framework makes a number of implicit and explicit assumptions about the correlation of various asset values, both within Pillar I risks and across them. Outside the trading book (where, as discussed in the point above, relatively liberal hedging assumptions are allowed), the most significant asset-correlation parameters are embedded in the Basel Committee's internal-ratings-based (IRB) formula. For a clear derivation of the formula on which the IRB approach is based see Vasicek (2002). Supervisors decided at the onset of Basel II that the values for this parameter should be specified by regulators rather than left to the

firms. And the Pillar I rules require that the three components of the capital charge (credit risk, market risk and operational risk) be simply added together. A commonly held view is that this additive treatment is conservative, with industry often arguing for diversification benefits under Pillar II. However, research has since indicated that this intuition does not necessarily hold when the individual components interact in a non-linear fashion. In some cases the simple additive approach can underestimate the overall risk (Basel Committee on Banking Supervision 2009a). In summary, there is a risk that the overall diversification benefits implicit in the Basel minimum may be overstated.

6. The behavioural aspects of crises are especially difficult to model, although they often have features in common such as a rush to exit, which leads to undesirable falls in asset values and uncertainty about individual institution insolvency. Thus we should not necessarily be surprised that risk-based approaches perform poorly in times of stress.

7. The risk-based regulatory framework has typically given benefits to the model-based approaches in terms of reduced capital requirements (compared with the standardised approaches). These are typically argued as being justified, since, in order to meet the more onerous model-based requirements, firms need to invest heavily. Regulators, it is argued, should therefore provide incentives to firms to make the necessary investments. The argument depends fundamentally on the premise that a more extensive use of models provides benefits to regulators that justify reduced capital. But these benefits can be overstated, and regulators need to be confident that any capital reductions associated with the regulatory recognition of models are truly warranted.

8. The risk-based approaches (and the model-based risk-based approaches in particular) can suffer from excessive complexity. Under conditions of stress, market participants can lose confidence in the framework and focus instead on simpler, more observable measures. This in turn undermines a fundamental objective of regulatory capital, which is that people must be confident in it as a measure of the soundness of individual institutions.

Taken together, these arguments indicate that a degree of healthy scepticism in the current risk-based framework may be justified, at least from the regulators' perspective.

There are, broadly speaking, two schools of thought in response to these issues associated with the risk-weighted assets. First, there is a fairly extensive body of work, often led by industry that takes the view that indeed there were shortcomings in the regulatory framework (and in firms' own models). However, in principle, it is possible to address these with improvements in the models, or improvements in the way (at least some) firms use the models or (at least some) regulators monitor them. Proponents of this school of thought will typically seek to argue that regulatory and private incentives are aligned in the sense that both regulator and firms want improved risk-management; also that there should be regulatory incentives in place to achieve this aim (this implies that the private benefits of good risk management, which presumably include improved financial performance, are insufficient and need to be augmented with regulatory incentives).

The second school of thought is more cautious, and recognises that public and private objectives are different. From this perspective, it may seem surprising that private-based modelling approaches should serve regulatory objectives at all, given that presumably the purpose of regulation is to address the negative consequences associated with allowing private market participants to pursue their own interests in an unfettered manner.

The Basel Committee remains committed to the risk-based regulatory architecture. The leverage ratio is a backstop to the risk-based measures, rather than a replacement for them, and the 3% calibration announced in September 2010 following the agreement of the Group of Central Bank Governors and Heads of Supervision (GHoS) reflects this objective.

7.3 REGULATORY AND MARKET DEFINITIONS OF LEVERAGE

This section discusses various definitions of leverage, focusing mainly on regulatory practice in a number of jurisdictions, and highlighting some of the key differences between the approaches.

Probably the most common definition of leverage used by the market is the simple balance-sheet definition relating total assets to equity. The main benefit of this definition is its simplicity and ease of calculation from public data. It suffers, however, from a number of deficiencies. First, accounting treatments vary across jurisdictions, notably between International Financial Reporting Standards (IFRS) and US Generally Accepted Accounting Principles (US GAAP) in the treatment of derivative exposures (of which, more later). Second, a bank's equity contains many items that may not be sufficiently robust, at least for regulatory purposes, so analysts and regulators have often stripped out "intangibles" (notably goodwill and deferred tax assets). Section 7.4 provides a fuller discussion of the appropriate leverage ratio capital measure. Finally, these measures exclude off-balance-sheet leverage, such as leverage due to derivatives, and off-balance-sheet commitments.

7.3.1 US, Canadian, Swiss and German leverage ratios

The United States and Canada have relatively long-standing leverage ratios in place, whereas the Swiss and the Germans have introduced it into their respective jurisdictions only after the financial crisis.

The following paragraphs demonstrate that, in a number of major jurisdictions, leverage is regarded as a key component of effective banking supervision. However, there is diversity in the design and implementation of measures in different jurisdictions.

In the US, the Board of Governors of the Federal Reserve System has established leverage limits to apply to certain bank holding companies (BHCs). The limits apply to all BHCs with assets greater than US$500 million and certain other BHCs if other tests are met. The ratio is defined as Tier 1 capital to total average on-balance-sheet assets, and is applied on a consolidated basis. The limits are 3% for "strong" BHCs, and for BHCs that have implemented the Board's risk-based capital measure, and 4% otherwise. The Federal Reserve does not deem a BHC with a leverage ratio below this level to be in compliance with minimum capital adequacy standards.

The leverage ratio is also used in the "Prompt Corrective Action" (PCA) regime, in which progressively greater restrictions are applied to depository institutions as the leverage ratio and risk-based capital ratios deteriorate through various PCA "categories". The categories are established for national banks, state-chartered banks that are members of the Federal Reserve, and other state-chartered banks by the Office of the Comptroller of the Currency, the Federal Reserve

Board and the Federal Deposit Insurance Corporation (collectively, "primary federal supervisors") respectively. Each agency is responsible for applying the required and discretionary restrictions under the regime to the institution, for which it is the primary federal supervisor.

The PCA categories are "well capitalised" (which requires a leverage ratio above 5%), "adequately capitalised" (a leverage ratio above 4%, or above 3% if the bank has been rated "1" in the most recent bank examination), "undercapitalised" (a leverage ratio below 4%, or below 3% if the bank has been rated "1"), "significantly undercapitalised" (a leverage ratio below 3%) and "critically undercapitalised" (a tangible equity-to-total-assets ratio below 2%). Except for the last category, each category also has thresholds for Tier 1 and total risk-based capital ratios.

The US leverage ratio is calculated using average assets to avoid window-dressing or intra-period gaming. Goodwill and certain other assets that have been deducted from Tier 1 are also deducted from the total assets figure. However, the US definition is often criticised for failing to capture off-balance-sheet items such as commitments and guarantees.

The Canadian regulator, the Office of the Superintendent of Financial Institutions Canada (OSFI), has an "assets to capital multiple test" (OSFI 2007) – this is in effect a (inverse) leverage ratio, although domestically it is not typically referred to as such directly. The calculation, which is applied on a consolidated basis, relates the institution's total assets (including certain off-balance-sheet items such as direct credit substitutes, letters of credit, guarantees and repurchase agreements at their notional amount) to the sum of adjusted Tier 1 and Tier 2 capital. On-balance-sheet amounts arising from derivative transactions are included and may be netted provided certain criteria are met. Similar to the US leverage ratio, items that have been deducted from capital are also deducted from total assets. The limit that applies in Canada is a multiple of 20 times (as noted above, equivalent to a 5% ratio of capital to total assets); but this limit can be increased to an amount of up to 23 times at the discretion of the regulator. Alternatively, the regulator may prescribe a lower limit.

The Swiss authorities acted in advance of the Basel Committee's proposals, and in November 2008 introduced their own leverage requirement for their two largest banks by decree, to be implemented progressively to move the country's banks to compliance by January 1, 2013.

The Swiss calculation is a Tier 1 capital-to-adjusted-assets measure, with a limit of 3% at group and 4% at individual institution level, rising to 5% in good times (ie, allowing less leverage in good times). The most interesting feature of the definition is the calculation of total adjusted assets. Apart from an adjustment to the IFRS derivative replacement values designed to make allowance for netting, the main adjustment is to exclude loans to Swiss (non-bank) clients (cash and balances with central banks are also excluded). The rationale for the Swiss lending exemption was to render the leverage ratio "more politically acceptable" by mitigating the domestic economic effect of the measure (FINMA 2009). A flavour of the political debate in Switzerland can be seen from the following excerpt from a speech by a senior official (Zuberbühler 2009):

> At that time our proposals seemed quite radical and were opposed by both banks [UBS and Credit Suisse], to varying degrees but chiefly using the standard argument of disadvantages in global competition. A majority of Swiss politicians were also sceptical. Our colleagues in the Basel Committee responded to our unilateral approach with a mixture of incomprehension and admiration.

In terms of impact, the end-2008 figures published by each institution, and the author's calculations, indicate that the Swiss assets exemption improved the reported leverage ratio by around 30 basis points for each institution.

Officials from from the Swiss Financial and Market Supervisory Authority (FINMA), have subsequently indicated that they expect to adapt their approach for consistency with the Basel standards.

The German authorities have imposed (via the German Act for Strengthening of the Financial Markets and Insurance Supervision) a requirement for institutions to calculate a leverage ratio and report the results to the authorities.[3] This requirement has subsequently been clarified in 2010 with guidance to firms issued by the regulator, the Bundesanstalt für Finanzdienstleistungsaufsicht (BaFin 2010). The focus of the regulation is not only on the absolute level of leverage, but also on reporting changes in leverage greater than 5% to the authorities. The definition is based on accounting own funds, on-balance-sheet items and certain off-balance-sheet commitments such as guarantees. Also of note is the fact that the ratio does not represent a binding restriction, which distinguishes it from the approach in other jurisdictions.

7.3.2 Banks' own disclosure of leverage

In response to increased market interest in bank leverage, banks have started to disclose leverage to the market; typically each bank has a preferred measure that differs slightly from others. For example, Unicredit has disclosed a leverage ratio calculated as "the ratio of total assets net good will and other intangible assets (the numerator) and net equity (including minorities) net goodwill and the other intangible assets (the denominator)" (UniCredit 2010). Meanwhile, Barclays (2009) disclosed their leverage ratio as "the multiple of adjusted total tangible assets over total qualifying Tier 1 capital". Deutsche Bank reported figures using a US GAAP-based definition of total assets and accounting equity adjusted for fair-value gains and losses on own debt (Deutsche Bank 2010a). While these disclosures are undoubtedly to be welcomed, the diversity of definition makes like-for-like comparison between banks difficult. Furthermore, banks' current definitions often omit off-balance-sheet commitments, which risks giving a partial view of the leverage of the institution.

We have seen that international regulatory and market practice is relatively diverse, not just with respect to the definition of leverage, but, within the regulatory community, also with respect to the role of a leverage ratio within prudential supervision. In the next section, we shall examine the Basel Committee's proposals for an internationally agreed standard.

7.4 THE G20 REFORMS AND THE BASEL COMMITTEE'S PROPOSALS

This section discusses the Basel Committee's development of an internationally agreed definition for the leverage ratio, and highlights the major areas of policy debate.

During the Basel reform process, the G20 took a considerable and detailed interest in proceedings, and made a number of supportive remarks about the importance of supplementing the risk-based capital requirements with a leverage ratio. It is worth charting the progress of the leverage ratio through the G20 summits.

- ❏ The London Summit declaration in April 2009 agreed that "risk-based capital requirements should be supplemented with a simple, transparent, non-risk-based measure which is internationally comparable, properly takes into account off-balance-sheet exposures, and can help contain the build-up of leverage in the banking system".
- ❏ Following further statements from the Pittsburgh and Toronto summits in September 2009 and June 2010 respectively, the Seoul declaration in November 2010 endorsed "the landmark agreement reached by the BCBS on the new bank capital and liquidity framework, which ... includes an internationally harmonized leverage ratio to serve as a backstop to the risk-based capital measures".

The Group of Governors and Heads of Supervision (the oversight body of the Basel Committee on Banking Supervision) reached agreement in July 2010 (Basel Committee on Banking Supervision 2010b) on the design of the leverage ratio, following a public consultation in December 2009 (Basel Committee on Banking Supervision 2009b).

The December 2009 Basel consultation clearly set out the rationale for a leverage ratio as being to "help contain the build-up of excessive leverage in the banking system, introduce additional safeguards against attempts to game the risk based requirements, and help address model risk". The document stated that the twofold objective of the leverage ratio was to

> put a floor under the build-up of leverage in the banking sector, thus helping to mitigate the risk of the destabilising deleverage processes which can damage the financial system and the economy; and introduce additional safeguards against model risk and measurement error by supplementing the risk based measure with a simple, transparent, and independent measure of risk that is based on gross exposures

The document went on to state that the leverage ratio would be adjusted across jurisdictions for accounting differences and that there would be appropriate testing of its interaction with the risk-based measure.

The main elements of design are set out in Paragraphs 202–38 in the December 2009 consultation and the Basel Committee's subsequent decisions following consultation are set out in the Annex to the July 2010 press release. The industry gave fairly extensive feedback on the leverage ratio in its responses to the consultation process. As ever, the consultation process elicited a range of responses from the political to the technical. The main arguments put forward can be separated into high-level comments about the idea of a leverage ratio, or the desirability or practicability of implementing one, plus more technical detail.

The Committee's July 2010 statement recapped the objective of the leverage ratio as providing a simple, transparent, non-risk-based measure that is calibrated to act as a credible supplementary measure to the risk-based requirements. As a non-risk-based measure, the leverage ratio definition disallowed certain elements incorporated in the risk-based measure, such as credit-risk mitigation and collateral.

The main policy issues addressed during the work on the leverage ratio design, which were set out in the December Consultation Paper (Paragraph 238), are discussed below; at the end of each subsection the final Basel Committee decision on the relevant issue is recalled.

7.4.1 Measure of capital

As noted above, a leverage ratio requires a measure of capital or equity as a base on which to calculate leverage. The starting point for those who favour simplicity might be to use the bank's common equity. However, this suffers from the obvious drawback that by including items of dubious loss absorbency (at least in stressed times) in the numerator, this would allow banks to leverage non-absorbent capital items such as goodwill and deferred tax assets. So some modification is needed. It would seem possible to use "tangible common equity" (equity but with intangible items and preference shares removed), but rather than create a separate definition of capital for the leverage ratio numerator, the Committee decided instead to align the numerator with the new regulatory capital framework, with a focus on Tier 1.

Having selected a regulatory definition of capital, which should ensure non-loss-bearing items have been deducted, the next policy question is: which quality of capital should be used. The alternatives to Tier 1 are common equity (using a regulatory definition with deductions applied) or total capital. A desire to constrain leverage as tightly as possible and avoid gearing within the numerator might lead naturally to a conclusion that common equity (less regulatory deductions) would be the best solution. However, one of the policy concerns about the leverage ratio (which was expressed forcibly in the feedback) is the worry that it could force deleveraging in bad times, leading to procyclical side effects. Using a wider definition of capital could mitigate this concern, the argument goes, by allowing banks to issue a lower quality of capital to meet the requirement in bad times. Provided the bank has sufficient common equity during bad times to maintain credibility and meet the minimum risk-based requirement, it should be easier (less expensive) to issue non-core Tier 1.

The Committee has agreed that the capital measure should be based on the new definition of Tier 1 capital, although the Committee also agreed to track the impact of total capital and common equity.

7.4.2 Traditional off-balance-sheet items

One of the major charges levelled at (some) pre-existing leverage ratio definitions is that, by failing to include off-balance-sheet items, they are vulnerable to elementary arbitrage. Indeed, the G20 London statement specifically referred to the need to "take into account" off-balance-sheet items in the leverage ratio design.

There are a variety of exposures that can be referred to as "traditional" off-balance-sheet items. These include commitments, unconditionally cancellable commitments, direct credit substitutes, acceptances, standby letters of credit, trade letters of credit, failed transactions and unsettled securities.

Having decided that this category of items needs to be included, the major policy question is how to do it. There are two main options: either include them all at 100% (on the basis that the leverage ratio is not risk-based and therefore should not seek to incorporate probability of draw or credit-conversion factors), or find some system of converting the full commitment amount to a (lower) figure for inclusion in the leverage ratio. This in turn could take the form of standardised factors (such as the standardised CCFs) or firms' own estimates. However, the obvious problem with using firms' own estimates is that these are in large part based on modelled assumptions; and a key part of the Committee's intention in introducing a leverage ratio is to guard against model risk.

With regard to trade finance, firms argued that these types of exposures did not really constitute leverage, were collateralised, and that inclusion at 100% might affect the price and/or supply of trade finance arrangements, with consequences for international trade.

Regulators, however, were concerned about too many exceptions, and the consequence for regulatory arbitrage, especially in the non-risk-based, simple, backstop measure designed to shore up the risk-based requirements.

The December 2009 Basel consultation proposed inclusion of all OBS items at 100%; subsequent industry feedback concentrated on unconditionally cancellable commitments, and on trade-related items. Subsequently, the Committee responded to the consultation by allowing a 10% conversion factor for the unconditionally cancellable items.

The Committee agreed to include off-balance-sheet items for the purposes of the leverage ratio by applying a uniform 100% credit conversion factor (CCF). For any commitments that are unconditionally cancellable at any time by the bank without prior notice, banks are to apply a CCF of 10%, although this figure is subject to further Committee review.

7.4.3 Treatment of liquid assets

One of the more controversial issues associated with the Basel discussions on leverage ratio design was the treatment of liquid assets.

During the consultation process, a number of industry participants argued that there was a conflict between the liquidity rules, specifically the Liquidity Coverage Ratio, which requires banks to hold high-quality liquid assets, often attracting low risk-based requirements (see Chapter 8), and the leverage ratio (which could discourage holdings of those assets).

On the other side of the argument, regulators felt these concerns could be overstated. They also worried about the "slippery slope" problem: it is one thing to exempt central bank cash, but what about riskier government bonds, covered bonds or securitisations? Weren't these potentially exactly the kinds of assets that have very low risk-based capital requirements and contributed significantly to balance-sheet leverage during the good times?

Ultimately, the Committee agreed to include all assets within the leverage ratio.

7.4.4 Treatment of derivatives and repos

There are two key questions with respect to derivative activity: first, the calculation of exposure value and, second, whether or not to allow netting.

(a) Exposure value

In general, derivatives contribute to leverage with two types of exposure: an economic exposure to the underlying instrument or reference, and, depending on the current position of the derivative, a counterparty credit-risk exposure to the counterparty arising from the positive value of the contract. Either, or both, of these exposures can be regarded as sources of leverage.

It is worth considering the options for seeking to include the economic leverage of derivative transactions. It could be tempting to take a "non-risk-based" approach to calculating derivative leverage, and seek to include all derivative transactions at notional. However, a quick inspection of bank balance sheets illustrates why this is not feasible. The sheer notional size and volume of the contracts is in many cases very much larger than the banks' balance sheets. Figure 7.2 illustrates the effect for Barclays: at the end of 2009, the derivative exposures outstanding were £39 trillion, of which £33 trillion was accounted for by interest-rate derivatives. In relative terms, the total notional contract sizes were 28 times the IFRS balance sheet. In comparison, the derivative assets (ie, the positive fair-value amounts recorded under IFRS) of £416 billion were approximately 1% of the total derivative notional. Whether or not it would be desirable to limit derivative total notional values, the practical effect of simplistic inclusion would be to achieve a leverage ratio that acted almost entirely on interest rate derivatives, and effectively ignored all other types of exposure.

There are possible theoretical frameworks that seek to provide a robust framework for measuring derivative leverage (Breuer 2000). However, the main drawback of these approaches is that they can be hard to reconcile with the idea of a simple, non-risk-based backstop. On the other hand, most people would agree that the economic leverage of derivatives can be significant; and it would seem odd to set it aside in formulating a regulatory leverage ratio.

Therefore a more simplistic treatment is needed. The Committee has opted for the "Current Exposure Method" (CEM). This is an

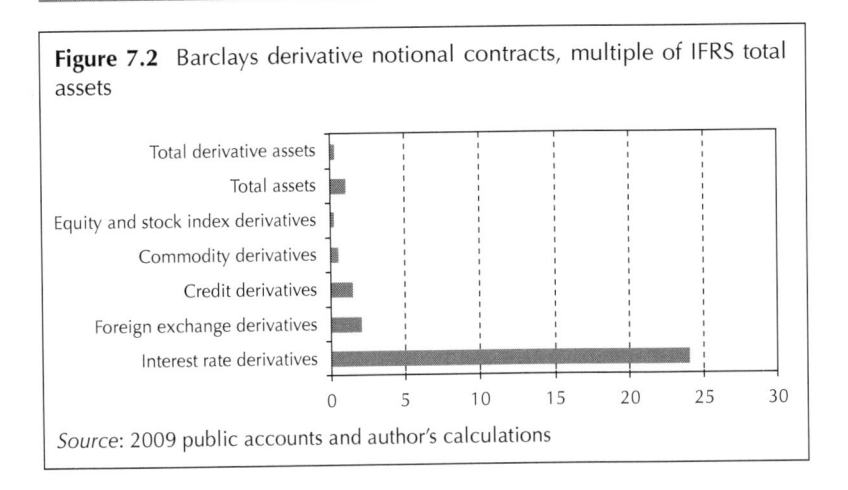

Figure 7.2 Barclays derivative notional contracts, multiple of IFRS total assets

Total derivative assets	
Total assets	
Equity and stock index derivatives	
Commodity derivatives	
Credit derivatives	
Foreign exchange derivatives	
Interest rate derivatives	

Source: 2009 public accounts and author's calculations

existing counterparty-credit-risk exposure method set out in Annex 4 of the current Basel framework. Under the Current Exposure Method, banks calculate the current replacement cost of a derivative position by marking contracts to market, and then adding a factor (the "add-on") to reflect the potential future exposure. The add-on factors are themselves based on a percentage of the notional value, with the percentages based on asset class and (residual) maturity of the notional principle. For example, interest rates between one and five years are weighted at 0.5% of notional.

There was some support during the consultation process from those banks that have been more enthusiastic promoters of models-based approaches that the Internal Models Method (IMM) might be suitable for inclusion within the leverage ratio total exposures calculation. This would be an alternative to the CEM and avoid requiring banks to perform parallel calculations. However, it is difficult to reconcile the IMM with a simple, non-risk-based "backstop" measure.

The question of netting was thrown into sharp relief by the very large differences between the size of banks' US GAAP and IFRS balance sheets. A few banks report figures for both IFRS and US GAAP, and the difference in size of the derivative assets can be very considerable.

For example, as of the June 30, 2010, interim report (Deutsche Bank, 2010a interim report) Deutsche Bank reported leverage using an IFRS balance sheet of 45 times equity compared with just 23 times equity under US GAAP pro forma. This indicates that the accounting treatment makes a difference of a factor of approximately two times the measured leverage. Three adjustments are made to the €1,926 billion IFRS balance sheet to transform it to the US GAAP value – adjustments to derivatives, pending settlements and repos in accordance with US GAAP. The reductions in balance-sheet size for each adjustment are €735 billion, €135 billion, and €9 billion respectively. Taken together, the effect of applying US GAAP netting reduced the balance sheet by 46% to €1,043 billion. A similar picture may be observed for other large banks with significant derivative positions.

The underlying distinction in the accounting standards that gives rise to this significant difference can initially appear quite slight, since both allow netting provided there is legal ability to settle on a net basis, but IFRS additionally requires the intention to settle net, which is not generally present with derivative contracts.

From a policy perspective, the main argument against recognising netting within a non-risk-based leverage ratio is that it is a key part of the risk-based requirements; having a (small) net exposure is not the same as having no exposure at all; and there is still a residual risk and as such the non-risk-based supplementary measure should not incorporate risk-based netting. On the other hand, a restrictive treatment of netting would give a considerable focus on derivative assets within the leverage ratio denominator (in the example above, 42% of Deutsche Bank's total assets under IFRS were derivative assets). It could be difficult to calibrate such a leverage ratio in a way that applied as a backstop across a wide category of banks, including those with low levels of derivative activity.

The Committee agreed to apply Basel II netting (based on legally enforceable netting agreements but not requiring intent to settle on a net basis) for derivative and repo-transactions, plus a simple measure of potential future exposure based on the standardised factors of the current exposure method.

7.5 DISCUSSION ON UNDESIRABLE SIDE EFFECTS AND PROCYCLICALITY

This section discusses possible undesirable side effects of a binding regulatory leverage ratio.

The major undesirable side effect of a leverage ratio put forward is generally that it produces incentives for firms to take on additional risk. This argument can be overstated. The leverage ratio has not been proposed as a standalone regulatory requirement: instead, it has been proposed as a supplement to the risk-based measures. So the incentives problem is more limited, and the focus should be on circumstances under which the leverage ratio and not the risk-based ratio is the binding constraint. As a general maxim, whenever a firm is under these circumstances it is probably a good idea for both the firm and supervisor to ask whether there is the possibility of risk underestimation.

It has also been argued that a binding leverage ratio accompanied with a one-size-fits-all calibration could unduly affect banks with safe but low-risk-weight business – for example, smaller mortgage banks. The evidence appears to indicate that, overall, larger banks are more affected by the Basel leverage ratio than smaller ones. Both the Basel (Basel Committee on Banking Supervision 2010c) and the CEBS (Committee of European Banking Supervisors 2010) Quantitative Impact Study (QIS) results indicated that (on average) leverage was significantly higher for larger (Group 1) banks than smaller (Group 2) ones (2.8% for the Group 1 banks versus 3.8% for the Group 2 banks in the Basel study, and 2.5% for the Group 1 banks versus 3.5% for the Group 2 banks in the CEBS study). Recall that a higher-leverage ratio in percentage terms indicates less leverage; a leverage ratio of 2.5% indicates a leverage multiple of 40 times. The CEBS study notes that this indicated that "large banks are considerably more leveraged than smaller banks". It is certainly true that there is a range of bank leverage across different jurisdictions and business models, and any consistently applied leverage ratio will likely affect some more than others. But nevertheless it seems inherent to the Committee's purpose as an international standard setter that the same minimum standard be applied to all.

Firms have argued that a leverage ratio is volatile, and that such volatility is difficult to manage. This could be an issue where derivatives are included without netting. For Deutsche Bank, for example, the quarterly standard deviation of 'Positive market values from derivative instruments' – derivative assets – over the eight quarters to Q3, 2010, was 19.1%. This compares with 13.1% standard deviation for total balance-sheet assets and just 9.1% for non-derivative assets (Deutsche Bank 2010b). As discussed earlier, netting is recognised in the Committee's final leverage measure, so perhaps these concerns have been mitigated if not eliminated.

It has also been argued that a binding leverage ratio could cause damaging deleveraging (either of individual firms or of the system). Although in concept the leverage ratio should seek to constrain leverage in good times (when asset growth is often strong and risk can be underestimated), leverage can also increase during bad times when losses erode the capital base. To the extent that the leverage ratio is binding for a particular institution, this could cause deleveraging. Set against this, it should be noted that any binding minimum capital standard – including the risk-based requirement – will cause firms either to raise capital or reduce the capital requirement as the requirement starts to bite. Indeed, it is fundamental to prudential supervision that there be a minimum requirement. A bank that has the leverage ratio as the binding constraint rather than the risk-based requirement might well be under market pressure to deleverage irrespective of the regulatory requirements. Where the leverage ratio is the binding requirement, the firm has the choice of raising capital or deleveraging; where the risk-based ratio is binding, the choice is between raising capital and a range of techniques to reduce the risk-weighted assets – including deleveraging but also potentially purchasing credit-risk mitigation, taking collateral, etc. But it is not necessarily wise to operate on the assumption that future purchase of credit-risk mitigation or taking of collateral will be both possible and economically feasible, at least not on a system-wide basis. So it is not clear that a binding leverage ratio will cause deleveraging effects any more than the risk-based minimum requirements. And allowing Tier 1 as the capital measure rather than common equity could allow banks to improve their leverage ratio using Tier 1 rather than having to issue common equity.[4]

7.6 CONCLUSION

The debate over the desirability of a leverage ratio and its possible negative consequences seems set to continue for the foreseeable future. The Committee has clearly decided – with GHoS and G20 support – to migrate to a binding measure by 2018. This follows a four-year parallel run period, disclosure from 2015, and the possibility of final adjustments in 2017.

Confidence in risk-based capital requirements has been badly shaken; the task of rebuilding it (in which the leverage ratio plays an important role) is a difficult one.

The author is writing in a personal capacity and the views expressed do not necessarily represent either those of the Financial Services Authority or of the Basel Committee on Banking Supervision.

1. The term "banking" is used here to describe all types of institution that take deposits and make loans.
2. This type of construction can be referred to as a "stock-based" leverage ratio, to distinguish it from a "flow-based" ratio, which relates, for example, revenue or profit to a measure of capital.
3. The requirement applies domestically to all credit institutions except Bürgschaftsbanken.
4. There is a limit, however, to the extent to which lower-quality forms of capital will maintain credibility with the market during stressed times.

REFERENCES

Alessandri, P., and A. Haldane, 2009, "Banking on the State", *The Future of Finance: The LSE Report*, (London: LSE).

BaFin, 2010, "Circulation Letter 2010/03, BA".

Barclays Bank, 2009, "Balance Sheet commentary", in Annual Report, available at http://www.barclaysannualreport.com/ar2009/index.asp?pageid=68.

Basel Committee on Banking Supervision, 2009a, "Findings on the interaction of market and credit risk", BCBS Working Papers No. 16, May.

Basel Committee on Banking Supervision, 2009b, "Consultative proposals to strengthen the resilience of the banking sector announced by the Basel Committee", December, available at http://www.bis.org/press/p091217.htm.

Basel Committee on Banking Supervision, 2010a, "Adjustments to the Basel II market risk framework announced by the Basel Committee", June, available at http://www.bis.org/press/p100618.htm.

Basel Committee on Banking Supervision, 2010b, "The Group of Governors and Heads of Supervision reach broad agreement on Basel Committee capital and liquidity reform package", July, available at http://www.bis.org/press/p100726.htm.

Basel Committee on Banking Supervision, 2010c, "Results of the comprehensive quantitative impact study", December, available at http://www.bis.org/publ/bcbs186.pdf.

Breuer, Peter, 2000, "Measuring Off-Balance Sheet Leverage", WP00/002, IMF Working Paper Series.

Committee of European Banking Supervisors, 2010, "Results of the comprehensive quantitative impact study", December, available at http://www.c-ebs.org/cebs/media/Publications/Other%20Publications/QIS/EU-QIS-report-2.pdf.

Deutsche Bank, 2010a interim report, Q2, available at http://annualreport.deutsche-bank.com/2010/q2/notes/otherinformation/targetdefinitions.html.

Deutsche Bank, 2010b, "Financial Data Supplement", October, available at http://www.db.com/ir/en/download/FDS_3Q2010.pdf.

FINMA, 2009, "Financial market crisis and financial market supervision", September, p. 40, available at http://www.finma.ch/e/aktuell/Documents/Finanzmarktkrise-und-Finanzmarktaufsicht_e.pdf.

OSFI, 2007, "The Assets to Capital Multiple", *Capital Adequacy Requirement (CAR) No A-1*.

Santos, J., 2000, "Bank Capital Regulation in Contemporary Banking Theory; a Review of the Literature", BIS Working Papers No. 90, available at http://www.bis.org/publ/work90.pdf.

Tiner, John, 2006, "UK's Leading Role in the Adoption of International Initiatives", speech to the BBA's 10th Annual Supervision Conference, available at http://www.fsa.gov.uk/pages/Library/Communication/Speeches/2006/1011_jt.shtml.

UBS, 2008, "Shareholder Report on UBS's Write-Downs", April, available at http://www.ubs.com/1/ShowMedia/investors/releases?contentId=140331&name=080418ShareholderReport.pdf.

UniCredit, 2010, "The UniCredit Group in 2009", press release, available at http://www.unicreditgroup.eu/en/pressreleases/PressRelease1425.htm.

Vasicek, Oldrich, 2002, "The Distribution of Loan Portfolio Value" *Risk Magazine*, December 2002.

Walter, Stefan, 2010, "Basel III and Financial Stability", speech to the 5th Biennial Conference on Risk Management and Supervision.

Zuberbühler, D., 2009, "The Swiss regime for large banks: setting the pace for international capital regulation", speech, March.

8

The New Framework for Liquidity Risk

Gianluca Trevisan
Bank of Italy

8.1 INTRODUCTION

Liquidity risk management has become a fast-evolving discipline. The reassessment of management practices and techniques to identify, measure and monitor this risk is strictly intertwined with the regulatory reform introduced by the Basel Committee under the political input of G20 leaders and the high-level commitment of the Financial Stability Board (FSB). This chapter will discuss the new regulations as they relate to liquidity risk.

Liquidity risk can be defined as "the ability to fund increases in assets and meet obligations as they come due, without incurring unacceptable losses" (BCBS 2008a). It generally manifests itself in the form of a failure to meet payment obligations, which may be caused by an inability to raise the necessary funds (funding liquidity risk) or the existence of limitations on the liquidation of assets (market liquidity risk). Liquidity risk also includes the risk of having to meet payment obligations at non-market costs, ie, incurring high funding costs or (and sometimes at the same time as) capital losses where assets have to be liquidated.

One of the lessons learnt from the 2007–08 financial crisis is that minimum capital requirements are a necessary but not sufficient condition for the stability of the financial system. Despite high capital levels, many financial institutions have experienced serious difficulties – when not shifted into solvency troubles – because they struggled to maintain adequate liquidity too. The Northern Rock default, for example, has quickly become a case study.[1]

The new regulations that have ensued represent a reasonable balance between incentivising prudent liquidity risk management and containing the potential restrictive impact on the financial system and the economy as a whole. However, the fact cannot be ignored that the new framework may be further adjusted according to the results of the observation phase that international regulators have imposed before the final rules can enter into force. This chapter is based on the draft of the initiatives led by the Basel Committee as of December 2010.

The chapter is organised as follows. After an overview of the regulatory response to the financial crisis contained in Section 8.2, Sections 8.3 and 8.4 analyse the new regulation of liquidity risk issued by the Basel Committee. Section 8.5 describes the principal issues that are still open. Finally, Section 8.6 contains a preliminary assessment of the new regulatory framework. Section 8.7 contains our concluding remarks.

8.2 THE REGULATORY RESPONSE TO THE FINANCIAL CRISIS: AN OVERVIEW

Liquidity risk played a key role in the dynamics of the financial crisis, especially in its first phase. As discussed in Chapter 1, the announcements made by an increasing number of financial institutions of larger-than-expected losses due to subprime mortgages and subsequent profit cuts led to a liquidity shortage, which quickly spread to interbank markets. As a consequence, since the first analyses were carried out, the attention of policymakers has been very much focused on better understanding of banks' practices with regard to liquidity risk management, and on the shortcomings of current regulation. The need for a harmonised framework for measuring and managing liquidity risk, which had previously been recognised but largely neglected until then, became a top priority on the international agenda.

Early in 2008, the Basel Committee carried out a first survey of pre-crisis liquidity regulations in the major countries (BCBS 2008b). This survey found several common features, notably in the broad regulatory objectives (eg, in terms of proportionality, liquidity policies, stress tests and contingency funding plans), but also highlighted several differences in implementation at a national level, which gave rise to different supervisory approaches to liquidity risk, intended as the methodology used by the supervisor to control the liquidity risk of the banking system.

These approaches can be grouped into three main categories: quantitative, qualitative and mixed. Quantitative approaches hinge on indicators and tolerance ranges with respect to specific maturities;[2] qualitative methods focus on risk management and internal controls of the bank, providing criteria for effective liquidity controls; and mixed approaches combine the former in an attempt to obviate their weaknesses. Although most approaches fall into the mixed-approaches category, with varying weights assigned to quantitative vis-à-vis qualitative aspects, in the late 2000s international regulations have particularly emphasised the importance of stronger internal controls rather than overly prescriptive quantitative requirements. It was indeed assumed that an approach based on a combination of liquidity risk parameters (quantitative measures) and internal management systems (qualitative measures) would be the best suited to reflect the ongoing evolution of financial markets.

The crisis clearly highlighted the need for a stronger supervisory approach. At national level, new laws and regulations were enacted and new supervisory practices established.[3] As market tensions rose to a global scale, regulators set out to strengthen international coordination and cooperation, in order to establish a common operational approach to crisis response.

In April 2008 the Financial Stability Forum (FSF)[4] issued recommendations aimed at creating a financial system with more capital, less debt and stronger rules (see also Chapter 2) (FSF 2008). In September 2008 the Basel Committee, "in recognition of the need for banks to improve their liquidity risk management and control their liquidity risk exposure", issued guidelines for sound liquidity risk management and supervision which are analysed in Section 3. In Europe the Committee of European Banking Supervisors (CEBS)[5] published a series of recommendations for liquidity risk management and, within the European Central Bank (ECB); the Banking Supervision Committee performed a survey of the banking industry's stress-testing techniques and contingency plans used by banks (European Central Bank 2008).

Following the bankruptcy of Lehman Brothers in 2008, international cooperation intensified further, as regulators recognised the need for a coherent and internationally consistent regulatory framework on liquidity. In December 2009, the Basel Committee proposed regulations introducing specific quantitative rules for liquidity (the so-called Consultative Document). Meanwhile CEBS issued guidelines on the composition of the mandatory liquidity buffer to be held by banks. In February 2010, the European Commission began consultations on a proposed amendment to the Capital Requirements Directive (CRD4) that would endorse, among other things, the new Basel liquidity framework. In December 2010 the Basel Committee finalised the new liquidity framework (see Table 8.1).

8.3 THE PRINCIPLES FOR SOUND LIQUIDITY RISK MANAGEMENT AND SUPERVISION

The "Principles for Sound Liquidity Risk Management and Supervision" (BCBS 2008a), originally issued in 2000 and then reviewed in 2008, have the ultimate objective of strengthening liquidity risk management for both banks and supervisors. Particular attention is given to the principle of proportionality: although the paper focuses on medium and large complex banks, the practices deemed to be sound can be widely applied to all types of banks. Each measure of sound practice should be proportional to the size and complexity of each bank and to the role it plays in the financial sector of the jurisdictions in which it operates. Furthermore the

Table 8.1 Regulatory initiatives on liquidity risk

Feb 2008	Basel Committee	Liquidity Risk: Management and Supervisory Challenges
Sep 2008	Basel Committee	Principles for Sound Liquidity Risk Management and Supervision
Dec 2009	Basel Committee	International framework for liquidity risk measurement, standards and monitoring – Consultative document
Jun 2008	CEBS	Second part of CEBS' Technical Advice to the European Commission on Liquidity Risk Management
Dec 2009	CEBS	CEBS Guidelines on Liquidity Buffers
Feb 2010	European Commission	Consultation regarding further possible changes to the Capital Requirements Directive (CRD)
Dec 2010	Basel Committee	Basel III: International framework for liquidity risk measurement, standards and monitoring

principles emphasise the importance of establishing a robust liquidity risk management framework that is well integrated into the bank-wide risk management process.[6] Among other things, the principles aim to raise standards in the following areas: governance of liquidity risk; management of liquidity risk, including stress testing and the definition of a contingency funding plan (CFP); transparency and public disclosure; and the role of supervisors.

Governance of liquidity risk. A key operational parameter of the Basel Committee paper is "liquidity risk tolerance" – this is to be determined by the higher echelons of bank management, alongside the broader liquidity management strategy. The paper also calls for explicit transfer pricing rules, so as to ensure that the incentives of individual risk-taking units internalise the impact of such risk-taking on the risk exposure of the bank as a whole. Effective liquidity risk governance, in the Committee's view, rests crucially on the steady exchange of information between treasury units, risk-control units and business lines. Finally, the paper advocates routine audits of the liquidity risk management system by an independent internal auditing.

Management of liquidity risk. Sound liquidity risk management must be run on a consolidated basis, covering all on- and off-balance-sheet items and encompassing all meaningful currency positions (separately and as a whole). Intraday liquidity risk stemming from payment and settlement systems is singled out for specific monitoring. No metric or reference model was explicitly recommended. However, whatever the measurement system, banks must adopt dynamic risk measures, for instance by estimating expected cashflows based on their balance sheet and identifying offsetting items based on their ability to tap different funding sources.

This analysis must be complemented by stress tests covering a variety of bank-specific and market-wide scenarios, with a view to developing effective contingency funding plans. Results of stress tests must also inform strategic planning, cashflow monitoring and concentration limit setting (on both liquid assets and short-term liabilities matching them). The Basel paper also lists some examples of circumstances where stress tests are recommended.[7]

Stress tests must be an input into a strong contingency funding plan. The decision-making process underpinning the CFP must include a time-bound list of tasks and actions, with triggers and people responsible for such actions clearly identified.

Transparency and public disclosure. Disclosure is key to offering interested parties a truthful picture of banks' liquidity risk management system: it increases transparency, reduces uncertainty and ultimately strengthens market discipline.

Information on the organisational aspects and the methodology of liquidity risk management within banks is essential: the respective roles and responsibilities of board members and senior management should be described, as well as those of relevant business units. Banks' funding structure and limits on both notional and risk-adjusted liquidity positions should also be discussed. Last but not least, liquidity positions should be publicly disclosed on a regular basis.

The role of supervisors. Basel guidelines also raise the bar for supervisors, urging them to request prompt removal of weaknesses in banks' liquidity risk management systems and to maintain constant communication with other domestic or foreign authorities (above all under systemic stress). In particular, supervisors should routinely review the liquidity risk management of banks and assess their resilience under stress, taking into account the systemic relevance of different institutions. Supervisors must be equipped with a suite of powers and tools commensurate with the significance of identified deficiencies,[8] and use such powers and tools to seek remedial action from banks.

Following the publication of the "Principles", the Basel Committee launched an assessment of their implementation, at the level of both authorities and firms.

8.4 THE NEW QUANTITATIVE LIQUIDITY STANDARDS

The Basel Committee (BCBS 2010) set out two complementary quantitative standards on liquidity risk, with different time horizons and objectives: the liquidity coverage ratio (LCR) and the net stable funding ratio (NSFR); the new framework also proposes additional monitoring tools. The rules will be applied to all internationally active banks on a consolidated basis but they may also be used to monitor the liquidity position of individual legal entities, foreign branches and subsidiaries, in keeping with Principle 6 (of 17) of the "Principles" (BCBS 2008a): "A bank should actively manage liquidity risk exposures and funding needs within and across legal entities, business lines and currencies, taking into account legal, regulatory and operational limitations to the transferability of liquidity".[9]

8.4.1 The liquidity coverage ratio

The LCR measures the ability of a banking group to survive under a significant stress scenario in the short run, "by which time it is assumed that appropriate corrective actions can be taken by management and/or supervisors, and/or the bank can be resolved in an orderly way" (BCBS 2010). It is aimed at covering possible short-term mismatches, through the comparison of expected cumulative net cash outflows for a 30-calendar-day time horizon, calculated taking into account a predetermined scenario, with high-quality unencumbered liquid assets at the bank's disposal. Table 8.2 illustrates the LCR, ie, the ratio of the "stock of high-quality liquid assets" to the "total net cash outflows over the next 30 calendar days", which must be no lower than 100%. The ratio will come into full force on January 1, 2015.

8.4.1.1 Stock of high-quality liquid assets

The definition of the liquidity buffer was undoubtedly one of the most debated items on the Committee agenda. The final definition of high-quality liquid assets, which represents a reasonable compromise between the narrow and the broad definitions proposed in the Consultative Document, is driven by the criteria of an asset's marketability in the financial markets under a stress situation and of its ideal eligibility at central banks.[10] On the one hand, all these assets should be ideally central-bank-eligible for intraday liquidity needs and overnight liquidity shortages in the jurisdiction where the liquidity risk is incurred; on the other hand, the central bank

Table 8.2 The liquidity coverage ratio

$$\frac{\text{Stock of high-quality liquid assets}}{\text{Total net cash outflows over the next 30 calendar days}} \geq 100\%$$

eligibility does not by itself constitute the basis for the categorisation of an asset as "high-quality".

The liquidity buffer includes (1) Level 1 assets, which can be held on an unlimited basis, composed of:

❏ cash;
❏ central bank reserves, to the extent that these reserves can be drawn down in times of stress;
❏ under certain criteria,[11] marketable securities representing claims on or claims guaranteed by sovereigns, central banks, non-central-government public-sector entities (PSEs), the Bank for International Settlements, the International Monetary Fund, the European Commission, or multilateral development banks;
❏ government or central-bank debt for non-zero-risk-weighted sovereigns, issued in domestic currencies by the country in which the liquidity risk is being taken or the bank's home country; and
❏ domestic sovereign or central-bank debt for non-zero-risk-weighted sovereigns, issued in foreign currency, to the extent that this currency matches the currency needs of the bank's operations in that jurisdiction.

(2) a Level 2 liquidity buffer, adequately diversified, with a cap that allows up to 40% of the stock, represented by:

❏ government and PSEs assets qualifying for the 20% risk weighting under the standardised approach for credit risk; and
❏ high-quality, non-financial, corporate and covered bonds not issued by the bank itself, among other characteristics, rated at least AA–.[12]

Assets belonging to Level 2 should be subject to a 15% haircut.[13] In order to avoid that the buffer captures assets artificially generated through secured funding or collateral swaps transactions, the 40% cap should be calculated taking into account the impact on cash or other Level 1 or Level 2 assets caused by secured funding transactions (or collateral swaps) maturing within 30 days undertaken with any non-Level 1 and non-Level 2 assets. In this regard, for the purpose of calculating the buffer, short-term secured funding or lending backed by Level 1 and Level 2 assets should be considered rolled off. Finally, in order to mitigate cliff effects that could arise from some eligible liquid assets becoming ineligible (eg, due to rating downgrade), a grace period of 30 days has been given to allow banks additional time for replacing the assets.[14]

8.4.1.2 Treatment for jurisdictions with insufficient liquid assets
The new rules also introduce an alternative definition of liquidity buffer more suitable to jurisdictions with insufficient supply of government debt.[15] This concern was one of the main arguments for the adoption of the broad instead of the narrow (baseline)[16] definition of the liquidity buffer. Three carve-out options are proposed. The first option allows access to contractual, committed central-bank liquidity facilities. The central bank would charge a fee that ensures that the holding cost of the unencumbered assets used as collateral on the facility equals the holding cost of a representative portfolio of Level 1 and Level 2 assets, which are in turn adjusted for any material differences in credit risk. The second option allows jurisdictions to hold liquid assets in a currency different from that of the liquidity risk exposure, provided that the resulting currency mismatch is justifiable and kept within limits approved by supervisors.[17] The third option, provided sufficient Level 2 assets are available, allows use of a limited amount of additional liquid assets, with a higher haircut, that are eligible as Level 2. During the observation period,[18] the Basel Committee will develop prescriptive quantitative thresholds (known as tests of insufficiency) to identify jurisdictions with insufficient Level 1 and Level 2 assets. The quantitative thresholds should be such as to minimise the number of jurisdictions which qualify for alternative treatment.

8.4.1.3 Net cash outflows
With regard to net cash outflows under a stress scenario, the Basel Committee has identified a set of risk factors and severity levels that should be applied by all jurisdictions to ensure cross-border comparability.[19] The proposed stress scenario considers a crisis in the broader market combined with firm-specific difficulties. In particular, the scenario envisages: a sizeable downgrade of the bank's rating (three-notch downgrade); a partial withdrawal of deposits and a contraction of wholesale funding; the impossibility of

renewing unsecured interbank operations due to the closure of the unsecured market; increases in margins related to derivative transactions; and other off-balance-sheet operations. These include the potential need for the bank to buy back debt or honour non-contractual obligations in the interest of mitigating reputational risk. Stress parameters are largely set within the framework and national supervisors can only make them tighter. The amount of net cash outflow is represented by the difference between the cumulative expected cash outflows and the inflows. The cumulative sum of the latter cannot exceed 75% of the former.

In what follows, we describe the main components of the "total net cash outflows over the next 30 calendar days" and the denominator of the LCR and highlight major amendments to the Consultative Document.

8.4.1.4 Retail and small-business customers' deposits

The two classes are treated as equivalent provided that total aggregated deposits from each individual small-business customer (SBC) is below €1 million.[20] Minimum run-off rates for both classes of depositors are 5% or 10% (versus 7.5% and 15% in the December 2009 Consultative Document), depending on the relative stability of the underlying funding categories. Criteria to identify stable funding categories include, as a necessary condition, the existence of an effective deposit insurance scheme; however, low minimum run-off rates apply only to long-standing deposits and accounts whose transactional nature makes the withdrawal highly unlikely. Such broad principles, while suitable for encompassing a spectrum of banks with different levels of depositor loyalty, involve a degree of judgement and discretion by financial institutions. As mentioned in Chapter 13, quantitative impact study (QIS) results show broad variations between stable and volatile funding, even among banks with similar business models. This, in turn, affects the calculated net flows under stress and, ultimately, liquidity buffer needs, as stable and volatile deposits are assumed to carry different shocks.

8.4.1.5 Unsecured wholesale funding provided by banks, non-financial corporates, central banks and PSEs

Different run-off rates to deposits are envisaged depending on whether the accounts are operational (25%) or have different purposes (at least 75%) (BCBS 2010). The most notable changes in the assertions of the December 2009 Consultative Document affect the treatment of unsecured interbank transactions. While the standard run-off rate for these deposits stays at 100%, operational deposits, or those between affiliates within cooperative bank networks, qualify for lower rates. In particular, a 25% outflow can be assigned to financial and non-financial deposits for demonstrable relationships of clearing, custody or cash management, wherein the bank is given control of the deposit as an independent third party. These relationships were clearly defined in the final text of the rules (BCBS 2010, Paragraphs 75–7). Only the specific amount of deposits used for these operational functions qualifies for such preferential treatment. Balances, in excess of said operational requirements, that can be withdrawn receive the ordinary run-off rates. The depositor bank would receive a 0% inflow recognition for operational balances, which are expected to be locked in the other bank at times of stress, such as, for instance, the shocks experienced during the initial stage of the crisis in 2007. Deposits from correspondent banking or prime-brokerage services are not eligible for preferential treatment as operational balances.[21]

As already mentioned, preferential treatment is also granted to deposits from banks within the same cooperative network, ie, banks within "a group of legally autonomous institutions with a statutory framework of cooperation with common strategic focus and brand where specific functions are performed by central institutions and/or specialised service providers" (BCBS 2010). A lower run-off rate of 25% is assessed on deposits from banks to the central institution of the same cooperative network made under: "a) statutory minimum deposit requirements, which are registered at regulators or b) common task sharing and legally, statutory or contractual arrangements so long as both the bank that has received the monies and the bank that has deposited participate in the same institutional network's mutual protection scheme against illiquidity and insolvency of its members. As with other operational deposits, these deposits would receive a 0% inflow assumption for the depositing bank, as these funds are considered to remain with the centralised institution." Table 8.3 illustrates the treatment of financial deposits.

The run-off rate of non-operational deposits from sovereigns, central banks and PSE counterparties is set at 75% versus 100% in the

Table 8.3 Treatment of financial deposits

		Outflows Run-off rates			Inflows Eligible share*
	Banks	**Banks belonging to a cooperative network**		**Banks**	**Banks belonging to a cooperative network**
Deposits from banks	for clearing, custody or cash-management purposes 25%		**Deposits held in other banks**	for clearing, custody or cash-management purposes 0%	
	for correspondent banking and prime-brokerage purposes 100%			for correspondent banking and prime-brokerage purposes 100%	
	for other purposes			for other purposes	
	100%	25% if as per para 79 applies		100%	0% if as per para 79 applies

* Eligible shares and all other inflows are capped at 75% of gross outflows.

proposal. The lower rate is somewhat more realistic, as central banks, unlike private-sector financial institutions, are not likely to cut back their liquidity provision, especially secured lines, during a period of market stress. Deposits provided by non-financial corporate customers, sovereigns, central banks and PSEs with operational relationships fully covered by deposit insurance may receive the same treatment as stable retail deposits with 5% run-off rates.

8.4.1.6 Secured funding and reverse repo

The treatment of repos (repurchase agreements) and reverse repos reflects the eligibility of the underlying collateral as liquid asset reserves; in other words, banks should assume that repos and reverse repos maturing within 30 days (ie, the time horizon for calculation of the LCR) will be rolled over in full (if the security put up as collateral is "Level 1"), at 85% rate ("Level 2"), at 0 rate (other securities). In the last case, however, an exception is made for outstanding repos with sovereigns, central banks and PSEs; indeed repo funding

THE NEW FRAMEWORK FOR LIQUIDITY RISK

Table 8.4 Treatment of secured funding and reverse repos

	Outflows				Inflow*		
	Secured funding and repo maturing within 30 days				Secured lending and reverse repo maturing within 30 days		
	backed by				backed by		
	L1 assets	L2 assets	All other collateral		L1 assets	L2 assets	All other collateral
with domestic sovereigns, central banks and PSEs	0%	15%	25%	with all counterparties	0%	15%	100%
with other counterparties	0%	15%	100%				

* Eligibility rates, together with all other inflows, are capped at 75% of the gross outflows. According to Paragraph 109 of BCBS 2010, if the collateral obtained through reverse repo, securities borrowing or collateral swaps, which matures within 30-day horizon, is reused and is tied up for 30 days or longer to cover short positions, a bank should assume that such reverse repo or securities borrowing arrangements will be rolled over and will not give rise to any cash inflows.[22]

from such counterparties benefited from a major amendment to the Consultative Document (which was the initial proposal by the Basel Committee regarding the new liquidity rules), namely a 75% rollover assumption based on the low likelihood that these entities would "pull the plug" on banks at crisis times. Table 8.4 illustrates the outflows and inflows from, respectively, secured funding and reverse repos maturing within 30 days.

For transactions maturing beyond 30 days, cash received for a repo qualifies for the liquidity buffer if, and only if, it is held by the bank on the day of reporting. The associated securities, instead, are obviously ineligible since they are held by the counterparty.[23] Securities received for a reverse repo, if eligible, qualify for the liquidity buffer.

The treatment of the secured funding and the broader definition of the liquidity buffer could create a regulatory arbitrage between eligibility of securities against the minimum LCR and for repos with central banks.[24] The regulation provides an incentive for European banks, in particular, to refinance less liquid, higher-market-risk assets (such as asset-backed securities (ABSs)) from self-securitisation and eligible loans, with the ECB while holding liquid assets to meet minimum LCR.[25] Banks would then have an incentive to reinvest ECB liquidity in LCR-eligibile liquid assets, which would *de facto* artificially strengthen liquid reserves (albeit only

219

temporarily). The incentive would obviously be stronger for banks that fail to meet the minimum LCR, but it could also become widespread, if there were rigidities in restructuring balance sheets.

Additional requirements have been introduced for the increased liquidity needs as they relate to downgrade triggers embedded in short-term financing transactions, derivatives and other contracts, or to the potential changes in the valuation of posted collateral-securing derivative transactions. A bank should also maintain sufficient liquidity to cover the loss of funding on asset-backed commercial paper, conduits, securities investment vehicles, ABSs, covered bonds and other structured financing instruments. An adequate buffer should also guarantee a bank from drawdowns on committed credit and liquidity facilities. The rules distinguish the run-off rates by counterparty and by financing instrument. In particular, drawdowns on committed credit and liquidity facilities to retail and small-business clients, compared with the Consultative Document, were reduced to 5% from 10% of the currently undrawn portion of these facilities. Run-off rates stay at 100% on facilities granted to financial institutions. For the committed facilities granted to non-financial corporate customers, sovereigns, central banks and PSEs, the regulatory framework set out different run-off rates for the credit (10% from 100% contained in the December 2009 proposal) and for the liquidity facilities (unchanged at 100%). Finally, banks are asked to maintain a sufficient level of liquidity to cover other contingent funding liabilities both contractual (eg, guarantees, letter of credit, unconditionally revocable "uncommitted" credit and liquidity facilities) and reputational (eg, requests for bank debt repurchases).

8.4.1.7 Inflows

Assumptions on inflows have also undergone major changes since the Consultative Document. The Basel III framework document (BCBS 2010) now provides more detail and it limits considerably banks' leeway in estimating the aggregate. QIS evidence showed large differences across banks in terms of new lending, which affected inflow estimates; hence the results of the prescriptive stress tests of the LCR in estimating cash outflows. As a result, inflows and outflows would cancel each other out and make liquidity buffers unnecessary.

THE NEW FRAMEWORK FOR LIQUIDITY RISK

The new rules of the BCBS paper do clarify that qualifying inflows from fully performing outstanding exposures are only those that are "contractual" (ie, not those that are merely "planned"). Overall inflows are also capped at 75% of total cumulative cash outflows, which limits inflows' recognition and forces banks always to maintain some amount of liquid assets stock. Also, while 100% of all maturing and performing assets qualify as inflows, it is now assumed that some lending to certain counterparties is maintained. On a net basis, the new rules recognise, as inflows, 100% of repayments from financial institutions and 50% of those from non-financial corporate, retail and small-business clients. These numbers reflect either the rollover of existing business or new loan origination.

The treatment of inflows from other classes of transactions included in LCR calculations (ie, deposits for clearing, custody, cash management, deposits within cooperative networks, reverse repos, secured lending) was described earlier in the chapter.

8.4.2 The net stable funding ratio

The NSFR aims at coping with possible structural mismatches in the composition of balance-sheet liabilities and assets over a one-year horizon. It compares the total of sources of funds with maturity greater than one year and of the portion of "stable" non-maturity deposits (available amount of stable funding), on the one hand, and the less liquid assets (required amount of stable funding), on the other hand. Similarly to the LCR, the ratio must be at least 100%. Table 8.5 illustrates the NSFR, ie, the ratio of the "available amount of stable funding" to the "required amount of stable funding", which must be no lower than 100%. The NSFR will have full force on January 1, 2018.

For the NSFR, as well as for the LCR, both the consultation process and QIS results led the Basel Committee to modify the initial proposal so as to better address the trade-off between the severity of the new standards and the potential negative impact on financial

Table 8.5 Net stable funding ratio

$$\frac{\text{Available amount of stable funding}}{\text{Required amount of stable funding}} > 100\%$$

markets. The main concerns were the relative incentives of retail vis-à-vis wholesale business models. This is the reason that it was decided to carry out an "observation phase" to address any unintended consequences across business models or funding structures.

In what follows, we discuss the main components of the NSFR and the major amendments to the Consultative Document.

8.4.2.1 Available amount of stable funding

The numerator (ie, the available amount of stable funding) is made up of different forms of stable funding, identified by associating different weights to the various balance sheet items, each reflecting potential changes under stress situations, although less severe than the ones assumed for the LCR.[26]

Decreasing weights are assigned to the following liabilities according to their presumed stability: capital items and liabilities with effective maturities greater than one year (100%); "stable" deposits (raised from 85% to 90% after the consultation process); "less stable" deposits (from 70% to 80%); and unsecured wholesale funding or deposits with maturity below one year (50%), as long as they are provided by non-financial corporates, sovereigns, central banks and PSEs. Interbank funding with maturity below one year, also for operational purposes, is not taken into account by the rule. A possible favourable treatment could be recognised for deposits held from banks that belong to a cooperative network (BCBS 2010, Footnote 32).

8.4.2.2 Required amount of stable funding

The denominator contains assets weighted inversely to their liquidity degree. The more liquid an asset is, the less required amount of stable funding is needed:

❑ cash and money market instruments (0%);
❑ unencumbered marketable securities with maturities greater than one year towards sovereigns, central banks, supranational bodies or multilateral development banks that are assigned a 0% risk-weight under the Basel II standardised approach (5%);
❑ unencumbered corporate and covered bonds and marketable securities representing claims on public entities or multilateral development banks that are rated AA– or higher or are assigned a

20% risk weight under the standardised approach with maturities greater than one year; these are respectively traded in liquid markets and have shown themselves in the past to be adequately liquid under stress situations, and an active repo-markets exist for these securities (20%);
❏ gold, unencumbered listed equity securities, unencumbered corporate and covered bonds rated A+ to A and loans to non-financial corporate, sovereigns, central banks and PSEs clients having a residual maturity of less than one year (50%); and
❏ loans to retail clients having a residual maturity of less than one year (85%); the weight associated with required stable funding for residential mortgages and other loans that would qualify for the 35% or better risk weight under the standardised approach is set to 65% (which was 100% in the Consultative Document); for off-balance sheet commitments to 5% (originally from a proposed 10%).

8.4.3 Monitoring tools
The additional monitoring tools suggested in the new framework include the analysis of data related to the cashflows of banks, balance-sheet structure, available unencumbered collateral and certain market indicators. These should enable supervisors to capture the information needed for monitoring both the resilience of individual financial institutions and the stability of the market and the banking system as a whole. These tools could also be used in communicating liquidity exposures among home and host supervisors. All such tools should enable supervisors to achieve the following.

❏ Identify a maturity mismatch between the contractual inflow and outflow of liquidity for defined time bands (contractual maturity mismatch). This metric provides a simple baseline of contractual commitments and it is useful in comparing liquidity risk across institutions, as well as flagging emerging liquidity shortages.
❏ Evaluate the concentration of funding, particularly in counterparties, instruments and currencies in the wholesale market (concentration of funding).
❏ Measure the amount of unencumbered assets that each reporting bank can pledge against secured funding either in the market and

with the central bank (available unencumbered assets). This should make institutions more aware of their potential to raise additional secured funds, although at time of stress such ability would inevitably be diminished.
❏ Calculate LCR by relevant currencies, and, in so doing, track potential currency mismatch (LCR by significant currency).
❏ Consider market-related monitoring tools in order to have a source of instantaneous data on potential liquidity difficulties (so-called market-related monitoring tools). They could include data on asset prices and liquidity and other bank-specific information (such as the banks' ability to fund themselves in various wholesale markets).

8.5 OPEN ISSUES

Unresolved, residual issues not dealt with by the Basel III discussions and the possible ramifications of this are discussed in this section. As for the other components of the Basel III package, the definition of the new liquidity standards has followed a relatively quick process. The final calibration – which has benefited from the consultation and the QIS evidence – clearly reflects the twofold objective of international regulators to address the shortcomings of the current regulatory framework and, at the same time, avoid a negative impact on financial markets and economic growth.

However, it cannot be guaranteed that such rules will not be further adjusted in the future "The Committee will put in place rigorous reporting processes to monitor the standards during the observation period and will continue to review the implications of these standards for financial markets, credit extension and economic growth, addressing unintended consequences as necessary . . . The observation period will be used to monitor the impact of the standards on smaller institutions versus larger, and on different business lines, especially focusing on the impact on retail versus wholesale business activities" (BCBS 2010, Paragraphs 9 and 196). The observation phase (which began in 2011 and will finish at the end of 2014 for the LCR and began in 2011 and will terminate at the end of 2017 for the NSFR) will represent the opportunity for verifying, on a continuous basis, the impacts of the new rules on the banking system and for resolving the open issues.

Reference is made, as an example, to the in-depth examination of quantitative criteria that, in conjunction with use of the external rating, could be employed for estimating the inclusion of an asset in the Level 2 buffer of the LCR. Regarding this aspect, the Basel Committee has identified some additional parameters of comparison (for instance, the bid–ask spread, the trading volume and the turnover during past stress periods), which, if adequately developed, will be able in the future to reduce the emphasis assigned to the rating. However, the above-mentioned new parameters will have to be considered as supplementary and not alternative to the external rating. In addition to the potential changes listed above, the Committee will continue to consider whether to apply to the NSFR some amount of recognition to matched funding within the one-year time frame, as well as some other structural changes to the proposal. In particular, the Committee will gather data to allow analysis on time bands of both assets and liabilities maturing within the one-year horizon. Finally, there are open issues aimed at guaranteeing a minimum degree of consistency between the LCR and the NSFR with reference to the treatment of the inter-bank deposits with an operational relationship and from banks that belong to cooperative networks that (in calculating the short-term liquidity ratio) are subject to a more favourable weight than that established in the structural indicator.

Several issues have remained open. On these the observation period will allow more inputs to be gathered for their clearer understanding. Among others, they are the degree of flexibility for banks in meeting the new ratios on a continuous time (8.5.1); the relationship between the LCR and stress test (8.5.2); and disclosure (8.5.3).

8.5.1 Liquidity buffer or contingent liquidity buffer?

The new regulation states that banks shall meet the proposed standards continuously. Moreover, securities considered highly liquid that are included in the buffer shall be managed with the clear and sole intent of being used as "contingent funds". Such provisions would not consider liquidity reserves held to comply with the rules as resources that could be used to cover liquidity outflows. For banks hit by a liquidity shock, in fact, it would be impossible to use the regulatory buffer since they should comply with the rules on liquidity even in a stress situation. Therefore, it seems desirable that the buffer required by the new regulation could be considered an adequately flexible tool, giving banks the ability to draw on it in case of need.

Without prejudice to the need for compliance with the rules on an ongoing basis, it could be envisaged, in case the reserves are used to cover outflows in a stress situation, that the buffer could be restored, for instance after the application of a specific penalty,[27] over an adequate period of time, as set out in the CRD Proposal published for consultation by the European Commission.

8.5.2 Are stress tests on LCR enough?

The new framework highlights, compared with the initial proposal, a loosening of the (in some cases, excessive) severity of some risk factors considered in the scenario for the calculation of the LCR. The regulatory stress makes no explicit distinction between banks' business models, assuming that the same stress situation applies to all banks in the calculation of liquidity net position.[28]

Therefore, the question is whether the new rules are sufficient to ensure a prudent management of liquidity risk or, considering the above, should be supplemented by banks' own analyses to account for the activities that are specific to them only. This seems to be the auspice of the Basel Committee, as, in illustrating the new regulation, it states that "this stress test should be viewed as a minimum supervisory requirement for banks. Banks are still expected to conduct their own stress tests to assess the level of liquidity they should hold beyond this minimum, and construct scenarios that could cause difficulties for their specific business activities".[29]

Considering what is mentioned above, the regulatory stress test could be a valuable starting point for the development of further scenarios that would allow defining the exposure to liquidity risk more accurately than through a one-size-fits-all regulatory approach. The following issues represent possible refinements, aimed at improving the assessment of the liquidity risk profile of a financial institution made through a stress-testing framework: relationship between stress test and business model and time horizon, the scope of application of a liquidity stress test exercise, the concept of stress test on liquidity buffer.

8.5.2.1 Stress test and business model

The stress scenario should take into account the main risk factors of a specific business model. For instance, a traditional bank focused on retail customers could supplement the regulatory stress test through a change in the assumptions concerning the demand deposits behaviour and the cash inflows related to reimbursement of loans. In the new regulatory framework, in fact, it is probable that the intermediaries, and especially traditional banks, in order to minimise liquidity reserves and their subsequent impact on profitability,[30] focus their choices on funding sources that are less penalised in the calculation of LCR, such as retail deposits. The acquisition of new deposits could determine an increase in the competition level, eventually causing an increase in the level of responsiveness under a stress situation and a change in the ratio between stable and unstable components. In this regard it could therefore be useful to increase shock percentages of demand deposits, which were strongly reduced with respect to the proposal of the Consultative Document. In this context, to some particularly volatile items, such as internet deposits, a further increased percentage of change could be given.[31]

Moreover, the increased competition in the market could reduce the level of customer loyalty and retention. In this case, it would be appropriate to reduce the stable part of deposits, increasing the unstable part. As for cash inflows, considering the worsening of the macroeconomic context, a bank could assume a lengthening of the maturities greater than one month of planned reimbursements or an increase in the arrears rate. According to the Basel regulatory proposal, these conditions would not produce any inflows for the LCR calculation, thus requiring an increase in the liquidity buffer to cover outflows.

The investment-bank business model is based mainly on bond funding with institutional investors whose funds are lent to corporate customers through loans or bond underwriting. These medium/long-term operations are not fully caught by the stress scenario proposed for the LCR and, as a consequence, their cash outflows do not contribute to the formation of the LCR, at least for maturities greater than 30 days. The stress defined by the Basel Committee does not take into account liquidity positions over maturities spanning from one month, regulatory minimum for the short-term indicator, to one year, beyond which the banks' liquidity position is monitored through the structural ratio. As a result, the moment a bond residual maturity is lower than one month, an investment bank could suddenly need to manage a strongly negative liquidity position and the available buffer could be insufficient to cover outflows.[32] Considering this peculiarity, the scenario proposed by the Basel Committee could be complemented with an extended stress time horizon to represent the concentration of bond reimbursements across some time slots and, meanwhile, to enable the bank to find funds to face cash outflows.[33] However, the use of longer time-horizon results in lower reliability of the projections of cashflows to stress. The choice of a time horizon up to at least three months would allow the adequate trade-off between the exposure to model risk and the forecast capacity of the estimate. In order to define the survival horizon under stress and, theoretically, the time available for adopting emergency actions, it is essential to appreciate all the maturities of the maturity ladder.

8.5.2.2 Stress test and time horizon
A stress scenario should consider the impact of a shock of risk factors on the liquidity position of a bank as to different time horizons, including the intraday horizon. In the section on the connection between the stress test and business models some comments have already been made about the necessity to lengthen the observation period considered by the LCR. This section focuses on the management of liquidity within the 30-day time horizon, with particular reference to the intraday horizon, a subject that is given attention by the Basel Committee. In the final version of the new discipline the necessity of banks and supervisors being made aware of any potential mismatches within the 30-day period is recognised; they must also ensure that sufficient liquid assets are available to meet any cashflow gaps throughout the month and develop in the near future monitoring tools related to intraday liquidity risk.

As the stress scenario for the LCR does not take into account intraday liquidity risk, it can be noted that the liquidity buffer cannot be deemed sufficient for covering this risk, although for their inclusion in the buffer assets should be central-bank-eligible (ie, assets can be used as collateral to obtain liquidity from the central bank) for intraday liquidity needs.[34] It is therefore necessary that, while awaiting the definition of a clearer reference frame on intraday liquidity risk management, banks supplement the stress scenario for LCR with hypotheses accounting for intraday difficulties and add to the liquidity buffer envisaged by the regulation further liquid reserves to cover possible shortfalls occurring in the course of the business day.

The intraday stress scenario should consider not only critical payments to be met by the bank, putting them in sequence and planning outflows according to the assigned priority,[35] but also payments deriving from operations with customers related to services within the payments system (eg, when a banks acts as contingency liquidity provider).[36] It is a good practice to measure inflows and outflows expected daily with the purpose of anticipating as much as possible any liquidity needs that could rise.[37] A frequent monitoring of the most relevant positions during the business day could contribute to identifying further intraday liquidity needs or to limiting cash outflows to meet critical payments. It is also necessary for a bank's intraday sources to be sufficient for each exposure's currency, especially if the bank has limited access to intraday credit from the central bank for activities in foreign currency. It is also important to be aware of the time necessary for liquidating the various types of collateral for obtaining intraday credit, among which collateral held abroad is particularly relevant.

Finally, it is necessary that the risk of a gradual shortening of funding maturities for all time horizons be taken into account. The Basel document assumes only a reduction of the rollover percentage, with no indications as to the term of the renewed collection operations. In this regard it could be beneficial to reflect in the stress tests – besides the reduction of renewed operations – a gradual decrease in funding maturities, the object of renegotiation in the course of time.

8.5.2.3 The scope of application of a liquidity stress test
Stress tests should allow you to analyse the impact of tense situations on both the consolidated and individual liquidity positions. The regulatory stress test will apply to the consolidated level, with possible extensions to individual components according to local regulations. The scope of consolidation is the same for the overall regulation issued by the Basel Committee, thus including banking and financial companies, with no regard to other group entities that could affect the liquidity position of a bank, such as insurance companies. Banking groups in which insurance companies are

present could therefore modify the baseline scenario, by changing both risk factors and applied shock percentages, taking into account the impact on the liquidity position of a tense situation in the insurance sector.[38] The necessity to perform stress tests on individual components of the group basically concerns cross-border groups (ie, banking groups that have legal entities in different countries), considering possible limitations to liquidity transfer between different countries; in this case the definition of the scenario for the individual legal entity should be adapted to catch possible peculiarities of the host country, such as shock percentages of retail deposits.

8.5.2.4 The concept of stress tests on the liquidity buffer
The LCR focuses the application of the stress test only on the ratio's denominator: net cashflows. As for the numerator, the liquidity buffer, no assumption is made about possible variations on the market value of its components, which could reduce, in a tense situation (such as the sovereign debt crisis that began in 2010), the amount of available liquidity to cover cash outflows.[39] Considering the conditions for the eligibility of an asset within the buffer, banks could further refine the regulatory test by assuming severe yet plausible changes in the market value of securities included within the liquid reserves in a stress situation. The objective would be to verify, besides the impact of the stress on the overall amount of liquidity obtainable from the market, that the requirements for the inclusion in the buffer are still met.[40]

Finally, considering that a large part of the liquidity buffer will consist of government bonds, in the light of the 2010 sovereign debt crisis it might be appropriate to verify the effects of hypothetical crisis scenarios on government bonds held in portfolio, by simply replicating those that have already occurred, also with regard to possible contagion effects.[41]

8.5.3 Disclosure

The need for a strengthening of the disclosure to the market is deemed necessary at international level. The Financial Stability Forum (2008), the Basel Committee (2008a, Principle 13) and the CEBS (2009a) have all highlighted the need to ensure that banks' liquidity situation is properly disclosed to the market. An adequate degree of disclosure should, eventually, determine an overall strengthening of the financial system, even though the market is not always able to distinguish the sound banks from the weaker ones on the basis of an assessment of risk management or organisational framework on liquidity risk. Information asymmetries[42] coupled with negative external factors linked to the spreading of tensions at systemic level would make you wonder whether it is advisable to accomplish disclosure on the liquidity condition of an intermediary.[43] In a going-concern situation, the incentive represented by the market supervision could properly function, but a situation of systemic crisis in which were grafted idiosyncratic difficulties could represent a further element of instability (ie, the contagion risk of liquidity shortages at one bank causing shortages at others). However, it is possible to object that the financial crisis worsened just because of the uncertainty resulting from a lack of clear information on the banks' liquidity conditions. Adequate disclosure of the management procedures and of the liquidity situation, besides giving more insight as to the context, would have also represented an incentive for banks to adopt risk-adverse behaviours.

Without prejudice to the need for an increase in the degree of disclosure, it is necessary to define the granularity level and completeness of information to disclose in order to allow the market to reasonably appreciate the banks' liquidity risk. This necessity seems also relevant in order to ensure an adequate level playing field among intermediaries belonging to different countries and to minimise potential regulatory arbitrages that could develop within cross-border groups, due to the discretionary power given to each country for the definition of some parameters referred to by the rules (eg, run-off percentages of retail deposits, which could even be stricter than those set out as minimum regulatory requirements, or the assumptions related to contingent liabilities).[44]

Therefore, it seems crucial to reach the right balance between accuracy and comprehensibility of the information, thus avoiding either over concise or extremely detailed information. Obviously, this level of disclosure should involve not only the regulatory standards that will become effective in coming years, but also qualitative information such as governance structures, policies, liquidity risk measurement and management procedures, funding strategies, collateral management, internally run stress tests and contingency funding plans.

Another particularly relevant aspect of disclosure is the frequency of reporting the information described in the regulatory standards. In order to prevent "window-dressing" operations in the imminence of the information disclosure to the market (for instance, by increasing the liquidity buffer the day before the calculation of the LCR), in this case with specific reference to the LCR, it would also be advisable to create mechanisms to communicate the daily/monthly average with reference to LCR and NSFR respectively.[45]

Another issue is the time lag in reporting the information requested. In this case, the pros and cons of a time-lag provision can be identified too. The assumption of market speculation regarding indicators not perfectly compliant with the regulation would tend towards a 6–12-month postponement of the reporting. In this period, on the one hand, the banks would be motivated to change their liquidity position to prevent market panic; on the other hand, the supervisory authorities would have enough time to take all necessary actions to assist intermediaries experiencing difficulties. However, this mode of operating would increase uncertainty, in case of a new crisis, as to the soundness of the liquidity situation of a bank that in the past had experienced tensions, and it could also undermine the reliability of supervisory authorities on the subject of interventions to ensure financial stability. The most reasonable assumption would be to limit as much as possible the time lag in reporting the standards, trying, in the meantime, to tailor the supplied information so as to allow the market to understand the actual liquidity situation of a bank and of the whole financial system.

Considering all the issues highlighted above, the role that banks will play seems, therefore, pivotal. The actions related to disclosure will aim to educate all the stakeholders so to allow the market to correctly distinguish the strong intermediaries from the weak ones (CEBS 2009a).

8.6 A PRELIMINARY ASSESSMENT OF THE NEW RULES

A full assessment of the likely impact of the new standards on liquidity on both institutions and financial markets is not straightforward. At the time of writing many technical details were still to be defined in the implementation phase. For this reason, the quantitative evidence gathered in the QIS has to be interpreted with caution (see Chapter 13). However, a preliminary qualitative assessment is still possible, with regards to banking strategies (8.6.1), their risk tolerance (8.6.2), the possible crowding-out effect (8.6.3) and the incentives for banks (8.6.4).

8.6.1 Possible impact on banking strategies

The enforcement of the new regulation is likely to strengthen the process of changing company strategies, already partially started, returning to businesses more focused on traditional activities (so-called back-to-basics)[46] with a possible downsizing of trading activities. Many banks are gradually carrying on a process of deleveraging and are reducing the part of assets less pertinent to the core business (for example, sale of foreign branches or insurance companies). The need to extend funding maturities and to strengthen the stable component of the funding will cause a considerable reduction in the margin of interest and an increase in the competitive pressures on retail deposits. In this case, smaller banks, even if they themselves are not subject to the liquidity regulation,[47] may see some cost pressure as bigger banks compete with them for deposits or pass on higher costs when lending to them.

The inclusion of highly liquid assets in the buffer will imply an increase in the opportunity cost, which will inevitably determine a decrease in profits. The extraordinary levels of profitability reported in the past, favoured by a market that rewarded extreme financial innovation, can hardly recur.

Finally, the liquidity regulation could lead to a strong market innovation in order to provide new instruments that could help banks to comply with the standards or alternative ways of channelling funds. In a context where banks will not hold securities that are designated as non-liquid or will not provide long-term funds, the affected borrowers may need to seek new lenders among non-bank entities (eg, the shadow banking system). As a consequence, risks may be simply disguised or shifted around, with implications not only for market functioning but also for financial stability.

8.6.2 Banks' liquidity risk tolerance

The above-mentioned Principles on liquidity risk set by the Basel Committee provided for, among other things, the banks to set out the liquidity risk tolerance in light of the characteristics of their own business model and of their role in the financial system (BCBS 2008a,

Principle 2). The new liquidity regulation, in defining in a very detailed and prescriptive manner the two standards (LCR and NSFR) aimed at mitigating banks' liquidity risk, implicitly sets a level of risk tolerance strongly limiting a bank's decision power in this respect. As a consequence, banks can modify the liquidity risk tolerance threshold only in a more conservative sense, within the time horizons defined by the Liquidity Regulation.[48] The bank's decision power can thus be expressed – as well as by changing the values of the two proposed standards, to make them more averse to risk – by defining tolerance thresholds related to periods different from those already prescriptively set out by the Basel document. Banks can, for instance, set out liquidity risk tolerance levels on an intra-daily basis or on a medium-to-long-term horizon greater than one year, a period that has not explicitly taken into account by the new rules. However, the banking system is expected to start to set out risk appetite levels consistent with the evolution of the framework at international level, during the provisional period aimed first at defining and then applying the new rules.

8.6.3 Crowding-out effect

The new rules on liquidity are also likely to generate a crowding-out effect (ie, any reduction in private consumption or investment that occurs because of an increase in government spending) on corporate bonds and covered bonds with a rating under AA–, benefiting government bonds ("segmentation" between liquid and non-liquid securities).[49] The magnitude of the crowding-out will be determined by the regulation's impact on the balance-sheet structure of banks and by the depth of the corporate bond market.

In all likelihood an increase in spreads between government bonds and corporate bonds, to the former's advantage, will occur once the regulation is in force. The increase in yield spread should be noticed also with regard to government securities, among which those assets with a weighting factor of 0% and 20% according to the Basel II regulations on credit risk will be rewarded, to the detriment of the others.

Particularly interesting is the crowding-out effect that the new regulation would produce with regard to bank bond issuances underwritten or purchased on secondary markets by other banks. For instance, these liabilities, provided that they satisfy the minimum requirements set out by the euro system in terms of rating and cash-flows structure, are currently eligible for repos with the central bank if they are not presented by the issuer or by a company belonging to the same group as the issuer. With the new rules, these securities would be even more severely treated, in comparison with corporate bonds, with further pressure on spreads.[50] This change in relative pricing implies more favourable conditions for borrowers such as governments and high-rated non-financial corporates. By contrast, the borrowing cost for financial-sector issuers and lower-rated corporates will rise. The results would be a general increase in banks' funding cost. Eventually, credit rationing to companies could develop.

The regulation could also create a crowding-out effect on short-term instruments benefiting long-term ones (so-called segmentation between maturities). The potential shift towards longer-term funding might lead to a decline in activity in the unsecured short-term funding market. As a consequence the cost of long-term funds could rise relative to short-term funds, resulting in a steepening of the money-market yield curve, with repercussions on the financing cost for the economy as a whole. This may also have implications for monetary policy implementation, since many central banks currently use the overnight or short-term market rates as their operating targets and may undermine the central bank's ability to implement monetary policy.[51]

8.6.4 Rules and incentives

The strengthening of methodologies for liquidity management postulated by the new regulation can determine costs not provided for by the company budgets.[52] Potential moral-hazard phenomena[53] could lead banks to minimise interventions with the purpose of restraining the related costs. These possibilities led to a review of the incentive mechanisms for banks, including those for bank treasury's functions.

Liquidity risk could originate in any banking sector and so calls for a shared managerial approach. Compensation policies encouraging treasuries to take on excessive risks strongly weaken the incentives to pursue a prudent and mindful risk management. Prior to the crisis, the main objective of treasuries was to minimise funding cost. Pursuing this objective is still advisable. What has been changed by the crisis is how to quantify this price, since it must now take into account the higher costs the bank could bear in a stress situation. The distribution of the liquidity across the various bank business units, in parallel with the capital allocation techniques, will thus be carried out by means of methodologies comparing, through a transfer price system, the expected profitability resulting from an operation with its liquidity risk, so as to include also the cost related to the need for further liquid resources under a stress situation. The liquidity risk should also be taken into account by the New Products Approval Committee, the body in charge of assessing the various risks related to the entrance into a new segment or into the trading of a new instrument. Unlike in the past, this would mean that, for example, in assessing expected profitability before making a deal, a trader would have to take into account not only market risk but also liquidity risk. This would be necessary, for example, when the treasury needs to renew its funding at higher rates due to worsening market conditions, or when the conditions for activating the contingency funding plan occur, in case rollover is not possible. This mode of operating would make all company functions more aware of their responsibilities in managing liquidity risk.

8.7 CONCLUDING REMARKS

The liquidity rules introduced by Basel III provide the necessary framework for a more prudent management of such a risk by financial institutions and enrich the supervisory toolkit with a range of quantitative metrics that will support the Principles introduced by the Basel Committee some months earlier.

In a few years, the Committee designed a sound and articulate liquidity risk framework. This undoubtedly represents a strong answer to the financial crisis. However, the journey towards a "safe harbour" is still long, and difficulties will still pave the way in the coming years. It is desirable, for the future, that all banks introduce an even stricter monitoring system, based on a prompt control of liquidity that also includes future cash outflow projections. It is in fact necessary for banks to have a forward-looking view on some assets and liabilities. Static analyses are useful, but contingency funding plans linked to scenario analyses are essential. By this time, banks are aware of the necessity of stress tests, but there is still the need for an effective outline of the tests.

Improvements need to be made with respect to several issues. First of all, the stress scenarios have to take into account the close links between liquidity risk and other risk types. Risk-mitigating measures – such as collateral management under contingent situations, the arrangement of a contingency funding plan and of the diversification of funding sources – need to be strengthened. Similarly, the identification of the most fitting metrics for pricing the internal transfer of funds represents a significant challenge for banking groups (particularly for cross-border ones) in terms of ensuring consistency between risk taking on the part of individual business units (or financial institutions) and overall liquidity risk (maturity mismatch, contingent and market liquidity risk) generated for the institution.

International regulators and supervisory authorities will have to address several topics in coming years, so as to finalise all technical details of the new rules and ensure a rigorous and homogeneous enforcement of the new standards. This is the only way to pursue the ultimate objective of the new framework: provide banks with a credible set of rules for managing a key risk in their day-to-day activity and allow supervisors to monitor such a risk in a timely and effective way.

> I wish to thank Paolo Corradino for his comments. Thanks also to Angelo Francesco Carriero and Edmondo Ferrigno for their final revision. Remaining errors are obviously my own. The opinions expressed are those of the author and do not necessarily reflect those of the Bank of Italy.

1 Northern Rock had a business plan that involved borrowing in the UK and in international money markets from institutional counterparties. Mortgages were extended to customers based on this funding. These mortgages were then resold on international capital markets (so-called securitisation). When the demand from investors for securitised mortgages dropped in August 2007, the bank became unable to repay loans from the money market. The bank sought and received a liquidity support facility from the Bank of England to replace funds it was unable to raise from the money market. This led to panic among individual depositors, which led to a bank run. According to the press release published by the Bank of England on September 14, 2007, "The FSA judges that Northern Rock is solvent, exceeds its regulatory capital requirement and has a good quality loan book. The decision to provide a liquidity support facility to Northern Rock reflects the difficulties that it has had in accessing longer term funding and the mortgage securitisation market, on which Northern Rock is particularly reliant." See http://www.bankofengland.co.uk/publications/news/2007/090.htm.

2 For example, among quantitative indicators, it is possible to identify so-called stock-based indicators, those more oriented to cashflows according to a maturity mismatch approach, and so-called hybrid indicators that take into account both aspects.

3 Reference is made, for instance to the amendments to the regulation in Great Britain through the publication of the Turner Review (March 2009). In Italy, since the turmoil began, Bank of Italy introduced a weekly liquidity monitoring (even daily monitoring for more distressed situations and for systemic intermediaries), of the major banking groups first, and later of almost all the Italian banks and the foreign banks' branches, which allowed prompt detection of possible difficult situations and implementation of the subsequent corrective actions.
4 Since 2009, Financial Stability Board.
5 Since 2011, European Banking Authority (EBA).
6 According to BCBS 2008a, "a primary objective of the liquidity risk management framework should be to ensure with a high degree of confidence that the firm is in a position to both address its daily liquidity obligations and withstand a period of liquidity stress affecting both secured and unsecured funding, the source of which could be bank-specific or market-wide".
7 For instance according to Paragraph 101 of BCBS 2008a, a bank needs to consider the appropriateness of a number of assumptions such as the asset market illiquidity and the erosion in the value of liquid assets; the run-off of retail funding; the (un)availability of secured and unsecured wholesale funding sources; additional margin calls and collateral requirements; potential draws on committed lines extended to third parties or the bank's subsidiaries, branches or head office; the liquidity absorbed by off-balance-sheet vehicles and activities (including conduit financing); liquidity drains associated with complex products/transactions; the ability to transfer liquidity across entities, sectors and borders, taking into account legal, regulatory, operational and time-zone restrictions and constraints; the access to central bank facilities; and the operational ability of the bank to monetise assets.
8 For instance, the liquidity risk management is not robust or well integrated into the bank-wide risk-management process; a bank does not hold an adequate liquidity cushion composed of readily marketable assets to be in a position to survive such periods of liquidity stress.
9 To ensure consistency in applying the consolidated standards across jurisdictions, BCBS 2010 provides two guidelines for their application: (1) when calculating the liquidity standards on a consolidated basis, a cross-border banking group should apply the liquidity parameters adopted in the home jurisdiction to all legal entities being consolidated except for the treatment of retail/small-business customers' deposits, which should follow the relevant parameters adopted in host jurisdictions in which the entities operate; (2) no liquidity should be recognised by a cross-border banking group in its consolidated LCR if there is any doubt about the availability of the liquidity.
10 In the December 2009 proposal, the basic definition of the liquidity buffer included cash, central banks' reserves, high-quality government securities and debt issued in domestic currencies by the country in which the liquidity risk is being taken or the bank's home country (this is the so-called narrow definition of the liquidity buffer). The alternative option, the so-called "broad buffer", contemplated high-quality non-financial corporate bonds and covered bonds (in addition to securities included in the narrow definition). As underlined by the Committee, finding an equilibrium between the necessity for the intermediaries to maintain prudent funding liquidity profiles, and the need for keeping the costs for the financial system at an acceptable level, has represented a determining factor in finalising these rules.
11 The eligibility criteria are: (i) low credit risk, ie, assets are assigned a 0% risk weight under the Basel II standardised approach; (ii) traded in large, deep and active repo or cash markets characterised by a low level of concentration; (iii) proven record as a reliable source of liquidity in the markets (repo and sale) even during stressed market conditions; (iv) not an obligation of a bank, investment or insurance firm.
12 According to Paragraph 42 (a) and (b) of BCBS 2010, in addition to the characteristics mentioned in the main text of this chapter, in order to include public securities, corporate and covered bonds in the Level 2 buffer, assets should be traded in large, deep and active

THE NEW FRAMEWORK FOR LIQUIDITY RISK

repo and cash markets that are characterised by a low level of concentration and proven record as a reliable source of liquidity in the markets (repo and sale) even during stressed market conditions (for instance, a maximum decline of price or increase in haircut over a 30-day period during a relevant period of significant liquidity stress not exceeding 10%). In addition, as stated by the Basel Committee, during the observation period a number of quantitative criteria, such as bid–ask spread (in its December 2010 draft this was not included in the criteria, although it was in the December 2009 proposal), trading volume, turnover and other possible criteria will be tested in order to use them with rating to determine the eligibility of Level 2 assets. As the new criteria become more robust, there should be less emphasis placed on external ratings and more on these additional criteria.

13 This refers to the formulas used in the valuation of securities for the purpose of calculating a broker-dealer's net capital. The haircut varies according to the class of a security, its market risk and the time to maturity. For example, cash-equivalent government could have a 0% haircut, equities could have an average 30% haircut, and fail positions (securities with past due delivery) with little prospect of settlement could have a 100% haircut.

14 In case of the unexpected absence of the characteristics required for inclusion of a bond in the liquidity buffer (for instance in case of a downgrading of a covered bond below a AA_ rating), there is the possibility of maintaining the bond in the buffer for 30 days in order to give a bank the possibility of finding another bond in substitution. Otherwise the buffer could suddenly fall (this is the cliff effect).

15 This is particularly true for domestic banks that have significant liabilities in the currency of the jurisdiction concerned.

16 For a definition of narrow buffer see Endnote 11.

17 At the moment the Basel Committee has not yet identified a parameter to consider what constitutes a "justifiable" currency mismatch. When the rules come into force the supervisor will decide if a currency mismatch should be consider justifiable.

18 In particular, with reference to the LCR the observation period will finish at the end of 2014; the observation period of the NSFR will terminate at the end of 2017.

19 However, a few of the parameters contain elements of national discretion to reflect jurisdiction-specific conditions. According to the new rules, these parameters should be transparent and clearly outlined in the regulations of each jurisdiction, to provide clarity both within the jurisdiction and internationally.

20 The definition of small-business customers is in accordance with Paragraph 231 of the Basel II framework: "Loans extended to small businesses and managed as retail exposures are eligible for retail treatment provided the total exposure of the banking group to a small business borrower (on a consolidated basis where applicable) is less than ⇔1 million. Small business loans extended through or guaranteed by an individual are subject to the same exposure threshold."

21 According to Footnote 17 of Paragraph 74 of BCBS 2010, "Corresponding banking refers to arrangements under which one bank (correspondent) holds deposits owned by other banks (respondents) and provides payment and other services in order to settle foreign exchange transactions. Prime brokerage is a package of services offered to large active investors, particularly hedge funds. These services usually include: clearing, settlement and custody; consolidated reporting; financing (margin, repo or synthetic); securities lending; capital introduction; and risk analytics."

22 Despite the rollover assumptions, a bank should manage its collateral to such a degree that that it is able to fulfil obligations to return collateral whenever the counterparty decides not to roll over any reverse repo or securities lending transaction.

23 This is in line with Paragraph 53 of BCBS 2010, which states that banks are not be permitted to double-count items.

24 The nature and the magnitude of such consequences depend crucially on the current design of the operating framework, which varies considerably across central banks. For central

239

banks that accept only a narrow range of collateral similar to the Level 1 definition for open market operations, this concern about collateral liquidity does not apply.

25 However, the overall effect on the risk transferred to the ECB is not easy to calculate. While market risk will likely increase, above all in terms of volatility in collateral's valuation (eg, for ABSs and eligible loans), credit risk for counterparties enjoying broader access to repos with central banks is likely to decline. The new rules, in fact, by strengthening controls on liquidity risk, should increase the safety of the overall financial system.

26 The stress scenario is based only on an extended firm-specific, and not also on a market-wide scenario, "where a bank encounters, investors and customers become aware of: 1) a significant decline in profitability or solvency arising from heightened credit risk, market risk or operational risk and/or other risk exposures; 2) a potential downgrade in a debt, counterparty credit or deposit rating by any nationally recognised credit rating organisation and/or 3) a material event which calls into question the reputation or credit quality of the institution" (BCBS 2010).

27 For instance, if a bank uses the liquidity buffer in a stressful situation that leads to a lowering of the LCR below 100%, the bank may be required to maintain an LCR, for example, equal to 110% for the year following of the overrun.

28 Actually, following the consultation process, the Group of Governors and Heads of Supervision, at the meeting of July 26, 2010, decided to reduce the run-off percentage of interbank deposits from financial institutions carrying out custodian, cash management and clearing functions, acknowledging the greater stability of these components as long as they are correlated to a specific business model. The final version of the regulation also provides for a favourable treatment for banks belonging to cooperative networks.

29 See Point 19 of the new regulation.

30 Besides the impact related to the opportunity cost linked to the acquisition of government bonds versus the use of liquidity for investments, it is probable that market competition will push banks to offer ever higher returns on deposits, which as a consequence will reduce overall income.

31 In this regard the Basel document seems to hypothesise greater stress percentages.

32 After all, the sole application of the LCR in the 30 preceding days would have not allowed for identification of the need for buffer strengthening in the following month, due to limitations related to the time horizon.

33 This provision is also desired by the Basel Committee in the "Sound Principles on Liquidity", which state that banks should consider the possibility of performing stress tests on time-extended scenarios.

34 According to Paragraph 31, "... banks and regulators should be aware that the LCR stress does not cover expected or unexpected intraday liquidity needs that occur during the day and disappear by the end of the day".

35 For example, critical payments could be those presenting a specific maturity during the business day, those settling transactions in other payment and settlement systems and those related to market activities (delivery or return-of-money market transactions or margin payments).

36 The stress scenario should take into account the connections between different payment and settlement systems, contemplating interventions that could allow management of possible simultaneous disruptions.

37 Furthermore, it must be noted that the concept of the business day has different dimensions according to the country in which the payment and settlement systems used by the bank are located. For example, for an international bank operating mainly in Asia, Europe and America, it seems important to monitor the intraday liquidity position on an ongoing basis, considering the different time zones.

38 The presence of insurance companies within the group necessarily requires a change in the scenario, as the assumptions of the new international regulation are focused on the banking business model.

THE NEW FRAMEWORK FOR LIQUIDITY RISK

39 It must be noted, moreover, that the choice of securities to be included within the liquid reserves implicitly involves those components that, given the assumed tense situation, should present a limited decrease of value and as a consequence minimise the unsteadiness of funds that can be possibly obtained to cover expected outflows.

40 It can be considered, for example, a crisis scenario determining a downgrading of a corporate or covered bond below the AA– rating.

41 Consider, for instance, the market-value reduction of a Spanish government bond during the sovereign debt crisis.

42 In economics and contract theory, information asymmetry deals with the study of decisions in transactions where one party has more or better information than the other. This creates an imbalance of power in transactions that can sometimes cause the transactions to go awry. Examples of this problem are adverse selection and moral hazard. Most commonly, information asymmetries are studied in the context of principal-agent problems.

43 In fact, if a bank with some difficulties were forced to reveal its liquidity position there would be the risk of worsening the situation and, in the extreme case, of encouraging investor and depositor flight, thus achieving an objective exactly opposite to the one supposed by the new regulation (the so-called stigma effect).

44 Although the new liquidity regulation identifies the necessity of improving the comparability of liquidity situations at international level among the purposes of the introduction of the two standards, the national discretion provided for, if not clearly expressed, could determine disadvantages for the banks whose supervisory authorities chose more conservative solutions in endorsing the new regulations.

45 With regard to LCR, some banks could temporarily strengthen, in the imminence of the deadline, their liquidity buffer, giving the market a distorted view of their actual situation. This behaviour could potentially accentuate the yield-spread and yield-curve effects around reporting dates, especially in the case of inelastic supply of liquid assets. Periodic shocks that make banks alternate between compliance and non-compliance are likely to induce volatility in prices for liquid assets and yields on stable sources for bank funding.

46 The new rules, and in particular the net stable funding, encourage a reduction of the level of maturity mismatch transformation and a reduction of the ratio assets/deposits by virtue of the necessity to ensure more stable funding to the bank's management.

47 According to Paragraph 187 of BCBS 2010, "The standards and monitoring tools should be applied to all internationally active banks."

48 Either for the LCR and for the NSFR the minimum risk appetite level is already set by regulation, being equal to 100%.

49 Government bonds and high-quality corporate bonds are considered liquid by the rules. The rest of securities are considered not liquid.

50 In addition to that, banks that are subject to the global liquidity regulation are often also the key market makers; compliance may affect their capacity to trade as an intermediary.

51 In addition, according to the new regulation, there will be a tendency to prefer longer-term operations over short-term ones, though the reduced roll-off rates for short-term central bank lending operations should mitigate it.

52 Particular reference is made to the strengthening of liquid assets whose holding would determine an opportunity cost, to the subsequent reduction of assets, to the extension of funding maturities or to the increase in the stable part of the stable funding, all things that will determine a decrease in the margin of interest.

53 Moral hazard arises because a bank does not take the full consequences and responsibilities of its actions, and therefore has a tendency to act less carefully than it otherwise would, leaving the central bank to hold some responsibility for the consequences of those actions. For example, for profitability reasons, a bank could minimise the liquidity buffer, having in mind that, in case of trouble, the central bank will intervene without any doubt.

REFERENCES

Basel Committee on Banking Supervision, 2008a, "Principles for Sound Liquidity Risk Management and Supervision", September.

Basel Committee on Banking Supervision, 2008b, "Liquidity Risk: Management and Supervisory Challenges", February.

Basel Committee on Banking Supervision, 2009, "International framework for liquidity risk measurement, standards and monitoring – consultative document", December.

Basel Committee on Banking Supervision, 2010, "Basel III: International framework for liquidity risk measurement, standards and monitoring", December.

CEBS, 2008, "Second part of CEBS' Technical Advice to the European Commission on Liquidity Risk management", June.

CEBS, 2009a, "Disclosure guidelines: Lessons learnt from the financial crisis", October.

CEBS, 2009b, "Guidelines on Liquidity buffer", December.

European Central Bank, 2008, "EU Banks' Liquidity stress testing and Contingency Funding Plans", November.

European Commission, 2010, "Consultation regarding further possible changes to the Capital Requirements Directive", February.

Financial Services Authority, 2009, "The Turner review. A regulatory response to the global banking crisis", March.

Financial Stability Forum, 2008, "Actions to Enhance Market and Institutional Resilience", April.

9

The Discipline of Credit Rating Agencies

Luca Giordano, Valerio Novembre, Neomisio Susi
CONSOB

9.1 INTRODUCTION

Credit rating agencies (CRAs) play an important role in global securities and banking markets, as their credit ratings are used by investors, borrowers, issuers and governments as part of making informed investment and financing decisions. Credit institutions, investment firms, insurance undertakings, reinsurance undertakings, undertakings for collective investment in transferable securities (UCITS) and institutions for occupational retirement provision may use those credit ratings as the reference for the calculation of their capital requirements for solvency purposes or for calculating risks in their investment activity. However, their function had been increasingly questioned, especially with regard to the role credit ratings for structured finance had played in prompting the crisis. Many observers have argued that CRAs hold key responsibility for the crisis. In particular, they have been accused of oligopolistic behaviour, and of reacting slowly when downgrading to market trends. Also, their conflicts of interest and sometimes over-optimistic creditworthiness opinions have been increasingly questioned.[1]

The reaction to these failures has mainly been based on re-regulation and supervision. New rules regarding CRAs were introduced in 2009 within the EU. As a consequence, an important role of supervision and enforcement has been assigned to national competent authorities (designed by each member state). Subsequently, in an amended version of the regulation was approved in December 2010 and published at the end of May 2011, this has been assigned to the European Securities and Markets Authority (ESMA).[2] In the US, the existing system of recognition for CRAs has been strengthened by the introduction of *ex post* supervision and by making the requirements for recognition more stringent. Several efforts to reduce the regulatory reliance on credit ratings have also been put in place. New rules were slated to be in place by the end of 2011, with a Securities and Exchange Commission (SEC) rule due to finish public consultation in July of the same year.

This chapter aims to describe how the regulation of CRAs has been changing in the aftermath of the financial crisis. It is organised as follows. Section 9.2 analyses to what extent the credit rating market is affected by market and regulatory failures and how these failures can be tackled. Section 9.3 reviews the main re-regulatory initiatives both at the international and supranational levels, namely in the EU and in the US. Section 9.4 will look at the important issues for the EU rating agencies' regulation and supervision in the future. Section 9.5 concludes.

9.2 ECONOMIC ANALYSIS AND REGULATORY INTERVENTION
9.2.1 The credit rating industry: market or regulatory failures?

A key characteristic of the world credit rating market is its oligopolistic structure.[3] On the global scenario there are only three main players: Moody's (a widely held company specialising in rating activities), Standard & Poor's (owned by McGraw-Hill and a big provider of financial information services, of which credit activities are only a part) and Fitch Ratings (a merger of smaller agencies currently owned by Fimalac, a French holding operating in financial services). In the past, this number has never risen higher than five and Standard & Poor's and Moody's still hold alone around 80% (Hill 2004; *Economist* 2007) of the total market share, with their services being provided all around the world.[4] In addition to these three major firms, it is possible to identify almost 30 fairly small rating agencies (BIS 2000) that largely provide local services around the world. A new large rating agency owned by the Chinese government, named Dagong,[5] has started operating in the global market. However, at the time of writing, it has not been authorised to operate in some jurisdictions, namely in the US.

Many authors have questioned why the market is so concentrated, and proposed two possible explanations.[6] One stream of literature[7] argues that the presence of significant economies of scale, scope and standardisation in the process whereby ratings are produced may explain the small number of incumbents.[8] In particular, they claim that investors prefer to have a few standardised ratings (and raters, ie, rating agencies) to compare (White 2001, p. 11), so reputation is vital and firms need to cover the market extensively if they want to establish their name among investors. Indeed, the greater the number of issuers an agency is able to cover, the more useful the comparison is. According to this school of thought, the rating market is not able to hold many competitors, and thus is naturally oligopolistic.

A second scholarship[9] hypothesises that regulation has played a big role in shaping the structure of the market: while the recognition system[10] might have kept the market oligopolistic,[11] the US "two-ratings norm" (whereby bond issues are required to have at least two ratings) (Coffee 2006, p. 300) might have been crucial in empowering Standard & Poor's and Moody's as the two market leaders.[12] The underlying view is that ratings have virtually no information content (Partnoy 2001) (ie, they don't add any new creditworthiness information to that which is already incorporated by market prices) and agencies simply sell regulatory licences, ie, "the right to be in compliance with various rules and regulations" (Partnoy 2001, p. 80). In their opinion this is mainly because a significant number of investors are required by law to purchase only investment-grade instruments, while there is evidence that professional investors and issuers rely on grades only partially, both for quality (Kent Baker and Mansi 2002) and time-effectiveness (Ellis 1998; Hill 2004, p. 43) problems. In the particular case of structured finance, regulatory licences are said to be an even more compelling reason to explain the structure and functioning of the securitisation market, in that deals can be structured *ad hoc* by rating agencies to provide investors with the ratings they are looking for (see next section).

The regulatory licence thesis (as described above) has been challenged on several grounds, mainly referring to the evidence that, regardless of the presence and level of regulation, rating agencies have never been numerous;[13] most of the time issuers buy Moody's and S&P grades, despite the fact that Fitch has been empirically proven to be cheaper and more favourable (White 2001); and that several issuers ask for a rating even when they expect it to be under investment grade (Cantor and Packer 1997, pp. 1395–1417). Still, as

245

the 2007 financial crisis has clearly demonstrated, it is very difficult for rating agencies to ignore the regulatory effects of their decisions, especially when downgrading under investment grade and thereby changing the way financial firms treat the bond. On the other hand, it is not possible for the market to ignore the regulatory relevance of rating agencies' choices (ie, their ratings), therefore it has been argued that "the new information that the change in a rating brings to the financial markets might be only about the change in the regulatory status rather than any new information about the likelihood of default" (White 2001, p. 21).[14] But the picture is mixed and later studies have shown instead, that rating changes provide new and significant information to the markets.[15]

This problem aside, the economic literature has identified two other main market failures affecting the rating market. First, ratings are not provided in the desired quality and/or quantity because they show typical public good features,[16] ie, they are non-rival and non-excludable. Second, rating agencies are affected by conflicts of interest that are built into their institutional structure:[17] on one hand, there is an inevitable overlap between the actual credit assessment and the consulting activity on how to structure a bond issue;[18] on the other hand, rating agencies are often overcautious when bringing their grades down. This is because they recognise that their prophecies might easily prove self-fulfilling. Whether these failures naturally arise from the market's inherent features or they are at least in part a consequence of the regulatory framework remains contentious. In particular, the "issuer pays" rule[19] may be one key reason why ratings maintain typical public-good and conflicts-of-interest problems.[20] However, an "investor pays" rule would probably also prove inefficient in that it would easily give rise to strong free-riding problems (Coffee 2010; Sangiorgi, Sokobin and Spatt 2008).[21]

Consequently, while it is clearly evident that the credit rating market is affected by failures, it is not entirely understood whether these failures are intrinsic in the nature of the rating market (market failures) or represent a direct consequence of regulation itself (regulatory failures). What we can be sufficiently sure about is that regulation has had and still has an influence on the rating market. Thus market consequences should be carefully assessed before enacting new legislation.

9.2.2 Credit ratings' regulatory relevance

Credit ratings have a twofold regulatory importance for financial intermediaries: on the one hand, ratings are key for determining the amount of regulatory capital used under the Basel capital adequacy rules; on the other hand, in most jurisdictions they are relevant for asset-management purposes.

Regarding securities, regulation makes use of credit ratings for regulatory purposes mainly in the area of mutual funds. As for Europe, the Undertakings for Collective Investments in Transferable Securities IV Directive (UCITS IV Directive)[22] refers to external ratings as one of three possible parameters for the determination of the eligible assets that a mutual fund can hold.[23] As for the US, the investments of certain mutual funds are restricted on the basis of the credit ratings assigned to their purchased assets.[24] The US regulatory system provides for a pure "reserve system" (ie, the rating activity can be performed only by recognised rating agencies), with the Securities and Exchange Commission being assigned extensive regulatory powers and the possibility to use external ratings for regulatory purposes. As an example, the offer and listing process of a new financial instrument is much simpler when a grade issued by a recognised rating agency (ie, Nationally Recognised Statistical Rating Organisation – NRSRO) is available (Ferri and Laticignola 2009, p. 163). However, in the EU only ratings issued by registered rating agencies can be used for regulatory purposes,[25] which in turn are mainly set by the law and in the field of securities are essentially limited to the above-mentioned UCITS IV Directive.

As for the banking sector, the Basel standardised approach for credit risk relies extensively on credit ratings to assign risk weights to various exposures. Exposures are classified into a set of asset classes and a different risk weight is assigned to each one in light of its relative degree of risk. Risk weights are in turn determined according to external credit ratings: while in Basel I all corporate exposures were weighted at 100%, since the advent of Basel II weights have been widely differentiated according to firms' rating, with, at the extremes, a 20% weight assigned to AAA credits and 150% weight given to firms rated below B–.[26] Unrated firms maintain instead the same 100% risk weight as originally set under Basel I. Regarding interbank claims, the Basel I distinction between OECD and non-OECD banks was later cancelled and two possible external-rating-based approaches have been left at the discretion of national supervisors. Overall, the standardised approach yields capital charges that are more sensitive to credit risk than what used to be under Basel I rules and that strongly rely on rating agencies' judgement. Similarly, the treatment of securitisations in the internal-rating-based approaches is based on external ratings, where available (BCBS 2004, pp. 606–9).

Gearing banks' capital requirements to the external credit ratings of their borrowings was often supposed a safe choice that simply improved the risk-sensitivity of capital requirements in respect to Basel I. In reality, rating agencies (for these purposes also named external credit-assessment institutions, or ECAIs) have been given by regulators a key power in that they can indirectly determine (as explained above) the amount of capital, banks using the standardised approach, are asked to keep aside. Thus ECAIs have reinforced their quasi-regulatory role, which is not limited any more to the ability to sell "investment-grade" licences but allows them to influence the banking sector's capital-adequacy level. This new role has relevant implications also for the way responsibilities are assigned in case of banks' capital shortages, leading to boundaries between regulators and "quasi-regulators" becoming more blurred. The assignment of a "quasi-regulatory" role to rating agencies is particularly problematic in that credit ratings are the result of a subjective assessment in which the methodology, rating scale and evaluation factors might differ substantially. The differing credit evaluations of CRAs may in turn be able to bias[27] not only capital requirements but also the lending policies of banks and thus the efficiency of the overall process of credit allocation (Tabakis and Vinci 2002).

A cross-sector area in which credit ratings' regulatory relevance has proved particularly problematic is structured finance (Committee on the Global Financial System 2005; IOSCO 2008a). In a standard securitisation scheme, the special-purpose vehicle is financed through a complex issue of bonds with different seniority. Senior tranches are often provided with an AAA rating and many observers have argued that this happens because all parties' interests (namely, the originator's, the issuer's and institutional investors') converge to the same objective.[28] Actually, "good ratings ... attract lower capital requirements[29] and expand the range of products eligible for investments or credit protection" (BCBS 2009, p. 55). As a consequence of these interests' convergence in the past, the securitisation process has often made it possible to easily transform subprime bonds into supersafe ones (Hull 2010), something that should not be feasible even for the most sophisticated financial engineers. A more compelling explanation for these transformations is then the presence and abuse of the well-known conflicts of interest[30] between rating agencies and their clients (Benmelech and Dlugosz 2009; Bolton, Freixas and Shapiro 2009). In particular, there is evidence that issuers have used the same rating agencies' credit models to structure their bonds on a first place. This process of "reverse engineering" has further enhanced the inherent flaws of the credit models, leading to a systematic underestimation of the actual credit risk (Danielsson 2008).[31]

9.2.3 Regulatory options

Given that the credit market is affected by market and regulatory failures, there are two main possible solutions to overcome these problems.[32] A first one is strengthening the role of current rules through tighter public enforcement. A second one is reducing the regulatory relevance of ratings in favour of a more market-based system. Aside from these two options, leaving some space for wider possibilities of private enforcement may be of help, too. Actually, these three options (or two of them) could also work together: even if regulatory reliance on external ratings is reduced, public supervision could still strengthen the reliability and/or the signalling role of agencies' grades. Private enforcement would then provide further incentives for agencies to prevent potential conflicts of interest being exploited.

9.2.3.1 Public supervision

One method for reducing the negative consequences of rating agencies' market and regulatory failures is public supervision. This entails public authorities verifying the regularity of agencies' ratings. There are two main ways to do so:

- ❑ a qualitative input or process-oriented analysis (ie, looking at which information is used and with which methodology and procedures it is processed to verify whether ratings issued by CRAs are trustful); and

❏ a more quantitative output-oriented analysis (ie, looking at how effective a certain rating system and methodology has proved, for example by crossing rating time series with actual defaults by rated companies to understand whether they constitute an effective proxy for credit worthiness).

Reforms are mainly (but not only) following the first solution (see Section 9.3), which is easier to implement and has clear advantages in terms of flexibility and adaptability to single circumstances. However, monitoring qualitative process-oriented standards might be tricky on several grounds. First, in order to enact a process-oriented supervision, independent authorities have to look closely at CRAs' methods and procedures and to the information they are processing. This postulates that they are provided with clear-cut supervisory powers that allow them to carefully assess whether the internal process is compliant with standards. In their absence, mistakes can easily be made, with the risk of supervisors being blamed by exterior forces such as media outlets and politicians. Also, process-oriented supervision might bias the CRAs' incentives structure because, by (subjectively) judging their methodologies, supervisors in fact share with them the responsibility for possible mistakes.[33] Finally, when regulation is qualitative, developing material rules to be used in the supervisory process is definitely not easy[34]. Consequently, despite the fact that qualitative standards are more flexible by nature, quantitative standards are easier to monitor and ensure a more consistent supervisory assessment. A balanced system that takes advantage of some quantitative rules but is still able to verify the standards required by the law on more qualitative grounds would be ideal, but finding a good balance between the two is not easy.

If an input-based system (ie, the above-mentioned qualitative input or process-oriented analysis) is established, ensuring that supervision is internationally homogeneous by building up smoother cooperative arrangements becomes particularly relevant. Given the international dimension of the rating market, a supervisory regime can then be shaped in two main different ways:

1. a first option is coordination and cooperation at the international level, while national authorities are responsible for authorisation, supervision and sanctioning; and

2. a second option is to combine the establishment of a centralised agency (at least at continental level) that is solely responsible for the authorisation process, with partial reliance on state-level authorities and colleges of national supervisors for supervision and sanctioning purposes.

A model of coordination might work well for big international players but it cannot guarantee that the same standards are consistently applied by domestic authorities to small local players. Differently, if opting for the second option (ie, a centralised authorisation), consistency appears easier to achieve not only for international CRAs, but also for smaller local players.

From a more theoretical standpoint, the dichotomy between output-based and process-based regulation echoes the long-lasting debate between the advocates of "principle-based" and (detailed) "rule-based" regulation. While flexibility is associated with general rules ("principle-based"), certainty, consistency and predictability are generally believed to come together with more detailed rules ("rule-based"). So, when international regulatory regimes are linked with local supervision, objective rules seem the only way to guarantee consistency in implementation and thus avoid regulatory arbitrage. On the other hand, when qualitative and more principle-based rules are established, only a supervisory conglomeration (or strong coordination) might be able to ensure a shared approach to supervision.

9.2.3.2 Deregulatory option

A second possibility to make the market work better would be simply to reduce the relevance of credit ratings for regulation. This would force issuers to ask for rating services only when they believe in their own creditworthiness and, at the same time, investors would take ratings into account only if they constitute a real effective proxy for the probability of default. As mentioned, many academics endorse this thesis by arguing that rating agencies have become increasingly powerful after public authorities incorporated them into their substantive regulation.[35] Incorporating credit ratings into legislation does in fact generate regulatory licences that have a value (Partnoy 2001), and these are key in constituting "private authority" (Kerwer 2001) for credit agencies. What it is striking here is that even

CRAs seem to agree with this point. As argued by Moody's, "the widespread use of ratings in regulation threatens to undermine the quality of credit over time by increasing rating shopping, decreasing rating agency independence, and reducing incentives to innovate and improve the quality of ratings" (Moody's Investors Service 2004, p. 10). Within this framework, regulating rating agencies may alter CRAs' structure of incentives by reducing the degree of accountability in front of the market and exposing supervisors to political criticism. As White (2001) argues, "these suggestions do not mean that the credit rating firms should be prevented from playing a continuing role in helping issuers and investors pierce the fog of asymmetric information in financial markets. But that role should be determined by the market participants themselves, not by additional regulation that artificially increases demand and restricts supply. The latter is a recipe for shortages, rents, and distortions. This is not a welcome prospect."

9.2.3.3 A market solution

An additional solution that could work in tandem with the others to reduce the rating market's failures and foster innovation could be based on the introduction of a private liability system for agencies, such as that which is currently in force in the US for auditors (Enriques and Gargantini 2010, p. 492). Such an approach has never been accepted by the US jurisprudence, mainly on the basis of the freedom-of-speech principle,[36] and it has often been criticised as being an undue help to rating agencies (together with a system of strengthened direct regulation and supervision of CRAs, see Subsection 9.3.7). In any case, the Dodd–Frank Act of 2010 has extended the auditors' liability system to rating agencies[37] so it will soon be possible to assess whether a private liability system for ratings agencies is the right way forward. In particular, the costs arising from a stronger liability system will need to be monitored so as to verify whether, by imposing a further cost on CRAs, the new regulation has negative consequences on prices and market contestability.

9.3 AFTER THE FINANCIAL CRISIS: RE-REGULATING AND SUPERVISING RATING AGENCIES

9.3.1 From the crisis to the FSF report

As described in Section 9.2, one of the most important triggers of the 2007–8 turmoil was the precipitous decline of confidence in the ratings assigned to structured credit products. After assigning high ratings to subprime-related residential mortgage-backed securities (RMBSs) and collateralised debt obligations (CDOs) between 2004 and 2007, thus contributing to the phenomenal growth of subprime lending, since mid-2007 CRAs have announced an inordinate number of rapid multi-notch downgrades (ie, double or triple change in the rating scale evaluation) of these instruments. This has raised questions about the quality of credit ratings with regard to structured products.[38]

In October 2007, the G7 ministers and central bank governors asked the Financial Stability Forum (FSF) to undertake an analysis of the causes and weaknesses that had led to the financial crisis and to set out recommendations for increasing the resilience of markets and institutions in the future. On April 7, 2008, the FSF presented to the G7 finance ministers and central bank governors a report (FSF, 2008) that included a chapter titled "Change in the role and uses of credit ratings". It stated that "CRAs assigned high ratings to complex structured subprime debt based on inadequate historical data and in some cases to complex flawed models. As investors realised this, they lost confidence in ratings of securitised products more generally."

The report recognises that CRAs have undertaken a series of actions to draw lessons for their internal governance and operational practices to strengthen ratings quality, enhance the rating process, manage conflicts of interest and enhance the information they provide on rating methodologies and the meaning and limitations of ratings. However, the attention of regulators was also drawn to the need to do more.[39]

In particular, it set out recommendations relating to:

1. the quality of the rating process;
2. differentiated ratings and expanded information on structured products;
3. CRAs' assessment of underlying data quality; and
4. the uses of rating by investors and regulators.

9.3.1.1 *The quality of the rating process*

With regard to the quality of the rating process and the conflicts of interest in structured products, one issue that received attention is whether CRAs' poor ratings performance in structured products might reflect the existence of more intense conflicts of interest for these products. While the issuer-pays model – in which the entity issuing the debt pays for the rating – applies to all products rated by these CRAs, including corporate bonds, conflicts of interest may be more acute for structured-finance ratings, because structured products are designed to take advantage of different investors' risk preference and they are typically structured for each tranche[40] to achieve a particular credit rating.[41]

The severe underestimation by CRAs of the credit risks of instruments collateralised by subprime mortgages resulted in part from flaws in their rating methodologies. One issue is the limited set of historical data available for subprime lending activities, while another is the underestimation of the correlation in the defaults that would occur during a broad market downturn. Of particular interest is the fact that many CRAs did not publish verifiable and easily comparable historical performance data regarding their ratings, thus preventing competition by not allowing customers to assess the accuracy of the CRAs' past ratings.

9.3.1.2 *Differentiated ratings and expanded information on structured products*

As regards the policies of investment managers, CRAs are expected to differentiate ratings on structured finance from those on bonds, and expand the initial and ongoing information provided on the risk characteristics of structured products.

Many investors took CRAs' ratings opinion of structured credit products as a seal of approval and looked no further, but structured-finance ratings differ from traditional corporate debt ratings in that they are model-based and to a larger degree assumption-driven. This condition results from an "inverted" ratings process in which a structured credit product is fitted into a desired rating, often relies on non-public information about the underlying assets, and has the potential for significantly higher ratings volatility in certain circumstances. While structured products have more stable ratings than corporate bonds during times of overall economic and financial calm, they suffer from a higher risk of severe downgrade than corporate bonds during difficult conditions. When an economy-wide event occurs that influences the creditworthiness of many assets at once, correlated defaults in the asset pool eliminate much of the benefit of diversification.[42] Despite these differences, CRAs applied the same rating categories to both structured products and corporate bonds. Many investors did not understand or fully appreciate the differences in risk characteristics between those products. Clearly, additional information therefore needs to be provided on the different risk characteristics of structured products.

9.3.1.3 CRAs' assessment of underlying data quality

Another important area of intervention is the improvement of the quality of input data.[43] In achieving this goal CRAs are supposed to enhance their review of the quality of the data input and of the due diligence performed on underlying assets by originators, arrangers and issuers involved in structured products. To this end, CRAs are required to (i) adopt reasonable measures to ensure that the information they use is of sufficient quality to support a credible rating; (ii) establish an independent function to review the feasibility of providing a credit rating for new products materially different from those currently rated; (iii) refrain from rating a security in case the complexity or structure of a new type of structured product, or the lack of robust data about the underlying assets, raises serious questions as to whether they can determine a credit rating.

9.3.1.4 The uses of rating by investors and regulators

The last recommendation concerns the use of ratings by investors and regulators. In order to prevent "overreliance" risk (ie, the attitude to delegate any risk assessment only to the CRAs), investors' associations should consider developing standards of due diligence and credit analysis for investing in structured products. Ratings should not replace appropriate risk analysis and management on the part of investors. They should conduct risk analysis that is commensurate with the complexity of the structured product and the materiality of their holding, or refrain from such investments.[44] Authorities should check that the roles they have assigned to ratings in regulations and supervisory rules are consistent with the objectives of having investors make independent judgement of risks and perform their own due diligence, and that they do not induce uncritical reliance on credit ratings as a substitute for that independent evaluation.

9.3.2 The FSB principles

As a further step to tackle CRAs' criticalities, on October 27, 2010, the Financial Stability Board (FSB)[45] published "Principles for Reducing Reliance on Credit Rating Agency (CRA)" (FSB 2010). The new principles were drawn from the recognition that the use of CRA ratings in regulatory regimes for banks and other financial institutions had contributed significantly to mechanistic market reliance on ratings. This, in turn, is a cause of herding and cliff effects[46] from CRA ratings changes that can amplify procyclicality[47] and cause systemic disruption. More widely, the regulatory use of CRA ratings had contributed to an undesirable reduction in banks', institutional investors' and other market participants' own capacity for credit risk assessment and due diligence.

The goal of the FSB principles is consequently to reduce mechanistic reliance on ratings and to promote improvements in independent credit-risk assessment and due-diligence capacity. Banks, market participants and institutional investors should be expected to make their own credit assessment, and not rely solely or mechanistically on CRA ratings.[48] The design of regulations and other official actions should support this. Accordingly, authorities should assess references to CRA ratings in laws and regulations and, whenever possible, remove them or replace them by suitable alternative standards of creditworthiness.

The new principles (FSB 2010) aim to catalyse a significant change in existing practices. They cover the application of the aforementioned broad objectives in five areas:

1. prudential supervision of banks;
2. policies of investment managers and institutional investors;
3. central bank operations;
4. private-sector margin requirements; and
5. disclosure requirements for issuers of securities.

9.3.2.1 Prudential supervision of banks
Banks are required not to rely mechanistically on CRA ratings for assessing assets' creditworthiness. This implies that banks should

have the capability to conduct their own assessment of the creditworthiness of, as well as other risks relating to, the financial instruments they are exposed to and should convince supervisors that they possess that capability.[49] Larger, more sophisticated banks within each jurisdiction should be expected to assess the credit risk of everything they hold (either outright or as collateral), whether it is for investment or for trading purposes. Smaller, less sophisticated banks may not have the resources to conduct internal credit assessments for all their investments, but still should not mechanistically rely on CRA ratings and should publicly disclose their credit assessment approach.

9.3.2.2 Policies of investment managers and institutional investors

As regards policies of investment managers and institutional investors, the above principles contain explicit advice on the need for investment managers to conduct risk analysis commensurate with the complexity and other characteristics of the investment and the materiality of their exposure, or else refrain from such investments. They should publicly disclose information about their risk-management approach, including their credit-assessment processes. Where CRA ratings are used as input, investment managers should understand the basis on which the CRA opinion has been formed.

9.3.2.3 Central bank operations

Central banks are expected to reach their own credit judgements on the financial instruments they will accept in market operations, both as collateral and as outright purchases. Central bank policies should avoid mechanistic approaches that could lead to unnecessary abrupt and large changes in the eligibility of financial instruments and the level of haircuts that may exacerbate cliff effects.[50] Central banks should avoid mechanistic use of CRA ratings by making independent determinations of whether financial instruments should be eligible in its operations, or by reserving the right to apply risk-control measures such as additional haircuts to any individual financial instruments or classes of collateral based on an internal risk assessment.

9.3.2.4 Private-sector margin requirements

Market participants and central counterparties should not use changes in CRA ratings of counterparties or of collateral assets as automatic triggers for large, discrete collateral calls in private sector margin agreements on derivates and securities financing transactions.

9.3.2.5 Disclosure requirements for issuers of securities

Finally, regarding disclosure requirements for issuers of securities, these are required to disclose comprehensive, timely information that may enable investors to make their own independent investment judgements and credit risk assessments of those securities. In the case of publicly traded securities, this should be a public disclosure.[51]

The FSB also asked standard setters and regulators to consider the next steps that could be taken to translate the principles into more specific policy actions and reduce reliance on CRA ratings in laws and regulations. This implies the need to incentivise a transition to a system of reduced reliance over a reasonable timeframe extending into the medium term, while taking into account the need for market participants to build up their own risk-management capabilities to replace reliance on CRA ratings and the particular circumstances of different products, market participants and jurisdictions.

The FSB was expected to report to the G20 finance ministers and governors on the progresses made throughout 2011.

9.3.3 The role of the IOSCO and the Basel Committee

Throughout the 2008–2010 crisis, financial authorities performed a deep analysis on the implementation of effective regulatory policies aimed to promote financial stability. The FSB (and previously the FSF) has been one of the most important forums where this work has been done. Separately, other relevant work on the securities and banking sides has been performed by the International Organisation of Securities Commissions (IOSCO) and the Bank of International Settlements (BIS), respectively.

On the securities side, it was the IOSCO that took the initiative to undertake a critical review of the regulatory standard setting concerning the impact of credit ratings on financial stability. It was just when the crisis was starting that the IOSCO published (on May 28, 2008) the final report containing amendments to the "Code of Conduct Fundamentals for Credit Rating Agencies"[52] (IOSCO 2008b). The changes to the Code of Conduct were introduced after a public consultation process involving regulators, CRAs and financial market stakeholders. These changes were intended to address the issues that had arisen in relation to the activities of CRAs in the market for structured-finance products.

The following amendments were made to the Code of Conduct.

The main areas of interventions adopted, in order to protect the integrity of the ratings process, ensure that investors and issuers are treated fairly and safeguard confidential material information, focus on the following.

1. Quality and integrity of the rating process: CRAs are required to (a) prohibit CRA analysts from making proposals or recommendations regarding the design of structured-finance products that the CRA rates, (b) adopt reasonable measures so that the information they use is of sufficient quality to support a credible rating, (c) establish and implement a rigorous and formal review function responsible for periodically reviewing the methodologies and models and significant changes to the methodologies and models it uses, (d) ensure that adequate resources are allocated to monitoring and updating its ratings.

2. CRA independence and avoidance of conflicts of interest: CRAs are required to (a) disclose whether any issuer, originator, arranger, subscriber or other client and its affiliates make up more than 10% of the CRA's annual revenue, (b) establish policies and procedures for reviewing the past work of analysts that leave the employ of the CRA, (c) conduct formal and periodic reviews of remunerations policies and practices for CRA analysts to ensure these policies and practices do not compromise the objectives of the CRA's rating process, (d) define what it considers and does not consider to be an ancillary business.

3. CRA responsibilities to the investing public and issuers: CRAs are required to (a) publish verifiable, quantifiable historical information about the performance of their ratings opinions, (b) differentiate ratings of structured-finance products from other ratings, preferably through different rating symbols, (c) provide investors with sufficient information about their loss and cashflow analysis of structured-finance products so that an investor allowed to invest in the product can understand the basis for the CRA's rating, (d) disclose the principal

methodology or methodology version in use in determining a rating.

4. Disclosure of the code of conduct and communications with market participants: A CRA should publish in a prominent position on its home webpage links to its code of conduct, a description of the methodologies it uses and information about its historic performance data.

After the peak of the financial crisis had subsided in March 2009 "A review of implementation of the IOSCO code of conduct fundamentals for credit rating agencies" (IOSCO 2009) was published. It reviews the codes of conduct of various CRAs around the world to determine whether they have incorporated the IOSCO CRA Code. As a result, in May 2010 the Technical Committee (TC) of IOSCO published a paper titled "Regulatory implementation of the Statement of principles regarding the activities of credit rating agencies" (IOSCO, 2010).[53]

On the banking side, the Basel Committee has been the main actor of the re-regulatory process. Soon after the financial crisis started it prompted a redraft of the Basel II rules in favour of a more comprehensive and up-to-date agreement, which was then renamed Basel III Accord. With regard to CRAs, Paragraph 91 and 565(b) of the Basel II text have been amended as follows. First, it was clearly stated that, when determining whether an external credit-assessment institution (ECAI) meets the criteria for recognition, national supervisors should refer to the IOSCO Code of Conduct (IOSCO 2008b). Second, two of the six eligibility criteria (namely transparency and disclosure) were strengthened, providing for greater clarity on methodologies, assumptions, outputs (ie, transition matrixes), etc. Third, new operational criteria for the use of external credit assessment for securitisation purposes were put forward. In particular, enhanced disclosure duties apply to ECAIs whose loss and cashflow analyses (as well as the sensitivity of ratings to changes in the underlying ratings assumptions) should be publicly available (ie, not only to the parties to a transaction). Finally, given that different ECAIs assign different ratings when faced with similar situations (because credit ratings are a subjective assessment in which the methodology, the rating scale and the evaluation factors might differ substantially), banks are no longer allowed to cherry-pick the assessments provided by different ECAIs, but they need to use the chosen ECAIs and their rating consistently for each type of claim.

9.3.4 The European Commission's intervention

At the European level the initiative to carry out a legislative measure on CRAs was first taken in 2004 by the European Commission, which opened a dialogue with the Committee of European Securities Regulators (CESR) by requesting technical advice in shaping a new regulatory framework.

The CESR undertook several analyses on how to deal with CRAs in the new regulatory context. In particular, it assessed whether there was any market failure and whether there was a need for the introduction of some sort of recognition and/or regulation of rating agencies, as these were generally not regulated in Europe at that time.

Starting from 2004, many consultation papers or reports focused on these topics and promoted an ongoing debate about the need for regulatory intervention on CRAs' activity. In particular, the CESR issued on March 2005 a "Technical Advice" to the European Commission on possible measures concerning CRAs (CESR 2005): this Advice concluded that it did not seem appropriate, at that moment, to introduce a regulation on CRAs in the EU, especially because the IOSCO Code of Conduct had just been elaborated and the effects of its introduction had to be carefully considered and assessed. The Technical Advice also highlighted that, should self-regulation fail to deliver, there might be subsequently a need for statutory regulation. After this report, other documents essentially dealt with the issue to monitor the implementation of the IOSCO Code of Conduct by the CRAs and to analyse the possible need for regulatory intervention.

On September 11, 2007, the CESR presented the work that was under way to monitor the compliance of CRAs with the IOSCO "Code of Conduct Fundamentals for Credit Rating Agencies" (IOSCO 2008b), and updated the Commission on progress made on the in-depth study of rating of structured-finance products. This study follows findings by the CESR during its first review of the application of the Code by rating agencies under its voluntary framework. In addition, the CESR received a letter from the European Commission on May 7, 2007, asking for further analysis to be undertaken in relation to structured finance. Therefore, the CESR launched a Call for Evidence in the form of a questionnaire on June 22, 2007, the final date for the completion of which was September 10, 2007.

In October 2007 EU finance ministers agreed to a set of conclusions on the crisis (the "ECOFIN Roadmap", which was mentioned for the first time in Annex II of the ECOFIN Council's press release of October 2007), which included a proposal to assess the role played by CRAs and to address any relevant deficiencies. Specifically, the Commission was asked to examine possible conflicts of interest in the rating process, transparency of rating methods, time lags in rating reassessments, and regulatory processes. The EU Council of June 20 and October 16, 2008, called for a legislative proposal to strengthen the rules on CRAs and their supervision at EU level, considering it a priority to restore confidence and proper functioning of the financial sector.

In February 2008, the CESR published a consultation paper (CESR 2008a) on the role of CRAs in structured finance to seek market participants' views before the end of March 2008 on the main issues arising from the activity of the CRAs in the structured-finance market and, in particular, on their views on possible policy options. The CESR received 26 responses to its consultation before the closing date.

In July 2008 the European Commission published two consultation documents on CRAs, seeking views from all interested parties: the first document relates to the conditions for the authorisation, operation and supervision of CRAs (EC 2008a); the second proposes policy options in order to tackle what is felt to be an excessive reliance on ratings in EU legislation[54] (EC 2008b).

The consultation papers suggested the adoption of a set of rules introducing a number of substantive requirements that CRAs needed to respect for the authorisation and exercise of their rating activity in the EU. The main objective of the Commission proposal was to ensure that ratings were reliable and accurate pieces of information for investors. CRAs would be obliged to deal with conflicts of interest, have sound rating methodologies and increase the transparency of their rating activities.

The consultation document also proposed two options for an efficient EU oversight of CRAs. The first was based on a reinforced coordination role for the Committee of European Securities Regulators (CESR) and strong regulatory cooperation between national regulators. The second option combined the establishment of a European agency (either the CESR or a new agency) for the EU-wide registration of CRAs and the reliance on national regulators for the supervision of CRA activities.

As a result of the aforementioned efforts, in November 2008 the European Commission put forward a proposal for a regulation on credit rating agencies[55] (EC 2008c). This proposal was part of a package of proposals to deal with the financial crisis and adds to the Commission's proposals on Solvency II, Capital Requirements Directive, Deposit Guarantee Schemes and Accounting. The new rules were designed to ensure high-quality credit ratings that are not tainted by the conflicts of interest inherent in the ratings business.

The proposal drew from the verification – contained in CESR (2008b) – that self-regulation based on voluntary compliance with the IOSCO code (IOSCO 2008b) does not appear to offer an adequate reliable solution to the structural deficiencies of the business, laying down conditions for the issuance of credit ratings that are needed to restore market confidence and increase investor protection. It introduced a registration procedure for CRAs to enable European supervisors to control the activities of agencies whose ratings are used by credit institutions, investment firms, insurance, assurance and reinsurance undertakings, collective investment schemes and pension funds within the Community.

CRAs were expected to comply with rigorous rules in order to (i) make sure that they avoid conflict of interest in the rating process or at least manage them adequately, (ii) improve the quality of the methodologies used by them and the quality of ratings, (iii) increase transparency by setting disclosure obligations for CRAs, (iv) ensure an efficient registration and surveillance framework, avoiding "forum shopping" and regulatory arbitrage between EU jurisdictions. The proposal also included an effective surveillance regime whereby European regulators will supervise CRAs.

Some of the proposed rules were based on the standards set in the IOSCO code (IOSCO 2008b). The proposal gave those rules a legally binding character. Also, in those cases where the IOSCO standards were considered insufficient to restore market confidence and ensure investor protection, the Commission proposed stricter rules.

9.3.5 Regulating rating agencies in Europe

Following the public consultation and the proposal from the European Commission described above, in July 2009 the European Parliament and the European Council approved a proposed regulation on CRAs[56] (henceforth called "the Regulation" for the purposes of this chapter). The Regulation (European Parliament and the Council of the European Union 2009) has a major impact on the activity of CRAs, which issue opinions on creditworthiness of companies, governments and sophisticated financial structures. CRAs will be expected to comply with strict standards of integrity, quality and transparency and will be subject to ongoing supervision of public authorities. Consequently, users of credit ratings in the EU would be in a better position to decide if the opinions of a specific CRA are trustworthy and to what extent those opinions should impact their investment choices.

9.3.5.1 Registration process

The EU regulation introduced a legally binding registration and surveillance regime for CRAs issuing credit ratings mainly intended for use for regulatory purposes by credit institutions, investment firms, insurance, assurance and reinsurance undertakings, collective investment schemes and pension funds. The activity of CRAs whose ratings are intended to be used within the European Community will be subject to prior registration. The regulation lays down the conditions and the procedure for granting or withdrawing that registration.

The Regulation establishes a mechanism for CRAs to be registered with their "home" member states' (ie, the member states in which the CRA has its registered offices) competent authorities, and for their EU affiliates to be supervised through a "college of supervisors" (coordinated and moderated by the CESR) where decisions on registration must be taken unanimously.[57] The Regulation applies to CRAs that are legal persons established in the Community.[58] These competent authorities will have supervisory and investigatory powers, but may not interfere with the content of credit ratings.[59]

In certain circumstances registration must be withdrawn by the competent authority of the home member state. This may happen when the CRA expressly renounces its registration, has provided no credit ratings for the preceding six months, has made false statements in obtaining the registration, no longer meets the conditions under which it was registered, or has infringed the provisions of the regulations that deal with operating conditions.[60]

9.3.5.2 Disclosures

In order to enhance the transparency of the credit rating process and enable investors to make a more informed investment decision, the Regulation requires CRAs to make various disclosures to the public. CRAs must disclose any credit rating on a non-selective basis and in a timely manner (unless the credit ratings are distributed by subscription). Under the Regulation, registered CRAs must publish an annual transparency report detailing their legal structure and ownership, financial information and internal systems. Registered CRAs must also make full and public disclosure of matters relating to conflicts of interest (both actual and potential), policies relating to the publication of credit ratings, and any services ancillary to their core rating business, amongst other matters.

9.3.5.3 Independence

One of the aims behind the Regulation is to ensure that conflicts of interest are avoided or adequately managed in order to uphold the quality and objectivity of credit ratings.

The key independence requirements are as follows.

❏ Management: CRAs must have an administrative or supervisory board, responsible for ensuring the independence of the rating process. The board also needs to ensure that conflicts of interest are properly identified, managed and disclosed, and check the compliance of the CRA with the requirements of the Regulation. The senior management of a CRA is expected to be of good reputation and sufficiently skilled and experienced. There must be at least two independent non-executive members on the board, and their term of office must not be longer than five years. They can be dismissed only in cases of professional misconduct or underperformance. The remuneration of the independent members of the board cannot be linked to business performance of the CRA. Where a CRA rates structured-finance instruments, at least one of the independent members and one other member of the board should be an expert in securitisation and structured finance.

- Services provided: CRAs should limit their activity to credit ratings and related operations, excluding consultancy or advisory services.
- Monitor credit ratings: CRAs must have information of a sufficient quality (and from reliable sources) on which to base their ratings and an internal function must be created to review the quality of the ratings.
- Records: CRAs must keep records of all their activities for at least five years. If the registration is withdrawn, the records should be kept for an additional three years.

9.3.5.4 Enforcement

In order to ensure effective enforcement, the Regulation stipulates that member states should lay down penalties for infringement that are effective, proportionate and dissuasive, and must notify the provisions so enacted to the EU Commission.

The Regulation requires cooperation between the competent authorities of different member states. A mediation mechanism will be established by the CESR to resolve any disagreement between competent authorities. There are also provisions for an exchange of information with non-EU countries, provided that guarantees of professional secrecy are in place.

9.3.5.5 Endorsement

Specific and sufficiently exacting treatment is envisaged, and may be extended, on a case-by-case basis, to CRAs operating from non-EU jurisdictions provided that they comply with a series of requirements that make the supervision on those third countries' CRAs comparable with the level of supervision at the EU level. For recognising the ratings of instruments and entities given by CRAs outside the European Community, registered CRAs can endorse the ratings of entities or instruments given by their affiliates outside the European Community, provided that (among other things) (a) the registered CRA is able to demonstrate on an ongoing basis that the conduct of the third-country CRA operates under no less stringent requirements than those of the EU regulation; (b) there is an objective reason for the rating to be performed in the third country rather than within the European Community; and (c) there is an "appropriate" cooperation agreement in place between the national regulator of the registered CRA and the third country CRA's regulator.

9.3.6 Supervising rating agencies in Europe: the role of ESMA

As rating services are not linked to a particular territory and the ratings issued by a CRA can be used by financial institutions all around Europe, the Commission has proposed a more centralised system for supervision of CRAs at EU level. Heads of state and government called the Commission to come forward with proposals in June 2010.[61]

Following the announcement of the creation of the European Securities and Market Authority (ESMA), the CRA regulation was then revised in December 2010 and published in May 2011 (henceforth "the amended Regulation" for the purposes of this Chapter). The amended Regulation (European Parliament and the Council of the European Union 2011) – while not changing all the substantial requirements and measures of the Regulation approved in 2009 – gives to ESMA an exclusive responsibility for the registration, supervision and enforcement of credit rating agencies in the European Union. According to the amended Regulation, ESMA is also required to discharge important coordination and advisory functions alongside its traditional role of promoting convergence through Level 3 guidelines and recommendations.[62] Furthermore, the Regulation mandates ESMA to maintain a central repository where information on the past performances of CRAs and information about credit ratings issued in the past are to be kept and made public.

The creation of ESMA as an EU Authority as of January 1, 2011, through the ESMA regulation, has resulted in some relevant changes of the four-level (so-called "Lamfalussy") legislative procedure: at Level 1, directives and regulations continue to set out the high-level political objectives on the area concerned by the legislation. Occasionally, at this early stage, ESMA may be asked for technical advice by the Commission as it develops its legislative proposal. At Level 2, ESMA has been given a greater role in drafting what can be considered subordinate acts (known as delegated acts and implementing acts).[63] At Level 3 ESMA will develop guidelines and recommendations with a view to establishing consistent, efficient and effective supervisory practices within the European System of Financial Supervision, and to ensure the common, uniform and consistent application of Union Law. Finally, at the request of a national competent authority, the European Parliament, Council, Commission or the Stakeholder Group, ESMA can be requested at

Level 4 to launch an enquiry into the enforcement of some aspects of the Regulation, and can issue a recommendation addressed to the national authority, within two months of launching its investigation. ESMA will also be able to launch investigations on its own initiative.

With regard to supervision on CRAs, ESMA has been given powers to request information, to launch investigations and to perform onsite inspections. These changes mean that CRAs would operate in a much simpler supervisory environment than the existing national environments and would have easier access to the information they needed. Users of ratings would also be better protected as a result of centralised EU supervision of all CRAs and increased competition among CRAs.

The amended Regulation, published on May 31, 2011, came into force the day after that of its publication in the *Official Journal of the European Union* (European Parliament and the Council of the European Union, 2011). The transfer of powers from national competent authorities to ESMA was due to take place from July 1, 2011.

9.3.7 Work in progress: the European Commission Consultation Paper and the US initiatives

9.3.7.1 The European Commission Consultation Paper

During the sovereign debt crisis in the European Union at the beginning of 2010, CRAs were again criticised for the way they issued ratings for sovereign debt. Consequently, it was questioned whether the EU regulatory framework for CRAs needed to be further strengthened in order to ensure higher transparency and enhance the quality of sovereign debt ratings.

Actually, the Regulation required (Art. 39, Para. 1) that the European Commission make an assessment, by December 2012, "of the application of the regulation, including an assessment of the reliance on credit ratings in the Community, the impact on the level of concentration in the credit rating market, the cost and benefit of impacts of the regulation and of the appropriateness of the remuneration of the credit rating agency by the rated entity (issuer-pays model)", and submit a report to the European Parliament and the Council on these issues.

With regard to these aspects, the European Commission issued on June 2, 2010, a Communication ("Regulating Financial Services for Sustainable Growth") announcing that it would examine the above-mentioned issues, in order to assess whether further regulatory measures are needed. In parallel, other international organisations (ie, the International Monetary Fund – IMF - and the FSB) have dealt with these issues.[64]

Consequently, on November 5, 2010, the European Commission issued a Consultation Paper (CP) (European Commission 2010), dealing with the above matters to gather the views of market participants, regulators and other stakeholders on possible future initiatives to strengthen the EU regulatory framework for credit rating agencies. Issues raised in this public consultation are the following.

1. *Measures to reduce overreliance on external credit ratings and increase disclosure by issuers of structured-finance instruments*: It is highlighted that this sovereign debt crisis in the European Union, as well as other crises such as that which occurred with regard to structured-finance instruments in 2007 and 2008,[65] has raised the concern that financial institutions and institutional investors may be relying too much on external ratings and do not carry out sufficient internal credit risk assessments.

    The proposed solutions aimed at alleviating this overreliance are essentially twofold: first, references to ratings in the regulation should be reconsidered in light of the risk that these ratings are implicitly regarded as "publicly endorsed" and of their potential to influence behaviour in an undesirable way, for instance by producing sudden increases of capital requirements following some rating downgrades. Second, financial firms should be requested or incentivised to undertake their own due diligence and internal risk management rather than indiscriminately relying on external ratings.

    The areas that are considered in the aforementioned CP to reduce the overreliance on credit ratings are (i) the use of external ratings in regulatory capital frameworks for credit institutions, investment firms, insurance and reinsurance undertakings; (ii) the use of external ratings for internal risk management purposes; (iii) the use of external ratings in the mandates and investment policies of investment managers.

2. *Improvements to transparency, monitoring, methodology and process of sovereign debt ratings in EU*: The Regulation provides, as

described in Subsection 9.3.5, stringent rules that aim to increase the level of transparency of the rating process and the quality of credit ratings and their methodologies. These rules fully apply also to sovereign ratings. However, the sovereign ratings may have a particular importance for the economic systems of different countries – especially when some financial crises and/or concerns on the public debt occur, with regard to a specific country – and present some specificities. Therefore, the CP considers the possibility of providing specific measures for these kinds of ratings (similarly to what was introduced by the Regulation for structured-finance ratings), in order to increase the level of transparency and add some specific procedural requirements that CRAs have to comply with when rating sovereign debt.

In particular, those measures concern an enhanced disclosure of the rating reports, of the staff allocated to these kinds of ratings, and of the methodologies, models and key rating assumptions. Moreover, the CP provides (for sovereign ratings) for an "enlargement" (the time period for disclosure would be, according to the proposal, larger for sovereign ratings) compared with the general rule referred to all credit ratings,[66] of the time period, before the publication of a credit rating, to disclose its content to a rated entity. This previous disclosure would allow the rated entity to check and to draw the attention of the CRA to any factual errors and new developments that may influence the rating. Therefore, whereas the general rule for all kinds of ratings provides a period of 12 hours before the publication, the CP proposed that this period be longer for sovereign ratings. Finally, some measures referring to the timing of the disclosure of a sovereign rating to the market will also be designed.

3. *Measures to enhance competition in the CRA market*: The CP also provides some measures aimed at increasing the degree of competition in the rating market, which has historically been characterised by the presence of a few big players. These entities (Standard and Poor's, Moody's and FitchRatings) issue most of the corporates' and financial institutions' ratings, as well as the ratings of structured-finance products and the sovereign ratings. By reducing competition, the oligopolistic

structure of the ratings market may negatively impact on the quality of credit ratings and/or increase their cost.

The measures that should increase competition are concerned with the possibility of, and the incentive for, the European Central Bank, or national central banks, to issue ratings to be used for regulatory purposes; the introduction of incentives for member states in order to facilitate the entrance of new players at national level; the creation of a new EU-based CRA using either public or private funding or a combination of both; and the establishment of a European network of small and medium-sized CRAs, able to share best practices and resources in order to improve their expertise and the quality of their ratings. Moreover it should be considered that the new regulation itself can contribute to the increase in the level of competition within the rating market, as the need to fulfil the registration requirements provided by the regulation can help new market entrants to enhance public confidence in their capacity to issue quality credit ratings and consequently to overcome the reputational barrier to entry or to expand the scope of their ratings activities.

4. *Introducing a civil liability regime for CRAs*: Current regulation does not cover civil liability itself but states that any claim against CRAs in relation to any infringement of the provisions of the regulation should be made in accordance with the appropriate national law on civil liability. The CP provides for the possibility of considering the introduction of a civil liability regime in the CRA regulation, at EU level, in order to improve legal certainty for investors, prevent forum shopping and have a preventive disciplining effect on CRAs. This regime could ensure that, for example, CRAs are held liable if they intentionally or negligently infringe the provisions of the CRA regulation, leading to an incorrect rating on which investors have based an investment decision.

5. *New measures to reduce conflicts of interest due to the issuer-pays model and preventing rating shopping*: Finally, the CP provides possible measures designed to reduce the conflicts of interest that are inherent to the issuer-pays model (which is prevalent in the credit rating market), according to which the issuers solicit and pay for the ratings of their own debt instruments.

The possible measures that are considered in order to reach this goal are to stimulate the introduction, as a possible alternative to the issuer-pays model, of other models, such as the subscriber/investor-pays model, the payment-upon-results model, the trading-venues-pay model, the government-as-hiring-agent model and the public-utility model.[67]

9.3.7.2 The new US regulation on CRAs

On October 5, 2010, a new version of the Securities and Exchange Act was published, following the introduction of the Dodd–Frank Act provisions (US Senate and House of Representatives 2010). The Dodd–Frank Act provided new rules in several different areas of the financial market regulation, aimed at strengthening financial stability and the investors' protection.

These are mainly "self-executing" provisions, which are already part of the US law and do not require the SEC to add any additional rules. In addition, there are a number of provisions that make reference to the need for the SEC to "adopt rules"; these provisions will be fully implemented only once these rules have been adopted. In this regard, the SEC published its proposed rule changes for consultation in May 2011, in addition to any other amendments that may be made to the NRSRO requirements.

In particular, the Dodd–Frank Act also modified rules on CRAs in several areas.

❏ As for corporate governance, some new requirements have been introduced, the most important of which are (i) the provision to have independent members of the board, (ii) the requirement dealing with the effectiveness of the internal quality control system and (iii) the requirement that the compliance officer to be independent.

❏ Regarding the management of conflicts of interest, important new provisions have been introduced, mainly referring to (i) reinforcing requirements regarding the organisation of CRAs' business in relation to conflicts of interest, (ii) specific disclosure requirements in rating reports regarding conflicts of interest, (iii) specific requirements dealing with reporting illegal conduct to the compliance officer without negative consequences, (iv) new requirements introduced to review the work of analysts that leave

the employment within a CRA, (v) broadening the prohibition on rating analysts from being involved in negotiations of fees/payments.
❏ Some new organisational requirements have also been provided on procedures for risk assessment, internal control and the independence of the compliance officer.
❏ Further, new requirements have been introduced to ensure the quality of methodologies and regarding the constant monitoring of credit ratings in order to assess whether or not new information has an impact on the ratings themselves. In addition, the SEC is requested to issue new rules regarding the monitoring and disclosure of credit rating methodologies. A general obligation for the board of the CRA has also been instituted to establish, maintain and enforce policies and procedures for determining credit ratings, and to assess the effectiveness of the internal control system on these policies and procedures. With regard to the quality of ratings and analysis of the information used in assigning credit ratings, new requirements have been introduced providing an obligation for a CRA to publish information about the reliability, accuracy and quality of the data relied on in determining the rating.
❏ As for the disclosure of credit ratings, new requirements have been introduced with regard to the disclosure of unsolicited ratings, the explanation of key elements underlying a credit rating, the information about the sources that were specifically material in determining the ratings, the limitations and attributes of ratings and the disclosure relating to structured-finance instruments.
❏ Finally, the powers of the SEC in this area were strengthened by the enlargement of the perimeter of the persons against whom sanctions can be taken and the expansion of the kind of actions that can be implemented.

9.4 THE WAY FORWARD IN EUROPE

9.4.1 The effectiveness of supervisory controls: can they open the black box?

One of the most important aspects of the regulation on CRAs concerns the nature and depth of supervisory controls. These are particularly relevant in that, until the introduction of the Regulation 1060/2009, CRAs were not subject to any supervision other than supervisory inquiries related to possible market-abuse offences (which clearly refer also to CRAs).

Currently, European CRAs – both the international and the national entities, which have applied for registration since June 7, 2010 – are under an assessment process by colleges of national competent authorities (or by the home competent authority in case of a national CRA operating in only one country), whereas the day-to-day supervision on compliance with the Regulation will start in a subsequent phase, ie, after granting the registration.

Therefore, the characteristics and depth of the supervisory controls will be concretely tested in this subsequent phase and will be carried out essentially by ESMA, which according to the amended Regulation, approved in December 2010 (European Parliament and the Council of the European Union 2011) has been entrusted since July 2011 with powers and responsibilities to issue enforcement measures and penalties, to adopt supervisory actions and also to take the responsibility in the registration process.[68]

With regard to the nature of supervisory controls to be implemented, the amended Regulation provides ESMA (or national competent authorities until July 1, 2011, according to the Regulation currently in place) with a broad range of supervisory powers. These powers enable them to (i) access any document in any form and to receive or take a copy thereof; (ii) demand information from any person and if necessary to summon and question a person with a view to obtaining information; (iii) carry out onsite inspections with or without announcement; (iv) request records of telephone and data traffic. Competent authorities also assess CRAs' compliance by considering all the documents and information that are provided within the application process for registration, and CRAs should also notify competent authorities, without delay, of any material changes to the conditions for initial registration.

The scope and the "philosophy" of the supervisory controls and assessments provided by the Regulation are mainly based on the monitoring of the procedures and the organisational aspects of CRAs. When applying for registration, and also during the day-to-day supervision, CRAs should comply with requirements and measures regarding the procedures that they need to have in place to issue ratings, to identify, eliminate, manage and disclose conflicts of interest and on the corporate governance and control aspects (independent members of the board, compliance function, etc).

Therefore, the Regulation mainly refers to supervisory controls, which can be defined as "process-based" (see Section 9.2.3) because they are based on the assessment of the procedures and organisational requirements that a CRA has in place. Moreover, Art. 23, Para. 1, of the Regulation clearly states that "neither the competent authorities nor any other public authorities of a Member State shall interfere with the content of credit rating or methodologies", providing in this way a clear limit to the supervisory powers of the national competent authorities (and, later on, of ESMA).

However, CRAs should also comply with requirements and measures that are more "output-based" (see Section 9.2.3), such as those referred to the disclosure of credit ratings data and to some characteristics of the rating methodologies themselves.

There are essentially two aspects that represent a form of "output-based" supervision and can both be considered crucial when defining the effectiveness of the supervisory controls that will be in place for CRAs:

1. the kind of ratings data to request to the CRAs as periodical data; and
2. the supervision of credit rating methodologies, with particular regard to the activity of backtesting, based on historical data.

Concerning Point i above, the Regulation attributes to the competent authorities quite broad powers in terms of supervisory actions. These include the power to request data and information whose content and frequency are the most appropriate for the goals of supervision. With regard to Point ii above, the Regulation dictates (in Art. 8, Para. 3) that the rating methodologies used by CRAs should be "rigorous, systematic, continuous and subject to validation based on historical experience, including back-testing". Of course, this last provision needs to be coordinated, in the phase of ongoing supervision, with Art. 23, Para. 1, which stresses the non-interference of the supervisors with regard to the content of credit ratings or rating methodologies.

9.4.1.1 Ratings data

On August 30, 2010, the CESR issued a Guidance on the enforcement practices and activities to be conducted under Art. 21.3(a) of the Regulation (CESR 2010a). Among operational data to be provided by the CRAs, this Guidance also includes monthly ratings data (lists of new issues, rating transitions and reviews, withdrawals; number of issuers/transactions rated/monitored and broken down by type of credit rating). Because the responsibility of the supervision of the CRAs has been attributed to ESMA since July 1, 2011, the exact content and format of this monthly ratings data will be defined by the ESMA Technical Standards Committee within seven months of the entry into force of the amended Regulation.

This issue is quite contentious within ESMA members, as there is a need to choose between two possible policy options: (i) to ask for analytical monthly data concerning rating actions – which would allow competent authorities to have information on the main elements and the timing of each rating action adopted by the CRAs; (ii) to ask for more aggregated monthly data, which would allow us to identify the trends of the rating market, but not to collect data on rating actions to be used for supervisory purposes.

The reasons for supporting the request of periodical analytical data about rating actions is that ESMA needs to have a continuous flow of micro-data available in order to implement an effective and efficient supervision on CRAs. If, on the basis of this information, some criticalities are then identified, further information would still be requested by competent authorities from CRAs.

On the contrary, those supporting the alternative option highlight the fact that the burden for the CRAs to provide analytical information on a monthly basis could be excessive. Aggregated data would be sufficient to identify the trends of the ratings market (for example, a high number of downgrading from investment-grade ratings to ratings below this level) so that appropriate actions may be adopted. However, the lack of analytical data would make it necessary to ask for further information on single rating actions and to make requests to CRAs from the very first phase of supervision, thereby making the supervision itself less effective.

9.4.1.2 The supervision on credit rating methodologies

As previously discussed, one of the most important provisions of the regulation of CRAs is that competent authorities must not interfere with the content of credit rating or methodologies. In fact, limiting the ability of CRAs to determine their own methodologies or models would signal to the market that competent authorities, by the registration process and the subsequent supervision, are in some way endorsing the methodologies elaborated by the CRAs, and this would produce very negative effects in terms of investors' overreliance on credit ratings.

However, as mentioned above, Art. 8, Para. 3, of the Regulation also provides that the rating methodologies used by CRAs should be "rigorous, systematic, continuous and subject to validation based on historical experience, including back-testing". To deal with these issues, the CESR published on August 30, 2010, the "Guidance on common standards for assessment of compliance of credit rating methodologies with the requirements set out in Article 8.3" (CESR 2010b). On the same subject, ESMA were due to issue (according to Art. 21, Para. 3, of the amended Regulation – see Para. 3.6) regulatory technical standards seven months after the entry into force of the amended Regulation itself. These technical standards will represent the implementing measures of some provisions of the amended Regulation; their content is binding and they may use, if appropriate, the content of the previous CESR Guidance.

The approach followed by the CESR in its Guidance is to provide a detailed description of written policies and procedures that the CRAs should implement concerning the different aspects of their methodologies. Competent authorities (see Subsection 9.3.5.1) will assess – during the application process for registration and, later on, by their supervisory activity – whether these policies and procedures are complete, exhaustive and consistent. If they verify that some elements are missing or incomplete, they may request that the CRAs integrate the methodologies or make them more consistent in order to better comply with the regulation. Moreover, by the activity of backtesting, the competent authorities will assess the reliability of credit rating methodologies on the basis of historical data (thereby also performing an "output-based" supervision).

However, this assessment by the competent authorities must not interfere with the content of the methodologies, ie, supervisors will not express any judgement or evaluation on the quality or appropriateness of the methodologies and models adopted by the CRAs. These aspects would be left to the autonomous decisions of the CRAs.

9.4.2 National and supranational powers: which equilibrium?

As described above, the amended Regulation approved in December 2010 transfers to ESMA the powers and responsibilities that were previously attributed to the national competent authorities – also organised in Colleges (see Subsection 9.3.5.1.) – for international CRAs having more than one registered office in Europe.

This means that, according to the amended Regulation, since July 1, 2011 ESMA will have the exclusive power to issue supervisory measures and penalties and to adopt all the supervisory actions provided for by the regulation, including adopting decisions on registration. However, a transitional measure (Art. 40a, Para. 1, of the amended Regulation) provided that, for the CRAs that applied between June 7, 2010, and September 7, 2010 (ie, those CRAs that, according to the Regulation are considered as "existing credit rating agencies"[69]), the registration process will be completed by the current Colleges of competent authorities. These will therefore take the decision on whether to grant the registration.

Moreover, the amended Regulation provides for various areas of cooperation between ESMA and the national competent authorities.

First, with regard to onsite inspections, the amended Regulation envisages cooperation between ESMA and the national competent authority of the country where the inspection will be carried out. ESMA could delegate the national competent authority to conduct the inspection or part of it; additionally, the national competent authority can request ESMA to participate in the inspection. In any case, ESMA would maintain the final responsibility for the inspection and for any decision concerning it.

Second, a more general power of delegation of "specific tasks" of supervision by ESMA to national competent authorities is also foreseen. The determination of these specific tasks should be the object of previous consultations between ESMA and the relevant national competent authorities, with particular regard to (a) the scope of the tasks to be delegated; (b) the schedule for their implementation; (c) the reciprocal exchange of information between ESMA and the relevant competent authority. The use of this delegation of powers is particularly important because it would allow ESMA to use the expertise and knowledge of the national markets belonging to the competent authorities in order to identify more precisely and effectively the cases to which the supervisory activity should be addressed.

Finally, the amended Regulation also provides for cooperation mechanisms between ESMA and the national competent authorities based on the initiative of the latter. Competent authorities should signal to ESMA possible breaches of the regulation that they identify. If this breach is considered serious and persistent, in that it could have a significant impact on the investor protection or on the financial stability of a member state, the national competent authority may also request that ESMA suspend the use for regulatory purposes of ratings issued by the involved CRA.

In any case, the decision regarding whether or not to adopt single actions or supervisory measures remains under ESMA responsibility; if ESMA decides not to carry out an action that was signalled by a national competent authority, it should appropriately justify this decision and inform the relevant competent authority.

9.5 CONCLUSION

CRAs have been considered a key trigger for the financial crisis. Their overoptimistic opinions on creditworthiness (especially with regard to securitisations schemes) and their slow reactions, when downgrading, to market trends, have been increasingly questioned. These shortcomings have mainly been considered as a consequence of some well-known market failures (especially arising from conflicts of interests or oligopolistic behaviour). However, both credit ratings' regulatory relevance and investors' overreliance on credit ratings have also been put under scrutiny. Consequently, the solutions to the problems of CRAs are diverse to say the least.

At the international and supranational levels, the response to the market and regulatory failures of CRAs has been based on both re-regulation and supervision, in parallel with some efforts aimed at reducing regulatory reliance on credit ratings. Time will tell whether both the EU (the Regulation introduced in 2009 and its subsequent amendments) and US initiatives (the strengthening of the regulation and supervision on CRAs introduced by the Dodd–Frank Act) will be successful. As for Europe, where the supervision of CRAs is brand-new, two issues appear key for the future. First, supervisors will need to demonstrate that they can open the black box of the agencies' data and methodologies without interfering with their contents. Second, the envisaged cooperation and delegation of powers between ESMA and national supervisors will need to be carefully fine-tuned day by day to make this first area of consolidated European supervision completely efficient and effective.

Opinions expressed are exclusively the authors' and do not necessarily reflect those of CONSOB. Although the chapter is the result of a teamwork, Sections 9.1, 9.2 and 9.5 can be attributed to Valerio Novembre, Subsections 9.3.1, 9.3.2, 9.3.3, 9.3.4 and 9.3.5 to Luca Giordano and Sections and Subsections 9.3.6, 9.3.7 and 9.4 to Neomisio Susi.

1   See Section 9.2.
2   The amended regulation was published on the 31 May 2011 in the *Official Journal of the European Union* and came into force on the 1st June 2011.
3   A market is oligopolistic when each firm keeps a close eye on the decisions made by other firms in the industry (maintaining interdependence). Oligopolistic firms are reluctant to change prices, but instead try to attract customers using incentives other than prices and they are inclined to cooperate formally and legally (ie, through mergers) or informally and illegally (ie, through collusion) with their competitors.
4   There are so few ratings agencies partly because of network effects, insofar as investors want consistency of ratings across issuers.
5   See http://www.dagongcredit.com/dagongweb/english/index.php.
6   The argument that the market is oligopolistic and the two incumbents are able to exercise market power seems to be confirmed by the supranormal profits that rating agencies' balance sheets show, as well as by the almost proportional fee structure (while the costs to analyse small and big issuers do not necessarily differ too much) (White 2001).
7   See, for example, White (2001).
8   There are some aspects of the industry that suggest natural monopoly. Other than the structure of the CRAs' cost function it is worth mentioning the "regulatory licence", which represents a barrier to entry.
9   See, for example, Partnoy (2001).
10 See below at Section 9.2.2.
11 See, for instance, Cochran (2005).
12 Also, both fund managers and issuers' CEOs have a vested interest in keeping this system intact, as it reduces the responsibilities for the former and helps the latter in dealing with the market. See Hill (2004).
13 It should be noted that with more agencies we might see a race to the bottom as issuers seek the agency that will rate them most favourably.
14 Knowing that they are able to fulfil the future prospect of the rated issuer themselves, rating agencies face a conundrum between forbearing and providing issuers with incentives for moral hazard.
15 See for instance Jewell and Livingston (1999).
16 For non-technical readers, an explanation for most of the technical terms referred to in this chapter can be found in Varian (1992).

17 Conflicts of interest often arise because rating agencies are paid by the companies issuing the securities or in general whenever their business interest impairs the independence or accuracy of the credit rating activities.
18 This failure proves particularly problematic in the area of structured finance because the asymmetric information existing between the issuer and investors is higher and the boundaries between rating and consulting are more blurred.
19 Of course, if a CRA is paid by the same issuer of the debt it has to assess (ie, "issuer pays" rule), this latter might provide the CRA's executives with strong incentives to shade their forecast in a more favourable light (eg, by promising a further mandate for rating services). This is not likely to happen when it is up to the investors to pay for the service they benefit from (ie, "investor pays" rule).
20 To be sure, unsolicited ratings have been heavily criticised as well (Partnoy, 2006). For a more innovative proposal to reward rating agencies through the same bond issues they rate see Listokin e Talbleson (2010).
21 However, no relevant free-riding problems have been reported for Egan Jones, a relatively small agency based on the "investor pays" model, which has often proved more reliable than Moody's, Standard & Poor's and Fitch (Beaver, Shakespeare and Soliman 2006, pp. 303–34). As it was accepted for registration in the US as an NRSRO (nationally recognised statistical rating agency) only in 2008, it is still to be assessed whether the NRSRO status has reduced its grades' reliability. The answer to this research question would provide useful evidence on whether it is regulation or the pricing model that matters.
22 Art. 50.1 of Directive 2009/65/CE (see also Art. 6 of Directive 2007/16/CE).
23 Also, (non-binding) guidelines on a common definition of European money market funds (CESR 2010) ask that this kind of funds invest only in highly rated issues (ie, those that are assigned at least the second-highest notch).
24 SEC Rule 2a-7.
25 See Art. 4.1, Art. 2 and Art. 14 of regulation (EC) No. 1060/2009 of the European Parliament and of the Council on credit rating agencies.
26 The way risk weights are allocated is questioned by Resti and Sironi (2005), who argue that the risk–rating relationship might be steeper than the one approved by the Basel Committee and suggest some adjustments on this matter.
27 Different creditworthiness evaluations assigned by different agencies might allow banks to choose the most optimistic rating, thus obtaining a relief in terms of capital requirement.
28 See more below at Section 9.3.
29 As in BCBS (2004), Part II (4). However, "The Committee also is conducting a more fundamental review of the securitisation framework, including its reliance on external ratings" (BCBS 2010, p. 15).
30 In general, issuers can push for better ratings by leveraging on the possibility of changing rating provider and/or by promising other advisory fees. Structured issues often pose even more significant problems in two respects. "First, it is a business that has been earning supernormal profits, not only for the investment bank proposing the issues, but also (in a smaller way) for the CRAs. With fees generally higher in relation to marginal costs than is the case for a corporate rating, the incentive to over-rate to secure a fee is much greater. Secondly, whereas a company would normally want to be rated by all the major agencies – or at least two of them – structured issues are often rated by only one or two agencies." Consequently, "the proposers seek out the agency that will give the highest rating (or demand the least credit-enhancement to achieve the desired ratings); the other agencies are then not used. That indicates a *prima facie* case for bias" (Goodhart 2008, p. 13 onwards).
31 Issuers have used the creditworthiness of rating agencies' mathematical models to structure their bonds *ex ante*. This process can be seen as a "reverse engineering", as economists say, to mean that the same models as are supposed to assess securities' creditworthiness have been used to build-up the securities themselves.

32 As a caveat, it should be mentioned here that in pointing out possible regulatory solutions we are not addressing the issue of systemic effects arising from credit ratings' "chain reactions". "While it is perfectly rational for individuals, firms and institutional investors to be guided by a rating when making their investment decisions, these decisions can destabilize the financial markets at a systemic level if downgrades and rating triggers result in mass selling, write-downs, and additional capital requirements." However, credit ratings provide information on the credit quality of a specific company or financial product but they say nothing on systemic risk. Thus, the objective of regulating CRAs can only be to make ratings more reliable and mitigate conflicts of interest (Utzig 2010, p.5 onwards).

33 In such a system, CRAs maintain quite a comfortable position: on one side issuers are expressly required by regulators to use CRAs' services; on the other the same regulators act as certifier of CRAs' work.

34 "Should there be stronger public supervision of rating agencies, the public supervisors will have to develop their own material rules; and this is an extremely challenging task", in Kerwer (2001, p. 27).

35 See above at 9.2.2.

36 First Amendment to the United States Constitution.

37 SEC 933(a). Other rules such as 933(b)(1) also go in the same direction (Coffee 2010, p. 46).

38 A theoretical background supporting the existence of CRAs is based on the causality assumption, which states that financial markets will develop more strongly if, all things being equal, a country increases the number of rated companies. It relies on the hypothesis that the availability of more rated companies will improve the information available to intermediaries and investors. In turn, market failures depending on information asymmetries will be reduced and financial markets will be boosted by expanding both demand and supply.

39 Another problem to deal with was the limited price competition among agencies, despite the fact that the rating agencies share some of the problems of the analysts. The most obvious is conflicts of interest. Not only are the agencies beholden for their fees to companies whose securities they rate: they often sell the same clients a parcel of advisory services. Just as for audit firms, which did likewise until Sarbanes–Oxley (2002) prevented them, the temptation is to keep up ratings in return.

40 A tranche is one of a number of related securities offered as part of the same transaction.

41 To the extent that CRAs discuss with issuers during this structuring process the rating implications of particular structures, the potential for conflicts of interest becomes greater.

42 Given the uniformity of CDO structures and their highly leveraged nature, any mistakes embedded in the credit rating model have been compounded over the many CDOs structured by issuers using these models.

43 Input data is data on which CRAs' elaborate their evaluations, they include data concerning issuer characteristics and macroeconomic data.

44 While ratings play a useful role in limiting, monitoring and communicating the credit risks that investors and asset managers take, they clearly do not cover the full range of risks investors face.

45 The FSB has been established as the successor of the FSF to coordinate at the international level the work of national financial authorities and international standard-setting bodies, and to develop and promote the implementation of effective regulatory, supervisory and other financial sector policies in the interest of financial stability. It brings together national authorities responsible for financial stability in 24 countries and jurisdictions, international financial institutions, sector-specific international groupings of regulators and supervisors, and committees of central bank experts.

46 CRA rating changes may cause simultaneous and imitative reaction by investors.

47 An economic variable moves in the same direction as the others.

48 Firms should ensure that they have appropriate expertise and sufficient resources to manage

THE DISCIPLINE OF CREDIT RATING AGENCIES

the credit risk that they are exposed to. They may use CRA ratings as an input to their risk management, but should not mechanistically rely on CRA ratings. Firms should publicly disclose information about their credit-assessment approach and processes, including the extent to which they place any reliance on CRA ratings. Supervisors and regulators should closely check the adequacy of firms' own credit-assessment processes, including guarding against any upward biases in firms' internal ratings.

49 In order to provide market discipline, banks should publicly disclose information about their credit-assessment approach, and the proportion of their portfolio (or of particular asset classes) for which they have not conducted an internal credit assessment. Banks using the standardised Basel II approach currently have minimum capital requirements based on CRA credit ratings. As long as some banks continue to have capital requirements based on CRA ratings, supervisory processes should be put in place to check the understanding of the appropriate uses and limitations of CRA ratings by these banks' risk managers.

50 Haircut is a percentage that is subtracted from the par value (face value) of assets that are being used as collateral. Cliff effect refers to the risk that market participants tend to lose confidence in the solvency of financial instruments and regain it only after a very long and painful adjustment.

51 In some cases, investors have weaker access to issuer information than CRAs, thus adding to their reliance on CRA ratings. Improved disclosure by issuers to investors will facilitate the build-up of capabilities of banks, investment managers and institutional investors to conduct their own assessment of the creditworthiness of the financial products they invest in and thus enhance their ability to avoid mechanistic reliance on CRA ratings.

52 The IOSCO CRA Code, first drafted in 2004, was designed to protect investors and enhance market efficiency by improving the transparency by which CRAs decide on ratings.

53 The paper reviews CRA supervisory initiatives in the EU, Japan, Mexico and the US in order to evaluate whether, and if so how, these regulatory programmes implement the four principles set forth in the 2003 IOSCO paper "Statement of the Principles Regarding the Activities of Credit Rating Agencies".

54 The EC's press release stated that: "The documents published today aim at ensuring the highest professional standards for rating activities. They do not intend to interfere with rating methodologies or rating decisions which will remain the sole competence and responsibility of CRAs. The envisaged proposals also take account of existing standards and developments at international level. The US has had rules on CRAs since the mid-seventies and is at present also considering changes to its rules" (Brussels, July 31, 2008).

55 In the US, where most of the CRAs with significant EU activities have their parent companies, the regulation on CRAs was changed in June 2007. The US Credit Rating Agency Reform Act of 2006 entered into force on 27 June 2007, establishing a stronger legal framework for the registration of NRSROs (Nationally Recognised Statistical Rating Organisations). Given the global nature of rating business, it was important to level the playing field between the EU and the US by setting up a regulatory framework in the EU comparable to that applied in the US and based on the same principles.

56 The EU Regulation 1060/09 on CRAs entered into effect on December 7, 2009.

57 The college must comprise the competent authority of the home member state – this means the member state in which the credit rating agency has its registered office – and other competent authorities that decide to become a member of the college provided that (a) a branch that is a part of the credit rating agency or of one of the undertakings in the group of CRAs is established within its jurisdiction; or (b) the use for regulatory purposes of credit ratings issued by the credit rating agency or the group of CRAs concerned is widespread or has or is likely to have a significant impact within its jurisdiction.

58 Once registered, a CRA will be entered on an updated list in the *Official Journal of the European Union*.

59 The competent authority must be designed by each member state. The competent authority

283

must have all the supervisory and investigatory powers that are necessary for the exercise of its functions.
60 If a CRA is removed from the register, ratings made by it may still be used for regulatory purposes for three months if no other CRA has rated the same instrument or entity. The competent authority can extend this period in exceptional circumstances in the interests of financial stability.
61 The Commission had two main objectives: ensuring efficient and centralised supervision at European level, and increased transparency on the entities requesting the ratings so that all agencies have access to the same information. These changes would improve supervision, increase competition in the CRA market and improve investor protection.
62 Based on the recommendations of the Committee of "Wise Men" chaired by Baron Alexandre Lamfalussy, the four levels of the Lamfalussy framework were designed to speed up the legislative process. They are as follows: Level 1: framework legislation, voted on by the Council and Parliament; Level 2: implementing measures for the Level 1 legislation, led by the Commission; Level 3: supervisory committees facilitating the convergence of regulatory outcomes; Level 4: enforcement of all EU measures, led by the Commission.
63 The lawmakers can give the EU Commission the option to supplement or amend certain nonessential elements of the EU law or framework law by delegating authority. The Lisbon Treaty (2007) introduced delegated acts as a special category of law in addition to EU directives and regulations. For example, delegated acts may specify certain technical details or they may consist of a subsequent amendment to certain elements of a legislative act. The legislator can therefore concentrate on policy direction and objectives without entering into overly technical debates.
64 In particular, the IMF released a global financial stability report with a specific focus on sovereign debt ratings (International Monetary Fund 2010), whereas the FSB endorsed principles to reduce on financial institutions' reliance on CRA ratings FSB (see the press release of October 20, 2010, available at http://www.financialstabilityboard.org/press/pr_101 020.pdf).
65 The crisis, defined as the "subprime mortgage crisis" (as discussed in Subsection 9.3.1), burst at the end of 2006 and continued in 2007 and 2008. It originally involved the sector of the subprime mortgages and, subsequently, it expanded to other areas of the financial market and to other financial instruments.
66 According to Article 10 in conjunction with Annex I, Section D I.3, of the Regulation 1060/2009, a CRA must inform the rated entity at least 12 hours before publication of the credit rating and of the principal grounds on which the rating is based in order to give the entity an opportunity to draw the attention of the credit rating agency to any factual errors.
67 To have quite a detailed description of each of this possible model, see the Consultation Paper of the European Commission (November 2010). As mentioned above (see Section 9.2.1), each model is affected by its own failure.
68 This last responsibility refers only to CRAs having applied after September 7, 2010.
69 The concept of "existing credit rating agencies" is quite important because only these agencies, which have applied by September 7, 2010, can use their ratings within the EU also during the registration process (therefore, even if the CRA is not registered yet), whereas the CRAs that are not considered as "existing" can use their ratings within the EU only after they are registered.

REFERENCES

BCBS, 2004, "International convergence in capital measurement: new regulatory framework", Basel, June.

BCBS, 2009, "Strengthening the resilience of the banking sector", Basel, December.

BCBS, 2010, "Basel III: a global regulatory framework for more resilient banks and banking systems", Basel, December.

Beaver, W. H., C. Shakespeare and M. T. Soliman, 2006, "Differential properties in the ratings of certified versus non-certified bond-rating agencies", *Journal of Accounting and Economics* 42.

Benmelech, E., and J. Dlugosz, 2009, "The Credit Rating Crisis", NBER working paper.

BIS, 2000, "Credit ratings and complementary sources of credit quality information", Working Paper No. 3, August.

Bolton P., X. Freixas and J. Shapiro, 2009, "The Credit Ratings Game", NBER working paper.

Cantor, R., and F. Packer, 1997, "Differences of opinion in the credit rating industry", *Journal of Banking and Finance*, 21(10), pp. 1395–417.

CESR, 2005, "Technical Advice to the European Commission on possible measures concerning credit rating agencies", March.

CESR, 2008a, "The role of credit rating agencies in structured finance", February.

CESR, 2008b, "Second Report to the European Commission on the compliance of credit rating agencies with the IOSCO code", May.

CESR, 2010a, "Guidance on the enforcement practices and activities to be conducted under Article 21.3(a) of the Regulation", August, available at http://www.esma.europa.eu.

CESR, 2010b, "Guidance on common standards for assessment of compliance of credit rating methodologies with the requirements set out in Article 8.3", August, available at http://www.esma.europa.eu.

Coffee J. C. Jr, 2006, "Gatekeepers: the professions and corporate governance".

Coffee J. C. Jr, 2010, "Ratings Reform: The Good, The Bad, and The Ugly", working paper, available at http://www.ssrn.com.

Committee on the Global Financial System, 2005, "The role of ratings in structured finance: issues and implications", Basel.

Danielsson, J., 2008, "Blame the Models", *Journal of Financial Stability* 4(4), December 2008.

EC, 2008a, "Proposal for a regulatory framework for CRAs", July.

EC, 2008b, "Policy options to address the problem of excessive reliance on ratings", July.

EC, 2008c, "Proposal for a Regulation of the European Parliament and of the Council on Credit Rating Agencies", November.

EC, 2010a, "Communication from the Commission to the European Parliament, the Council, the European Economic and Social Committee and the European Central Bank, Regulating Financial Services for Sustainable Growth", June.

EC, 2010b, "Public Consultation on Credit Rating Agencies", November.

Economist, 2007, "Measuring the measurers", May 31.

Ellis, D. M., 1998, "Different sides of the same story: investors' and issuers' views of rating agencies", *Journal of Fixed Income* 35(7).

Enriques, L., and M. Gargantini, 2010, "Regolamentazione dei mercati finanziari, rating e regolamentazione del rating", *Analisi Giuridica dell'Economia*, December.

European Parliament and the Council of the European Union, 2009, "Regulation (EC) No. 1060/2009 of the European Parliament and of the Council of 16 September 2009 on credit rating agencies", November.

European Parliament and the Council of the European Union, 2011, "Regulation (EU) No 513/2011 of the European Parliament and of the Council of 11 May 2011 amending Regulation (EC) No 1060/2009 on Credit Rating Agencies", May.

Ferri, G., and P. Laticignola, *Le agenzie di rating*, Bologna: Il Mulino p. 163, 2009.

FSB, 2010, "Principles for Reducing Reliance on Credit Rating Agency (CRA)", October.

FSF, 2008, "Report of the Financial Stability Forum on Enhancing Market and Institutional Resilience", April.

Goodhart C. A. E., 2008, "How, if at all, should Credit Ratings Agencies (CRAs) be Regulated?", special paper, London Business of Economics, No 181.

Hill, C. A., 2004, "Regulating the Rating Agencies", *Washington University Law Quarterly* 82.

Hull J., 2010, "Credit Ratings and the Securitization of Subprime Mortgages", working paper, available at http://www.frbatlanta.org/documents/news/conferences/10fmc_hull.pdf.

International Monetary Fund, 2010, "World Economic and Financial Surveys Global Financial Stability Report".

IOSCO, 2008a, "The Role of Credit Rating Agencies in Structured Finance Markets", final report, May.

IOSCO, 2008b, "Code of Conduct Fundamentals for Credit Rating Agencies", May.

IOSCO, 2009, "A review of implementation of the IOSCO code of conduct fundamentals for credit rating agencies", March.

IOSCO, 2010, "Regulatory implementation of the Statement of principles regarding the activities of credit rating agencies", May.

Jewell, J., and M. Livingston, 1999, "A comparison of bond ratings from Moody's, S&P and Fitch", *Financial Markets, Institutions and Instruments*, 8(4), 1999.

Kent, Baker H., and S. A. Mansi, 2002, "Assessing credit rating agencies by bond issuers and investors", *Journal of Business, Finance and Accounting* 29.

Kerwer D., 2001, "Standardising as governance, the case of credit rating agencies", Max-Planck-Projektgruppe Recht der Gemeinschaftsgüter (working paper), Bonn, 2001.

Listokin, Y., and B. Talbleson, 2010, "If You Misrate, Then You Lose: Improving Credit Rating Accuracy Through Incentive Compensation", *Yale Journal on Regulation*.

Moody's Investors Service, 2004, "Response of Moody's Investors Service to the Committee of European Banking Supervisors' Consultation Paper on the recognition of External Credit Assessment Institutions", September.

Partnoy, F., 2001, "The Paradox of Credit Ratings", University of San Diego Law & Econ Research Paper No. 20.

Partnoy, F., 2006, "How and Why Credit Rating Agencies Are Not Like Other Gatekeepers", in Y. Fuchita and R. Litan (eds), *Financial Gatekeepers: Can They Protect Investors?* (Washington: Brookings Institution Press).

Resti, A., and A. Sironi, 2005, "The Basel Committee approach to risk – weights and external ratings: what do we learn from bond spreads?", Temi di discussione del Servizio Studi, Bank of Italy, Rome.

Sangiorgi, F., J. Sokobin and C. Spatt, 2008, "Credit-Rating Shopping, Selection and the Equilibrium Structure of Ratings", Carnegie Mellon working paper.

Tabakis and Vinci, 2002, "Analyzing and combining multiple credit assessments of financial institutions", Working Paper No. 123, European Central Bank, 2002.

US Senate and House of Representatives, 2010, "Dodd–Frank Wall Street Reform and Consumer Protection Act", January, available at http://www.sec.gov/about/laws-/wallstreetreform-cpa.pdf.

Utzig, S., 2010, "The financial crisis and the Regulation of Credit Rating Agencies: A European Banking Perspectives", ADBI Working Paper Series, January.

Varian H. R., 1992, Microeconomic Analysis, 3th edition, Norton.

White, L. J., 2001, "The Credit Rating Industry: An Industrial Organization Analysis", NYU Center for Law and Business Research Paper No. 01–001.

10

Systemically Important Banks

Daryl Collins, David Rule

UK Financial Services Authority

10.1 INTRODUCTION

During the 2007–2009 financial crisis, a number of systemically important financial institutions in different jurisdictions experienced significant distress or failure with several requiring unprecedented levels of government support. This chapter sets out the international policy response, as it has developed so far, towards systemically important banks (SIBs). Policy in this area is still being developed and the purpose of the chapter is to describe the current international debate. It does not set out the position of the UK Financial Services Authority.

A joint report by the International Monetary Fund (IMF), Bank for International Settlements (BIS), and Financial Stability Board (FSB) to the G20 finance ministers and governors in 2009 defined systemic risk as "a risk of disruption to financial services that is (i) caused by an impairment of all or parts of the financial system and (ii) has the potential to have serious negative consequences for the real economy" (IMF, BIS, FSB 2009). While this chapter focuses on the policy response to SIBs, it is worth noting that distress or failure of other types of financial institutions and infrastructures can also be a source of systemic risk, making them potentially "systemically important".

Central to the definition of systemic risk, and by extension a SIB, is the potential for the distress or failure of the bank to disrupt the provision of financial services, thereby generating significant "negative externalities", ie, economic or social costs to people beyond the shareholders, creditors and employees of the bank in question. Developing policies to specifically address these externalities represents an important departure from the historical focus of bank regulation, which has hitherto been targeted primarily towards mitigating risks that could lead to individual bank failure.

A SIB can generate negative externalities in a number of ways, including the following.

❏ If the SIB is large enough, its distress or failure has the potential to reduce the availability of financial services or the supply of credit to an economy directly, to such an extent that other banks could not quickly fill the void.
❏ The distress or failure of a SIB could cause a wider loss of confidence and fears of contagion, in turn leading to a wider tightening of bank funding.
❏ The failure of a SIB may disrupt financial markets if it provides critical services to other financial institutions that are not easily replaced, such as payments, settlement and custody.

Importantly, a SIB does not need to fail in order to generate negative externalities. Actions it may take in an attempt to recover its position in response to stress can also have wider disruptive effects. For example, a SIB may seek to rebuild its capital ratios rapidly by cutting back new lending on a scale that affects the supply of credit to the real economy. Or it may conduct a "fire sale" of its assets to an extent that depresses wider market prices, in turn weakening the balance sheets of other financial institutions holding similar assets.

The negative externalities associated with SIB distress or failure tends to be greater in times of economic weakness and financial fragility, which is of course when failures are more likely. In order to limit wider damage during the crisis, governments in a number of countries stepped in to support failing SIBs by investing public money and guaranteeing their liabilities.[1] This government guarantee for SIBs – whether explicit or implicit – creates moral hazard by encouraging SIBs to take greater risks due to the fact that shareholders and creditors benefit from the potential rewards, but also may have a limited exposure to any downside. It also introduces competitive distortions in banking markets.

Policies to address the risks associated with SIBs can be targeted towards:

❏ reducing the negative externalities associated with the distress or failure of SIBs directly by making it possible for them to fail without doing intolerable wider damage to the economy and financial system; and/or
❏ further reducing the probability of SIBs experiencing distress or failure in the first place by toughening existing bank regulatory and supervisory requirements for SIBs vis-à-vis non-SIBs.

At the time of writing, an internationally agreed policy response to these risks is still to be finalised. The FSB has outlined how it intends to work together with the Basel Committee on Banking Supervision (BCBS) to arrive at an agreed policy framework by the end of 2011 (FSB 2010a). There are a wide range of views internationally. In this context, we have attempted to focus this chapter on the most relevant issues and options.

Section 10.2 outlines factors to consider when seeking to identify systemically important banks, in particular size, interconnectedness, and substitutability. Section 10.3 outlines how non-SIB-specific policies will help to reduce SIB risk. Sections 10.4 and 10.5 outline a wide range of possible policy measures to reduce the impact and probability of SIB distress/failure. Section 10.6 summarises the characteristics a coherent policy framework would display.

10.2 IDENTIFICATION OF SYSTEMICALLY IMPORTANT BANKS

In order to implement a policy framework targeted at SIBs, policymakers need first to identify which banks are systemically important. This is not straightforward since the potential wider costs associated with a bank's failure or distresses are by their nature difficult to measure, dynamic and time-varying. Systemic risk can depend on the economic environment. For example, under weak economic conditions the failure of even a relatively unimportant financial institution could trigger a more general loss of confidence. In addition, assessments of the systemic risk posed by a particular bank will be conditioned by the financial infrastructure and crisis management arrangements that are in place at the time (IMF, BIS, FSB 2009).

Systemic risk can be defined at a number of different geographical levels. A bank can be systemic at a local, national, regional and global level depending on how far-reaching the negative externalities of its distress or failure would be. This in turn depends on the nature of both its assets and its liabilities. For example, the failure of a large domestic bank may still have a global impact if its liabilities are held by investors around the world.

Any approach to identifying SIBs is likely to employ a mix of quantitative indicators and supervisory judgement. This is especially so in light of the limitations of current data, for example, to measure interconnections between banks. Improved data would help refine the ability of regulators to identify SIBs and target policies appropriately. An FSB group has been formed to consider what data gaps need to be filled to conduct effective global financial stability analysis.

The joint report to the G20 (IMF, BIS, FSB 2009) identified three key criteria that are helpful in identifying the systemic importance of an institution: size, interconnectedness, and substitutability.

10.2.1 Size

A bank's distress or failure is more likely to damage an economy or a financial market if its loans comprise a large share of credit provided, its deposits a large proportion of the money supply or its trading and settlement activities a large part of the relevant overall markets. For example, if a failed bank's loans comprised a significant proportion of credit in an economy, the continuing supply of credit to that economy would be adversely affected as it is unlikely that other banks would have the capacity to quickly fill the void. The failure of a big bank is also more likely to reduce confidence in the financial system as a whole. Size is therefore a key measure of systemic importance.

Total balance sheet is the simplest proxy for size and both on-balance-sheet and off-balance-sheet exposures can be considered. But other measures are also relevant, such as market shares or positions in "league tables" in key retail and wholesale markets.

10.2.2 Interconnectedness

If a bank has strong interconnections with other financial institutions, its failure could lead to contagion to these other financial institutions and a significant disruption to the provision of financial services in aggregate. In extreme, large interbank liabilities could spark a chain of failures. But, short of that, market uncertainty about the scale of exposures to a failing bank can lead to a loss of confidence in other firms. Liabilities to the rest of the financial system are a proxy for the direct impact of failure on creditors, while claims on the rest of the financial system measure the potential impact through a reduction in the supply of credit to other firms.

10.2.3 Substitutability

Significant costs may arise if customers of a failed bank are suddenly denied access to a service that is critical for the operation of financial markets or the wider economy. Moving to an alternative provider may be difficult if switching is costly or time-consuming or if the bank is a dominant provider of the service: for example, some payments, settlement and clearing activities are close to being natural monopolies with strong economies of scale and scope. The ability of customers to substitute another provider for any critical services provided by a bank is therefore another important measure of systemic importance.

10.3 NON-SIB-SPECIFIC POLICIES WILL HELP TO REDUCE SIB RISK

The Basel III package of reforms, agreed in September 2010, should help to reduce the systemic risk posed by SIBs by reducing the likelihood of their stress or failure. Indeed some measures will have a larger relative impact on many SIBs: for example, the strengthening of capital requirements for counterparty credit exposures arising from banks' derivatives, repo, and securities financing transactions; the introduction of a leverage ratio; and higher capital requirements for the trading books of banks.[2]

These initiatives are primarily intended to address inadequacies in the allocation of capital to risk (the microprudential dimension), rather than tackle directly the potential for the distress or failure of SIBs to damage the wider economy (the macroprudential dimension). The latter will require further measures to limit the wider impact of SIB distress or failure directly and/or to reduce further the probability of SIB distress or failure to a degree that reflects the associated negative externalities.

10.4 POLICY MEASURES TO LIMIT THE IMPACT OF SIB DISTRESS/FAILURE ON THE WIDER ECONOMY

10.4.1 Removing impediments to an orderly resolution

The G20 leaders' stated ambition is that no firm should be too big or complicated to fail (G20 leaders 2010). Making orderly resolution a viable option for every firm would effectively address moral-hazard issues and aim to ensure minimal disruption to the wider provision of financial services following firm failure.[3] In order to achieve an orderly resolution, the relevant authorities in each of the jurisdictions in which a firm is active need appropriate powers and tools, adequate information and arrangements to work together coherently.

The FSB is working closely with the BCBS to outline a common set of features that resolution regimes in all jurisdictions should have (FSB 2010a; BCBS 2010a). These include:

- identification of a designated resolution authority;
- ensuring that this authority has a wide range of legal powers to ensure resolution options exist to prevent disruption to the financial system (for example, powers to establish a temporary bridge institution, or enable a sale, merger or acquisition of all or part of a firm's operations);
- ensuring the authority has the appropriate mandate and powers, for example, to replace management, suspend shareholder rights and transfer assets and liabilities as required;
- ensuring the authority can access appropriate sources of funding for an orderly resolution;
- ensuring the authority can act with the necessary speed and flexibility to restore public confidence while maintaining adequate safeguards for creditors etc; and
- a requirement that relevant financial institutions should have robust *ex ante* recovery and resolution plans (RRPs) that are reviewed regularly and stress-tested.

RRPs, sometimes referred to as "living wills", set out the bank's *ex ante* plans for recovering from a period of significant stress, in addition to the information authorities would need to resolve the bank should the stress be so severe that the bank cannot recover. In particular, such plans could include: how a bank would recover its liquidity and capital positions following a severe stress; how it would deal with the failure of its largest counterparties; an outline of the data necessary to assess resolution options and reassurance of how that could be made available to relevant resolution authorities within required timescales; an explanation of the relationships among the different entities of a group; and an outline of how the firm would make an orderly exit from the market and payment infrastructure systems to which they are connected (FSA 2009).

In order to make viable the orderly resolution of globally active SIBs, effective cross-border coordination mechanisms between national authorities are needed. Resolution authorities need the freedom to cooperate with equivalent bodies in other jurisdictions and to share information across borders. The FSB has outlined that relevant resolution authorities, supervisors and central banks should all put in place cooperation agreements for the management of crises affecting individual global SIBs. These agreements should define the roles and responsibilities of each authority; establish crisis-management groups to agree common objectives and processes and regularly review the firm's RRP; and set out the legal basis for information sharing under relevant national laws during normal times and in crisis.

10.4.2 Large exposures

As discussed above, the more interconnected a firm is to other financial institutions, the more easily distress or failure can spread. To help limit contagion and the impact a firm's failure could have on other financial institutions, restrictions could be placed on the maximum size of exposures that can exist between financial firms. Currently, there is no internationally agreed large-exposure regime. Despite differences, however, most regimes define a large exposure as an exposure of 10% or more of the institution's capital base with limits in the region of 15–25%. One option to limit the impact of SIB failure is therefore to consider specifying a stricter limit for SIBs. That would recognise not only the greater potential for harm in failure but also the bigger absolute size of large exposures for such banks.

10.4.3 Structural solutions

On one view, even with the best resolution procedures, some SIBs are too large and complex to fail without causing intolerable costs.

This view supports the case for restructuring SIBs to make them easier to resolve. That might involve breaking up banks to make them smaller. Or it might mean reorganising banking groups, for example, by putting critical functions into subsidiaries that are ring-fenced from the rest of the group, or aligning group structure with national boundaries so that group companies in each country can stand or fall alone. Structural solutions could involve legislating to separate bank types according to their business models (for example, separating commercial and investment banking as was the case in the United States from 1933 to 1999[4]). Another approach is to limit a bank's permission to undertake certain types of activity, such as proprietary trading or ownership of hedge funds; see Annex A.[5]

10.4.4 Bank levies

A further option is to use tax policy to try to incentivise SIBs to rebalance their activities. In 2010 the UK announced plans to levy a tax on the balance sheets of UK banks and building societies, and the UK operations of banks from abroad, if their total balance-sheet size (less a proportion of high-quality liquid assets) exceeded £20 billion. The levy is higher on wholesale funding with a maturity of less than one year – this is in order to encourage a shift towards more stable and longer-term funding. Germany and France have also announced plans for similar levies.

Both a bank levy and a capital surcharge make it more costly for banks to undertake the activities to which they are related. There are important differences, however. In particular, a capital surcharge increases a bank's loss-absorbing capacity and ability to withstand shocks, whereas a bank levy reduces them. A bank levy instead provides funding for government – to be used either for general expenditure or alternatively to finance specific initiatives such as a bank resolution fund.

10.5 POLICY MEASURES TO REDUCE THE PROBABILITY OF SIB DISTRESS/FAILURE

10.5.1 Capital surcharge/extra loss absorbency

Alongside policies to reduce the impact on the financial system and wider economy, international policy-makers are also committed to reducing the likelihood of SIB distress or failure by requiring them to have greater loss-absorbing capacity than other banks.

10.5.1.1 Common equity

Common equity is the difference between a firm's assets and liabilities. When a firm makes a loss it effectively reduces its common equity by the amount of the loss. Common equity by its nature therefore will always be able to absorb losses. Requiring SIBs to hold higher common equity than other banks will therefore provide them with greater loss absorbency.

Because negative externalities can arise when a SIB is in distress as well as when it fails, additional common equity should ideally be available to absorb losses prior to resolution while the bank remains a going concern. Setting a higher "buffer" of common equity for SIBs above the minimum regulatory capital requirement would give the bank more breathing space if it suffered losses (see Chapter 3), avoiding the necessity for abrupt deleveraging that has the potential to cause wider damage. The SIB could eat into its "buffer" without breaching regulatory minimum capital requirements, although it might incur restrictions on distributions to shareholders until the buffer was rebuilt.

10.5.1.2 Contingent convertible capital

"Early trigger". Other more innovative capital instruments may also be able to provide SIBs with greater loss-absorbency capacity. Contingent convertible capital instruments (Cocos) are instruments that would convert into common equity at some predefined trigger point (see Annex B). Once triggered, the loss-absorbency capacity of the relevant firm would increase (Huertas 2010).

To ensure its use as a loss absorber on a going-concern basis, the trigger would need to be set at a point when the firm is still clearly a going concern (an "early trigger"). The trigger could potentially be market-based (ie, when the share price reaches a certain level) or regulatory-based (when the capital ratio reaches a certain level or the regulatory authority determines it to be appropriate). One risk with a going-concern trigger point is that in seeking to avoid the trigger point in a time of stress a firm takes drastic management action (ie, distress-type actions), limiting its usefulness in avoiding the wider damage associated with such actions.

Another issue about this type of instrument is that the market for it is untested and it is not clear that sufficient demand would exist. It is also unclear what the market reaction would be if conversion of one of these instruments were triggered – would the extra loss absorbency increase confidence in the firm or the triggering of conversion undermine it?

"Late trigger". Alternatively, the trigger for conversion could be set at the point at which regulators determine that the bank is no longer viable (a "late trigger"). That would reduce the probability of a bank being wound up or needing public support. But the additional loss absorbency would not be available before the firm became severely distressed. One possible approach would therefore be a combination of:

❏ requiring additional common equity, available to absorb losses both in distress and at the point of failure; and
❏ making a further category of liabilities able to absorb additional losses in order to avoid the wider costs of failure, either contractually through a creditor-based recapitalisation (also known as a "bail-in") or as part of the statutory resolution process.

In August 2010 the BCBS published a proposal that all regulatory capital should either be common equity or be convertible to common equity at the point of non-viability (BCBS 2010b). This was agreed in January 2011 and from 1 January 2013 all classes of capital instruments should be capable of absorbing losses prior to insolvency.[7]

Creditor-based recapitalisation (or bail-in) refers to unsecured and uninsured claims converting into common equity in order to absorb losses and attempt a recovery of the firm or aid in its orderly resolution. Conversion triggers could be set out in the contractual terms of debt instruments, or resolution authorities could be granted the powers to impose this via statute, or both. In order effectively to recapitalise the firm and restore confidence, it is likely that there would need to be a significant amount of such claims capable of being converted to equity. The FSB and BCBS have committed to working further on the legal and operational aspects of both contractual and statutory bail-in mechanisms providing for debt-to-equity conversions, as outlined above, and/or the write-down of claims in resolution (FSB 2010a).

10.5.2 Liquidity surcharge

In some cases distress or failure is not caused by lack of capital or capacity to absorb losses, but by a lack of liquidity. In particular, in the case of a run on deposits or a significant drop in confidence, a firm may be unable to borrow on a scale or liquidate sufficient assets in time to pay its debts as they become due. In order to reduce the probability of this type of scenario causing a SIB to suffer distress or failure, a liquidity surcharge might be appropriate.

10.5.3 More intensive supervision

Increasing the intensity of supervision of SIBs can also help to reduce the probability that a SIB experiences distress or failure. The FSB has produced "SIFI Supervisory Intensity and Effectiveness Recommendations" covering the mandates, powers, and resourcing of national supervisors; techniques supervisors should employ; and recommended approaches to home/host information sharing and macroprudential surveillance (FSB 2010b). Implementing these recommendations in all jurisdictions will help ensure that regulatory policies relating to SIBs are supported by effective risk assessments and enforcement.

10.6 CONCLUSIONS

The FSB and BCBS plan to work further on the policy options outlined above over the course of 2011 and 2012. The overall package will need to be coherent and ideally should display a number of other desirable characteristics, including:

- being well targeted, relating to firms whose distress or failure has the greatest potential to cause systemic risk;
- being capable of application consistently across jurisdictions and being applied consistently in practice;
- creating incentives for firms to reduce the systemic impact of their distress or failure; and
- reducing the impact that the distress or failure of a SIB could have on the real economy.

This chapter has described the international work under way to address the risks to financial stability posed by the distress or failure of SIBs. It has outlined the policy options being considered both to reduce the potential impact of SIB distress or failure on the wider financial system and economy – from making orderly resolution a viable option to limiting the size of individual interconnections – and to further reduce the probability of a SIB experiencing distress or failure, for example, by requiring greater loss-absorbency capacity. Gaining international agreement to a comprehensive set of policies that meet all the characteristics detailed in this chapter will require significant cooperation and focused determination from the respective jurisdictions.

The opinions expressed are those of the authors and do not necessarily reflect those of the UK Financial Services Authority.

1 See also Chapter 1.
2 For the impact of the different measures, see Chapter 13.
3 See also Chapter 12.
4 This was due to the Banking Act of 1933, often referred to as the Glass–Steagall Act.
5 The United States has adopted an approach along these lines in the Dodd–Frank Act of 2010, a move underpinned by advice from the former United States Federal Reserve chairman Paul Volcker.
6 See Chapters 3 and 12.

REFERENCES

Basel Committee on Banking Supervision, 2010a, "Report and Recommendations of the Cross-border Bank Resolution Group".

Basel Committee on Banking Supervision, 2010b, "Proposal to Ensure the Loss Absorbency of Regulatory Capital at the Point of Non-Viability".

Financial Services Authority, 2009, "Turner Review Conference Discussion Paper: A regulatory response to the global banking crisis: systemically important banks and assessing the cumulative impact", FSA Discussion Paper 09/4.

Financial Stability Board, 2010a, "Reducing the moral hazard posed by systemically important financial institutions".

Financial Stability Board, 2010b, "Intensity and Effectiveness of SIFI Supervision: Recommendations for enhanced supervision".

G20 leaders, 2010, "The Seoul Summit Document".

Huertas T. F., 2010, "*Crisis: Cause, Containment and Cure*". Palgrave MacMillan.

International Monetary Fund, Bank for International Settlements and Financial Stability Board, 2009, "Guidance to Assess the Systemic Importance of Financial Institutions, Markets and Instruments: Initial Considerations".

11

Regulating Remuneration Schemes in Banking

Isabel Argimón, Gerard Arqué, Francesc Rodríguez

Bank of Spain

11.1 INTRODUCTION

In the wake of the current financial crisis, compensation schemes in financial firms have received heightened attention. The reason is that executive compensation packages have been regarded as one of the key drivers in the generation of the crisis, although a causal link has not been established. The discussion has not been limited to the role played by executive pay arrangements but it also covered remuneration practices applied to a broader group of employees, and especially to personnel undertaking activities that are regarded as involving risk taking. This chapter reviews the proposals that have been designed to reform remuneration practices in financial services.

Shareholders, regulators, and academics have been re-examining the decision-making process in financial firms and have proposed changes to reduce the risks inherent in the inadequate incentives of firms. This refers particularly to those related to compensation policies and structures[1] that have neither fostered commercial success over time nor discouraged short-run excesses in risk taking.

The arguments put forward to link the crisis with poor incentives for employees have been formulated in terms of there being too weak a relationship between compensation and the long-term performance of a firm, inadequate metrics to measure performance and risk, too little transparency with regard to remuneration schemes and policies in financial firms, excessive risk-taking due to the structure of option compensation and poor governance and management practices in the area of incentives. With this in mind, most measures proposed have aimed at aligning executives' incentives not only with those of the shareholders but also with those of other stakeholders, such as taxpayers, who, in most countries, have eventually financed the losses.

Up to the crisis, guidance in relation to remuneration practices was mostly embedded in different codes of good practice, which were usually targeted at firms traded in the stock market, regardless of their economic sector. Those codes traditionally set a series of principles for the good governance of such firms, including recommendations relative to the firm's compensation policy.

However, financial institutions present some features that make them different from firms in unregulated industries, such as the manufacturing sector, and that may explain why their governance may differ (Adams and Mehran 2003). For instance, the number and heterogeneity of stakeholders is greater in financial firms, as they do not include only investors but also depositors, regulators and, eventually, taxpayers. Thus, the question in the light of the crisis is whether these recommendations were adequate for financial institutions and in particular for banks. The relevance of risk considerations in the design and implementation of remuneration policies has been regarded as one of the specific features of the financial sector that up to the crisis had received too little attention.

In section 11.2 we present a brief overview of the theoretical framework that links remuneration to risk taking. Section 11.3 is devoted to discussing the arguments put forward to regulate compensation schemes in the banking sector, distinguishing between the regulation's objective as defined in terms of consumer protection, and the objective defined in terms of financial stability. Section 11.4 describes the different proposals that have been put forward by the international forums, national authorities and the industry for improving remuneration policies. We finish with some concluding remarks on implementation issues (section 11.5).

11.2 REMUNERATION AS AN INCENTIVE MECHANISM

The remuneration scheme that defines an employee's pay in many economic sectors is basically made of a base salary and bonus, which may materialise in cash or be equity-based, in the form of shares, share-linked instruments or stock options, or even include pension benefits. The bonus or variable component of compensation aims to align the interests and motivation of the employee with the firm's overall objectives. Deferral and retention of part of such compensation is a common practice, which results from the difficulty in forecasting future results and the uncertainty associated with risk measurement, especially in the financial sector. As for the payout processes, they may be rather complex, combining explicit *ex post* risk adjustments with implicit (market) adjustments to motivate employees to work harder and to have a positive contribution to the shareholders' wealth.

There is both a theoretical and empirical debate over what determines the level and structure of executive pay packages and what their effect is. The field is academically dominated by the contracting approach of agency theory as introduced by Jensen and Meckling (1976).

Agency theory explains that, if managers operate independently, they may take decisions that are detrimental to shareholders. Traditionally, economic theory states that managers' interests are better aligned with those of shareholders if a manager's compensation increases when shareholders gain and falls when shareholders lose. Therefore, under this approach, there is a need to increase pay performance sensitivity, through, for instance, the use of stock options that allow executives' compensation to be properly related to long-term performance.[2]

However, it has also been argued that undesired effects appear with option compensation, as this gives incentives to CEOs to take more risks than would have been optimal from a shareholder's point of view, or that could be detrimental to debtholders (John and Qian 2003). While stock-based compensation may favour decisions that enhance the long-term value of a firm, in the case of banking firms or high-leveraged institutions the effects on risk-taking need to be factored in, especially when financial stability is being considered.[3] An inadequate design of compensation with stock options may conflict with the interests of depositors or debt-holders, as well as with supervisors' objectives.

The fact that some traditional external governance mechanisms, such as the threat of hostile takeovers in the industry, are absent – or less common – in the case of banking firms, which are regulated, needs to be factored in when addressing the adequacy of the firm's incentive mechanisms. The disciplinary capacity of markets is thus more limited and supervision, in this case, may play a complementary role in the governance of banking firms.

Empirical research focusing on executive pay and its role in the banking crisis does not provide clear support for a specific line of action. For instance, the analysis carried out by Fahlenbrach and Stulz (2011) on a sample of 98 US banks provides some evidence that banks with chief executive officers (CEOs) whose incentives were better aligned with the interests of shareholders had higher returns during the crisis, but no evidence that they had better stock returns and better return on equity. They also show that bank CEOs did not reduce their holdings of shares in anticipation of the crisis or during the financial turmoil. Consequently, they suffered extremely large wealth losses in 2007–2009.[4]

11.3 RATIONALE FOR THE REGULATION OF COMPENSATION POLICIES AND PRACTICES

There is rather a large consensus that remuneration policies were at the root of the crisis that hit the markets in 2007 (see Chapter 1). The remaining questions are whether the shortcomings are likely to be removed by market participants themselves or if, rather, there is a need for public measures and which sort of intervention will produce the best outcomes.

The high losses experienced in the financial sector and, above all, the more-than-likely reduction in the number of institutions engaged in the "originate to distribute" business model, will certainly lead to the correction of some of the practices that contributed to excessive risk taking. Those related to remuneration policies are among them.

However, there are some doubts about the dimension of the corrections in compensation policies that could take place if only market forces are at play. The existence of shareholders with short-term interests, the current existing practice in labour markets that favour risk-taking strategies, and the cyclicality of risk-taking behaviour in financial firms are three of the reasons that may limit the size of the market-led adjustment. The moral hazard enhanced by the massive rescue programmes will certainly contribute to the limitation of changes voluntarily undertaken by financial firms. In fact, shareholders of a banking organisation in some cases may be willing to tolerate a degree of risk that is inconsistent with the organisation's safety and soundness, as shareholders are factoring in the existence of public safety nets such as deposit guarantee schemes,[5] or the possibility of a bail-out (see Chapters 10 and 12). Incentive compensation arrangements and related corporate governance practices that are adequate from the standpoint of shareholders do not necessarily have to be aligned with financial stability.

The dynamics of total real staff expenses per employee in the banking sector in Organisation for Economic Co-Operation and Development (OECD) countries between 2006 and 2009, as reported in Figure 11.1, seem to support the idea that the market reaction has been rather ambiguous.

The ratios show a systematically decreasing pattern from 2006 up to 2008 only in Germany and the Netherlands. On the other hand, the average cost per employee in 2008 is below the levels seen in 2006 in many countries, a fact that can be taken as an indicator of the adjustment that may have taken place in employees' remuneration. The increase in the ratio for the USA in 2009 may be an indicator of the temporary nature of the correction in some jurisdictions.

However, there is a need to distinguish between the level of executive compensation and the mechanisms for determining its amount and composition. We will argue that, from the point of view of a risk-based regulation, the second aspect is the more relevant one. However, it is clear that from the point of view of a

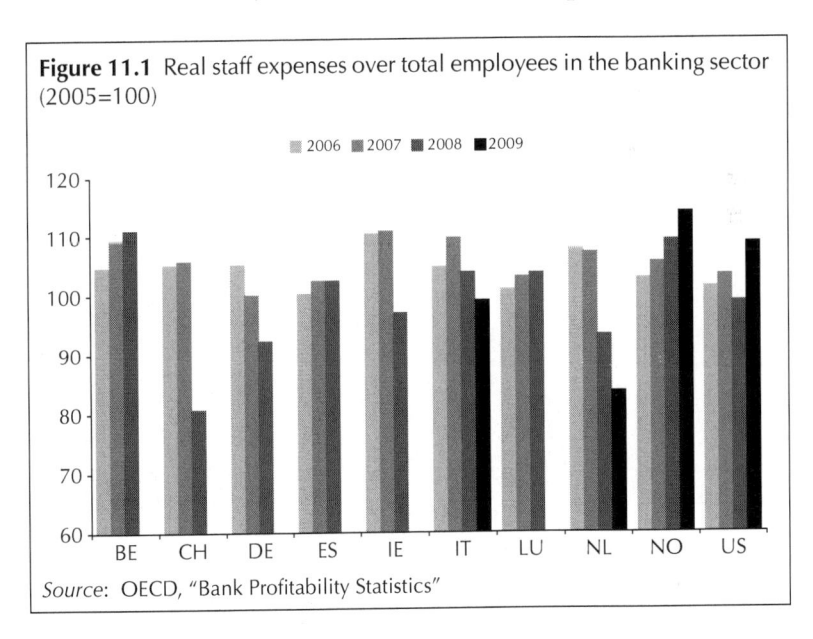

Figure 11.1 Real staff expenses over total employees in the banking sector (2005=100)

Source: OECD, "Bank Profitability Statistics"

consumer-protection regulation, the level and not simply the compensation structure may be important, if we consider the possibility of expropriation by managers. Moreover, it is also relevant to discuss whether the nature of the issue requires a regulatory approach or if it is a matter of supervisory activity only.

11.3.1 Consumer protection

The level of compensation in the financial sector may be considered excessive in relation to its own productivity or in comparison to the one received by workers in equivalent positions in other economic sectors. In fact, the average income received in the financial sector is larger than the average one received in other sectors such as manufacturing, renting or business activities, as recorded in Figure 11.2 with 2007 data regarding average housing income. In some countries the difference seems to be much higher than 50%.

The level may also be regarded as excessive by taxpayers if the firm paying such compensation has received public money as part of a rescue or assistance plan, without the variable remuneration of employees having been adjusted accordingly. The absolute amount received by some of the managers who have stepped down from firms that in turn have experienced major losses (and that may even

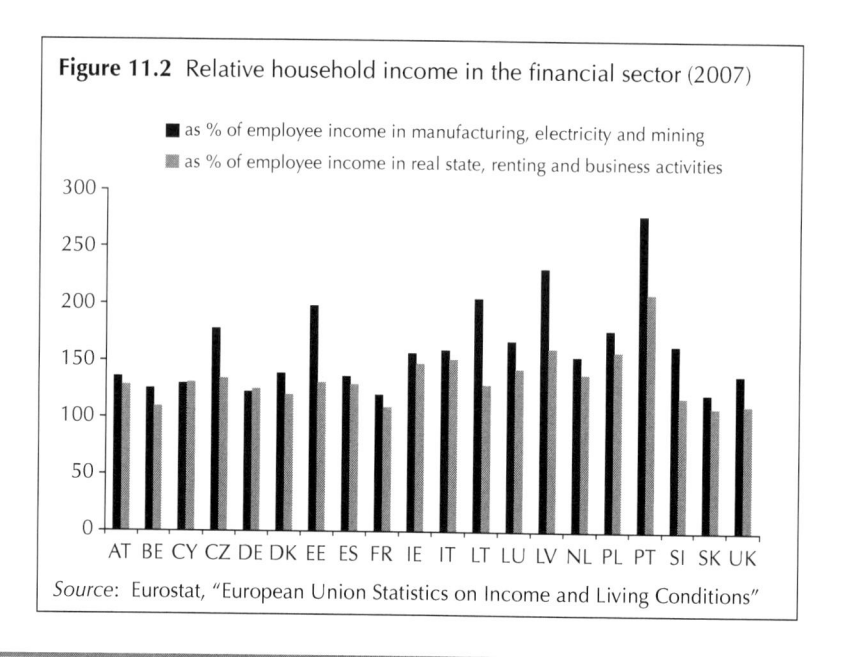

Figure 11.2 Relative household income in the financial sector (2007)

■ as % of employee income in manufacturing, electricity and mining
■ as % of employee income in real state, renting and business activities

Source: Eurostat, "European Union Statistics on Income and Living Conditions"

have received important resources from the public sector) has been regarded as unfair and may be explained only by contract agreements signed during better times.

There is neither evidence on talent gathering in the financial sector particularly nor data to support the view that objective factors such as average education or expertise may explain the level of the difference in pay between this sector and other economic sectors. However, neither the social unrest generated by such difference nor such difference itself justifies the intervention of a risk-based regulator aiming at financial stability, as it does not necessarily entail greater risk taking. In fact, compensation contracts are private agreements between the firm and the employees. Therefore, as far as all stakeholders are empowered with enhanced board oversight and there is transparency in relation to compensation policy, a high remuneration level on its own cannot justify public intervention on fiscal stability grounds.

However, from a consumer-protection perspective it could be argued that minority shareholders are not always properly represented in governance arrangements in these institutions; that the complexity of the sector ensures that monitoring is a professional task; and, most importantly, that top managers can influence their own pay for their own financial interest, thus effectively expropriating shareholders. Therefore, the important information asymmetry that characterises the functioning of these markets may be the main factor behind such high remuneration in the financial sector.

In general, the existence of conflicts of interest between several players of the financial system and the fact that such players have only partial information upon which they may take their decisions justifies regulatory intervention with the objective of protecting consumers and investors. The relatively poor knowledge that the owners may have about the functioning of the firm in addition to the complexity of the financial instruments could support the existence of generous remuneration structures. These may be, generally speaking, inadequate for the shareholders' interests. Therefore, corporate control mechanisms that limit such distortions would need to be established so as to protect small shareholders and depositors.

Excessive risk taking is also an issue in the face of consumer protection but we will properly deal with it when we address the issue of incentive structure in remuneration policies. However, we need to take into account the fact that rescue packages designed by governments have precisely been addressed to those institutions whose risk management has been poorest. Given that rescue plans have been financed not by the ailing sector that is benefiting from the stability provided by these plans, but by taxpayers' money, the issue of stakeholders' protection becomes relevant in this case.

11.3.2 Financial stability

Traditionally, the area of management compensation policies has been beyond the scope of solvency regulation. Codes of good governance, which define best practices in this area, were designed to protect consumers and investors in different countries. Although consumer protection may be included as a statutory objective of prudential regulators, financial stability or the containment of systemic risk, which are usually the main focus of such regulators, are not the primary objectives of these codes.

As a result of the 2007 financial crisis, concerns were raised in relation to the impact that remuneration policies may have on the risk assumed by financial firms. To the extent that compensation schemes are designed in such a way that employees who have the power and responsibility to take decisions enjoy the benefits that arise in boom times, but do not suffer the losses associated to the bad times, there is an encouragement of excessive risk taking. Such behaviour may put at risk not only the solvency of the institution that is incurring such risk but, because of the externalities it may generate, the overall system stability. For both reasons, there may be a case for prudential regulators to intervene.

It is not the fixed part but the design and functioning of the variable component of the compensation package that may generate such negative externalities, as it is the latter that may distort behaviour. If inadequate parameters to define the variable part are used, inadequate incentives will result in undesired effects on the behaviour of staff.

It seems that there is no direct association between the risk in the short term and the risk in the long term that a financial institution may assume and that, in general, the existing remuneration policies seem to favour short-term considerations. Such short-term focus may lead institutions to generate systemic risk, which, as the current economic crisis has illustrated, will show up only in the long term.

The short-term focus arises because there are shareholders with a short-term perspective who see their interests aligned with employees, the whose bonuses depend on the short-term performance of the firm. Such a short-term focus generates asymmetries, so that while, during good times, a large proportion of stakeholders win, during bad times, losses are borne mostly by long-term shareholders. Indeed, in some cases (for example, the economic crisis), such losses are also borne by taxpayers and in fact by the economy as a whole, when lending is reduced below welfare enhancing levels (ie, when there is a credit crunch).

The short-term focus and the fact that remuneration is not adjusted by risk leads to risk taking that can be regarded as excessive in the sense that it gives rise to negative externalities. Decisions taken as a result of the incentives created by existing compensation schemes do not incorporate the potentially negative consequences for the firm and for the rest of the economy. Such risk is not only improperly priced, but it is also inadequately managed. The shortcomings in such risk management are a source of regulatory concern.

The design of compensation policies that align the incentives inherent in the system of compensation for executive managers with the financial institution's risk appetite is not a trivial task. The fact that compensation is an effect and not only a cause of the risk appetite and of excessive risk taking of financial firms is central to understanding the difficulty in regulating this area.

In fact, the lack of alignment of the interests and motivation of the employees with the risk appetite of the financial institution has characterised many of the financial-sector compensation schemes, which can generate a regulatory risk. If the approach to risk is not centralised, its management cannot be so, either, rendering its effectiveness rather poor. This may also be a concern from a prudential perspective.

However, the main issue that needs to be taken into account when designing an effective mechanism to align these incentives with the risk appetite of financial firms is that the mechanism must establish measures that cannot be subject to the arbitrage of managers (ie, through the assignment of losses to a unit of the firm that does not compute for bonus) or of markets. A market that operates efficiently will allow for covering the risks that have been assumed. Therefore, there is a need to explicitly prevent such hedging strategies.

Increased transparency, which implies greater dissemination of information relating to even low-rank executive compensation systems, would provide the market with a discipline tool. However, market discipline does not seem enough in the face of such undesired spillover effects. The good-governance guidelines and best practices that are already in place in many countries and institutions have emphasised aspects of compensation systems that can only partially reduce these negative externalities. Therefore, it seems that there is a complementary role available for public intervention and, moreover, that it has to include some binding requirements.

11.4 THE REGULATORY REPAIRS

Very early in the development of the crisis, national financial authorities, international institutions, experts from the financial industry, the public sector and academics devoted resources to analysing industry practices in the area of remuneration and its effects on the accumulation of risk. Many different initiatives were put in place and different approaches were proposed to deal with the undesired effects of the incentives within the compensation arrangements.

11.4.1 International initiatives: Financial Stability Board

As early as April 2008, and as a response to the mandate made in October 2007 by the G7 ministers and Central Bank governors, the predecessor of the Financial Stability Board (FSB), the Financial Stability Forum (FSF), pointed to incentive distortions as one of the weaknesses that contributed to the turmoil (see Chapter 2). The FSF argued that a striking feature of the financial turmoil had been that large payouts to staff had been devoted to areas that had incurred high losses, as risks materialised. They concluded that compensation schemes "encouraged disproportionate risk-taking with insufficient regard to longer-term risks" (FSF 2008) and pointed to shortcomings in risk-management systems in relation to risk taking as a source of such undesired behaviour.

Among the recommendations they made to increase the efficiency and resilience of the financial system, they included recommendation II.19, which stated that "regulators and supervisors should work with market participants to mitigate the risks arising from remuneration policies". They pointed to the need for compensation models within financial firms to take into account the long-term and firm-wide perspective.

Following this recommendation, the FSF published, in April 2009, the "FSF Principles for Sound Compensation Practices" (FSF 2009), directed at significant financial institutions (see Box 11.1). The FSF stressed the need to distinguish these Principles from the short-term measures that national authorities could implement to affect compensation in the firms that had received government support. They regarded these Principles as reinforcing the effectiveness of other proposed reforms. The FSF argued that, to spread sound compensation practices, the contribution of supervisors and regulators was required, as competitive pressure would prevent adequate voluntary change in ongoing practices, stressing the need to ensure that coordination among supervisors and practitioners took place.

The FSF stated that the nine Principles were intended to apply to significant financial institutions and were regarded as especially critical for large, systemically important firms. However, they defined neither what a significant institution was nor what characterised systemic firms, leaving the definition to national authorities (see Chapter 10). On the other hand, they dealt with governance, alignment of risk and compensation, and effective oversight and engagement by stakeholders, also aiming at covering compensation of relevant staff in those firms.

The FSF argued that a sound compensation system had both to be risk-adjusted and to include sensitivity to risk outcomes. They considered that, on the one hand, risk measures were not perfect and some risks were hard to capture so that loopholes may exist, but on the other, a purely outcome-based system could encourage the taking of tail risks.

BOX 11.1 FSF PRINCIPLES FOR SOUND COMPENSATION PRACTICES

Effective Governance of Compensation:

1. The firm's Board of Directors must actively oversee the compensation system's design and operation.
2. The firm's Board of Directors must monitor and review the compensation system to ensure the system operates as intended.

↓

> 3. Staff engaged in financial and risk control must be independent, have appropriate authority, and be compensated in a manner that is independent of the business areas they oversee and commensurate with their key role in the firm.
>
> Effective Alignment of Compensation with Prudent Risk Taking:
>
> 4. Compensation must be adjusted for all types of risk.
> 5. Compensation outcomes must be symmetric with risk outcomes.
> 6. Compensation payout schedules must be sensitive to the time horizon of risk.
> 7. The mix of cash, equity and other forms of compensation must be consistent with risk alignment.
>
> Effective Supervisory Oversight and Engagement by Stakeholders:
>
> 8. Supervisory review of compensation practices must be rigorous and sustained, and deficiencies must be addressed promptly with supervisory actions.
> 9. Firms must disclose clear, comprehensive and timely information about their compensation practices to facilitate constructive engagement by all stakeholders.
>
> Source: FSF (2009)

At the London summit, the G20 leaders endorsed these Principles and the Basel Committee on Banking Supervision (BCBS) incorporated them as guidance under Pillar II within the package of measures approved in July 2009, with an expectation that banks and supervisors begin implementing the new guidance immediately.

In order to ensure a coherent and determinant implementation of the Principles at international level, the FSB published in September 2009 the Implementation Standards Report (FSB 2009) and announced that it would carry out a peer review of implementation whose results would be published in March 2010.

The 19 Standards are directed only at significant financial institutions throughout the world and aim to ensure that implementation, with which the BCBS, the International Association of Insurance Supervisors (IAIS) and the International Organisation of Securities Commissions (IOSCO) were charged, is prompt and consistent with the Principles.

The Standards cover five areas: governance, compensation and capital, pay structure and risk alignment, disclosure, and supervisory oversight. In the area of governance, the Standards state that such financial institutions should have a board remuneration committee as an integral part of their governance structure. This would be in charge of the evaluation of the firm's compensation policy and would ensure that an independent annual compensation review would be carried out and submitted to the relevant national supervisory authorities, or disclosed publicly. The second area establishes that total variable compensation does not undermine the institution's ability to strengthen its capital base, emphasising that national supervisors should limit the variable component of compensation as a percentage of total net revenue when it is inconsistent with the maintenance of a sound capital base.

The area of "pay structure and risk alignment" is the most detailed one (Standards 4 to 14, see Box 11.2). The Standards provide examples of quantitative thresholds for certain variables (eg, Standard 6) and they suggest that the deferral period should not be less than three years. They also establish the need not to have a guaranteed bonus (with very few exceptions), and even that clawback arrangements should be in place for any unvested portions of deferred compensation. They also require that contractual payments related to a termination of employment should be re-examined and that, in the event of government assistance, the supervisor may restructure the compensation system. Financial firms are urged to immediately apply these Standards and prevent their employees from engaging in hedging strategies.

In the area of disclosure, the Standards support firms publishing an annual report on compensation, including both qualitative and quantitative information. Such a report should contain aggregate quantitative information on compensation, on amounts and form of variable remuneration, on amounts of deferred compensation (both awarded and outstanding) and on severance payments. It should also cover, among other areas, how compensation policy is designed.

Finally, with regard to "supervisory oversight" the Standards state that national supervisors should require financial institutions to demonstrate that their compensation schemes comply with the Principles. In case they do not, supervisors should take prompt remedial action or appropriate corrective measures according to national frameworks or under Pillar II of the Basel II framework. Supervisors are asked to coordinate internationally to ensure that these Standards are implemented consistently in all jurisdictions.

BOX 11.2 FSB IMPLEMENTATION STANDARDS ON PAY STRUCTURE AND RISK ALIGNMENT

4. For significant financial institutions, the size of the variable compensation pool and its allocation within the firm should take into account the full range of current and potential risks, and in particular:
   - the cost and quantity of capital required to support the risks taken;
   - the cost and quantity of the liquidity risk assumed in the conduct of business;
   - consistency with the timing and likelihood of potential future revenues incorporated into current earnings.
5. Subdued or negative financial performance of the firm should generally lead to a considerable contraction of the firm's total variable compensation, taking into account both current compensation and reductions in payouts of amounts previously earned, including through malus or clawback arrangements.
6. For senior executives as well as other employees whose actions have a material impact on the risk exposure of the firm:
   - a substantial proportion of compensation should be variable and paid on the basis of individual, business-unit and firm-wide measures that adequately measure performance;
   - a substantial portion of variable compensation, such as 40 to 60 percent, should be payable under deferral arrangements over a period of years; and
   - these proportions should increase significantly along with the level of seniority and/or responsibility. For the most senior management and the most highly paid employees, the percentage of variable compensation that is deferred should be substantially higher, for instance above 60 percent.
7. The deferral period described above should not be less than three years, provided that the period is correctly aligned with the nature of the business, its risks and the activities of the employee in question. Compensation payable under deferral arrangements should generally vest no faster than on a pro rata basis.
8. A substantial proportion, such as more than 50 percent, of variable compensation should be awarded in shares or share-linked instruments (or, where appropriate, other non-cash instruments), as long as these instruments create incentives aligned with long-term value creation and the time horizons of risk. Awards in shares or share-linked instruments should be subject to an appropriate share retention policy.

↓

9. The remaining portion of the deferred compensation can be paid as cash compensation vesting gradually. In the event of negative contributions of the firm and/or the relevant line of business in any year during the vesting period, any unvested portions are to be clawed back, subject to the realised performance of the firm and the business line.
10. In the event of exceptional government intervention to stabilise or rescue the firm:
    - supervisors should have the ability to restructure compensation in a manner aligned with sound risk management and long-term growth; and
    - compensation structures of the most highly compensated employees should be subject to independent review and approval.
11. Guaranteed bonuses are not consistent with sound risk management or the pay-for-performance principle and should not be a part of prospective compensation plans. Exceptional minimum bonuses should only occur in the context of hiring new staff and be limited to the first year.
12. Existing contractual payments related to a termination of employment should be re-examined, and kept in place only if there is a clear basis for concluding that they are aligned with long-term value creation and prudent risk-taking; prospectively, any such payments should be related to performance achieved over time and designed in a way that does not reward failure.
13. Significant financial institutions should take the steps necessary to ensure immediate, prospective compliance with the FSB compensation standards and relevant supervisory measures.
14. Significant financial institutions should demand from their employees that they commit themselves not to use personal hedging strategies or compensation- and liability-related insurance to undermine the risk alignment effects embedded in their compensation arrangements. To this end, firms should, where necessary, establish appropriate compliance arrangements.

Source: FSB (2009)

In October 2009, the FSB commissioned the BCBS a detailed guide for supervisors, to provide directions for reviewing individual firms' compensation practices and assessing their compliance with the FSB Principles and Standards. The Assessment Methodology (BCBS 2010a) finally published in January 2010 clarified some issues and provided a wide range of supervisory approaches consistent with the overall framework.

Table 11.1 Illustrative examples of remuneration practices in deferral and *ex post* risk adjustment

a) Types of *ex post* risk adjustments	**Example of a malus scheme used by a large retail bank***
	For the most senior executives, bonuses are deferred for three years, and vesting occurs only if none of the following events occur:
	❏ the employee leaves the firm; ❏ bad financial performance of firm (specific indicators are used); ❏ breach of code of conduct and other internal rules, especially concerning risks; ❏ material restatement of the firms's financial statements; and ❏ significant changes in the firm's economic capital and qualitative of risks.
	No malus for other employees of the firm
	Example of a clawback scheme used by a large universal bank**
	All remuneration awards for the year 2009 are subject to three clawback conditions:
	1. The first condition is based on the group earnings (relevant only for the most senior executives); 2. The second condition refers to the case of a violation of internal rules or external regulations (relevant for all employees); and 3. The third condition is based on "substantial decreases" in the value of specific positions on an individual level (relevant for all employees).
b) Designed risk adjusted deferred remuneration schemes	**Example: used by a large universal bank**
	For the senior executives, roughly 60% of the variable remuneration is deferred.
	The deferred part of the variable remuneration consists of two components: a stock-based "equity award" (75%) and a cash-based "incentive award" (25%)
	1. Stock-based equity award: ❏ deferred for 3¾ years; ❏ value tied to the sustained performance of the institution (stock price under the additional condition of a non-negative net income before tax of the institution); and ❏ pro-rata vesting and payment in shares, starting at the end of the first year of the deferral period (9 tranches).
	2. Cash-based incentive award: ❏ deferred for 3 years; and ❏ value tied to the sustained performance of the institution (based on the ROE less cost of funds under the additional condition of a non-negative net income before tax of the institution).
	Pro-rata vesting and payment in cash, annual payments starting at the end first year of the deferral period (3 tranches)

Source: Basel Committee on Banking Supervisors (2010b)

* According to CEBS (2010c) a malus is an arrangement that permits the institution to prevent vesting of all or part of the amount of a deferred remuneration award in relation to risk outcomes of performers. Malus is a form of *ex post* risk adjustment.

** According to CEBS (2010c) a clawback is a contractual agreement in which the staff member agrees to return ownership of an amount of remunerations to the institution under certain circumstances. This can be applied to both upfront and deferred variable remuneration. When related to risk outcomes, clawback is a form of ex post risk adjustment.

In March 2010 a peer-review report was published with information from 24 countries, in relation to the Principles and Standards implementation. It concluded that, while the Principles regarding governance of compensation schemes, disclosure and transparency were being applied, much work was still needed on the risk alignment of compensation. As a result, the FSB asked the BCBS to develop for consultation a report on methodologies for risk and performance alignment, which would also cover proportionality and the design of deferred compensation, which resulted in BCBS issuing a Consultative Document in October 2010[6] (BCBS 2010b). Two of the illustrative examples provided in the BCBS document, which show the balance between performance and *ex post* risk adjustments, are recalled in Table 11.1. In December 2010, the BCBS published a Consultation on Pillar 3 disclosure requirements for remuneration (BCBS (2010c)), which aimed to be consistent with the Pillar 2 guidance issued in July 2009 (BCBS (2009)) which integrated the FSB Principles and which was expected to be implemented by banks and supervisors immediately.

11.4.2 The European initiatives

Two weeks after the publication of the FSB Principles, the Committee of European Banking Supervisors (CEBS) – now the European Banking Authority (EBA) – published the high-level principles on remuneration policies,[7] whose objective was to provide general guidance as regards remuneration policies, based on a limited number of principles. In particular, the five high-level principles address the areas of risk alignment, transparency, governance, performance measurement and form of remuneration (See Box 11.3).

The set of principles were addressed to regulators and all regulated financial institutions, within the remit of CEBS, including all levels of the organisation and all categories of employees. They had to be implemented by the end of the third quarter of 2009 and they were completely consistent with FSB Principles, although they did not cover the area of supervisory review and evaluation process.

In the same vein, in April 2009, the European Commission published two Recommendations regarding compensation: Recommendation 2009/385/EC on Executive remuneration on quoted firms[8] and Recommendation 2009/384/EC on Remuneration Policies in the Financial Sector.[9] While the first one complemented

> ## BOX 11.3 CEBS HIGH-LEVEL PRINCIPLES FOR REMUNERATION POLICIES
>
> **General**
> 1. The financial institution should adopt an overall remuneration policy that is in line with its business strategy and risk tolerance, objectives, values and long-term interests. It should not encourage excessive risk-taking. The remuneration policy should cover the institution as a whole and contain specific arrangements that take into account the respective roles of senior management, risk takers and control functions. Control functions should be adequately rewarded to attract skilled individuals.
> 2. The remuneration policy should be transparent internally and adequately disclosed externally.
>
> **Governance**
> 3. The management body, in its supervisory function, should determine the remuneration of the management body in its management function. In addition the management body, in its supervisory function, should approve the principles of the overall remuneration policy of the institution and maintain oversight of their application. The implementation of the remuneration policy should be subject to central and independent review.
>
> **Measurement of performance**
> 4. Where the pay award is performance related, remuneration should be based on a combination of individual and collective performance. When defining individual performance, factors apart from financial performance should be considered. The measurement of performance, as a basis for bonus awards, should include adjustments for risks and the cost of capital.
>
> **Form of remuneration**
> 5. There should be a proportionate ratio between base pay and bonus. Where a significant bonus is paid, the bonus should not be a pure upfront cash payment but contain a flexible, deferred component; it should consider the risk horizon of the underlying performance.
>
> Source: CEBS (2009)

the previous recommendations issued in 2004 and 2005 in relation to this area, the second one, although much less exhaustive, covered all Principles, both FSB's and CEBS's. However, it did not request a compensation report and, while stating some quantitative limits to some remuneration concepts, it did not set explicit thresholds.

The next step taken by the Commission was part of the programme of financial services reform that it had set in its communication "Driving European Recovery".[10] In particular, the Commission published Directive 2010/76/EU[11] (CRD III) amending Directives 2006/48/EC and 2006/49/EC in December 2010. The so-called CRD III covered not only changes in capital requirements for the trading book and for resecuritisations, but also implied the inclusion of the supervisory review of remuneration policies. The new proposal in the Directive aimed at imposing a binding obligation on firms to have a remuneration policy consistent with sound and effective risk management (art. 22) and enabling supervisory authorities to impose capital "surcharges" on financial institutions, the remuneration policies of which were found to generate unacceptable risk (art. 43). Member states had to comply with these new provisions by January 1, 2011.

A detailed description of the principles and characteristics that remuneration policies are expected to display were included in a new section added to Annex V of the Directive. This incorporates the FSB Principles and Standards, and follows CEBS's High Level Principles, establishing them as requirements.

Under CRD III, supervisors are to require credit institutions to limit variable remuneration as a percentage of total net revenues when it is inconsistent with the maintenance of a sound capital base and can even require credit institutions to use net profits to strengthen the capital base (art. 136). The consideration of the appropriate level of own funds should also take into account remuneration policies that become subject to Pillar II requirements.

Also, as part of the amendment to Annex XII in the CRD III, which refer to technical criteria on transparency and disclosure, the Directive requires that annual updates be made to the public in relation to the remuneration policy and practices of the credit institution for those categories of staff whose professional activities have a material impact on its risk profile. The information required covers both qualitative and quantitative data, being more detailed for significant[12] credit institutions. In general, compliance with these disclosures must be proportionate, as to be adapted to the institution's size, nature and complexity.

In order to promote supervisory convergences in the assessment of remuneration policies and practices, the CRD III asked CEBS to develop "Guidelines on sound remuneration policies", which were published in December 2010 (CEBS 2010c). They were based on the findings of the Implementation study (CEBS 2010a) carried out by CEBS in the first semester of 2010 (see Box 11.4) regarding the national implementation of the High Level Principles by both supervisors and institutions alike.

The main goal of the Guidelines was stated in terms of overcoming "the discrepancies between requirements set by regulators

BOX 11.4 FINDINGS OF THE CEBS' IMPLEMENTATION STUDY REPORT

1. Governance
- A more extensive role is played by the management body in its supervisory function, but there is too little involvement of the management body in setting the overall remuneration policy and in the oversight of its implementation, and little or no involvement of the management body in the definition of the senior management compensation.
- An independent review of remuneration policies is usually carried out; differences emerge regarding the bodies in charge of the review.
- There is an improvement in setting up remuneration committees, mainly composed of non-executive and/or independent; important differences arise among countries.
- Not enough interaction is observed between control functions and the management body, although in some larger institutions, control functions provide input to remuneration committees.
- The majority of supervisors have not used specific oversight methods and tools for the review of governance arrangements.

2. Risk-adjusted performance measurement
- Extensive use of qualitative (such as customer satisfaction, cooperation skills, and compliance with core standards), risk sensitive criteria to determine individual compensation.
- Bonus pools are mostly determined by quantitative criteria (ROE, net operating income, or economic profit), and at the level of the institution and/or its business lines, in a "top-down" approach.
- In some countries, institutions started to take into account ex ante risks when measuring performances (based on expected losses, delinquency ratios/non-performing loans, or risk weighted assets).
- Some countries found unsatisfactory attempts to adjust performance measurement for risks (malus or clawback were not observed).

↓

3. Structure of remuneration
- Most institutions follow the open criteria, specified by CEBS principles, of a proportionate ratio between fixed pay and bonuses.
- Practices regarding this proportion are not typically formalised in detail; where proportions are stipulated, it mainly differs depending on seniority and the type of business line.
- Risk sensitive practices are emerging (although vary significantly among institutions) in relation to the proportion of remuneration to be deferred, the time horizon of deferral and the form of the deferred part.

4. Transparency
- Internal transparency of remuneration policies towards employees does not seem to be problematic in institutions.
- There is no detailed assessment of external transparency, although institutions are expected to provide information of their remuneration systems in their annual reports.

5. Discrepancies
- Discrepancies between supervisors and institutions under supervision are observed especially in new fields, like risk adjusted performance measurement (such as the measurement of liquidity risk), or by remaining uncertain on the dimensions of scope, proportionality and home/host relationships.
- There may be a lack of convergence between national adoptions by supervisors.

Source: CEBS (2010a)

and the practices observed in institutions" and remedying "the lack of convergence among supervisors" (CEBS 2010c). In particular, the Guidelines focused on corporate governance, alignment with risk and market disclosure, distinguishing between guidelines directed to institutions and those directed to supervisors.

In the area of governance, the Guidelines focus on three issues: the importance of the management body in its supervisory function to design, approve and oversee the remuneration policy; the creation of remuneration committees for significant institutions; and the independence of staff engaged in control functions from the business they oversee. In the area of risk alignment, they focus on the alignment of variable remuneration with risk. This implies, among other things, the measuring of risk and performance, the use of *ex ante* risk variables to adjust the awards, and the specification of the pay-out process. Within the pay-out process, the Guidelines specify the amount of remuneration that should be deferred (40–60%) and the recommendation to use both cash and instruments for variable remuneration, as well as *ex post* risk adjustments. Finally, in the area of transparency, the Guidelines point out the importance of quantitative information on remuneration, as well as that of internal disclosure for staff members.

The Guidelines also clarify concepts that had previously remained ambiguous, such as the institutions to be covered (all those falling under the Capital Requirements Directive (CRD)),[13] the staff to be identified (executive members, senior managers, staff responsible for control functions, other risk takers and other employees with remuneration similar to senior managers and other such risk takers), and the concept of proportionality (among institutions and categories of staff) that applies to all principles.

CEBS committed itself to carry out another implementation study in the fourth quarter of 2011, to observe the state of convergence in the application of the CRD III and the Guidelines within the European Economic Area.

11.4.3 Other initiatives

Many other initiatives have been developed in the area of remuneration since the beginning of the crisis. We will refer here, very briefly, to just four of them. Two were developed by different national authorities (the FSA and the Fed) and two by private institutions: an international organisation (the Institute of International Finance (IIF)) and a private Swiss bank (UBS[14]).

11.4.3.1 The FSA

The Financial Services Authority (FSA) in the UK was one of the first financial national authorities to explicitly incorporate into regulation issues of remuneration practices.[15] The first move of the FSA was to publish a "Dear CEO" letter in October 2008 explaining the work the FSA was doing on the matter and urging firms to start reviewing their remuneration policies. In this letter, the FSA expressed the view that remuneration structures had been inconsistent with a sound risk management.

The Turner Review (FSA 2009), published in March 2009, contained, among the 28 actions proposed to create a stable and effective banking system, one that stated that "remuneration policies should be designed to avoid incentives for undue risk taking; risk management considerations should be closely integrated into remuneration decisions. This should be achieved through the development and enforcement of UK and global codes." Not only that, but it also demanded that the FSA supervisory approach should focus on remuneration policies.

In August 2009 a "Code of practice on remuneration policies"[16] featuring one Rule and eight Principles was agreed upon, with the idea that it would come into force at the beginning of 2010 and would to be applied only to the 26 largest financial institutions. It is worth mentioning that the Consultative Document, initially issued, contained three more principles that were dropped in the final version. Those principles referred to the specific structure of remuneration: one focused on the need to have a fixed component large enough to allow for a fully flexible bonus policy; the second referred to the need to defer the majority of any significant bonus; the last one suggested the possibility of linking the deferred elements to the future performance of the firm. The industry argued that these principles would have adverse competitive effects for the UK's financial institutions, thereby ensuring that the final Code that was put into the Handbook did not contain them.

However, the Code was revised a year later to introduce, among other provisions, the changes that the CRD III required, also implying a broadening of the scope of application to all banks, building societies and investment firms under the CRD, changing guidance into rules, introducing the new regulation on the protection of the capital base, the deferral of payments and clawback provisions, and broadening the group of employees to whom it applied.

11.4.3.2 The Fed
The first action in the area of remuneration taken by the board of governors of the Federal Reserve System (Fed) in relation to the crisis was the publication in October 2009 of a proposed "Guidance on Sound Incentive Compensation Policies". This was initially directed only to banking organisations supervised by the Fed.[17] Its objective was to help ensure that incentive compensation policies at these organisations did not encourage excessive risk

taking and were consistent with the safety and soundness of said organisations.

In June 2010, after reviewing the comments of the industry and in cooperation with other US agencies (the Office of the Comptroller of the Currency (OCC), the Federal Deposit Insurance Corporation (FDIC) and the Office of Thrift Supervision (OTS)), the Fed published final guidance that was to be applied to all the banking organisations supervised by these agencies. The Guidance comprises three principles, which are consistent with FSB Principles and the related Implementation Standards.

The principles state that compensation arrangements at a banking organisation should (a) allow employees' incentives to balance risk and reward; (b) be compatible with effective controls and risk-management; and (c) be supported by strong corporate governance, including active and effective supervision by the organisation's board of directors. The Guidance made it clear that it was aimed at being applied not only to senior executives, who include, at minimum, executive officers, but also to "other employees who have the ability to expose the banking organization to material amounts of risk", clarifying that "other employees ..." are those employees whose activities "are material to the organization or are material to a business line or operating unit that is itself material to the organization".

In order to ensure some proportionality, the Guidance stated that the reviews, policies, procedures and systems implemented by a smaller banking organisation that uses incentive compensation arrangements on a limited basis would be substantially less extensive, formalised and detailed than those at a large banking organisation (LBO), which received a more detailed treatment. In particular, the Guidance highlights the types of policies, procedures and systems that LBOs should have and maintain, but that are not expected of other banking organisations. Supervisory reviews of incentive compensation should then be tailored to reflect the scope and complexity of the organisation. On the other hand, it is expected that, particularly in the case of LBOs, adoption of this principles-based approach will require an iterative supervisory process to ensure that the flexibility provided does not undermine the effective implementation of the Guidance.

Finally, with respect to US operations of foreign banks, the guidance establishes that "incentive compensation policies, including management, review, and approval requirements for a foreign bank's US operations should be coordinated with the foreign banking organization's group-wide policies developed in accordance with the rules of the foreign banking organization's home country supervisor".

The Federal Reserve also announced two supervisory initiatives: (a) a review of compensation practices to be carried out at large, complex banking organisations; and (b) a review of such practices carried out at other banking organisations.

11.4.3.3 The IIF

Having seen the damaging consequences of misaligned incentives, many financial institutions started re-examining their compensation structures. In particular, the Institute of International Finance, whose members account for a significant proportion of the global financial industry, published a long report in July 2008 on "Best Market Practices"[18] (IIF 2008), which contained principles of conduct, best-practice recommendations and considerations for the official sector in different areas such as compensation policies.

Seven "Principles of conduct" were set in the area of compensation. The first Principle states that compensation schemes should be based on performance and be aligned with both shareholders' interests and long-term firm-wide profitability, while the second one declares that compensation incentives must not induce risk taking in excess of the firm's risk appetite. Principle 3 states that the payout of incentives should be based on risk-adjusted profit and phased in to coincide with the risk-time horizon of such a profit. Principle 4 supports the view that part of the incentive components should reflect the impact of the business units' performance on the overall results of the organisation and/or firm. Principle 5 states that incentive components should also reflect the firm's overall result and achievement of risk management. Principle 6 states the importance of relating severance payments to performance over time, while the final Principle declares that the approach and objectives of compensation schemes should be transparent to stakeholders.

11.4.3.4 UBS

This was the first bank to announce a change in its remuneration policy, after having posted a SFr20 billion loss, the largest financial loss in Swiss corporate history. In particular, the 2008 UBS annual report (UBS 2009) recorded the compensation principles to be applied from 2009 onwards, explaining how the compensation policy and compensation components would affect the chairman, the executive board members, and independent board of directors (BoD) members.

Neither the chairman nor the independent BoD members are entitled to a variable compensation. The chairman's fixed base salary comprises cash and a predetermined fixed number of shares, which vest after four years and are subject to a "malus" during the vesting period. The executive board members' compensation comprises a fixed salary and also a variable cash (cash balance plan) and equity (performance equity plan) compensation. The variable compensation awarded is based on long-term performance, incorporates a "malus" system and addresses risk management.

The cash balance plan rewards long-term profitability by linking variable cash compensation to sustainable performance, including a "malus" or negative bonus to be applied under specific circumstances, such as incurring a financial loss, or taking excessive risk. The performance equity plan is dependent on results produced over a three-year period. A potential number of performance-linked shares for executives are subject to the achievement of predefined business targets. Two performance metrics, the so-called economic profit and the total shareholder return, are used to determine the final number of shares actually vesting.

11.4.3.5 Comparisons

The main difference between the proposals made by the private sector and those made by public authorities refers to the divergent role that supervisors and regulators are expected to play. In particular, the underlying idea behind the private approach is that there is no role for public intervention, particularly when it comes to regulation. The other major differences lie mainly in their respective proposals for remuneration structures and in the relevance that they give to deferral payments, which in the authorities' proposals is always mentioned while in the private proposals it is not. The reduced discretion that compulsory deferral implies is at the heart of such discrepancies, as the market for talent is regarded as very competitive. Finally, the private proposals contain only minor changes to governance.

As for comparisons between the approaches endorsed by the different public authorities, concerns have been raised over the tighter requirements for remuneration in the European Union that the CRD III and the associated CEBS' Guidelines implied in relation to the approach suggested by the FSB Principles or the one proposed by the Fed[19] (see Table 11.2).

On the one hand, principles and provisions have been recast by the EU into binding rules under the CRD III, except for the guidance by CEBS, which comes under the "comply or explain" approach that characterises the international attitude and that allows for deviations from the guidance that need to be justified. On the other hand, a broader scope of application of the new rules has been defined: not only do significant financial institutions need to comply with the new provisions, but also all those financial institutions falling under the CRD, which include credit institutions and investment firms. In the case of the UK, the broader scope of application has implied extending the initial coverage of the "Code of practice on remuneration policies" from 26 authorised firms to more than 2,500. Moreover, the group of employees who are considered relevant in the EU case is much larger than under the FSB Principles and needs to be properly identified. Finally, the applicability of the provisions contained in the CRD III to firms that operate also in non-EEA jurisdictions raises concerns over level-playing-field issues.

In fact, relevant guidance and rules in the area of remuneration for internationally active banks could overlap, as these could be subject to provisions issued by the G20, or in the European context by the European agencies and authorities as well as by national supervisory bodies from jurisdictions in which they have a substantial presence. The fact that there are no contradictory approaches from the different bodies that have issued guidance implies that these international banks will be in compliance if they manage to adhere to even the most stringent rule. However, strengthening coordination among different supervisors will be the way forward to reduce any overlaps, ie, through the work of colleges.

With regard to Europe, the fact that remuneration considerations are already included within Pillar II through CRD III implies that an unsound remuneration policy in breach of remuneration require-

Table 11.2 Comparison of remuneration approaches

	EU (CRD III–CEBS)	US (Fed)	International (FSB–BCBS)
To which institutions does it apply?	All institutions covered by the CRD (credit institutions and investment firms)	Banking organisations supervised by the Agencies[1] (national banks, state member banks, state nonmember banks, savings associations, US bank holding companies, savings and loan holding companies ...)	Significant financial institutions
To which employees does it apply?	Executive members, senior managers, staff responsible for control functions, other risk takers, other employees with remuneration similar to senior managers and other risk takers	Senior executives and employees who have the ability of expose the banking organisation to material amounts of risk	Senior management, material risk takers, staff performing risk management and control functions, groups of employees who may together (even if not individually) take material risks
Is there a concept of proportionality?	Yes (both on institutions and on staff)	Yes (only on institutions)	Implicitly (emphasis on the LCFI)
Does it detail a maximum % of variable remuneration?	No	No	No
Does it make mandatory an explicit % of retained/deferred? And how long?	Yes (between 40% and 60%)[2]; not less than 3 to 5 years	No	No, it provides examples such as: 40% to 60% for managers, most senior management above 60%, for a period of years
Does it make it mandatory to form a remuneration committee?	Yes (for significant institutions)	Yes	Yes
Does it make it mandatory to publish an annual report on remuneration?	Yes (to all stakeholders)	No	Yes (to the public)
Does it provide an explicit treatment of discretionary pension benefits?	Yes	No	No

[1] The OCC, Board of Governors of the Federal Reserve System, FDIC and OTS
[2] Only 30% of non deferred pay in cash

ments may give rise to additional capital requirements, penalties or other supervisory action. The fact that the BCBS has already integrated the FSB Principles in Pillar II of Basel II (BCBS 2009) suggests that it is only a matter of time before such an approach is extended across the board, as more jurisdictions incorporate such changes into their regulatory framework.

11.5 CONCLUSIONS

It is clear that flawed incentive schemes may lead to undesired behaviour by employees, resulting in outcomes that are not consistent with financial stability. Employees being rewarded for increasing the firm's revenue or short-term profit, without due consideration for the risks their activities pose to the firm, exacerbate risks and increase the probability of losses. Moreover, it is not only the design of compensation schemes that matters but also their governance. The effects of executive pay packages differ among firms, as their impact also depends upon the effectiveness of boards, so that there might be some substitution between different governance and incentive compensation arrangements. Most of the international bodies that have produced rules or guidance on sound remuneration practices have also committed to an implementation review of these rules and guidance so as to monitor convergence in their implementation among jurisdictions, which could help evaluate their effectiveness and detect any drawbacks.

Notwithstanding the benefits that the new remuneration framework will bring, its implementation will not come without a cost, which in turn will apply not only to firms. In accordance with the new rules and guidance, supervisors need to explicitly monitor remuneration policies and practices, ie, they would need to build compensation considerations into their activities, with the corresponding implications for one-off and continuous supervisory resources. Supervisors will need to be trained in these issues and their supervisory framework will need to be adapted to the new requirements. Moreover, time will need to be devoted to the analysis of the remuneration practices so that, if inappropriate policies are being implemented in this field, a response may be granted.

As for firms, many need to change all or part of their compensation schemes and governance. They need to ensure that their compensation practices comply with the relevant rules and guidelines, taking into account the proportionality approach that has been suggested in implementation and making the necessary changes in the contract terms. Many changes will arise because of the new quantitative requirements, especially those referring to payment deferral or retention and to performance-related bonuses. This is also due to the need to implement different forms of *ex post* risk adjustment, such as malus or clawback provisions that require the recipient to return all or part of the bonus if certain subsequent negative events occur, such as poor financial performance.

There are some concerns that, at the end of the day, the new regulation will result in an increase in the proportion of the fixed salary with respect to the variable part. If this were the case, fixed costs for all firms would be rising.

Compensation practices that resulted in excessive risk taking were mainly associated with the "originate-to-distribute" business model. Those firms with more traditional approaches to business either did not show such inadequate incentives or the impact of their variable compensation schemes on risk was much more moderate, as incentives associated with compensation were better aligned with risk taking and risk tolerance. It can therefore be expected that most large changes in remuneration policies and practices will mostly affect such business models, covering investment firms and the areas of investment banking activity. In particular, the requirements on long vesting periods may be particularly important for high-risk, high-volatility lines of business, where short-run surges in revenues and profits can be offset, if not reversed, in the longer term. However, the new regulatory framework covers all types of banks and business areas, therefore affecting all of them.

Most of the new rules and guidance reinforce the need for firms to publish annually their compensation schemes, either jointly with their annual statement or as a specific publication. This will certainly imply additional compliance costs for firms not already publishing such an analysis, especially if the new rules point out the need to analyse the risk implications of compensation schemes.

The new requirements on governance will imply that there will be a need to devote more time to compensation issues in the agendas of the board or other committees. Risk-management functions will be reinforced with additional focus on remuneration policies (which up to now were traditionally outside their scope) with time-resources implications.

Finally, another important source of costs for firms will be the renegotiation of contracts. In particular, there may be a need to amend existing private and collective agreements or to issue new ones in accordance with new rules.

Besides cost considerations, there are some challenges ahead in the implementation of the new regulatory and supervisory remuneration approach that are worth reviewing.

Consistency in different jurisdictions and firms is a necessary condition for the effectiveness of the new framework to make a change. To attain such convergence, there is a need for international commitment and enforcement of the principles that have been agreed. If supervisory authorities do not consistently apply these rules and principles, competition to attract and retain the very best talent may disadvantage those actually applying such rules. Peer-reviewing or any other initiative that may provide information on the implementation characteristics of the agreed principles may contribute to the necessary convergence in their application. In fact, as already discussed in the previous section, larger differences arise between jurisdictions that implement these principles through rules and regulations and those that use guidance and rely on the supervisory process.

Another issue arises for certain financial institutions, for example cooperatives, non-listed and savings banks whose capital structure does not seem to fit easily into the framework that has been proposed. In particular, these banks may find it difficult to fulfil the requirement to include shares or share-linked instruments in their variable remuneration, either because such instruments do not exist or because a dilution of the voting rights of existent shareholders should be avoided.[20] With this in mind, the proposal made by CEBS to use equivalent non-cash instruments for institutions that are not publicly traded requires further development.

Concerns over the tax treatment of the new arrangements have also been raised, with particular attention paid to the vested rights resulting from the instruments paid and belonging to the employee, but subject to a retention period when they cannot be sold. Given that retention arrangements for part of the vested instruments are compulsory and that tax falls on an accrual basis in some jurisdictions, it could be the case that a negative net current cashflow results. Generally speaking, there is a need to clarify the interaction between taxation and the clawback clauses, as such clauses may imply that the employee has to return ownership of an amount of variable remuneration, which may be either upfront or deferred, and that may imply lower cash or a lower number of instruments finally awarded.

Another issue is how the new information resulting from the disclosure requirements will be used by market players. As more detailed and comparable information becomes available in the market, recruiting and maintaining staff will need to take into consideration the strategies of competitors, thus enhancing competition in the labour market. However, while harmonisation will be facilitated by greater transparency, the coexistence of firms that have to comply with these new requirements with those that do not could have a negative impact on the ability of the former to attract and retain talent. In the case of board members, it may be even more difficult to find managers who can comply with all the enhanced roles that are now required. In particular, it could reduce the quality of management in the banking industry due to the expectation of lower or more risk-based salaries.

The effectiveness of some of the incentives embedded in the remuneration packages may be much weakened if institutions find elusive mechanisms (eg, through the creation of other legal entities that are not subject to regulation) to remunerate employees. It may also be weakened in relation to deferred payment, if the employee is able to negotiate a "golden handshake" arrangement with their new organisation. The fact that the new organisation may well be a non-regulated firm makes the issue more complex, although the extension of such weakening practices may be rather limited.

Finally, implementation dates for much of the new guidance and many of the rules have implied very tight deadlines to change policies and procedures. It could be the case that the approval of shareholders is required for such changes, or that new employment agreements need to be signed or old ones renegotiated and amended, resulting in extremely pressing time frames.

> The views expressed in this chapter are the authors', and do not reflect those of Bank of Spain. We would like to thank S. Carbó, J. M. Casado, C. Fernández Vidaurreta, J. L. López del Olmo, E. Palomeque and the editors for their suggestions and help.

1. See, for example, UBS (2008) and IIF (2008) for the initial industry reaction, the contributions of Delong, Portes and Zimmermann in Eichengreen and Baldwin (2008) for the corresponding academic one and Ferrarini and Ungureanu (2010) for a review of European national authorities' initiatives.
2. On the other hand, management preferences are for cash instead of options as depositors have seniority over compensation contracts.
3. Stock options and similar instruments provide upside rewards if share prices rise but no downside penalties if they fall. Consequently, the incentive is to take excessive risk.
4. Fahlenbrach and Stulz (2011) estimate that the mean dollar loss between 2006 and 2008 for the 80 CEOs included in their sample amounted to US$31.4 million, while the maximum loss attained US$368.4 million.
5. A deposit guarantee scheme is a rescue fund for depositors of failed banks.
6. The consultation period lasted up until December 31, and the BCBS is expected to publish the definitive document on the methodologies to align risk and remuneration during the second term of 2011.
7. See http://eba.europa.eu/getdoc/34beb2e0-bdff-4b8e-979a-5115a482a7ba/High-level-principles-for-remuneration-policies.aspx.
8. Commission Recommendation complementing Recommendations 2004/913/EC and 2005/162/EC as regards the regime for the remuneration of directors of listed companies (C(2009)3177/2).
9. Commission Recommendation on remuneration policies in the financial services sector (C(2009)3159/2).
10. See http://ec.europa.eu/commission_barroso/president/pdf/press_20090304_en.pdf.
11. See http://eur-lex.europa.eu/LexUriServ/LexUriServ.do?uri=OJ:L:2010:329:0003:0035:EN:PDF.
12. "Significant in terms of their size, internal organisation and the nature, the scope and the complexity of their activities" (CRDIII).
13. Credit institutions as defined under Article 4(1) of Directive 2006/48/EC; and investment firms as defined under Directive 2006/49/EC, which in turn refers to Directive 2004/39/EC on markets in financial instruments (MiFID).
14. The merger announced on December 8, 1997, between Union Bank of Switzerland (Zurich) and Swiss Bank Corporation (Basel) to form UBS AG became reality on July 1, 1998.
15. The Financial Supervision Authority in Finland had already published some standards affecting remuneration, where the need to take into account risk incentives was established (Rahoitustarkastus 2007) and Bank of Italy followed the initiative early on (Bank of Italy 2008).
16. See http://fsahandbook.info/FSA/html/handbook/SYSC/19A#DES1.
17. The American Recovery and Reinvestment Act of 2009 substantially tightened the executive pay restrictions on recipient firms of the Troubled Asset Relief Program (TARP) of October 2008. In particular, it imposed strict limitations on incentive payments and severance payments and added new corporate governance standards and requirements for those firms.
18. An interim report had already been released in April 2008.
19. In spite of the principles-based approach to regulation that the Fed has historically favoured, the Dodd–Frank Wall Street Reform and Consumer Protection Act (2010) requires banking regulators to "jointly prescribe regulations or guidelines that prohibit any types of incentive-based payment arrangement" that "create inappropriate risk". For this reason, the Fed is expected to announce during the first half of 2011 a more rules-based regulation on compensation that may explicitly limit bonuses and establish a minimum deferral component, which is more in line with EU regulation.
20. The latter could also affect other financial institutions.

REFERENCES

Adams, R., and H. Mehran, 2003, "Is Corporate Governance Different for Bank Holding Companies?", Federal Reserve Bank of New York Economic Policy Review, April, pp. 123–42.

Bank of Italy, 2008, "Regulation on Banks' Organisation and Corporate Governance", Bank of Italy, March.

BCBS, 2009, "Enhancements to the Basel II framework", Basel Committee on Banking Supervision, July.

BCBS, 2010a, "Compensation Principles and Standards. Assessment Methodology", Basel Committee on Banking Supervision. January.

BCBS, 2010b, "Range of Methodologies for Risk and Performance Alignment of Remuneration", Consultative Document, Basel Committee on Banking Supervision, October.

BCBS, 2010c, "Pillar 3 disclosure requirements for remuneration", Consultative Document, Basel Committee on Banking Supervision, December, available at http://www.bis.org/publ/bcbs191.pdf.

CEBS, 2009, "High-level principles for Remuneration Policies", Committee of European Banking Supervisors, April.

CEBS, 2010a, "Report on national implementation of CEBS High-level principles for Remuneration Policies", Committee of European Banking Supervisors, June.

CEBS, 2010b, "CEBS's guidelines for the joint assessment and joint decision regarding the capital adequacy of cross-border groups", Committee of European Banking Supervisors, December, available at http://www.eba.europa.eu/cebs/media/Publications/Standards%20and%20Guidelines/2010/JRAD/Guidelines.pdf.

CEBS, 2010c, "Guidelines on remuneration policies and practices", Committee of European Banking Supervisors, December, available at http://eba.europa.eu/cebs/media/Publications/Standards%20and%20Guidelines/2010/Remuneration/Guidelines.pdf

Eichengreen, B., and R. Baldwin (eds), 2008, "Rescuing our jobs and savings: What G7/8 leaders can do to solve the global credit crisis", a VoxEU.org publication, Centre for Economic Policy Research, London.

Fahlenbrach, R., and R. M. Stulz, 2011, "Bank CEO incentives and the credit crisis", *Journal of Financial Economics* 99, pp. 11–26.

Ferrarini, G. A., and M. C. Ungureanu, 2010, "Economics, Politics, and the International Principles for Sound Compensation Practices: An Analysis of Executive Pay at European Banks", ECGI Law Working Paper No. 169/2010.

FSA, 2009, "Turner Review: A Regulatory Response to the Financial Crisis", Financial Services Authority, UK, March.

FSB, 2009, "FSB Principles for Sound Compensation Practices. Implementation Standards", Financial Stability Board, September.

FSF, 2008, "Report of the Financial Stability Forum on Enhancing Market and Institutional Resilience", Financial Stability Forum, April.

FSF, 2009, "FSF Principles for Sound Compensation Practices", Financial Stability Forum, April.

IIF, 2008, "Final Report of the IIF Committee on Market Best Practices: Principles of Conduct and Best Practice Recommendations. Financial Services Industry Response to the Market Turmoil of 2007–2008", Institute for International Finance, July.

Jensen, M. C., and W. H. Meckling, 1976, "The Theory of the Firm: Managerial Behavior, Agency Costs and Ownership Structure", *Journal of Financial Economics* 3(4), pp. 305–60.

John, K., and Y. Qian, 2003, "Incentive features in CEO compensation in the banking industry", Federal Reserve Bank of New York Economic Policy Review 9, pp. 109–121.

Rahoitustarkastus (Finnish Financial Supervision Authority), 2007, "Standard 1.3 – Internal governance and organisation of activities", Financial Supervision Authority, Finland, October.

UBS, 2009, "Compensation principles 2009 and beyond for UBS senior executives", UBS, Annual report 2008, restated May 20.[1] Bank of Spain.

Part IV

The Emerging Regulatory Landscape

12

Crisis Management and Resolution

Giovanni Bassani; Maurizio Trapanese

UK Financial Services Authority; Bank of Italy

12.1 INTRODUCTION

On the occasion of the second anniversary of the bankruptcy of Lehman Brothers, a *Financial Times* columnist compared the date of September 15, 2008 (9/15 in American jargon), to the most eventful date in the recent history of mankind: September 11, 2001 (for ever 9/11). The main thrust of the article (Rachman 2010) was that the consequences of the collapse of Lehman Brothers Inc. will have a more lasting impact on the world's geopolitical framework than the infamous terrorist attacks in Manhattan. In the end, the columnist argued, while the 9/11 attacks did not shake the US's role as the world's only superpower, the global financial crisis will probably be remembered for ever as the beginning of the end of American global economic and financial dominance. Be this as it may, it is nonetheless unquestionable that the importance and the impact of the failure of Lehman Brothers on the global economy in general and global financial markets in particular cannot be overstated.

The Lehman insolvency represents the classic (and incredibly disruptive) coordination failure scenario between national authorities in dealing with the crisis of a cross-border financial group. The disruptive effects of the Lehman bankruptcy and its dramatic impact on financial and economic confidence around the world made sure that no other cross-border financial institution was allowed to fail during the 2008–2009 financial crisis.[1] The enhanced moral hazard that the too-big-to-fail assumption implies, is the most significant challenge that policymakers have been faced with in the wake of the global financial crisis.

In this regard, cross-border crisis-management arrangements (at global and European levels) are core to the topical macroprudential agenda. As is well known, macroprudential policy has two complementary dimensions: time series and cross-section.[2] The cross-sectional dimension deals with the uneven distribution of systemic risk across the financial system at a specific point in time and includes the identification, regulation and supervision of systemically important financial institutions (SIFIs).

In theory, there are three fundamental tools to deal with SIFIs (either in order to reduce their probability of default or mitigate the impact on the financial system given their default): enhanced supervision/regulation (eg, systemic capital surcharges); intervening on the structure of SIFIs (eg, Volcker rule, Glass–Steagall-type separation, cross-border standalone subsidiarisation); and efficient cross-border crisis-management and resolution arrangements (making these firms resolvable without causing disruption to financial stability and without the necessity to inject public money).

Theoretically, these three sets of intervention can be considered both as a substitute and as a complement. It is difficult to gauge *ex ante* the optimal policy mix between them, and we leave this discussion to Chapter 10.

But, in any case, we could safely assume that, if the cross-border resolvability of a SIFI could become a reality, then the whole too-big-to-fail issue would be significantly mitigated, if not completely resolved, and there would probably be no necessity to intervene on the structure of the group or with enhanced prudential regulatory requirements. On the other hand, if cross-border resolution is not a viable option, then enhanced supervisory, regulatory and structural tools are needed. Therefore, it is not possible to deal with the cross-section dimension of systemic risk, without preliminarily assessing, and improving if needed, the cross-border resolvability of the systemically important cross-border financial institutions.[3]

This chapter deals with the ongoing international policy initiatives on cross-border crisis management. Section 12.2 will discuss the current debate at the global level, notably in the Financial Stability Board (FSB) and the Basel Committee on Banking Supervision. Section 12.3 analyses the policy proposals at the European level and Section 12.4 concludes.

BOX 12.1 THE LEHMAN BROTHERS' BANKRUPTCY: SOME STYLISED FACTS ON INTERNATIONAL IN LIFE BUT NATIONAL IN DEATH

As the administrator of the Lehman bankruptcy in the US stated in a testimony before the US Financial Crisis Inquiry Commission, "at the time of the commencement of the bankruptcy case, Lehman Brothers Holdings Inc., LBHI, [the group's holding], directly and indirectly, had approximately 8,000 subsidiary entities and affiliates, of which over 100 were actively engaged in the various business activities of Lehman." After the American holding company filed for bankruptcy protection "approximately 80 insolvency proceedings affecting Lehman subsidiaries and affiliates were initiated in 18 foreign countries" within days (Miller 2010, pp. 11–12). According to Hughes (2008), the most important European subsidiary of LBHI, Lehman Brothers International Europe plc (LBIE), the UK subsidiary, tried to file for bankruptcy (administration) in London before the American filing in order to protect the European operations from any claims that the American parent company might have. LBIE was the holding company of the European operations of Lehman Brothers, which included more than 200 legal entities in many European jurisdictions. In the end, LBIE did file for bankruptcy in London at 7.56 am GMT on September 15, 2008, while LBHI had filed electronically in New York for bankruptcy protection approximately 50 minutes earlier (see Miller (2010) p. 10, who reports approximately 2 am in New York as the time of filing). Ross Sorkin reports the time of filing for bankruptcy protection with the United States Bankruptcy Court for the Southern District of New York at 1.45 am on Monday, September 15, when in London it was 6.45 am (Ross Sorkin 2009, p. 373, and related endnote). This rush for bankruptcy filing, even if successful, would not have significantly protected the UK subsidiary in any case. According to the matrix-structure business model, with significant business functions centralised at the holding company level, Lehman Brothers, among many other business functions, managed its liquidity centrally. As mentioned in Hughes (2008), "like many global corporations, the bank swept all the cash from its regional operations back to New York each night and released the funds the next day. The Friday sweep had taken about $8bn out of London. Without cash, the business could not meet its financial obligations on Monday morning. A thriving business [Lehman Brothers International Europe plc – LBIE]] of more than 5,000 staff and investments worth billions of dollars was suddenly flat broke." And again:

> "matters as simple as setting up a bank account caused problems. Having run most of its accounts through its New York parent, Lehman Europe [LBIE)] had few deposit accounts of its own. Nor

> could it set up any with another bank, since that bank was likely to be a creditor or debtor and could try to seize any money parked with it. In the end, the Bank of England came to the rescue. The bankrupt bank now [November 2008] has more than 60 accounts with the Central Bank ..."

12.2 THE GLOBAL AGENDA

12.2.1 The G20 and the FSB Principles for cross-border cooperation in crisis management

On April 2, 2009, the Financial Stability Board published "Principles for Cross-border Cooperation on Crisis Management" (Financial Stability Forum 2009). On the same day the G20 leaders' declaration on strengthening the financial system after the London summit included a clear commitment to implement the FSF principles immediately. The leaders also agreed that "home authorities of each major financial institution should ensure that the group of authorities with a common interest in that financial institution meet at least annually".

The main focus of the 15 principles is on cross-border cooperation between home and host authorities on crisis preparedness, management and resolution for the most significant cross-border banking groups (arguably, the too-big-to-fail institutions mentioned above).

In this regard, Principle 4 requires that national authorities

> meet at least annually to consider together the specific issues and barriers to co-ordinated action that may arise in handling severe stress at specific firms. Home supervisors will co-ordinate this process, which will directly involve the relevant authorities (including supervisors, central banks, finance ministries) in countries represented on a cross-border bank's core supervisory college. This process will be done for every bank with an FSF core supervisory college, but authorities may also co-operate around other specific cross-border firms as appropriate.

The Principle envisages a complete parallel between cross-border banking groups for which a global core supervisory college needs to be established and cross-border banking groups for which a crisis-management cooperative structure must be set up. More specifically, while the establishment of a crisis-management structure is mandatory for the banks with a core college, national authorities could extend their crisis-cooperation arrangements to other cross-border firms (also non-banks, such as insurance companies).[4] For obvious reasons of moral hazard and constructive ambiguity the FSB has never made public a list of cross-border financial groups that need a core supervisory college.

Therefore, the banks for which a global core supervisory college is required should also have a cross-border crisis-management cooperative structure in place. These cooperative structures have been named "Crisis Management Groups" (CMGs) and should include supervisory authorities, central banks, finance ministries and other authorities – such as special resolution authorities – from countries participating in the core supervisory college. Therefore, they are conceptually similar to supervisory colleges, but with a different membership (including all the national authorities from the home and host countries with an interest in crisis management) and a different focus and mandate.

Specifically, the most important tasks performed by CMGs involve improving information sharing and building trust and cooperation between national authorities in an out-of-the-crisis situation, in order to prevent coordination failures and noncooperative behaviour (first and foremost, ring-fencing of assets in host jurisdictions) in a crisis situation within one of those global banking institutions. With an analogy to game theory, the success of these groups will be measured against their ability to transform the management of the crisis of a cross-border banking group from a prisoner's dilemma type of game – with a noncooperative dominant strategy and a noncooperative equilibrium – into a cooperative, efficiency-enhancing game between national authorities. As already said, the final outcome should guarantee the cross-border resolvability of these banking groups, without the risk of disruption to financial stability and without the necessity of an injection of public money.

Taking into account what we have learned from the Lehman experience, much ground needs to be made up in the area of crisis management and these CMGs cannot be regarded as the panacea for firm specific cross-border crisis management. Some critical obstacles to cross-border cooperation (for instance, the presence of the national depositor preference rule in some jurisdictions or impediments to cross-border asset transferability) are embedded in national legal frameworks and cannot be overcome by firm-specific enhanced cooperation arrangements alone. Moreover, it is next to impossible to predict whether (and in which way) national courts will intervene for the protection of the creditors of branches or subsidiaries of the bank in a specific jurisdiction, *de facto* preventing the achievement of a group-wide solution. This is especially relevant if the operations in that jurisdiction are particularly significant for the whole banking group (not only in financial and economic terms, but also in order to preserve the franchise value of the banking group).

There is also the high likelihood of a political intervention in the host countries, given the social and political sensitivity of some critical financial functions provided by commercial banks (retail deposits, payment services, etc).

Above all, the burden-sharing issue is the most significant obstacle to cross-border cooperation between national authorities in the management of the crisis of a cross-border banking group. The basic problem is that neither home nor host authorities/countries face the full costs of dealing with a cross-border bank in trouble, so no authority/country has the correct incentives to minimise the overall cost of dealing with the crisis. This incentive misalignment matters because actions that one authority/country takes to resolve the crisis may simply shift costs to other countries, or, even worse, increase the overall cost of dealing with the crisis with net loss of social welfare. For example, a home country regulator that tries to save the cross-border banking group by forcing it to repatriate resources from branches/subsidiaries may slightly reduce the cost of saving the group from the home country's perspective, but acting in this way may impose significant costs on the host countries. The same is true of the reverse situation, when the host country ring-fences the assets of a branch or a subsidiary.

Therefore, without a framework for sharing (or discussing how to share) the costs of the crisis of a cross-border banking group between home and host countries, it is very difficult to envisage the possibility of cross-border cooperation on firm-specific crisis-management and resolution actions. But, if this is the case, we are, then, in the realm of national fiscal policies and more general political considerations, which are very difficult to discuss and assess *ex ante* with reference to a specific banking group, while wider bilateral and multilateral issues can also have a bearing on financial stability discussions between national governments.

BOX 12.2 CROSS-BORDER ASSET TRANSFERABILITY

It could be assumed that intra-group asset transferability within a group that is facing a liquidity crisis may assist in restoring viability by transferring resources from one entity of the group that is in surplus to another one in a different jurisdiction (especially at the parent-company level) that is in deficit in order to prevent a group-wide default. This should be easily achievable in a business-as-usual situation (apart from potential local regulatory requirements – eg, local liquidity and capital requirements – in the host jurisdictions, so-called supervisory ring-fencing) and is actually widely used in the cross-border, centralised-banking business model outlined above. Nonetheless, in a crisis situation, such free movement of assets across legal entities in different jurisdictions may be impeded by regulatory and supervisory actions such as asset maintenance requirements or ring-fencing in the branches and subsidiaries in the host countries. Moreover, national company law provisions can actually prevent intra-group asset transferability in a crisis situation. For example, the directors of one subsidiary may face legal restrictions on entering transactions with troubled/insolvent companies, even within the same group and even with the holding company. In fact, such asset transfers, if they failed to lead to a recovery or return to viability for the whole group, could in the end prejudice minority shareholders in the subsidiary and the creditors of the subsidiary. On the other hand, if we were dealing with a cross-border organisational structure based on a standalone subsidiarisation model, it could be argued that, while impediments to asset transfers may prevent recovery, the transfer of assets from one strong entity in the group to a weaker one might lead to intra-group contagion and thereby bring down a whole systemically important financial institution when in fact the "core" problem could have been isolated and resolved in a specific legal entity. As already seen, the standalone subsidiarisation model is virtually nonexistent. Therefore, the potential for the containment of the crisis of a large cross-border financial institution in a specific legal entity is very limited (assuming, as is often the case, that the legal entity affected is material and significant for the whole group).

The consultation paper from the European Commission (2011)[5] includes proposals for preventing regulatory and supervisory ring-fencing and remedial actions from creditors and minority shareholders, giving recognition to the concept of group interest. On the contentious issue of management responsibility towards creditors and minority shareholders it is proposed that shareholders sign a preliminary agreement, "which should set out the conditions for asset transferability and enable the management to carry out asset transfers when the conditions are met". It is then proposed that such an agreement be approved by the supervisory authority of the transferor entity and included in the ↓

> recovery plan of the transferee and in the group-wide recovery plan. A joint decision between home and host supervisory authorities within the supervisory college should make the preliminary agreement effective.

BOX 12.3 TERRITORIALITY VERSUS UNIVERSALITY IN NATIONAL INSOLVENCY PROCEEDINGS

As mentioned in this chapter the likelihood of national courts' intervention (or other national authorities' intervention) in host jurisdictions (basically through ring-fencing) is increased when national creditor preference is enshrined in the law of home jurisdictions. Moreover, different judicial systems have different approaches to cross-border insolvency. Courts in some jurisdictions have a more universal approach to insolvency (ie, applying the law of the home country to all the operations/assets of cross-border groups), while in some other jurisdictions they have a more territorial approach (ie, applying the law of the country of location to the operations/assets of cross-border groups). Strictly speaking, universality and territoriality are concepts that are applicable only to the foreign branch network of a cross-border group and not to its cross-border subsidiaries. In practice, a similar conceptual framework could be applied to insolvency of foreign subsidiaries through the concepts of ancillary and plenary insolvency proceedings. This is a general feature of the cross-border corporate insolvency framework but specific consequences arise for cross-border bank insolvency proceedings.

For a discussion of the territorial versus universal approach (also in their modified form) see Baxter, Hansen and Sommer (2004). These authors point out that the US, by far the most important jurisdiction in cross-border financial insolvency proceedings, has an asymmetric approach to banking insolvency: a universal approach when the United States is the home country (including also subsidiaries of foreign groups – the universal approach applies to all the US chartered banks); and a territorial approach for the branches of foreign banks in the US. In the authors' opinion this is an appropriate framework when it comes to financial markets, given the special features of financial firms subject to authorisation, regulation and supervision. Therefore, a speciality of insolvency proceedings is also in order. The authors' argument is based on the necessity for an early initiation of insolvency proceedings for banks. In this regard, only the local supervisors would have the right incentives and information to initiate an early intervention concerning branches and this would also put pressure on the home authorities to deal promptly with the problems at the holding/parent company level. In the authors' opinion this would create a healthy supervisory competition ↓

> between home and host authorities. But a jurisdiction that couples a universal approach when it is the home country with a territorial approach when it is the host country is the most uncooperative actor in cross-border insolvency proceedings. This is recognised in the article and the preference for a combination of territoriality and universality hinges more on the assumed pre-crisis superior supervisory outcomes (see, for instance, Baxter, Hansen and Sommer 2004, p. 79).
>
> With regard to cross-border bank insolvency proceedings, the 2010 Geneva Report on the World Economy (Claessens *et al* 2010) proposes a middle way between pure territoriality and pure universality (see Chapter 5 on resolution in an international context), given that the first approach has significant negative financial stability implications and the second one is unrealistic and unfeasible (it would, in the end, require an international treaty, an international insolvency court and/or an international special resolution authority). The proposed intermediate approach is labelled "modified universality". In a nutshell, modified universality does not seek to establish a global special resolution regime for banks and other financial institutions, but tries to foster international cooperation between home and host authorities, preventing ring-fencing actions in the host countries. This will require a framework similar to the ancillary proceedings in the host countries and to the main proceedings that run in the home country that are already adopted for corporate cross-border insolvencies in the 1997 UNCITRAL (United Nations Commission on International Trade Law) Model Law on Cross-border Insolvency. To this end, the report advocates more harmonisation between national special resolution regimes and a new concordat (supplementing the existing 1983 Basel Supervisory Concordat) "to improve crisis management arrangements between home and host countries, and, in the absence of a legally burden sharing agreement, provide better incentives for collaboration in supervision and resolution" (p. 96).

It is, then, very important to be realistic about the most significant, non-firm-specific, legal and political obstacles to cross-border cooperation on crisis management in order to be realistic about what can be practically achieved by those CMGs. Moreover, with specific reference to wider political issues that national governments can discuss alongside policies for dealing with the crisis of a cross-border financial group, it is important to bear in mind that many other bilateral and multilateral political forums come into play, while the CMGs are just technical arrangements.

It is also clear that these groups do not have a decision-making role.[6] Principle 2 clearly states: "While financial crisis management remains a domestic competence, the growing interactions between national financial systems require international cooperation by authorities." More broadly, the Financial Stability Board, like other international standard-setting bodies in the economic and financial sector,[7] does not issue legally binding rules, but its standards are "soft" law, in that they need the voluntary acceptance of their addressees in order to become effective with the only possible enforcement mechanism confined to peer review.

Therefore, Principle 2 continues, "home authorities should lead work with the key host authorities to look at the practical barriers to achieve coordinated action in the event of a financial crisis involving specific firms". The necessity of coordinated action is reiterated by Principle 11, which states that "in managing a financial crisis, authorities will strive to find internationally coordinated solutions that take account of the impact of the crisis on the financial systems and real economies of other countries, drawing on information, arrangements and plans developed *ex ante*".[8]

It is, then, mostly a planning exercise. And in order to plan accurately for the management of a crisis, the first task is identifying the (foreseeable) obstacles that can hamper the smooth execution of a cross-border cooperative solution. These obstacles can be broadly identified in:

❏ the business model and cross-border organisational structure of the banking groups, given the significant operational and financial interdependencies between legal entities in different jurisdictions[9]; and
❏ the national legal frameworks (especially insolvency laws, including special resolution regimes for banks, but also company laws or depositor-protection provisions) that involve (or can lead to) a territorial approach to insolvency.[10]

As far as crisis planning is concerned, Principle 8 provides that the authorities "strongly encourage firms to maintain contingency plans and procedures for use in a wind-down situation (e.g. factsheets that could easily be used by insolvency practitioners), and regularly review them to ensure that they remain adequate and accurate".

To be precise, Principle 8 focuses on resolution plans only ("for use in a wind-down situation"), while the subsequent debate has moved towards a more complex structure with regard to these plans, with a clear distinction between recovery (where the bank can still preserve its going-concern status with the implementation of some extraordinary restructuring actions) and resolution (where the bank is a gone concern and the authorities have to step in with resolution tools to try to prevent wider market disruptions).

The follow-up paper to the Turner Review, the Turner Review Conference Discussion Paper (Financial Services Authority 2009, Annex 1), lays out the main elements of a potential recovery and resolution plan. The recovery strategy is owned by the firm itself and, at the cross-border level, the authorities' members of the CMGs are entrusted with the task of evaluating the feasibility and viability of such a plan given a generic idiosyncratic or systemic crisis scenario.[11] Hence, the banking group has to submit a list of actions it will undertake in order to withstand a financial crisis, such as capital-raising activities, disposal of financial assets or entire business units, and liquidity contingency actions, which could be deployed in an emergency situation.[12]

A funding contingency plan is also mentioned in a separate principle. Principle 9 states that authorities will "ensure that firms maintain robust, up to date, funding plans that are practical to use in stressed market scenarios". This special place for a liquidity contingency plan is a direct consequence of the financial crisis, where many financial institutions ran into trouble for the significant maturity mismatch in their balance sheet and the simultaneous and mutually reinforcing drying-up of market liquidity and funding liquidity, which made it impossible to refinance their long-term assets.[13]

On the other hand, the cross-border resolution strategy is owned by the authorities represented in the CMG, which have to draw up a resolution plan and keep it updated. This plan would detail how the authorities intend to deal with the insolvency of the cross-border group: in substance, how they plan to alert each other about a crisis situation, how they will share information and cooperate (*ex ante* and in a crisis situation), which special resolution tool(s) will be most likely used by the authorities in the home jurisdiction and how this intervention can be made compatible with the powers of the authorities in the host jurisdictions. It is evident that such a plan needs a significant amount of information on the cross-border organisational structure and business model of the financial group in order to be drawn up and be operational. This vital information must be supplied by the financial group itself under the authorities' directions.

One crucial piece of information is how the provision of critical economic functions maps into the business units and the legal entities of the banking group on a cross-border basis. In a crisis situation, supervisory and financial authorities are mostly interested in safeguarding fundamental economic functions provided by the ailing financial group. Once again, while the authorities' emergency powers (such as partial property transfers, including the deposit book of a bank) apply on a legal-entity basis, the provision of core financial services by the banking intermediaries follows an organisational structure based on business units that cut across legal entities or with several business units in the same legal entity. This occurs both at the domestic and cross-border levels.

The Financial Stability Board has set up a Steering Committee on Resolution in order to coordinate the consistent implementation of the principles across the world.

12.2.2 The recommendations of the Basel Committee

In March 2010, the Basel Committee on Banking Supervision published a report of its Cross-border Bank Resolution Group.[14] The report carried 10 recommendations, mostly addressed to national authorities, "to address the challenges arising in the resolution of a cross-border bank".[15]

Recommendation 1. Effective national resolution powers. Each national jurisdiction should have effective special resolution regimes with appropriate tools (including bridge banks and partial transfers) in order to achieve an orderly resolution of all types of financial institutions. This recommendation calls for effective national resolution regimes with special resolution powers applicable also to non-depository financial institutions.[16] This is particularly important also for financial conglomerates.

Recommendation 2. Frameworks for a coordinated resolution of financial groups. Given the necessity to apply special resolution tools to every type of financial institution (also within a conglomerate) it is important to have a national framework for coordinating the interventions by the competent authorities, which can have powers over only a specific financial sector.

Recommendation 3. Convergence of national resolution tools. It is important to have consistency in national resolution tools for financial institutions and in their application (eg, similar intervention thresholds).

Recommendation 4. Cross-border effects of national resolution measures. Host country judicial or administrative recognition of resolution measures implemented in the home country is of the utmost importance.

Recommendation 5. Reduction of complexity and interconnectedness of group structures and operations. Given the significant organisational and financial complexity of the cross-border financial institutions (operational and financial interdependencies between legal entities in different jurisdictions), simplification of the group structure could be beneficial in achieving an orderly resolution.

Recommendation 6. Planning in advance for orderly resolution. Without making a clear distinction between a recovery plan and a resolution plan, this recommendation calls for firm-specific wind-down contingency plans on a cross-border basis.

Recommendation 7. Cross-border cooperation and information sharing. The authorities should cooperate and exchange information on a regular basis, especially on the specific responsibilities of national authorities for regulation, supervision, liquidity provision, crisis management and resolution.

Recommendation 8. Strengthening risk-mitigation mechanisms. This recommendation aims at improving the market mechanism for reducing risk in financial transactions, thus guaranteeing settlement finality (eg, enforceable netting agreements and central counterparties for OTC derivative contracts).

Recommendation 9. Transfer of contractual relationships. This recommendation tries to address the complicated issue of early-termination clauses on an event of default. Close-out clauses embedded in financial contracts (especially OTC derivative contracts) could have a destabilising effect and impair the ability of the authorities to impose an orderly wind-down of a financial institution. Preventing the counterparties from acting in the event of default (eg, the intervention of the authorities) even for a limited amount of time (eg, 24 hours, as in the US legislation under the Dodd–Frank Act) would give the authorities the opportunity to transfer the contracts to a third party or to a bridge firm. The report specifically recommends the review of ISDA master agreements to include conditions that contracts not be automatically terminated due to the intervention of the authorities.

Recommendation 10. Exit strategies and market discipline. National authorities should include in their crisis-management planning clear options for withdrawing public intervention after a crisis in order to guarantee minimum market discipline.

12.2.3 The US and EU approaches to cross-border crisis management

The following two subsections deal with two specific proposals that are at the centre of the current debate on cross-border financial crisis management. According to Gillian Tett (2010) from the *Financial Times* these two different approaches constitute the main topic of debate (and disagreement) between American and European policymakers on how to design a crisis-management framework for cross-border financial institutions.

Tett argues that, while the American authorities are in favour of expanding the special resolution tools (bridge banks, partial transfers, etc) to the whole financial system and to every kind of financial intermediary (including investment banks and insurance companies),[17] thus allowing an orderly liquidation of any financial institutions that could pose a threat to financial stability,[18] the European authorities would be sceptical of the practical feasibility of such an approach and advocate the necessity of new tools (ie, automatic debt conversion into equity) in order to allow the financial group in crisis to keep providing its critical financial functions. In substance, one approach favours an orderly liquidation of the cross-border group led by the home country authorities, while the other approach proposes a restructuring of the company still as a going concern.

12.3.2.1 The Dodd–Frank Act
President Barack Obama signed the Dodd–Frank Act on the Wall Street reform and consumer protection into law on July 21, 2010.

The new legislation is very complex and includes many other issues than just crisis management (including enhanced regulation and supervision for systemically important financial institutions and the introduction of the Financial Stability Oversight Council). As is widely known, many implementing secondary rules are necessary in order to make the new legislation completely operational.

Title 2 of the Dodd–Frank Act deals with the so-called "orderly resolution authority". Though many details of the implementing legislation are still not known, the two major novelties of the American special resolution regime for financial companies can be summarised as follows:

❏ a new special resolution regime for the whole financial group and non-bank-financial companies (not just for deposit-taking institutions within a bank holding company) with the power for the Federal Deposit Insurance Corporation (FDIC) to take in receivership the bank holding company itself and all the major financial subsidiaries (eg, broker-dealers and insurance companies); and
❏ the impossibility for the American authorities to provide open bank assistance to an insolvent bank under any circumstances; to be clear, it will not be possible to provide capital injections to ailing banks invoking the systemic risk exemption, as available in the previous special resolution framework, but the banking entity must be immediately put in receivership.

As far as the new resolution powers for non-deposit-taking institutions are concerned, the Act provides[19] that the Board of Governors of the Federal Reserve System and the FDIC may recommend that the secretary of the Treasury, in consultation with the president, make a determination that the failure of the financial company (that, as already said, could be a bank holding company or a financial subsidiary non-deposit-taking institution) would have an adverse systemic effect. Where the financial company is a broker-dealer (investment bank) or an insurance company, the recommendation will be made by the SEC and the director of the Federal Insurance Office respectively (in both cases jointly with the Fed Board).

A financial company (bank holding company or financial subsidiary) for which the determination has been made becomes a "covered financial company".

There is a procedural requirement[20] under which, after the determination has been made, the secretary of the Treasury must petition the US District Court for the District of Columbia for an order authorising the secretary to appoint the FDIC as the receiver of the covered financial company. The order must be granted within 24 hours, after which the FDIC is appointed by operation of law.[21] The Federal Court must determine whether the Treasury secretary's determination is arbitrary and capricious. There is a right to appeal the court's decision, but without automatic stay of the actions of the receiver; therefore, the appointment of the FDIC as receiver is immediately executed after the Court's order.

Insolvent deposit-taking institutions can be taken into receivership following the old special resolution rules. There is still a systemic risk exemption that trumps the least-cost resolution rule, but, as we saw above, the open bank assistance procedure is no longer available also for deposit-taking institutions. This means that government's recapitalisation of banks (or of any other financial institution) is no longer permitted.

On September 27, 2010, the FDIC published a Dodd–Frank Act Notice of Proposed Rulemaking, which opened a public consultation on the secondary rules implementing the orderly resolution powers. In the remarks accompanying the publication, the chairman of the FDIC stated: "With the enactment of the Dodd–Frank Act ..., the FDIC was given the tools to resolve a failing financial company that poses a significant risk to the financial stability of the United States. We now have the framework in place to resolve any financial institution, no matter how large or complex. Implementation of Dodd–Frank is designed to end 'too big to fail', and the new resolution authority is a major reason why it will do so."

The chairman went on, "If appointed as a receiver for a failing systemic financial company,[22] the FDIC has broad authority under the Dodd–Frank Act to operate or liquidate the business, sell the assets and resolve the liabilities of the company immediately after its appointment as receiver or as soon as conditions make this appropriate. This authority will enable the FDIC to act immediately to sell assets of the company to another entity or, if that is not possible, to create a bridge financial company to maintain critical function as the entity is wound down."

12.2.3.2 Bail-inable debt

In an article in the *Economist* (Calello and Ervin 2010) two Credit Suisse executives proposed the fast conversion of debt (including senior debt) into equity as the best means of managing the financial crisis of a financial institution, while avoiding the injection of public money. The main rationale is that the bankruptcy of a financial institution acts as a loss amplifier, which in turn creates increased market disruption and loss of confidence. Roughly speaking, the proposal involves the conversion into capital of all the preferred stocks and subordinated debt, wiping out all the existing shareholders, while converting into capital also a variable amount of senior unsecured debt. The equity capital in the new structure would be equally divided between holders of preferred stock and subordinated debt and senior unsecured creditors.

The article almost immediately sparked a global debate on the feasibility and desirability of such an approach. While some policymakers received the suggestion with enthusiasm, hailing this approach as an effective and innovative way to deal with moral hazard, other policymakers warned of the legal and practical obstacles to the bail-in proposal. Above all, it is by no means clear why market participants should invest in debt instruments,[23] which would automatically convert (at a variable rate and with different likelihood according to the rank of the instruments) into equity, exactly when the equity ownership is practically facing mostly, if not exclusively, significant downside risks in relation to the par value of the debt instrument. It will probably take a significant amount of time before market participants will be able to correctly price debt financial instruments with these conversion features at the time of their issuance.[24] It will also be interesting to see how they will trade in the secondary market, especially in the run-up to the conversion event. Another issue to monitor will be the performance of bail-inable debt as opposed to contingent capital financial instruments.

Moreover, it is not clear from a market-efficiency point of view whether the conversion should be triggered by the intervention of the authorities, which would be entrusted with discretionary (even if constrained by some prudential parameters) powers, or whether the conversion should only have a contractual basis.[25] On the one hand, it can be argued that the availability of a bail-in solution as a contractual clause would probably make it easier for market participants to price the financial instruments, provided that the trigger events can be easily and univocally determined. On the other hand, the availability of public powers would probably better take into account and protect wider financial-stability concerns. It is difficult to imagine an orderly conversion of debt into equity based only on contractual terms during a financial crisis. Many legal actions seem to be easily predictable.

Another complicated issue is the evaluation of the losses, which should give an estimate of the capital needed to keep the bank as a going concern and, in turn, of the amount of debt to be converted. As we have seen, the rationale behind the bail-in proposal is that bankruptcy acts as a loss amplifier. Even though this is easily agreeable, it is by no means certain that in the midst of a severe financial crisis the real losses that impair the capital position could be accurately evaluated, especially in the short time frame available. This could trigger a suite of staggered conversions of debt into equity (starting from the most junior to the most senior) with increasing uncertainty among bondholders of different classes. It is, then, incredibly complicated to distinguish within the liability structure of a banking institution which types of claim would be better excluded in order to avoid run-type behaviours in the market, not to mention concerns about equal treatment of creditors, which could generate numerous legal suits.

Last, it should be carefully examined whether the conversion of debt into equity (especially if triggered by the authorities) during the crisis of a financial institution could ultimately spread panic and contagion to many other financial institutions, thus bringing about the very event it was supposed to prevent.

A bail-in tool is clearly mentioned in the FSB report on SIFIs to the G20 leaders in October 2010 (Financial Stability Board 2010) as one of the tools that would make the resolution of a SIFI a viable option. The report recommends that "national authorities should consider restructuring mechanisms to allow recapitalisation of a financial institution as a going concern by way of contractual and/or statutory (ie, within resolution) debt-equity conversion and write-down tools, as appropriate to their legal frameworks and market capacity". It must be noted also that debt write-down is mentioned alongside the debt-equity conversion option. It is worth underscoring that debt write-down does not automatically address the capital provision issue. It seems only fair that equity shareholders be wiped out, but, if creditors are not automatically converted into equity holders, it would not be possible to keep the bank operating as a going concern. In this regard, debt write-down seems a tool that needs to be coupled with other ordinary resolution tools (such as temporary public ownership, partial transfer to a private-sector purchaser or a bridge bank, and a liquidation procedure).

The report announced that a "working group will be established to examine the legal and operational aspects of both contractual and statutory bail-in mechanisms providing for debt to equity conversions and/or write-downs in resolution". The working group had expressed its intension to present its findings and recommendations by mid-2011.

Also the working document of the European Commission (European Commission 2011) mentioned bail-in or debt write-off mechanisms as a necessary addition to the resolution toolkit available to the authorities. The Commission makes a distinction between a "comprehensive approach", where potentially every type of debt (even if with several proposed exclusions[26]) could be converted into equity and a "targeted approach", where only special issuances of debt would have an embedded conversion clause. The latter proposal seems to blur even more the distinction between contingent capital and bail-inable debt, while also connecting the "targeted approach" to contractual bail-in and the "comprehensive approach" to statutory bail-in.

12.2.4 The G20 leaders summit in Seoul and the way ahead

The Communiqué of the G20 Leaders' Summit in Seoul (November 11–12, 2010) reaffirmed that "G-SIFIs should be subject to a sustained process of mandatory international recovery and resolution planning". Moreover, the leaders agreed "to conduct rigorous risk assessment on these firms through international supervisory colleges and negotiate institution-specific crisis cooperation agreements within crisis management groups".[27]

The latest Financial Stability Board document on systemically important financial institutions (FSB 2010), indicates the way ahead for the two actions on firm-specific crisis-management arrangements identified by the G20 leaders:

1. cross-border, firm-specific recovery and resolution plans; and
2. cross-border, firm-specific cooperation agreements on crisis management.

The FSB was slated to assess and report by the end of 2011 on the progress in the development of institution-specific recovery and resolution plans for G-SIFIs. It was expected to report on practical measures taken to improve resolvability, addressing obstacles associated with booking practices, global payments, intra-group guarantees and information systems.

Moreover, it was agreed that by the end of 2011, relevant home and host authorities should have drawn up for all G-SIFIs institution-specific cooperation agreements that specify the respective roles and responsibilities of the authorities at all stages of a crisis.

In order to give guidance to these two firm-specific work streams, the FSB is carrying out an analysis of the current national legal frameworks for the resolution of financial institutions with the aim of identifying the legal changes needed in order to accomplish effective resolution. It was envisaged that by mid-2011 the FSB would have set out criteria for the resolvability of financial institutions and the key attributes of effective national resolution regimes.

12.3 THE FINANCIAL CRISIS: WHICH LESSONS FOR THE EU SINGLE MARKET?

12.3.1 The European supervisory framework after the crisis

The financial crisis has revealed the inadequacy of the pillars on which the European single market has been built during the last decades. The building blocks of the EU regulatory framework have been the following: (i) the minimum harmonisation of national laws; (ii) the shared recognition of the competences and powers of the national authorities; (iii) the principle of the home-country control in the provision of financial services across borders; (iv) the cooperation and exchange of information among the national authorities based on voluntary agreements (ie, memoranda of understanding) that bear no binding rules for the enforcement process.

The crisis has also shown that the distribution of responsibilities of the current supervisory framework in the EU between the home- and host-country authorities is not aligned with the cross-border structures of the banking groups.

The principle of free establishment, which is one of the guiding forces of the European regulatory and supervisory framework, has allowed financial intermediaries to ensure the cross-border provision of financial services without limits and within very complex corporate structures or different business models. In many cases the development of the activities carried out in foreign countries by the largest banking groups has been undertaken without considering the possible negative externalities on the financial sectors of the host member states and the likely cross-border spillover effects.

A number of factors hampered the cooperation between the home- and the host-country authorities. We can refer at least to the following. First, there is a lack of clarity on which of the authorities is deemed at the end of the process responsible for financial stability, given the different reach of supervisory responsibilities in the case of foreign subsidiaries or branches, the different scope of central banking remit for liquidity support to market and single institutions, and the entire nationally based fiscal powers. This situation is exacerbated by the lack of harmonised frameworks for asset transfers and the winding-up of cross-border institutions.

Second, national authorities have limited incentives to undertake a smooth exchange of information in periods of stress because of the absence of burden-sharing agreements. These would allow a fair and equitable distribution of the costs stemming from the crisis among member states. Without such a commitment, national authorities tend, naturally, to pursue national interests first.

Third, host authorities have limited powers (and information) to preserve financial stability due to unsound practices developed by foreign branches in their markets. This is increasingly the case for local banks that are foreign-owned institutions as well, since cross-border banking groups are used to centralise key management functions, for the monitoring of which the flow of the relevant information is directed mainly towards the consolidating supervisor.

Finally, the lack of an explicit mandate in the EU legislation for national authorities to monitor financial-stability developments from an EU-wide perspective was a contributing factor to the subsequent reductions of incentives to introduce information-sharing practices. This led to suboptimal outcomes in some cases during the crisis.

The above-mentioned drawbacks in the supervisory framework help to explain the limited role that has been played by the supervisory colleges in reaching a coordinated response to the crisis affecting some EU cross-border banking groups. This is because colleges have not been in a position to provide the needed platform for meaningful coordination and information-sharing among supervisors. Some host authorities stated that the colleges have not been fully informed by their consolidating supervisors about the adverse developments faced by important cross-border institutions. This lack of information sharing has been often motivated by the need to safeguard market-sensitive information. This is a clear case for the definition of burden-sharing agreements, which have the potential – *inter alia* – to increase the incentives to exchange relevant information among the involved actors.

On the contrary, the actual management of the crises took place through either bilateral relations between the supervisors or other informal and *ad hoc* structures, including also the central banks and the ministers of finance of the countries where cross-border banking groups has been established.

12.3.2 The experience of the 2008 EU-wide MoU for crisis management during the crisis

The same arguments can be applied to the effective functioning of the framework for cooperation that has been provided by the Memorandum of Understanding (MoU) on financial stability. This was signed in 2008 by all the central banks, financial supervisors and finance ministries of the European Union, but has not played a strong role in guiding the actions of the authorities during the emergency (see Box 12.4).

The crucial point for the efficient management of a cross-border crisis was identified in the interaction between the new structures for cooperation proposed in the MoU (namely the Cross-Border Stability Groups) and the existing cross-border networks for cooperation among authorities (supervisory colleges and networks of central banks). In this respect, it is important to mention Paragraph 4.4 of the

BOX 12.4 THE 2008 EU MEMORANDUM OF UNDERSTANDING ON FINANCIAL STABILITY

The 2008 EU-wide Memorandum of Understanding on financial stability – signed by the financial supervisors, central banks and finance ministers of the EU – outlines basic common principles for cross-border crisis management and contains procedures and arrangements for information sharing and coordination.

The common principles are aimed at facilitating the management and resolution of cross-border systemic financial crises in a way that facilitates private-sector solutions and minimises the economic and social costs of a crisis while promoting market discipline and limiting moral hazard. They do not provide *ex ante* solutions for burden sharing, but recognise that achieving a least-cost solution (ensuring taxpayers' interests) may require the use of public funds. In this case, the MoU includes a commitment that fiscal costs should be shared in an equitable and balanced manner, taking into account the economic impact of the crisis and the distribution of supervisory powers between home and host authorities

The Memorandum defines procedures and practical arrangements for the involvement of all relevant parties in a crisis situation, based on the existing legal responsibilities and building on existing networks of authorities, including the supervisory colleges. It contains provisions for cooperation between authorities not only in crisis situations but also for enhancing crisis preparedness in normal times, through the development of simulation exercises, stress tests and contingency plans.

The MoU also introduces the concept of a coordinating authority in the management of a cross-border crisis. This coordinating authority should be, as a rule, from the home country of the banking group. Accordingly, the MoU states that, as a rule, the national coordinator of the home country will be the cross-border coordinating authority. Depending on the type of crisis, the authority assuming the role of cross-border coordinator may vary. These provisions do not imply any transfer of responsibilities: each member state remains fully in charge for its budgetary decisions, and division of powers between home and host authorities remains unchanged (in line with the current EU legislation).

The MoU commits all central banks and supervisors to develop a common framework for systemic assessment of a crisis. This framework will be applied by the authorities in defining the depth of a crisis and in agreeing on policy responses. It thus contributes to the timeliness of actions. The MoU sets out principles and procedures for realising in practice information sharing and cooperation among responsible authorities. The MoU also includes the commitment of the parties to develop, as well as to test and update on a regular basis, at national and EU levels, contingency arrangements for managing crisis situations and to conduct stress-testing exercises.

MoU, where it says that the responsibility for the coordination and involvement of the different authorities may vary according to the legal competencies and the specific features of the crisis.

Moreover, in several paragraphs of the MoU, it is affirmed that the Cross-Border Stability Groups are aimed at contributing to the management of a crisis – when deemed necessary according to specific circumstances – taking into account the roles of the other existing channels of cooperation among authorities at the cross-border level (colleges of supervisors and networks of central banks). All these provisions were aimed at requiring that the different authorities may be involved at different stages of the crisis-management process according to the specific features of the crisis situation.

The limited use national authorities have made of the provisions of the MoU during the crisis can be partly explained by the fact that it was not conceived as a tool to deal with global and systemic crises, since its main rules are directed towards authorities in charge of the supervision/oversight of individual cross-border financial institutions; others have outlined the difficulties in applying its provisions during the crisis, since its implementation is ongoing.

However, in our opinion it is fair to admit that the substantial failure of the 2008 EU MoU has demonstrated the limitations of any coordination framework based on voluntary and non-binding mechanisms; moreover, coordination would have been as effective as needed during the crisis if based on a high degree of harmonisation of national laws in the field of crisis management and resolution.

Moreover, we believe that some provisions included in the MoU have not facilitated their smooth adoption. For instance, during the effective management of the crises that hit some important EU banking groups, it had been quite impossible to give operational terms to the distinctions between crisis prevention, crisis management and crisis resolution. These terms were devised in the MoU in order to assign particular responsibilities to each authority and to determine the interaction among supervisors, central banks and finance ministries.

The experience referred to above on the limitations of cooperation agreements that are not binding has the potential to indicate some possible ways forward on how to improve the conditions for a coordinated response by the several authorities that can be involved in a crisis situation.

The first building block of more efficient and effective arrangements for the supervision of cross-border banking groups relies on the significantly enhanced role of the supervisory colleges. These structures should be reinforced and seen as the main forum through which to address the risks affecting a large cross-border banking group, risks that could jeopardise the financial stability of the countries where the banking group has relevant subsidiaries.

In order to make the process manageable, a core supervisory college, comprising authorities from the most important countries where the group is present, should be the foundation for the supervisory response to a crisis affecting a cross-border financial group.

For the largest banking groups a core college should be set up, including the supervisory authorities directly involved in the management of a crisis, in line with any burden-sharing agreements among member states. These core colleges would cooperate with the respective central banks and finance ministries, within the framework of the Cross-Border Stability Groups foreseen in the 2008 MoU, where appropriate.

It is really crucial that the functioning of supervisory colleges be based on written agreements. These agreements should not only set modalities for the ongoing coordinated supervision of the group but also clarify the responsibilities of individual supervisors and the procedures for cooperation in crisis situations.

We believe these specific agreements for crisis situations should, in particular, (i) be confidential in order to provide practical criteria for a clear attribution of responsibilities while preserving the flexibility to adapt to different circumstances; (ii) set out the division of labour between home- and host-country supervisors regarding the different layers of supervision (consolidated and at the level of subsidiaries); (iii) clarify what kinds of coordination of resolution/reorganisation measures are feasible; and (iv) be regularly reviewed to keep them updated with the developments in the structure of the financial group.

The written agreements among college supervisors should fit into wider agreements for cooperation involving central banks and ministries of finance of the countries where the cross-border financial group has subsidiaries or significant branches; these agreements should include criteria for burden sharing.

The supervisory colleges should have the specific responsibility of translating the identification of macroprudential risks – as detailed by the European Systemic Risk Board (ESRB), central banks and supervisors – into measures with regard to the financial group as a whole. In this context, supervisors within colleges, working in close cooperation with the central banks of the involved countries, should ensure that measures are taken to reduce the risk that the activities of branches and subsidiaries of financial groups fuel macroeconomic imbalances in local markets.

In order to make the detection of vulnerabilities more effective, the microprudential analysis of risks carried out at the level of each supervisory college should be part of the wider macro-analysis undertaken at the EU level.

The new EU Supervisory Authorities should coordinate the activities of colleges in this area, in order to ensure the microprudential analysis of risks carried out at the level of colleges, feeds the wider macro-analysis undertaken at the EU level. They should also ensure that the detection of macroprudential risks is adequately used by colleges to identify the implications for their respective financial group.

The supervisory colleges should enhance the preparedness for managing a crisis of a financial group. The fundamental duties that colleges should discharge for this purpose are: (i) to produce a periodic risk assessment capable of detecting both current weaknesses and vulnerabilities to adverse scenarios of the financial group as a whole and its main components; (ii) to draw up and implement a supervisory activity programme based on such risk assessment, setting priorities and activities to be undertaken by each supervisor and identifying corrective actions for the financial group; (iii) work with other authorities (central banks, finance ministries) to prepare a contingency plan, possibly based on the banking groups' own planning, which would consider how the reorganisation and/or winding-up of branches and subsidiaries in member states would be handled and coordinated.

In order for home- and host-country authorities to share a common assessment of cross-border financial groups, these groups should maintain contingency plans covering scenarios of increasing severity, including how the reorganisation and/or winding-up of branches and subsidiaries in different countries would be handled and coordinated as well as on how the crisis-management and resolution tools would operate.

These plans, and the organisational structures, should be defined and implemented on the basis of supervisory guidance and subject to home- and host-country scrutiny.

12.3.3 Crisis management in the new EU supervisory architecture

The European financial architecture that came into force at the beginning of 2011 is aimed at addressing the most important regulatory and supervisory failures that have been outlined by the crisis. In this section we describe the role of the new architecture in crisis management, while we leave other issues to Chapter 15. As we mentioned, one of the most relevant issues contained in the global package refers to the recommendations issued by the FSB for a policy framework to reduce the risks and externalities associated with the SIFIs. For the time being, the FSB recommendations are focused on global systemic banks; further work will be needed with respect to "domestic" systemic institutions and to those SIFIs that operate in other financial sectors.

The policy measures that the FSB has identified to address the problems stemming from the failure of the SIFIs are: (i) higher loss absorbency, by considering a combination of instruments, ie, the imposition of a capital surcharge, the introduction of bail-in arrangements (either statutory or contractual) and of contingent capital, debt that converts into equity when some triggers are hit; (ii) reinforcing and harmonising national resolution regimes in order to make it feasible to resolve financial institutions without taxpayer support, through the mechanism enabling shareholders and unsecured creditors to absorb losses; (iii) strengthening cross-border cooperation between resolution authorities through firm-specific arrangements based on the recovery-and-resolution plans (RRPs) prepared and periodically reviewed – in collaboration – by the banks and all the involved authorities (supervisors, central banks and ministries of finance); (iv) strengthening SIFI supervision through the definition of clear supervisory mandates, a full suite of supervisory powers, an improved set of standards for supervisors and a stricter risk-assessment regime.

It would be advisable to differentiate the issues that can be dealt with in the short term and more radical reforms that would require more time to be finalised. In the short term, we could envisage national implementation of those principles that allow for higher contributions, in the form of contingent capital and bail-inable instruments, by the private sector to the banking crisis through changes of contractual arrangements used in financial markets.

At the same time national authorities should review and update their domestic crisis-management toolbox (ie, special administration, power of appointing directors and setting up bridge banks) and develop firm-specific cooperation agreements for crisis management for all major financial institutions.

In the medium term, more demanding legal reforms could be planned (more binding procedures for cross-border coordination and statutory bail-in). This would lead to the consideration of a new international concordat, which could better define home–host relationships in crisis management, allow for group-wide approaches to crisis management and resolution, and introduce the legal basis for cooperation among authorities and for recognition of foreign administrative and judicial decisions in appropriate circumstances.

The new European Banking Authority (EBA) should have a leading role in strengthening supervision and crisis-management tools for the EU cross-border banking groups. This would allow for an appropriate implementation of the policy proposals put forward by the FSB for global SIFIs at the EU level. In this respect the EBA can play an important role by deploying the new tools envisaged by the reform: common and centralised databases with information on the colleges; the conduct of stress tests based on harmonised methodologies and effective peer reviews.

The mechanism for achieving this objective relies on an enhanced role of the colleges of supervisors as the instrument for an effectively integrated supervision on cross-border groups, by developing: (i) common methodologies for risk assessment and their convergent application across colleges, also in the perspective of early intervention measures (thus enhancing the prevention of crises); (ii) coordinated actions in the context of the Supervisory Review Process; (iii) joint decisions in the capital-adequacy process. Up to the time of writing this chapter, supervisory methodologies have been found to differ in very significant respects and we have missed clear guidance on how to achieve a more integrated model of supervision to be consistently applied to groups operating cross-border.

Correcting this is a necessity in order to ensure the success of the entire reform.

The crisis determined a substantial refocusing during 2008–2010 of the Committee of European Banking Supervisors' (CEBS) activities towards the analysis of the risks and vulnerabilities facing the largest European cross-border groups.

The three pillars of the CEBS's approach in 2008–2010 were: the monitoring of the establishment and functioning of supervisory colleges with the aim of fostering coordination among home and host authorities; the development of regular risk assessments on the largest cross-border banking groups; the coordination of EU-wide stress tests to help identifying vulnerabilities and the need for supervisory actions.

In 2008 and 2009 colleges of supervisors were established by the home competent authorities for a large number of the largest cross-border EU banking groups, and for an additional number of (smaller) cross-border European banking groups. Moreover, objectives were established for a coordinated risk assessment under Pillar II in line with the provisions of the revised capital requirements directive.

Since 2006 the CEBS has submitted twice a year to the Economic and Financial Committee (EFC) a Financial Stability Table, a risk-assessment report aimed at detecting the main risks arising at the level of the largest cross-border banking groups. This exercise combines the identification of system-wide risks and vulnerabilities for the EU banking sector as a whole, to which the ECB contributes through colleges of supervisors of the involved banking groups.. In addition, in 2009–2010 the CEBS successfully coordinated two EU-wide stress-testing exercises that have involved the EU major banking groups with the aim of providing policy information for assessing the resilience of the EU banking system. Also here, a bottom-up approach has been used and stress-testing scenarios have been developed in close cooperation with the ECB and the EU Commission.

An important aspect of the new financial architecture concerns the role of the EBA in the supervision of the EU's largest cross-border banking groups. In this respect the new tasks assigned to the EBA by the European Parliament are really significant and have the potential – if interpreted with a high level of ambition – to substantially improve the supervision of the largest banking groups.

The EBA will monitor and foster coherence in the functioning of colleges of supervisors. It will also do the following: collect and share all relevant information to facilitate the work of the colleges; coordinate Union-wide stress tests to assess the resilience of banking groups, ensure that a consistent methodology is applied; where appropriate, address a recommendation to the competent authority to undertake mitigating actions on issues identified in the stress test and promote effective supervisory activities, including evaluating the risks to which financial institutions are or might be exposed. A legally binding mediation role will allow the EBA to solve disputes between competent authorities.

The EBA will have a key role in providing an IT infrastructure for the information exchange between supervisors in colleges, and for providing peer-group information about large financial institutions for supervisors. This is a condition for the EBA to develop periodic assessments of the resilience of the EU banking sector, complementary to the macroprudential analyses that will be developed by the ESRB.

First, the EBA should enhance crisis prevention by developing common methodologies for risk assessment and promoting their consistent application between the home and the host supervisors within colleges, thus increasing the capability of supervisors to intervene early and in a coordinated way. It is important that supervisory risk-assessment processes be based on a commonly agreed set of indicators that effectively capture the risk profile of the parent bank and its subsidiaries.

To this end the work on the joint risk-assessment process within colleges under the Pillar II should constitute a useful starting point. The new powers assigned by the Regulation to the EBA will contribute to fostering convergence among supervisory practices and achieving more ambitious results in terms of common approaches to onsite/offsite analysis, early-warning systems and information exchange.

Second, the role the EBA can play in ensuring the adequate implementation of the FSB proposals on crisis management and resolution for SIFIs depends on the actual definition of the EU legislation. This is particularly relevant in the areas where the EBA has been provided with the power to develop technical standards or to exercise binding mediation. In this respect the proposal on the EU crisis-management framework that was put forward by the EU Commission goes into the right direction.

The role of the EBA should be reinforced in the following area: the development of technical standards for recovery and resolution plans, with the aim of increasing the degree of preparedness to deal with crisis situations by authorities and firms in a coordinated way.

Common approaches in this area will increase the feasibility of these plans and the speed at which the planned actions will be implemented across the different jurisdictions affected by the crisis. If statutory haircuts – which are being considered at international level – are introduced as an additional tool at the disposal of the authorities for preserving the going-concern perspective, it is worth exploring the role of the EBA in defining at regulatory level the triggers for their application. Moreover, the role of the EBA is also crucial for the definition of standards in the field of deposit protection schemes; this is in order to introduce common methodologies for calculating contributions to be paid by banks according to their risk profile

12.4 CONCLUSIONS

The most severe financial crisis since the Great Depression has brutally exposed the weaknesses of a global financial system that is based on international financial institutions but with national jurisdictions. The extraordinary policy interventions needed after the collapse of Lehman Brothers have brought about an increased moral hazard in the financial sector.

The Financial Stability Board (under the aegis of the G20), along with the Basel Committee and the European Union, has put forward significant policy proposals for the establishment of a cross-border crisis-management and resolution framework based on *ex ante* information sharing and cooperation between national authorities on firm-specific crisis planning and resolution. Other policy proposals (such as bail-inable debt) are still under consideration, while the United States with Title II of the Dodd–Frank Act has taken the lead in a major overhaul of national special resolution regimes. It is probably still too early to assess the efficiency and effectiveness of such policy proposals and legislative changes, and the general hope is that they will never need to be tested in such a severe and systemic crisis as the one that rose in the aftermath of the Lehman demise.

It is nonetheless clear that only the availability of such a framework will allow the national authorities to properly address the moral hazard stemming from the too-big-to-fail issue. In this regard, an international consensus on cross-border banking crisis management and resolution is too important to fail.

The opinions expressed here are those of the authors only and do not necessarily represent the views of either the UK FSA or the Bank of Italy. The chapter is the outcome of a shared assessment and decision; however, Sections 12.1 and 12.2 are by G. Bassani, while Section 12.3 is by M. Trapanese.

1   See Huertas (2010c): "But monetary and fiscal stimulus was not the full story. Just as important in arresting the slide into the Great(er) Depression was the revision of resolution policy. At the start of October governments made strong statements, soon backed up by convincing actions that they would not allow systemically important institutions to fail."
2   See, for instance, Borio (2003) and Chapter 2.
3   The fundamental importance of an effective and efficient resolution framework for cross-border financial institutions in order to mitigate the too-big-to-fail problem has been easily acknowledged by the Financial Stability Board in its report to the G20 leaders. Section III on resolution of SIFIs as a viable option starts with a clear statement: "Any effective approach to addressing the 'too big to fail' problem needs to have effective resolution at its base. Such a regime must be able to prevent the systemic damage caused by a disorderly collapse without exposing the taxpayer to the risk of loss" (see Financial Stability Board 2010, p. 3).
4   The origin of both core global colleges (at least in a formal way) and crisis-management groups was the Financial Stability Forum report on enhancing market and institutional resilience (FSF 2008). Among the many recommendations on how to fix the global financial system, Rec. V.5 mandated that "the use of international colleges of supervisors should be expanded so that, by end-2008, a college exists for each of the largest global financial institutions"; while Rec. VI.10 stated: "for the largest cross-border financial firms, the most directly involved supervisors and central banks should establish a small group to address specific cross-border crisis management planning issues. It should hold its first meeting before end-2008." Therefore, these two recommendations dealt with firm specific international cooperation in a business-as-usual and crisis situation respectively. It is important to bear in mind this common origin between global core colleges and crisis-management groups for the most important cross-border financial institutions. The FSF principles, one year after the first FSF report, narrowed down firm specific cross-border cooperation on crisis management and resolution to banking groups only, but the set of institutions has always been the same (ie, the largest cross-border financial groups).
5   This consultation paper expands the issues and proposals already discussed in the Commission Communication October 20, 2010, on a new EU framework for crisis management in the financial sector (see European Commission 2010).
6   While decision-making powers rest with the competent national authorities, the crisis-management groups should allow the national decision makers to take better informed decisions.
7   The most significant exception being probably the World Trade Organisation with a significant legal enforcement framework of its rules.
8   A global cooperative solution for the crisis in the banking groups included in the FSB's list

CRISIS MANAGEMENT AND RESOLUTION

(slated to be 2011 for G-SIFIs) is clearly the first best objective for the crisis-management groups. If there were any doubts on this, Principle 14 clearly lays out the second-best objective: "If a fully coordinated solution is not possible [the authorities will] discuss as promptly as possible national measures with other relevant authorities." The primacy of a globally coordinated resolution strategy is predicated on the assumption that a cooperative unified solution maximises the overall economic value (or, better, minimises the overall economic costs) of the resolution, while also taking into account the legitimate financial stability concerns of the different jurisdictions (both home and host).

9 The Financial Stability Board report to the G20 leaders on systemically important financial institutions (Financial Stability Board 2010) has identified some intra-group business practices or transactions that can impede the cross-border resolvability of a financial group, because they produce cross-border operational or financial interdependencies. In particular the report mentions intra-group guarantees, global payment and settlement services, and service-level agreements (for the provision of operational services, for instance IT services).

10 We have already mentioned some examples of national legal rules with a specific territorial bias. As already said, it is next to impossible to predict *ex ante* how the numerous provisions that can have a bearing on the insolvency proceedings of a cross-border bank will be applied in specific cases by national courts (see Box 12.3 for rather introductory remarks on territoriality and universality in cross-border insolvency).

11 The distinction between an idiosyncratic and a systemic crisis scenario is fundamental in the evaluation of the robustness of the recovery plan. It is obvious that in a systemic crisis situation, where many financial institutions tried to implement their recovery plans simultaneously, it would be much more difficult to have a successful implementation of the measures included in the plans (eg, capital raising actions and asset disposals). Unfortunately, it seems next to impossible to plan for a recovery in a systemic crisis scenario. The assumptions made about timeframe and returns of the planned actions are almost unavoidably made in an idiosyncratic crisis scenario. This seems to be an insurmountable drawback of any recovery plan.

12 A significant part of the recovery plan (especially the asset disposal actions or more general balance-sheet management actions) can also be termed a de-risking plan, where the financial institution tries to refocus its business to achieve a more manageable size.

13 In this regard, though asset valuation in a crisis situation is a very difficult, and highly uncertain, exercise, it can be argued that most of the banks and financial institutions that ran into trouble during the financial crisis were struck by liquidity insolvency (incapacity to pay their debts when they are due) rather than balance-sheet insolvency (value of the liabilities higher than the value of the assets).

14 The group was set up by the Basel Committee in December 2007. The original mandate of the group mentioned an analysis of "the existing resolution policies, allocation of responsibilities and legal frameworks of relevant countries, as a foundation to a better understanding of the potential impediments and possible improvements to cooperation in the resolution of cross-border banks". The group includes representatives of the G10 countries, plus Spain, Luxembourg, Switzerland, Argentina and Brazil. The Offshore Group of Banking Supervisors (an umbrella organisation for the financial supervisory authorities of many offshore centres) is also a member of the Cross-border Bank Resolution Group. The mandate of the group was extended in December 2008 "to expand its analysis to review the developments and processes of crisis management and resolutions during the financial crisis". The group was hence asked to submit to the Basel Committee a report on the lessons learned from the ongoing financial crisis on the special-resolution regimes in place with recommendations aimed at strengthening cross-border resolution mechanisms. Its works are currently highly intertwined with the workstream on cross-border crisis management of the Financial Stability Board (see above in the text).

15 See also Box 12.3 for the general framework of "modified universality" recommended in the same report.
16 It will be clearer below that the American authorities have taken the lead in the national implementation of this recommendation with Title II (orderly liquidation authority) of the Dodd–Frank Act.
17 Current national special resolution regimes generally apply only to deposit-taking institutions.
18 It is well known that after the Lehman collapse the most serious threat to the global financial system was represented by an insurance company, AIG (American International Group Inc), even if the real danger was stemming from its role as counterparty in many derivative transactions (carried out by its subsidiary AIG Financial Products) rather than from the traditional insurance business. In the end, AIG needed to be rescued with financial assistance from the Federal Reserve, which provided up to US$182 billion in funding in order to cover the burgeoning losses that emerged during the crisis.
19 See Section 203 of the Act.
20 This procedural requirement is operational in the case that the board of directors of the covered financial company does not acquiesce or consent to the appointment of the FDIC as receiver. If the board of directors acquiesces or consents to the appointment of the FDIC as receiver it is immediately effective upon the determination of the Secretary of the Treasury.
21 This means that, if the Court does not grant the order within 24 hours from the petition, the FDIC is automatically appointed as the receiver by operation of law.
22 With the procedure described in the text.
23 In principle the debt-to-equity conversion feature could be applicable to every class of unsecured debt (subordinated debt, mezzanine debt, senior debt, etc).
24 It is likely that bail-inable debt instruments will be issued and trade at a significant discount to their par (face) value.
25 In the original proposal (Calello and Erwin 2010) the regulatory authorities would be given the powers to decide the timing and the terms of the conversion.
26 The Commission's document states that "to ensure proper functioning of credit markets" (ie, to avoid panic and contagion or driving the prices of some essential funding or hedging instruments to unsustainable levels) "certain exclusions might be necessary . . .: swap, repo and derivatives counterparties and other trade creditors; short term debt (defined by a specified maximum maturity); retail and wholesale deposits and secured debt (including covered bonds). It is also questionable whether the power could in practice be exercised to claims that are covered by master netting agreements (even if uncollateralised)."
27 The conclusions of the Seoul G20 leaders' summit followed up on the G20 leaders' summit held in Toronto on June 26–27, 2010. In Toronto the G20 leaders reiterated their commitment "to design and implement a system where [the authorities] have the powers and tools to restructure or resolve all types of financial institutions in crisis, without taxpayers ultimately bearing the burden".

REFERENCES

Basel Committee on Banking Supervision, 2010, "Proposal to ensure the loss absorbency of regulatory capital at the point of non viability", consultative document, August, available at http://www.bis.org.

Basel Committee on Banking Supervision, 2011, "Basel Committee issues final elements of the reforms to raise the quality of regulatory capital", press release, January 13, available at http://www.bis.org.

Baxter T. C., 2010, "Statement by the General Counsel of the Federal Reserve Bank of New York before the Financial Crisis Inquiry Commission", September 1, available at http://fcic.gov/.

Baxter, T. C., J. M. Hansen and J. H. Sommer, 2004, "Two cheers for territoriality: An essay on international bank insolvency law", *American Bankruptcy Law Journal* 78, pp. 57–91.

Borio, C., 2003, "Towards a macroprudential framework for financial supervision and regulation?", BIS Working Paper 128, February, available at http://www.bis.org.

Calello, P., and W. Ervin, 2010, "From bail-out to bail-in", *Economist*, January 30–February 5, p. 95.

Claessens, S., R. J. Herring and D. Schoenmaker, 2010, "A safer world financial system: improving the resolution of systemic institutions", Geneva Report on the World Economy, International Center for Monetary and Banking Studies.

European Commission, 2011, "Technical details of a possible EU framework for bank recovery and resolution", DG Internal Market and Services Working Document, January, available at http://www.europa.eu.

Financial Services Authority, 2009, "A Regulatory Response to the global banking crisis: systemically important banks and assessing cumulative impact", Turner Review Conference Discussion Paper, October, available at http://www.fsa.gov.uk

Financial Stability Forum, 2008, "Report of the Financial Stability Forum on enhancing market and institutional resilience", April 7, available at http://www.financialstabilityboard.org.

Financial Stability Forum, 2009, "Principles for Cross-border Cooperation on Crisis Management", April 2, available at http://www.financialstabilityboard.org.

Financial Stability Board, 2010, "Reducing the moral hazard posed by systemically important financial institutions. FSB recommendations and timeline", October 20, available at http://www.financialstabilityboard.org.

Financial Times, 2008, "Terror law used for Iceland deposits", October 9.

Goodhart, C., and D. Schoenmaker, 2009, "Fiscal Burden Sharing in Cross-Border Banking Crises", *International Journal of Central Banking* 5(1), March, pp. 141–65.

Goodhart, C., and D. Schoenmaker, 2010, "Improve banks' survival with living wills", *Financial Times*, August 10, 2010.

Huertas, T., 2009, "Too big to fail, too complex to contemplate: What to do about systemically important firms", speech at the FMG–LSE Conference, "Too big to fail, too interconnected to fail?", London, September 15, available at http://www2.lse.ac.uk/fmg/documents/events/conferences/2009.

Huertas, T., 2010a, "Living wills, how can the concept be implemented?", speech at the Wharton School of Management, University of Pennsylvania, February 12, available at http://www.fsa.gov.uk.

Huertas, T., 2010b, "Policy of too big to fail is too costly to continue", in *Financial Times*, March 23.

Huertas, T., 2010c, "Ending too big to fail: Why it should be done and how to do it", speech at the 12th Geneva Conference on the World Economy, Geneva, May 7.

Huertas, T., 2010d, "The road to better resolution: from bail-out to bail-in", paper presented at the London Financial Regulation Seminar Series at the Financial Markets Group of the London School of Economics, November 15, 2010, available at http://www2.lse.ac.uk/fmg/events/financialRegulation/home.aspx.

Hughes, J., 2008, "Winding up Lehman Brothers", *Financial Times*, November 7.

Jenkins, P., and P. J. Davies, 2009, "Thirty financial groups on systemic risk list", *Financial Times*, November 30, 2009.

Miller, H. R., 2010, "Testimony before the Financial Crisis Inquiry Commission", September 1, available at http://fcic.gov/.

Rachman, G., 2010, "Why 9/15 changed more than 9/11", *Financial Times*, September 14.

Ross Sorkin, R., 2009, *Too Big to Fail: Inside the Battle to Save Wall Street* (London, New York: Penguin Books).

Tett, G., 2010, "Transatlantic differences split debate on banks", *Financial Times*, October 1.

Turner, A., 2009, "The Turner Review. A regulatory response to the global banking crisis", Financial Services Authority, London, March, available at http://www.fsa.gov.uk.

13

The Impact of the New Regulatory Framework

Francesco Cannata; Ulrich Krueger
Bank of Italy; Deutsche Bundesbank

13.1 INTRODUCTION

The definition of the Basel III framework has been accompanied by a wide range of economic analyses aimed at assessing the likely effects of the new rules on banks and the economy as a whole. On the one hand, impact assessment is a working tool that is widely used in regulatory processes, not limited to the financial sector. On the other hand, the fact that the introduction of the new prudential rules followed the most severe economic crisis since 1929 has made such analyses crucial from a policy point of view.

This chapter aims at providing an overview of the main results of these analyses, highlighting the key aspects as well as the more controversial issues. The text is organised as follows. Section 13.2 discusses the role of impact assessment in the Basel III regulatory process. Section 13.3 summarises the results of the Comprehensive Quantitative Impact Study (C-QIS) for international banks, following the same methodology and presentation adopted by the Basel Committee and the Committee of European Banking Supervisors (CEBS – now the European Banking Authority – EBA); Section 13.4 reports the main results of the macro analyses, looking at the effects during the transitional period (Subsection 13.4.1) and in the long run (Subsection 13.4.2). Section 13.5 contains the concluding remarks.

13.2 IMPACT ASSESSMENT IN THE BASEL III REFORM

Regulatory initiatives are generally accompanied by discussions and analyses on their likely impact on relevant stakeholders. Regulators are interested in identifying possible costs and benefits of the available options, given the policy objectives to be pursued. Meanwhile, market counterparties are interested in assessing in a timely manner the likely impact of the rules on their business.

Impact assessment has become a key component of the regulatory process of the Basel Committee. As regards prudential regulation, the crafting of the Basel II framework had been supported by a series of quantitative impact studies (QIS), conducted on the basis of the data provided by banks. The evidence gathered in the QIS has been used for calibrating the capital requirements for credit and operational risks and for addressing key policy issues, such as the prudential treatment of loans to small and medium-sized enterprises (SMEs).

Like for Basel II, the Basel III reform has been accompanied by a wide debate on its possible impact on banks and the economy as a whole. Such a discussion started at the very moment when the G20 and the Financial Stability Board designed the roadmap for a global reform of the regulatory framework as it stood. This process intensified once the Basel Committee got close to finalising the new package. Considering the final objective of providing a severe and homogeneous response to the financial crisis without jeopardising the economic recovery, the views expressed among regulators, market practitioners and academics on the likely effects of the reform are diverse and sometimes extreme.

A key issue in the debate has been the stringent criteria in terms of eligible capital instruments and the high level of risk-weighted assets (RWAs) that – in combination – have been supposed to represent an excessively severe calibration of the new standards. However, some regulators also felt that the new requirements would not be sufficiently restrictive, given the severe losses and liquidity shortages that many banks have experienced during the crisis. After the Basel Committee agreed on the calibration of the new capital and liquidity standards, some observers said the Basel III reform moved in the right direction but was not enough as a response to the most severe financial crisis since 1929. They therefore called on banks to hold higher minimum capital levels as a cushion against risk, arguing that the cost to banks of maintaining more capital is associated with significant benefits for the financial system, due to lower risks to creditors and taxpayers. "The regulators are trying to make the existing financial system less unsafe, incrementally. That is better than nothing. But it will not create a safe system. The world cannot afford another such crisis for at least a generation. By these standards what is emerging is simply insufficient. This mouse will never roar" (Wolf 2010).

The banking industry's stance on the impact of the reform has generally been quite diverse, highlighting the restrictive effects on lending and the economy as a whole. According to the Institute of International Finance (IIF), the implementation of the framework proposed in December 2009 for the US, euro area and Japan would have implied in the period 2011–15 a reduction of real GDP with respect to a baseline scenario of 3.1 percentage points. The effects of unemployment would have been even harsher: almost 9 million jobs would be lost in the same period (IIF 2010).

Financial authorities at the G20 and the European level themselves carried out a series of articulated impact assessments, focused both on the effects on banks and on the economy. The impact analysis carried out by the Basel Committee – also referred to as the "Comprehensive Quantitative Impact Study" (C-QIS) in public documents – has been considered an indispensable part of the Basel III reform. Due to the degree of complexity and the wide range of issues addressed in the framework, a comparison of policy options under discussion on the basis of banking data and the fine-tuning of the consultative proposals were essential in the reform process.

The survey was conducted throughout 2010; the aggregate results for the international banking system, based on 2009 data, were published in December 2010 together with the rules text (BCBS 2010a); a similar exercise has been conducted by the Committee of European Banking Supervisors on European banks (CEBS 2010). Such "bottom-up" exercises have been integrated by analyses aimed at assessing the macroeconomic impact of the regulatory reform, both in the transitional period and in the long run (BCBS 2010e, 2010d). These exercises, carried out together with the FSB, are based on a theoretical framework but, given the objective they pursue, are built on a high number of assumptions.

13.3 THE IMPACT ON BANKS: EVIDENCE FROM THE C-QIS

The structure of the C-QIS exercise reflects the main components of the new framework as proposed in the 2009 BCBS Consultative Document (2009a, 2009b): the changes to the definition of capital; the increases in RWAs resulting from changes to the definition of capital, securitisation, trading book and counterparty credit risk (CCR); the data items necessary to calculate a leverage ratio and those needed to compute the new liquidity standards.

The evidence in this section is presented, for both the Basel Committee on Banking Supervision (BCBS) and EU banks, in the following way: the general features of the exercise are described in Subsection 13.3.1 while Subsection 13.3.2 describes the results of the simulation of the new rules on capital requirements, both risk- and non-risk-based. The impact of the two liquidity standards is reported in Subsection 13.3.3.

13.3.1 Features and scope of the exercise

The sample of participating banks is very large. A total of 263 banks from 23 countries participated in the BCBS exercise, including 94 Group 1 banks and 169 Group 2 banks.[1] Country coverage, (ie, the share of total assets represented in the sample) was very high for Group 1 banks, while coverage for Group 2 banks was lower and varied across countries. As regards European banks, 246 institutions from 21 CEBS member countries participated in the EU-QIS, including 48 Group 1 banks and 182 Group 2 banks.[2]

Banks were asked to provide data as of December 31, 2009, at the consolidated group level. Subsidiaries of other banks were excluded from the analyses to avoid double counting.

Overall data quality (defined by compliance to reporting instructions and on the reliability of banks' estimates) was adequate, even though the degree of complexity of the new rules suggests considering many caveats in the interpretation of the results. In that respect, national supervisors have carefully checked the quality of the data submitted by banks headquartered in their jurisdictions and challenged them when data issues needed to be clarified.

The estimated impacts of the new regulatory framework do not take into account either the transitional arrangements introduced in the framework[3] or the possible adjustments of the banking sector to the changing economic and regulatory environment. "The QIS results do neither consider banks' profitability nor make any assumptions about banks' behavioural responses, such as changes in capital or portfolio composition and strategy as well as other management actions, to the policy changes since end-2009 or in the future" (BCBS 2010a).

13.3.2 The impact on capital

This subsection focuses on the rules regarding capital. The evidence is presented by discussing, first, the effects of the changes of the definition of capital; second, the impact of the new rules to calculate the RWAs, then the overall impact on risk-based capital requirements; and, finally, the impact deriving from the introduction of a leverage ratio.

The analysis made in the C-QIS compares the level of the three capital aggregates defined in Basel III – common equity Tier 1 (CET1), Tier 1 (T1) and total capital (TC) – as calculated under the Basel II regime and their Basel III-compliant version. The focus is on CET1, the predominant component of banks' capital. Given that under Basel II a regulatory definition of CET1 did not exist, the Basel Committee has defined CET1 under this framework – only for QIS purposes – as capital and reserves gross of all deductions.[4] For this reason, the comparisons, which provide an overestimated measure of the impact, must be interpreted with caution.

Table 13.1 shows the change in the CET1 ratio for Group 1 and Group 2 banks, distinguishing the impact of the different deductions applied to gross CET1. As explained in Chapter 3, one of the major improvements to the definition of regulatory capital comes from the calculation of deductions, as regards both the items to be deducted and the capital layers from which deductions are to be applied.

For deferred tax assets (DTA), the figure includes the impact of items fully deducted from CET1 (eg, loss carry forwards) as well as those in excess of the 10% individual threshold under the basket (eg, timing differences). For holdings in other financial institutions, impacts include reciprocal cross-holdings in common equity as well as small investments and significant investments in the common equity of other financial institutions where these investments exceed the 10% individual thresholds. The category "Excess above 15%" refers to the deduction of the amount by which the aggregate of the three items subject to the 10% limit for inclusion in CET1 capital exceeds 15% of a bank's common equity component of Tier 1, calculated after all deductions from CET1. Deductions from CET1 are also required for investments by banks in their own shares,[5] shortfall of provision to expected losses, cashflow hedge reserves, cumulative changes in own credit risk, pension-fund assets and securitisation gains on sale. Minority interests, ie, the portions of a bank subsidiary's stock that are not owned by the parent and are not included in the total deductions.

For both BCBS and EU Group 1 banks, the reduction in CET1 capital is driven primarily by deductions of goodwill, holdings in other financial institutions and DTA. Minority interests have a larger impact in countries – as in the EU – where these interests were included in the predominant form of Tier 1 capital. Generally, other deductions, for example those related to own shares, pension-fund assets and securitisation gains on sale, are less significant. The corresponding figures for BCBS and EU Group 2 banks are broadly in line with those for Group 1. The main exception is represented by a lower impact of the goodwill (due to a lower involvement of these institutions in M&A transactions).

These results are significantly affected by the policy decisions taken during the negotiations: after the consultation and based on the C-QIS results, some significant amendments to the original proposals have been made in the direction of making the impact of the new rules less severe. Under the 2009 Consultative Document the impact would have been more sizable. As discussed in Chapter 3, the main changes deal with: (i) the inclusion of minority interests in CET1 to the extent that the minority interests support the risks in a subsidiary that is a bank and exclude the surplus; (ii) the offsetting of long and short positions relating to investments in the capital instruments of other financial institutions, eliminating restrictions on CCR

Table 13.1 Impact on CET1: main drivers as of end-2009 (%)[6]

		\multicolumn{8}{c}{CET1 deductions and minority interest as a percentage of new CET1 gross of deductions}
		Goodwill	Intangibles	Financials	DTA	MSRs	Excess above 15%	Other	Total	Minority interest
BCBS	Group 1	−19.0	−4.6	−4.3	−7.0	−0.4	−2.4	−3.6	−41.3	−2.0
	Group 2	−9.4	−2.3	−5.5	−2.8	0.0	−1.0	−3.7	−24.7	−2.1
EU	Group 1	−19.8	−4.4	−5.0	−6.3	0.0	−1.8	−4.8	−42.1	−3.7
	Group 2	−12.4	−3.1	−8.9	−2.9	0.0	−1.4	−4.7	−33.4	−3.0

Source: BCBS (2010a), CEBS (2010)

in hedging and introducing an underwriting exemption; (iii) instead of a full deduction, the limited recognition in CET1 of holdings in financial companies, some types of deferred tax assets (DTAs) and mortgage servicing rights (MSRs).

As regards changes to how RWAs are computed, the impact is reported by disentangling the following items:

1. definition of capital, ie, the change in RWAs as a result of the application of a risk-weighting treatment to exposures currently being deducted from capital or vice versa;
2. CCR, which measures the impact of the changes introduced to the calculation of the capital charge against CCR and also reflects the higher capital charge against exposures to financial institutions under the internal ratings-based (IRB) approach to credit risk (see Chapter 5);
3. securitisation in the banking book (Sec BB);
4. stressed value-at-risk (sVaR), ie, the impact of the new stressed value-at-risk capital requirement in the trading book (see Chapter 4);
5. equity standard measurement method (Equity SMM), ie, the impact of the higher capital charge for certain equity exposures subject to the standardised measurement method in the trading book; and
6. incremental risk charge and securitisations in the trading book (IRC and Sec TB), ie, the effect of the incremental risk capital charge and the increase in capital charges for securitisations held in the trading book.

Assuming full implementation of all these measures, overall RWAs would increase by approximately 23% for BCBS Group 1 banks; as for capital, also for RWAs, the final rules text has introduced a less severe treatment of some items with respect to the consultative proposals. The main changes deal with: (i) the adoption of a bond-equivalent approach for the Credit Value Adjustment (CVA) charge for counterparty credit risk (instead of the EAD method), without the five-times multiplier initially proposed; (ii) the increase from a US$25 to US$100 billion threshold for applying the increased asset-value correlation parameter to exposures towards regulated financial institutions in the internal ratings-based approach for credit risk; (iii) RWAs associated with changes to the definition of capital. These last items, in particular, are larger under the final accord than the December 2009 proposal. In fact the limited recognition for significant investments in financial institutions', MSRs' and DTAs' timing differences results in at least a portion of these assets being risk-weighted rather than deducted from capital (ie, deductions fall, but RWAs rise).

The main drivers of the results are the charges against CCR, the definition of capital and trading-book exposures.

As regards CCR, it is very important to highlight that, given the ongoing discussion at the Basel Committee on the final prudential treatment of counterparty risk, the figures reported in the C-QIS do not reflect all revisions since the initial proposal. A follow-up quantitative assessment has been carried out in the first months of 2011 on the impact of changes to the proposed rules on the prudential treatment of CVA and exposures to central counterparties. The revised treatment of securitisations in the banking book would increase RWAs of BCBS Group 1 banks by 1.7% (3.3% for EU Group 1 banks).

SVaR determines an average increase of risk-weighted assets of 2.3%. The elimination of the preferential risk-weight for equity exposures subject to the standardised measurement method has almost no impact on Group 1 banks. The incremental and comprehensive risk capital charges and the capital charges for securitisation exposures in the trading book contribute to the overall increase of RWAs with a 5.1% average increase.

Since Group 2 banks are less affected by the revised CCR and trading-book rules, their RWAs would increase by about 4%. The figures for European banks are broadly in line with the BCBS figures.

As regards the overall impact on risk-based ratios, ie, considering changes on both numerator and denominator, the BCBS weighted

Table 13.2 Basel III impact on RWAs: main drivers as of end-2009 (%)

		Overall	Def. of capital	CCR	Sec BB	sVaR	Equity SMM	IRC and Sec TB
BCBS	Group 1	23.0	6.0	7.6	1.7	2.3	0.2	5.1
	Group 2	4.0	3.2	0.3	0.1	0.3	0.1	0.1
EU	Group 1	24.5	6.0	9.7	3.3	2.0	0.4	3.2
	Group 2	4.1	3.1	0.2	0.1	0.6	0.2	0.0

Source: BCBS (2010a), CEBS (2010).

Table 13.3 Basel III versus Basel II capital ratios as of end-2009 (%)

		CET1 ratio	Tier 1 ratio		Total capital ratio	
		Basel III	Basel II	Basel III	Basel II	Basel III
BCBS	Group 1	5.7	10.5	6.3	14.0	8.4
	Group 2	7.8	9.8	8.1	12.8	10.3
EU	Group 1	4.9	10.3	5.6	14.0	8.1
	Group 2	7.1	10.3	7.6	13.1	10.3

Source: BCBS (2010a), CEBS (2010).

average CET1 ratio would be 5.7% for Group 1 banks and 7.8% for Group 2 Banks. The impact on CET1 ratios for European banks is higher, for both Group 1 and 2 banks.

The impact is also significant for Tier 1 and total capital ratios: the Tier 1 capital ratios of BCBS Group 1 banks would on average decline from 10.5% to 6.3%, while total capital ratios would decline from 14.0% to 8.4%. The decline in other capital ratios is also less pronounced for Group 2 banks. European banks would experience a higher decrease in capital ratios.

The capital shortfall for BCBS Group 1 banks in the QIS sample would be between €165 billion for the CET1 minimum requirement of 4.5% and €577 billion for a CET1 target level of 7% (which includes also a 2.5% CET1 target for the Capital Conservation Buffer). The impact on Group 2 banks would be significantly lower. The corresponding figures for European banks in the sample are lower in relative terms for Group 1 banks; conversely they are higher for Group 2 banks, mirroring the number of EU versus non-European countries in the BCBS sample.

As a point of reference, the sum of profits after tax prior to distributions across the BCBS and EU Group 1 banks in 2009 was respectively €209 billion and €80 billion. This suggests that, assuming on average the same profitability as reported in the past, profit retention should allow most institutions to strengthen to a large extent their capital base in order to meet the Basel III capital standards.

As regards the introduction of a leverage ratio, ie, a non-risk-based tool aimed at supplementing the solvency standards (see Chapter 7), the data gathered in the C-QIS have allowed regulators to assess a wide range of policy options regarding the treatment of some

Table 13.4 Capital shortfall in CET1 as of end-2009 (€bn)

		Min. req. 4.5%	Min. + CCB 7%
BCBS	Group 1	165	577
	Group 2	8	25
EU	Group 1	53	263
	Group 2	9	28

Source: BCBS (2010a), CEBS (2010)

specific types of exposures in order to identify a proper definition of the items needed to compute the ratio.[7] However, the need to get a more in-depth understanding of all functioning aspects of such a tool has prompted the Basel Committee to introduce a monitoring period up to 2017.

The average value of the leverage ratio as of end-2009 would be 2.8% for BCBS Group 1 banks and 3.8% for BCBS Group 2 banks. Approximately 42% of the Group 1 banks and 20% of the Group 2 banks in the sample would have been constrained by a 3% leverage ratio as of December 31, 2009. This is assuming that the new definition of Tier 1 capital was already in place (see Chapter 3). As shown in Figure 13.1 for the BCBS sample, dispersion of values around the mean is quite high, especially for Group 2 banks.

Table 13.5 Basel III leverage ratio as of end-2009 (%)

	Group 1	Group 2
BCBS	2.8	3.8
EU	2.5	3.5

Source: BCBS (2010), CEBS (2010)

13.3.3 The impact on banks' liquidity

As widely discussed in Chapter 8, the Basel III reform envisages two new quantitative standards for liquidity risk: the liquidity coverage ratio (LCR) and the net stable funding ratio (NSFR). The policy debate on the calibration of these new rules has been very intense, given the implications that strategies adopted by banks in order to meet the new standards might have on financial markets (eg, through a different composition of the portfolio of financial instruments). For this reason, the C-QIS exercise has represented a key

Figure 13.1 BCBS sample: dispersion of leverage ratio around the mean

Source: BCBS (2010a)

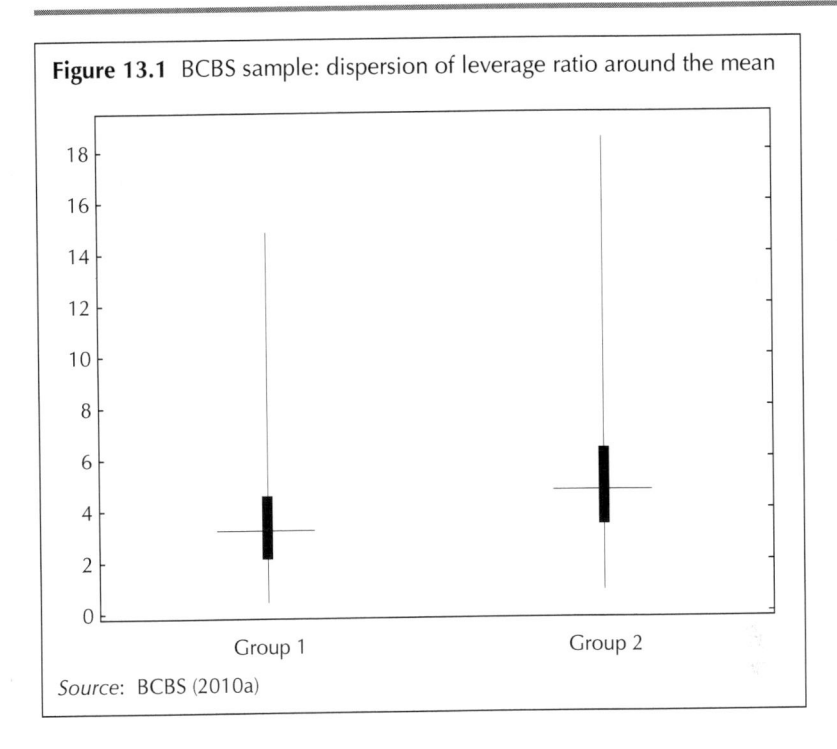

step for the design and the calibration of the liquidity standards; indeed, significant changes have been introduced only in the final rules text.

The main differences that have been introduced in the definition of the LCR since the 2009 Consultative Document are: (i) the reduction of the run-off-rate floors of retail and SMEs' deposits to 5% (stable) and 10% (less stable),[8] respectively from 7.5% and 15%; (ii) the introduction of a 25% outflow bucket for custody and clearing and settlement activities, as well as selected cash-management activities for deposits held with financial institutions counterparties; (iii) the reduction of the drawdown percentage on committed credit facilities to sovereigns, central banks and public-sector entities (PSEs) from 100% to 10%; (iv) the reduction of the run-off percentage of sovereigns', central banks' and PSEs' deposit to 75% from 100%; (v) as regards inflows, the recognition of 50% retail, small-business customers and corporate and 100% financial institutions inflows, capped at 75% of gross outflows; (vi) the assumption of a 25% roll-off of secured funding backed by assets that would not be included in the stock of liquid assets with domestic sovereigns, central banks and

PSEs; (vii) the reduction of the draw down percentage to committed lines to retail and SME from 10% to 5%.

The main changes to the NSFR are: (i) the reduction of the required stable funding (RSF) factor to 65% (from 100%) for residential mortgages and other loans that would qualify for the 35% or better risk weight under the standardised approach for credit risk; (ii) the increase of the available stable funding (ASF) factor for stable and less stable retail and SME deposits from 85% and 70% to 90% and 80%, respectively; (iii) the reduction of RSF of off-balance sheet items from 10% to 5% and (iv) the reduction of the RSF factor to 20% for securities issued by sovereigns with a 20% risk weight, securities directly issued by non-central-government PSEs (20% risk weight) and securities guaranteed by non-central-government PSEs (20% risk weight).

As regards data quality, banks have put much effort into trying to map the requested information with their internal databases. However, quality of information has not always been as high as expected. In addition, "the Committee identified some areas where there may be differences between jurisdictions in interpreting the instructions and the additional guidance published. While these differences in interpretation led the Committee to work on clarifications of definitions and reporting instructions, some differences remain. As a result, not all elements of the data are comparable across banks" (BCBS 2010a).

BCBS banks show an average value of the LCR to be 83% and 98% for Group 1 and Group 2 banks, respectively. Lower figures (67% and 87%) are shown by European banks.[9] The associated shortfall of liquid assets (due to 54% of banks included in the sample) – computed with regard to a 100% minimum value of the ratio – would amount to €1.73 trillion (1 trillion for EU banks). As shown in

Table 13.6 Average LCR and associated shortfall (€bn) as of end-2009

		LCR	Shortfall[10]
BCBS	Group 1	83%	1,730
	Group 2	98%	
EU	Group 1	67%	1,000
	Group 2	87%	

Source: BCBS (2010a), CEBS (2010)

Figure 13.2 BCBS sample: dispersion of LCR around the mean

Source: BCBS (2010a)

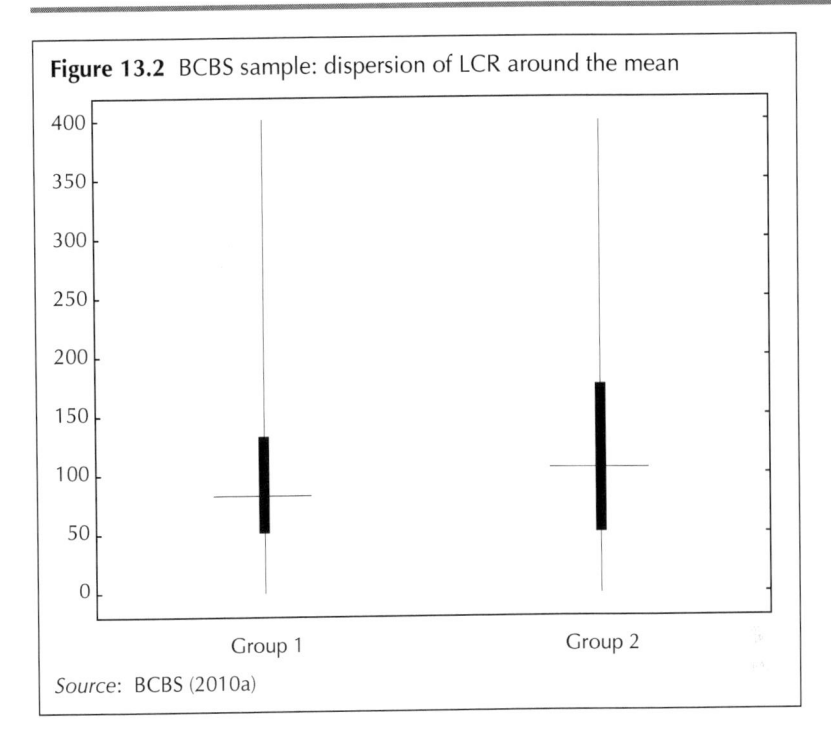

Figure 13.2 for BCBS only, the dispersion around the mean is quite high, ranging from values close to zero to maximum 400% (capped for methodological reasons).

A key issue for the LCR, very much discussed during the consultation, is the composition of the liquidity buffer, ie, the numerator of the ratio. In this area significant changes have been introduced in the final rules text, with the aim of reducing the likely impact of this standard. Figure 13.3 shows the composition of liquid assets for all BCBS banks (both Group 1 and Group 2): the major share of the buffer is represented by "Level 1" assets (among which sovereign with a 0% risk weight represent the main security type).

As regards the NSFR, the average value would be 93% and 103% respectively for BCBS Group 1 and Group 2 banks. Lower figures are reported by European banks. The shortfall in liquid assets (due to 64% of banks included in the sample, with 37% below 85%) would amount to €2.88 trillion. As shown in Figure 13.4, dispersion is also very high for the NSFR, especially for Group 2 banks.

A key question is how banks can meet the new standards. In this respect, institutions might rely on a range of different options: in

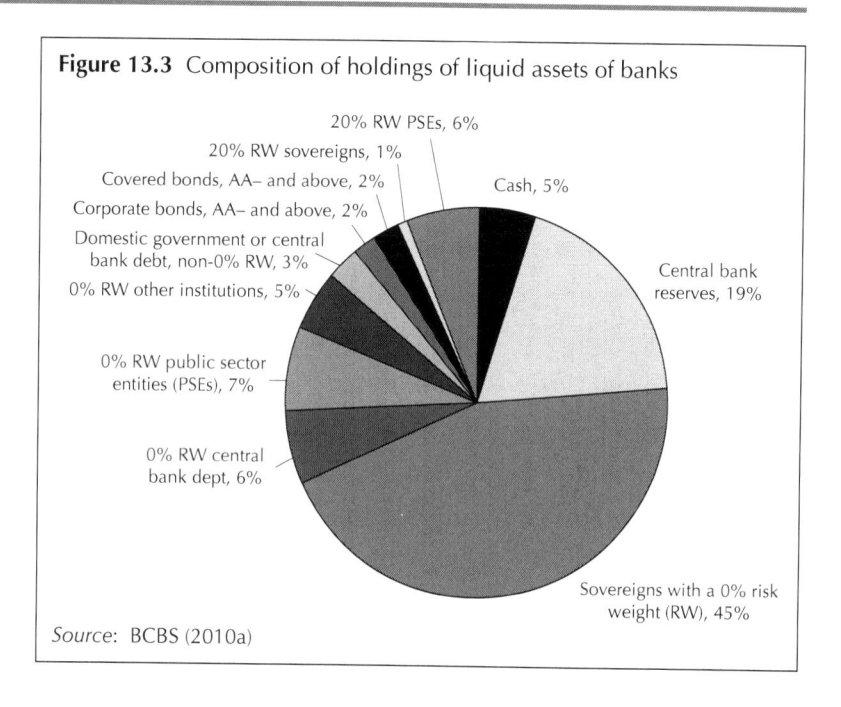

Figure 13.3 Composition of holdings of liquid assets of banks

- 20% RW PSEs, 6%
- 20% RW sovereigns, 1%
- Covered bonds, AA− and above, 2%
- Corporate bonds, AA− and above, 2%
- Domestic government or central bank debt, non-0% RW, 3%
- 0% RW other institutions, 5%
- 0% RW public sector entities (PSEs), 7%
- 0% RW central bank dept, 6%
- Cash, 5%
- Central bank reserves, 19%
- Sovereigns with a 0% risk weight (RW), 45%

Source: BCBS (2010a)

addition to strengthening capital or funding sources with maturities higher than one year, they could increase retail deposits, either stable or volatile; they could also rely on the wholesale funding market. In this regard, the beneficial effect deriving from the recomposition of the liquidity buffer that banks might be willing to make in order to meet the LCR must also be considered.

Table 13.7 Average NSFR and associated shortfall (€bn) as of end-2009

		NSFR	Shortfall[11]
BCBS	Group 1	93%	2,890
	Group 2	103%	
EU	Group 1	91%	1,800
	Group 2	94%	

Source: BCBS (2010a), CEBS (2010)

13.4 THE MACRO ASSESSMENT

In addition to the C-QIS, the Committee has conducted articulated analyses on the possible macroeconomic impact of the prudential reform (BCBS 2010d, 2010e). This section summarises the main

Figure 13.4 BCBS sample: dispersion of NSFR around the mean

Source: BCBS (2010a)

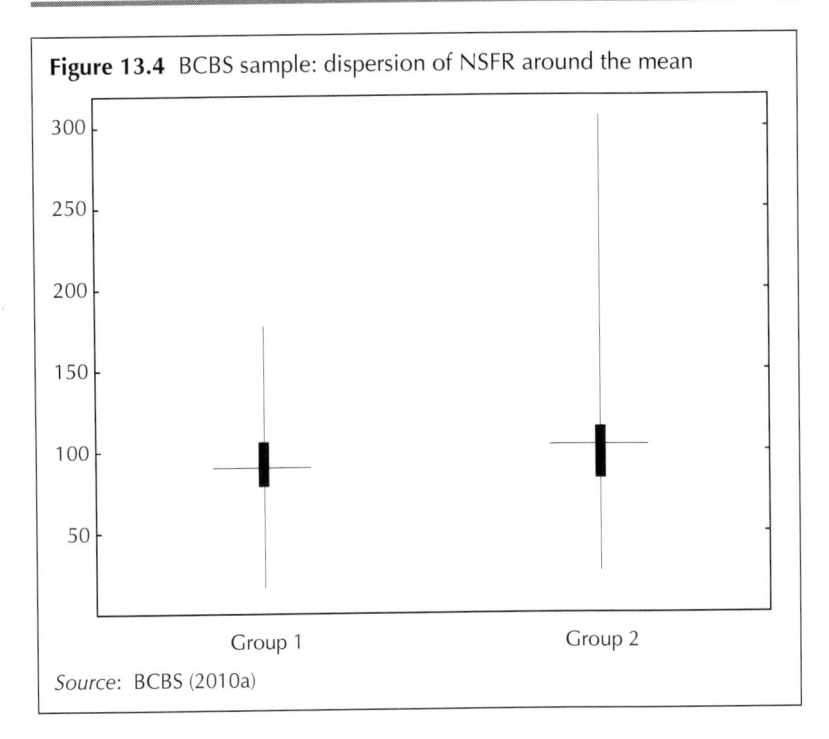

evidence from these workstreams, focusing first on the analysis of the impact in the transitional period (Subsection 13.4.1) and in the long run (13.4.2).

13.4.1 Macroeconomic assessment of Basel III in the transitional period

A first piece of analysis on the possible macroeconomic effects of the prudential reform focuses on the transitional period: as described in Chapters 3 and 8, rules on both capital and liquidity will be phased-in gradually, up to 2019 (in some cases preceded by an observation period), so as to allow banks a smooth transition towards the new prudential targets.

A specific working group, the Macroeconomic Assessment Group (MAG), composed of BCBS and FSB members, was established to develop and apply a framework for assessing the transitional macroeconomic impact of the implementation of the new framework. The group was asked to assess the costs associated with a range of transition paths.

The project involved the estimation of the impact of changes in the capital and liquidity holdings of banks on GDP through the application of a wide range of modelling approaches to a common set of scenarios.[12] For bank capital and liquidity, it was decided to model increases in target ratios (including voluntary capital buffers), and not the required minimum levels set by regulators. This approach allows for ready comparison of results across economies, avoiding the need to incorporate assumptions about how regulatory minimums affect desired capital and liquid asset holdings in national models.

A first piece of analysis, published in the MAG Interim Report in August 2010, applied this analytical framework to a generic 1-percentage-point increase in target capital ratios, since the evidence coming from C-QIS was not available at that time. In the last months of 2010 such analysis was extended along two dimensions. First, by using the QIS results in terms of actual capital shortfall of banks (see Section 13.2); second, by implementing more accurately the length of the transitional arrangements agreed in the final rules text.

In this context, it was estimated that bringing the global common equity capital ratio to a level that would meet the agreed minimum and the capital conservation buffer would result in a maximum decline in GDP, relative to baseline forecasts, of 0.22%, which would occur after 35 quarters. In terms of growth rates, annual growth would be 0.03 percentage points (or 3bp) below its baseline level. This is then followed by a recovery in GDP towards the baseline. These results include the impact of spillovers across countries, reflecting the fact that many or most national banking systems would be tightening capital levels at the same time as simultaneously responding to changes in exchange rates, commodity prices and shifts in global demand.[13]

As in the C-QIS, many caveats must be considered when interpreting the results. As highlighted in the final MAG report, there are a number of reasons why the actual impact could be different from the one reported. On the one hand, banks may attempt to meet – also under market pressure – the stronger requirements ahead of the timetable set out in the final rules text. If they choose to implement the higher requirements in four years, for example, the impact on the level of GDP will be more severe and the impact on growth will be greater. Banks may also choose to hold an additional, voluntary buffer of common-equity capital above the amounts set out in the new framework. On the other hand, it must be considered that banks have a number of options for responding to the stronger requirements, including reducing costs or shifting their portfolios towards safer assets, which in most cases were not explicitly modelled in the estimations performed in the analysis. These might reduce the need for them to increase loan spreads or cut back on lending volumes, thereby reducing the impact on real activity.

13.4.2 The implications of Basel III in the long run

The assessment of the macroeconomic implications of Basel III in the long term aims at quantifying the benefits of stronger capital and liquidity buffers and comparing them with the long-term costs, assuming that banks have completed the transition to the new levels of capital and liquidity.

To do this, the exercise has compared two steady states, with and without the proposed regulatory enhancements. The benefit at the top of the list is that, with more capital and liquidity, the probability of crises is reduced. On the other hand, it is a well-established finding that crises imply serious costs in terms of GDP losses in the form of recessions or even depressions. Evidence strongly suggests that, following a crisis, there is a significant impact on economic growth.

However, the longer-term effects of crises can vary substantially, with some countries returning to earlier growth rates rather quickly, while others stagnate. The analysis concludes that in most countries serious financial crises occur every 20 to 25 years and the median estimate for the GDP loss is around 60% of annual GDP. This means that reducing the probability of a crisis by even 1 percentage point each year should yield benefits of 0.6% of GDP.

Raising the capital ratio by 1 percentage point and meeting the Basel Committee's new liquidity standard should cut the probability of crises in half, from 4.6% to 2.3%. Using estimate of GDP gains, that translates into a benefit of 1.4% of GDP. The marginal impact of tighter standards diminishes as capital levels increase. But, even if the ratio of TCE/RWA rises as high as 10%, the benefits of further increases in capital remain considerable.

The long-run costs of higher capital and liquidity requirements on output have been assessed using a variety of macroeconomic models, such as dynamic stochastic general equilibrium (DSGE) models, semi-structural models and reduced-form models. In brief, the higher cost of bank credit lowers investment and consumption, in turn influencing the steady-state level of output. The mapping of changes in regulatory requirements into lending spreads relies on a representative bank's balance sheet for several national banking systems. Assuming that the whole adjustment is absorbed by lending rates – ie, any increase in funding costs or reductions in returns on investments are fully passed through, and that the cost of capital does not fall as banks become less risky – it is possible to calculate the increase in lending spreads necessary to recover the additional costs of the higher standards.

Considering the median across countries, two key results follow: each 1-percentage-point increase in the capital ratio raises lending spreads by 13bp. Second, the additional cost of meeting the liquidity standard amounts to around 25bp in lending spreads when RWAs are left unchanged; however, it drops to 14bp or less after taking account of the fall in RWAs and the corresponding lower regulatory capital needs associated with the higher holdings of low-risk assets.

Not surprisingly, these results are sensitive to the return on equity (ROE) that banks are assumed to target.[14] Similarly, the results are very sensitive to the strategies that banks might adopt to adjust to changes in required capital and liquidity requirements. For example, on average across countries, a 4% reduction in operating expenses, or a 2-percentage-point fall in ROE, is sufficient to absorb a 1-percentage-point increase in the capital-to-RWA ratio. In practice, banks are likely to follow a combination of strategies.

Based on this intermediate step, it is then possible to estimate the impact of tougher regulatory requirements on output across the full set of macroeconomic models. A 1-percentage-point increase in the capital ratio translates into a median 0.09% decline in the level of output relative to the baseline. The median impact of meeting the liquidity requirement is of a similar order of magnitude, at 0.08%.

The various measures just described are then put together to quantify the net benefits: on balance, there is considerable scope to increase capital and liquidity standards while still yielding positive net benefits.

13.5 CONCLUSIONS

Impact assessment has played a central role in the definition of the Basel III rules. The degree of complexity of the new prudential framework and its potential impact on the real economy has led international authorities to accompany the "bottom-up" exercises run with banks' data QIS with "top-down" simulations of the possible macroeconomic effects. Both types of exercise have benefited from a remarkable effort by supervisors and institutions themselves in providing the data and checking their quality. However, the results have to be interpreted with caution, given the "static" nature of the simulations (ie, they do not take into account future profits).

In addition, some key pieces of the global regulatory reform are still under discussion at international level: among others, the prudential treatment of systemically important financial institutions (SIFIs) and the review of the prudential rules on market risk. All of these are likely to have an impact on the capital level of some financial institutions. Finally, on some specific areas of the reform (mainly leverage and liquidity) the Basel Committee has stated that the data available in the C-QIS is not enough to fully investigate all relevant issues. For this reason, a monitoring period on these new rules will precede their actual implementation.

Notwithstanding these important caveats, the evidence gathered in the impact analyses discussed in this chapter suggests that the final objectives of the global reform – ie, addressing the shortcomings of the current regulatory framework and ensuring a more sound and prudent financial system in the next years – can be fully met. The capital and liquidity shortfalls simulated on a global level in the C-QIS shows that the effort requested to the international banking system is not negligible, even though the long transitional period will allow most institutions to target the new standards in a smooth and ordered way.

Most of the impact on the capital side seems to arise from the more severe definition of capital, namely as regards the treatment of deductions and the new stricter criteria for the eligibility of capital instruments in supervisory capital. In relative terms, the changes introduced to the way RWAs are computed are likely to have a less substantial effect on capital ratios, even though its materiality will significantly change across institutions depending on size, complexity and exposure to derivatives business. On the liquidity side, the shortfalls simulated for the two new regulatory standards indicate the need for most banks in main jurisdictions to increase their liquidity buffer and find a better balance in the structure of the balance sheets.

As discussed in other chapters of the book, a quantitative assessment is not exhaustive as regards the analysis of all possible implications of the global reform. The strategies of banks, the effects on financial markets and the interaction with the development of the economic situation will certainly affect the final impact of the new rules. In this regard, the analysis that international and national financial authorities will undertake in the following years will allow them to get a more reliable picture of the likely effects of the new framework and make any refinement deemed necessary.

The opinions expressed here are those of the authors only and do not necessarily represent the views of the Bank of Italy or the Deutsche Bundesbank.

1   Participating banks have been divided into two groups, based on three criteria: Tier 1 capital higher than €3 billion, activity at international level and wide diversification of assets (Group 1); all other institutions (Group 2).
2   Out of 21 CEBS member jurisdictions that participated to the C-QIS, 9 of them are also included in the BCBS QIS (Belgium, France, Germany, Italy, Luxemburg, Netherlands, Spain, Sweden and United Kingdom).
3   The transitional arrangements for non-correlation trading securitisation positions in the trading book are exemptions to this.
4   More precisely, changes in CET1 were computed as gross CET1 (without deductions) with net CET1, where gross CET1 consists of paid-in capital, retained earnings and accumulated other comprehensive income and other reserves.
5   Stock that is reacquired by the issuing bank.
6   Figures reported in the tables and figures may contain rounding differences.
7   A second goal of the C-QIS was to assess the dynamics of the indicator through the economic cycle. However, due to data quality, such analysis (including the interaction of the leverage ratio with the risk-based ratio) is going to be fully analysed during the observation period, which – as discussed in Chapter 7 – will last until 2017.
8   Run-off-rate floors reflect the assumed minimum amount of deposits that is expected to be withdrawn.
9   The final results of the analysis, however, are biased by a discretionary criterion used by banks to identify the stable and volatile components of retail and SME deposits. In this regard, in fact, the regulation does not set a specific composition percentage. Considering the various shocks to which the core and unstable parts of deposits are subjected by the proposed stress scenario, the adoption of different composition percentages affects the overall amount of net cashflows.
10 It should be noted that the shortfalls in the LCR and the NSFR are not additive, as decreasing the shortfall in one standard may equal a similar decrease in the shortfall of the other standard, depending on the steps taken to decrease the shortfall.
11 See footnote 10.11.
12 The main method was a two-step procedure in which members first estimated the impact of capital requirements on lending spreads and volumes based on econometric and accounting relationships, and then used these results as inputs to the macroeconomic forecasting models

in use at central banks and regulatory agencies. This analysis was complemented by estimations using other approaches, including dynamic, stochastic, general equilibrium (DSGE) models that incorporate a banking sector and reduced-form models that focus on the historical statistical relationships among capital, growth and other variables.

13 The estimated maximum GDP impact per percentage point of higher capital was 0.17%, which is slightly less than the 0.19% figure estimated for four-year implementation in the Interim Report. The point at which this maximum impact is reached, the 35th quarter, is quite a bit later than the maximum-impact point estimated for four-year implementation in the Interim Report (the 18th quarter). As a result, the projected impact on annual growth rates is lower.

14 For example, if the average ROE is assumed to be 10% (rather than the 1993–2007 average of nearly 15% but consistent with a range of academic studies), then each percentage-point increase in the capital ratio can be recovered by a 7bp rise in lending spreads.

REFERENCES

BCBS, 2009a, "Strengthening the resilience of the banking sector", December.

BCBS, 2009b, "International framework for liquidity risk measurement, standards and monitoring", December.

BCBS, 2010a, "Results of the comprehensive quantitative impact study", December.

BCBS, 2010b, "Basel III: A global regulatory framework for more resilient banks and banking systems", December.

BCBS, 2010c, "Basel III: international framework for liquidity risk measurement, standards and monitoring", December.

BCBS, 2010d, "An assessment of the long-term economic impact of stronger capital and liquidity requirements", August.

BCBS, 2010e, "Assessing the macroeconomic impact of the transition to stronger capital and liquidity requirements", December.

CEBS, 2010, "Results of the comprehensive quantitative impact study", December.

Institute of International Finance, 2010, "Interim Report on the Cumulative Impact on the Global Economy of Proposed Changes in the Banking Regulatory Framework", June.

Wolf M., 2010, "Basel: the mouse that did not roar", *Financial Times*, 14 September.

14

A Brazilian Perspective on Basel III

Lucio Rodrigues Capelletto, Paula Cristina Seixas de Oliveira
Central Bank of Brazil

14.1 INTRODUCTION

As examined in Chapter 3, the Basel III reform has been discussed and endorsed (with the FSB and the G20 addressing the problems that resulted from the financial crisis) under a stronger institutional ground and a more expanded constituency than the Basel II Accord. This contributed to strengthening the decision-making process at the global level, with the aim of promoting greater homogeneity in the subsequent implementation of the new standards.

The publication of the new Basel Accord was a landmark for banking systems. Many countries have changed their prudential framework and implemented new procedures to guarantee the regular functioning of their financial systems. Among them, Brazil can be seen as an example of an emerging market that has strengthened its financial system in the midst of a transitional social environment, migrating from an unstable to a stabilised economy.

During the 2007 financial crisis, when economic fundamentals and financial systems were put under an enormous amount of stress, Brazil showed great resilience, as demonstrated by the fact that it was one of the last countries to suffer the effects and the first to present true signals of recovery from the worldwide recession.

After the crisis, with Brazil having evolved into the seventh-largest economy – with social and economic stabilisation and the very strong promise of further development – the prudential framework and supervisory procedures adopted by its financial system has become a financial model that needs to be better understood.

Understanding the reasons behind this process will certainly avoid the undesirable consequences of another crisis.

Furthermore, Brazil has intensively participated in international forums, fomenting more integration, better health distribution, and sharing its experiences from an emerging-country perspective. In short, Brazil has provided significant contributions to the development of new international Basel standards. For example:

- the proposal of conservative rules to define the capital adequacy required and capital;
- making rules more consistent with heterogeneous financial systems;
- providing the perspective of high-growth countries and their relative problems;
- highlighting the importance of supervisory agencies having access to timely information from the financial system, including cross-border operations; and
- sharing experiences with regard to the implementation of Basel II and III.

In short, this chapter describes the experience of a major player, ie, Brazil, with regard to the decision-making process of the Basel reform in the new institutional setting discussing why the reform was needed and the consequences it may have on the Brazilian financial system.

In Brazil, the Central Bank of Brazil (BCB) is responsible for carrying out monetary and financial-stability policies.[1] This is directly correlated to the financial system's soundness – that is to say why the supervision of financial institutions is under the responsibility of the BCB. With regard to its supervisory duties, it has discretionary power to authorise, regulate (by issuing prudential rules), supervise and apply enforcement tools, including intervention and extraordinary liquidation, over financial institutions and other entities under supervision.

In order to have a broader understanding of the evolution and the context of the Basel Accord's implementation in Brazil, it is important to have a brief historical overview. Prior to the Real Plan,[2] launched in July 1994, the Brazilian banking sector operated under a high and unstable inflationary environment. It is not surprising, therefore, that the main source of income was the "inflationary revenue" obtained by the banks through "floating".[3]

In this period, industrial, sector and regional policies were mostly implemented by making financial institutions absorb corporate risks in certain circumstances. An environment of increasing inflation and greater dependence on banking resources was formed, with loans granted by banks to corporates exposed to the natural devaluation of the national currency. Longer maturity represented higher risk.

In parallel, the deterioration of public-sector finance (due to non-performing loans) and the need to enlarge the market for government debt instruments required banks to hold increasing amounts of government securities. At that time, federal, state and municipal government issued bonds to finance their development. Banking institutions were viewed as the favourite targets of governments' financing, as they were sometimes compulsorily obliged to acquire specific government debt securities. The number of federal- and state-owned banks at that time facilitated the process of funding public policies.

All these features of the Brazilian banking sector led to an overgrown structure, which was put to a real "stress test" with the monetary stabilisation initiated in the second half of 1994.

Along with the economic measures established by the Real Plan, the Basel Accord (BCBS 1988) was introduced to the Brazilian financial system.

These above-mentioned measures in a different economic scenario (ie, after the implementation of the Real Plan) featuring low inflation, a strong and stabilised currency and rigorous prudential rules for the banking system, represented a "new era" for the banking system, which required deep adjustments to maintain profitability. Between 1994 and 2000 more than 60 banks stopped operating, being incorporated, merged or liquidated.[4]

For the purpose of detailing the implementation of the Basel Accords in Brazil, Section 14.2 describes the implementation from a chronological viewpoint, highlighting the impact on the banking system. Section 14.3 details the evolution of the financial system before the crisis, under a risk and supervision perspective. Section 14.4 analyses the effect of the financial crisis on the Brazilian financial sector, and how this affected Basel proposals. Section 14.5 contains a discussion of Basel III and how it will be implemented in Brazil. Section 14.6 evaluates the potential impact of Basel III and Section 14.7 concludes.

14.2 THE IMPLEMENTATION OF BASEL ACCORDS IN BRAZIL

The strengthening of the Brazilian financial system has been supported by the prudential rules implemented during the period that followed the first Basel recommendations of 1988.

By the end of 1994, the Brazilian financial system had introduced capital requirements along the lines of the first Basel Agreement (Resolution 2099) to all kinds of financial institutions. The minimum capital requirement was imposed according to the type of financial institution.

Capital adequacy requirement compares on- and off-balance-sheet risks and denominated risk-weighted assets (RWA), with equity and other types of long-term liabilities not chargeable at any time by the investor. The relationship between risk and capital is expressed by a ratio called the Basel Index or Capital Adequacy Ratio.[5]

Internationally, the Basel Committee recommends 8% as a minimum capital requirement (MCR). In Brazil, according to the National Monetary Council (CMN) Resolution 3490/07, the minimum capital requirement (MCR) is 11% Initially, the limit of capital required against risks inherent to financial activities was set at 8% (Resolution 2099/94), but it was increased to 10% (Resolution 2399/97), and subsequently to 11% (Resolution 2606/99), due to the unstable international economic conditions that were observed between 1994–1999.[6]

In the year 2000 other important measures adopted were provisions stating that capital requirements and other operational limits should be met at the consolidated basis (Resolution 2723/00), which encompassed all kinds of financial institutions (banking and non-banking), their subsidiaries, domestic and abroad, and other non-financial enterprises controlled by financial institutions.

Until the implementation of Basel II in 2004 (BCBS 2004), capital was charged solely against credit and market-risk exposures, specifically those related to fixed interest rate and foreign-exchange rate.

Basel II introduced the concept of promoting a self-risk-management approach. The intention was not to restrict operational activities, but to keep risk assets and capital at a proportionate level (ie, proportionate to capital), by providing incentives to have better understanding and more comprehensive risk management within the financial institutions (for example, if you adequately manage your risks, less excess to capital is needed to be held). In this way, a higher operational level is not a problem itself, since there is enough capital to cover all risks involved.

The minimum capital requirement was set at 11% of RWA, above Basel's minimum of 8%, and it covered credit, market and operational risks.

Analysing the risk composition, credit risk represents 90% of the total capital requirement by the financial system. Regarding credit risk, it is important to mention that the Brazilian regulation established very conservative measures to avoid any exposures (ie, credit risk) not covered by provisions.[7]

Since 2000, the provisioning rules established by Resolution 2682/00 have charged provisions based on expected and incurred losses, in a mix comprehensive model. This takes into account a prospective view of the borrower payment capacity and the loan's delinquencies (credit default). In this sense, banks have been required to make provisions at the very moment when any loans are granted, using an "expected model"[8] approach. Depending on the loan quality classification,[9] in default or not, there is a provision requirement. Obviously, if the loan is non-performing, a provision is required according to the number of days in default. Other conservative measures include the treatment of defaults, which require provisions for the whole loan (ie, the total credit amount), in spite of provisioning just the overdue payments, and the limit of 60 days to keep revenue accrual for non-performing loans.

For the Brazilian system, market risk represents around 5% of the total capital requirement of the financial system. The broader scope introduced by Basel II has incorporated new capital requirements for volatility in interest-rate coupons (ie, foreign exchange, price index and interest rate), commodities and stocks prices,[10] and also for non-trading portfolios (ie, banking books). However, the new requirements have not changed the market-risk composition, as fixed-interest-rate risk and foreign-exchange risk (less than 3% of capital) have been the most relevant components due to the fact that there is no exposition in other risks such as equity, commodities or prices index.

401

Operational risk has been introduced into the banking system by charging capital, as recommended in the Basel II Accord. Nowadays, it represents approximately 5% of the total capital requirement at the financial system.

The use of internal risk models for credit, market and operational risk is part of the BCB's regulatory plan, to be implemented gradually, in a medium-time horizon (ie, from three to five years).

Internal model regulation (which determines what is needed to have an internal model for market risk approved by BCB, and also establishes how to apply to it) for market risk has been approved and it is expected that some banks will present their application to the BCB. Internal models for operational risk are still under discussion. As of March 2011, no bank had been authorised to employ internal models.

Looking ahead, most banks will continue to use the standardised approach, which is set up by the BCB for every bank that does not use an internal model (this approach requires 11% of capital) for credit, market and operational risk. Just a select group of banks, with efficient internal controls, are able to readily implement internal models, and they will need to have their internal models validated by a due supervisory process.

The capital of banks is composed of Tier 1 and Tier 2, which is eligible up to 100% of Tier 1. Tier 1 is composed of high-quality capital such as common stocks and hybrid instruments accepted by BCB. Tier 2 is composed of subordinated debt, hybrid instruments not eligible in Tier 1, fair-value adjustments of securities and derivatives, and redeemable and cumulative stocks.

Considering the eligibility criterion (ie, the quality of capital) of loss-absorbency, the following items are deducted from Tier 1:

- deferred tax assets not realised on future profitability (five years);
- investments in other financial institutions, including subordinated debt and hybrid instruments;
- excess of immobilisation, which is calculated based on money invested in assets that are not financial assets, such as fixed and intangible assets (the limit for which is 50% of capital); it aims to avoid investments in fixed assets, in other companies, or in intangible assets;
- investments in non-consolidated financial institutions; and

❏ loans to public-sector operations that exceed 45% of the banks' capital.

Although Pillar I has been a landmark in implementing Basel II in Brazil, other measures related to Pillar II have also been adopted to strengthen the supervision function. These measures contributed (by providing power to supervisory action) to the assessment of regulatory capital and management structures for operational, credit and market risks implemented by all types of financial institutions, particularly by banks.

Pillar III has received less attention in Basel II. Still, both the old and new regulations have enhanced the market discipline through a higher level of disclosure concerning capital regulatory composition and risk management structure.

The regulation establishes that financial institutions must have formal policies of disclosure, including information related to the internal control systems, a continuous process to validate the information disclosed, evaluating the contents adequacy and assessing the relevant criteria used to define what will be disclosed. All the information disclosed by Brazilian financial institutions must be on a consolidated basis, taking into consideration all kinds of institutions (ie, both financial and non-financial).

Besides capital, the prudential framework issued by the CMN and BCB includes several regulations related to internal controls; credit risk, including management, classification, provisioning and data information; deposit insurance fund; consolidated financial statements, including non-financial companies abroad, liquidity and market risk; operational limits; and capital disclosure.

For all exposures, Brazil presents sound regulation regarding credit, market and operational risk, and its regulation guidelines to liquidity risks follow the sound practices recommended by Basel in all its permutations.

14.3 THE EVOLUTION OF THE FINANCIAL SYSTEM

During the 2000s, Brazil gained more importance in the world economy through its commercial balance, which shows that it has steadily increased exports of manufactured goods, commodities and services, as shown in Table 14.1, and its import potential, thanks to a huge internal market, as well as its ability to become a significant

Table 14.1 Brazil balance of payments (in US$ million)

Year	1995	2000	2001	2002	2003	2004	2005	2006	2007	2008	2009	2010
CURRENT ACCOUNT	-18384	-24225	-23215	-7637	4177	11679	13985	13643	1551	-28192	-24302	-47518
Commercial balance (FOB)	-3466	-698	2650	13121	24794	33641	44703	46457	40032	24836	25290	20267
Exports of goods	46506	55086	58223	60362	73084	96475	118308	137807	160649	197942	152995	201915
Import of goods	-49972	-55783	-55572	-47240	-48290	-62835	-73606	-91351	-120617	-173107	-127705	-181649
Services and Rents	-18541	-25048	-27503	-23148	-23483	-25198	-34276	-37120	-42510	-57252	-52930	-70630
Unilateral Transfers 4/	3622	1521	1638	2390	2867	3236	3558	4306	4029	4224	3338	2845
Capital and Financial Accounts	29095	19326	27052	8004	5111	-7523	-9464	16299	89086	29352	71301	100102
Capital Account	352	273	-36	433	498	372	663	869	756	1055	1129	1119
Financial Account	28744	19053	27088	7571	4613	-7895	-10127	15430	88330	28297	70172	98983
Direct Investments	3309	30498	24715	14108	9894	8339	12550	-9380	27518	24601	36033	36962
Brazilian direct investments	-1096	-2282	2258	-2482	-249	-9807	-2517	-28202	-7067	-20457	10084	-11500
Foreign direct investments	4405	32779	22457	16590	10144	18146	15066	18822	34585	45058	25949	48462
Portfolio investments	9217	6955	77	-5119	5308	-4750	4885	9081	48390	1133	50283	64458
Brazilian portfolio investments	-1155	-1696	-795	-321	179	-755	-1771	6	286	1900	4125	-3337
Foreign portfolio investments	10372	8651	872	-4797	5129	-3996	6655	9076	48104	-767	46159	67795
Derivatives (net)	17	-197	-471	-356	-151	-677	-40	41	-710	-312	156	-112
Other investments	16200	-18202	2767	-1062	-10438	-10806	-27521	15688	13131	2875	-16300	-2324
Other Brazilian investments	-1819	-2989	-6585	-3211	-9752	-2085	-5035	-8416	-18552	-5269	-30376	-51490
Other foreign investments (net)	18019	-15213	9353	2150	-686	-8721	-22486	24104	31683	8143	14076	49166
ERRORS	2207	2637	-531	-66	-793	-1912	-201	628	-3152	1809	-347	-3484
Balance net income	12919	-2262	3307	302	8496	2244	4319	30569	87484	2969	46651	49101
Monetary authority rights (- = increasing)	-12919	2262	-3307	-302	-8496	-2244	-4319	-30569	-87484	-2969	-46651	-49101

Source: The Central Bank of Brazil, available at http://www.bcb.gov.br/?ENGLISH

Table 14.2 Main economic and banking indicators in Brazil (in R$ million and percentages)

Year	1995	2000	2005	2006	2007	2008	2009	2010
GDP	705,641	1,179,482	2,147,239	2,369,484	2,661,344	3,031,864	3,185,125	3,674,964
Assets	598,379	962,677	1,674,624	1,997,736	2,559,108	3,295,992	3,610,296	4,385,829
Loans	205,893	329,714	608,010	737,678	917,947	1,182,423	1,410,666	1,740,290
Loans/GDP	29%	28%	28%	31%	34%	39%	44%	47%
Deposits	246,337	324,567	682,703	781,486	926,734	1,274,828	1,325,663	1,491,305
Equity	50,003	89,097	164,235	198,834	249,920	299,140	345,065	432,934
Profits	−940	3,638	18,291	19,873	31,370	21,163	31,000	37,094

Source: Top 50 banks in Brazil by total assets, available at http://www.bcb.gov.br/?ENGLISH

receiver of foreign investments (the highlighted rows in the table are related to foreign currency inflows). Its rapidly growing economy in a stabilised situation has attracted more and more capital inflows.

Higher private investments, along with the availability of public resources in infrastructure, technology and education, have enhanced the development process and wage distribution. As a natural consequence of this social growth, there has been an inclusion of a huge mass of low-wage classes into the financial system (35 million people ascended to middle class and 20 million people left in poverty).

As shown in Table 14.2, the financial system's assets have improved steadily since the beginning of the Real Plan (1994), mainly because of loans from banks, following GDP growth, except in 2008, due to the last financial crisis, reaching 47% of GDP by the end of 2010.

In terms of solvency, capital has also increased and strengthened in quality, providing good conditions for its consistent expansion. The Basel ratio has been on average 17%, much higher than the minimum requirement set by BCB (11%).

On the liability side, deposits have been the banks' core funding, providing stable resources for loans. There is a proportionate growth between deposits and assets, as we can see from Table 14.1. This shows a high level of confidence in the banking system and no mismatch between liabilities and assets.

Estimates suggest a growth trend for the Brazilian financial system – encompassing the economy's blooming and relevant investments needed to support infrastructure projects such as the FIFA World Cup and Olympic Games, which begin in 2014 and 2016, respectively – becoming larger, more complex and riskier. Potential growth, based on economic and social statistics, with better wealth distribution (see the Emerging Consumer Survey 2011 (Curtis 2011, p. 9)), will be reflected in the volume of loans to individuals and small- to medium-sized enterprises. In this way, there is a strong perception that credit risk will keep its position as the main risk in the financial system.

Since 1997, the BCB has been collecting credit operations information, including the classification risk, from all types of financial institutions, on a monthly basis, in order to adequately evaluate credit risk. Through the subsequently created database, it is possible to know the creditworthiness of all borrowers that owe above

R$5,000 (US$3,000, approximately). The data collected from credit above R$5,000 represents almost 90% of the total credit operations, in terms of total amount. The information for borrowers who owe less than R$5,000 is collected on aggregate manner, without identifying the borrower.

Besides credit risk, priority has been given to liquidity risk. In this particular, Brazilian monitoring systems have used properly developed instruments to evaluate the risks inherent in the bank's activities promptly. This is possible; due to the broad information collected from clearings, register centres, and financial institutions that is only 24 hours old.

After 2002, the monitoring process, which occurs after the aforementioned information collection, has been conducted by using daily information with a one-day lag (ie, the information was obtained from operations negotiated on the previous day). This is possible because all types of financial instruments must be registered in an organised system or in a clearinghouse, and the BCB has the power to request data from these organisations on a daily basis.

The collected data allows the daily measurement of the Liquidity Ratio for each bank, which denotes the ratio between the amount of liquid assets and the estimation of the cash flow, for a three-week time horizon, under a stress scenario (Stressed Cash Flow). This ratio, although calculated on a daily basis, does not have a mandatory minimum level which institutions are obliged to maintain. Its monitoring is designed to provide timely information to the Central Bank's board of directors and the supervisors.

Figure 14.1 shows the Liquidity Ratio behaviour for the Brazilian Banking System in an aggregate level.

The BCB liquidity monitoring system provides supervision with timely and updated information at moments of liquidity crisis, which leads to a greater capacity for taking decisions. This system also provides updated information regarding the liquidity risk of the financial system as a whole, identifying its main characteristics and fragilities.

14.4 FINANCIAL CRISES AND BASEL II

The global financial crisis raised doubts about the Basel II implementation. In terms of capital, there was clear evidence that an important part of the regulations was missed in the Basel Committee on

Figure 14.1 Liquidity ratio

Liquid assets/Stressed cash flow

Source: Financial Stability Report, April 2011

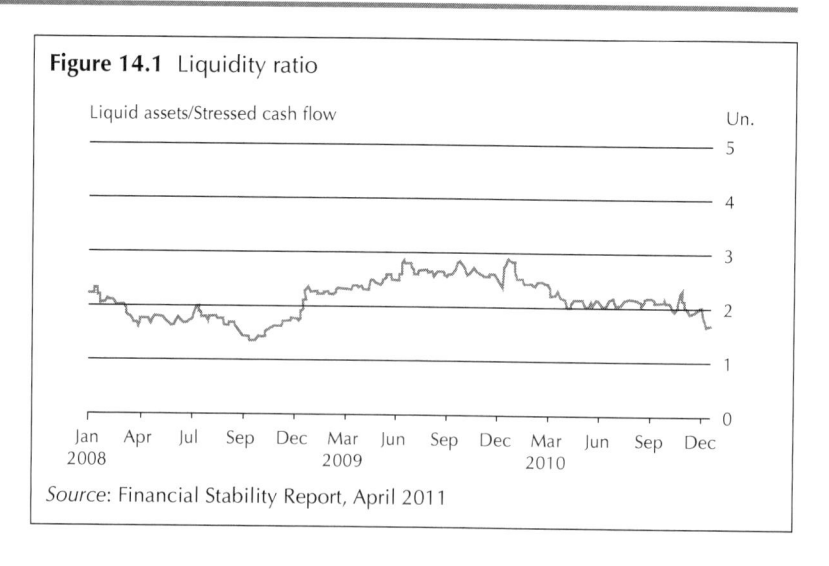

Banking Supervision's (BCBS) recommendations, especially those dealing with capital quality.

The BCBS pointed out several inefficiencies in Basel II, highlighting the inadequate internal banking process to measure risk and to evaluate capital adequacy (see Chapter 2). The deficiencies of these internal controls, added to a dynamic environment with many complex financial innovations (especially in derivatives), undermined any supervisory action or market discipline to protect the financial system against itself.

Basel II was excessively focused on risk measurement, using models and statistical tools. But it did not pay adequate attention to the quality and composition of capital, which is the true defence against risks.

During the crisis period, the Brazilian financial sector, especially banking, was strong and very well capitalised. As shown in Figure 14.2, detailed in the Financial Stability Report (BCB 2010b, p. 42), the solvency situation has been improved by accumulated profits and new capital inflow. While leverage dropped from 9.2 to 8.8, the Basel ratio (total capital ratio – TCR) increased from 18.4% to 18.6%.

Therefore, there were no signs of excessive exposure or leverage on and off the balance sheet. The dependence on foreign currency has been low, which can be shown by the foreign-exchange exposure. The Brazilian financial system does not use foreign currency as a main type of funding or asset. Although, it is not immunized against the

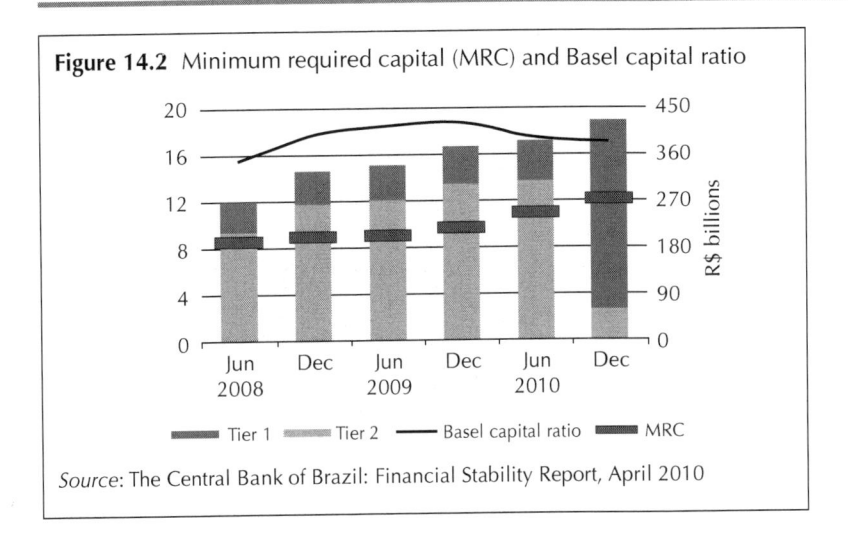

Figure 14.2 Minimum required capital (MRC) and Basel capital ratio

Source: The Central Bank of Brazil: Financial Stability Report, April 2010

international liquidity flood observed at the time of writing. There is no shadow banking system, since all types of financial instruments are registered, independently of the financial institution holding them, and BCB has complete access to this information.[11]

This aside, the liquidity shortage experienced during the crisis affected the Brazilian companies and the financial institutions (due to the fact that international banks cut off all available credit lines), mainly those involved in commercial operations abroad. The drastic reduction of credit lines provided internationally by foreign banks induced the Brazilian companies to look for credit at Brazilian banks.

Internally, the largest private banks imposed restrictions to the granting of loans in order to face any as yet unknown consequences of the crisis by keeping the liquidity level high. Small banks with business models highly dependent on liquidity suffered the worst impact, lacking confidence and funding resources.

Therefore, the BCB had to offer adequate responses to address any threat that emerged from the crisis, adopting prompt actions to maintain the confidence level and to strengthen the Brazilian financial system. In this regard, measures related to capital quality, funding and liquidity issues were essential to promote stability. The following measures were adopted:

❏ capital flow to finance the external commerce was re-established by BCB;

- ❏ the largest banks had an incentive to provide liquidity for small banks, by reducing reserve requirements (ie, if a bank provided liquidity to a smaller bank, it would have its reserve requirement reduced);
- ❏ small and medium banks were allowed to issue a special Certified of Deposit (CD) guaranteed by the Credit Funding Guarantee (FGC)[12] in case of the bank's bankruptcy. Each investor would have this special CD guarantee, worth up to R$20 million (US$12 million). This was very well accepted and reached the objective of providing liquidity to such banks. In fact, it restored the credibility and recovered their funding capacity;
- ❏ public banks kept providing loans, both for big companies and for individuals; and
- ❏ additional provisions were implemented that were considered as capital.[13] The additional provision was considered to be a counter-cyclical instrument that led to higher provisioning without affecting equity.

These measures have been quickly adopted thanks to the existence of the collected information at the BCB. During the crisis, Brazil did not experience the uncertainty with regard to the distribution of losses that other countries did: the collected data could identify on a daily basis who was carrying out the risk or where risk was. The information collected by BCBS from the financial system provided risk disclosure, especially with regard to credit, market and liquidity risk. It surely made the difference in the adoption of prompt corrective measures.

14.5 TOWARDS BASEL III

As the BCBS pointed out (2010a, p. 1), "Basel III is a comprehensive set of reform measures, developed to strengthen the regulation, supervision and risk management of the banking sector."

These measures are meant to be applied at the microprudential level, focusing on individual banking institutions, as well as at the macroprudential level, reducing the system risks that can build up across the banking sector as well as its procyclical amplification over time.

14.5.1 Capital

The implementation of Basel III in Brazil will complement Basel II recommendations, improving the financial institution's capacity to absorb losses resulting from its regular activities or in stressed conditions. A number of measures are proposed.

14.5.1.1 (a) Redefinition of the regulatory capital

Tier 1 capital must be sufficient to absorb losses on a going-concern basis and it will be fixed in 6% of RWA, (risk-weighted assets) divided into two parts (see also Chapter 4). The main part, established at a minimum level of 4.5% of RWA, represents the Common Equity Tier 1 (CET1) and it will be composed of common stocks, retained earnings, and non-redeemable preference stocks without any clause of cumulative dividends. The rest of Tier 1, considered additional Tier 1, will be composed of hybrid instruments that fulfil requirements of loss-absorbing, perpetuity, subordination, and non-cumulative dividends.

Tier 2 capital absorbs losses in a going-concern basis and it will be fixed at a minimum of 2%. The regulatory capital will be formed by the sum of Tier 1 and Tier 2, totalling 8%.

Considering the capital composition, at the time of writing, Tier 1 capital must be at least 5.5% of RWA, representing 50% of the minimum capital required (11% of RWA). Looking for a smooth transition, the proposal is to initiate the implementation by fixing Tier 1 at 5.5% in 2013, with CET1 at 4.5%, and the additional Tier1 at 1% of RWA.

14.5.1.2 (b) Conservation and countercyclical capital

Beyond the regulatory minima (ie, the 6% of RWA referred to above), Basel III introduces also two capital buffers: denominated conservation capital and countercyclical capital (see Chapter 6).

The conservation capital (CCO), fixed in 2.5%, aims to increase the absorption loss function established to the minimum required (Tier 1 + Tier 2). It should be accumulated in periods of growing economic cycles. The beginning of its composition will be in January 2016, increasing 0.625% steadily, reaching 2.5% of RWA in January 2019, as established by Basel III timetable.

The main objective of countercyclical capital (CCC) is to protect the financial system from periods of excess aggregate credit growth, avoiding a build-up of systemic risk in this phase of the credit cycle. Through this mechanism, there is an expectation of credit growth adjustment, by constraining it in periods of excessive expansion and fomenting it (ie, by liberating capital to expand activities) in periods of depression. It will work as a macroprudential tool, keeping the credit flow at a controlled level, adjusted by the economic cycle. The additional capital required in periods of credit expansion in a specific jurisdiction will reduce the bank's capacity for granting new loans.

Considering the credit growth verified in Brazil, there is the possibility that countercyclical capital will be implemented earlier than was proposed by Basel III. This will be charged gradually (at 0.625% of RWA) and will be calculated according to the difference between GDP and its trend (ie, the common increase in the credit over GDP in the previous ten years) but this must not exceed 2.5 % of RWA.

If there is a consensus that CCC will be needed earlier, its implementation will be anticipated in Brazil according to BCBS recommendations (BCBS 2010c).

Unlike with regulatory capital, failure to achieve any one of these two types of capital (ie, CCO and CCC) will not impose operational restrictions on banking activities, but limits in dividends and bonus distribution. In this regard, Brazilian law establishes a minimum obligatory dividends distribution (ie, there must be dividends if there are profits), which should be considered in the implementation process of Basel III.

14.5.1.3 (c) Leverage ratio
In addition to the RWA, Basel III reintroduces the leverage ratio. Before 1994, the Brazilian financial system had a limit of 15 times (by this we mean that liabilities could be at a maximum of 15 times the amount of capital) between liabilities and equity (see Chapter 7). The purpose of the leverage ratio is to fix a limit of 3% between Tier 1 and total assets, without any deduction, including off-balance-sheet items.

Financial institutions will begin to calculate their leverage ratio in 2013, disclosing it in 2015, as recommended by Basel III. In the same way, BCB will evaluate during the transition period (from 2013 to 2018, at most) whether the ratio is suitable to be carried over a full credit cycle and for different types of business model. Adjustments, if any are necessary, would be carried out in the first half of 2017.

Leverage ratio represents an additional safeguard to the banking operations, since it imposes an operational limit disregarding the assets risks, by taking into account the total amount of assets.

14.5.2 Liquidity

The shortage of liquidity observed in the last financial crisis affected without distinction all financial systems, especially those with banks internationally active. This was the case even if they were holding adequate capital levels, causing serious damage to the economy and generating a lack of confidence and an instability scenario. This proves that capital by itself is not sufficient to guarantee stability.

With this in mind, Basel III envisages two minimum quantitative requirements related to liquidity (see Chapter 8). One is the liquidity coverage ratio (LCR), established to prove the existence of liquid assets with high quality (ie, the "numerator") to face withdrawals in 30 days, under a significant severe liquidity stress scenario (ie, the "denominator"). Conceptually, this ratio is fully aligned with the Brazilian liquidity monitoring metrics: the Liquidity Ratio. This similarity will help the Basel III implementation process in Brazil, facilitating the identification of the main problems and points for discussion, as well as providing high-quality data for impact studies.

The other liquidity ratio, the Net Stable Funding Ratio (NSFR), is meant to quantify the availability of long-term stabilised funding, compared with its need, ie, the amount of assets without prompt liquidity, plus off-balance-sheet items, which requires funding resources. Brazil has no monitoring metrics similar to this ratio.

According to the Basel III implementation plan, financial institutions must start to calculate and inform LCR and NSFR components in 2012, for monitoring purpose. The minimum LCR and NSFR requirements will be charged in 2015 and 2018, respectively.

14.6 THE IMPACT OF BASEL

The Brazilian financial system has participated in the comprehensive quantitative impact study (QIS) promoted by BCBS in order to better evaluate the consequences of Basel III (see Chapter 13). Considering the conditions specified for participation in this study, few Brazilian banks were qualified to be part of the sample. This notwithstanding, internal simulations have been conducted for all banks in order to evaluate and put right any unforeseen consequences of applying

Basel III. Particularly to the LCR, Brazilian Liquidity Ratio is a good proxy of its behaviour.

The presumptions are aligned with Basel III recommendations, with all adjustments fully applied immediately.

14.6.1 Capital

As shown in Table 14.3, CET1 reaches 8.2% after all deductions required by Basel III, evidencing a comfortable margin when it is compared with the minimum of 4.5%, and also with the results of the QIS, which showed an average CET1 of 5.7% for Group 1 banks,[14] and 7.8% for Group 2 banks.

In terms of deductions, it is important to mention that the most significant item of deductions refers to deferred taxes, which represent around 50% of the total amount, followed by intangible assets, which represent 19%. Deferred taxes in Brazil are a consequence of a legal discrepancy between fiscal law and accounting rules. While the fiscal law does not allow deductions over provisions made on a yearly basis, deferred taxes are generated due to the anticipated payment.

The inter-temporal deferred taxes[15] represent more than 90% of the total amount of the deferred taxes registered in the assets of the Brazilian financial system. Taking into account that the financial institutions have demonstrated a capacity, through profit generation, to use them in an average period of less than five years, there is no reason to integrally deduct their value from capital, even if there is a full understanding that they are is worthless in the case of bankruptcy, as going-concern capital.

Similar to CET1, the banking system leverage ratio presents an average of 5.3%, superior to the minimum of 3%. In the same manner, comparing with the results of the QIS, which showed a leverage ratio of 2.8% for Group 1 banks and 3.8% for Group 2 banks,

Table 14.3 Impact of Basel III in Brazil – proxy calculated based on accounting variables (in R$ million)

	Equity	Deductions	CET1	Risk-weighted assets – proxy	Total assets	CET1 to RWA	Leverage ratio
Banking system	405,147	170,623	234,524	2,875,617	4,385,829	8.2%	5.3%

Source: Top 50 banks in Brazil by total assets, December 2010. available at http://www.bcb.gov.br/?ENGLISH

the Brazilian banking system has enough capital to expand its operations. The low leverage ratio was expected, since the relation credit to GDP is just 47%. This characteristic of the Brazilian banking system is a consequence of the hyperinflation period and high interest rates.

On this perspective, capital adjustments will not be a big concern for the Brazilian banking system. Even in those institutions (such as medium and small banks) that present a shortfall after the adjustments applied in the simulation process, there is a confident perspective that retained future profits during the transition period will be enough to achieve the new level of capital required.

14.6.2 Liquidity

The quantitative impact study on liquidity (BCBS 2010d) demonstrates that the internationally active Brazilian financial institutions are very liquid. Figure 14.1 shows the liquidity ratio behaviour for the Brazilian Banking System in an aggregate level, and confirms that, in a systemic perspective, this conclusion is also true. In fact, large Brazilian institutions maintain liquidity levels that far surpass the requirements established by Basel III, this will certainly help facilitate the implementation of the liquidity minimum standards.

BCB has already begun the process of implementing Basel III. The main tasks are the following:

- the revision of regulation with directives for sound liquidity risk management;
- the establishment of specific regulation for the Basel III liquidity standards;
- the elaboration of impact studies; and
- the revision of current liquidity reporting[16] (Liquidity Risk Statement – DRL), in order to include LCR and NSFR data collection in its template.

Broad discussions with the banking industry will be conducted throughout the implementation process, observing the BCBS' implementation calendar, which establishes the following main steps:

- 2011: the revised regulation on directives for sound liquidity risk management;
- 2012: the revised liquidity reporting template, with specific buckets for the calculation of LCR and NSFR;

❏ 2015: the LCR minimum requirement; and
❏ 2018: the NSFR minimum requirement.

14.7 CONCLUSIONS

The Brazilian perspective is important because it is representative of those of many countries that, while very significant to the world economy, were not effectively involved in drafting Basel II. One reason why Basel III has the potential to be more effective than Basel II is that more countries are committed to its implementation.

The main goal of the Basel reform is to improve the financial system's ability, especially the banking sector, to absorb shocks arising from financial and economic stress, whatever the source. Through this, it is expected that financial institutions will become more resilient, by enhancing their capability to support the consequences of stressing situations. This chapter has analysed how the new framework will be implemented and how it will affect Brazilian banks in particular, as a possible model for how this will work globally.

Consistently with the BCBS decisions, the implementation of Basel III in Brazil will include:

1. definition of capital, enhancing its ability to absorb losses;
2. creation of two new types of capital – one to absorb losses in stress periods (capital conservation buffer), and other to reduce the banking sector's exposure derived from an excessive credit growth to GDP (countercyclical buffer);
3. harmonisation of capital regulatory adjustments with international standards;
4. implementation of a leverage ratio, as a complementary measure of the minimum regulatory capital;
5. implementation of minimum liquidity requirements (LCR and NSFR); and
6. greater capital disclosure (achieved by establishing what must be disclosed).

The Basel III recommendations in Brazil aim to maintain a sound financial system in order to promote sustainable economic growth. Higher-quality capital level and minimum liquidity requirements will certainly mitigate the effects of future banking crises. In addition, Basel III intends to improve risk management, corporate governance and the information disclosure.

In that respect, the Brazilian prudential regulation (which has been implemented step by step since the introduction of the Basel I rules, in tandem with Basel) is much more restrictive than those recommended by the international standards, for example the provisioning rules for credit operations (which were established by Resolution 2682, 2000). Furthermore, the Brazilian financial institutions have shown higher liquidity, mostly composed of government bonds, and higher capital quality level, capable of absorbing losses.

Other relevant matters include the informational superiority of the Brazilian financial system, which permits more confidence in intermediaries' conditions. This has been achieved by the BCB, who have collected all the necessary information to evaluate financial risks. The BCB, as supervisor, can quickly access all kinds of market securities operations and other financial instruments - especially loans - evaluating the risk level at any time. The assessment of such risk information has made all the difference in supervising the system.

Banking supervisors do not deal with any restriction on data collection from the financial institutions and other market players, such as clearings and credit bureau centres. For supervisory purposes, information can be shared with other supervisors, including cross-border on an aggregate basis. This sharing of information is imperative in order to maintain international financial stability. This puts Brazilian banks in a comfortable situation and provides them with a competitive advantage with respect to other jurisdictions.

The process of capital quality improvement is expected to be smooth, following the timetable agreed with the banking system, without undesirable impacts. For this reason, any significant measure, with its implementation schedule, has been discussed and disclosed, permitting the adoption of timely measures to attend capital and liquidity needs by each financial institution.

> The views and opinions expressed in this work are exlusively those of the authors and do not necessarily reflect or represent those of the Central Bank of Brazil or its members.

1. The Central Bank of Brazil was created by Law 4595, in 1964. Its main purpose is to ensure the stability of the national currency. Its mission statement includes: (i) formulation and management of the monetary and foreign-exchange policies; (ii) regulation and supervision of the National Financial System; and (iii) currency supply and support for financial transactions.
2. The "Real Plan" was a monetary plan, composed of several economic measures, implemented to reduce and control inflation in order to strengthen the national currency. This plan led to "remonetisation" (BIS 1999, p. 108) in the economy.
3. Inflationary revenue is generated by non-interest-bearing liabilities such as demand deposits and resources in transit. By the early 1990s, banks' "inflationary revenue" had grown to around 4% of GDP, accounting for almost 40% of the revenue from financial intermediation and other services (BIS 1999, p. 106). This applies to any country with high inflation.
4. More information is available at http://www.bcb.gov.br/?ENGLISH.
5. Capital Adequacy Ratio (CAR) is a ratio that regulators in the banking system use to evaluate bank's health, specifically bank's capital to its risk. Regulators in the banking system track a bank's CAR to ensure that it can absorb a reasonable amount of loss. *Capital adequacy ratio* is the ratio which determines the capacity of a bank in terms of meeting the time liabilities and other risk such as credit risk, market risk, operational risk, and others. It is a measure of how much capital is used to support the banks' risk assets. Definition available at http://www.maxi-pedia.com/capital+adequacy+ratio+CAR
6. Any financial crisis is interconnected. See, for example, the 1994 economic crisis in Mexico and the so-called "tequila effect". Because it was an emerging country, the Mexico crisis affected the credibility of other financial systems located in emerging countries. In fact, it began a kind of test in each financial system, verifying whether the fundamentals of each were strong.
7. Resolution 2682, 2000, establishes a mix of expected and incurred model for provisioning.
8. The IASB (International Accounting Standards Board) has adopted this concept by issuing IFRS9 (International Financial Reporting Standard 9).
9. Resolution 2682, 2000, establishes a credit-risk classification, with nine categories. AA is the lowest risk and requires zero provisioning. A requires 0.5; B – 1%; C – 3%; D – 10%; E – 30%; F – 50%; G – 70%; and H – 100%.
10. Although implemented together with Basel II directives, the capital requirements for market risk introduced in 2004 refer to the standard model from Basel I Capital Accord.
11. Financial institutions must register all their financial instruments in any centre of registers. This is a bureau where the financial instruments used in negotiations by financial institutions are registered. It can also serve as a clearing centre. However, the difference between a register centre and a clearing centre is that the latter provides conditions to liquidate the operation by transferring money.
12. Private fund controlled by the banks, which was created by regulation, as a safeguard for the depositors. The resources are collected from deposits and other kinds of obligations.
13. During the crisis, financial institutions had an incentive to make more provisions than needed. This additional provision was not deducted from their capital.
14. Group 1 is composed of 94 banks, which have Tier 1 capital in excess of €3 billion, are well diversified and are internationally active. Group 2 is composed of all other 169 banks.
15. This refers to an estimated loss that is not tax-deductible *now*. It will be deductible in the future, following specific tax rules.
16. "Demonstrativo de Risco de Liquidez" ("DRL"), the monthly Liquidity Risk Report, is an important source of information not registered in clearing houses or other organised systems. It contains data from the liquidity risk manager's perspective regarding the amount of liquid assets, the contractual cashflow for the next 30, 60 and 90 days, the off-balance-sheet commitments, other sources of liquidity (such as available liquidity lines), the estimated losses due to stress tests, the funding concentration and the liquidity contingency plan.

REFERENCES

The Central Bank of Brazil, December, 2010c "Top 50 banks in Brazil by total assets", available at *http://www.bcb.gov.br*.

The Central Bank of Brazil, 2004, "Procedures for the implementation of a new capital structure – Basel 2", Comunicado No. 12,746, November.

The Central Bank of Brazil, 2007, "Procedures for the implementation of a new capital structure – Basel 2", Comunicado No. 16,137, September.

The Central Bank of Brazil, 2011a, "Financial Stability Report", April 2011, available at *http://www.bcb.gov.br*.

The Central Bank of Brazil, 2010a, "Financial Stability Report", September, available at *http://www.bcb.gov.br*.

The Central Bank of Brazil, 2009, "Relatório de Estabilidade Financeira", May, Disponível available at *http://www.bcb.gov.br*.

The Central Bank of Brazil, 2010b, "Financial Stability Report", April, available at *http://www.bcb.gov.br*.

The Central Bank of Brazil, 2011b, "Inform preliminary guidelines and timetable for Basel 3 implementation in Brazil", Comunicado No. 20,615, February.

BCBS, 1988, "International convergence of capital measurement and capital standards".

BCBS, 1996, "Amendment to the capital accord to incorporate market risks".

BCBS, 2000, "Sound practices for managing liquidity in banking organisations".

BCBS, 2004, "Principles for the management and supervision of interest rate risk".

BCBS, 2010a, "Basel III: A global regulatory framework for more resilient banks and banking systems".

BCBS, 2010b, "Basel III: International framework for liquidity risk measurement, standards and monitoring".

BCBS, 2010c, "Guidance for national authorities operating the countercyclical capital buffer".

BCBS, 2010d, "Results of the comprehensive quantitative impact study".

BIS, 1999, "Bank Restructure in Practice" BIS Policy Papers, BIS Policy Papers No. 6, August.

Curtis, Mary, Richard Kersley and Mujtaba Rana, 2011, "Emerging Consumer Survey 2011", Credit Suisse Research Institute, Zurich, Switzerland.

15

A New Institutional Framework for Financial Regulation and Supervision

Andrea Enria; Pedro Gustavo Teixeira

European Banking Authority; European Central Bank

15.1 INTRODUCTION

This final chapter deals with the institutional framework for financial regulation and the conduct and supervision at the global, European and national levels. The financial crisis had many causes (as detailed in Chapter 1) and provided the basis for a sweeping regulatory reform (Section 15.2). The new rules can however be effective only if accompanied by a new institutional architecture that is geared towards fulfilling the regulatory objectives, scope and approaches.

Accordingly, the chapter describes and comments upon the bodies, structures and processes that are emerging for the implementation of the regulatory reform with regard to both micro- and macroprudential supervision (Sections 15.3 and 15.4).

At the global level, the focus is on the roles of the FSB and the IMF in the formulation, implementation and enforcement of regulatory policies under the guidance of the G20, as well as in the monitoring of the global financial system.

The chapter then analyses at length the established European System of Financial Supervision (see Table 15.2), which comprises three European Supervisory Authorities (ESAs) with wide-ranging powers of rule making and supervisory coordination, as well as the European Systemic Risk Board (ESRB), responsible for macroprudential oversight.

A comparison with the frameworks being set up or foreseen for the US, the UK and other countries is also made to assess the extent to which a common regulatory agenda is being pursued by similar structures. This is essential to ensure international coordination in financial reform to prevent regulatory arbitrage, avoid loopholes and ensure a level playing field for market participants.

The chapter also highlights (Section 15.5) the major gap in the institutional framework for an orderly resolution of systemically important financial institutions. The "too big to fail" problem cannot be sufficiently mitigated without crisis resolution regimes that, if not harmonised or uniform, are at least consistent on a cross-border basis.

The conclusion (Section 15.6) indicates the areas that deserve particular attention in the future implementation of the regulatory agenda.

15.2 LESSONS FROM THE CRISIS FOR FINANCIAL REGULATION AND SUPERVISION

15.2.1 The sources of regulatory and institutional reform

The lessons from the crisis are reflected in the series of comprehensive reviews of the frameworks for safeguarding financial stability, which provided the blueprint for regulatory and institutional reform.

At the global level, the Financial Stability Forum (FSF) put forward in April 2008 the first roadmap for reform with the Report on Enhancing Market and Institutional Resilience, which was prepared in cooperation with standard-setting bodies and the G7 jurisdictions.[1] It included proposals for, alongside other such measures, strengthening capital standards and the supervision of liquidity risks, increasing the disclosure of risks by financial institutions; improving the credit ratings process; putting in place colleges of supervisors for the largest financial institutions; and improving crisis management arrangements. Each proposal had a given timetable – mostly within 2008 – with a well-defined allocation of responsibilities with reporting obligations. The FSF report is very much at the origin of the major global regulatory initiatives since the crisis, including the Basel III framework, the infrastructure for OTC derivatives, the supervision of systemically important financial institutions, the convergence of accounting standards and the development of macroprudential frameworks and tools.

The FSF report was endorsed by the G7 finance ministers and

central bank governors, also in April 2008, and its recommendations provided the basis for the Action Plan for Reform agreed at the G20 Summit in Washington, DC, on 15 November 2008, as well as for subsequent declarations and agreements on the global financial regulatory system at the summits of London and Pittsburgh in April and September 2009, respectively.[2] The re-foundation of the FSF, through the establishment of the Financial Stability Board (FSB), was enlarged to encompass all the G20 jurisdictions, and the enhancement of the role of the IMF in safeguarding global financial stability was decided at the London Summit (EMF Independent Evaluation Office 2011a).

At the European level, the Commission mandated in October 2008 a High-Level Group, chaired by Jacques de Larosière, with the mandate to put forward proposals to improve the financial supervision arrangements in the EU (High-Level Group on Financial Supervision in the EU 2009). The de Larosière Report of February 2009 provided the basis for an overhaul of the institutional framework, as analysed in the following subsections (most notably 15.3.2). It also submitted a number of recommendations on regulation in line with the guidance provided by the FSF and standard-setting bodies in areas including capital standards for banks and insurance companies, accounting rules, hedge funds, securitised products and derivatives, investment funds and corporate governance. The report also addressed financial crisis management, recommending that member states need to agree on detailed criteria for burden sharing. The Lars Nyberg Report, requested by the Economic and Financial Committee and presented to the Economic and Financial Affairs (ECOFIN) Council in October 2009, elaborated further on the lessons related to financial crisis management, which was taken into account in a roadmap of measures to underpin the coordination among Member States of policy actions in a systemic crisis (ECOFIN 2009).

The reviews made of experiences such as those with the bank run on Northern Rock on September 15, 2007, and problems in other UK banks (UK House of Commons Treasury Committee, 2008), the failures of Icelandic banks, and the impact of the crisis on the Belgian, German and Irish banking systems also provided impetus for regulatory reform.

The Turner Review in the UK highlighted issues such as the need for countercyclical capital buffers, tighter regulation of liquidity, regulation of "shadow banking", containment of remuneration practices and changes in the approach to regulation by the FSA (Financial Services Authority 2009) In Germany, the Issing Report proposed the creation of a "global risk map", which would consist of a unified database containing the risk exposures of financial institutions and markets in order to allow properly assessing systemic risk (Issing 2009). In Belgium, the Lamfalussy Report led to the overhaul of the institutional framework on the basis of a "twin peaks" model (see Subsection 15.3.3) (High-Level Committee on a New Financial Architecture 2009). The Honohan Report, a report by Regling and Watson, and the Peter Nyberg Report, pointed out the lack of macroprudential measures and early warnings to contain the build-up of vulnerabilities that eventually led to the major crisis of the Irish banking system (Nyberg 2011; Honohan 2010).

Finally, the academic community, including the research carried out by the staff of institutions such as the BIS, ECB, IMF, Commission and national authorities, also played a decisive role in the design of regulatory reform, for instance in areas such as macroprudential policies, capital standards, liquidity risk and institutional models for supervision (Galati and Richhild 2011). A number of collective works were particularly influential.

The Geneva Report titled "The Fundamental Principles of Financial Regulation" proposed a framework based on the distinction between micro- and macroprudential regulation, which would be carried out by separate institutions: financial services authorities for the former and central banks for the latter (Brunnermeier *et al* 2009).

The so-called Squam Lake Report advocated macroprudential regulation and a special resolution regime for systemically important institutions as corollaries of two principles: (1) "when developing and enforcing regulations, government officials must consider the implications not only for individual institutions but also for the financial system as a whole"; and (2) "regulators must create conditions that minimize the likelihood of bailouts of financial firms by forcing them to internalize the costs of failure they have been imposing on taxpayers and the broader economy" (French *et al* 2010).

The volume *Restoring Financial Stability*, authored by academics from the Stern School of Business, argues for four changes in regulation, which include changing the compensation incentives of financial managers to foster longer-term perspectives, imposing systemic risk levies on large financial institutions, and preventing regulatory arbitrage by making institutions pay for the safety net, and enforcing greater transparency of trading of derivatives (Acharya and Richardson 2009).

Lastly, the LSE report on "The Future of Finance" (Turner *et al.* 2010) concludes that the reform of the financial system should aim at preventing the financial system from destabilising the economy, protecting the taxpayers from the costs of bail-outs and reducing the share of income for the economy from the financial sector.Enhanced regulation, along the lines of other reports, and the implementation of a "Volcker Rule" (further discussed in Annex I of this book) in the form of narrow banking, where only deposit-taking institutions are insured by the state, are called for (Turner *et al* 2010).

15.2.2 Insufficient restraint of regulatory competition

Specific lessons from the crisis provided the rationale for the main building blocks of the new institutional framework for financial regulation and supervision. The first lesson that is important to highlight relates to the insufficient restraint of the dynamics of regulatory competition in ever more integrated financial markets, both globally and in Europe.

Following a long period without major financial crises, since the late 1990s the focus of policymakers has been mainly on the competitiveness of local financial markets, on their ability to attract business, generate new employment opportunities and support sustained economic growth. Under this perspective, the regulatory framework was often seen as a key element to prop up the competitive position of national players. In several countries there had been official reports pushing for further efforts to "cut the red tape", thus reducing compliance costs for national champions and favouring the localisation of business in the national financial marketplaces. Once some jurisdictions successfully promoted their financial institutions and markets, the pressure on regulators in other countries to follow suit became very strong.[3]

International standard setting was supposed to create a common floor to regulatory competition, so as to prevent a healthy pressure to avoid overregulation from ending up supporting a race to the bottom and a weakening of the safeguards against financial instability. In the EU, this process was enshrined in an even stronger institutional setting, the so-called Lamfalussy framework, set up in the early 2000s, whereby committees of national regulators had to ensure consistent implementation of the common rules, convergence of supervisory practices and cooperation among competent authorities.

In banking, neither the international standards set by the Basel Committee nor the tighter regulatory framework built around the Committee of European Banking Supervisors (CEBS) managed to effectively contain regulatory competition on the definition of capital, which is the landmark of risk-based, prudential supervision. An impressive process of financial innovation brought up a wide variety of capital instruments, combining elements of debt and equity (hybrid capital instruments). A number of complex contractual clauses were crafted to formally respect the basic requirements that an instrument needs to be loss-absorbent and permanent and allow for flexibility in payment to qualify as regulatory capital, while *de facto* circumventing the requirements. Once an innovative instrument was accepted as regulatory capital in a country, banks in neighbouring jurisdictions immediately started lobbying their national regulators, complaining that their competitors were enjoying a competitive edge thanks to the lower cost of capital. The pressure to lower the standards was very high, but, after the enormous effort of completing the Basel II package, regulators had little willingness to engage in yet another major effort to review the definition of capital.

It has to be acknowledged that CEBS identified the issue as a major loophole in regulatory framework, hampering the level playing field in the single market. Already in 2005, CEBS started working to take stock of the difference in the regulatory treatment of hybrids, with a view to promoting convergence. The process took quite a long time, due to the difficulty in finding consensus among regulators. The new, stronger criteria were eventually included in the so-called CRD2 (Capital Requirements Directive), which came into force in January 2011, with long transitional arrangements. As a result, when the crisis burst, many instruments still included in regulatory capital proved capable of neither absorbing losses nor suspending the payment of coupons, even in cases where taxpayers' money had to be injected into the banks. International standards lost their function as benchmarks for market participants: when assessing the resilience of a bank no one referred any more to the Basel Committee's definition of regulatory capital, but to much tighter aggregates such as tangible common equity, including only ordinary shares and reserves, net of all intangibles.

The crisis brought about the awareness that a much stronger framework for international standard setting was needed. Standards cannot be a broad umbrella under which a variety of practices then develop. They need to have teeth, if possible by giving sufficient details and leaving little, if any, room for interpretations at the national level. They have to be supplemented with close peer reviews on rule making at the national level to ensure real harmonisation and prevent competition in laxity. Finally, mechanisms have to be put in place to have a better control of financial innovation, so as to make sure that regulatory standards are maintained through time and remain effective in front of new products and business practices engineered by the industry to contain compliance costs.

15.2.3 Inadequate standards for the conduct of prudential supervision

A second lesson relates to the insufficiency of existing standards for the conduct of prudential supervision and of effective cooperation in the day-to-day supervision of cross-border groups. After the crisis the regulatory community, under the guidance of the G20 and the FSB, engaged in a massive effort of regulatory repair, but less attention has been devoted to identifying and addressing the shortcomings in the actual conduct of supervision. The UK Financial Services Authority singled out loopholes in the "light touch" approach to supervision that was adopted in the years leading to the crisis and has argued in favour of a move to a more intrusive supervisory approach.

However, in the monetary-policy field the exit from the period of high inflation that characterised the 1970s and the early 1980s was associated with the emergence of a broadly agreed international benchmark for central banking, focused on the experience of those central banks that were more effective in maintaining price stability. The same process has not yet taken off in the supervisory field. National approaches remain quite far apart in a number of key areas, such as the reliance on onsite versus offsite examinations, the data intensity of the supervisory analysis of risks, the qualitative versus quantitative approaches adopted to assess risks at financial institutions, the tools for supervisory interventions, sanctions, etc.

Even in cases where the rules are exactly the same, they are processed by quite different supervisory apparatuses and could lead to quite different supervisory outcomes. For instance, clear rules have been set up under International Financial Reporting Standards (IFRS) and the relevant prudential requirements to define whether a certain contract or the transfer of assets to a special-purpose vehicle determines a significant transfer of risk, so that those assets and risks can be taken off the institution's balance sheet and disregarded in the calculation of prudential requirements. In the EU the IFRS are implemented through a regulation, which is directly applicable in all member states, without requiring national implementation. However, exactly the same rules, apparently unambiguous in their intended result, have been associated with quite different attitudes by supervisors.

As a result, the so-called shadow banking system developed in different forms and to a different extent across countries. In some jurisdictions, the onus of proving that a significant risk transfer had effectively occurred was placed on the financial institutions, and supervisors were quite difficult to convince; in others, once external auditors validated the firm's assessment that a significant risk transfer had occurred or that a special-purpose vehicle was an independent entity that should not have been consolidated into the group's balance sheet, there was little the supervisor was entitled to do.

There are many other areas in which different supervisory traditions and methodologies deliver quite different outcomes. The supervisory review process under Pillar II of the Basel framework is another clear example. Notwithstanding the exchanges of experiences conducted at the global tables and the guidelines issued by CEBS in the EU, the approaches followed by supervisors are still quite diverse. Most apparent differences concern the type of information required of the banks to comply with the Pillar II requirements, the degrees of freedom left to financial institutions in conducting their Internal Capital Adequacy Assessment Programme (ICAAP) and the instruments used by the supervisors to assess the risks at the bank and review the outcome of the ICAAP – the measures adopted as a result of the Supervisory Review and Evaluation Programme (SREP). Again, CEBS has conducted valuable work to achieve a common understanding of the respective roles of the ICAAP and the SREP and to integrate supervisory processes for groups operating across the EU. It has also issued guidelines aimed at creating a common language for risk assessment, allowing the translation of assessments conducted in one country into scoring systems adopting in another. But on the field where line supervisors operate, the differences in national approaches are still wide. In a medium-term perspective, it looks difficult to accept that, while regulators agree to impose the same rules on financial institutions, they cannot move to a common manual to be used by supervisors in their day-to-day job, so as to ensure consistency in supervisory outcomes.

The differences in national approaches have hindered a truly joined-up approach to the supervision of cross-border groups. Supervisory colleges, bringing together home and host authorities responsible for the various components of a banking group, have worked mainly as forums for discussions and exchange of information, but are still lagging behind in terms of joint work, joint risk assessment, delegation of tasks, coordination of action and crisis management.

There is therefore a need for an institutional framework that is truly conducive to convergence in supervisory practices and genuine cooperation, especially in the assessment of risks and in the crafting of remedial actions.

15.2.4 Lack of effective macroprudential oversight

The third lesson regards the lack of effective macroprudential oversight, which could have detected at an early stage – as well as prompted actions to prevent or mitigate – the build-up of the main vulnerabilities that led to the financial crisis and its wide propagation.

Macroprudential oversight in the form of the monitoring and assessment of the stability of the financial system as a whole were mainly performed by central banks. The findings on potential risks were made known in Financial Stability Reviews in order to raise the awareness of both policymakers and market participants. However, the analysis relied mostly on market intelligence and central banking statistics, and seldom benefited from bottom-up supervisory input gathered through the ordinary risk assessments and results of onsite examinations. Moreover, the findings had for the most part an analytical nature and often stopped short of putting forward hard-hitting policy messages or recommendations for specific supervisory measures, particularly since central banks had no institutional mandate to encroach in supervisory matters – on the contrary, central banks were being more and more detached from supervision with the widespread establishment of separate supervisory authorities (IMF 2010a).

Also, in cases where central banks correctly pinpointed the emergence of risks and called for action, their pleas would go unanswered, since there was no mechanism of enforcement. As a result, there were no incentives for public authorities and market participants to scale down activities that provided substantial profit opportunities. This was, for example, the case of securitisation and credit-risk transfer activities, whose opaqueness on the actual distribution of risks had been highlighted in several studies many years before the financial crisis.[4]

At the same time, the task of raising awareness of risks was made harder by the conviction that the evolution of internal risk-management models and practices in financial institutions, the development in market infrastructures and the overhaul of prudential standards with the Basel II framework made the global financial system much more resilient to potential shocks and their propagation. This was confirmed by the relative absorption capacity demonstrated in events such as the 1998 Russian crisis, the debacle of Long-Term Capital Management (also in 1998), or the burst of the dotcom bubble in 2000. There were also some episodes where the warnings on risks were possibly overstated, such as those related to exposures to the telecoms industry in 2003. Furthermore, the period of strong economic growth supported the view that the financial sector could in any case sail through a crisis with ever increasing profitability (a "soft-landing"). The example of the Irish crisis is paradigmatic in this respect.[5]

Accordingly, the outcome of financial-stability analysis could be easily dismissed by the expectations that the financial system as a whole would withstand the materialisation of risks. This also justified the rationale for light-touch regulation, which gained ground in the period before the financial crisis. A narrow approach to the scope of the regulatory perimeter was also favoured, which implied that important parts of the financial system were left lightly regulated or unregulated, such as the off-balance-sheet activities of banks and bank-like activities developed by unregulated institutions. All of this was accompanied by the confidence that the use of taxpayers' funds would not be required in a crisis, since large and complex financial institutions that were likely to pose a systemic threat were perceived as being widely diversified and able to absorb even extreme shocks.

As a result, the outcome of financial-stability analysis consisting of warnings about the emergence of risks and assessing the probability of their crystallisation went largely unheeded. A well-functioning, profitable and ever-growing financial sector could not be restrained on the basis of mere warnings without the mechanism of translation into concrete policies. They were not even acknowledged in the institutional framework as an instrument for safeguarding financial stability. Thus, it would have been naïve to assume that such warnings would persuade public authorities and market players to address decisively the build-up of risks, particularly in an effective and coordinated manner as required in an integrated global and European financial system. Furthermore, the toolkit of central banks and supervisory authorities did not include the sorts of measures required to prevent or mitigate vulnerabilities in the financial system as a whole, such as imposing limits to leverage, countercyclical capital buffers, liquidity regulations, crisis-resolution instruments or powers to expand the regulatory perimeter. Therefore, the warnings represented essentially a communication tool of central banks, which could aim only at a mild influence on market behaviour.

In conclusion, following the crisis, there is a broad consensus on elevating macroprudential supervision as a pillar of the financial stability framework and to empower the bodies entrusted with this policy with new and effective tools to address systemic risk.[6] In this context, *macroprudential policy* was defined by the FSB, IMF and BIS as follows (FSB, IMF and BIS 2011):

> a policy that uses primarily prudential tools to limit systemic or system-wide financial risk, thereby limiting the incidence of disruptions in the provision of key financial services that have serious consequences for the real economy by (i) dampening the build-up of financial imbalances and building defences that contain the speed and sharpness of subsequent downswings and their effects on the

economy; and (ii) identifying and addressing common exposures, risk concentrations, linkages and interdependencies that are sources of contagion and spillover risks that may jeopardise the functioning of the system as a whole.

15.3 THE FRAMEWORK FOR REGULATORY REPAIR
15.3.1 The global policy response

With the deepening of the crisis after the failure of Lehman Brothers in September 2008 it became increasingly clear that that there was a need for a globally coordinated action to reform the prudential rules that had failed to contain the overall risks in the world financial system (see Chapter 1, "The Big Financial Crisis").

The first issue to address was to identify the right forum to bring this reform process forward. The institutional architecture for standard setting in financial markets was built around G10 structures, at least in the prudential field, most notably the Basel Committee on Banking Supervision (BCBS). IOSCO – the International Organisation of Securities Commissions, the forum for cooperation between securities regulators – has always had a global membership. This was not tenable, as the crisis originated from developed markets and spread worldwide. An enlargement of the structures for supervisory cooperation was essential.

Accordingly, the G20 London Summit of April 2009 redefined the institutional framework for financial stability and regulation (London Summit 2009).[7] It established in particular the FSB to replace the Financial Stability Forum, which had been set up 10 years before by the G7 to foster international cooperation and information-sharing among authorities. The FSB was placed in a strong institutional position. It has a wide membership underpinning its legitimacy, which comprises the G20 countries, Spain and the major standard-setting bodies – including the BCBS, the IOSCO, the Committee on the Global Financial System, the Committee on Payment and Settlement Systems, the International Association of Insurance Supervisors, and the International Accounting Standards Board. The FSB reports directly to the G20. As an umbrella organisation responsible for international coordination, it undertakes reviews of the work of the standard-setting bodies and evaluations of national jurisdictions regarding the compliance with global financial standards. Other specific tasks of the FSB include the establishment of supervisory colleges for systemically important financial institutions (SIFIs) and the development of contingency planning for cross-border crisis management.[8]

The establishment of the FSB led to a structured process for regulatory repair and supervisory convergence at the global level. Five main layers may be distinguished in such a process (see Table 15.1).

The first two layers in Table 15.1 regard the surveillance of the global financial system by the IMF, and the conduct of macroprudential oversight, which is undertaken jointly by the FSB and the IMF, especially through Early Warning Exercises. These are analysed in Subsection 15.4.1. The outcome of these processes then feeds into the formulation of policies by the FSB, standard-setting bodies and national authorities.

The third layer relates to the formulation and coordination of regulatory and supervisory policies. The FSB soon took up the role of the policy engine for the regulatory reform, providing overall direction and ensuring coordination among standard-setting bodies and jurisdictions. The standard-setting bodies develop the more technical work. In the prudential field, and as part of the Basel III framework, the Basel Committee on Banking Supervision issued ambitious standards on bank capital, leverage, liquidity and risk capture – the last aimed in particular at toughening the requirements for trading and

Table 15.1 The global financial stability and regulation architecture

Functions	Authorities
1. Surveillance of the global financial system	IMF through its World Economic Outlook and Global Financial Stability Report
2. Macroprudential oversight	FSB and IMF through Early Warning Exercises (see Section 15.4 below)
3. Formulation and coordination of regulatory and supervisory policies	FSB and standard-setting bodies (reporting to and under the guidance of the G20)
4. Implementation of policies	National authorities
5. Assessment of implementation	• IMF, through FSAPs[9] (with the World Bank), ROSCs[10] and Article IV consultations • FSB, through peer reviews regarding the follow-up to FSAP recommendations • Standard-setting bodies through monitoring of implementation

derivatives business, which were at the centre of the crisis (BCBS 2010a). The Senior Supervisors Group also contributed to the prudential work by conducting a number of reviews, namely on risk management and best market practices, as well as on counterparty exposures, on the basis of surveys and self-assessments among global institutions. The findings were conveyed to the FSB (Senior Supervisors Group 2009).[11]

The content of the regulatory reform is discussed in details in previous chapters. It is important to stress, however, that the policy momentum generated by the crisis and the reshaping of the infrastructure for international standard setting delivered very far-reaching outcomes in a fairly short period of time. The Basel III framework was developed and endorsed in the space of two years, while almost eight years were needed for the finalisation of the previous Basel II package. Moreover, such results were achieved by consensus, although the subject matter was extremely contentious and implied major adjustment costs for banks in most jurisdictions.

The FSB has a direct role in the formulation of policies regarding cross-border systemic matters. The main example is addressing the risks associated with SIFIs. The FSB fostered the creation of supervisory colleges and developed a complete policy framework for SIFIs, including requirements for crisis management and resolution, increased loss-absorbency capacity and more intensive supervisory oversight (FSB 2010a, 2010b). This framework is, at the time of writing, being elaborated further by the FSB and standard-setting bodies. The FSB also undertakes work on whether the boundaries of the perimeter for financial regulation should be expanded so as to address any gaps that may give rise to systemic risk, such as the potential migration of financial activities to the so-called shadow banking sector.

The fourth layer of the global architecture is the implementation by national jurisdictions of the policies agreed at the global level, which ensures supervisory convergence. The fifth regards the assessment as to whether such implementation is done appropriately. In several areas, a clear understanding has been achieved that significant differences in national implementation cannot be tolerated, as they would generate competitive distortions that are considered unacceptable in front of the global effort to strengthen the regulatory framework. Accordingly, there has been a major push for supervisory convergence. For instance, there has been a clear policy steer from the FSB that the new standards on compensation should be applied in all jurisdictions in a very similar fashion. Otherwise, the most skilled managers and staff would be attracted by foreign banks that, thanks to laxer implementation of the standards, can offer richer remuneration and bonus packages.

The FSB plays a role in assessing the implementation of standards through the conduct of peer reviews among its members. The reviews may be thematic, eg, on compensation or risk-disclosure practices, or consist of country reviews where the objective is to follow up on the recommendations of the IMF stemming from Financial Sector Assessment Programmes (FSAP).

In conclusion, the new global setting has already achieved significant results in regulatory repair, notably through the swift adoption of the Basel III framework and the policy guidance coordinated by the FSB to close the regulatory gaps evidenced by the financial crisis. The new setting puts a strong emphasis on ensuring regulatory and supervisory convergence. This is pursued essentially by narrowing down the choices available to supervisors in the interpretation and application of rules through more detailed policy guidance by the FSB and standard-setting bodies. Such implementation is then assessed by the IMF in the context of FSAP exercises and through the peer reviews conducted by the FSB. There is, therefore, a significant potential in the new architecture to deliver a consistent and complete regulatory framework at the global level.

15.3.2 The European supervisory authorities

In the EU there was a strong commitment to change gear and move towards a new institutional setting that would address the weaknesses found in the conduct of financial supervision. The starting point was the de Larosière Report. This report identified several shortcomings in the institutional setting, which was based on committees of national supervisors without enforcement powers. This led to (1) regulatory failures with regard to financial institutions; (2) the impossibility of challenging regulatory practices on a cross-border basis; (3) a lack of frankness and cooperation between regulators; (4) a lack of consistent powers across regulators; and (5) a lack of means for regulators to take common decisions (Larosière 2009, Paragraphs 152–66; European Commission 2009). As a result, the single financial market ended up being regulated by a patchwork of national requirements. During the financial crisis, this led to the primacy of national solutions in addressing EU-wide disturbances.

The central premise of the de Larosière Report was to argue in favour of an EU-wide single rulebook, taking up a policy concept first put forward by Tommaso Padoa-Schioppa, at the time a member of the executive board of the ECB, as early as 2004, consisting of a streamlined, uniform and flexible regulatory framework for addressing the challenges of supervising the increasingly pan-European financial institutions and services. More concretely, the single rulebook would be composed of EU regulations directly applicable throughout the single market. This would prevent standard setters, with a view to achieving consensus, from agreeing on "umbrella standards", defining broad principles under which a wide variety of rules and supervisory practices can prosper. In the core area of regulation, the rules should be exactly the same for all financial institutions operating in the single market, without any possibility for adding layers of national regulation or watering down the standards through domestic implementation and interpretation. As Padoa-Schioppa put it, "Competition among rules, standards and business practices can be an important force for the integration process, but it should not be at the expense of an adequate supervision" (Padoa-Schioppa 2004; Padoa-Schioppa 2007).

Accordingly, the de Larosière Report recommended the establishment of a European System of Financial Supervision comprising three sectoral authorities regarding banking, insurance and securities markets, respectively, which would take over the tasks of the so-called Level 3 Committees (see Table 15.2). The key step forward in the institutional setting would be to attach to the powers of the authorities the concept of "binding": the authorities would be able to adopt binding supervisory standards, exercise binding mediation among supervisors and issue binding technical decisions applicable to individual financial institutions. These enforcement powers would be exercised only when required for the effective functioning of the single financial market, in line with the principle of subsidiarity, thus preserving a largely decentralised framework for the conduct of supervision.

The new European Supervisory Authorities (ESAs) were established on January 1, 2011: the European Banking Authority (EBA), the European Insurance and Occupational Pensions Authority (EIOPA) and the European Securities Markets Authority (ESMA), acting together on issues of common interest through a Joint Committee.[12] These, the European Systemic Risk Board (ESRB) and the national supervisors form the European System of Financial Supervision, whose parties are bound by the obligation of sincere cooperation among them.

The ESAs have a largely common set of tasks, which fall under a wide range of categories, including (1) rule making, (2) enforcement of EU law, (3) supervisory convergence, (4) consumer protection, (5) financial stability, (6) crisis management, (7) crisis resolution and (8) international and advisory tasks. Specific instruments are provided for the fulfilment of each task (see Table 15.3).[13]

Starting with the rule-making powers, they allow the ESAs to issue technical standards for financial regulation and supervision, which may be either legally binding or have a soft-law nature. The EU financial services law – comprising legislation adopted by the Council and the European Parliament – contains a number of provisions delegating to the Commission the power to issue specific regulations to implement or complement legislation (Articles 290 and 291 of the Treaty).[14] In these areas of delegation, the ESAs can issue draft regulatory technical standards, which are then submitted to the Commission for adoption so as to provide for binding legal effects across the EU. These powers should provide the basis for the

Table 15.2 The European system of financial supervision

Microprudential supervision	Macroprudential supervision
Joint Committee of European Supervisory Authorities	European Systemic Risk Board
European Banking Authority	
European Insurance and Occupational Pensions Authority	*Voting authorities:* ECB, EU-27 national central banks, Commission, ESAs
European Securities and Markets Authority	*Non-voting authorities:* EU-27 national supervisors, President of the Economic and Financial Committee
National supervisors (including colleges of supervisors for banking and insurance groups)	

development of a single rulebook, directly applicable throughout the single market, regarding the key areas of financial regulation.

The more soft rule-making powers consist of the issuance of guidelines and recommendations to national supervisors and financial institutions with a view to ensuring consistent and effective supervisory practices and application of EU law. Although they are not legally binding, these guidelines and recommendations will be supported by a "comply or explain" mechanism. National supervisors should provide reasons for non-compliance and financial institutions may be required to report whether they comply with the guidelines or recommendations that are addressed to them. Cases of non-compliance should be published by the ESAs and reported to the Parliament, Council and Commission. Accordingly, these powers will also underpin the development of the single rulebook. Guidelines and recommendations may also represent first initiatives, which if unable to deliver satisfactory supervisory convergence, may later be translated into regulatory standards for adoption by the Commission.

The powers of the ESAs to build up a single rulebook will progressively reduce the scope for national supervisors to either issue additional layers of rules or to water down EU standards through national options and discretions, which have been quite numerous in EU legislation thus far. There will be, however, room for national rulebooks to persist, covering areas not falling under the EU regulations, in order to reflect specific features of national markets. Also, due to the fact that in some areas the rules are becoming quite complex (in order to reflect the business practices of the most sophisticated players), some flexibility will be allowed with regard to the application of the rules for smaller institutions, adopting simpler business models. But the core rules should become uniform, exactly the same for all market participants. The goal is to contain duplication of compliance costs for cross-border business activities and eliminate the possibility of regulatory competition and a weakening of safeguard to stability.

The ESAs' direct rule-making powers should also return benefits in terms of due process and accountability. Until now, the EU legislative process was perceived as quite distant by most financial institutions since, eventually, what mattered in terms of compliance was the collation of national rulebooks. Although a large part of these rulebooks was derived from (often very detailed) EU legislation, they remained very different in terms of the nature of the rules (primary legislation, regulations, administrative rules of the national supervisors), actual content of the obligations imposed on the industry, and reporting requirements. For cross-border groups, the national segmentation of compliance meant high compliance costs – often perceived as dead-weight costs – which were generated by the differences in national implementation and reporting, often leading to different databases and IT platforms. However, it was not uncommon that, when the rules and the weight of compliance were criticised, the responsibility was passed on to the EU legislator.

In the new institutional framework, it will be possible to better differentiate the EU rules vis-à-vis the national rulebooks. The different layers of rule making will be much more distinctive, allowing a clearer allocation of responsibilities and, as a consequence, improved accountability of EU and national authorities for their respective part of the rulebook. For example, this implies that impact assessments and due consultation processes can be enhanced significantly. The financial industry and the wider public will be engaged directly in the consultation processes of the ESAs. It will not be possible any more to argue at the national level for or against rules that have been adopted at the European level.

Coupled with rule making, the ESAs have substantial enforcement powers akin to the exercise of "federal" competences, which is one of the major innovations of the new institutional framework. In particular, the ESAs may take legally binding decisions addressed to specific national supervisors or financial institutions in a number of instances, when this is justified by the need to safeguard the single financial market as a whole from threats to its functioning, integrity or stability.

One of such instances is in the context of policing the breaches by national supervisors of EU financial-services law, including of the standards issued by the ESAs themselves. Breaches are defined as a failure to ensure that a financial institution fulfils the requirements set by EU law. The enforcement procedure is initiated when an ESA takes the initiative or is requested by national supervisors, the European Parliament, the Council, the Commission or its own stakeholder group, to investigate an alleged breach or non-application of EU law by a national supervisor. If the ESA finds such infringement, it may issue a recommendation to the supervisor setting out the action necessary for complying with EU law. If there is no compliance, the Commission may issue a formal opinion requiring the supervisor to take action. When action is nevertheless not taken, the ESA will be able, under certain conditions, to issue a legally binding decision addressed directly to a financial institution to remedy the infringement of EU law. The conditions for activating this instrument include the need to remedy the non-compliance (1) in a timely manner, (2) to maintain or restore competition in the market or (3) to ensure the orderly functioning of the financial system.

This ability of the ESAs to take directly applicable decisions is also foreseen for addressing disagreements among supervisors on cooperation, coordination or joint decision making, including within supervisory colleges and also among supervisors of different financial sectors (in this case, the Joint Committee decides). The ESAs may take a legally binding decision, after an attempt for conciliation, requiring one or more supervisors to take or refrain from taking action. If the supervisors do not comply, the ESA may also address a decision to a financial institution, directing it to comply with its obligations under EU law. A similar framework for decisions applies in crisis situations. When the Council declares an emergency situation – on a recommendation by the ESRB or an ESA – the ESAs may also take decisions to coordinate national supervisors when this is necessary to respond to adverse developments, which may seriously jeopardise the orderly functioning and integrity of financial markets or the stability of the whole or part of the EU's financial system. In case of non-compliance by supervisors, decisions may then be directed at individual financial institutions.

In this context, an important element of the ESAs legislation is the introduction of a safeguard clause relating to the fiscal responsibilities of Member States. Given the federal nature of the ESAs' powers to take directly applicable decisions, it was considered important to create mechanisms to prevent such decisions – namely those adopted in emergency situations (including in this context the temporary prohibition or restriction of financial activities) and for settling disagreements among national supervisors – to potentially give rise to a fiscal burden on member states, for instance in a financial crisis.[15] In order to ensure that this is respected, it is provided that, where a member state considers that a decision by an ESA impinges on its fiscal responsibility, it may notify that the national supervisor does not intend to implement the decision, together with a justification. The ESA will then inform the member state as to whether it maintains its decision or whether it amends or revokes it. When the decision is maintained, the member state may refer the matter to the Council and the decision of the ESA is suspended. The Council must, within two months, decide whether the decision should be maintained or revoked.

Accordingly, the federal-type powers of the ESAs are confined in terms of scope to last-resort situations and may also be challenged by member states in terms of their potential implications. However, such powers provide a decisive role to the ESAs in safeguarding the single financial market in the case of regulatory or coordination failures among national supervisors. This, in turn, may represent a powerful dissuasive factor against attempts to undermine the effective and consistent implementation of financial regulation across the EU.

The other tasks of the ESAs, in contrast to rule making and the enforcement of EU law, may be considered as less incisive and relating to broader objectives. This is the case for supervisory convergence, where the aim is to ensure, in line with the needs of the single financial market, that national regulatory practices are consistent and as much as possible uniform across the EU. Very diverse tools are at the disposal of the ESAs for this purpose, ranging from the promotion of a common supervisory culture, facilitating the delegation of tasks among supervisors, to the conduct of peer reviews. The latter, if interpreted extensively, could be a very effective tool, particularly since the outcome of the reviews may then provide the basis for regulatory standards to achieve further convergence.

The ESAs also play a role in the functioning of colleges, especially to ensure consistency in the supervision of cross-border financial institutions. They may exercise their rule-making powers with regard to colleges, participate in colleges, receive all relevant information, and request a college to review any decision leading to an incorrect application of EU law or not contributing to supervisory convergence. This is a major task to the extent that differences in supervisory approaches have hindered the truly joined-up conduct of the supervision of cross-border groups. Supervisory colleges, where they were established, have worked mainly as forums for discussions and exchange of information and have lagged behind in their ability to promote joint work, through shared assessments of the risk profile of the firm, ample recourse to the delegation of tasks, coordination of corrective action and crisis management.

In the field of financial stability, the ESAs were entrusted with a number of instruments for dealing with systemic risk. The ESAs should monitor and assess risks and vulnerabilities with regard to their respective financial sectors. For this purpose, the ESAs will develop in cooperation with the ESRB a "risk dashboard", comprising a set of indicators to identify and measure systemic risk. Moreover, the ESAs will develop criteria for measuring the systemic risk of financial institutions. The institutions posing such risk will be subject to strengthened supervision. In this context, the ESAs will be able to contribute to the repair of the financial system by conducting stress-testing exercises, in cooperation with the ESRB, to assess the resilience of individual financial institutions and the financial system as a whole, identifying possible vulnerabilities such as recapitalisation or restructuring needs.

Although the financial stability tasks of the ESAs are justified by the need also to consider the build-up of risks in microprudential supervision, there is potential for a certain degree of overlap with the mission of the ESRB (see Subsection 15.4.2). For this reason, the ESAs and the ESRB have obligations of mutual cooperation, notably with regard to the follow-up on the warnings and recommendations of the ESRB addressed to the ESAs or national supervisors, and to the sharing of information.

Finally, the ESAs have a statutory task to promote consumer protection. They will monitor new and existing financial activities and may issue warnings in case a financial activity poses a serious threat to the stability and effectiveness of the financial system. In addition, they may temporarily prohibit or restrict certain financial activities on the same basis and advise the Commission on permanent measures in this respect.

In conclusion, the setting-up of the ESAs is a major component of the EU's regulatory reform to achieve a deepening of the single financial market through more integrated regulation, enforcement and supervision, as well as an increased level of financial stability and consumer protection. For this purpose, the ESAs are entrusted with broad and significant powers to be exercised with independence, some largely of a coordinating nature, while others have federal-like features.[16] At the same time, this is achieved without disenfranchising national authorities of their competences. In the words of the de Larosière Report, the new system is "a largely decentralised structure, fully respecting the proportionality and subsidiarity principles of the Treaty. So existing national supervisors, who are closest to the markets and institutions they supervise, would continue to carry-out day-to-day supervision and preserve the majority of their present competences" (Larosière 2009, Paragraph 184). Furthermore, the decisions related to the tasks and powers of the ESAs are made by their respective Boards of Supervisors, which comprise the heads of the national supervisors of each EU member state. Accordingly, the future life of the ESAs will likely consist of a "learning by doing" process in striking the right balance in the exercise of EU and national competences for achieving EU-wide objectives such as a single rulebook and supervisory convergence.

15.3.3 Common trends in supervisory reforms

The reforms in national supervisory structures, that aim at addressing the regulatory failures which lay at the heart of the financial crisis, involve some common trends regarding the institutional models for the conduct of supervision.

The first trend relates to the preference to follow the so-called "twin peaks" model, according to which responsibilities for financial supervision are allocated according to one of two objectives: (i) prudential supervision or (ii) conduct of business and consumer protection. In this model, the financial system is supervised independently of sectors or legal form of the regulated entities (banks, insurance companies or securities firms). This model has been adopted in France, in addition to the existing ones in the Netherlands and Italy.[17] The proposed reform in the UK also adopts this model explicitly by establishing a Prudential Regulatory Authority and a Financial Conduct Authority (HM Treasury 2011). It may also be considered that the Dodd–Frank Act of July 2010 in the US takes up elements of a twin-peaks approach by better differentiating between the different objectives. It creates the Consumer Financial Protection Bureau within the Federal Reserve as a new independent authority responsible for consumer protection, and it establishes the Financial Stability Oversight Council, which can

Table 15.3 The tasks and instruments of the European supervisory authorities

Tasks	Instruments
1. Rule making	Draft regulatory technical standards and implementing standards
	Guidelines and recommendations for consistent supervisory practices and application of EU law
2. Enforcement of EU law	Specific recommendations to national supervisors failing to ensure compliance of financial institutions with EU law
	Last-resort decisions to financial institutions not in compliance
	Mediation of disagreements between national supervisors, including decisions for taking or refraining from taking action
3. Supervisory convergence	Promotion of a common supervisory culture
	Conduct of peer-review analyses among national authorities
	Participation in and contribution to the functioning of colleges
	Facilitating the delegation of tasks among supervisors
	Issuing opinions on prudential assessment of cross-border mergers
4. Consumer protection	Promoting transparency, simplicity and fairness in the market
	Guidelines and recommendations on safety of markets
	Warnings on financial activities
	Temporary prohibition or restriction of financial activities
5. Financial stability	Follow-up to ESRB warnings and recommendations
	Monitoring and assessment of risks and vulnerabilities and development of a risk dashboard
	Enquiries and recommendations into institutions or products
	Collection of information and setting-up of central database
	Indicators and criteria for assessing systemic risk
	Conduct of stress-testing exercises
6. Crisis management	Issuing a confidential recommendation to the Council regarding an emergency situation
	General coordination role of supervisors in crisis situations
	Decisions addressed to supervisors in crisis situations
	Last-resort decisions on individual financial institutions
7. Crisis resolution	Development and coordination of recovery and resolution plans
	Contribution to strengthening of deposit guarantee schemes
	Developing methods for resolution of failing institutions and contributing to a European resolution framework
8. Advisory and international	Opinions to the Parliament, the Council or the Commission
	Relations with third-country authorities

recommend prudential standards to the Federal Reserve (see Subsection 15.3.3. below).

(The sectoral approach followed for the ESAs is largely the result of the evolution of EU law and of the format of the committees of supervisors preceding the ESAs. To address the shortcomings of the sectoral approach, the ESAs' regulations include a number of mechanisms to ensure coordination among them, including the Joint Committee mentioned above for addressing cross-sectoral matters. Upon a request of the European Parliament, the review of the ESAs, which will first take place by January 2014, should examine, among others, the appropriateness of the sectoral model.)

A second trend regards the strengthening of the role of central banks in financial supervision. In particular, it is clear that the twin-peaks approach is usually coupled with the attribution of prudential responsibilities to the central bank. In some countries, supervision over the whole financial sector has been attributed to the central bank. Following the lessons from the financial crisis, the greater involvement of central banks corresponds to the need to oversee the financial system as a whole as well as to take into account the interaction of the financial system with the real economy in order to properly address systemic risk.[18]

The third trend is the enhanced public accountability of regulatory and supervisory functions. Previously, extensive accountability and transparency in the conduct of regulation and supervision was seen to be at odds to some extent with the independence of authorities. The financial crisis, and in particular the costs involved for taxpayers from regulatory failures, has contributed to a more balanced approach where effective public accountability is a pillar of the framework, ensuring better performance of regulatory functions, while maintaining the necessary independence.

This trend is well illustrated by the ESAs' framework. The ESAs are explicitly accountable to the European Parliament and the Council. The Parliament, in particular, plays a wide-ranging role in the functioning of the ESAs. It is involved in the nomination and removal of the chairpersons and executive directors, in the rule making by the ESAs, in the compliance by national supervisors with rules issued by the ESAs and in the regular review of the operation of the overall framework. The chairpersons of the ESAs may also be requested to participate in hearings and to provide information to the Parliament.

Somewhat similarly, the Dodd–Frank Act (2010) also created a vice chairman for supervision in the Federal Reserve with the specific duty of reporting to the Congress semiannually on regulation and supervision matters. The governance of the Federal Reserve Banks will also be reviewed to enhance the representation of the public. In the UK, the accountability and transparency of the new regulatory authorities will be ensured through mechanisms such as reporting to the Treasury and the Parliament (also through hearings), mandatory publications relating to financial stability and regulatory developments, and a specific new duty to report when there is a regulatory failure, including the disclosure of confidential information when this is in the public interest.

In most frameworks, it is now common practice and a requirement for regulators to consult widely with the financial industry and the public on the preparation of draft rules and implementation of policies. In the case of the ESAs, stakeholder groups have been established specifically for this purpose. Impact assessments of the proposed standards should also accompany any decision.

In conclusion, the lessons from the financial crisis and the ensuing regulatory reform brought about a sea change in the institutional structures. They had to be adapted to implement properly the new approaches to the regulation and supervision of the financial system for supervision, and also to fulfil the strengthened requirements for public accountability.

15.4 THE FRAMEWORK FOR MACROPRUDENTIAL POLICY
15.4.1 The global setting

The FSB was given a broad mandate for safeguarding financial stability, which may be likened to a macroprudential function. One of its key responsibilities is to assess vulnerabilities affecting the global financial system, and to identify the regulatory and supervisory actions required for addressing them, as well as review the outcome of such actions.

The main analytical tool of the FSB for this purpose is the conduct of Early Warning Exercises (EWEs) together with the IMF (Atish *et al* 2009). The EWE is a semiannual exercise that aims at assessing the extent to which the global financial system may be vulnerable to systemic risk. It consists of an analytical process that starts with the identification of major risks, vulnerabilities and key trends in the global financial system. These are then ranked according to systemic importance in view of their respective expected likelihood and potential impact on the financial system as a whole. The IMF takes the leading role in the identification of economic, macrofinancial and sovereign risk vulnerabilities, while the FSB addresses regulatory and supervisory issues, drawing mainly on the analyses of its members. For this purpose, the FSB operates mainly through its Standing Committee on Assessment of Vulnerabilities (SCAV), which monitors financial system vulnerabilities and discusses the possible policy responses.

The methods used for the risk identification and ranking processes include both quantitative assessments, drawing on statistical data and on the analytical toolkit of the IMF and national authorities represented in the FSB, and expert judgements collected from market participants, academics and financial stability authorities. The outcome is compiled in an Early Warning List of major risks and vulnerabilities. The final analytical step is then taken by the FSB and IMF staff, who elaborate recommendations for policy actions to mitigate such risks and vulnerabilities, and may also make suggestions for further analysis to be undertaken in the next EWE.

The EWE is concluded when the risks and vulnerabilities, as well as the recommendations for action, are presented at the International Monetary and Financial Committee (IMFC) during the IMF's annual and spring meetings. The aim of the presentation is to raise the awareness of the IMFC members for the policies, and the related coordination of such policies across financial sectors and countries, that may be required to contain the potential systemic risks brought to light by the EWE. Accordingly, the presentation normally focuses on the risk clusters and channels for contagion that increase the likelihood of spillovers through the financial system. The results from the EWE and the IMFC discussions then trickle down to inform the FSB tasks and the IMF's multilateral and bilateral surveillance activities, thus having a bearing on the formulation of policies at both global and national levels. The outcome of the EWE also remains confidential to safeguard the privileged information on which it is based and also due to the potential market-sensitivity of its outcome.[19]

The EWE can, therefore, be equated to the exercise of a macroprudential function at the global level due to two defining features: (i) it aims at identifying the building-up of risks and vulnerabilities for the financial system as a whole; and (ii) it aims at prompting timely policy responses to address and mitigate such risks and vulnerabilities. In this sense, the EWE may be considered as one of the main components of the regulatory architecture of the global financial system, together with the surveillance conducted by the IMF, the formulation and coordination of regulatory policies by the FSB and the assessment of national implementation of policies by both the FSB and the IMF (see Table 15.1).

Looking forward, the conduct of an effective macroprudential function for the global financial system faces a number of challenges. These include analytical challenges, namely the ability to gather and process a meaningful set of data, information and indicators across jurisdictions and across regulated and non-regulated financial sectors, as well as to develop reliable models and tools to capture systemic risk, particularly with regard to the linkages between the financial system and the real economy.[20] Institutionally, the fulfilment of such a macroprudential function hinges on the interplay between the FSB and the IMF, especially in the EWE, and among the FSB, standard-setting bodies and national jurisdictions. In particular, translating the outcome of the EWE into coordinated and consistent policies across jurisdictions is a significant challenge. In the same context, it will be crucial to track the extent to which the implementation of macroprudential policies formulated at the global level is effective in addressing the risks and vulnerabilities identified in the EWE. The main instruments for this purpose are the peer-review process by the FSB and the IMF's assessments of compliance with standards. They should therefore be well integrated within the overall surveillance of the global financial system in order to better support the performance of macroprudential oversight (see Table 15.1 above summarising the global financial stability architecture).[21]

15.4.2 The European Systemic Risk Board

Similarly to the response at the global level to the financial crisis, the EU established a new function regarding the macroprudential oversight of the European single financial market as a whole. The de Larosière Report recommended the establishment of a European Systemic Risk Council (ESRC) for macroprudential supervision, which would be tasked with the following: "[to] form judgements and make recommendations on macroprudential policy, issue risk warnings, compare observations on macro-economic and prudential developments and give direction on these issues." Taking into account the role of central banks in preserving financial stability,[22] the ESRC would be primarily composed of the members of the General Council of the ECB and it would also be set up under the auspices of the ECB. The ECOFIN Council of June 9, 2009, renamed the ESRC as European Systemic Risk Board (ESRB), possibly to follow the terminology used for the FSB. On this basis, the Commission presented in September 2009 two legislative proposals, which were then adopted by the Council and the European Parliament on November 24, 2010, leading to the formal establishment of the ESRB.[23]

The ESRB is responsible for the macroprudential oversight of the EU's financial system, defined as contributing to the prevention or mitigation of systemic risks that arise from developments within the financial system and taking into account macroeconomic developments, so as to avoid periods of widespread financial distress. The ESRB tasks include: (1) the collection and analysis of all information relevant for macroprudential oversight; (2) the identification and prioritisation of systemic risks; (3) the issuance of warnings where such risks are deemed to be significant; (4) the issuance of recommendations for remedial action; (5) the monitoring of the follow-up to warnings and recommendations; (6) the cooperation with the ESAs, including the development of indicators of systemic risk and the conduct of stress-testing exercises; (7) the issuance of a confidential warning on an emergency situation addressed to the Council; and (8) the coordination with the IMF and the FSB, as well as other macroprudential bodies.

In terms of governance, the ESRB comprises a General Board as its decision-making body, a Steering Committee, which sets the agenda and prepares the decisions, a Secretariat, an Advisory Technical Committee and a Scientific Committee. The governance structure has three key features.

First, it follows the recommendation of the de Larosière Report to give a prominent role to central banks. The majority of the voting members of the General Board are central banks, the chair is the ECB president, and the ECB also provides the Secretariat and analytical, statistical, administrative and logistical support to the ESRB.

Second, at the same time, supervisors are an integral part of the ESRB in view of their responsibilities to address systemic risk. The chairs of the ESAs are members with voting rights of the General Board and the ESRB has a second vice-chair, who corresponds to the chair of the Joint Committee of the ESAs. In addition, all the EU national supervisors are members without voting rights of the General Board and members of the Advisory Technical Committee.

Third, the ESRB also benefits from advice stemming from the unofficial sector through its Advisory Scientific Committee, which comprises independent experts from academia and other areas. The chair and vice-chairs of this committee are members of the General Board and Steering Committee.

Eventually, the ESRB operates through a number of structures with a very wide and diverse membership. This aims at enabling an all-encompassing perspective on systemic risk, although it may potentially involve a certain cost in terms of efficiency and effectiveness in the performance of the ESRB tasks.

Regarding the analytical process of the ESRB's macroprudential oversight, the starting point is the surveillance and monitoring phase, which involves the collection of all relevant information for detecting and assessing systemic risk. The ESRB will need to determine which sets of information it requires from the vastness of potentially relevant data taken from the regulated and non-regulated financial sectors and also the EU economy. In particular, the ESRB will require both aggregate macrofinancial information to perform top-down analysis of system-wide risks, and microfinancial information to perform bottom-up analysis of the risks that firms may pose for the system as a whole, for instance through common exposures and linkages.[24]

For top-down analysis, the ESRB will be able to rely to a large extent on the wide range of macrofinancial statistical information already compiled by central banks. In addition, the ESRB can draw on market-based information, such as prices and volumes of financial transactions, as well as regular market intelligence on potential risks and vulnerabilities. For bottom-up analysis, it will need to access information on individual financial institutions through supervisory authorities (Constâncio 2010). In this context, there are specific provisions in EU legislation, according to which the ESRB may either request information from the ESAs in summary or collective form, such that financial institutions cannot be identified, or address a reasoned request to the ESAs to provide data on individual financial institutions. If the requested data is not available, the ESRB may address a request to supervisors, central banks, statistics authorities or ultimately member states.[25]

The wide-ranging collection of information on sources of systemic risk will be a challenging task of the ESRB. Information gaps were a major constraint in the ability of authorities to anticipate the build-up of vulnerabilities at the core of the financial crisis. Such gaps stem from the fragmentation and non-harmonisation of certain macro- and microfinancial data across, for instance, financial sectors, from the fact that data may not be updated at a sufficient and timely frequency, and particularly from insufficient coverage of non-regulated sectors, such as shadow banking. In this sense, the broad mandate given to the ESRB to collect all information on sources of systemic risk should contribute a significant strengthening of the capacity to detect risks at the EU level. This will improve the quality of financial data and support the conduct of more in-depth macroprudential analysis, similar to the objective underpinning the creation of the Office for Financial Research in the US.

After the gathering of information, the next step in the ESRB's macroprudential process concerns the identification of potential systemic risks. These are assessed in terms of the probability of their materialisation as well as the severity with which they may impact the financial system. A host of analytical tools can support such assessment, such as models to gauge the possible extent of contagion and spillovers, indicators of systemic risk, and the conduct of stress-testing exercises. For this purpose, the ESRB and the ESAs are mandated to develop a "risk dashboard" (as discussed in Subsection 15.3.2). The ESAs are also tasked to develop a stress-testing regime and criteria for the identification and measurement of systemic risk, including that posed by financial institutions.[26] Therefore, the conduct of macroprudential oversight in Europe will require the development of an analytical framework and toolkit, which will underpin risk identification and assessment, as well as the calibration of the potential policy instruments to address systemic risks.

The analytical assessment of the probability and potential severity of systemic risks will provide the basis for a prioritisation or ranking of such risks. The ESRB will consider the ranking and judge whether to issue risk warnings and/or policy recommendations.

A risk warning is a formal instrument of the ESRB. It may be addressed to the EU as a whole, to one or more member states, to one or more of the ESAs or to one or more national supervisors. In principle, warnings will not be addressed to financial markets or institutions. The aim of the warnings is to raise the awareness of authorities to the potential materialisation of systemic risk, which may warrant a policy response. In this context, the ESRB is requested to elaborate a colour-coded system distinguishing between different risk levels, which are then applied to warnings (and recommendations) in order to support their effectiveness. The legislation also foresees the possibility that the ESRB issues a specific confidential warning addressed to the Council on an emergency situation. This warning would provide the Council with a basis to assess whether to determine the existence of an emergency, which in turn would trigger the use of certain powers by the ESAs (see Subsection 15.3.2).

When contemplating the issuance of a risk warning, the ESRB will need to consider a series of factors. First, by its nature, macroprudential analysis involves large confidence intervals due to the time lag in the build-up of imbalances. It may be quite challenging to pinpoint the period in which risks may materialise. Second, as with any other public policy, the effectiveness of macroprudential policy relies to a large extent on its credibility over time. The ESRB may thus take into account the need to safeguard its credibility by avoiding falling into either type 1 (false alarm of risks that did not materialise) or type 2 (failure to alarm on risks that materialised) errors. Third, the communication strategy is also a component of macroprudential policy. The effectiveness of risk warnings may depend on their frequency, justification and timing in terms of influencing the behaviour of authorities and financial institutions. Accordingly, although risk warnings will be evidence-based, they will likely not be issued as an automatic reaction to the output of macroprudential analysis. They will involve instead a considerable degree of judgement and discretion by the ESRB.

On the basis of the risks identified, the ESRB may also issue recommendations on the policies required to prevent or mitigate the materialisation of such risks. These policy recommendations may have the same addressees as for the risk warnings and also, in addition, the European Commission when the recommendations concern initiatives for EU legislation. The recommendations should identify the appropriate policy actions and specify a timeline for their implementation.[27]

Accordingly, the ESRB may recommend which macroprudential instruments are suitable to address a concrete source of systemic risk. Such instruments may include a wide range of measures and tools. A major part will consist of microprudential tools that are adjusted to strengthen the resilience of the financial system as a whole and that may also be subject to calibration in line with the findings of macroprudential assessments. Examples of these tools include the capital buffers and leverage ratio, as well as rules to address potential liquidity shocks under the Basel III framework.[28]

On the other hand, there are also instruments developed to address specifically the emergence of systemic risk, such as countercyclical capital buffers or capital surcharges on systemically important institutions. A report by the CGFS concludes that the choice of instruments will very much depend on the balance to be found by policymakers between the macroprudential aims of ensuring the resilience of the system and countering the financial cycle to prevent the build-up of imbalances. It advises a pragmatic approach, according to which the macroprudential regime should start by relying on existing microprudential instruments that are refocused for reducing systemic vulnerabilities (Committee on the Global Financial System 2010).

The addressees of recommendations, which given the nature of the instruments may often be the ESAs and national supervisors, will have the obligation to communicate to the ESRB their policy response or to explain why they have not acted – an "act or explain" compliance mechanism. If the ESRB decides that its recommendations have not been followed and that the addressees have failed to explain their inaction appropriately, it must inform the Council and, where relevant, the ESA concerned. In this context, the ESAs will play a crucial role, since they are required to use their powers to ensure a timely follow-up by national supervisors to ESRB recommendations. In addition, when a supervisor does not follow-up, it has to inform the respective ESA and, in its reply to the ESRB, it has to take into account the input of the ESA.

The degree of effectiveness of the risk warnings and recommendations will be decisive for the functioning of macroprudential supervision. The effectiveness will be measured by the extent to which risk warnings and policy recommendations are implemented and the mitigating effects on systemic risk. Since the ESRB will have no legally binding powers to ensure compliance, it will need to rely on the quality and credibility of its macroprudential analysis and policies. In addition, the warnings and recommendations will be supported by the ESRB's institutional framework, which provides for regular reporting to the Council, close cooperation with the ESAs, and the act-or-explain mechanism. The ESRB will also have the right to publish the warnings and recommendations on a case-by-case basis, which may increase the pressure for the prompt actions. Given the sensitivity of such a publication, it will be expected that the decision of the ESRB would be taken on an exceptional basis, when serious threats to financial stability are not being addressed to the extent necessary.

In conclusion, the establishment of the ESRB, together with the ESAs, introduced an explicit regulatory public good for the single financial market: the stability of the European financial system. The ESRB's risk warnings and recommendations have the potential to influence and guide the design and implementation of regulation with a truly European scope. It will therefore be an essential ingredient for a truly European-based financial regulation and supervision, in the same way that the emergence of the public good of European monetary stability was a precursor to European Monetary Union (EMU).

15.4.3 Comparison with other macroprudential bodies

The pursuance of macroprudential oversight is also being incorporated into national frameworks as a core pillar of financial regulation.

In the United States, one of the main objectives of the Dodd–Frank Act is to address systemic risk. For this purpose, it established the Financial Stability Oversight Council (FSOC) with the mandate to identify risks and respond to emerging threats to financial stability, including eliminating regulatory gaps and weaknesses. The Secretary of the Treasury chairs it and the members comprise the Federal Reserve, the federal financial regulators and also state regulators (as non-voting members). Alongside the FSOC, the Office for Financial Research (OFR) was also set up within the Treasury to

Table 15.4 The ESRB tools for macroprudential oversight

1. Issuing warnings on significant risks to financial stability
2. Issuing recommendations with a specified timeline for policy response
3. Publishing risk warnings and recommendations
4. Monitoring the follow-up to the ESRB recommendations on the basis of a comply or explain mechanism
5. Informing the Council and the ESAs concerned when the ESRB recommendations have not been followed and the addressees have failed to explain their inaction
6. Requesting information from the ESAs, also on individual financial institutions, and under certain conditions from the ESCB, supervisors, statistics authorities or the member states
7. In cooperation with the ESAs, using indicators of systemic risk and conducting stress-testing exercises
8. Issuing a confidential warning to the Council in an emergency situation

improve the quality of financial data and conduct systemic-risk analysis.

The tasks of the FSOC may be summarised as comprising three sets of powers: coordination, advisory and systemic. First, the FSOC has the duty to support the coordination among its members. This concerns regulatory policy, supervisory examinations, reporting requirements and enforcement. Furthermore, it should coordinate information sharing and collection of information. If the information available is insufficient to assess potential systemic risks, the FSOC can instruct the OFR to collect information from individual institutions. Second, the FSOC may issue recommendations for regulatory policy. In particular, it may recommend new or stricter standards for interconnected institutions including non-banks, as well as financial products and markets posing a threat to financial stability. The FSOC may also issue recommendations to the US Congress to close regulatory gaps. Third, the systemic powers include the possibility to require consolidated supervision of non-bank financial institutions and to designate specific financial market infrastructures (eg, payment, clearing and settlement) as systemic so as to subject them to regulatory oversight. Finally, the FSOC also plays a role in the possible breaking up of institutions that pose a "grave threat" to financial stability; for instance, under Section 121 of the Dodd–Frank Act, the Federal Reserve can take action against such institutions only if supported by an affirmative vote of at least two-thirds of the voting members of the FSOC.

The UK is in the process of establishing a body akin to a macroprudential authority. The Financial Policy Committee (FPC) will contribute to the pursuance of the financial stability mandate of the Bank of England. The FPC will have two main functions. The first is to monitor the financial system in view of identifying and assessing systemic risks. In this context, the FPC will be responsible for the preparation of the Financial Stability Review. The second function is to select the most appropriate policy tools to address such systemic risks. The instruments of the FPC to conduct macroprudential policy will include public pronouncements and warnings; influencing macroprudential policy in Europe and internationally; recommendations to the Treasury, the Bank of England, the financial sector and international or European organisations; recommendations to the Prudential Regulatory Authority and the Financial Consumer Authority on the basis of a comply or explain mechanism; and instructions to these regulators to implement the specific macroprudential tools entrusted to the FPC by legislation. According to the latest policy paper published by the UK Treasury, a broad macroprudential toolkit is being considered for the FPC, including tools such as countercyclical buffers, leverage limits, liquidity ratios, and collateral requirements.[29]

The ESRB, the FSOC and the proposed FPC have a number of broad similarities. They all have analytical functions regarding the monitoring of the emergence of systemic risks and in this context the ability to share and collect information on the financial system. While the FSOC is supported by the OFR, it may be considered that the ECB has a similar supporting function to the ESRB. The Bank of England supports the FPC. All can also make recommendations for policy and regulatory action from regulators and legislatures. However, while the ESRB's and the FPC's recommendations can rely on a number of mechanisms for compliance, as mentioned above, the Dodd–Frank Act does not address the issue of compliance for the FSOC other than what can be expected from its members. The main difference between the three macroprudential bodies concerns, therefore, their ability to intervene directly in the financial system. The ESRB does not have such ability. The FSOC can bring institutions and market infrastructures within the scope of regulatory oversight and determines whether the Federal Reserve can act in the context of its important new power to break up financial institutions. The FPC is possibly the body that will have a deeper power of intervention, since it is foreseen in the consultation by HM Treasury that it will become fully responsible for a set of macroprudential tools.

Similar initiatives to strengthen the capacity to address systemic risk are also being undertaken in many other countries. For instance, this is the case in France, where a Financial Regulation and Systemic Risk Council, chaired by the Finance Minister and comprising the central banks and regulators, will play a coordinating role and be entrusted with macroprudential tasks.

15.4.4 Challenges in the implementation of macroprudential policies

As a fundamentally new public policy field, the effective implementation of macroprudential oversight and the attainment of its objectives face a number of challenges. It is often questioned whether macroprudential oversight will have "real teeth" to deliver a more resilient and stable financial system.

A first set of challenges regards the definition of what macroprudential policy aims at achieving. This is highlighted by a CGFS report and relates in particular to the two macroprudential aims of, on the one hand, ensuring the resilience of the financial system and, on the other hand, leaning against the financial cycle to prevent at an early stage the build-up of vulnerabilities (Committee on the Global Financial System 2010). These aims are not mutually exclusive, but are complementary and to a certain extent can also replace each other. Pursuing resilience, for instance through capital standards, may allow for less concern about the effects of the financial cycle on the soundness of financial institutions. Conversely, countering the cycle, for instance through countercyclical buffers, may allow for less stringent measures for resilience and also support the conduct of other policies, such as monetary policy. Achieving the right balance between the two aims is challenging given the limited experience in implementing macroprudential policies, the complexity of determining the potential impact of vulnerabilities on the financial system and institutions, and also the uncertainty as to the real effectiveness of macroprudential tools, particularly with regard to countering the financial cycle without also affecting economic growth in a longer-term perspective.

The balance between objectives has implications for the development and activation of macroprudential tools. Tools aiming at resilience may draw to a large extent on microprudential frameworks, which may be refined to pursue stability for the system as a whole. Leaning against the cycle, although it may also rely to some extent on microprudential approaches, requires the development of specific tools, which may be targeted to address vulnerabilities in the financial system as a whole, specific sectors, markets or a set of institutions. It should also be possible to readjust continuously such tools in accordance with the dynamics of the financial cycle. There are, however, very few existing tools in this domain, which poses limits to macroprudential policy.

This context also explains some of the common features of the governance of the macroprudential frameworks analysed above. They normally consist of structures grouping the three sets of financial authorities – central banks, financial regulators and treasuries – not only on account of their expertise but also because the macroprudential objectives and tools may both depend and impact on their respective policies. Ensuring resilience is closely associated with the functions of financial regulators; leaning against the cycle is closer to the central banking field; and both objectives are of interest to treasuries due to the potential links to fiscal policies. Accordingly, macroprudential structures may often need to tackle and find agreement among the potentially very diverse perspectives of the structures members, notably on how to translate macroprudential analysis into concrete policies and measures. This could hinder decisive and timely decision making and actions.

Moreover, the statutory tasks allocated to macroprudential structures are for the most part analytical and advisory, so as to be complementary and enhancing of the responsibilities of the financial authorities. The implementation of macroprudential objectives through binding impositions on financial authorities would risk impinging on the conduct of other policies and also blurring or diluting responsibilities. The approach chosen is relying on more soft instruments, such as warnings and recommendations based on a shared assessments of systemic risk. Accordingly, the challenge of compliance is particularly prominent. Mechanisms such as comply-or-explain, peer pressure and public pronouncements will play a decisive role in this respect.[30]

Finally, macroprudential policy will also be challenged by the need to ensure adequate coordination among financial authorities at several levels. As analysed in this section, macroprudential structures may be depicted as a Russian doll involving global, regional and national layers. The policy guidance emerging at global and regional levels from the FSB and the IMF or the ESRB aims at being reflected in policy implementation in individual jurisdictions. However, the effectiveness of macroprudential tools will depend on the extent to which they are sufficiently granular – ie, tailored to addressing specific vulnerabilities that are often related to the structural features of financial systems, markets and institutions. This level of granularity will be difficult to achieve at the global or regional level, leading to a certain detachment between macroprudential analysis and implementation. Jurisdictions may tend to develop their own specific instruments and policy stance on how to address systemic risk within their respective borders. This may pose the risk that the overall implementation of macroprudential policies is made on a country-by-country basis and not following a consistent framework. The lack of such consistency would have the significant shortcoming of neglecting to capture adequately major threats to financial stability arising from cross-border systemic linkages, such as those relating to interconnectedness among financial institutions or the activities of systemically important financial institutions.

15.5 THE CRISIS-RESOLUTION FRAMEWORK

One of the main gaps that remain in the institutional framework regards the ability of authorities to ensure the orderly resolution of systemically important financial institutions, which may be deemed as "too big to fail". While there is a broad agreement that supervision of systemically relevant institutions needs to be strengthened (FSB 2010a, 2010b), there is no convergence of approaches on how to safeguard – and, in particular, make compatible – public interests such as financial stability and the integrity of taxpayers' funds in a crisis situation, particularly when the crisis has potential cross-border externalities. This lack of convergence has two consequences.

The first relates to the fact, which the financial crisis has made evident, that national taxpayers provide the ultimate backstop to prevent the materialisation of systemic risk when a major financial institution is at the brink of failure. This has the implication that the default crisis mode means that each single jurisdiction is solely responsible for domestically chartered firms (ie, cross-border groups are a constellation of firms). In turn, this means that the main incentive in such a crisis mode is to safeguard the national taxpayers' funds from the immediate direct costs of the crisis. This could lead to suboptimal solutions for financial stability both domestically and cross-border. For example, the ring-fencing of assets of subsidiaries may provoke the insolvency of a whole cross-border financial group with significant spillovers across countries and possibly even increased second-round costs for national taxpayers. It may also have detrimental effects from a crisis-prevention perspective, such as less integrated, group-wide management of risks. And, most importantly, it prevents national authorities from coordinating crisis-management and -resolution procedures across borders. The primacy of national taxpayers' interests hinders a potential mutualisation of the costs of a financial crisis, also known as "burden sharing" among the countries where a banking group has significant business. Accordingly, the "non-cooperative solution" among jurisdictions is the most likely outcome in a crisis.

The second consequence is that, in the lack of an orderly resolution framework, authorities are left with no choice but to indeed deploy taxpayers' funds to bail out financial institutions that are deemed too big to fail. The uncertainty as to a systemic crisis stemming from the disorderly failure of such an institution prompts the use of taxpayers' funds as the least costly option, given the severe costs of contagion to the wider financial system and the real economy. As a result, systemically important institutions have long enjoyed a competitive advantage in terms of funding costs due to their perceived too-big-to-fail status. This has been confirmed *ex post*, with few investors (even sub-debtholders) suffering capital losses or suspension in payments in a financial crisis affecting major institutions.

Closing this gap in the institutional framework is quite challenging. It requires, among other things, providing an enhanced common set of resolution tools to authorities, despite the differences among national regimes. These tools should allow authorities to intervene expeditiously, for example to maintain an institution as a "going concern" in order to ensure continuity to essential services while the institution is restructured or wound up to prevent market disruption, also avoiding greater losses than immediate bankruptcy. Cross-border coordination arrangements between home- and host-country authorities should be developed to address prisoner's-dilemma types of occurrences. For instance, this could include allowing the transfer (rather than ring-fencing) of liquidity or assets within a financial group or enabling the delegation of resolution powers to the home jurisdiction with safeguards ensuring equitable treatment of all (home and host countries') creditors. Burden-sharing agreements could also be put in place to align the incentives of the countries involved in the eventuality that the use of public funds is decided. Mechanisms should also be put in place to limit the need to rely on taxpayers' funds to address the failure of a major institution. Resolution funds could be set up on the basis of contributions by the financial sector. Financial institutions should also develop their own recovery-and-resolution plans. And there is also an ongoing debate over the desirability (and legal feasibility) of introducing contractual or statutory bail-in debt, which would avoid or reduce the use of taxpayers' funds by providing sources of capital from existing equity and debt.

The FSB is promoting the development of a globally consistent approach to bank recovery and resolution (FSB 2011). However, the latest developments still present very divergent approaches.

In the US, the most striking development was the introduction of the principle that large financial institutions that fail should be resolved. The Dodd–Frank Act prohibits the use of taxpayers' funds for either bailing out or liquidating a financial institution, in particular by the Federal Deposit Insurance Corporation (FDIC). Systemically important financial institutions should be allowed to fail and should then be wound down. Institutions cannot be maintained as a "going concern" but immediately become a matter of "gone concern". Any costs should be borne by shareholders and then the unsecured creditors in the liquidation process. The costs that cannot be repaid from the assets of the institution should then be covered by the rest of the financial sector through contributions to a deposit insurance fund or liquidation fund.

A somewhat different approach is followed in the framework being currently considered for the EU by the European Commission (European Commission 2011). The general rule should be the orderly resolution without risks for financial stability and costs for taxpayers.

However, financial institutions could be allowed to be maintained as a "going concern" if their liquidation would not be appropriate due to systemic risk. A similar regime is followed in the UK, where the Banking Act provides that authorities should select the most suitable resolution tools to fulfil statutory objectives, such as protecting financial stability, depositors or public funds, thus allowing an institution to be kept as a "going concern" (Brierley 2009).

Given that the EU regime is a cross-border framework, which has to integrate the complexities of dealing with several national regimes, the ultimate aim is to build up consistent and uniform resolution procedures as much as possible. In this context, the ESAs are provided with the task of contributing towards a European system of bank resolution, namely through the coordination of resolution plans, the development of preventive measures to minimise the systemic impact of any failure, and the assessment of the need for funding mechanisms. The ESAs are in addition responsible for overseeing the adequate funding and functioning of depositor, investor and insurance holder guarantee schemes throughout the EU. The European Commission has proposed the further harmonisation of these schemes within the EU.[31]

In conclusion, the component of the institutional framework regarding crisis resolution is still very much in a state of flux, given in particular the sensitive link with the potential use of taxpayers' funds as a matter of national sovereignty. Further evolution towards a consistent regime at the global and European levels will likely consist of a very gradual process, possibly relying in the first phases on softer instruments, such as dissemination of best practices and methods of resolution, coordination agreements among home- and host-country authorities, contractual mechanisms to ensure bail-in, or arrangements among resolution funds.

15.6 OUTLOOK

The financial crisis has prompted a deep and wide-ranging reform of the institutional framework for the conduct of financial regulation and supervision at the global, European and national levels, as described in this chapter. The policy response to the lessons from the crisis was therefore impressive. A more integrated and complete body of rules was developed, which provides more restraint for regulatory competition and is conducive to convergence in supervisory practices and genuine cooperation among the supervisory authorities. Moreover, the new policy function relating to macroprudential supervision was institutionalised widely as a core pillar of the institutional framework. Particular efforts were made to ensure appropriate coordination between micro- and macroprudential authorities. The new European System of Financial Supervisors (ESFS) addresses this issue through the broad composition of the ESRB, which fosters a constructive two-way dialogue between central banks and supervisory authorities, and through provisions to ensure a smooth exchange of information. In addition, considerable efforts are being made to set up a framework that allows for the orderly exit of any financial institution, however large and systemic, with mechanisms allowing for cross-border interoperability in crisis management and resolution.

There are issues that require further consideration in ongoing regulatory reforms. These include, first, the remaining relative complexity of the institutional architecture. Although emphasis has been put on mechanisms of coordination, there is possibly some room for duplication or overlap of tasks between authorities both nationally and across jurisdictions, with potential blurring of responsibilities.

Second, there is the risk that too high expectations have been placed on the conduct of macroprudential supervision and on the effectiveness of cross-border microprudential supervision. In particular, macroprudential supervision does not function as a panacea for stemming the emergence of systemic risk as highlighted in Subsection 15.4.4. While the development of a more uniform rulebook and convergent supervisory practices will support more effective cross-border supervision, this will rightly represent a process of progressive and ongoing enhancement among supervisors rather than an instantaneous outcome.

Third, the potential build-up of systemic risk outside the regulated sector, in the so-called "shadow banking sector", will remain one of the most important items of the current regulatory agenda. In particular, tightening the regulatory framework for banking activities will provide incentives to innovate and move risky business outside regulated entities. Addressing this challenge is a shared objective for microprudential and macroprudential supervision, which requires concerted action. The regulatory perimeter may need to be enlarged so as to capture new financial activities and new sets of financial institutions. However, it may be challenging to build a convincing case for extending the scope of regulation, also taking into account the potential limitations in data availability in unregulated areas. More importantly, financial innovation could be so fast that there is the risk that the extension of the regulatory coverage is realised only when risks have already moved to another unregulated area. In the EU, the powers of the ESAs regarding consumer protection and financial innovation, as well as the macroprudential oversight of the ESRB, will help to highlight areas of financial activity that need to be brought under the regulatory umbrella.

In conclusion, the new institutional framework put in place in the course of 2010 and 2011 provides the conditions for a better and more consistent regulation and supervision of the financial system. This opportunity should now be reaped for achieving the best possible effect.

> The views expressed in this chapter are those of the authors and do not necessarily reflect those of the EBA or the ECB. The chapter takes account of developments until 30 April 2011.

1 Available at http://www.financialstabilityboard.org.
2 See the leaders' statements from these summits, available at http://www.g20.org.
3 A good example can be found in the so-called Bloomberg report (http://www.nyc.gov/html/om/pdf/ny_report_final.pdf), which a few months before the bursting of the subprime crisis pointed to the loss of competitiveness of New York and US markets vis-à-vis London and emerging markets, calling for a drastic streamlining of the rulebook in the US to cut compliance costs.
4 See, for example, Committee on the Global Financial System (2003), which already in January 2003 expressed concerns about the lack of transparency and information on the distribution of risk resulting from these activities, as well as the role of credit rating agencies and the increased counterparty risk.
5 As repeatedly pointed out in the reports reviewing the Irish financial crisis, which are mentioned above.
6 For an overview, see G30 (2011).
7 See also Chapter 2, "The Policy Response . . ."
8 See the FSB Charter, available at http://www.financialstabilityboard.org.
9 Financial Sector Assessment Programmes.
10 Reports on the Observance of Standards and Codes.
11 See, in particular, Senior Supervisors Group (2009). The Group includes the Canadian Office of the Superintendent of Financial Institutions, the French Banking Commission, the German Federal Financial Supervisory Authority, the Japanese Financial Services Agency, the Swiss Financial Market Supervisory Authority, the UK Financial Services Authority, and, in the US, the Office of the Comptroller of the Currency, the Securities and Exchange Commission and the Federal Reserve.
12 The Commission put forward on 23 September 2009 legislative proposals, which were then adopted on 24 November 2010: Regulation (EU) No 1093/2010 establishing a European

Supervisory Authority (European Banking Authority), OJ L 331, 15.12.2010, p.12; Regulation (EU) No 1094/2010 establishing a European Supervisory Authority (European Insurance and Occupational Pensions Authority), OJ L 331, 15.12.2010, p.48; Regulation (EU) No 1095/2010 establishing a European Supervisory Authority (European Securities and Markets Authority), OJ L 331, 15.12.2010, p. 84.

13 There are certain powers that are specific to each of the ESAs, such as the registration and supervision of credit-rating agencies by ESMA. See Regulation No. 1060/2009 of the European Parliament and the Council of 16 September 2009 on credit rating agencies, OJ L 302/1, 17.11.2009. In addition, EU legislation may attribute further powers and tasks to the ESAs.

14 The Commission committed explicitly to continue to consult experts appointed by member states in the preparation of delegated acts in the area of financial services. See Declaration 39 on Article 290 of the Treaty, annexed to the Final Act of the Intergovernmental Conference.

15 The recitals of the ESAs regulations clarify that the safeguard clause should be invoked only when a decision taken by an ESA leads to a significant material fiscal impact, and not in cases such as a reduction of income linked to the temporary prohibition of specific activities or products in order to protect consumers.

16 The ESAs may be characterised as EU agencies with significant independence and autonomy, particularly vis-à-vis the Commission.

17 The references to national supervisory structures in Europe are based on the information provided in ECB, "Recent developments in supervisory structures in the EU Member States (2007–2010)", available at http://www.ecb.europa.eu.

18 The argument towards a stronger involvement of central banks in prudential supervision for providing a stronger focus on systemic risk in the context of EMU was made in 2001 by the ECB (ECB 2001).

19 For an overview of the EWE, see IMF (2010b).

20 The Independent Evaluation Office of the IMF found that one of the reasons for the lack of a clear warning by the IMF on the financial crisis resulted from the inadequate linking of macroeconomic and financial sector analysis. See EMF Independent Evaluation Office (2011b).

21 For an overview of the challenges to the FSB from a political economy perspective, see Helleiner (2010).

22 On the role of central banks in financial stability, see Padoa-Schioppa (2004).

23 Regulation (EU) No. 1092/2010 of the European Parliament and of the Council of 24 November 2010 on European Union macroprudential oversight of the financial system and establishing a European Systemic Risk Board, OJ L 331, 15.12.2010, p.1 (henceforth, "the ESRB Regulation"); and Council Regulation (EU) No 1096/2010 of 17 November 2010 conferring specific tasks upon the European Central Bank concerning the functioning of the European Systemic Risk Board, OJ L 331, 15.12.2010, p.162.

24 A "global risk map" has been suggested to obtain a picture of mutual exposures among the large and complex financial institutions and also their counterparties. See Issing (2009).

25 See Article 15 of the Regulation on EU macroprudential oversight of the financial system and establishing a European Systemic Risk Board (see above).

26 See Article 3 (2) (g) of the ESRB regulation as well as Article 23 of each of the ESAs regulations. An example of such indicators is the "Systemic Risk Ranking" developed by the Stern Business School of New York University, which is a calculation of the expected capital shortage faced by a financial firm in a potential future financial crisis, available at http://vlab.stern.nyu.edu.

27 Article 16 of the ESRB Regulation.

28 For a description of the Basel III framework, see Basel Committee (2010).

29 Available at http://www.hm-treasury.gov.uk/d/consult_newfinancial_regulation170 211.pdf.

465

30 For a legal analysis, see Alexander Ferran (2010).
31 Proposal for a directive of the European Parliament and of the Council on deposit guarantee schemes (recast) and on a proposal for a directive amending Directive 97/9/EC of the European Parliament and of the Council on investor-compensation schemes, COM(2010)368 final, 12.7.2010.

REFERENCES

Acharya, Viral, and Mathew Richardson (eds), 2009, *Restoring Financial Stability: How to Repair a Failed System* (New York, John Wiley & Sons).

Alexander, Kern, and Eilis Ferran, 2010, "Can soft law bodies be effective? The special case of the European Systemic Risk Board", *European Law Review* (6), December, pp. 751–76.

Basel Committee, 2010, "Basel III: A global regulatory framework for more resilient banks and banking systems", December, available at http://www.bis.org.

BCBS, 2010a, "The Basel Committee's response to the financial crisis: report to the G20", October, available at http://www.bis.org.

BCBS, 2010b, "Basel III: A global regulatory framework for more resilient banks and banking systems," December, available at http://www.bis.org.

Bloomberg, Michael, 2010, "Sustaining New York's and the US' Global Financial Services Leadership", available at http://www.nyc.gov/html/om/pdf/ny_report_final.pdf.

Brierley, Peter, 2009, "The UK Special Resolution Regime for failing banks in an international context", Financial Stability Paper No. 5, Bank of England, July.

Brunnermeier, Markus, *et al*, 2009, "The Fundamental Principles of Financial Regulation", *Geneva Reports on the World Economy* 11, 2009.

Committee on the Global Financial System, 2003, "Report on Credit Risk Transfer", January, available at http://www.bis.org.

Committee on the Global Financial System, 2010, "Macroprudential instruments and frameworks: a stocktaking of issues and experiences", CGFS Papers No. 38, May, available at http://www.bis.org.

Constâncio, Vítor, 2010, "Information requirements for macroprudential oversight and the role of central banks", speech, October, available at http://www.ecb.europa.eu.

ECB, 2011, "Recent developments in supervisory structures in the EU Member States (2007–2010)", available at http://www.ecb.europa.eu.

ECB, 2001, "The role of central banks in prudential supervision", available at http://www.ecb.europa.eu.

ECOFIN 2009, "Council Conclusions of 20 October 2009", available at http://www.se2009.eu and http://www.consilium.europa.eu.

European Commission, 2009, "European Financial Supervision", COM (2009) 252 final, May.

European Commission, 2011, "Technical details of a possible EU framework for bank recovery and resolution," June, available at http://ec.europa.eu/internal_market/consultations/docs/2011/crisis_management/consultation_paper_en.pdf.

Financial Services Authority, 2009, "The Turner Review: a regulatory response to the global banking crisis", March, available at http://www.fsa.gov.uk.

French, Kenneth R., et al, 2010, *The Squam Lake Report: Fixing the Financial System* (Princeton, NJ: Princeton University Press), 2010.

FSB, 2010a, "Reducing the moral hazard posed by systemically important financial institutions", October, available at http://www.bis.org.

FSB, 2010b, "Intensity and Effectiveness of SIFI Supervision – Recommendations for enhanced supervision", November, available at http://www.bis.org.

FSB, 2011, "Progress in the Implementation of the G20 Recommendations for Strengthening Financial Stability – Report of the Financial Stability Board to G20 Finance Ministers and Central Bank Governors", February, available at http://www.financialstabilityboard.org.

FSB, IMF and BIS, 2011, "Macroprudential policy tools and frameworks – Update to G20 Finance Ministers and Central Bank Governors", February, available at http://www.financialstabilityboard.org.

G30, 2011, "Enhancing Financial Stability and Resilience: Macroprudential Policy, Tools and Systems for the Future", available at http://www.group30.org.

Galati, Gabriele, and Richhild Moessner, 2011, "Macroprudential Policy – A literature review", BIS Working Paper No. 337, February.

Ghosh, Atish R., Jonathan D. Ostry and Natalia Tamirisa, 2009, "Anticipating the Next Crisis", *Finance & Development* 46(3), September.

Helleiner, Eric, 2010, "What role for the new Financial Stability Board? The politics of international standards after the crisis", *Global Policy Journal* 1(3), October, pp. 282–90.

High-Level Committee on a New Financial Architecture, 2009, Report, June, available at http://www.docufin.fgov.be.

High-Level Group on Financial Supervision in the EU, 2009, Report, February, available at http://ec.europa.eu.

HM Treasury, 2011, "A new approach to financial regulation", February.

Honohan, Patrick, 2010, "The Irish Banking Crisis Regulatory and Financial Stability Policy 2003–2008", available at http://www.bankinginquiry.gov.ie.

IMF Independent Evaluation Office, 2011a, "IMF Performance in the Run-Up to the Financial and Economic Crisis", February, available at http://www.ieo-imf.org.

IMF, 2010a, "Central Banking Lessons from the Crisis", May, available at http://www.imf.org/external/np/pp/eng/2010/052710.pdf.

IMF, 2010b, "The IMF-FSB Early Warning Exercise, Design and Methodological Toolkit", September, available at http://www.imf.org.

Issing, Otmar, 2009, "New Financial Order: Recommendations by the Issing Committee, Part I and Part II", Center for Financial Studies, University of Frankfurt, White Papers Nos 1 and 2, February, available at http://www.ifk-cfs.de.

Larosière, Jacques de, 2009, "de Larosière Report", available at ec.europa.eu/internal_market/finances/docs/de_larosiere_report_en.pdf.

London Summit, 2009, "Declaration on Strengthening the Financial System", April, available at http://www.londonsummit.gov.uk.

Nyberg, Peter, 2011, "Misjudging Risk: Causes of the Systemic Banking Crisis in Ireland", report of the Commission of Investigation into the Banking Sector in Ireland, available at http://www.bankinginquiry.gov.ie.

Padoa-Schioppa, Tommaso, 2004, regulating "How to deal with emerging pan-European financial institutions?", speech at The Hague, November, available at http://www.ecb.europa.eu.

Padoa-Schioppa, Tommaso, 2004, *Regulating Finance* (Oxford University Press).

Padoa-Schioppa, Tommaso, 2007, "Europe Needs a Single Financial Rule Book", *Financial Times*, December 11.

Regling, Klaus, and Max Watson, 2010, "A Preliminary Report on the Sources of Ireland's Banking Crisis", available at http://www.bankinginquiry.gov.ie.

Senior Supervisors Group, 2009, "Risk Management Lessons from the Global Banking Crisis of 2008", October, available at http://www.newyorkfed.org.

Turner, Adair, *et al*, 2010, "The Future of Finance – The LSE Report", London School of Economics and Political Science.

UK House of Commons Treasury Committee, 2008, *"The Run on the Rock"*, January, available at http://www. parliament.uk.

Annex A

Structural Regulation Redux: The Volcker Rule

Marco Bevilacqua

Bank of Italy

A.1 INTRODUCTION

In the current search for measures to eliminate or reduce the negative externality generated by systemically important financial institutions (SIFIs), prospective options available to regulators include structural solutions. These are mandated constraints and limits on the activities that a financial institution may exercise, on the investments it may undertake and on its size and financial structure.

However, this approach has not enjoyed much consensus among policymakers thus far. Indeed, as described in Chapter 10, most efforts in the ongoing process of reforming the international regulatory framework have been focused on the enhancement of the loss-absorbing capacity of financial firms (in order to reduce the likelihood of distress) and on the development of better resolution mechanisms (to limit the spillover effects of any single default event on the financial system as a whole). Risk-based prudential measures remain at the forefront, as the starting point, to tackle the issue of systemically important institutions.

The Financial Stability Board endorsed this view in its latest Recommendations (FSB 2010), contending that more stringent prudential requirements on SIFIs are needed, while reckoning that additional measures, including structural ones, might prove useful in some circumstances and could be considered on a case-by-case basis.

The US represents a notable exception to the global policy trend towards non-structural solutions. The Dodd–Frank Wall Street

Reform and Consumer Protection Act (often called the Dodd–Frank Act and hereafter referred to as the DFA), enacted by President Obama on July 21, 2010, contains both prudential regulatory tools, along the lines of Basel's Committee work, and significant structural provisions. These provisions, concerning restrictions to proprietary trading and speculative investments by commercial banks, partially borrow from the proposal by the Economic Recovery Advisory Council (ERAC), presented in January 2010 and officially endorsed by the White House. The Council was headed by the former Fed chairman Paul Volcker; acknowledgement of his intellectual role in devising the suggested regulatory innovations is implied by the widespread recognition of this proposal as "The Volcker Rule".

This annex introduces the core of this part of the new regulation, stressing some key aspects concerning its actual implementation. Section A.2 briefly summarises some relevant points of the debate[1] about functional separation in the financial services industry, outlining the rudimentary cost-benefit framework. This may prove useful to characterise the policy rational behind proposed regulations, which comes under scrutiny in more detail in Section A.3. Section A.4 concludes.

A.2 COSTS AND BENEFITS OF FUNCTIONAL SEPARATION
A.2.1 Potential macroprudential benefits of separation
Functional separation, meaning the prohibition to exercise some activities (eg, credit intermediation and trading on own account) within the same financial institution, might, in the first place, reshape the structure of the financial system, entailing positive benefits for systemic stability. Looking at the counterfactual for separation (ie, integration), and stressing its revealed weaknesses, is a useful starting point to outline this argument. It is, however, necessary to point out that further research is needed to sharply depict causal mechanisms potentially linking separation and financial stability.

Size, interconnectedness and substitutability are agreed-upon proxies for the systemic importance of a financial institution (see Chapter 10). Large and complex intermediaries appear to be clear candidates for generating relevant negative externalities, through any of the above-mentioned drivers. These institutions typically operate across both the regulated banking sector and the shadow banking system, putting together traditional credit intermediation with investment banking and asset-management businesses, often serving the role of market makers in a wide range of standardised and OTC financial instruments, lead underwriters for primary market offers, and broker-dealers, both on own and third parties' accounts. Increasing integration with capital markets and orientation to an originate-to-distribute banking model are important features of this paradigm (see Chapter 1).

The cross-sector diversification and integration strategy, pursued by many players, has been driving considerable balance-sheet expansion,[2] modifying not only the asset structure but also liabilities composition. As deposits are poorly responsive to the evolution of funding needs, short-term market funding, often in the form of repurchase agreements, gained importance as a primary financing source for universal banks. "Steeper" leverage, increased maturity mismatch and dependence on overnight debt rollover emerged as noteworthy features of the conglomerate model.

The introduction of some degree of separation in the financial services industry may serve the purpose of at least partially disentangling liquidity provisioning from risk sharing, setting a border between regulated deposit taking institutions and the players of the former shadow banking environment, thus spinning off non-bank activities from the explicit and implicit safety net enjoyed by commercial banks. This would likely increase the funding cost faced by non-bank intermediaries, reducing the incentive for higher leverage and the volume of funds channelled outside the regulated banking system. This second aspect is particularly salient, as many authors have pointed out the role of shadow banking in feeding asset bubbles. Furthermore, limiting the "market arm" of the traditional banking sector could limit the opportunities for banks to accumulate excessive risks, reducing their access to structured finance for speculative purposes, also by means of increased transaction costs.[3]

Functional separation does not address directly the well-known problem of moral hazard for SIFIs: it tries to restrict the perimeter of moral hazard and the opportunities, for players still within this perimeter, to engage in opportunistic, excessive risk-taking behaviours paid for by the society as a whole.

As a consequence of mandated separation, forced spin-offs of forbidden activities would follow and this could also reduce the size of financial institutions, at least in the short term. It is, however, ambiguous what the financial system might look like in the long term, as financial innovation and new intra-sector waves of mergers among newly minted specialised intermediaries could push again towards an increase in size, unless moral hazard for too-big-to-fail institutions is effectively tackled, by means of prudential regulation or pigouvian taxation on the externalities they beget.

A.2.2 Potential costs

We have argued so far about the potential benefits of functional separation in financial services. On the other hand, potential costs should also be discussed. Traditional arguments in favour of horizontal and vertical consolidation in the financial services rely on the existence of scale and scope economies and on the allegedly wider risk-mitigation opportunities that diversified firms could exploit. These claims were particularly popular in the 1990s, in the debate that led to the repeal of the Glass–Steagall Act (eg, Benston 1990; Saunders and Walter 1994).

Concerning scale and scope economies, however, no clear consensus has emerged. Since the seminal work of Berger and Humphrey (1997), which does not identify any evidence of scale economies, several analyses followed, sharing similar views. Amel *et al* (2004), for instance, contend that scale economies exist in commercial banking but are marginally decreasing and disappear pretty quickly, after the threshold of US$10 billion in total assets. The evidence of scope economies is similarly elusive. DeLong (2001) actually argues in favour of diseconomies of scope.

Greater managerial complexity is in general deemed to erode the benefits from cross-selling, because of, for instance, increased management costs, poorer oversight over operations and potential losses of productivity. Schmidt and Walter (2009) claim that scope economies exist between commercial banking and underwriting or insurance businesses, due to cross-selling, but do not find any evidence for other business combinations. The analysis by Elsas *et al* (2009) stands as one of the few attributing the greater profitability observed in financial conglomerates to scale economies. Stiglitz (2010) and Acharya *et al* (2010) argue, on the other hand, that this competitive advantage descends from monopolistic power, lobbying and the rent-extraction ability of institutions considered too big to fail or too interconnected to fail.

Focusing on risk mitigation opportunities, the issue can be tackled at both individual and systemic levels. Again, Benston (1990) and Saunders and Walter (1994) stressed how the promise of diversification would mean better risk sharing in the financial system, implying both more solid institutions and increased financial stability. Events fostered a thorough reflection on the issue. Boot and Thakor (2009), borrowing from network theory concepts, contend that, while increased interconnections between intermediaries might reduce the individual default probability, this does not imply more systemic stability, as individual shocks could trigger widespread and quicker spillover effects. Wagner (2010) is along the same lines. De Jonghe (2009) and Stiroh and Rumble (2006) provide empirical evidence of the augmented financial fragility associated with diversification.

It is worth pointing out that, in light of the evidence provided by the last financial crisis, the assumed individual benefits from diversification came under question as well. Demirgüç-Kunt and Huizinga (2009) analyse a pool of more than 1,000 banks, concluding that more diversified business models, featuring an increased dependence on short-term funding and a higher contribution from non-interest income, are highly associated with increased idiosyncratic risk.

A.2.3 Side effects and caveats

Several authors argue that additional benefits occur as a result of functional separation. Deterring the adoption of originate-to-distribute business models and reducing the use of structured finance might help to sustain lending standards, limiting the incentives for risky lending to marginal borrowers. Wilmarth (2009) and Brunnermeier (2009) stress the role of securitisation in lowering the standards for credit allocation.[4] Other popular arguments in favour of separations claim that a system featuring specialised intermediaries fosters financial innovation (Boot and Thakor 1997) and that the presence of universal banks impairs the development potential of capital markets, as relationship lending in a long-term framework satisfies the financial needs of firms, thus reducing the role of markets. Furthermore, functional separation can partially soothe the unavoidable conflict of interest between clients and intermediaries.

Other potential drawbacks that should be taken into account include the fact that banning proprietary trading activities, which will impact on the market-making capacity of large financial firms, could reduce the liquidity of some markets. Additionally, limiting the access of banks to capital markets would arguably have negative effects on the ability to effectively hedge against risk. Both these issues are analysed in the next section in the discussion of the Volcker rule framework.

Brunnermeier (2009) sheds light on the possibility that imposing a hiatus (ie, sharp separation) between a regulated sector and a less or non-regulated one, promising higher yields, could incentivise procyclical capital flow, as agents' risk aversion changes through the cycle. In other words, while in good times capital might shift towards the riskier, unregulated sector, searching for higher return, when things turn bad, investors could prefer the safer, insured deposit, thus triggering substantial capital outflow from the non-bank sector. Intermediaries would then be forced to divest their assets, feeding fire sales. This would in turn exert downward pressure on prices, worsening the downturn through the subsequent depreciation of assets still held on balance sheets. The experience of the 2007–2010 financial crisis seems to confirm the danger of "fire sales spirals".

A.3 THE VOLCKER RULE

Section 619 of the DFA, better known as the Volcker Rule, states that banking entities are not allowed to engage in proprietary trading;[5] to acquire or retain any ownership interest in hedge funds and private equity funds;[6] to sponsor[7] such entities, with the exceptions detailed in Table A.1. For the purposes of this provision by the DFA, "banking entity" is defined as any insured depository institution (12 USC 1813), any company controlling an insured depository institution, and any affiliate or subsidiary of any such entity.[8]

The Volcker rule restrictions apply only to banking entities. Non-bank financial companies supervised by the Federal Reserve Board[9] and engaged in proprietary trading activities or hedge funds investment may be subject to additional prudential requirements and quantitative limits on the activity volumes.

It is worth noting that a further structural provision is included in the DFA. Section 622 states that no financial institution can hold liabilities exceeding the limit of 10% of total financial system liabilities. This rule complements the already existing 10% limit on deposit taking, over the overall amount of deposits, as provided for by the Riegle–Neal Interstate Banking and Branching Efficiency Act of 1994.

Table A.1 Exemptions from the Volcker Rule

Proprietary trading	Hedge funds and private equity
✓ Proprietary trading in connection with **underwriting and market-making** activities, to the extent that such activities do not exceed the reasonable near term demand of customers and counterparties	✓ Banking entities are allowed to organise and offer hedge funds and private equity funds under the joint evidence of the following:
✓ Proprietary trading in connection with **underwriting and market-making** activities, to the extent that such activities do not exceed the reasonable near term demand of customers and counterparties	❏ the banking entity provides bona fide trust, fiduciary services, investment advisory services;
✓ Proprietary trading for the purpose of **risk-mitigating hedging**, designed to reduce the specific risks to the banking entity	❏ the fund is organised and offered in connection with the above services, and offered only to customers of such services;
✓ Any activity in connection with **securitisation and sale of loans** (by *rule of construction*)	❏ the banking entity does not hold any ownership interesting the fund, except for a *de minimis*; and
✓ Purchase, sale, acquisition or disposition (short: proprietary trading) of **US government obligations**	❏ no "covered transaction" takes place between the banking entity and the affiliate fund, including the grant of any guarantee.
✓ Proprietary trading of obligations, participations or other **instruments issued by government agencies** (eg, Government National Mortgage Association)	✓ The banking entity is allowed to invest in the fund it organises and offers under the following limits:
✓ Proprietary trading of obligations issued by States or other political entities, like municipalities	❏ one year after the establishment of the fund, the banking entity cannot hold more than 3% of fund's assets; and
✓ Investments in the so called *small business investment companies* (SBI Act, 1958)	❏ the sum of the quotas the banking entity holds in such funds cannot exceed 3% of Tier 1 Capital.
✓ Investment with the recognised purpose of promoting public welfare, as defined by law (12 USC 24)	
✓ Some investment by insurance companies	

A.3.1 Implementation process

With the approval of the DFA, the US Congress made room for regulatory innovations. It is now a task for regulatory agencies to fill up the room, thus shaping the renewed US financial landscape. At the time of writing it is difficult to foresee what exactly this landscape is going to look like.

The effectiveness of the new regulatory scheme, in limiting excessive risk taking and generating negative externalities, largely depends on the future implementation choices of the regulators, which were delegated powers from Congress to enable them to lead the study and rulemaking phase.

According to some commentators (Acharya et al 2010) the full implementation of the DFA process would require more than 200 decrees and involve as many as 11 agencies. It was envisaged that the Federal Reserve Board (FRB), which in late 2010 released its yearly rulemaking plan[10] for 2011, would play a prominent role in the process. A draft of implementing provisions for the Volcker Rule was expected to be submitted for public consultation in the second quarter of 2011. Along with the FRB, the Securities Exchange Commission (SEC) and the Commodities Futures Trading Commission (CFTC) were slated to be involved as rule-makers.

October 2011 was made the deadline for regulatory drafting. The timeline for the process is embedded in the DFA, which said the study and rulemaking phase should be completed before July 2012, 24 months after the enactment of the statute. A transition period of two years would then be granted to the banks, in order to comply with the new legislation, which was intended to be fully effective after July 2014.

In January 2011, the Financial Stability Oversight Council (FSOC), in compliance with the DFA, issued its "Study and Recommendations on prohibitions on proprietary trading and certain relationships with hedge funds and private equity funds"[11] (FSOC 2011). The document contains binding policy recommendations which the agencies will have to take into account when exercising their rulemaking duties. Some relevant aspects of FSOC policy advice are addressed in the following subsection.

A.3.2 The challenges for regulators

There are several difficulties that the regulatory agencies will face when implementing the Volcker Rule. The keystone of the entire framework lies in the definition of proprietary trading, ie, in devising a border between admitted activities and activities that are banned.

For the purposes of this exposition, it is useful to consider the two-fold dimension of every trade, meaning:

❏ type of financial instruments involved; and
❏ aim of the transaction.

Some financial instruments, by virtue of their presumed riskless nature, are excluded from the scope of application of the proprietary trading ban. They include, for instance, government securities (see Table A.1).

For the remaining securities, the purpose of the transaction is the most pertinent point. Three main purposes fall outside the scope of the Volcker Rule: market making, hedging and underwriting. The rationale behind these exemptions is quite clear. The legislation implicitly acknowledges the importance of these above-mentioned functions for the smooth functioning of markets and for their liquidity (market making and underwriting) and for the risk management of any individual financial institution (hedging). Preserving market liquidity and firms' risk-management capabilities are primary, agreed-upon objectives to be safeguarded.

A similar approach is used with relation to securitisation. An explicit rule of construction[12] is included in the statute, stating that no provision included in the Volcker rule should prevent banks from securitising and selling loans. This is meant to avoid penalising the troubled securitisation market, whose functioning is considered necessary to sustain credit expansion and economic growth.

Henceforth, several top-down constraints will restrict the policy range available to regulators. The preferred approach seems to be lightening the regulatory load on those activities deemed critical from the application of the Volcker rule, shifting the burden of verifying compliance with the legal norms onto the supervisors. Market making, underwriting and hedging, as well as the management of related inventories of financial instruments, offer the opportunity to assume risks on own capital, taking proprietary positions. Selective hedging, for instance, is a typical way to take a position with respect to underlying market factors.

Section 622 (d) (1) (B) clarifies that market making and underwriting activities are admissible "to the extent that any such activities ... are designed not to exceed the reasonably expected near term demands of clients, customers, or counterparties". Several discretionary elements appear in this statement. The task for the regulatory agencies is to identify clear metrics to overcome any dangerous ambiguity, restricting the room for regulatory arbitrage.

The complex, dynamic nature of the trading positions to be monitored makes enforcement very difficult and will require considerable resources. The Financial Stability Oversight Council (FSOC), in its aforementioned study, suggests a quadripartite enforcement framework:

1. INTERNAL CONTROLS: Banks should be required to set up an appropriate compliance regime, which would include any policies and procedures necessary to ensure compliance with the norms. Testing by internal or external auditors should also be required, as well as a public attestation by the CEO that regulatory standards are met.
2. ANALYSIS AND REPORTING OF QUANTITATIVE METRICS: In particular, the FSOC recommends the mandatory recording and periodic communication to the authorities of (a) revenue-based measures, (b) revenue-to-risk measures, (c) inventories measures and (d) clients flow measures.
3. SUPERVISORY REVIEW: The agencies should be in charge of periodic review and testing of the internal controls and procedures, and of reviewing the quantitative metrics for red flags, allowing ambiguous situations to be further analysed. Within this pillar, the FSOC also says that "agencies should strongly consider conducting regular monitoring of trading activity in order to identify impermissible proprietary trading". Hence, at the time of writing, the analysis of trading data on a continuous base is considered, just as an option.
4. ENFORCEMENT PROCEDURES FOR VIOLATIONS: The uncertainty about the recourse to direct monitoring of trading activities, which would be extremely resource-consuming, pushes the analysis of quantitative measures to the forefront of supervisory actions. The FSOC suggests a particular scheme for analysis, indicating for market making, underwriting and hedging a series of indicia of impermissible activity, and providing examples of measurable, observable phenomena, to be monitored, to quantitatively and objectively gauge evidence of possible anomalies. Both cross-section data analysis (within homogeneous peer groups) and

Table A.2 Main measures suggested by FSOC for detection of impermissible trading activity

Revenue-based metrics	Revenue-to-risk metrics	Inventory metrics	Customer-flow metrics
✓ Historical revenues comparison ✓ Day One profit and loss	✓ Profitable trading days as percentage of total days ✓ Sharpe Ratios ✓ Revenues to VaR ✓ VaR	✓ Inventory turnover ✓ Inventory ageing	✓ Customer-initiated trade ratio ✓ Inventory to customer-initiated trades ✓ Revenues to customer-initiated trades

time-series analysis (for a single intermediary) can provide valuable insights into the evolution of operations, revealing forbidden activities.

Concerning market making, for instance, the FSOC suggests verifying the size of inventories held through the declaration of market-making purpose, thus monitoring the relationship between inventory levels and client-driven transactions. Other indicators can relate to inventory turnover, to inventory ageing or to "first-day-profits". The underlying assumption is that proprietary trading desks look for gains over a longer horizon, while market makers tend to profit from inventories in the short term, also showing a more stable revenue stream, a higher ratio of revenues to risk and a higher frequency of profit days. A similar approach is suggested for underwriting and hedging.

The monitoring of risk-mitigation trades seems to be the biggest challenge, as it is difficult to trace out a direct connection that would link a single exposure to its hedging, since exposures are often hedged for on an aggregate basis. Moreover, imperfect hedging could itself allow for impermissible risk-taking, through the strategic accumulation of basis risk. Table A.2 summarises some of the measures suggested by the Council.

A.4 CONCLUSIONS

This appendix has outlined some features of the new regulatory framework that is to be realised in the United States under the provisions of Section 619 of the Dodd–Frank Act – the so-called Volcker Rule. Attention has been devoted also to the rationale behind a structural approach to the new regulations and to the key implementation challenges.

A definitive framework was scheduled to be finalised by October 2011, when preliminary drafting and public consultations would have taken place.

The effectiveness of the rules as a complementary macroprudential tool will crucially depend on the implementation choices of the regulatory agencies. The framework outlined by Congress and the advice provided by the FSOC highlight that the protection of market liquidity, the guarantee of the risk-mitigating capacity of banks and the necessity to revive securitisation are considered primary needs by the legislator. They will represent constraints to be taken into account by regulators, thus restricting the policy options available and shifting the burden of proving the exercise of impermissible activities onto the supervisors. This is particularly relevant, as proprietary positions are often assumed within the activity of market making, underwriting and hedging, which are in principle excluded from the application of the rule. Moreover, the treatment of securitisation, protected by an explicit rule of construction in the DFA, seems very mild and arguably does not fully address some criticalities that emerged from the 2007–2010 crisis.

The development of a precise and unambiguous oversight framework is necessary. At the moment, it is unclear whether or not the supervisory review will include direct monitoring of trading data or will just rely on periodic analysis of quantitative metrics provided by firms. Direct monitoring of dynamic trading positions for several intermediaries could prove extremely resource-consuming. Excessive reliance on internal controls and self-attestations of compliance, on the other hand, leaves considerable room for opportunistic behaviours.

It is in the end worth emphasising that additional factors may affect the effectiveness of the norm, concerning in particular the expulsion of non-bank firms from the implicit and explicit safety net granted to deposit-taking banks. It is reasonable to expect that direct linkages between the regulated banking sector and other financial firms, as well as cross-sector exposures, will continue to be significant. Hence, there is a strong need for a sound prudential framework for non-bank institutions and for further efforts to be employed in strengthening central counterparties for OTC derivatives. Exposure concentration limits for these kinds of contracts should also be considered.

Unless these concerns are properly tackled by regulatory action, substantial room would remain for moral hazard and excessive risk taking, with particular regard to the less regulated non-bank institutions.

The opinions herein expressed are those of the author and do not necessarily reflect the position of the Bank of Italy.

1 This dates back as far as 1933 and enjoyed new life in the 1990s, when many commentators, from both business and academia, exerted strong pressures towards the repeal of the Glass–Steagall Act (1933), thus against the separation of investment and commercial banking, in favour of the emergence of the universal banking model in the US.
2 At the end of 2009, the six US largest financial conglomerates, all of them being bank holding companies (Bank of America, Citigroup, JP Morgan, Wells Fargo, Goldman Sachs, Morgan Stanley) totalled assets for US$6.2 trillion, with a 135% increase over the figure of 1999, when the Glass–Steagall Act was repealed.
3 The use of securitisation over the last decade can be considered as a bright example of how the integration between banking and market operations may not only serve the purpose of risk mitigation, but also offer new and cheaper opportunities for risk accumulation. Shin (2009) analyses the issue in depth.
4 This does not necessarily refer to the idea that banks can lower the lending standards since they can they transfer their "bad loans" to third parties. Shin (2009) points out that credit supply has an endogenous nature, and that securitization has also served the purpose of creating assets, to enlarge balance sheets, increase leverage and profitability, once the prime credit market was saturated. An example of this is the fact that when the asset bubble burst on real estate in the US, most of the credit risk was concentrated inside of the financial system.
5 DFA, Section 619 (h), Definitions, Point 4: "The term 'proprietary trading' ... means engaging as a principal for the trading account of the banking entity or nonbank financial company supervised by the Board in any transaction to purchase or sell, or otherwise acquire or dispose of, any security, any derivative, any contract of sale of a commodity for future delivery, any option on any such security, derivative, or contract, or any other security or financial instrument ..."
6 Concerning the definition of hedge fund and private equity fund the DFA refers to the Investment Company Act (1940), providing that such funds are characterized as exclusion cases from the category of investment management companies, by 3.c.1 (fewer than 100 investors; no public offering or intention to offer) and 3.c.7 (only qualified investors; no public offering or intention to offer).
7 DFA, Section 619 (h), Definitions, Point 5: "The term to 'sponsor' a fund means (A) to serve as a general partner, managing member, or trustee of a fund; (B) in any manner to select or to control (or to have employees, officers, or directors, or agents who constitute) a majority of the directors, trustees, or management of a fund; or (C) to share with a fund, for corporate, marketing, promotional, or other purposes, the same name or a variation of the same name."
8 The definition also includes any company that is treated as a bank holding company for purposes of Section 8 of the International Banking Act of 1978.

9   The Financial Stability Oversight Council is empowered to decide which non-bank financial institutions should be supervised by the FRB.
10 See http://www.federalreserve.gov/newsevents/reform_milestones201104.htm.
11 http://www.treasury.gov/initiatives/Documents/Volcker%20sec%20%20619%20study%20final%201%2018%2011%20rg.pdf.
12 In the legal context, a "rule of construction" is an explicit interpretation clause included in the statute.

REFERENCES

Acharya, V. V., T. Cooley, M. P. Richardson and I. Walter, 2010, *Regulating Wall St. – The Dodd Frank Act and the new architecture of global finance* (Hoboken, NJ: John Wiley & Sons).

Amel D., C. Barnes, F. Panetta and C. Salleo, 2004, "Consolidation and Efficiency in the Financial Sector: A Review of the International Evidence", *Journal of Banking and Finance*.

Benston, G. J., 1990, *The Separation of Commercial and Investment Banking* (London: Macmillan).

Berger, A. N., and B. Humphrey, 1997, "The dominance of inefficiencies over scale and product mix economies in banking", *Journal of Monetary Economics* 28.

Boot, A. W. A., and A. V. Thakor, 1997, "Financial system architecture", *Review of Financial Studies*.

Boot, A. W. A., and A. V. Thakor, 2010, "The accelerating implications of banks and markets and its implications for regulation", in Berger, A.N., Molyneux, P., Wilson, J. *The Oxford Handbook of Banking*. (Oxford University Press)

Brunnermeier, M. K., 2009, "Deciphering the liquidity and credit crunch 2007–2008", *Journal of Economic Perspectives*.

De Jonghe, O., 2009, "Back to the basics in banking? A micro analysis of banking system stability", forthcoming, *Journal of Financial Intermediation*.

DeLong, G., 2001, "Stockholder gains from focusing versus diversifying bank mergers", *Journal of Financial Economics* 29, pp. 221–52.

Demirgüç-Kunt, A., and H. Huizinga, 2009, "Bank activity and funding strategies: the impact on risk and return", European Banking Centre Discussion Paper 2009–01, January.

Elsas, R., A. Hackethal and M. Holzhaüser, 2009, "The anatomy of bank diversification", *Journal of Banking and Finance*.

Financial Stability Board, 2010, "Reducing the moral hazard posed by systemically important financial institutions – FSB recommendations and Time Lines".

Financial Stability Oversight Council, 2011, "Study and recommendations on prohibitions on proprietary trading & certain relationship with hedge funds & private equity funds", January, available at http://www.treasury.gov/initiatives/Documents/Volcker%20sec%20%20619%20study%20final%201%2018%2011%20rg.pdf.

Laeven, L., and R. Levine, 2007, "Is there a diversification discount in financial conglomerates?", *Journal of Financial Economics* 85(2).

Saunders, A., and I. Walter, 1994, *Universal Banking in the United States* (NY and Oxford: Oxford University Press).

Schmidt, M., and I. Walter, 2009, "Do financial conglomerates create or destroy economic value?", *Journal of Financial Intermediation* 18.

Shin, H. S., 2009, "Securitisation and Financial Stability", *Economic Journal*.

Stiglitz, J., 2010, *Freefall: Free Markets and the Sinking of the Global Economy* London: Penguin).

Stiroh, K., and A. Rumble, 2006, "The dark side of diversification: the case of US financial holding companies", *Journal of Banking and Finance*.

Wagner, W., 2010, "Diversification at financial institutions and systemic crisis", forthcoming, *Journal of Financial Intermediation*.

Wilmarth, A., 2009, "The dark side of universal banking: financial conglomerates and the origins of the subprime financial crisis", *Connecticut Law Review*, May.

Annex B

The Changing Uses of Contingent Capital under the Basel III Framework

Massimo Libertucci
Bank of Italy

B.1 INTRODUCTION

The Basel III framework places great emphasis on both the quantity and quality of the regulatory capital endowment of banks. The post-crisis experience illustrated that market participants focused primarily on common equity in periods of systemic distress. Nevertheless, it may be the case that different capital instruments can still play a role. Among these instruments, contingent capital – that is, a security that converts into equity when a predefined event occurs[1] – has gathered increasing attention. This annex provides an evaluation of the debate among regulators, academics and market participants surrounding the possible implementation of contingent capital under the Basel III framework.

Several variants of contingent capital have been proposed over the years. The post-crisis debate has focused on forms of debt that – more or less automatically – transform to common equity after a given signal is issued – for example, in the form of a given level of a predefined variable, commonly referred to as the "trigger".[2]

The idea of requiring banks to issue special capital instruments – tools that encompass features of both debt and equity, thereby bridging the gap between the two – is not a new one. For instance, the issue of subordinated notes and debentures[3] has been advocated as a valuable tool for improving the market discipline of larger intermediaries, and for identifying market-based triggers that would enable prompt supervisory corrective action.[4] In fact, subscribers of subordinated debt would have an incentive to monitor the operations of the debt issuer since their investment would be wiped out in the case of failure. Indeed, subordinated debtholders, while unaffected in business-as-usual scenarios, would bear losses in the case of default.

The disciplining impact of subordinated debt (ie, the incentives it provides to both debt and equity subscribers) crucially depends on the likelihood of an external bailout. Indeed, expectations of an external intervention – in the form, for example, of a public-money injection that would spread losses among a wider base – would limit the downside risk for subordinated bondholders, greatly reducing their monitoring effort (ie, the willingness to look after an agent's actions).

The introduction of contingent capital could therefore be viewed as an evolution of subordinated debt, without its shortcomings. In its basic design, contingent capital is a hybrid security that contains triggers that convert it into common equity. The differences between contingent capital and subordinated debt are subtle: Sections B.2 and B.3 will discuss them in detail, particularly with regard to their use in bank default situations. The advantages of contingent capital are twofold. On the one hand, while contingent capital would maintain the benefits of debt instruments, subscribers would also be exposed to the consequences of excessive risk taking and would thus be more willing to monitor the bank. Contingent claim structure efficiently provides a market mechanism that counteracts the excessive risk taking of common shareholders, which stems from the limited liability of the latter.

On the other hand, shareholders themselves would also have a strong incentive to monitor risk exposures in order to avoid a massive dilution of their rights when debt is converted to capital and subsequently a new voting majority can emerge; the threat of a punitive dilution for existing shareholders can in turn provide incentives for bank management to avoid excessive risk taking. Moreover, contingent capital can be included as a part of a manager's compensation scheme: with an appropriate design, based on performance variables, it can introduce a downside to risk-taking. Simply put, excessive risk-taking can result in the following sequence: (i) a bank's bad performance, (ii) because of this the conversion of contingent capital, (iii) because of this a manager to bear losses caused by their excessive risk-taking.

Not only would contingent capital introduce a more balanced distribution of risks between bond holders and equity holders (achieving this through allowing investment by both fixed-income institutional investors – such as pension funds and asset managers – and retail investors), but it may also enlarge the investor base and through this the distribution of risk among different sectors.[5]

An additional attractive feature of contingent capital is that it adds a different strand to bank capital management. By choosing trigger variables that ensure an early, timely conversion of contingent capital into equity, this process becomes transparent for investors; at the same time, room for regulatory forbearance is drastically reduced by anchoring the decision to convert to a fixed ruler, rather than to a discretionary choice by an authority. Moreover, the market value of contingent capital itself provides additional knowledge about the state of health of a bank. This knowledge may be used to assess the riskiness of a bank and thus to spur on proactive activities in order to avoid the occurrence of adverse events.

Although theoretically sound, appetite for contingent convertibles has been driven by the post-crisis regulation focus on capital quality increase. It is fair to acknowledge that, from a market-participant perspective, the most powerful necessity is to develop a capital tool that, while able to cover losses when needed, is less expensive than common equity for banks. Thus, there is clearly an appetite for instruments that, while satisfying supervisors' requests, are also able to keep funding costs under control.

The use of contingent capital has been proposed under two different settings. The first one relates to a bank's default (ie, gone concern). In this circumstance, the role of contingent capital is clear-cut: as a component of regulatory capital, it has to ensure loss-absorbency at the point of non-viability (BCBS 2010a). With respect to the analogous function performed by subordinated debt, a stricter definition of non-viability (that includes situations that go beyond a bank's default, such as public-money injection) represents a major difference.

On the contrary, the role of contingent capital in a business-as-usual (going-concern) situation is less well defined. At different stages of the debate this kind of contingent security has been proposed in association with measures aiming at tackling procyclicality, providing systemically important financial institutions (SIFIs) with additional loss-absorbency, or meeting bank-specific Pillar II requirements (BCBS 2010b).

This annex provides an evaluation of the debate among regulators, academics and market participants surrounding the possible implementation of contingent capital under the Basel III framework. Section B.2 discusses the use of contingent capital in gone-concern scenarios.[6] Section B.3 illustrates the possible applications of going-concern contingent capital. Section B.4 concludes after presenting some of the more relevant issues still under debate.

B.2 CONTINGENT CAPITAL IN A GONE-CONCERN SCENARIO

After a lively debate, the possible role of contingent capital in a gone-concern scenario has gathered a general consensus. For instance, in its consultative document, the BCBS (2010b) outlines a proposal to enhance the entry criteria of regulatory capital to ensure that all regulatory capital instruments issued by banks are capable of absorbing losses in the event that a bank is unable to support itself in the private market.

Among the components of regulatory capital, prudential regulation has traditionally assigned Tier 2 capital the role of absorbing losses on a gone-concern basis, helping to ensure that depositors and senior creditors can be repaid should a default occur.[7]

However, as the experience gathered from the 2007 crisis has shown, the presence of too-big-to-fail institutions violates this assumption: the liquidation of large, systemically relevant institutions does not take place since this is typically anticipated (and thus avoided) by public bailouts. Therefore, subordinated debtholders do not bear (and do not expect to bear) any loss and they do not require higher risk premiums.[8]

For these reasons, contingent capital should be seen as a more credible variant of subordinated debt, which guarantees that subscribers will also bear losses in spite of the size and the relevance of institutions. In its proposal, the BCBS (2010) considers the capacity to bear a loss to be a precondition for financial instruments to be treated as regulatory capital.

To expand upon this, the first element of the proposal requires all non-common Tier 1 instruments and Tier 2 instruments of internationally active banks to have a clause in their terms and conditions that requires them to be written off or converted to common equity should a "trigger event" occur. With respect to this, BCBS (2011) proposes it should be the earlier of the following: a discretionary decision by the relevant supervisory authority; a public-sector injection of capital.[9]

Requiring such a contractual clause is one of the possible options that would ensure loss absorption. In fact, either developing a bank resolution regime that would enable losses to be allocated to capital instruments issued by too-big-to-fail banks, or banning these banks from using Tier 2 instruments, represents an effective alternative. Nevertheless, both options present undesirable features. While an effective resolution regime appears to be highly desirable but unlikely to be implemented in the short run, the ban on subordinated debt for a certain category of banks would suffer several drawbacks in terms of moral hazard[10] and distorted incentives.

B.3 CONTINGENT CAPITAL IN A GOING-CONCERN SCENARIO

The role of contingent capital in going-concern conditions is unclear. Under this scenario, contingent capital generally converts into common equity before the point of non-viability. In different stages of the debate these kinds of contingent securities have been associated with different aims: meeting bank-specific Pillar II requirements; tackling the procyclicality of risk-sensitive capital requirements; and providing large internationally active financial institutions with additional loss-absorbency. The subsequent paragraphs discuss the main issues related to these aims.

B.3.1 Stress test

Contingent capital can be used in Pillar II stress test buffers. In such a circumstance, a bank is asked to maintain a capital cushion above its core requirements, in order to mitigate the risk that a shock, either systemic or idiosyncratic, may cause a bank to breach the common equity Tier 1 ratio. An adequately designed contingent convertible can meet the additional capital requirements linked with a forecast stressed scenario. The conversion of contingent capital is required either when the stress event materialises, or, when as a consequence of the stress event itself, a bank suffers losses that pose the risk of breaching capital requirements.

The issuance of contingent debt by Lloyds Banking Group (LBG) represents a case study of contingent capital for a stress test capital exercise. In its November 2009 capital plan, LBG offered a new contingent capital instrument in the form of a lower Tier 2 dated subordinated note, ie, denominated enhanced capital notes (ECNs).[11] For regulatory purposes, the ECNs are treated as Tier 2 for ongoing capital-adequacy calculations, but they have been granted Core Tier 1 quality for stress test capital calculations. In this particular implementation, contingent capital can be counted as Core Tier 1 when assessing the bank's capital adequacy in the stress test exercise required by the UK regulator.

B.3.2 Countercyclical buffer

From a theoretical perspective, contingent capital would be a good candidate for meeting the countercyclical buffer requirement.[12] In this framework, in good times banks would be allowed to issue contingent capital in order to build up their capital buffer; in bad times contingent capital would be converted into common equity, thus providing banks with sufficient resources for avoiding a credit crunch in the real sector (De Martino et al, 2010). Under this assumption, the introduction of contingent capital in a countercyclical setting would establish a clear distinction between microprudential and macroprudential policy objectives and, accordingly, a precise partition between different forms of regulatory capital.

The notion that contingent capital could serve in a countercyclical toolkit is adequate if it is thought to bear the increased losses a bank faces during a slowdown. On the contrary, if the predominant target of the countercyclical toolkit is to maintain an adequate credit supply to the real sector during a slowdown, it is straightforward to acknowledge that room for the use of contingent capital becomes drastically smaller.

On the back of this, the BCBS reviewed the questions of permitting other fully absorbing capital beyond common equity and identifying the form it would take.[13] As of the time of writing, the countercyclical buffer should be met with common equity only, although further debate may determine a change in the future.

B.3.3 SIFIs

The policy framework for SIFIs includes a variety of measures (such as a more pervasive supervisory oversight, stress-resilient core infrastructure and a dedicated resolution regime). In this instance, the adequacy of loss-absorbency capacity plays a leading role.[14]

Regulators state the need for SIFIs to have additional loss-absorption beyond the already increased minimum Basel III standards[15] (that is, a capital surcharge). This additional loss-absorbing capacity is in the pursuit of several targets: reducing the likelihood of adverse events; minimising its impact in case of a SIFIs failure; reducing its burden for taxpayers in case of a public rescue; and levelling the playing field by eliminating competitive advantage with respect to non-SIFIs in terms of market conditions.

Contingent capital can be tested in its ability to meet these targets with respect to common equity that represents a baseline option.[16] The incentive structure of contingent capital imposes a punitive conversion for the shareholder in case of conversion, thereby reducing risk taking. This feature represents a major advantage with respect to common equity, because it can directly affect the likelihood of adverse events. On the other hand, contingent capital performance crucially hinges on its effectiveness in providing additional resources when needed. This is possible when the trigger is able to identify adverse situations consistently, without "false negative" signals.[17]

Contingent capital does not differ from common equity in terms of reducing both the impact of a SIFIs failure and the taxpayers' burden. As long as its conversion takes place promptly (for example, acting as a backstop in the gone-concern scenario described above), both instruments provide the same amount of additional resources.

SIFIs can exploit their competitive advantage (ie, their implicit rescue guarantee) over capital markets. The ability of contingent capital to level the playing field is questionable: the more the entire engineering of the instrument is devoted to this goal, the more likely for it to be effective.

The first plan to globally apply a specific capital surcharge for systemically important banks involves Switzerland's biggest banks, UBS and Credit Suisse (FINMA 2010). Remarkably, the plan is the first to propose a fully fledged use of contingent capital. In the October 2010 proposal by a Swiss government-appointed panel, the two banks should hold total capital equal to at least 19% of risk-weighted assets by 2019, nearly twice as much capital as required by Basel III regulations; notably, while the common equity component should be limited to 10%, the rest can be covered by contingent capital.

Under this proposal, the use of contingent capital is invoked in two circumstances. The first one involves a conservation capital buffer:[18] compared with the 2.5% proposed by the Basel Committee, the two banks may in fact need to increase their buffers to 8.5%. Of that, at least 5.5% has to be in the form of common equity, and the rest can be made up of contingent capital.

Moreover, the proposals call for an additional capital buffer, currently calibrated at 6%, but with the option to change over time, depending on some bank- and market-specific indicators. All of this should be in the form of contingent capital.

In the proposed agreement, the first contingent capital buffer should convert into equity once the common equity ratio breaches a 7% threshold. The second buffer could convert at a 5% common equity ratio and may be used to support the systemically important parts of a bank's business, while the rest is wound down in a crisis.

B.4 CONCLUSIONS

The Basel III framework places a greater emphasis on both the quantity and quality of regulatory capital endowment of banks than that proposed by Basel I and Basel II. While the experience of the crisis illustrated that market participants focused primarily on common equity in periods of systemic distress, it may be the case that different capital instruments – including contingent capital – can still play a role. This annex has described the debate concerning the possible uses of contingent capital in the Basel III framework, explaining the perspectives of regulators, academics and market participants. While some aspects are quite clear, there are some issues that remain unresolved.

The choice of an appropriate trigger represents the first logical step in contingent capital design. The debate around the trigger has followed two dimensions. The first (more relevant) dimension differentiates between the choice of a prudential variable and a market one. As the case studies provided in Sections B.3.3 and the Basel III consultative process bear witness, banking industry preferences seem to lie closer to prudential variables. Although the calibration of triggers is not univocal, it must be acknowledged that the breaching of the newly established 7% threshold, given by the sum of common equity Tier 1 ratio and capital conservation buffer, seems to represent a watershed.

A major weakness of triggers based on capital ratios is that they provide a lagging signal: while conversion into equity would require a more timely approach in order to be effective, these ratios need time before they can be computed.[19] This undesirable feature has been used as a reason for the introduction of market-based triggers that ensure a timely signal of impeding distress. In spite of this attribute, a fully fledged application of market triggers is treated with scepticism. The value of market variables cannot be 100% immune from manipulation, although some structures – for example, relying on the long-term moving average – reduce the likelihood of manipulation. Besides the explicit risk of manipulation, market triggers raise additional concerns in terms of dynamic, death-row spiral, volatility, statistical errors and multiple equilibria.[20]

All these concerns set the stage for the second question, regarding the use of single versus multiple triggers. Using two variables rather than a single one may represent a straightforward way to cope with most of the previous issues.[21] Moreover, the adoption of a double trigger may provide an additional advantage in systemic crisis situations.[22] Such advantages have a cost in terms of increased complexity, especially regarding the pricing of the instrument, which depends on the state of the two variables.

Suggested prudential treatment of contingent capital implies that, if it is used to meet specific requirements (such as additional loss-absorption, countercyclical buffer, and Pillar II stress test requirements), it would not be eligible to meet regulatory capital requirements. Moreover, for banks investing in contingent capital, the same deduction regime as applies for the investments of banks in common stocks investment under Basel II applies to contingent capital. By deducting the contingent capital component from common equity Tier 1 capital, regulators seek to avoid both contagion among financial institutions and double counting of capital within the banking system.

Deducibility regimes, as well as other "debt-alike" contractual features, have undesirable side effects in terms of prudential outcome, in the form of loss-absorbency capacity.[23] If the equivalence between common equity and contingent capital does not hold, the related issue of an appropriate exchange rate between the two arises. While a par exchange rate would represent a fairly simple solution (without the additional evidence of a lower loss-absorbing capacity of contingent capital with respect to common equity), a higher exchange rate would have an advantage in terms of the more-than-proportional creation of common equity.

By the same token, the proportion of additional loss-absorption met with contingent capital is a close issue. In fact, only a fraction of this additional capital surcharge can be met by contingent capital: its proportion with respect to common equity may range from 0 to 100%. The final decision about the actual size is intimately related to the perceived ability for contingent capital to perform at least as effectively as common equity in loss-absorption.

All in all, contingent capital has many attributes, but the possibility that it will be implemented by market participants is still debatable. As some contingent capital sceptics outline (Standard & Poor's 2009), these kinds of securities represent one potential answer to a well-defined capital-management question. While it has proven useful when managing capital structure in periods of distress, contingent capital is not fit, nor is it expected, to replace common equity in all of its functions.

> The opinions herein expressed are those of the author and do not necessarily reflect the position of the Bank of Italy.

1 Because of this feature, contingent convertible ("Coco") is widely used as a synonym for contingent capital.
2 Contingent capital has gather increasing attention by both academic and regulators. For instance, Flannery (2005) proposes the use of reverse-convertible debentures triggered by a bank-specific variable, focusing on an idiosyncratic crisis. The risk of price manipulation by interested parties would be reduced by averaging market prices over a given time interval. Conversely, Hancock and Passmore (2009) suggest mandatory convertible subordinated debt, issued in good times and automatically converted into common equity during a systemic crisis. Therefore, they specify a single trigger that is totally independent of firm-specific risks and calibrated in order to be pulled very infrequently (once-in-a-lifetime).
3 In general terms, these are debt securities of different maturities, which can be changed into common stock – for example, after a predetermined period of time – and which rank below other liabilities.
4 See Turner (2010) for an exhaustive survey.
5 Nevertheless, the gain from the extension of investor base to fixed-income institutional investors is debateable. A major issue is represented by the post-conversion behaviour (ie, the behaviour after the transformation of debt to equity) of these investors. In case of a sudden liquidation of their positions, the risk of a fire sale (ie, emergency selling at a very discounted price) may be significant.
6 See also Chapter 3.
7 In a gone-concern scenario, subscribers of subordinated debt require higher risk premiums (compared with other bondholders), since they bear the losses in the case of default. As such,

THE CHANGING USES OF CONTINGENT CAPITAL UNDER THE BASEL III FRAMEWORK

Tier 2 subordinated debt is an efficient component of a bank's capital structure and arguably there is no need for contingent capital.

8 In other words, the distinction between going and gone concern is not meaningful since it fails to acknowledge that too-big-to-fail institutions never go through a "formal" default status.

9 As outlined in the Basel III consultation process, the relevant degree of discretion that characterises the "triggering phase" can have relevant drawbacks in terms of regulatory forbearance and market pricing.

10 For instance, such a proposal would in turn imply the disclosure of a list of those institutions that are judged as too big to fail.

11 ECNs are subordinated notes with bullet maturities of at least 10 years, no issuer call and no coupon deferral. ECNs have the form of a par-for-par exchange into LBG carrying a coupon equal to the coupon of the existing securities (fixed rate or floating rate for life depending on the existing securities), plus a premium subordinated note with bullet maturities of at least 10 years, no issuer call and no coupon deferral.

12 See also Chapter 6.

13 BCBS (2010b) initially allowed other fully loss-absorbing capital instruments to meet the countercyclical buffer.

14 See also Chapter 10.

15 FSB (2010) states, "G-SIFIs should have loss absorption capacity beyond the minimum agreed Basel III standards. They should have a higher share of their balance sheets funded by capital and/or by other instruments which increase the resilience of the institution as a going concern."

16 This additional loss-absorbency capacity can derive from different sources. FSB (2010) states, "Depending on national circumstances, this greater capacity could be drawn from a menu of viable alternatives and could be achieved by a combination of a capital surcharge, a quantitative requirement for contingent capital instruments and a share of debt instruments or other liabilities represented by 'bail-inable' claims, which are capable of bearing loss at the point of non-viability, ie, within resolution, thus enabling creditor recapitalisation and recovery while maintaining vital business functions."

17 In this context, a false negative arises when a bank was not supposed to face a problem, but eventually it ended up facing a period of serious distress. This concept is equivalent to a Type I error in statistics.

18 This is a capital cushion that aims at preserving the breaching of the core capital requisite.

19 McDonald (2010) states that market variables are preferable to accounting ratios because the latter are updated less frequently and are backward-looking; moreover, accounting rules may be subject to arbitrage.

20 For a comprehensive discussion of these aspects, see Sundaresan and Wang (2010).

21 The Squam Lake Working Group (2009) propose that banks issue mandatory long-term debt instruments in good times; during a crisis, they would be automatically converted into equity. Conversion would be determined subject to two conditions: (a) the financial system incurred a systemic crisis, as announced by the supervisory authority; and (b) a bank-specific variable – such as the capital adequacy ratio – is triggered. McDonald (2010) also opts for a set of triggers relying on market-based indicators. In his proposal, contingent capital would be converted if both the firm's stock price and a financial sector index drop below predefined values.

22 In fact, by limiting conversion to the occurrence of systemic crisis, contingent capital would provide the same benefit – in terms of a disciplining factor for managers – as debt in all but the most extreme periods. Moreover, even sound banks, would be forced to convert in a crisis. The use of a second, bank-specific, trigger would enable the identification of a quasi-default status: the bank is still able to meet regulatory requirements, but a need for additional capital injection emerges since generalised problems are incoming.

23 As debt instrument, there is the possibility for a bank to subtract part of the interest paid from the end-year income, thus reducing profits and by this loss absorption.

REFERENCES

BCBS, 2010a, "Proposal to ensure the loss absorbency of regulatory capital at the point of non-viability", consultative document, August.

BCBS, 2010b, "Group of Governors and Heads of Supervision announces higher global minimum capital standards", press release, September 12.

De Martino, G., M. Libertucci, M. Marangoni and M. Quagliariello, 2010, "Countercyclical contingent capital (CCC): possible use and ideal design", Bank of Italy Occasional Paper No. 71, September.

FINMA, 2010, "Committee of experts on 'too big to fail' issue – FINMA and SNB recommend rapid implementation of measures" press release, October 4.

Flannery, M., 2005, "No Pain, No Gain? Effecting Market Discipline via Reverse Convertible Debentures", in H. S. Scott (ed.), *Capital Adequacy beyond Basel: Banking, Securities, and Insurance* (Oxford University Press).

FSB, 2010, "Reducing the moral hazard posed by systemically important financial institutions", FSB Recommendations and Time Lines, October 20.

Hancock, D., and W. Passmore, 2009, "Mandatory Convertible Subordinated Debt and Systemic Risks", slides presented at Methods of Implementing Systemic Risk Regulation, Symposium, New York Federal Reserve Bank.

McDonald R. L., 2010, "Contingent Capital with a Dual Price Trigger", Northwestern University mimeo.

Squam Lake Working Group on Financial Regulation, 2009, "An Expedited Resolution Mechanism for Distressed Financial Firms: Regulatory Hybrid Securities", 2009.

Standard & Poor's, 2009, "Contingent Capital is Not a Panacea for Banks", *Research*.

Sundaresan, S., and Z. Wang, 2010, "Design of Contingent Capital with a Stock Price Trigger for Mandatory Conversion", *Federal Reserve Bank of New York Staff Reports* (448).

Turner, A., et al, 2010, "The Future of Finance: The LSE Report", London School of Economics and Political Science.

Index

(page numbers in italic type refer to figures and tables)

A
American International Group
 (AIG) 26, 31
arbitrage of deposit insurance
 13–14

B
Bank of America 27, 37
Banco Central do Brasil (BCB), see
 Central Bank of Brazil
Bank of England 24, 25, 342, 456
Bank for International Settlements
 (BIS) 48
Barclays 27, 28, 195, 200, *201*
Basel Committee on Banking
 Supervision (BCBS) 48, 74–5,
 131, 133
 additional comparison
  parameters identified by 225
 ambitious standards set out by
  433
 amendment of January 1996 12, 13
 Assessment Methodology of 315
 banks encouraged by, on
  securitisation products 108
 and "Basel 2.5" 105–12; see also
  "Basel 2.5"
 and Brazilian financial system,
  see Brazil
 commitment of, to risk-based
  regulatory architecture 191
 and Comprehensive Risk
  Measure floor 123
 consultative documents of 106–7,
  126, 141, 167, 216, 219, 220,
  317, 323, 377, 488
 countercyclical framework of
  167–78
 eligibility criteria devised by 79,
  86
 expanded membership of 50
 guidelines for sound liquidity
  risk management issued by
  209
 important part of regulations
  missed by 407–8
 interventions of 138
 IRB formula of 189
 IOSCO publishes joint survey
  with 103
 level of regulatory floor set by 111
 monitoring period introduced by
  384
 and national resolution powers
  51
 new guidelines introduced by 77
 new liquidity framework
  finalised by 210

497

new regulation on liquidity risk issued by 208
1998 Press Release of 75
proposal on regulatory capital by 298
role of IOSCO and 258–61
quantitative standards on liquidity risk set out by 21
Cross-border Bank Resolution Group report published by 350–2
risk factors and severity levels identified by 215
stress-testing guidance published by 122
survey of pre-crisis liquidity regulations in major countries carried out by 208
proposals of, and G20 reforms 195–202
and regulatory capital definition, changes to 74
rules on capitalisation of bank exposures pubished by 150
updated "revisions to the Basel II market risk framework" published by 111
working towards proposals of 45–67
"Basel 2.5" 105–12
versus Basel III phase-in 111–12
July 2005 105–6
July 2008 to January 2009 106–10
and correlation trading carve-out 109–10
final proposal 110–11
"Incremental Default Risk" to "Incremental Risk Charge" 107
proposed treatment for TV securitisations 107–9
Bear Stearns 22, 26, 27, 28
Brazil 397–418
and Basel III, movement towards 410–13
and capital 411–13
and liquidity 413
and Basel III's implementation 400–3
Basel III's impact on 413–16
capital 414–15
liquidity 415–16
and financial crises and Basel II 407–10
and financial system, evolution of 403–7
perspective of, on Basel III, 397–418, *404, 405, 408, 409, 414*
British Bankers' Association 13

C
Capital Adequacy Directive 12, 13
capital conservation buffer 93, 170, 171–3, 177, 178, 390, 492
capital ratio, evolution of 100
capital surcharge/extra loss absorbency 296–8
common equity 297
contingent convertible capital 297–8
Central Bank of Brazil 398, 402, 406, 407, 409, 412, 417
Citibank 26
Citigroup 22, 27
Committee of European Banking Supervision (CEBS) (later European Banking

INDEX

Authority, *q.v.*) 34, 87, 169, 203, 209, 210
  high-level principles of, on remuneration policies 317–18
  implementation study of 320–1, 367
Committee on Payment and Settlement Systems (CPSS) 149
Comprehensive Quantitative Impact Study (C-QIS), evidence from 377–88
  and bank liquidity 384–8
  features and scope 378
  and impact on capital 379–84
contingent capital:
  changing uses of 485–96
  in going-concern scenario 489–92
    countercyclical buffer 490–2
    SIFIs 490–1
    stress test 489–90
  in gone-concern scenario 488–9
contingent convertible capital instruments (Cocos) 297, 487, 489
corporate law and prudential regulation 82
correlation trading carve-out 109–10, 119–26
countercyclical buffer 93, 170, 173–8, 490
  industry reaction to 175
counterparty credit risk (CCR) 137–53
  before financial crisis, regulatory capital for 138–40
    under Basel I 138–9, *139*
    under Basel II 139–40

charges, revisions to 141–7
  and default risk charge, changes to 142–4
  in financial crisis 141–2
and credit valuation adjustment charges, capitalisation of 144–7
enhanced requirements for 150–1
other measures for improving coverage of 147–51
  central counterparties 149–50
  collateralised counterparties and margin period of risk 149
  increased asset-value correlation for financial counterparties 148
credit crunch, *see* financial crisis
credit rating agencies (CRAs):
  assessment by, of underlying data quality 255–6
  discipline of 243–84
  and economic analysis and regulatory intervention 244–52
  and market v regulatory failures 244–6
  and ratings' relevance 247–9
  regulatory options concerning 249–52
  in Europe, way forward 273–9
  effectiveness 273–8
  national and supranational powers 278–9
  and IOSCO, role of, and Basel Committee 258–61
  nationally recognised, statistical 247
  post-crash re-regulation and supervision of 253–73

499

ESMA's role in 267–8
in Europe 264–8
and European Commission
   Consultation Paper and US
   initiatives 268–73
and European Commission's
   intervention 261–3
and FSB principles 256–8; *see
   also* Financial Stability
   Board: principles of
and IOSCO, role of, and Basel
   Committee 258–61
and underlying data quality,
   assessment of 255–6
US regulation on 272–3
Credit Suisse 22, 26, 194, 491
credit valuation adjustment (CVA)
   141–2, *142*, *147*, 381, 382
   charges, capitalisation of
   144–7
crisis management 339–72
   and bail-inable debt 355–7
   and Basel Committee
      recommendations 350–2
   and cross-border asset
      transferability 345–6
   cross-border cooperation in, G20
      and FSB principles for
      342–50
   cross-border, US and EU
      approaches to 352–7
   and Dodd–Frank act 252–5
   and financial crisis 358–69
   and G20 summit, Seoul, 357–8
   and global agenda 342–58
   and Memorandum of
      Understanding 360–5
   in new EU supervisory
      architecture 365–9

and post-crisis European
   supervisory framework
   358–60
and territoriality versus
   universality in national
   insolvency proceedings
   346–7
cyclicality *19*
   and Basel II countercyclical rules
      161–3
   and less-cyclical borrowers
      162
   and Pillar II and stress tests
      162–3
   risk parameters 161–2
   and Basel III countercyclical
      framework 167–78, *172*, *176*
   and capital conservation
      buffer 171–3
   and countercyclical buffer
      173–8
   and minimum capital
      requirements, tools for
      mitigating cyclicality of
      168–70
   in Basel I 157–8, *157*
   in Basel II 158–61
   and borrowers, treatment of 162
   credit 19
   and post-crisis debate 163–7
      and binding rules on
         estimation of probabilities of
         default 164
      and countercyclical
         provisioning 166–7
      and smoothing output of
         capital function 166
      and strengthening stress tests
         164–5

and time-varying capital
functions 165
procyclicality born of 155
see also procyclicality of financial
regulation

D

depletion of capital buffers 7–9
deposit insurance, arbitrage of
13–14
derivatives and repos, treatment of
200–2
Dodd–Frank Act 252–5, 272, 352,
353–5, 446, 454, 455, 470
dynamics of financial crisis 20–35,
*21, 23, 24, 25, 29, 30, 31, 32,
34, 35*
  subprime losses 25–6
  and systemic shock 21–7
    and creditors, rescue of 26–7
    and depositors, rescue of 24–5
    and losses, crystallisation of
    22–3
  see also financial crisis

E

Economic Recovery Advisory
Council (ERAC) 470
European Banking Authority
(EBA) (formerly Committee
of European Banking
Supervision, *q.v.*) 317, 366,
367–9
European Central Bank 24, 25, 33,
65, 209, 219, 367, 456
European Securities and Markets
Association (ESMA) 244,
267–8, 274–5, 276, 277,
278–9, 437

European Systemic Risk Board
448–54

F

Federal Reserve (Fed) 24, *24*, 28, 34,
192–3, 323–5, 455–6
  Consumer Financial Protection
  Bureau within 443
financial safety net, rapid
detriment to 5–16, *8, 9, 10,
11, 15*
  and early intervention, lack of
  14–16
  and deposit insurance, arbitrage
  of 13–14
  and provisions, shortfalls of 6–7,
  6, 7
  and capital buffers, depletion of
  7–9
  and capital charges, reduction of
  9–13
  and trading book, invention of
  12–13
Financial Accounting Standards
Board (FASB) 59, 60
financial crisis 3–41, *16, 17, 18, 20,
21, 23, 24, 25, 29, 30, 31,
32*
  counterparty credit risk in 141–2;
  see also counterparty credit
  risk (CCR)
  debate after 163–7
    and binding rules on the
    estimation of probabilities of
    default 164
    and countercyclical
    provisioning 166–7
    and smoothing output of
    capital function 166

501

and strengthening stress tests
164–5
and time-varying capital
functions 165
dynamics of 20–35, *21, 23, 24, 25, 29, 30, 31, 32, 34, 35*
and systemic shock 21–7
estimates of length of 3
European supervisory
framework after 358–60
and financial safety net, rapid
detriment to 5–16, *8, 9, 10, 11, 15*
and lessons for EU single market
358–69
lessons from, for financial
regulation and supervision
422–32
and effective macroprudential
oversight, lack of 429–32
and prudential supervision,
inadequate standards for the
conduct of 427–9
and regulatory competition,
insufficient restraint of
425–7
sources of regulatory and
institutional reform 422–5
main lessons from 47
and market confidence,
restoration of 31–5
shareholders, rescue of 32–5
new institutional arrangements
following 47–54
and FSB "peer reviews" 53–4
G20 process and membership
of international groups 48–51
national authorities'
interaction 51–2

origins of 4–20
panic caused by 27–31
Lehman Brothers' collapse 28
systemic crisis 28–31
policy response to 45–67
changes to regulation and
supervision 54–64
and provisions, shortfalls of 6–7, *6, 7*
and early intervention, lack of
14–16
and deposit insurance,
arbitrage of 13–14
and capital buffers, depletion
of 7–9
and capital charges, reduction
of 9–13
and trading book, invention of
12–13
regulatory response to, an
overview 208–10
re-regulation and supervision of
credit rating agencies after
253–73
and agencies' assessment of
underlying data quality
255–6
and differentiated ratings and
expanded information on
structured products 254–5
Financial Stability Forum
(FSF) report 253–6
and rating process, quality of
254
shock of 16–20
credit cyclicality 19, *19*
global imbalances 17–18
systemic 21–7
yield-curve distortions 18–19

financial regulation, procyclicality of
  and Basel I 157–8
  and Basel II, 158–61
  and Basel II countercyclical rules 161–3
    and less-cyclical borrowers 162
    and Pillar II and stress tests 162–3
    risk parameters 161–2
  how cyclicality becomes 155
  and impact of different rating systems 160
  and leverage ratio 202–4
  tools for mitigating 155–80, *157, 158, 159*
  see also cyclicality
Financial Sector Assessment Programme (FSAP) 435
  "peer reviews" 53–4
Financial Stability Board (FSB) 45, 49–50, 51–2, 54–5, 56–7, 58, 62–5 *passim*
  and crisis management 342
  and G20 48–9, 50
  "peer reviews" by 53–4
  principles of 256–61
    central bank operations 257
    disclosure requirements for issuers of securities 258
    policies of investment managers and institutional investors 257
    private sector margin requirements 257–8
    prudent supervision 256–7
  and regulatory repairs 310–17

Financial Stability Oversight Council (FSOC) 454–6, 476, *479*
  enforcement framework suggested by 478
Financial Times 163, 339
FINMA 194
fiscal regimes and prudential regulation 86

G
G20 46, 48–9, 53, 64, 149–50, 312, 423, 432
  and Basel Committee proposals 195–202, *201*
    and derivatives and repos, treatment of 200–2
    and liquid assets, treatment of 199
    measure of capital 197–8
    traditional off-balance-sheet items 198–9
  FSB and FSB Principles for cross-border cooperation in crisis management 342–50
  stated ambition of 294
  way ahead, after Seoul summit 357–8
Glass–Steagall Act 12, 472
global credit crunch, *see* financial crisis
Goldman Sachs 28, 31
Goodhart, Charles 163
grandfathering mechanisms and transitional arrangements 93–5
Group of Governors and Heads of Supervision (GHoS), 179, 191, 196

503

I

IKB Deutsche Industriebank 22
Incremental Risk Charge (IRC) 102, 107–8, 112–19, 125–6, 146
  assumptions and regulatory parameters for computing 116–18
  and liquidity horizon, maturity mismatches within 119
  and offsetting and hedging 118–19
  and optionality 119
  rationale for 114
  risks captured by 115–16
  scope of 115
International Accounting Standards Board (IASB) 59, 60, 64
International Monetary Fund (IMF) 48, 50, 269, 289, 447–8
International Organisation of Securities Commissions (IOSCO) 48, 105, 149
  role of, and Basel Committee 258–61

K

Korea Development Bank 28

L

Lehman Brothers 20, 22, 26, 27–9, 209, 369
  immediate effect of collapse of 29
  international in life but national in death 341–2
  lasting effect of collapse of 339
  second anniversary of collapse of 339

leverage:
  banks' own disclosure of 195
  ratio 185–205, *188*
  regulatory and marketing definitions of 191–5
  risk-based, reliance on 186–91
  in US, Canada, Switzerland and Germany 192–5
liquidity buffer:
  concept of stress tests on 230
  or contingent liquidity buffer? 225
liquidity coverage ratio (LCR) 213–21, *218*
  inflows 220–1
  net cash outflows 215–16
  retail and small-business customers' deposits 216
  secured funding and reverse repo 218–20, *219*
  stock of high-quality liquid assets 213–15
  stress tests on 226–30
    and business model 227–8
    concept of, on liquidity buffer 230
    scope of application of 229–30
    and time horizon 228–9
  treatment for jurisdictions with insufficient liquid assets 215
  unsecured wholesale funding provided by banks, nonfinancial corporates, central banks and PSEs 216–18
liquidity horizon, maturity mismatches within 119
liquidity risk:
  banks' tolerance to 233–4

new framework for 207–41, *210*
new quantitative standards for 212–24
  coverage ratio 213–21; *see also* liquidity coverage ratio
  monitoring tools 223–4
  net stable funding ratio 221–2, *221*
open issues concerning 224–32
  disclosure 230–2
  and LCR stress tests 226–30
  liquidity buffer or contingent liquidity buffer 225–6
preliminary assessment of 232–6
  crowding-out effect 234–5
  possible impact on banking strategies 233
  rules and incentives 235–6
  tolerance of banks 233–4
and regulatory response to financial crisis, overview of 208–10
sound management and supervision of, principles of 210–12
  governance 211
  management 211–12
  and supervisors, role of 212
  transparency and disclosure 212
loss absorption 37, 57, 79, 80, 87–8, 197, 296–8, 402, 426, 469, 487, 489, 493–4

M

Macroeconomic Assessment Group (MAG) 389–91
market confidence, restoration of 31–5

Market Risk Amendment (MRA) 100, 104, 113
Market Risk Framework:
  main changes to *101*, 102–3
  specific risk in:
    new treatment for 112–26, *127*
    specific VaR 112–14
    treatment for 104–5
  and trading book (TB) 99–135
market v regulatory failures 244–6
Memorandum of Understanding 360–5
Merrill Lynch 22, 26, 27
Morgan Stanley 22, 26, 28, 31, 37

N

net stable funding ratio 221–2, *221*
  available amount of stable funding 222
  required amount of stable funding 222–3
new quantitative standards for liquidity risk 212–24
  coverage ratio 213–21; *see also* liquidity coverage ratio
  monitoring tools 223–4
  net stable funding ratio 221–2, *221*
Northern Rock 24, 207

O

Obama, Barack 353, 470
Office for Financial Research (OFR) 454–5, 456
Organisation for Economic and Cooperation Development (OECD) 48

P

Persaud, Avinash 163
Peruvian bonds 4
Pillar I 78, 126, 190, 403
Pillar II 164–5, 172, 190, 313, 319, 327, 367, 403
  and countercyclical buffer 175
  and stress tests 162–3, 489
Pillar III 403
Pillar IV 178
preliminary assessment of liquidity risk framework 232–6
  crowding-out effect 234–5
  possible impact on banking strategies 233
  rules and incentives 235–6
  tolerance of banks 233–4
procyclicality of financial regulation:
  and Basel II countercyclical rules 161–3
    and less-cyclical borrowers 162
    and Pillar II and stress tests 162–3
    risk parameters 161–2
  and Basel I 157–8
  and Basel II, 158–61
  how cyclicality becomes 155
  and impact of different rating systems *160*
  and leverage ratio 202–4
  tools for mitigating 155–80, *157, 158, 159*
  see also cyclicality
prudential regulation:
  and corporate law, 82
  and fiscal regimes 86

R

regulation, scope of 57–9
regulation and supervision
  changes to 54–64
  macroprudential 60–4
  and systemic risk 61–3
  microprudential 55–60
  and accounting standards 59–60
  capital and liquidity requirements for the banking sector 56–7
  and scope of regulation 47–9
  SIFIs 55–6
regulatory capital 73–96, *93*
  and corporate law 82
  for counterparty credit risk before the financial crisis 138–40
  definition of, under Basel I and II 74–7, *78*
  definition of, under Basel II 77–92, *78*
  and fiscal regimes 86
  new structure 77–9, *78*
  quantity of 92–3
  raising quality of 79–92
    Additional Tier 1, new eligibility criteria for 87–8, *88*
    Common Equity Tier 1 79–87, *85*
    Common Equity Tier 1, eligibility criteria for 81
    Tier 2, new eligibility criteria for 89–92
  and transitional arrangements and grandfathering mechanisms 93–5
  see also regulatory framework

regulatory framework 375–95, *380, 382, 383, 384, 385, 386, 387, 388, 389*, 421–66
  C-QIS study concerning 377–88
  and bank liquidity 384–8
  features and scope 378
  and impact on capital 379–84
  for crisis resolution 459–62
  and European supervisory authorities, tasks and instruments for *444*
  impact of, assessment in Basel III reform 375–7
  impact of, on banks 377–88
  on liquidity of 384–8
  lessons from financial crisis for 422–32
    and effective macroprudential oversight, lack of 429–32
    and prudential supervision, inadequate standards for the conduct of 427–9
    and regulatory competition, insufficient restraint of 425–7
    sources of regulatory and institutional reform 422–5
  macro assessment of 388–92
    and Basel III long-term implications 391–2
    and Basel III in transitional period 389–91
  macroprudential policy on 446–59, *455*
    challenges in implementation of 457–9
    and European Systemic Risk Board 448–54
    global setting for 446–8
    macroprudential bodies for, comparison of 454–7
  repair, *see* regulatory repair
regulatory options and credit rating agencies 249–52
  deregulatory 251–2
  market solution 252
  public supervision 249–50
  see also regulatory framework
regulatory repair 310–29
  European initiatives 317–22
  Financial Stability Board 310–17
  framework for 432–46
    and common trends in supervisory reforms 443–6
    and European supervisory authorities 435–43
    global policy response 432–5
  other initiatives 322–9
    comparisons 326–9, *328*
    Fed 323–5
    FSA 322–3
    IIF 325
    UBS 325–6
  see also regulatory framework
remuneration schemes in banking *305, 306*
  comparison of *328*
  as incentive mechanism 302–4
  regulation of 301–33
    and consumer protection 306–8
    and financial stability 308–10
    rationale for 304–10
    and regulatory repairs 310–29; *see also* regulatory repairs
rescue of shareholders 32–5
  bank 32–3
  non-bank 33–5

S

Securities and Exchange Act, new version of 272–3
securitisation treatment:
   correlation trading carve-out 119–126
   additional requirements 121–3
    ad hoc stress tests 122
    and application of standardised approach for TB securitisations 123
    internal stress tests 123
    regulatory floor 123
    and short positions, treatment of 123–4
    and unrated securitisations 124–6
   and Comprehensive Risk Measure, scope of 120–1
   correlation trading business, description of 120
shock of financial crisis 16–20
   credit cyclicality 19, *19*
   global imbalances 17–18
   systemic 21–7
   yield-curve distortions 18–19
   see also financial crisis
shortfalls of provisions 6–7, *6*, *7*
SIB distress:
   policy measures to limit impact of, on wider economy 294–6
    bank levies 296
    an impediments to orderly resolution, removing 294–5
    large exposures 295
    structured solutions 295–6
   policy measures to reduce probability of 296–9
    capital surcharge/extra loss absorbency 296–8
    liquidity surcharge 299
    more intensive supervision 299
Société Générale 22, 26
specific risk in market risk framework 112–26
   and incremental risk charge 114–19
    assumptions and regulatory parameters for computing 116–18
    and liquidity horizon, maturity mismatches within 119
    and offsetting and hedging 118–19
    and optionality 119
    rationale for 114
    risks captured by 115–16
    scope of 115
   and securitisation treatment, correlation trading carve-out 119–26
    additional requirements 121–3
    and "Comprehensive Risk Measure" Positions, scope of 120–1
    correlation trading business, description of 120
   and VaR, changes in 112–14
specific risk in the market risk framework, new treatment for 112–2
   and incremental risk charge 114
   and specific VaR 112–14
stress tests 150–1, 211, 489–90
   ad hoc 122–3

and business model 227–8
concept of, on liquidity buffer 230
and contingency capital 489–90
internal 123
on LCR 226–30
liquidity, scope and application of 229–30
and Pillar II 162–3
strengthening 164–5
and time horizon 228–9
Supervisory Capital Assessment Program (SCAP) 34
Swiss National Bank 25
Systemically Important Financial Institutions (SIFIs) 52, 55–6, 340
systemically important banks (SIBs) 289–300
   distress, policy measures to limit impact of, on wider economy 294–6
      capital surcharge/extra loss absorbency 296–8
   distress, policy measures to reduce probability of 296–9
   identification of 291–3
      interconnectedness 292–3
      size 292
      substitutability 293
   risk to, and non-SIB policies 293

T
TARP 34, 37
trading book (TB):
   and "Basel 2.5" 105–12; *see also* "Basel 2.5"
   and capital ratio, evolution of 100
   developments in, under 1996 framework 103–5
   and banks' portfolios, evolution of 103
   specific risk 104
   link between Market Risk Framework and 100–2, *101*
   new framework for 99–135; *see also* Market Risk Framework
   main changes to *101*, 102–3
   and specific risk in the market risk framework, new treatment for 112–2
   and incremental risk charge 114
   and specific VaR 112–14
trading book, invention of 12–13
transitional arrangements and grandfathering mechanisms 93–5
Troubled Asset Relief Program (TARP) 34, 37

U
UBS 22, 26, 187, *188*, 194, 325–6

V
value-at-risk (VaR):
   and event risk 113–14
   specific, changes in 112–14
   specific, positions subject to 112–13
   stressed (sVaR) 126–31
      and implementation issues 129–31
      and industry concerns 126–7
      rationale 126
      specificities of 128

Volcker Rule 425, 469–82, *479*
   and challenges for regulators 476–9
   and costs and benefits of functional separation 470–4
   macroprudential 470–2
   potential costs 472–3
   side effects and caveats 473–4
   exemptions from *475*
   implementation of 475–6

W

Walter, Stefan 187